Presentation Book A

Level 4

Siegfried Engelmann
Susan Hanner

A Division of The McGraw·Hill Companies

Columbus, Ohio

www.sra4kids.com

SRA/McGraw-Hill

*A Division of The **McGraw·Hill** Companies*

Send all inquiries to:
SRA/McGraw-Hill
8787 Orion Place
Columbus, OH 43240-4027

Printed in the United States of America.

ISBN 0-07-569140-X

2 3 4 5 6 7 8 9 BCM 06 05 04 03

Table of Contents

Lessons 1–5 · Planning Page

	Lesson 1	Lesson 2	Lesson 3	Lesson 4	Lesson 5
Lesson Events	Reading Words Comprehension Passage Written Items Story Reading Paired Practice Written Items Independent Work Workcheck Language Arts	Reading Words Comprehension Passage Written Items Story Reading Paired Practice Written Items Independent Work Workcheck Language Arts	**Vocabulary Sentence** Reading Words Comprehension Passage Written Items Story Reading Paired Practice Written Items Independent Work Workcheck Language Arts	Vocabulary Sentence Reading Words Comprehension Passage Story Reading Paired Practice Written Items Independent Work Workcheck Language Arts	Vocabulary Sentence Reading Words Comprehension Passage Story Reading Paired Practice Written Items Independent Work Workcheck Language Arts
Vocabulary Sentence			**#1: The horses became <u>restless</u> on the dangerous <u>route</u>.**	#1: The horses became <u>restless</u> on the dangerous <u>route</u>.	#1: The horses became <u>restless</u> on the dangerous <u>route</u>.
Reading Words: Word Types	modeled words words with endings mixed words	words with endings mixed words	modeled words words with underlined parts	modeled words words with endings	–s words multi-syllable words mixed words
New Vocabulary	female select migration Florida male	flocks	equator glided	receive	dangers foolish trout sprang
Comprehension Passage	*Facts About Geese*	*More Facts About Geese*	*Directions on Maps*	*Facts About the Earth*	*Facts About the Equator*
Story	*Old Henry*	*Henry Meets Tim*	*Tim's Questions*	*Tim Has a Flying Lesson*	*Tim Practices Flying*
Skill Items					Vocabulary Sentence
Special Materials					
Special Projects/ Activities					

Lesson 1

Materials: For lessons 1–140, each student will need a pencil, a colored pen or pencil for marking, a textbook, worksheets, and lined paper.

EXERCISE 1

READING WORDS

Column 1

a. You're starting a new reading program today. For most lessons, you'll need a textbook, a worksheet, a pencil, and lined paper.
  - **Find lesson 1 in your textbook.** ✓
  - Touch column 1. ✓
  - (Teacher reference:)

1. **female**	3. **migration**
2. **select**	4. **Florida**

b. Word 1 is **female.** What word? (Signal.) *Female.*
  - Spell **female.** Get ready. (Tap for each letter.) *F-E-M-A-L-E.*
  - Girls and women are females. Everybody, what do we call girls and women? (Signal.) *Females.*

c. Word 2 is **select.** What word? (Signal.) *Select.*
  - Spell **select.** Get ready. (Tap for each letter.) *S-E-L-E-C-T.*
  - When you **select** something, you **choose** it. Everybody, what's another way of saying **She chose the small salad?** (Signal.) *She selected the small salad.*

d. Word 3 is **migration.** What word? (Signal.) *Migration.*
  - Spell **migration.** Get ready. (Tap for each letter.) *M-I-G-R-A-T-I-O-N.*
  - A migration is a long journey that animals make every year. Animals migrate to the same place year after year.

e. Word 4 is **Florida.** What word? (Signal.) *Florida.*
  - Spell **Florida.** Get ready. (Tap for each letter.) *F-L-O-R-I-D-A.*

- Florida is one of the states in the United States.

f. Let's read those words again, the fast way.
  - Word 1. What word? (Signal.) *Female.*
  - Word 2. What word? (Signal.) *Select.*
  - Word 3. What word? (Signal.) *Migration.*
  - Word 4. What word? (Signal.) *Florida.*

g. (Repeat step f until firm.)

Column 2

h. Find column 2. ✓
  - (Teacher reference:)

1. **months**	4. **lonely**
2. **yearly**	5. **markings**
3. **ponds**	

- All these words have endings.

i. Word 1. What word? (Signal.) *Months.*
  - Word 2. What word? (Signal.) *Yearly.*
  - Word 3. What word? (Signal.) *Ponds.*
  - Word 4. What word? (Signal.) *Lonely.*
  - Word 5. What word? (Signal.) *Markings.*

j. (Repeat step i until firm.)

Column 3

k. Find column 3. ✓
  - (Teacher reference:)

1. **Henry**	4. **geese**
2. **chest**	5. **flapping**
3. **goose**	

l. Word 1. What word? (Signal.) *Henry.*
  - Word 2. What word? (Signal.) *Chest.*
  - Word 3. What word? (Signal.) *Goose.*
  - Word 4. What word? (Signal.) *Geese.*
  - Word 5. What word? (Signal.) *Flapping.*

m. (Repeat step l until firm.)

Column 4

n. Find column 4. ✓
  - (Teacher reference:)

1. **male**	3. **shorter**
2. **migrate**	4. **hatch**

o. Word 1. What word? (Signal.) *Male.*
  - Men and boys are males. Everybody, what do we call men and boys? (Signal.) *Males.*

- Word 2. What word? (Signal.) *Migrate.*
- Word 3. What word? (Signal.) *Shorter.*
- Word 4. What word? (Signal.) *Hatch.*
p. Let's read those words again.
- Word 1. What word? (Signal.) *Male.*
- Word 2. What word? (Signal.) *Migrate.*
- Word 3. What word? (Signal.) *Shorter.*
- Word 4. What word? (Signal.) *Hatch.*
q. (Repeat step p until firm.)

Individual Turns

(For columns 1–4: Call on individual students, each to read one to three words per turn.)

EXERCISE 2

COMPREHENSION PASSAGE

a. Find part B in your textbook. ✓
- You're going to read a story about a goose named Henry. First you'll read the information passage. It gives some facts about geese. I'll call on different students to read. Everybody else follow along, and point to the words that are being read. If you don't have your place when I call on you to read, you lose your turn.
b. Everybody, touch the title. ✓
- (Call on a student to read the title.) *[Facts About Geese.]*
- Everybody, what's the title? (Signal.) *Facts About Geese.*
c. (Call on individual students to read the passage, each student reading two or three sentences at a time. Ask the specified questions as the students read.)

Facts About Geese

(Student reads:)

> You're going to read a story about geese. Both geese and ducks are water birds, but geese are a lot bigger than ducks.

(You read:)
- Everybody, which are bigger, geese or ducks? (Signal.) *Geese.*

> There are many different kinds of geese. Snow geese are white. The geese in the story you'll read are Canada geese. They are gray, black and white.

> The picture shows a person standing near ducks, snow geese and Canada geese.

- Everybody, touch the ducks. ✓
- Touch the snow geese. ✓
- What color are they? (Signal.) *White.*
- Touch the Canada geese. ✓
- (Repeat until firm.)

> Male geese and female geese have the same color and markings. But male geese are bigger than female geese.

- Everybody, look at the ducks in the picture. Does the male duck look like the female duck? (Signal.) *No.*
- But the female goose and the male goose look the same. Touch the male Canada goose. ✓
- How do you know which goose is the male? (Call on a student. Idea: *The male is bigger.*)

> Baby geese hatch from eggs that are a lot bigger than chicken eggs. The babies are born in June. They are yellow, but as they grow older they change color. Geese are not full-grown by the time they are a year old.

- Everybody, in which month are geese born? (Signal.) *June.*
- What color are they? (Signal.) *Yellow.*
- Are they full-grown at the end of one year? (Signal.) *No.*

> When geese are three years old, they mate for the first time. Each female goose selects a mate, and the two geese stay together until one of them dies. As you will find out in the story, it may be a long time before one of them dies.

- Everybody, how old are geese when they mate for the first time? (Signal.) *Three years old.*
- After a male and female goose mate, how long do they stay together? (Call on a student. Idea: *Until one of the geese dies.*)

WRITTEN ITEMS

> **Note:** Students will need worksheet lesson 1, regular pencils, and marking pens or pencils of a different color.

a. **Find part A on your worksheet.** ✓
  • The questions in part A are about geese. I'll read each question and call on someone to answer it. Follow along. Don't write anything until I tell you to write.

b. (For each item: Read the item. Call on a student to answer it.)
  • Item 1: What's the name of geese that are all white? *[Snow geese.]*
  • Item 2: What's the name of geese that are gray and black and white? *[Canada geese.]*
  • Item 3: Both geese and ducks are water birds, but <u>blank</u> are a lot bigger. What's the answer? *[Geese.]*
  • Item 4: You can tell male geese from female geese because <u>blank</u>. The choices are **male geese have brighter colors, male geese are larger,** and **male geese have longer feathers.** What's the answer? *[Male geese are larger.]*
  • Later you'll underline that answer.
  • Item 5: What color are all geese when they are born? *[Yellow.]*
  • Item 6: How old are geese when they mate for the first time? *[3 years old.]*
  • Item 7: After male and female geese mate, they stay together <u>blank</u>. The choices are **for the summer, for a full year,** and **until one goose dies.** What's the answer? *[Until one goose dies.]*
  • Later you'll underline that answer.

c. Now you're going to write the answers for part A without looking at the passage. Read item 1 to yourself, and write the answer. Raise your hand when you've done that much.
  (Observe students and give feedback.)

d. Now read item 2 to yourself and write the answer. Raise your hand when you've done that much.
  (Observe students and give feedback.)

e. Now read the rest of the items to yourself and answer them. Raise your hand when you've finished part A.
  (Observe students and give feedback.)

f. We're going to check your answers for part A. Here are the rules: Use your marking pencil to make an **X** next to any item that is wrong. If the answer is right, don't make any mark. If it's wrong, make an **X** next to it. Don't change any answers, and don't mark over any answers.

g. (For each item: Read the item. Call on a student to answer it. If an answer is wrong, say the correct answer.)
  • Item 1: What's the name of geese that are all white? *[Snow geese.]*
  • Everybody, make an **X** next to item 1 if you got it wrong. ✓
  • Item 2: What's the name of geese that are gray and black and white? *[Canada geese.]*
  • Item 3: Both geese and ducks are water birds, but <u>blank</u> are a lot bigger. What's the answer? *[Geese.]*
  • Item 4: You can tell male geese from female geese because <u>blank</u>. What's the answer? *[Male geese are larger.]*
  • Item 5: What color are all geese when they are born? *[Yellow.]*
  • Item 6: How old are geese when they mate for the first time? *[3 years old.]*
  • Item 7: After male and female geese mate, they stay together <u>blank</u>. What's the answer? *[Until one goose dies.]*

h. Now use your marking pencil to fix up any items you got wrong. Do not erase anything you wrote. Write the correct answer close to the answer that is wrong. (Observe students and give feedback.)

i. You'll do items 8 through 16 later.

STORY READING

a. Find part C in your textbook. ✓
  • You're going to read this story. The error limit for this story is 5 errors. If you make more than 5 errors, you'll read the story again. Remember to follow along when someone else is reading.

b. Everybody, touch the title. ✓
  • (Call on a student to read the title.) *[Old Henry.]*
  • Everybody, what's the title? (Signal.) *Old Henry.*
  • So what's this story about? (Signal.) *Old Henry.*

c. (Call on individual students to read the story, each student reading two or three sentences at a time. Ask the specified questions as the students read.)

- (Correct errors: Tell the word. Direct the student to reread the sentence.)
- (If the group makes more than 5 errors, direct the students to reread the story.)

Old Henry

The other geese called him Old Henry. His name tells you one thing about him. He was old. Most geese live about 30 years. That's a long time for a bird. But Old Henry was 35 years old.

- Why was he called Old Henry? (Call on a student. Idea: *Because he was old.*)
- Everybody, what kind of animal was Old Henry? (Signal.) *A goose.*
- How old do most geese get? (Call on a student. Idea: *About 30 years old.*)
- Everybody, how old was Old Henry? (Signal.) *35.*

You couldn't tell he was that old by looking at him. He was sort of a gray color with a white chest, just like the other Canada geese. If you saw Old Henry swimming on Big Trout Lake with the other geese on a warm summer day, you would not be able to tell that he was the oldest goose in the flock.

- Everybody, what's the name of the lake where Old Henry was during the summer? (Signal.) *Big Trout Lake.*
- What kind of goose was Old Henry? (Signal.) *Canada goose.*
- Tell how Canada geese look. (Call on a student. Idea: *Gray body with a white chest, black neck, black and white face.*)
- Everybody, could you tell that Old Henry was the oldest goose in the flock? (Signal.) *No.*

If you saw Old Henry three months later that year, you might get the idea that he was an old goose. ✭ **He was the only goose that was still on Big Trout Lake. All the other geese in the flock had gone south for the winter. They wanted Old Henry to go with**
them. But he told them, "No, I'm getting too old to fly two thousand miles. I've done it too many times, and I'm just too tired."

The other geese told him, "But if you stay here, you may never make it through the winter. The lakes will freeze and you'll die."

Henry replied, "Maybe I won't die," but he didn't really believe that at all. So, he waved goodbye to the other geese as they took off from the lake, and he watched them form a great V that moved slowly south.

- Everybody, how far were the geese going to fly on their trip south? (Signal.) *Two thousand miles.*
- Was it still summer when the geese left Big Trout Lake? (Signal.) *No.*
- What season was it? (Signal.) *Fall.*
- Why didn't Old Henry fly with the rest of the flock? (Call on a student. Ideas: *Because he was too old; too tired.*)
- Everybody, where had the rest of the flock gone? (Signal.) *South.*
- What was going to happen to the lakes during the winter? (Call on a student. Idea: *They'd freeze.*)
- Why do you think a goose would die if it had to spend the winter where the lakes were frozen? (Call on a student. Idea: *Because it would be so cold.*)
- Everybody, did Old Henry really believe that he would make it through the winter? (Signal.) *No.*

EXERCISE 5

PAIRED PRACTICE

a. As part of most lessons, you're going to work in pairs.
- (Assign an **A** member and a **B** member in each pair.)
- (After assigning all students:)
- All **A** members raise your hand. ✓
- All **B** members raise your hand. ✓
- (Repeat until firm.)

b. You're going to read aloud to your partner. Today, the **A** member of each pair will read first. Then the **B** member will read.
- The **A** members will read from the beginning of the title to the star in the story. Everybody, touch that star. ✓

- The **B** members will start at the star and read to the end of the story.

c. Here are the rules: The student who is not reading follows along. If there is a mistake, that student points out the error and tells the correct word. If there is a problem, raise your hand, and I'll help you.

- **A** members, start reading. Raise your hand when you've read to the star. (Observe students and give feedback.)
- (Direct **B** members to read from the star to the end of the story. Praise teams that follow the rules.)

EXERCISE 6

WRITTEN ITEMS
Story Items

a. Find part B on your worksheet. ✓
- These questions are about today's story. Today's story told about Old Henry. I'll read each item and call on someone to answer it. Follow along. Don't write anything until I tell you to write.

b. (For each item: Read the item. Call on a student to answer it.)
- Item 8: Most geese live for about <u>blank</u> years. What's the answer? *[30.]*
- Item 9: How old was Old Henry? *[35.]*
- Item 10: What was the name of the lake the flock stayed at during the summer? *[Big Trout Lake.]*
- Item 11: In which season did the flock leave the lake? *[Fall.]*
- Item 12: In which direction did the flock fly? *[South.]*
- Item 13: How far was the flock going? *[2000 miles.]*
- Item 14: Who didn't want to make the trip? *[Idea: Henry.]*
- Item 15: He said that he was too <u>blank</u> to fly so far. What's the answer? [Ideas: *Old; tired.]*
- Item 16: What will happen to Big Trout Lake during the winter? [Idea: *It will freeze.]*

End-of-Lesson Activities

INDEPENDENT WORK

Now you're going to complete the worksheet without looking at the story. Read the items to yourself and answer them. Raise your hand when you've finished.
(Observe students and give feedback.)

WORKCHECK

Note: Students will need marking pens or pencils of a different color.

a. We're going to check the rest of the answers on your worksheet. Here are the rules: Use your marking pencil to make an **X** next to any item that is wrong. If the answer is right, don't make any mark. If it's wrong, make an **X** next to it. Don't change the answers and don't mark over any answers.

b. (For each item: Read the item. Call on a student to answer it. If the answer is wrong, say the correct answer.)
- Item 8: Most geese live for about <u>blank</u> years. What's the answer? *[30]*
- Everybody, write **X** next to item 8 if you got it wrong. You should have written the number or the word **30** in the blank.
- Item 9: How old was Old Henry? *[35.]*
- Item 10: What was the name of the lake the flock stayed at during the summer? *[Big Trout Lake.]*
- Item 11: In which season did the flock leave the lake? *[Fall.]*
- Item 12: In which direction did the flock fly? *[South.]*
- Item 13: How far was the flock going? *[2000 miles.]*
- Item 14: Who didn't want to make the trip? [Idea: *Henry.]*
- Item 15: He said that he was too <u>blank</u> to fly so far. What's the answer? [Ideas: *Old; tired.]*
- Item 16: What will happen to Big Trout Lake during the winter? [Idea: *It will freeze.]*

c. Now use your marking pencil to fix any items you got wrong. Do not erase anything you wrote. Write the correct answer close to the answer that is wrong. Before you hand in your independent work, all the items you missed must be fixed. (Observe students and give feedback.)

d. (At the end of the workcheck, have students record the total number of errors they made at the top of their worksheet.)

LANGUAGE ARTS

(Present Language Arts lesson 1 after completing Reading lesson 1. See Language Arts Guide.)

READING WORDS

Column 1

a. **Find lesson 2 in your textbook.** ✓
- Touch column 1. ✓
- (Teacher reference:)

1. flocks	4. flapping
2. migration	5. fliers
3. answers	6. shorter

b. All these words have endings.
c. Word 1. What word? (Signal.) *Flocks.*
- A flock of birds is a group of birds that lives together and flies together. Everybody, what do we call a group of birds that lives together and flies together? (Signal.) *A flock.*
- Word 2. What word? (Signal.) *Migration.*
- Word 3. What word? (Signal.) *Answers.*
- Word 4. What word? (Signal.) *Flapping.*
- Word 5. What word? (Signal.) *Fliers.*
- Word 6. What word? (Signal.) *Shorter.*
d. Let's read those words again.
- Word 1. What word? (Signal.) *Flocks.*
- Word 2. What word? (Signal.) *Migration.*
- Word 3. What word? (Signal.) *Answers.*
- Word 4. What word? (Signal.) *Flapping.*
- Word 5. What word? (Signal.) *Fliers.*
- Word 6. What word? (Signal.) *Shorter.*
e. (Repeat step d until firm.)

Column 2

f. Find column 2. ✓
- (Teacher reference:)

1. Florida	4. breeze
2. yearly	5. migrate
3. sudden	6. lonely

g. Word 1. What word? (Signal.) *Florida.*
- Word 2. What word? (Signal.) *Yearly.*
- Word 3. What word? (Signal.) *Sudden.*
- Word 4. What word? (Signal.) *Breeze.*
- Word 5. What word? (Signal.) *Migrate.*
- Word 6. What word? (Signal.) *Lonely.*
h. (Repeat step g until firm.)

Individual Turns

(For columns 1 and 2: Call on individual students, each to read one to three words per turn.)

COMPREHENSION PASSAGE

a. Find part B in your textbook. ✓
- You're going to read the next story about Old Henry. First you'll read the information passage. It gives some more facts about geese.
- I'll call on individual students to read. Everybody else follow along, and point to the words that are being read. If you don't have your place when I call on you to read, you lose your turn.
b. Everybody, touch the title. ✓
- (Call on a student to read the title.) *[More Facts About Geese.]*
- Everybody, what's the title? (Signal.) *More Facts About Geese.*
c. (Call on individual students to read the passage, each student reading two or three sentences at a time. Ask the specified questions as the students read.)

More Facts About Geese
Most wild geese are born in Canada and spend every summer in Canada.

- Everybody, where are they born? (Signal.) *Canada.*

- The map shows Canada. It is a very large country that is north of the United States. Touch Canada. ✓

Geese live in flocks that may have more than 50 geese in them. In the fall, flocks fly south to their winter home. Then in the spring, they return to their summer home in Canada.

- Everybody, in which direction do the flocks fly in the fall? (Signal.) *South.*
- In which direction do the flocks fly in the spring? (Signal.) *North.*

This yearly flying to the south and to the north is called a migration.

- Everybody, what is the yearly trip north and south called? (Signal.) *Migration.*

When geese migrate in the fall, they fly south. In which direction do they migrate in the spring?

- Everybody, what's the answer? (Signal.) *North.*

The geese that you're reading about migrate to a place in Florida. The map shows the path of the migration from Big Trout Lake in Canada to Crooked Lake in Florida.

- Listen: The flock we're reading about migrates from Big Trout Lake in Canada to Crooked Lake in Florida.
- Everybody, at which lake does the migration start? (Signal.) *Big Trout Lake.*
- Which lake does the migration go to? (Signal.) *Crooked Lake.*
- (Repeat until firm.)

- Touch Big Trout Lake on the map. ✓
- What country is Big Trout Lake in? (Signal.) *Canada.*
- Now follow the path to Crooked Lake. ✓
- What state is Crooked Lake in? (Signal.) *Florida.*
- Which direction did your finger go from Canada to Florida? (Signal.) *South.*
- In which season would the geese go in that direction? (Signal.) *Fall.*

Geese migrate south in the fall because the lakes and rivers freeze in Canada. Farther south, lakes and rivers do not freeze.

- Why do geese migrate south? (Call on a student. Idea: *Lakes freeze in Canada, don't freeze farther south.*)
- Everybody, in the wintertime, are the lakes in Canada frozen? (Signal.) *Yes.*
- Are the lakes in Florida frozen? (Signal.) *No.*
- Yes, the winter in Florida is very warm.

Not all flocks migrate to the same place in the south. Some flocks migrate over three thousand miles to their winter home. Some migrate only a thousand miles.

- Everybody, do all flocks migrate south to the same place? (Signal.) *No.*
- You can find geese spending the winter wherever the lakes don't freeze in the winter.

EXERCISE 3

WRITTEN ITEMS

Note: Students will need worksheet lesson 2, regular pencils, and marking pens or pencils of a different color.

a. You're going to write the answers to items about what you just read.
- **Find part A on your worksheet.** ✓
b. I'll read each item in part A and call on someone to answer it. Follow along. Don't write anything until I tell you to write.

c. Look at the map. Item 1: Make an **R** on Big Trout Lake. Everybody, touch Big Trout Lake. Keep touching it. ✓
- Item 2: What country are you touching? *[Canada.]*
- Item 3: Make an **F** on Crooked Lake. Everybody, touch Crooked Lake. ✓
- Item 4: Which lake is farther north? *[Big Trout Lake.]*
- Item 5: Make a **Y** next to the lake that freezes in the winter. Everybody, touch the lake that freezes in the winter. (Students touch Big Trout Lake.)
- Item 6: Geese live in large groups called <u>blank</u>. What's the answer? *[Flocks.]*
- Item 7: In what country are most wild geese born? *[Canada.]*
- Item 8: Where do these geese spend every summer? *[Canada.]*
- Item 9: In which direction do the geese fly in the fall? *[South.]*
- Item 10: What is this trip called? The choices are **mating, migration,** and **hibernation.** What's the answer? *[Migration.]*
- Later, you'll underline that answer.
- Item 11: Why do the geese leave Canada in the fall? The choices are **There is no snow, The lakes freeze,** and **The flock needs to fly.** What's the answer? *[The lakes freeze.]*
- Later, you'll underline that answer.
- Item 12: Every fall, Old Henry's flock went to the state of <u>blank</u>. What's the answer? *[Florida.]*

d. Now you're going to write the answers for part A without looking at the passage. Read the items to yourself and write the answers. Raise your hand when you've finished part A.
(Observe students and give feedback.)

e. We're going to check your answers for part A. Here are the rules: Use your marking pencil to make an **X** next to any item that is wrong. If the answer is right, don't make any mark. If it's wrong, make an **X** next to it. Don't change any answers, and don't mark over any answers.

f. (For each item: Read the item. Call on a student to answer it. If an answer is wrong, say the correct answer.)
- Item 1: Make an **R** on Big Trout Lake. Everybody, touch Big Trout Lake. ✓
- Everybody, write **X** next to item 1 if you got it wrong. ✓

- Item 2: What country is the **R** in? *[Canada.]*
- Item 3: Make an **F** on Crooked Lake. Everybody, touch Crooked Lake. ✓
- Item 4: Which lake is farther north? *[Big Trout Lake.]*
- Item 5: Make a **Y** next to the lake that freezes in the winter. Everybody, touch the lake that freezes in the winter. (Students touch Big Trout Lake.)
- Item 6: Geese live in large groups called <u>blank</u>. What's the answer? *[Flocks.]*
- Item 7: In what country are most wild geese born? *[Canada.]*
- Item 8: Where do these geese spend every summer? *[Canada.]*
- Item 9: In which direction do the geese fly in the fall? *[South.]*
- Item 10: What is this trip called? *[Migration.]*
- Item 11: Why do the geese leave Canada in the fall? *[The lakes freeze.]*
- Item 12: Every fall, Old Henry's flock went to the state of <u>blank</u>. What's the answer? *[Florida.]*

g. Now use your marking pencil to fix up any items you got wrong. Do not erase anything you wrote. Write the correct answer close to the answer that is wrong. **(Observe students and give feedback.)**

EXERCISE 4

STORY READING

a. Find part C in your textbook. ✓
- You're going to read this story. The error limit for this story is 5 errors. If you make more than 5 errors, you'll read the story again.

b. Everybody, touch the title. ✓
- (Call on a student to read the title.) *[Henry Meets Tim.]*
- What's going to happen in this story? (Call on a student. Idea: *Henry will meet Tim.*)

c. (Call on individual students to read the story, each student reading two or three sentences at a time. Ask the specified questions as the students read.)

- (Correct errors: Tell the word. Direct the student to reread the sentence.)
- (If the group makes more than 5 errors, direct the students to reread the story.)

Henry Meets Tim

Henry stayed in Canada while the other geese in the flock went south for the winter. It was lonely being all alone on Big Trout Lake, but Henry had felt lonely for the last five years. That was when his wife died. Henry still missed her. She had been his mate since they were both three years old.

- Everybody, what country was Henry in? (Signal.) *Canada.*
- In which direction had the flock gone? (Signal.) *South.*
- How long ago had Henry's wife died? (Signal.) *Five years ago.*
- The story said that she had been his mate since they were both how many years old? (Signal.) *Three years old.*
- That means that every year they had baby geese and took care of them—from the time they were both three years old until they were both thirty years old.

So Henry waited for winter. He spent time walking, swimming and looking at the sky. Every now and then a flock of geese would fly by. Henry would listen to the leader as he honked directions to the other geese.

The days were getting shorter and colder. Henry knew that very soon Big Trout Lake would freeze. Nine days after the others had left, Old Henry saw another Canada goose walking along the shore. Old Henry could tell that it was a very young goose. ⭐ It wasn't very big, and it didn't seem to know where it was going.

- The story told how the days were changing. How were they changing? (Call on a student. Idea: *They were getting colder and shorter.*)
- What would happen soon? (Call on a student. Idea: *Big Trout Lake would freeze.*)
- Everybody, how long was Henry alone on the lake before he saw someone else? (Signal.) *Nine days.*

- Who did he see? (Call on a student. Idea: *A goose.*)
- How did Henry know that it was a **young** goose? (Call on a student. Ideas: *It wasn't very big; it didn't seem to know where it was going.*)

"Hey, there," Henry called. "What are you doing here? You're supposed to be on your way to Florida."

- Everybody, where were the other geese going? (Signal.) *Florida.*

The young goose said, "Oh, I couldn't learn to fly because my leg was hurt."

Old Henry knew about that problem. When young geese learn to fly, they start out by running faster and faster. They hold their wings out to the side as they run. Then they flap their wings and fly. But if they can't run fast, they can't fly. Later, geese learn to take off from the water, but that's not the first thing they learn about flying.

- Tell what young geese do when they learn to fly. (Call on a student. Idea: *They run faster and faster with their wings out to the side, then flap their wings and fly.*)
- Why would a goose that had a bad leg have trouble learning to fly? (Call on a student. Idea: *Because it wouldn't be able to run.*)

"Well," Henry said. "If you don't have anything better to do, swim out here and join me. I would be glad to have your company."

EXERCISE 5

PAIRED PRACTICE

a. You're going to work in pairs.
   - All **A** members raise your hand. ✓
   - All **B** members raise your hand. ✓
   - (Repeat until firm.)
b. Today, the **B** member of each pair will read first. The **B** member will read from the beginning of the title to the star in the middle of the story. Everybody, touch that star. ✓

- The **A** members will read from the star to the end of the story.
c. Remember the rules. The student who is not reading follows along. If there is a mistake, that student points out the error and tells the correct word. If there is a problem, raise your hand, and I'll help you.
- **B** members, start reading. Raise your hand when you've read to the star. (Observe students and give feedback.)
- (As **B** members complete their reading, direct **A** members to read from the star to the end of the story. Praise teams that follow the rules.)

EXERCISE 6

WRITTEN ITEMS

Story Items

a. Find part B on your worksheet. ✓
- These questions are about today's story. Today's story told about Henry meeting Tim. I'll read each item and call on someone to answer it. Follow along. Don't write anything until I tell you to write.
b. (For each item: Read the item. Call on a student to answer it.)
- Item 13: Henry first mated with his wife when they were both <u>blank</u> years old. What's the answer? *[3.]*
- Item 14: Henry's wife had died <u>blank</u> years ago. *[5.]*
- Item 15: How had Henry felt ever since she had died? The choices are **free, tired,** and **lonely.** What's the answer? *[Lonely.]*
- Later, you'll underline the answer.
- Item 16: After the flock had been gone for <u>blank</u> days, Henry saw another goose. What's the answer? *[9.]*
- Item 17: Was that goose **old** or **young?** *[Young.]*
- Item 18: The goose told Henry, "I couldn't learn to fly because <u>blank</u>." The choices are **my leg was hurt, my wing was hurt,** and **I was too small.** What's the answer? *[My leg was hurt.]*

- Item 19: When geese learn to fly, do they start **in the water** or **on the land?** *[On the land.]*
- Item 20: They run with their <u>blank</u> out to the side. What's the answer? *[Wings.]*

Review Items

c. The rest of the items for today's lesson are in part D of your textbook. You'll write your answers on lined paper.
- **Take out a piece of lined paper.** ✓
- Write your name at the top of the paper. ✓
- Number your paper from 1 through 11. Skip every other line. Pencils down when you're finished. (Observe students and give feedback.)
d. Find part D in your textbook. ✓
- These items are review items. They're items from the last lesson.
- Item 1: What's the name of geese that are gray and black and white? *[Canada geese.]*
- Item 2: What's the name of geese that are all white? *[Snow geese.]*
- Item 3: What color are all geese when they are born? *[Yellow.]*
- Item 4: You can tell male geese from female geese because <u>blank</u>. The choices are **male geese have brighter colors, male geese have longer feathers,** and **male geese are larger.** What's the answer? *[Male geese are larger.]*
- Item 5: How old are geese when they mate for the first time? *[3 years old.]*
- Item 6: After male and female geese mate, they stay together <u>blank</u>. The choices are **for the summer, for a full year,** and **until one goose dies.** What's the answer? *[Until one goose dies.]*
- Item 7: Most geese live for about <u>blank</u> years. What's the answer? *[30.]*
- Item 8: What was the name of the lake where Henry's flock stayed during the summer? *[Big Trout Lake.]*
- Item 9: In which season did the flock leave the lake? *[Fall.]*
- Item 10: In which direction did the flock fly? *[South.]*
- Item 11: How far was the flock going? *[2000 miles.]*

End-of-Lesson Activities

Now you're going to complete the written work without looking at the story. Start with part B of your worksheet. Then finish the items in part D of your textbook, beginning with item 1. Read the items to yourself and answer them. Raise your hand when you've finished.

(Observe students and give feedback.)

WORKCHECK

Note: Students will need marking pens or pencils of a different color.

a. We're going to check the rest of the answers on your worksheet and the answers on your lined paper. Here are the rules: Use your marking pencil to make an **X** next to any item that is wrong. If the answer is right, don't make any mark. If it's wrong, make an **X** next to it. Don't change any answers and don't mark over any answers.

b. Let's start with part B of your worksheet. (For each item: Read the item. Call on a student to answer it. If the answer is wrong, say the correct answer.)

- Item 13: Henry first mated with his wife when they were both blank years old. What's the answer? *[3.]*
- Item 14: Henry's wife had died blank years ago. What's the answer? *[5.]*
- Item 15: How had Henry felt ever since she had died? *[Lonely.]*
- Item 16: After the flock had been gone for blank days, Henry saw another goose. What's the answer? *[9.]*
- Item 17: Was that goose **old** or **young?** *[Young.]*
- Item 18: The goose told Henry, "I couldn't learn to fly because blank." What's the answer? *[My leg was hurt.]*
- Item 19: When geese learn to fly, do they start **in the water** or **on the land?** *[On the land.]*

- Item 20: They run with their blank out to the side. What's the answer? *[Wings.]*

c. Now let's check the items on your lined paper.
- Item 1: What's the name of geese that are gray and black and white? *[Canada geese.]*
- Item 2: What's the name of geese that are all white? *[Snow geese.]*
- Item 3: What color are all geese when they are born? *[Yellow.]*
- Item 4: You can tell male geese from female geese because blank. What's the answer? *[Male geese are larger.]*
- Item 5: How old are geese when they mate for the first time? *[3 years old.]*
- Item 6: After male and female geese mate, they stay together blank. What's the answer? *[Until one goose dies.]*
- Item 7: Most geese live for about blank years. What's the answer? *[30.]*
- Item 8: What was the name of the lake where Henry's flock stayed during the summer? *[Big Trout Lake.]*
- Item 9: In which season did the flock leave the lake? *[Fall.]*
- Item 10: In which direction did the flock fly? *[South.]*
- Item 11: How far was the flock going? *[2000 miles.]*

d. Now use your marking pencil to fix up any items you got wrong. Do not erase anything you wrote. Write the correct answer close to the answer that is wrong. Remember, before you hand in your independent work, all the items you missed must be fixed. (Observe students and give feedback.)

e. (At the end of the workcheck, have students record the total number of errors they made at the top of their lined paper.)

LANGUAGE ARTS

(Present Language Arts lesson 2 after completing Reading lesson 2. See Language Arts Guide.)

EXERCISE 1

VOCABULARY

a. **Find page 352 in your textbook.** ✓
- These are sentences that you'll be working with in this program. They contain vocabulary words that you'll learn.
- Touch sentence 1. ✓
- It says: The horses became restless on the dangerous route. Everybody, read that sentence. Get ready. (Signal.) *The horses became restless on the dangerous route.*
- Close your eyes and say the sentence. Get ready. (Signal.) *The horses became restless on the dangerous route.*
- (Repeat until firm.)

b. When you feel **restless** you don't want to keep doing what you're doing. You are eager to do something else. When you feel restless in school, what do you want to do? (Call on a student. Idea: *Something else.*)

c. The different ways you can go to get to a place are the different **routes** that you can take to get there. If there's only one way to get to a place, there's only one route to get there. If there are a lot of different ways to get there, there are a lot of different routes.
- Tell me one of the routes you could take to get from school to where you live. (Call on a student. Accept reasonable responses.)
- Tell me another route to get from school to where you live. (Call on the same student.)

d. Listen to the sentence again: The horses became restless on the dangerous route. Everybody, say the sentence. Get ready. (Signal.) *The horses became restless on the dangerous route.*

e. What word tells how you feel when you want to do something different? (Signal.) *Restless.*
- What word tells how you get to a place? (Signal.) *Route.*
- (Repeat step e until firm.)

EXERCISE 2

READING WORDS

Column 1

a. Find lesson 3 in your textbook. ✓
- Touch column 1. ✓
- (Teacher reference:)

1. **equator**	4. **answers**
2. **flocks**	5. **above**
3. **breeze**	6. **fliers**

b. Word 1 is **equator.** What word? (Signal.) *Equator.*
- Spell **equator.** Get ready. (Tap for each letter.) *E-Q-U-A-T-O-R.*
- The equator is a make-believe line around the middle of the earth. The equator is the hottest part of the earth.

c. Word 2. What word? (Signal.) *Flocks.*
- Word 3. What word? (Signal.) *Breeze.*
- Word 4. What word? (Signal.) *Answers.*
- Word 5. What word? (Signal.) *Above.*
- Word 6. What word? (Signal.) *Fliers.*

d. Let's read those words again.
- Word 1. What word? (Signal.) *Equator.*
- Word 2. What word? (Signal.) *Flocks.*
- Word 3. What word? (Signal.) *Breeze.*
- Word 4. What word? (Signal.) *Answers.*
- Word 5. What word? (Signal.) *Above.*
- Word 6. What word? (Signal.) *Fliers.*

e. (Repeat step d until firm.)

Column 2

f. Find column 2. ✓
- (Teacher reference:)

1. <u>glide</u>d	4. <u>anymore</u>
2. <u>sudden</u>	5. <u>dived</u>
3. <u>training</u>	

- Part of each word is underlined. You'll read that part. Then you'll read the whole word.

g. Word 1. What's the underlined part? (Signal.) *glide.*
- What's the whole word? (Signal.) *Glided.*
- When a bird glides, it goes through the air without flapping or moving its wings.

- Everybody, what are birds doing when they go through the air without moving their wings? (Signal.) *Gliding.*
- Word 2. What's the underlined part? (Signal.) *sudd.*
- What's the whole word? (Signal.) *Sudden.*
- Word 3. What's the underlined part? (Signal.) *train.*
- What's the whole word? (Signal.) *Training.*
- Word 4. What's the underlined part? (Signal.) *any.*
- What's the whole word? (Signal.) *Anymore.*
- Word 5. What's the underlined part? (Signal.) *dive.*
- What's the whole word? (Signal.) *Dived.*

h. Let's read those words again the fast way.
- Word 1. What word? (Signal.) *Glided.*
- Word 2. What word? (Signal.) *Sudden.*
- Word 3. What word? (Signal.) *Training.*
- Word 4. What word? (Signal.) *Anymore.*
- Word 5. What word? (Signal.) *Dived.*

i. (Repeat step h until firm.)

Individual Turns

(For columns 1 and 2: Call on individual students, each to read one to three words per turn.)

EXERCISE 3
COMPREHENSION PASSAGE

a. Find part B in your textbook. ✓
- You're going to read the next story about Henry. First you'll read the information passage. It gives some information about directions on maps. I'll call on individual students to read. Everybody else follow along, and point to the words that are being read. If you don't have your place when I call on you to read, you lose your turn.

b. Everybody, touch the title. ✓
- (Call on a student to read the title.) *[Directions on Maps.]*
- Everybody, what's the title? (Signal.) *Directions on Maps.*

c. (Call on individual students to read the passage, each student reading two or three sentences at a time. Ask the specified questions as the students read.)

Directions on Maps
The geese in the story you're reading go from Canada to Florida in the fall. In which direction do they go?

- Everybody, what's the answer? (Signal.) *South.*
- Yes, the geese migrate south in the fall.

In which direction do they go when they go from Florida to Canada?

- Everybody, what's the answer? (Signal.) *North.*
- Yes, geese migrate north in the spring.

Maps always show four directions—north, south, east and west.

- Everybody, name the four directions. Get ready. (Signal.) *North, south, east, and west.*

North is always at the top of the map.
South is always at the bottom of the map.
East is always on this side of the map. →
West is always on this side of the map. ←
Map 1 shows the directions on all maps.
Touch the circle in the middle of the map and move your finger to the top of the map.

Map 1

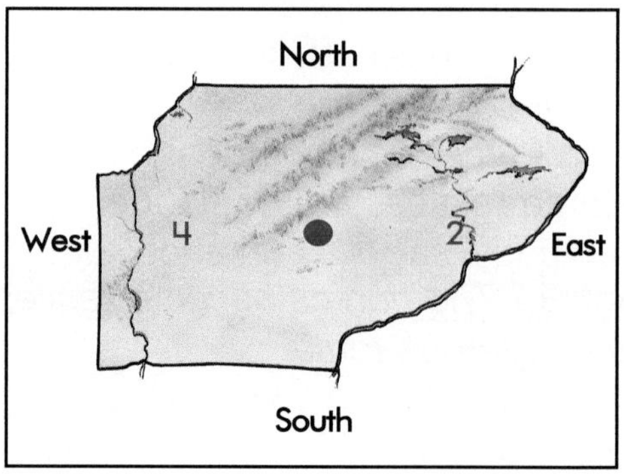

- Everybody, do it. ✓

In which direction did you go?

- Everybody, what's the answer? (Signal.) *North.*

Touch the circle and move to the bottom of the map.

- Everybody, do it. ✓

In which direction did you go?

- Everybody, what's the answer? (Signal.) *South.*

Touch the circle and move to the number 2.

- Everybody, do it. ✓

In which direction did you go?

- Everybody, what's the answer? (Signal.) *East.*

Touch the circle and move to the 4.

- Everybody, do it. ✓

In which direction did you go?

- Everybody, what's the answer? (Signal.) *West.*

Map 2 shows Canada, the United States and some other countries. Is the red dot in the United States, or in Canada?

Map 2

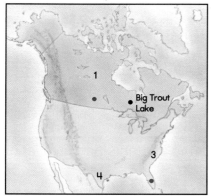

- Everybody, touch the red dot. ✓
- Is that dot in the United States or in Canada? (Signal.) *United States.*

In which country is the blue dot?

- Everybody, touch the blue dot. ✓

- In which country is that dot? (Signal.) *Canada.*
- Listen: Touch the blue dot and go to the number **1** on the map. ✓
- In which direction did you go? (Signal.) *North.*
- Yes, **north** is at the top of the map.

Touch the red dot and go to the 4 on the map.

- Everybody, do it. ✓

In which direction did you go?

- Everybody, what's the answer? (Signal.) *West.*

Touch the red dot and go to the 3.

- Everybody, do it. ✓

In which direction did you go?

- Everybody, what's the answer? (Signal.) *North.*

The red dot is in the United States. What's the name of the state the red dot is in?

- Everybody, what's the answer? (Signal.) *Florida.*

EXERCISE 4

WRITTEN ITEMS

> ***Note:*** Students will need worksheet lesson 3, regular pencils, and marking pens or pencils of a different color.

a. You're going to write the answers to questions about what you just read.
- **Find part A on your worksheet.** ✓
b. The questions in part A are about the directions on maps. I'll read each question and call on someone to answer it. Follow along. Don't write anything until I tell you to write.
c. (For each item: Read the item. Call on a student to answer it.)
- Item 1: Write the directions **north, south, east,** and **west** in the boxes on map 1.

- Touch the box for **north.** [Student touches top box.]
- Touch the box for **south.** [Student touches bottom box.]
- Touch the box for **east.** [Student touches right box.]
- Touch the box for **west.** [Student touches left box.]
- Item 2: In which direction do geese migrate in the fall? *[South.]*
- Item 3: In which direction do geese migrate in the spring? *[North.]*
- Item 4: Make a line that starts at the circle on the map and goes north. Trace with your finger to show where you'll draw the line. [Student moves finger from the circle toward top box.]
- Item 5: If you start at the circle and move to the number **4,** in which direction do you go? *[South.]*
- Look at map 2 on the next page. Item 6: What country is the **A** in? *[Canada.]*
- Item 7: What country is the **B** in? *[United States.]*
- Item 8: What **state** is the **B** in? *[Florida.]*
- Item 9: If you started at the **B** and went to the **A**, in which direction would you go? *[North.]*

d. Now you're going to write the answers for part A without looking at the passage. Read item 1 to yourself and write the answers. Raise your hand when you've done that much.
(Observe students and give feedback.)

e. Read the rest of the items in part A to yourself and answer them. Raise your hand when you've finished part A.
(Observe students and give feedback.)

f. We're going to check your answers for part A. Here are the rules: Use your marking pencil to make an **X** next to any item that is wrong. If the answer is right, don't make any mark. If it's wrong, make an **X** next to it. Don't change any answers, and don't mark over any answers.

g. (For each item: Read the item. Call on a student to answer it. If an answer is wrong, say the correct answer.)
- Item 1: Write the directions **north, south, east,** and **west** in the boxes on map 1.
- Touch the box for **north.** [Student touches top box.]
- Everybody, you should have written **north** in the top box.

- Touch the box for **south.** [Student touches bottom box.]
- Everybody, you should have written **south** in the bottom box.
- Touch the box for **east.** [Student touches right box.]
- (Hold up worksheet. Point to box on right.) Everybody, you should have written **east** in this box.
- Touch the box for **west.** [Student touches left box.]
- (Hold up worksheet. Point to box on left.) Everybody, you should have written **west** in this box.
- Everybody, write **X** next to item 1 if you got it wrong. ✓
- Item 2: In which direction do geese migrate in the fall? *[South.]*
- Item 3: In which direction do geese migrate in the spring? *[North.]*
- Item 4: Make a line that starts at the circle on the map and goes north. Use your finger to show me where you drew your line. [Student moves finger from the circle toward top box.]
- (Hold up worksheet and trace line that goes north from circle.) Everybody, this is where your line should be.
- Item 5: If you start at the circle and move to the number **4,** in which direction do you go? *[South.]*
- Look at map 2 on the next page. Item 6: What country is the **A** in? *[Canada.]*
- Item 7: What country is the **B** in? *[United States.]*
- Item 8: What **state** is the **B** in? *[Florida.]*
- Item 9: If you started at the **B** and went to the **A**, in which direction would you go? *[North.]*

h. Now use your marking pencil to fix up any items you got wrong. Do not erase anything you wrote. Write the correct answer close to the answer that is wrong.
(Observe students and give feedback.)

EXERCISE 5

STORY READING

a. Find part C in your textbook. ✓
- You're going to read this story. The error limit for this story is 8 errors. If you make more than 8 errors, you'll read the story again.

b. Everybody, touch the title. ✓
- (Call on a student to read the title.) *[Tim's Questions.]*
- Everybody, what's the title? (Signal.) *Tim's Questions.*

c. (Call on individual students to read the story, each student reading two or three sentences at a time. Ask the specified questions as the students read.)

- (Correct errors: Tell the word. Direct the student to reread the sentence.)
- (If the group makes more than 8 errors, direct the students to reread the story.)

Tim's Questions

Old Henry and a young goose were the only ones left on a pond in Canada. The young goose swam up to Old Henry and said, "My name is Tim. What's your name?"

Henry answered Tim's question, and then Tim said, "I have a lot of questions about geese. I was never able to ask my mom these questions because she was so busy getting my brothers and sisters ready for the flight down south."

Henry said, "So you have never made the trip to the south."

"That's right," Tim said. "I was born last June. So I'm less than half a year old."

- Everybody, what was the young goose's name? (Signal.) *Tim.*
- Why wasn't his mom able to answer the questions that he had about geese? (Call on a student. Idea: *She was very busy getting ready for the trip south.*)
- Everybody, when was Tim born? (Signal.) *June.*
- So he was less than half a year old.

"Well, ask me the questions," Old Henry said, "and I'll tell you the answers."

Tim said, "Well, Mom always told us that geese are the best high fliers there are. I don't know what she meant by that."

Old Henry laughed and said, "On the other side of the world are some mountains that are over five miles

high. There's only one kind of bird that can fly over those mountains, and that's a goose."

Tim shook his head. "Wow," he said. "Do the flocks fly that high when they go south for the winter?" ⭐

"No, no," Henry said. "You only go that high if you have to get over something. We fly pretty high, sometimes two or three miles high, but that's about as high as we go."

- How high do geese fly when they go to Florida? (Call on a student. Idea: *Two or three miles high.*)
- How high can geese fly to go over high mountains? (Call on a student. Idea: *Over five miles high.*)
- How many other types of birds can fly that high? (Call on a student. Idea: *None.*)

"I can see that geese fly pretty fast," Tim said, "but do you know how fast they go?"

"Of course I know," Old Henry said. "Geese can fly one mile a minute. That's sixty miles per hour, and geese can fly at that speed all day long."

- The story says that geese can fly one mile a minute. Everybody, how far would the geese go in one minute? (Signal.) *One mile.*
- If they fly one mile a minute, how many **miles per hour** do they fly? (Signal.) *Sixty.*
- (Repeat until firm.)

The geese stopped talking as a sudden breeze blew across the lake. It was very cold. Henry shook his head and said, "There will be some ice on Big Trout Lake tomorrow morning."

Tim said, "I wish I could fly south. My leg feels better now, but I don't know how to fly."

Henry said, "Well, if your leg is better, I could teach you how to fly." Henry shook his head. "And I suppose I could even tell you how to get to Florida."

- Everybody, was Tim's leg still hurt? (Signal.) *No.*
- Old Henry said he could do two things for Tim. What was the first thing? (Call on a student. Idea: *Teach him how to fly.*)
- What was the other thing? (Call on a student. Idea: *Tell him how to get to Florida.*)

> **"That would be great," Tim said. "It would be even better if you would come with me and show me the way."**
>
> **"No, no," Henry said. "I have flown to Florida for the last time. But I'll tell you how to get there."**
>
> **"Thank you," Tim said. "I would really love to go there."**

EXERCISE 6

PAIRED PRACTICE

a. You're going to work in pairs.
- All **A** members raise your hand. ✓
- All **B** members raise your hand. ✓
- (Repeat until firm.)
b. Today, the **A** member of each pair will read first. The **A** members will read from the beginning of the title to the star in the middle of the story. Everybody, touch that star. ✓
- The **B** members will start at the star and read to the end of the story.
c. Remember the rules: The student who is not reading follows along. If there is a mistake, that student points out the error and tells the correct word. If there is a problem, raise your hand, and I'll help you.
- **A** members, start reading. Raise your hand when you've read to the star. (Observe students and give feedback.)
- (As **A** members complete their reading, direct **B** members to read from the star to the end of the story. Praise teams that follow the rules.)

EXERCISE 7

WRITTEN ITEMS

Story Items

a. Find part B on your worksheet. ✓
- These questions are about today's story. Today's story told about Henry and Tim.

I'll read each item and call on someone to answer it. Follow along. Don't write anything until I tell you to write.
b. (For each item: Read the item. Call on a student to answer it.)
- Item 10: What was the name of the young goose? [*Tim.*]
- Item 11: When was that goose born? [Ideas: *In June; several months earlier.*]
- Item 12: How old was he? The choices are **more than a year, less than half a year,** and **more than half a year.** What's the answer? [*Less than half a year.*]
- Later, you'll underline that answer.
- Item 13: When young geese learn to fly, they hold their wings out as they blank. The choices are **walk, run,** and **swim.** What's the answer? [*Run.*]
- Item 14: Tim couldn't learn to fly because he couldn't blank. What's the answer? [*Run.*]
- Item 15: Was his leg still hurt? [*No.*]
- Item 16: **Underline** the 2 things that Henry said he would do for Tim. What will you underline? [*Teach him how to fly; tell him how to get to Florida.*]

Review Items

c. There are review items in part D of your textbook. You'll write those answers on lined paper.
- **Take out a piece of lined paper.** ✓
- Write your name at the top of the paper. ✓
- Number your paper from 1 through 13. Skip every other line. Pencils down when you're finished.
(Observe students and give feedback.)
d. Find part D in your textbook. ✓
- Item 1: What's the name of geese that are all white? [*Snow geese.*]
- Item 2: What's the name of geese that are gray and black and white? [*Canada geese.*]
- Item 3: What color are all geese when they are born? [*Yellow.*]
- Item 4: How old are geese when they mate for the first time? [*3 years old.*]
- Item 5: After male and female geese mate, how long do they stay together? [*Idea: Until one goose dies.*]
- Item 6: Most geese live for about blank years. What's the answer? [*30.*]
- Item 7: Geese live in large groups called blank. What's the answer? [*Flocks.*]

- Item 8: Where are most wild geese born? *[Canada.]*
- Item 9: In which direction do geese fly in the fall? *[South.]*
- Item 10: What is the trip called? The choices are **migration, mating,** and **hibernation.** What's the answer? *[Migration.]*
- Item 11: How had Henry felt ever since his wife had died? [Idea: *Lonely.*]
- Item 12: When geese learn to fly, do they start in the water or on the land? *[On the land.]*
- Item 13: They run with their <u>blank</u> out to the side. What's the answer? *[Wings.]*

End-of-Lesson Activities

INDEPENDENT WORK

Now you're going to complete the written work without looking at the story. Start with part B of your worksheet. Then do the items in part D of your textbook, beginning with item 1. Read the items to yourself and answer them. Raise your hand when you've finished. (Observe students and give feedback.)

WORKCHECK

Note: Students will need marking pens or pencils of a different color.

a. We're going to check the rest of the answers on your worksheet and the answers on your lined paper. Here are the rules: Use your marking pencil to make an **X** next to any item that is wrong. If the answer is right, don't make any mark. If it's wrong, make an **X** next to it. Don't change any answers and don't mark over any answers.
b. Let's start with part B of your worksheet. (For each item: Read the item. Call on a student to answer it. If the answer is wrong, say the correct answer.)
   - Item 10: What was the name of the young goose? *[Tim.]*
   - Item 11: When was that goose born? [Ideas: *In June; several months earlier.*]

- Item 12: How old was he? The choices are **more than a year, less than half a year,** and **more than half a year.** What's the answer? *[Less than half a year.]*
- Item 13: When young geese learn to fly, they hold their wings out as they <u>blank</u>. The choices are **walk, run,** and **swim.** What's the answer? *[Run.]*
- Item 14: Tim couldn't learn to fly because he couldn't <u>blank</u>. What's the answer? *[Run.]*
- Item 15: Was his leg still hurt? *[No.]*
- Item 16: **Underline** the 2 things that Henry said he would do for Tim. What did you underline? *[Teach him how to fly; tell him how to get to Florida.]*

c. Now let's check the items on your lined paper.
   - Item 1: What's the name of geese that are all white? *[Snow geese.]*
   - Item 2: What's the name of geese that are gray and black and white? *[Canada geese.]*
   - Item 3: What color are all geese when they are born? *[Yellow.]*
   - Item 4: How old are geese when they mate for the first time? *[3 years old.]*
   - Item 5: After male and female geese mate, how long do they stay together? [Idea: *Until one goose dies.*]
   - Item 6: Most geese live for about <u>blank</u> years. What's the answer? *[30.]*
   - Item 7: Geese live in large groups called <u>blank</u>. What's the answer? *[Flocks.]*
   - Item 8: Where are most wild geese born? *[Canada.]*
   - Item 9: In which direction do geese fly in the fall? *[South.]*
   - Item 10: What is the trip called? The choices are **migration, mating,** and **hibernation.** What's the answer? *[Migration.]*
   - Item 11: How had Henry felt ever since his wife had died? [Idea: *Lonely.*]
   - Item 12: When geese learn to fly, do they start in the water or on the land? *[On the land.]*
   - Item 13: They run with their <u>blank</u> out to the side. What's the answer? *[Wings.]*
d. Now use your marking pencil to fix any items you got wrong. Do not erase anything you wrote. Write the correct answer close to the answer that is wrong.

Remember, before you hand in your independent work, all the items you missed must be fixed. (Observe students and give feedback.)

e. (At the end of the workcheck, have students record the total number of errors they made at the top of their lined paper.)

(Present Language Arts lesson 3 after completing Reading lesson 3. See Language Arts Guide.)

EXERCISE 1

VOCABULARY REVIEW

a. Here's the new vocabulary sentence: The horses became restless on the dangerous route.
- Everybody, say the sentence. Get ready. (Signal.) *The horses became restless on the dangerous route.*
- (Repeat until firm.)

b. What word tells about how you get to a place? (Signal.) *Route.*
- What word tells about how you feel when you want to do something different? (Signal.) *Restless.*

EXERCISE 2

READING WORDS

Column 1

a. **Find lesson 4 in your textbook.** ✓
- Touch column 1. ✓
- (Teacher reference:)

1. route	4. above
2. receive	5. equator
3. unfrozen	6. anymore

b. Word 1 is **route.** What word? (Signal.) *Route.*
- Spell **route.** Get ready. (Tap for each letter.) *R-O-U-T-E.*

c. Word 2 is **receive.** What word? (Signal.) *Receive.*
- Spell **receive.** Get ready. (Tap for each letter.) *R-E-C-E-I-V-E.*
- **Receive** means **get.** When you get a letter in the mail, you receive a letter in the mail. Everybody, what's another way of saying **She got a puppy for her birthday?** (Signal.) *She received a puppy for her birthday.*

d. Word 3 is **unfrozen.** What word? (Signal.) *Unfrozen.*
- The prefix **un** means **not.** So what does **unfrozen** mean? (Signal.) *Not frozen.*

e. Word 4 is **above.** What word? (Signal.) *Above.*
- (Repeat for words 5 and 6.)

f. Let's read those words again, the fast way.
- Word 1. What word? (Signal.) *Route.*
- (Repeat for words 2–6.)

g. (Repeat step f until firm.)

Column 2

h. Find column 2. ✓
- (Teacher reference:)

1. circles	4. training
2. glided	5. dived
3. barns	

- All these words have endings.

i. Word 1. What word? (Signal.) *Circles.*
- (Repeat for words 2–5.)

j. (Repeat step i until firm.)

Individual Turns

(For columns 1 and 2: Call on individual students, each to read one to three words per turn.)

EXERCISE 3

COMPREHENSION PASSAGE

a. Find part B in your textbook. ✓
- You're going to read the next story about Henry. First you'll read the information passage. It gives some facts about the earth. Remember to follow along.

b. Everybody, touch the title. ✓
- (Call on a student to read the title.) *[Facts About the Earth.]*
- Everybody, what's the title? (Signal.) *Facts About the Earth.*

c. (Call on individual students to read the passage, each student reading two or three sentences at a time. Ask the specified questions as the students read.)

Facts About the Earth
Some places on the earth are colder and some places are hotter. Here are some facts you need to know about the earth.
- **The earth is shaped like a ball.**

- Everybody, say that fact. Get ready. (Signal.) *The earth is shaped like a ball.*
- (Repeat until firm.)

It doesn't look like it's that shape because the earth is very large. Pictures of the earth that are taken from a spaceship show that the earth is shaped like a ball.

Picture 1

- Picture 1 shows the earth. This picture was taken from a spaceship that was near the moon. You can see the blue parts and white parts on the earth. The blue parts are water. Touch a blue part. ✓
- The white parts are clouds. Touch a white part. ✓
- Everybody, listen: What are the blue parts of the earth? (Signal.) *Water.*
- What are the white parts of the earth? (Signal.) *Clouds.*

The hottest part of the earth is called the equator. You can see the equator in picture 2.

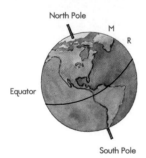

North Pole
M
R
Equator
South Pole

Picture 2

- Everybody, what's the name of the hottest part of the earth? (Signal.) *Equator.*
- Touch the equator in picture 2. ✓

The equator is a pretend line that goes around the fattest part of the earth.

- Everybody, say that fact. Get ready.

(Signal.) *The equator is a pretend line that goes around the fattest part of the earth.*
- Is the equator a real line that you would find on the earth? (Signal.) *No.*
- If you look at picture 1, you don't see an equator. It's just a pretend line around the fattest part of the earth.

The coldest parts of the earth are called the poles.

- Everybody, say that fact. Get ready. (Signal.) *The coldest parts of the earth are called the poles.*

You can see two poles in picture 2. The pole on top is called the North Pole. The pole on the bottom is called the South Pole.

- Everybody, what are the coldest parts of the earth called? (Signal.) *Poles.*
- How many poles are there? (Signal.) *Two.*
- What's the name of the pole on top of the earth? (Signal.) *North Pole.*
- What's the name of the pole on the bottom of the earth? (Signal.) *South Pole.*
- The poles are pretend marks. You don't see any poles on the earth in picture 1.

The farther you go from the equator, the colder it gets.

- Everybody, say that fact. Get ready. (Signal.) *The farther you go from the equator, the colder it gets.*
- Look at the letters R and M in picture 2. Raise your hand when you know which letter is farther from the equator.
- Everybody, which letter is farther from the equator? (Signal.) *M.*
- So which letter is at the colder place? (Signal.) *M.*
- How do you know it's not colder at place R? (Call on a student. Idea: *It's not farther from the equator.*)

The poles are the parts of the earth that are farthest from the equator.

- Everybody, which parts of the earth are farthest from the equator? (Signal.) *The poles.*

- That's why they are the coldest parts of the earth. If you wanted to live where it never got cold and never snowed in the wintertime, would you live **very close** to the equator or **not very close** to the equator? (Signal.) *Very close to the equator.*
- If you wanted to live where the winters were very cold, would you live **very close** to the equator or **not very close** to the equator? (Signal.) *Not very close to the equator.*

EXERCISE 4

STORY READING

a. Find part C in your textbook. ✓
- The error limit for this story is 9 errors.

b. Everybody, touch the title. ✓
- (Call on a student to read the title.) *[Tim Has a Flying Lesson.]*
- Everybody, what's the title? (Signal.) *Tim Has a Flying Lesson.*

c. (Call on individual students to read the story, each student reading two or three sentences at a time. Ask the specified questions as the students read.)

- (Correct errors: Tell the word. Direct the student to reread the sentence.)
- (If the group makes more than 9 errors, direct the students to reread the story.)

Tim Has a Flying Lesson
The morning was cold and still. Ice had formed all around the shore of the lake. Tim said, "Wow, it's really cold this morning."

"Yes," Old Henry said, "and if you're going to get on your way to Florida before it gets even colder, we'd better start on your training today."

- What was the weather like? (Call on a student. Idea: *Very cold.*)
- Everybody, did Henry think it was going to get even colder? (Signal.) *Yes.*
- What did Henry say they better start doing today? (Call on a student. Ideas: *Start Tim's training; start teaching Tim how to fly.*)

So Henry explained what Tim had to do. He had to run with his wings held straight out to the sides. Then Henry would honk. That honk told Tim to start flapping his wings. "I'll bet you can do it the first time we try," Henry said.

- What was the first thing Tim was supposed to do with his wings? (Call on a student. Idea: *Hold them straight out to the sides.*)
- What was Tim supposed to do when Henry honked? (Call on a student. Idea: *Start flapping his wings.*)
- Then what was supposed to happen? (Call on a student. Idea: *Tim would fly.*)

Henry and Tim went to a hill near the lake. Henry said, "Just run down this hill as fast as you can. Remember to keep those wings out to the side."
Then Henry took off and circled above Tim. "Go," Henry said, and Tim went—running as fast as he could.
Henry honked and Tim started flapping his wings. "That's it," Henry honked. "Keep flapping."
Tim took off, but as soon as he did, he became frightened and stopped flapping. Plop. He fell back down to the ground and tumbled over and over.

- Everybody, was Tim able to get into the air? (Signal.) *Yes.*
- Why did he stop flapping his wings? (Call on a student. Idea: *Because he got scared.*)
- What happened when he stopped flapping? (Call on a student. Idea: *He fell to the ground.*)

Henry landed next to him and laughed. "Well," Henry said, "at least you got into the air. Now all you have to do is learn how to stay up there. ✦ You have to keep flapping after you take off."
Tim said, "But I got scared."
Henry said, "Well, just remember: Geese are made for flying. It's nothing to be scared about. I'll fly in front of you. Just keep looking at me and do what I do."

- Everybody, did the fall hurt Tim? (Signal.) *No.*
- What did Henry tell Tim he had to do after taking off? (Signal.) *Keep flapping.*
- Where was Henry going to fly the next time Tim tried? (Call on a student. Idea: *In front of Tim.*)
- What was Tim supposed to do? (Call on a student. Idea: *Keep looking at Henry and do what Henry does.*)

> **So they tried again. This time, Henry made sure that he was right in front of Tim when he took off. Henry honked and honked. "Keep flapping and look at me."**
>
> **The two geese flew all the way across the lake and over the hill on the other side. Henry turned around to look at Tim. He didn't look scared anymore. He had a big smile on his face. He honked, "This is great. I love it."**

- Where did the geese go after they took off? (Call on a student. Idea: *Across the lake and over the hill on the other side.*)

> **"Well, just keep doing what I do," Henry said.**
>
> **Henry led Tim up higher and higher, more than a mile high. Then Henry held his wings out to the side and glided. Tim followed. The birds turned and swooped and dived and climbed. At last Henry said, "Now we're going to land. We'll go in the water. Remember to do what I do."**
>
> **Henry came down and made a perfect landing in the water. Tim also made a landing, but it was not perfect. He was going too fast, and he landed with a great splash. Both geese laughed. Tim shouted, "I can fly."**
>
> **"You sure can," Henry said.**

- How high did Henry and Tim go? (Call on a student. Idea: *Over a mile high.*)
- Where did the geese land? (Call on a student. Idea: *On the lake.*)
- Everybody, who made a perfect landing? (Signal.) *Henry.*
- Why wasn't Tim's landing perfect? (Call on a student. Idea: *He was going too fast.*)

- Everybody, was Tim pretty happy? (Signal.) *Yes.*

PAIRED PRACTICE

a. You're going to work in pairs. Today, the **B** member of each pair will read first. They will read from the beginning of the title to the star in the middle of the story. Then the **A** members will read from the star to the end of the story.

b. Remember: The student who is not reading follows along. If there is a mistake, that student points out the error and tells the correct word.

- **B** members, start reading. When you're done, **A** members read. Raise your hand when your pair is finished.
(Observe students and give feedback.)

WRITTEN ITEMS

Comprehension Passage Items

a. **Find part A on your worksheet.** ✓
- The questions in part A are about the earth. I'll call on individual students to read the items and say the answers. Follow along. Don't write anything until I tell you to write.

b. (For each item: Call on a student to read and answer the item.)
- Look at the map below.

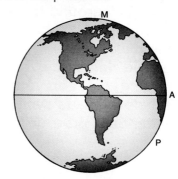

- Item 1. *[What's the name of the place shown by the letter **A**? Equator.]*
- Item 2. *[Which letter shows the coldest place? M.]*
- Item 3. *[Which letter shows the hottest place? A.]*
- Item 4. *[Which letter is farthest from the equator? M.]*
- Item 5. *[The earth is shaped like a ball.]*
- Item 6. *[The hottest part of the earth is called the equator.]*

- Item 7. *[What's the name of the line that goes around the fattest part of the earth?* **Equator.*]**
- Item 8. *[What's the name of the spot that's at the top of the earth?* **North Pole.*]**
- Item 9. *[What's the name of the spot that's at the bottom of the earth?* **South Pole.*]**
- Item 10. *[The <u>poles</u> are the coldest places on the earth and the <u>equator</u> is the hottest place on the earth.]*
- Item 11. *[How many poles are there? 2.]*
- Item 12. *[Are the equator and the poles* **real marks** *on the earth or* **pretend marks?** *Pretend marks.]*
- Item 13. *[The farther you go from the equator, the <u>colder</u> it gets.]*

Story Items

c. Find part B on your worksheet. ✓
- Items 14 through 22 are about today's story.
d. Item 14. *[Henry taught Tim to fly. Tim was supposed to run down <u>the hill</u> and hold his <u>wings</u> out to the side.]*
- Item 15. *[What was Tim supposed to do when Henry honked?* Idea: *Start flapping his wings.]*
- Item 16. *[Did Tim take off the first time he tried? Yes.]*
- Item 17. *[Did he keep on flying? No.]*
- Item 18. *[Why?* Idea: *He got scared.]*
- Item 19. *[Did Tim do better the second time he tried? Yes.]*
- Item 20. *[How high did the geese fly?* Idea: *More than a mile high.]*
- Item 21. *[Where did they land?* Ideas: *In the water; on Big Trout Lake.]*
- Item 22. *[Who was going too fast when they landed? Tim.]*

Review Items

e. The rest of the items for today's lesson are in your textbook. Find part D in your textbook. ✓
- These are review items. I'll read the items. Don't say the answers.
- Item 1: You can tell male geese from female geese because <u>blank</u>. The choices are **male geese are larger, male geese have brighter colors,** and **male geese have longer feathers.**
- Item 2: What was the name of the lake where Henry's flock stayed during the summer?

- Item 3: In which season did the flock leave the lake?
- Item 4: In which direction did the flock fly?
- Item 5: How far was the flock going?
- Item 6: Geese live in large groups called <u>blank</u>.
- Item 7: Where are most wild geese born?
- Look at the map.
- Item 8: What country is the red dot in?
- Item 9: What country is the blue dot in?
- Item 10: What **state** is the blue dot in?
- Item 11: If you started at the red dot and went to the blue dot, in which direction would you go?

End-of-Lesson Activities

INDEPENDENT WORK

Now finish the written work for lesson 4. Remember, don't look at the story. Start with your worksheet. Then do the items in your textbook. Write the answers for the textbook items on lined paper. Raise your hand when you're finished. (Observe students and give feedback.)

WORKCHECK

a. (Open Answer Key book to lesson 4 and direct students to take out their marking pencils.)
- We're going to check your independent work. Let's start with your worksheet. Remember, if you got an item wrong, make an **X** next to the item. Don't change any answers.
b. (For each worksheet item: Read the item. Call on a student to answer it. If the answer is wrong, say the correct answer. Refer to the Answer Key for the correct answers.)
c. Now let's check your textbook items.
- (Repeat step b for all textbook items.)
d. Now use your marking pencil to fix any items you got wrong. Remember, all mistakes must be fixed before you hand in your independent work.

LANGUAGE ARTS

(Present Language Arts lesson 4 after completing Reading lesson 4. See Language Arts Guide.)

Lesson 5

EXERCISE 1

VOCABULARY REVIEW

a. You learned a sentence that tells what the horses did.
- Everybody, say that sentence. Get ready. (Signal.) *The horses became restless on the dangerous route.*
- (Repeat until firm.)

b. What word tells about how you feel when you want to do something different? (Signal.) *Restless.*
- What word tells about how you get to a place? (Signal.) *Route.*

c. Once more. Say the sentence that tells what the horses did. Get ready. (Signal.) *The horses became restless on the dangerous route.*

EXERCISE 2

READING WORDS

Column 1

a. **Find lesson 5 in your textbook.** ✓
- Touch column 1. ✓
- (Teacher reference:)

1. dangers	4. circles
2. receives	5. lakes
3. barns	

- All these words end with the letter **S.**
b. Word 1 is **dangers.** What word? (Signal.) *Dangers.*
- Spell **dangers.** Get ready. (Tap for each letter.) *D-A-N-G-E-R-S.*
- Something that's a **danger** is something that is not safe. Icy roads are a danger. Who can name something else that's a danger? (Call on individual students. Accept reasonable responses.)
c. Word 2. What word? (Signal.) *Receives.*
- Spell **receives.** Get ready. (Tap for each letter.) *R-E-C-E-I-V-E-S.*
d. Word 3. What word? (Signal.) *Barns.*
- Spell **barns.** Get ready. (Tap for each letter.) *B-A-R-N-S.*

e. Word 4. What word? (Signal.) *Circles.*
- Spell **circles.** Get ready. (Tap for each letter.) *C-I-R-C-L-E-S.*
f. Word 5. What word? (Signal.) *Lakes.*
g. Let's read those words again, the fast way.
- Word 1. What word? (Signal.) *Dangers.*
- (Repeat for words 2–5.)
h. (Repeat step g until firm.)

Column 2

i. Find column 2. ✓
- (Teacher reference:)

1. foolish	3. daytime
2. below	4. unfrozen

- Part of each word is underlined. You'll read that part. Then you'll read the whole word.
j. Word 1. What's the underlined part? (Signal.) *fool.*
- What's the whole word? (Signal.) *Foolish.*
- Something that is **foolish** is the opposite of wise. Everybody, what's the opposite of **a wise choice?** (Signal.) *A foolish choice.*
- What's the opposite of **a foolish person?** (Signal.) *A wise person.*
- Word 2. What's the underlined part? (Signal.) *be.*
- What's the whole word? (Signal.) *Below.*
- Word 3. What's the underlined part? (Signal.) *day.*
- What's the whole word? (Signal.) *Daytime.*
- Word 4. What's the underlined part? (Signal.) *un.*
- What's the whole word? (Signal.) *Unfrozen.*
k. Let's read those words again, the fast way.
- Word 1. What word? (Signal.) *Foolish.*
- (Repeat for words 2–4.)
l. (Repeat step k until firm.)

Column 3

m. Find column 3. ✓

- (Teacher reference:)

1. trout	4. neck
2. sprang	5. confused
3. route	

n. Word 1. What word? (Signal.) *Trout.*
- A **trout** is a fish. Trout are good to eat.
o. Word 2. What word? (Signal.) *Sprang.*
- If a lion jumps at something today, we say the lion springs. If a lion jumped at something yesterday, we say the lion **sprang.** What do we say if a lion jumped at something yesterday? (Signal.) *The lion sprang.*
p. Word 3. What word? (Signal.) *Route.*
- (Repeat for words 4 and 5.)
q. Let's read those words again.
- Word 1. What word? (Signal.) *Trout.*
- (Repeat for words 2–5.)
r. (Repeat step q until firm.)

Individual Turns

(For columns 1–3: Call on individual students, each to read one to three words per turn.)

EXERCISE 3

COMPREHENSION PASSAGE

a. Find part B in your textbook. ✓
- In today's story, Tim gets better at flying. First you'll read the information passage. It gives more facts about the equator. Remember to follow along.
b. Everybody, touch the title. ✓
- (Call on a student to read the title.) *[Facts About the Equator.]*
- Everybody, what's the title? (Signal.) *Facts About the Equator.*
c. (Call on individual students to read the passage, each student reading two or three sentences at a time. Ask the specified questions as the students read.)

> **Facts About the Equator**
> You've learned about the poles and the equator. Let's see how much you remember.
> **How many poles are there?**

- Everybody, what's the answer? (Signal.) *Two.*

> **What are they called?**

- What's the answer? (Call on a student.) *[North Pole and South Pole.]*
- Everybody, touch the North Pole on the picture. ✓
- Touch the South Pole. ✓

> **What do we call the line that goes around the fattest part of the earth?**

- Everybody, what's the answer? (Signal.) *Equator.*

> **Where is the hottest part of the earth?**

- Everybody, what's the answer? (Signal.) *At the equator.*
- Touch the equator on the picture. ✓

> **Which parts of the earth are the coldest?**

- Everybody, what's the answer? (Signal.) *Poles.*

> **The heat that the earth receives comes from the sun.**

- That's an important rule. Everybody, say that rule. Get ready. (Signal.) *The heat that the earth receives comes from the sun.*

> **The equator is the hottest part of the earth because it receives more heat from the sun than any other place on the earth.**

- Why is the equator the hottest part of the earth? (Call on a student. Idea: *Because it gets more heat from the sun than any other place on the earth.*)

> **The poles are the coldest places on the earth because they receive less heat from the sun than any other place on the earth.**

- Why are the poles the coldest places on the earth? (Call on a student. Idea: *Because they get less heat from the sun than any other place on the earth.*)

STORY READING

a. Find part C in your textbook. ✓
- The error limit for this story is 11 errors.

b. Everybody, touch the title. ✓
- (Call on a student to read the title.) *[Tim Practices Flying.]*
- Everybody, what's the title? (Signal.) *Tim Practices Flying.*

c. (Call on individual students to read the story, each student reading two or three sentences at a time. Ask the specified questions as the students read.)

- (Correct errors: Tell the word. Direct the student to reread the sentence.)
- (If the group makes more than 11 errors, direct the students to reread the story.)

Tim Practices Flying
The two geese spent most of the next three days flying. Tim needed the practice, and Old Henry felt warmer when he was flying rather than swimming on that lake. There wasn't much room to swim anymore because most of the lake was frozen. Only some small circles near the middle were unfrozen.

- Everybody, what did Tim spend most of the next three days doing? (Signal.) *Flying.*
- Did Henry mind practicing with Tim? (Signal.) *No.*
- Why not? (Call on a student. Idea: *Because he felt warmer when he was flying.*)
- How much of the lake was frozen by the end of the third day? (Call on a student. Idea: *Most of it.*)

So Tim practiced and Old Henry gave him directions. By the third day, Tim could land on land and in the water. He still had trouble taking off from the water, but he could do it.
As the sun was setting on the third day, Old Henry said, "Well, my boy, the lake will be completely frozen tomorrow, so tomorrow is the time for you to go south."

- After they practiced for three days, what could Tim do well? (Call on a student. Idea: *Land on land and in the water.*)

- What could he do, but not well? (Call on a student. Idea: *Take off from the water.*)
- How much of the lake was frozen? (Call on a student. Idea: *Most of it.*)
- What did Henry say the lake would be like the following morning? (Call on a student. Idea: *Completely frozen.*)

Old Henry started to tell Tim how to get to Florida. The route was not simple. There were landing places about every 300 miles. Tim would have to land at each place and spend one or two nights. Then he would take off and go to the next landing place.

- Everybody, was the route to Florida simple? (Signal.) *No.*
- About how far apart were the landing places? (Signal.) *300 miles.*
- How long would Tim plan to stay at each landing place? (Call on a student. Idea: *One or two nights.*)
- Then what would he have to do? (Call on a student. Idea: *Fly on to the next landing place.*)

Old Henry started to tell Tim about each landing place. But Tim had trouble understanding the directions.
Old Henry started out by saying, "You take off from this lake and fly south and east. By about the middle of the afternoon, you'll come to a field that is next to a pond. The field has two barns. One is red and . . ."
Tim said, "I don't know which way south is."
"Of course you do," Henry said. "All geese know north from south."
"But I . . ." Tim said.

- What do you think Tim was going to say? (Call on a student. Idea: *I don't.*)
- Everybody, did he think he knew which direction south was? (Signal.) *No.*
- What did Henry say about north and south? (Call on a student. Idea: *That all geese know north and south.*)

Henry said, "Do this for me. ★ Take off, go high and go in the direction that feels really good. Fly in that direction for a little while and then come back here."

Tim went up and circled around and then he started flying directly south. Soon he came back and landed next to Henry.

Henry said, "You were flying south. All geese like that direction in the fall. In the spring, they like the opposite direction, north."

- Listen to that part again.
  Henry said, "You were flying south. All geese like that direction in the fall. In the spring, they like the opposite direction, north."
- Everybody, which direction do geese like in the fall? (Signal.) *South.*
- That's the direction they fly in the fall.
- Which direction do they like in the spring? (Signal.) *North.*
- That's the direction they fly in the spring.

Then Henry said, "Let's talk some more about the flight to Florida. The first stop is that field with the two barns. The next morning, you'll take off from that field but you won't fly exactly south. You'll go a little to the east."

Tim looked confused. He said, "I'm not sure I can remember all this. I don't know how you can remember it."

Old Henry said, "Oh, once you go to a landing spot, you'll remember it for the rest of your life. You'll know exactly how to get there and exactly what it looks like."

- Everybody, was Tim able to understand Henry's directions? (Signal.) *No.*
- Henry said that once Tim went to a landing spot, something would happen. What's that? (Call on a student. Idea: *He'd remember it for the rest of his life.*)

Then Old Henry tried again to tell Tim about the landing places. But by the time Henry had explained how to reach the third one, he could see that Tim was just about ready to start crying. "I'm sorry," Tim said, "but I just can't keep all this straight. How many landing places are there between here and Florida?"

Old Henry said, "Five," and Tim got a big tear in his eye.

"I can't do it," Tim said. "I'll never remember how to get there."

Old Henry said, "Well, we'll figure out some way to get you there."

- Why was Tim feeling sad? (Call on a student. Idea: *He didn't think he could remember enough to get to Florida.*)
- Everybody, how many landing places were there? (Signal.) *Five.*
- It would be hard to remember them if somebody told you about them but you hadn't seen them. Henry said, "We'll figure out some way to get you there." What do you think Henry could do to make sure Tim finds the landing places? (Call on individual students. Idea: Student preference.)

PAIRED PRACTICE

a. You're going to work in pairs. Today, the **A** member of each pair will read first. They will read from the beginning of the title to the star in the middle of the story. Then the **B** members will read from the star to the end of the story.
b. Remember: The student who is not reading follows along. If there is a mistake, that student points out the error and tells the correct word.
- **A** members, start reading. When you're done, **B** members read. Raise your hand when your pair is finished.
  (Observe students and give feedback.)

WRITTEN ITEMS

Comprehension Passage Items

a. **Find part A on your worksheet.** ✓
- The questions in part A are about the heat the earth receives. I'll call on individual students to read the items and say the answers. Follow along. Don't write anything until I tell you to write.
b. (For each item: Call on a student to read and answer the item.)
- Item 1. *[The heat that the earth receives comes from the <u>sun</u>.]*
- Item 2. *[The part of the earth that receives more heat than any other part is the <u>equator</u>.]*

- Item 3. [*The parts of the earth that receive less heat than any other part are called the <u>poles</u>.*]

Story Items

c. Find part B on your worksheet. ✓
- Items 4 through 11 in part B are about today's story.
d. Item 4. [*How many days did Tim practice flying? 3.*]
- Item 5. [*When Tim flew in the direction that felt best, in which direction did he fly? South.*]
- Item 6. [*How much of the lake was frozen by the end of the third day that Tim practiced? Almost all.*]
- Item 7. [*How much of the lake did Henry think would be frozen by the next morning? All.*]
- Item 8. [*Was Tim able to understand what Henry explained about the landing places? No.*]
- Item 9. [*How many landing places are there on the trip to Florida? 5.*]
- Item 10. [*The first landing place is a field next to a <u>pond</u>.*]
- Item 11. [*That landing place has <u>two barns</u> on it.*]

Skill Items

e. Items 12 and 13 are about the vocabulary sentence you learned. The sentence above item 12 says: The horses became restless on the dangerous route.
- Item 12: What word tells about how you get to a place? Everybody, what's the answer? (Signal.) *Route.*
- Item 13: What word tells how you feel when you want to do something different? Everybody, what's the answer? (Signal.) *Restless.*

Review Items

f. The rest of the items on your worksheet are review items. I'll read the items. Don't say the answers.
- Item 14: In which direction do geese fly in the fall?
- Item 15: What is this trip called?
- Item 16: In which direction do geese fly in the spring?
- Item 17: Write the directions **north, south, east,** and **west** in the boxes.
- Item 18: Make a line that starts at the circle on the map and goes east.

- Item 19: If you start at the circle and move to the number **3,** in which direction do you go?
g. Find part D in your textbook. ✓
- These are more review items. I'll read the items. Don't say the answers.
- Item 1: What country is the green dot in?
- Item 2: What country is the purple dot in?
- Item 3: What state is the purple dot in?
- Item 4: If you started at the purple dot and went to the green dot, in which direction would you go?
- Item 5: The earth is shaped like a <u>blank</u>.
- Item 6: The hottest part of the earth is called the <u>blank</u>.
- Item 7: What's the name of the line that goes around the fattest part of the earth?
- Item 8: What's the name of the spot that's at the top of the earth?
- Item 9: What's the name of the spot that's at the bottom of the earth?
- Item 10: The <u>blanks</u> are the coldest places on the earth and the <u>blank</u> is the hottest place on the earth.
- Item 11: How many poles are there?
- Item 12: The farther you go from the equator, the <u>blank</u> it gets.
- Item 13: What's the name of the place shown by the letter **C**?
- Item 14: Which letter shows the coldest place?
- Item 15: Which letter shows the hottest place?
- Item 16: Which letter is farthest from the equator?

End-of-Lesson Activities

INDEPENDENT WORK

Now finish the written work for lesson 5. Remember, don't look at the story. If an item has choices, you underline the right choice. Start with your worksheet. Then do the items in your textbook. Raise your hand when you're finished. (Observe students and give feedback.)

WORKCHECK

a. (Direct students to take out their marking pencils.)
- We're going to check your worksheet and textbook items. Let's start with your

worksheet. Remember, if you got an item wrong, make an **X** next to the item. Don't change any answers.

b. (For each worksheet item: Read the item. Call on a student to answer it. If the answer is wrong, say the correct answer. Refer to the Answer Key for the correct answers.)

c. Now let's check your textbook items.

• (Repeat step b for textbook items.)

d. Now use your marking pencil to fix any items you got wrong. Remember, all mistakes must be fixed before you hand in your independent work.

LANGUAGE ARTS

(Present Language Arts lesson 5 after completing Reading lesson 5. See Language Arts Guide.)

Lessons 6–10 · Planning Page

	Lesson 6	Lesson 7	Lesson 8	Lesson 9	Lesson 10
Lesson Events	Vocabulary Sentence Reading Words Comprehension Passage Story Reading Paired Practice Written Items Independent Work Workcheck Language Arts	Reading Words Comprehension Passage Story Reading Paired Practice Written Items Independent Work Workcheck Language Arts	Reading Words Comprehension Passage Story Reading Paired Practice Written Items Independent Work Workcheck Language Arts	Reading Words Comprehension Passage Story Reading Paired Practice Written Items Independent Work Workcheck Language Arts	Fact Game Reading Checkouts Test Marking the Test Test Remedies Literature Lesson Language Arts
Vocabulary Sentence	#1: The horses became <u>restless</u> on the dangerous <u>route</u>.				
Reading Words: Word Types	modeled words words with endings mixed words	–er words mixed words	two-syllable words mixed words	modeled words multi-syllable words proper nouns	
New Vocabulary	Michigan Kentucky crooked			constant sir	
Comprehension Passage	*The Sun Lights the Earth*	*Michigan and Kentucky*	*The Sun Heats the Earth*	*The Sun and the Earth*	
Story	*The Geese Leave Big Trout Lake*	*Old Henry Tests Tim*	*A New Plan*	*Flying With the Flock*	
Skill Items					Test: Vocabulary sentence #1
Special Materials					Thermometer charts, dice, Fact Game 10, Fact Game Answer Key, scorecard sheets, *materials for literature lesson
Special Projects/ Activities					Project after lesson 10

*Literature anthology; blackline masters 1A, and 1B; lined paper

EXERCISE 1
VOCABULARY REVIEW

a. You learned a sentence that tells what the horses did.
- Everybody, say that sentence. Get ready. (Signal.) *The horses became restless on the dangerous route.*
- (Repeat until firm.)

b. I'll say part of the sentence. When I stop, you say the next word. Listen: The horses became . . . Everybody, what's the next word? (Signal.) *Restless.*

c. Listen: The horses became restless on the dangerous . . . Everybody, what's the next word? (Signal.) *Route.*
- Say the whole sentence. Get ready. (Signal.) *The horses became restless on the dangerous route.*

EXERCISE 2
READING WORDS

Column 1

a. **Find lesson 6 in your textbook.** ✓
- Touch column 1. ✓
- (Teacher reference:)

1. **Michigan**	3. **crooked**
2. **Kentucky**	4. **triangle**

b. Word 1 is **Michigan.** What word? (Signal.) *Michigan.*
- Spell **Michigan.** Get ready. (Tap for each letter.) *M-I-C-H-I-G-A-N.*
- Michigan is one of the states that touches Canada.

c. Word 2 is **Kentucky.** What word? (Signal.) *Kentucky.*
- Spell **Kentucky.** Get ready. (Tap for each letter.) *K-E-N-T-U-C-K-Y.*
- Kentucky is a state you might go through if you went from Michigan to Florida.

d. Word 3 is **crooked.** What word? (Signal.) *Crooked.*
- Spell **crooked.** Get ready. (Tap for each letter.) *C-R-O-O-K-E-D.*
- **Crooked** is the opposite of **straight.** Everybody, what's the opposite of a straight line? (Signal.) *A crooked line.*
- What's the opposite of a straight arrow? (Signal.) *A crooked arrow.*

e. Word 4 is **triangle.** What word? (Signal.) *Triangle.*
- Spell **triangle.** Get ready. (Tap for each letter.) *T-R-I-A-N-G-L-E.*

f. Let's read those words again, the fast way.
- Word 1. What word? (Signal.) *Michigan.*
- (Repeat for words 2–4.)

g. (Repeat step f until firm.)

Column 2

h. Find column 2. ✓
- (Teacher reference:)

1. **foolish**	4. **sharper**
2. **dangers**	5. **lakes**
3. **rivers**	

- All these words have an ending.

i. Word 1. What word? (Signal.) *Foolish.*
- (Repeat for words 2–5.)

j. Let's read those words again.
- Word 1. What word? (Signal.) *Foolish.*
- (Repeat for words 2–5.)

k. (Repeat step j until firm.)

Column 3

l. Find column 3. ✓
- (Teacher reference:)

1. **trout**	4. **sprang**
2. **daytime**	5. **neck**
3. **below**	

m. Word 1. What word? (Signal.) *Trout.*
- (Repeat for words 2–5.)

n. Let's read those words again.
- Word 1. What word? (Signal.) *Trout.*
- (Repeat for words 2–5.)

o. (Repeat step n until firm.)

Individual Turns

(For columns 1–3: Call on individual students, each to read one to three words per turn.)

COMPREHENSION PASSAGE

a. Find part B in your textbook. ✓
- You're going to read the next story about Henry and Tim. First you'll read the information passage. It gives some facts about the sun and the earth.

b. Everybody, touch the title. ✓
- (Call on a student to read the title.) *[The Sun Lights the Earth.]*
- Everybody, what's the title? (Signal.) *The Sun Lights the Earth.*

c. (Call on individual students to read the passage, each student reading two or three sentences at a time. Ask the specified questions as the students read.)

> **The Sun Lights the Earth**
> **The sun shines all the time.**

- Everybody, say that rule. Get ready. (Signal.) *The sun shines all the time.*

> **But you can't see the sun all the time. Only half of the earth is in sunlight.**

- Listen to that rule again: Only half of the earth is in sunlight. Everybody, say that rule. Get ready. (Signal.) *Only half of the earth is in sunlight.*

> **You can see the sun if you're on the side of the earth that is closer to the sun.**

- Everybody, can you see the sun if you're on the side of the earth that is closer to the sun? (Signal.) *Yes.*
- Can you see the sun if you're on the side that is not closer to the sun? (Signal.) *No.*

> **It is daytime on the side of the earth where you can see the sun. It is nighttime on the side of the earth where you can't see the sun.**

- Everybody, is it **daytime** or **nighttime** on the side of the earth that is closer to the sun? (Signal.) *Daytime.*
- Touch the side of the earth that is closer to the sun in picture 1. ✓
- For the people who are on that side of the earth, it is daytime.

- Touch the dark side of the earth. ✓
- What time is it for the people on that side of the earth? (Signal.) *Nighttime.*

> **The earth turns around once every 24 hours.**

- Everybody, say that rule. Get ready. (Signal.) *The earth turns around once every 24 hours.*

> **If you lived on the equator, you would have one day and one night during that 24 hours.**

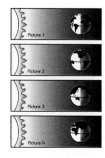

- Look at picture 1. It shows the earth as it turns.
- Everybody, touch the person in picture 1. ✓
- That person is on the equator below the United States.
- Everybody, touch the person in picture 2. ✓
- That is where the person would be six hours later. The earth has turned. For that person, it is now sunset. You can see that the person is still below the United States.
- Touch the person in picture 3. ✓
- This is where the person would be another six hours later. The earth has turned some more. What time of day is it for the person now? (Signal.) *Nighttime.*
- The person is still right below the United States.
- Touch picture 4. ✓
- We can't see the person in that picture because the person is on the part of the earth that we can't see. Where is the United States? (Call on a student. Idea: *On the part of the earth we can't see.*)
- Everybody, how long does it take for the earth to turn all the way around one time? (Signal.) *24 hours.*
- And during that time the person on the equator had one daytime and one nighttime.

STORY READING

a. Find part C in your textbook. ✓
  • The error limit for this story is 14 errors.
b. Everybody, touch the title. ✓
  • (Call on a student to read the title.) *[The Geese Leave Big Trout Lake.]*
  • Everybody, what's the title? (Signal.) *The Geese Leave Big Trout Lake.*
c. (Call on individual students to read the story, each student reading two or three sentences at a time. Ask the specified questions as the students read.)

> • (Correct errors: Tell the word. Direct the student to reread the sentence.)
> • (If the group makes more than 14 errors, direct the students to reread the story.)

The Geese Leave Big Trout Lake

Tim and Old Henry spent the night in a small woods near the lake. In the morning, the lake was completely frozen and the air was even colder than it had been.

Tim said, "I'm supposed to leave today. But I still don't know about all the landing spots. How long do you think it's going to take for me to learn about them?"

Henry said, "Oh, I thought of a different plan. I'll fly along with you part of the way. After we reach the third landing place, I'll head back here."

Tim smiled. "Thank you," he said. "I like this plan a lot better."

• Where did they spend the night? (Call on a student. Idea: *In some woods near the lake.*)
• What was the lake like in the morning? (Call on a student. Idea: *Completely frozen.*)
• What was Henry's new plan? (Call on a student. Idea: *To fly with Tim for the first part of the trip.*)
• Everybody, did Tim like that plan better than trying to learn about the landing places from Henry? (Signal.) *Yes.*

"Well, let's get going then," Henry said. "And remember to follow all the directions I honk out."

"I will," Tim said. And the two geese took off, circled above Big Trout Lake one time, and then headed south.

Old Henry led the way and Tim followed. But Tim got tired after the geese had flown about sixty miles. As they flew over a large lake, Tim said, "Let's land down there for a while. I see a few geese near the shore."

• Everybody, about how far had they gone? (Signal.) *Sixty miles.*
• Who was tired? (Signal.) *Tim.*
• Where did Tim want to land? (Call on a student. Idea: *On a large lake.*)
• Everybody, what did he see near the shore? (Signal.) *Geese.*

Old Henry laughed and said, "Never land where you see only a few geese. You'll find out they are not real geese at all. They are fake geese that hunters use to make other geese think it is safe to land there. But most of the geese that try to land there will get shot."

"Well, where can we land?"

"Two kinds of places are safe," Henry said. "One kind of safe place has hundreds of geese on the water. Another kind of safe place has no geese on the water."

• What are the two kinds of places that are safe? (Call on a student. Idea: *A place that has hundreds of geese and a place that has no geese.*)

Then Henry said, "Pick a safe place for us to land."

Tim said, "That's easy. There are lots of lakes down there, and I don't see ducks or geese on most of them."

"Well, lead the way to a safe place then." And that's what Tim did. The two geese rested there for a while. ⭐ They ate some water plants and took a nap in a field. Then they took off and flew south again.

A few hours later the two geese flew over the landing place where they would spend the night. Old Henry didn't say anything about where they were. He wanted to see if Tim would recognize the place. He didn't. Henry asked him, "Do you see anything interesting down below us?"

Tim looked at the trees, the pond and the two barns in the field. Then he said, "No, what's interesting down there?"

At that moment, Old Henry knew that he would have to do something more than just tell Tim about how to get to Florida on his own.

- What place did they fly over? (Call on a student. Ideas: *The place where they're supposed to spend the night; the place with two barns and a pond.*)
- Everybody, did Tim recognize the place? (Signal.) *No.*
- So Henry knew that he would have to do something more than just tell Tim about how to get to Florida on his own. What do you think he would have to do? (Call on a student. Idea: *Fly with Tim all the way to Florida.*)

The geese landed near the barns. They were empty except for some mice that lived in them. Something didn't smell right to Henry, however. Something told him to get out of this place. Just then, a red fox sprang from the grass and charged toward Tim. Before Tim could take off, the fox had grabbed his tail feathers. "Help," Tim yelled.

Old Henry put his head down and charged at the fox. He bit the fox on the neck and ears. The fox tried to attack Old Henry, but Old Henry kept biting the fox until it ran away.

- Everybody, what was in the barn? (Signal.) *Mice.*
- What was outside in the grass? (Signal.) *A fox.*
- Who did the fox attack? (Signal.) *Tim.*
- Who attacked the fox? (Signal.) *Old Henry.*
- What did the fox finally do when Old Henry kept biting it? (Signal.) *Ran away.*

Henry looked at where the fox had grabbed Tim to make sure that Tim was not hurt. Tim was all right.

Then Old Henry said, "That was a foolish fox. I guess she doesn't know that a full-grown goose is a much better fighter than a fox."

- Everybody, who is a better fighter, a fox or a full-grown goose? (Signal.) *A full-grown goose.*

What Henry didn't tell Tim was that an old goose that tries to fight a fox might hurt itself. Old Henry had a very sore wing. He was glad that he wouldn't have to fly until the morning.

- What was wrong with Henry? (Call on a student. Idea: *He had a sore wing.*)
- How did he get a sore wing? (Call on a student. Idea: *From fighting with the fox.*)

Tim and Henry walked all around to make sure that no other dangers were near the barn. Henry told Tim, "I think it will be safe here if we spend the night in one of these barns." And that's what the geese did.

- Everybody, where did they spend the night? (Signal.) *In one of the barns.*

EXERCISE 5

PAIRED PRACTICE

You're going to read aloud to your partner. Today the **B** members will read first. Then the **A** members will read from the star to the end of the story. (Observe students and give feedback. Praise teams that follow the rules.)

EXERCISE 6

WRITTEN ITEMS

a. **Find lesson 6 on your worksheet.** ✓
- The questions are about the sun and the earth. I'll call on individual students to read the items and say the answers. Follow along. Don't write anything until I tell you to write.
b. (For each item: Call on a student to read and answer the item.)
- Item 1. *[The sun shines <u>all of the time</u>.]*

- Item 2. *[Can you see the sun all day long and all night long? No.]*
- Item 3. *[If you can see the sun, you are on the side of the earth that is <u>closer to the sun</u>.]*
- Item 4. *[If you can see the sun, it is <u>daytime</u> on your side of the earth.]*
- Item 5. *[What is it on the other side of the earth? Nighttime.]*
- Look at the picture.
- Item 6. *[Shade the part of the earth where it is nighttime.]*
- Tell me the letter of the side you'll shade. *[A.]*
- Item 7. *[Which side of the earth is closer to the sun, A or B? B.]*
- Item 8. *[Which side of the earth is in nighttime? A.]*
- Item 9. *[Which side of the earth is in daytime? B.]*
- Item 10. *[The earth turns around one time every <u>24</u> hours.]*
- Item 11. *[Write the letter of the earth that shows the person in daytime. J.]*
- Item 12. *[Write the letter of the earth that shows the person 6 hours later. P.]*
- Item 13. *[Write the letter that shows the person another 6 hours later. F.]*
- Item 14. *[Write the letter that shows the person another 6 hours later. M.]*
- Item 15. *[Which letter shows the place that has the warmest winters? D.]*
- Item 16. *[Which letter shows the place that is closest to the equator? D.]*
- Item 17. *[Which letter shows the place that is closest to a pole? E.]*
- Item 18. *[Is the **North Pole** or the **South Pole** closer to that letter? South Pole.]*

Story Items

c. Find part D in your textbook. ✓
- The questions in part D are about today's story. Follow along. Don't write anything until I tell you to write.
d. (For each item: Call on a student to read and answer the item.)
- Item 1. *[Where did Henry and Tim spend their last night at Big Trout Lake? In the woods.]*
- Item 2. *[In the morning, Henry told Tim that he would <u>fly part of the way with him</u>.]*
- Item 3. *[Henry told Tim, "Don't land where you see <u>a few</u> geese."]*
- Item 4. *[Write the letters of the **2** kinds of places that are safe for geese. A, B.]*

- Item 5. *[When the two geese flew over the landing place, did Tim recognize it? No.]*
- Item 6. *[After they landed, which goose was attacked? Tim.]*
- Item 7. *[What attacked that goose? A fox.]*
- Item 8. *[What did Henry do? Attacked the fox.]*
- Item 9. *[Which is a better fighter, a full-grown goose or a fox? A full-grown goose.]*
- Item 10. *[After the fight, Henry had a sore <u>wing</u>.]*

Review Items

e. The rest of the items are review items from other lessons.

End-of-Lesson Activities

INDEPENDENT WORK

Now finish the written work for lesson 6. Do the worksheet first. For the textbook items, you'll write your answers on your lined paper. Raise your hand when you've finished the worksheet and textbook for lesson 6. (Observe students and give feedback.)

WORKCHECK

a. (Direct students to take out their marking pencils.)
- We're going to check your worksheet and textbook items. Let's start with your worksheet. Remember, if you got an item wrong, make an **X** next to the item. Don't change any answers.
b. (For each worksheet item: Read the item. Call on a student to answer it. If the answer is wrong, say the correct answer. Refer to the Answer Key for the correct answers.)
c. Now let's check your textbook items.
- (Repeat step b for all textbook items.)
d. Now use your marking pencil to fix any items you got wrong. Remember, all mistakes must be fixed before you hand in your independent work.

LANGUAGE ARTS

(Present Language Arts lesson 6 after completing Reading lesson 6. See Language Arts Guide.)

Lesson 7

READING WORDS

Column 1

a. **Find lesson 7 in your textbook.** ✓
- Touch column 1. ✓
- (Teacher reference:)

1. older	3. sharper
2. river	4. fewer

- All these words end with the letters **E-R.**
b. Word 1. What word? (Signal.) *Older.*
- (Repeat for words 2–4.)
c. Let's read those words again.
- Word 1. What word? (Signal.) *Older.*
- (Repeat for words 2–4.)
d. (Repeat step c until firm.)

Column 2

e. Find column 2. ✓
- (Teacher reference:)

1. **Reedy Lake**	4. **Michigan**
2. **Kentucky**	5. **triangle**
3. **crooked**	

f. The words in line 1 are the name of a place. What place? (Signal.) *Reedy Lake.*
g. Word 2. What word? (Signal.) *Kentucky.*
- (Repeat for words 3–5.)
h. (Repeat step g until firm.)

Individual Turns

(For columns 1 and 2: Call on individual students, each to read one to three words per turn.)

COMPREHENSION PASSAGE

a. Find part B in your textbook. ✓
- You're going to read the next story about Henry and Tim. First you'll read the information passage. It gives some facts about two states in the United States.
b. Everybody, touch the title. ✓
- (Call on a student to read the title.) *[Michigan and Kentucky.]*
- Everybody, what's the title? (Signal.) *Michigan and Kentucky.*

- (Call on individual students to read the passage, each student reading two or three sentences at a time. Ask the specified questions as the students read.)

Michigan and Kentucky
The map shows the migration path the geese are following. The map also shows the first three landing places.

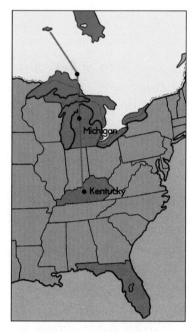

- Everybody, touch the place where the trip began. ✓
(Students should touch Big Trout Lake.)
- What's the name of the country in which the trip began? (Signal.) *Canada.*
- What's the name of the lake? (Signal.) *Big Trout Lake.*

Follow the path from Big Trout Lake to the first landing place.

- Everybody, do it. ✓

What country is that landing place in?

- Everybody, what's the answer? (Signal.) *Canada.*

Follow the path to the next landing place.

- Everybody, do it. ✓

> That landing place is in the United States. It is in a state named Michigan.

- Listen to that part again: That landing place is in the United States. It is in a state named Michigan.
- Everybody, is the landing place in Canada? (Signal.) *No.*
- What country is it in? (Signal.) *United States.*
- What **state** is it in? (Signal.) *Michigan.*
- (Repeat until firm.)

> Follow the path from the landing place in Michigan to the next landing place.

- Everybody, do it. ✓
- What **country** is that landing place in? (Signal.) *United States.*

> That landing place is not in the state of Michigan. It is in the state of Kentucky.

- Everybody, listen: What **state** is that landing place in? (Signal.) *Kentucky.*
- What **country** is that landing place in? *United States.*
- Yes, all the states from Michigan to Florida are in the United States.

EXERCISE 3

STORY READING

a. Find part C in your textbook. ✓
- The error limit for this story is 13 errors.
b. Everybody, touch the title. ✓
- (Call on a student to read the title.) *[Old Henry Tests Tim.]*
- Everybody, what's the title? (Signal.) *Old Henry Tests Tim.*
- (Call on individual students to read the story, each student reading two or three sentences at a time. Ask the specified questions as the students read.)

> - (Correct errors: Tell the word. Direct the student to reread the sentence.)
> - (If the group makes more than 13 errors, direct the students to reread the story.)

Old Henry Tests Tim
Old Henry's wing was very sore the next morning, but he didn't tell Tim about it. Before the geese took off, Old Henry tried to explain the next landing place to Tim. It was a field that had a stream running through it. The field was shaped like a triangle. It had a large grove of trees on the east side of the triangle. Old Henry even scratched a map in the dirt. It showed the landing place, the stream and the trees. "Remember, that's the place we're looking for this afternoon. I won't tell you when we're there. You'll have to tell me when we're there."

- Everybody, look at the picture. Touch the field that is shaped like a triangle. ✓
- Touch the stream in the picture. ✓

> **Henry didn't know how well Tim would do, but Henry had to find out. Henry knew that Tim didn't learn if Henry just described the place. But Henry hoped that Tim would do better if he saw a map.**

- Do you think he'll do better after he sees the map? (Call on a student. Idea: Student preference.)

So the geese took off and flew south. About an hour before they came to the landing place, Old Henry tested Tim. Old Henry said, "Look down there and tell me if you see anything that is interesting." Tim looked down and then looked at Old Henry. Tim said, "I think that's where we are supposed to land. Am I right?"

"No," Old Henry said. "That is not the place."

Tim said, "I'm sorry. I guess I am not very smart."

"You're doing fine," Henry said.

- Why did Tim think that they were over the landing place? (Call on a student. Idea: *Henry said the same thing he had said when they were over the first landing place.*)
- Why did Henry say that Tim was doing fine? (Call on a student. Idea: *Because he didn't want Tim to feel bad.*)

But Tim was not doing fine. An hour later the geese flew over the stream and the field shaped like a triangle. After they had flown past it, Old Henry said, "Our landing place is back there. Follow me." He knew that Tim would not be able to make the trip on his own.

After the geese had landed, Henry said, "What if we wanted to go back to our first landing place? ⭐ Could you find the way back?"

"Oh, sure," Tim said. "That's easy. You just fly back that way until you come to some blue hills, then you turn a little and go more north until you come to the place where the two rivers cross . . ." Tim went on to tell all the important facts about how to get there.

- Everybody, could Tim learn things from the maps that Henry drew and the things that he told about landing places? (Signal.) *No.*
- Did he know how to get back to the first landing place? (Signal.) *Yes.*
- So he had to go to a place before he really knew a lot about it.

Old Henry spent a lot of time thinking that night. And he thought a lot the next day. The geese did not fly on that day or on the day after that. On the first day, they rested and talked. It was warmer here than it had been farther north. The geese were not in Canada anymore. They were in Michigan. The trees were yellow and orange and the sun was warm.

- Everybody, did they fly on the day after they landed at the triangle-shaped field? (Signal.) *No.*
- What did they do? (Call on a student. Idea: *Rested and talked.*)
- Everybody, was this landing place in Canada? (Signal.) *No.*

- It was in the United States. Which state was it in? (Signal.) *Michigan.*
- The story says Henry spent a lot of time thinking. What do you think he was thinking about? (Call on a student. Idea: *How to help Tim get to Florida.*)
- Everybody, look at the picture.

- Does that look like a nice place? (Signal.) *Yes.*
- Are they still in Canada? (Signal.) *No.*
- Is this place **warmer** or **colder** than it was at Big Trout Lake? (Signal.) *Warmer.*

Old Henry knew that Tim could not remember a place unless he went to that place. So somebody would have to lead him all the way to Florida. Henry's problem was that his wing felt worse than ever. Henry didn't know how much more of the trip he would be able to make.

- When Henry left Big Trout Lake, how far did he plan to fly with Tim? (Call on a student. Idea: *The first three landing places.*)
- In Michigan, Henry changed his plans about helping Tim get to Florida. Henry knew that just showing Tim the first three landing places would not be enough. What would have to happen for Tim to get to Florida? (Call on a student. Idea: *Someone would have to lead Tim all the way to Florida.*)
- Why wasn't Henry sure that he'd be able to go all the way to Florida with Tim? (Call on a student. Idea: *Because his wing was so sore.*)
- If Tim can't use maps or descriptions to find landing places, what is Tim going to do if Henry can't fly with him? (Call on individual students. Idea: Student preference.)

Tim and Henry rested a second day. That day was the first time they saw another flock of geese. The flock formed a great V in the sky. Both Henry and Tim had eyes far sharper than human eyes. So they were able to see all the geese in that flock. Henry said, "There must be more than 60 geese in that flock."

"Are they going to the same place we're going?" Tim asked.

"No," Henry said. "They are heading a little bit to the west, so they are probably going to Mexico."

- Everybody, where did Henry think that flock was going? (Signal.) *Mexico.*
- How could he tell that it wasn't going to Florida? (Call on a student. Idea: *Because they were going a little to the west.*)

Tim asked, "Have you ever been to Mexico?"

Henry said, "No. The only place I've ever gone in the winter is to Crooked Lake in Florida. And that's what you'll do. Every year, you'll fly to Crooked Lake. Then in the spring you'll go back to Canada."

- Where had Henry gone every fall? (Call on a student. Ideas: *Florida; Crooked Lake.*)
- Where had he gone every spring? (Call on a student. Ideas: *Big Trout Lake; Canada.*)
- Everybody, if he was 35 years old, how many times had he made this trip? (Signal.) *35.*

EXERCISE 4

PAIRED PRACTICE

You're going to read aloud to your partner. Today the **A** members will read first. Then the **B** members will read from the star to the end of the story. (Observe students and give feedback. Praise teams that follow the rules.)

EXERCISE 5

WRITTEN ITEMS
Comprehension Passage Items
a. **Find part A on your worksheet.** ✓
- The questions in part A are about the geese's landing places. I'll call on different students to read the items and say the answers. Follow along. Don't write anything until I tell you to write.
b. (For each item: Call on a student to read and answer the item.)
- Item 1. *[Which letter on the map shows Big Trout Lake? C.]*
- Item 2. *[Which letter shows the landing place in Kentucky? A.]*
- Item 3. *[Which letter shows the landing place in Michigan? B.]*
- Item 4. *[Which letter shows the landing place in Florida? D.]*
- Item 5. *[Which letter shows the landing place in Canada? E.]*
- Item 6. *[Which letter shows Crooked Lake? D.]*
- Item 7. *[Which letter shows the first landing place? E.]*
- Item 8. *[Which letter shows the second landing place? B.]*
- Item 9. *[Draw the path the geese take on their migration south.]* Trace the path with your finger. ✓

Story Items
c. Find part B on your worksheet. ✓
- The questions in part B are about today's story. Follow along. Don't write anything until I tell you to write.
d. (For each item: Call on a student to read and answer the item.)
- Item 10. *[Did Henry tell Tim about his sore wing? No.]*
- Item 11. *[He got a sore wing when he fought with the fox.]*
- Item 12. *[Henry told Tim about the next landing place. He also made a map.]*
- Item 13. *[Did Tim recognize the next landing spot? No.]*
- Item 14. *[So what did Henry do? Led Tim to the landing place.]*
- Item 15. *[**Circle** the picture that shows the correct landing spot.]* Which picture? [C.]
- Item 16. *[This landing spot was in the state of Michigan.]*

- Item 17. [Was Tim able to tell Henry how to get back to the first landing place? Yes.]
- Item 18. [What did the two geese see on the second day they were at the triangle-shaped fields? Idea: Another flock of geese.]
- Item 19. [Was that flock going to **Florida** or **Mexico**? Mexico.]
- Item 20. [When Tim and Henry left Big Trout Lake, Henry had planned to take Tim to the first <u>3</u> landing places.]
- Item 21. [Now Henry realized that somebody would have to fly farther with Tim. How far? Idea: All the way to Florida.]
- Item 22. [Was Henry sure that he would be able to fly that far with Tim? No.]

Review Items

e. The items in your textbook are review items from other lessons.

End-of-Lesson Activities

INDEPENDENT WORK

Now finish the independent work for lesson 7. Do the worksheet first. For the textbook items, you'll write your answers on your lined paper. Raise your hand when you've finished the worksheet and textbook for lesson 7. (Observe students and give feedback.)

WORKCHECK

a. (Direct students to take out their marking pencils.)
- We're going to check your worksheet and textbook items. Let's start with your worksheet. Remember, if you got an item wrong, make an **X** next to the item. Don't change any answers.
b. (For each worksheet item: Read the item. Call on a student to answer it. If the answer is wrong, say the correct answer. Refer to the Answer Key for the correct answers.)
c. Now let's check your textbook items.
- (Repeat step b for textbook items.)
d. Now use your marking pencil to fix any items you got wrong. Remember, all mistakes must be fixed before you hand in your independent work.

LANGUAGE ARTS

(Present Language Arts lesson 7 after completing Reading lesson 7. See Language Arts Guide.)

READING WORDS

Column 1

a. **Find lesson 8 in your textbook.**
- Touch column 1. ✓
- (Teacher reference:)

1. <u>few</u>er	4. <u>cloud</u>y
2. <u>sea</u>son	5. <u>old</u>er
3. <u>hurt</u>ing	

- These words have more than one syllable. The first syllable is underlined.
b. Word 1. What's the first syllable? (Signal.) *few.*
- What's the whole word? (Signal.) *Fewer.*
c. Word 2. What's the first syllable? (Signal.) *sea.*
- What's the whole word? (Signal.) *Season.*
d. Word 3. What's the first syllable? (Signal.) *hurt.*
- What's the whole word? (Signal.) *Hurting.*
e. Word 4. What's the first syllable? (Signal.) *cloud.*
- What's the whole word? (Signal.) *Cloudy.*
f. Word 5. What's the first syllable? (Signal.) *old.*
- What's the whole word? (Signal.) *Older.*
g. Let's read those words again, the fast way.
- Word 1. What word? (Signal.) *Fewer.*
- (Repeat for words 2–5.)
h. (Repeat step g until firm.)

Column 2

i. Find column 2. ✓
- (Teacher reference:)

1. **Reedy Lake**	3. **Jackson Lake**
2. **Clarks Hill Lake**	4. **shown**

- Numbers 1 through 3 tell about different places.
j. Number 1. What place? (Signal.) *Reedy Lake.*
- Number 2. What place? (Signal.) *Clarks Hill Lake.*
- Number 3. What place? (Signal.) *Jackson Lake.*
- Word 4. What word? (Signal.) *Shown.*
k. (Repeat step j until firm.)

COMPREHENSION PASSAGE

a. Find part B in your textbook. ✓
- You're going to read the next story about Henry and Tim. First you'll read the information passage. It gives some facts about the sun heating the earth.
b. Everybody, touch the title. ✓
- (Call on a student to read the title.) *[The Sun Heats the Earth.]*
- Everybody, what's the title? (Signal.) *The Sun Heats the Earth.*
- (Call on individual students to read the passage, each student reading two or three sentences at a time. Ask the specified questions as the students read.)

> **The Sun Heats the Earth**
> **You can figure out which parts of the earth are hot and which are cold if you look at how the light from the sun gets to the earth.**
> **The picture shows lines of heat that are going from the sun to the earth. Those lines are the same distance apart.**

- Everybody, touch the lines that are going from the sun to the earth. ✓
- Are some of those lines closer together than other lines? (Signal.) *No.*
- Some of those lines are longer than other lines, but they are the same distance apart.

> **Here's a rule about the lines of heat:**
> <u>**Places on the earth that have more lines of heat are hotter than places that have fewer lines of heat.**</u>

- Listen to the rule again: Places on the earth that have more lines of heat are hotter than places that have fewer lines of heat.

- Everybody, say that rule. Get ready. (Signal.) *Places on the earth that have more lines of heat are hotter than places that have fewer lines of heat.*
- (Repeat until firm.)

> **Places A, B and C on the earth are the same size, but one of them is a very hot place and one is a very cold place.**

- Everybody, touch place A. ✓
- It is the same size as place B or C.

> **The hot place receives more lines of heat from the sun. So if you want to find out which place has more heat, you count the number of lines from the sun that hit that place.**
> **Count the lines that hit place C.**

- Everybody, do it. ✓
- How many lines of heat hit place C? (Signal.) *4.*
- If another place on earth had more lines of heat, would that place be **hotter** or **colder** than place C? (Signal.) *Hotter.*

> **Count the lines of heat at place B.**

- Everybody, do it. ✓
- How many lines of heat hit place B? (Signal.) *8.*
- Which place has more lines of heat, place C or place B? (Signal.) *Place B.*
- So which place is hotter? (Signal.) *Place B.*

> **Count the lines of heat at place A.**

- Everybody, do it. ✓
- Everybody, how many lines of heat hit place A? (Signal.) *10.*
- Which place has the **most** lines of heat? (Signal.) *A.*
- Which place has the **fewest** lines of heat? (Signal.) *C.*
- Which place is the coldest? (Signal.) *C.*

> **Remember, the sun heats the earth, and the equator receives more heat than any other part of the earth.**

- Everybody, where does the heat on the earth come from? (Signal.) *The sun.*
- Which part of the earth receives the most amount of heat? (Signal.) *The equator.*

STORY READING

a. Find part C in your textbook. ✓
- The error limit for this story is 13 errors.
b. Everybody, touch the title. ✓
- (Call on a student to read the title.) *[A New Plan.]*
- Everybody, what's the title? (Signal.) *A New Plan.*
- (Call on individual students to read the story, each student reading two or three sentences at a time. Ask the specified questions as the students read.)

> - (Correct errors: Tell the word. Direct the student to reread the sentence.)
> - (If the group makes more than 13 errors, direct the students to reread the story.)

> **A New Plan**
> **The next day's flight was very hard on Old Henry. His wing was sore, and the next landing place was a little more than 300 miles south of the landing place in Michigan. It would have made sense for the geese to travel only 200 miles and then spend the night at a new landing place. But geese don't always make sense. They always go to the same landing places. If those places are a little more than 300 miles apart, the geese fly a little more than 300 miles.**

- Everybody, about how far did the geese have to travel to the next landing place? (Signal.) *300 miles.*
- That's a long, long way. If you went on a freeway at sixty miles an hour, you would have to drive five hours without stopping to go 300 miles. Why didn't they just go about 200 miles and find a good place to land? (Call on a student. Idea: *Geese don't do it that way.*)

> **Tim and Old Henry reached the landing place by late afternoon. This landing place was between two lakes in Kentucky. One was large and one was small.**

- Everybody, what state was this landing place in? (Signal.) *Kentucky.*
- What state was the last landing place in? (Signal.) *Michigan.*

- This landing place was between how many lakes? (Signal.) *Two.*

Something about the large lake didn't seem right to Old Henry. There were some geese on the large lake, but they were too close to the shore.

Henry's wing was so sore that he really wanted to land and rest. So he told himself, "There's no problem down there," and he started to lead the way down to where the other geese were swimming. Tim flew up next to Old Henry and said, "I don't think we should land there."

"Why not?"

"You told me never to land in a place that had only a few geese on the water."

- Everybody, what was on the big lake? (Signal.) *A few geese.*
- Did Henry know better than to land where there were only a few geese? (Signal.) *Yes.*
- Then why was he going to land here? (Call on a student. Idea: *Because his wing was so sore.*)
- Everybody, who was trying to stop him? (Signal.) *Tim.*

Just then the geese heard a sound that was something like another goose calling, but Old Henry knew that it was not the sound of a real goose. He said, "You're right, Tim. There are hunters down there. Let's get out of here."

The geese made a great turn and started to climb higher and higher into the sky. Just then, there were loud banging sounds. Hunters were shooting at Tim and Old Henry, but they were too far away. "You may have saved our lives," Henry said to Tim. "You're a very smart young goose."

- What was the first sound that made Henry sure that there were hunters down below? (Call on a student. Idea: *A sound that was something like another goose calling.*)
- As Henry and Tim flew away from the lake, they heard other sounds. What were those? (Call on a student. Ideas:

Gunshots; banging sounds.)

- Why didn't the shooting hurt Tim or Henry? (Call on a student. Idea: *Because they were too far away.*)
- Tim remembered something important that Henry had told him. What was that? (Call on a student. Idea: *Not to land where there were only a few geese on the water.*)
- Why do you think Tim remembered **that** when he had trouble remembering what Henry told him about the landing places? (Call on a student. Idea: *Because he'd never been to the landing places.*)

The two geese found another landing place about five miles away. It was a field that had a small pond in the middle of it. The geese landed, took a nap and then ate some seeds. Old Henry wanted to go the rest of the way to Florida, but he knew that he could not travel as fast as flocks usually go. If Henry was to make it, he would have to fly one day and rest the next. He couldn't fly two days in a row.

- How far was the landing place from where the hunters were? (Call on a student. Idea: *About five miles away.*)
- What was Henry's new plan for helping Tim get to Florida? (Call on a student. Idea: *Fly one day, rest the next day.*)

When the sun was growing red in the west sky, the two geese were sitting near the pond. Tim said, "So where do we go tomorrow?"

Henry told him the plan. "We're going to rest tomorrow. Then we'll fly the next day."

Tim said, "But I'm not tired. I'll be ready to fly tomorrow."

"I won't be ready," Henry said.

Tim looked at Henry for a long time. Then he said, "Well, you're in charge. Anything you want to do is fine with me."

So the birds rested the next day. Late that afternoon, a large flock of more than eighty geese landed near the pond. The leader of the flock and three of the older geese came over and talked to Henry and Tim.

> **The leader asked, "Where's the rest of your flock?"**
>
> **Old Henry explained where the rest of the flock was and why Tim hadn't gone with them.**

- How many geese are in the other flock? (Call on a student. Idea: *More than eighty.*)
- Pretend you're Old Henry and I'm the leader of the other flock. Explain to me where the rest of the flock is and why Tim didn't go with them. (Call on a student. Idea: *The rest of the flock is in Florida. Tim couldn't fly with them because he had a sore leg and couldn't learn how to fly in time.*)

> **The leader of the other flock said, "We're from one of the big lakes between Canada and the United States."**

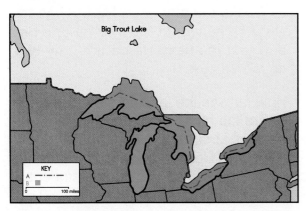

Big Trout Lake

KEY

0   100 miles

- Everybody, touch the map. ✓
- Below the map is a key. Touch the letter **A** in the key. ✓
- It shows the boundary line between the United States and Canada. Find that line on the map and trace it with your finger from one side of the map to the other side.
  (Observe students and give feedback.)
- The leader of the other flock lives on one of those big lakes between Canada and the United States. They are called the Great Lakes. Letter **B** in the key shows the color of the Great Lakes on the map. Touch the block in the key that shows that color.
  (Observe students and give feedback.)
- Count the Great Lakes and raise your hand when you know how many there are. Remember, the Great Lakes are just those big lakes between the United States and Canada. (Wait.)

- Everybody, how many Great Lakes are there? (Signal.) *Five.*
- You can see that some of those lakes are over 100 miles from one end to the other.

> **Tim said, "I know those big lakes. We flew over one of them, didn't we, Henry?"**
>
> **"Yes, we did," Henry said. Then he asked the leader, "Are you on your way to Florida?"**
>
> **"We are," the leader said. "We go to Reedy Lake."**
>
> **"That's wonderful," Old Henry said. "Tim is trying to go to Crooked Lake."**
>
> **"Oh," the leader said. "That's only a few miles from Reedy Lake."**
>
> **Old Henry said, "How would it be if Tim went with your flock? You could drop him off at Crooked Lake."**
>
> **"We could do that," the leader said.**

- What's Old Henry's latest plan? (Call on a student. Idea: *That Tim will fly with this flock to Florida.*)
- Everybody, is that plan all right with the leader? (Signal.) *Yes.*
- What do you think Henry will do if Tim goes with the others? (Call on individual students. Idea: *Student preference.*)
- How do you think Tim will feel about Henry's latest plan? (Call on individual students. Idea: *Student preference.*)
- We'll find out next time.

EXERCISE 4

PAIRED PRACTICE

You're going to read aloud to your partner. Today the **B** members will read first. Then the **A** members will read from the star to the end of the story. (Observe students and give feedback. Praise teams that follow the rules.)

EXERCISE 5

WRITTEN ITEMS

a. Find part D in your textbook. ✓
- Items 1 through 8 in part D are about the sun heating the earth. I'll call on individual students to read the items and say the answers. Follow along. Don't write anything until I tell you to write.

b. (For each item: Call on a student to read and answer the item.)
- Item 1. *[How many heat lines are hitting place A on the map? 10.]*
- Item 2. *[How many heat lines are hitting place B? 8.]*
- Item 3. *[How many heat lines are hitting place C? 4.]*
- Item 4. *[Write the letter of the place that's the hottest. A.]*
- Item 5. *[Write the letter of the place that's the coldest. C.]*
- Item 6. *[Write the letter of the place that has the warmest winters. A.]*
- Item 7. *[Write the letter of the place that's the farthest from the equator. C.]*
- Item 8. *[You know that place A is hotter than place C because place A <u>has more lines of heat</u>.]*

Story Items

c. Items 9 through 20 are about today's story. Follow along. Don't write anything until I tell you to write.
d. (For each item: Call on a student to read and answer the item.)
- Item 9. *[About how far was it from the landing place in Michigan to the one in Kentucky? 300 miles.]*
- Item 10. *[How did Henry feel by the end of that trip? Ideas: Sore; tired.]*
- Item 11. *[Which goose wanted to land at the regular landing place in Kentucky? Henry.]*
- Item 12. *[What kept them from landing there? Hunters were at that landing place.]*
- Item 13. *[Henry and Tim landed at a place that was about <u>5</u> miles away.]*
- Item 14. *[Did Henry plan to stay at this landing place* **one day** *or* **two days?** *2 days.]*
- Item 15. *[Another <u>flock</u> landed at the landing place the next day.]*
- Item 16. *[How many geese were in that flock? More than 80.]*
- Item 17. *[Where was that flock going? Ideas: Florida; Reedy Lake.]*
- Item 18. *[That flock spent summers on one of the <u>Great Lakes</u>.]*
- Item 19. *[Henry asked if <u>Tim</u> could fly with that flock.]*
- Item 20. *[Did the leader of that flock think this plan was okay? Yes.]*

e. There are more items about today's story on your worksheet.

Find item 1 on your worksheet. ✓
f. (For each item: Call on a student to read and answer the item.)
- Item 1. *[How many Great Lakes are there? 5.]*
- Item 2. *[Color the Great Lakes on the map.]* Touch the Great Lakes. ✓

Review Items

g. The rest of the items on your worksheet are review items from other lessons.

End-of-Lesson Activities

INDEPENDENT WORK

Now finish the independent work for lesson 8. Do the worksheet first. For the textbook items, you'll write your answers on your lined paper. Raise your hand when you've finished the worksheet and textbook for lesson 8.
(Observe students and give feedback.)

WORKCHECK

a. (Direct students to take out their marking pencils.)
- We're going to check your worksheet and textbook items. Let's start with your worksheet. Remember, if you got an item wrong, make an **X** next to the item. Don't change any answers.
b. (For each worksheet item: Read the item. Call on a student to answer it. If the answer is wrong, say the correct answer. Refer to the Answer Key for the correct answers.)
c. Now let's check your textbook items.
- (Repeat step b for textbook items.)
d. Now use your marking pencil to fix any items you got wrong. Remember, all mistakes must be fixed before you hand in your independent work.

LANGUAGE ARTS

(Present Language Arts lesson 8 after completing Reading lesson 8. See Language Arts Guide.)

Lesson 9

READING WORDS

Column 1

a. **Find lesson 9 in your textbook.** ✓
- Touch column 1. ✓
- (Teacher reference:)

1. **constant**	5. **daylight**
2. **sir**	6. **hurting**
3. **season**	7. **wintertime**
4. **seventy**	

b. Word 1 is **constant.** What word? (Signal.) *Constant.*
- Spell **constant.** Get ready. (Tap for each letter.) *C-O-N-S-T-A-N-T.*
- Something that is **constant** doesn't change. If a car goes at a constant speed, the speed does not change. What if something is a constant temperature? (Call on a student. Idea: *The temperature doesn't change.*)
c. Word 2. What word? (Signal.) *Sir.*
- An important man is sometimes called **sir.**
d. Word 3. What word? (Signal.) *Season.*
- (Repeat for words 4–7.)
e. Let's read those words again, the fast way.
- Word 1. What word? (Signal.) *Constant.*
- (Repeat for words 2–7.)
f. (Repeat step e until firm.)

Column 2

g. Find column 2. ✓
- (Teacher reference:)

1. <u>tilt</u>ed	4. <u>splash</u>ing
2. <u>cloud</u>y	5. <u>reach</u>es
3. <u>friend</u>s	6. <u>honk</u>ing

- Part of each word is underlined. You'll read that part. Then you'll read the whole word.
h. Word 1. What's the underlined part? (Signal.) *tilt.*
- What's the whole word? (Signal.) *Tilted.*
i. Word 2. What's the underlined part? (Signal.) *cloud.*
- What's the whole word? (Signal.) *Cloudy.*
j. Word 3. What's the underlined part? (Signal.) *friend.*
- What's the whole word? (Signal.) *Friends.*
k. Word 4. What's the underlined part? (Signal.) *splash.*
- What's the whole word? (Signal.) *Splashing.*
l. Word 5. What's the underlined part? (Signal.) *reach.*
- What's the whole word? (Signal.) *Reaches.*
m. Word 6. What's the underlined part? (Signal.) *honk.*
- What's the whole word? (Signal.) *Honking.*
n. Let's read those words again, the fast way.
- Word 1. What word? (Signal.) *Tilted.*
- (Repeat for words 2–6.)
o. (Repeat step n until firm.)

Column 3

p. Find column 3. ✓
- (Teacher reference:)

1. **South Carolina**	4. **Jackson Lake**
2. **Georgia**	5. **Clarks Hill Lake**
3. **Newmans Lake**	

- These are the names of different places.
q. Number 1 is South Carolina. What place? (Signal.) *South Carolina.*
- Number 2 is Georgia. What place? (Signal.) *Georgia.*
- Number 3. What place? (Signal.) *Newman's Lake.*
- (Repeat for numbers 4 and 5)
r. Let's read those words again. What place? (Signal.) *South Carolina.*
- Number 1. What place? (Signal.) *South Carolina.*
- (Repeat for numbers 2–5.)
s. (Repeat step r until firm.)

Individual Turns

(For columns 1–3: Call on individual students, each to read one to three words per turn.)

COMPREHENSION PASSAGE

a. Find part B in your textbook. ✓
- You're going to read the next story about Henry and Tim. First you'll read the information passage.

b. Everybody, touch the title. ✓
- (Call on a student to read the title.) *[The Sun and the Earth.]*
- Everybody, what's the title? (Signal.) *The Sun and the Earth.*
- (Call on individual students to read the passage, each student reading two or three sentences at a time. Ask the specified questions as the students read.)

The Sun and the Earth
Here's a rule about the earth and the sun. The earth is moving around the sun all the time.

- Everybody, say that rule. Get ready. (Signal.) *The earth is moving around the sun all the time.*
- (Repeat until firm.)

The earth makes a complete circle around the sun one time every year.

- Listen to the rule again: The earth makes a complete circle around the sun one time every year.
- Everybody, say that rule. Get ready. (Signal.) *The earth makes a complete circle around the sun one time every year.*
- (Repeat until firm.)

A year is 365 days, so it takes the earth 365 days to make a complete circle around the sun.

- Everybody, how many days are in a year? (Signal.) *365.*
- How many days does it take for the earth to circle the sun? (Signal.) *365.*
- How many **years** does it take for the earth to circle the sun? (Signal.) *One.*

The picture shows the earth at four different times of the year as it circles the sun.

- The picture shows four earths. Everybody, does that mean that there **are** four earths? (Signal.) *No.*

- The picture shows the **same** earth at different times of the year.

Touch the picture of the earth during winter.

- Everybody, do it. ✓

Notice how much of the earth is in shadow and how much is in sunlight.

- Half the earth is in sunlight. Everybody, how much of the earth is in shadow? (Signal.) *Half.*
- How much of the earth is in sunlight? (Signal.) *Half.*
- Is the part of the earth that is in sunlight **closer** to the sun or **farther** from the sun? (Signal.) *Closer to the sun.*

Follow the arrow around the sun and name the season that is shown by each earth. Start with the earth at wintertime.

- The season you'll start with is winter. Everybody, follow the arrow to the next picture. ✓
- If the first picture shows the earth during winter, what season does the second picture show? (Signal.) *Spring.*
- Follow the arrow to the third picture. ✓
- What season does that show? (Signal.) *Summer.*
- Follow the arrow to the next picture. What season does that show? (Signal.) *Fall.*
- Once more the fast way. Touch each earth and name the season, starting with winter. Get ready. (Signal.) *Winter, spring, summer, fall.*
- (Repeat until firm.)

Remember, the earth is in different places at different seasons of the year.

STORY READING

a. Find part C in your textbook. ✓
- The error limit for this story is 13 errors.

b. Everybody, touch the title. ✓
- (Call on a student to read the title.) *[Flying With the Flock.]*
- Everybody, what's the title? (Signal.) *Flying With the Flock.*

- (Call on individual students to read the story, each student reading two or three sentences at a time.) Ask the specified questions as the students read.

- (Correct errors: Tell the word. Direct the student to reread the sentence.)
- (If the group makes more than 13 errors, direct the students to reread the story.)

Flying With the Flock

After the geese from the large flock finished talking with Old Henry, they went over to their flock. As soon as they had left, Tim said, "When is that other flock going to fly?"

"Tomorrow," Henry said.

"We planned to fly tomorrow, didn't we?"

"Yes," Henry said.

"Well, why did you say I would fly with them? I thought I was flying with you."

Old Henry said, "Tim, I'm not sure I can make it all the way to Florida. If you go with them, they'll drop you off at Crooked Lake."

"But what will you do?" Tim asked. "Aren't you going to fly with them, too?"

"Well . . ." Old Henry said. He wanted to tell Tim that he didn't plan to go any further south, but Tim looked very sad. So Old Henry said, "Well, I'll go with them as far as I can. I'll fly with them tomorrow and then I'll see how I feel at the end of the day."

- Henry didn't tell Tim what he really wanted to do. What did Henry really want to do? (Call on a student. Idea: *Not fly any farther south.*)
- What did he tell Tim he would do? (Call on a student. Ideas: *Fly with them the next day; go as far as he could.*)
- So Henry changed his plans again, didn't he?

"Well, I'm going where you go," Tim said. "If you fly with them after tomorrow, I'll fly with them. But if you don't fly with them after tomorrow, I won't fly with them."

"We'll see how it goes tomorrow," Henry said.

- What was Tim going to do if Henry kept flying with the other flock? (Call on a student. Idea: *Keep flying with the flock.*)
- What was Tim going to do if Henry didn't keep flying with the other flock? (Call on a student. Idea: *Not keep flying with the flock.*)

So the next morning, more than eighty geese took off from that pond in Kentucky and formed a great V in the sky. The leader was near the front of the V, but he was not at the very point of the V. He was back a few places so he could see the front of the V and honk out orders to the other geese. Old Henry and Tim were far behind the leader. Tim was right behind a young goose. Old Henry was in front of one of the older geese.

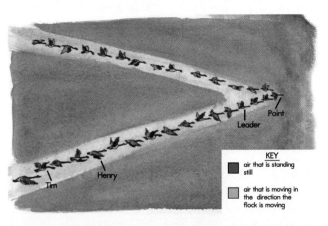

KEY
air that is standing still
air that is moving in the direction the flock is moving

- Everybody, look at the picture. Touch the point of the V.
  (Observe students and give feedback.)
- Is the leader at the point of the V? (Signal.) *No.*
- Touch the leader. ✓
- Why is the leader back a little from the point? (Call on a student. Idea: *So he can see the front of the V and give orders.*)
- Everybody, touch Tim and Henry. ✓
- Are they **close** to the leader or **pretty far behind?** (Signal.) *Pretty far behind.*

After the flock stopped climbing, it was nearly two miles high. ★ Tim called out to Henry, "I notice that it is a lot easier to fly than it was when you and I were alone."

"Right," Henry said. "It's easier flying in a large flock."

"Why?"

✿ Old Henry explained. "We are behind a lot of other geese. Those geese fly through the air and leave a trail of wind that moves in the same direction the geese are moving. We're flying through that air, so we don't have to work as hard as the geese up front."

- Listen to that part again:
  "We are behind a lot of other geese. Those geese fly through the air and leave a trail of wind that moves in the same direction the geese are moving. We're flying through that air, so we don't have to work as hard as the geese up front."
- The picture shows dark blue air and light blue air. The key shows that the dark blue air is standing still. The light blue air is moving in the direction the flock is moving. Everybody, hold your finger on your book and point to show the direction the light blue air is moving.
  (Observe students and give feedback.)
- Going through the light blue air is just like riding your bike with the wind. It's a lot easier than riding against the wind. So Tim and Henry didn't have to work as hard to fly with the flock.

Tim said, "That's good for us, but I sure wouldn't want to be one of those geese up front."

- Everybody, touch the goose at the point of the V. ✓
- You can see that that goose has to fly through air that is not moving, so that goose has to work harder than any other goose in the flock.

Henry said, "All the geese that are up front take turns at being the first goose in the V. They fly at the point for an hour or more and then change places with another goose."

Then Henry noticed that his wing wasn't as sore ✿ as it had been. He hadn't been thinking about that wing because it hadn't been hurting. Henry realized that it hadn't been hurting because it didn't have to work as hard as it did when he and

Tim flew alone. Henry said to himself, "If it doesn't get any harder than this, maybe . . ."

- How was Henry's wing feeling? (Call on a student. Ideas: *Better; not as sore as it had been.*)
- Why wasn't Henry's wing hurting? (Call on a student. Idea: *Because it didn't have to work so hard.*)
- If his wing keeps feeling good, what do you think he'll do? (Call on a student. Idea: *Keep flying with the flock.*)

He still wasn't sure how he would feel the next morning when the rest of the flock was ready to fly again.

Later that afternoon, when the sky was starting to get very cloudy, the great V of geese went lower and lower through the clouds and came out of them above a beautiful green lake. Tim asked Henry, "What's that lake?"

Henry said, "I don't know. This is not on the route I've taken. We always land at Clarks Hill Lake. It's much bigger than this lake and it's farther east."

Then Henry asked the old goose behind him, "What's the name of that lake?"

"Jackson Lake."

About ten minutes later the flock landed on Jackson Lake.

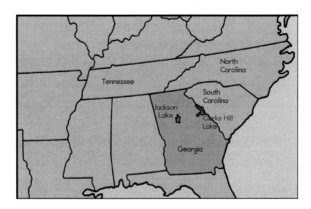

- Everybody, what's the name of the lake they landed at? (Signal.) *Jackson Lake.*
- Had Henry ever landed here before? (Signal.) *No.*
- Why not? (Call on a student. Idea: *It wasn't on the route he'd taken.*)
- Everybody, look at the map. Find Jackson Lake. It's one of the dark blue lakes.

Raise your hand when you know what state it is in. ✓
- Everybody, what state is that lake in? (Signal.) *Georgia.*
- Find Clarks Hill Lake. It's a dark blue lake. ✓
- That lake is in two states. What states? (Call on a student.) *[Georgia, South Carolina.]*
- Which lake is farther east, Clarks Hill Lake or Jackson Lake? (Signal.) *Clarks Hill Lake.*
- Which lake is bigger? (Signal.) *Clarks Hill Lake.*

EXERCISE 4

PAIRED PRACTICE

You're going to read aloud to your partner. Today the **A** members will read first. Then the **B** members will read from the star to the end of the story. (Observe students and give feedback. Praise teams that follow the rules.)

EXERCISE 5

WRITTEN ITEMS

Comprehension Passage Items

a. Find part A on your worksheet. ✓
- The questions in part A are about the earth moving around the sun. I'll call on individual students to read the items and say the answers. Follow along. Don't write anything until I tell you to write.

b. (For each item: Call on a student to read and answer the item.)
- Item 1. *[The earth makes a circle around the sun one time every <u>year</u>.]*
- Item 2. *[How many days does it take the earth to make one full circle around the sun? 365.]*
- Item 3. *[Fill in the blanks to show the four seasons. Winter, <u>spring</u>, summer, fall, <u>winter</u>, spring, <u>summer</u>, <u>fall</u>.]*
- Item 4. *[Write the missing seasons on the picture below.]* Touch earths B, C, and D and tell the season for each earth. *[B, spring; C, summer; D, fall.]*
- Item 5. *[Shade half of earth A and half of earth C.]*
- Touch the half of earth A that you'll shade. (Student touches left half of earth A.)

- Touch the half of earth C that you'll shade. (Student touches right half of earth C.)

Story Items

c. Find part B on your worksheet. ✓
- The questions in part B are about today's story. Follow along. Don't write anything until I tell you to write.

d. (For each item: Call on a student to read and answer the item.)
- Item 6. *[When Tim and Henry were in Kentucky, did Henry want to fly farther south? No.]*
- Item 7. *[Tim said he'd fly with the flock if Henry . . . Idea: flew with the flock.]*
- Item 8. *[Was it **easier** or **harder** to fly with a large flock? Easier.]*
- Item 9. *[Were Tim and Henry **near** or **far** from the point of the V? Far.]*
- Item 10. *[Flying near the back of a large flock is like riding your bike <u>with the wind</u>.]*
- Item 11. *[Look at the picture. Write **H** on the goose that has to work the hardest.]* Touch the goose that has to work the hardest. (Student touches goose at point of V.)
- Item 12. *[Color the air that is moving in the same direction the flock is moving.]* Show me with your finger where the air is. (Student traces the V.)

e. There are more items about today's story in your textbook. Everybody, find part D in your textbook. ✓
- Item 1. *[Henry noticed that his wing felt <u>better</u> because it didn't have to work very <u>hard</u>.]*
- Item 2. *[What's the name of the lake where the flock landed? Jackson Lake.]*
- Item 3. *[In what state is that lake? Georgia.]*
- Item 4. *[Had Henry landed there before? No.]*
- Item 5. *[At what lake did Henry's flock usually land? Clarks Hill Lake.]*
- Item 6. *[Which lake is farther east? Clarks Hill Lake.]*
- Item 7. *[Do you think Henry will be able to continue flying south with the flock?]* (Student preference.)

End-of-Lesson Activities

Now finish the independent work for lesson 9. Do the worksheet first. For the textbook items, you'll write your answers on your lined paper. Raise your hand when you've finished the worksheet and textbook for lesson 9. (Observe students and give feedback.)

WORKCHECK

a. (Direct students to take out their marking pencils.)
 • We're going to check your worksheet and textbook items. Let's start with your worksheet. Remember, if you got an item wrong, make an **X** next to the item. Don't change any answers.
b. (For each worksheet item: Read the item. Call on a student to answer it. If the answer is wrong, say the correct answer. Refer to the Answer Key for the correct answers.)
c. Now let's check your textbook items.
 • (Repeat step b for textbook items.)
d. Now use your marking pencil to fix any items you got wrong. Remember, all mistakes must be fixed before you hand in your independent work.

LANGUAGE ARTS

(Present Language Arts lesson 9 after completing Reading lesson 9. See Language Arts Guide.)

Note: You will need to reproduce blackline masters for the Fact Game in lesson 10 (Appendix G in Teacher's Guide).
A special project occurs after lesson 10. See page 57 for the materials you'll need.

Materials: For all test lessons, each student will need a pencil, a textbook, and lined paper.

Fact Game

For each team (4 or 5 students):
- pair of number cubes (or dice)
- copy of Fact Game 10

For each student:
- their copy of the scorecard sheet (at the end of workbook A)

For each monitor:
- a pencil
- Fact Game 10 answer key (at end of textbook A)

Reading Checkout

Each student needs their thermometer chart.

Literature Lesson 1

See Literature Guide for the materials you will need.

EXERCISE 1

FACT GAME

a. You're going to play a game that uses the facts you have learned. You will take turns. When it is your turn, you'll read a question out loud and then you'll answer it. If you answer all parts of the question correctly, you earn a point.

b. I'll show you how to play the game.
- (Choose four students to sit at a table.)
- I'll be the monitor for now. First the monitor hands the number cubes to the person to the left. That person rolls the number cubes.
- (Hand the number cubes to the student on your left. Tell the student:) Roll the number cubes.

c. The person who rolls the number cubes tells the number of dots that are showing.
- (Tell the student who rolled the number cubes:) Count up the dots and tell us how many. ✓

d. Now the person who rolled the number cubes reads the question for that number out loud.
- (Ask the student who rolled the number cubes:) What question are you going to read out loud? ✓
- Read your question and then answer it. ✓

e. The monitor uses the Fact Game Answer Key. The monitor compares the player's answer with the correct answer. If the answer is correct, the monitor tells the player that the answer is correct. Then the monitor gives the player one point by putting a check mark on the player's scorecard. The first check mark goes in box 1. Every time a player answers a question correctly, the monitor puts a check mark in the next box on the player's card. If the player's answer is not correct, the monitor says the correct answer. The player does not get a point.
- (If the student answered the item correctly, say:) That's the right answer. (Then record one point on the student's scorecard.)
- (If the student answered the item incorrectly, say:) That's the wrong answer. The answer is _____.

f. The player passes the number cubes to the person to the left and that player rolls the number cubes. Remember, roll the number cubes, figure out the number of the question, read that question out loud, and answer it. The monitor gives the points and tells the correct answers. Do not argue with the monitor. If you argue, you lose your next turn.

g. (Divide the students into groups of four or five each. Identify a monitor for each group. Give each group a pair of number cubes.)

h. (Direct each monitor to the lesson 10 Fact Game Answer Key at the back of textbook A. Tell each monitor:) That page gives the correct answers for this game. Don't show the answers to the other players.

i. **Everybody, write your name on your scorecard and find lesson 10.** ✓

- You have 10 minutes to play the game. Keep taking turns until I tell you to stop.
- (Permit the game to be played for 10 minutes. When 5 minutes have elapsed, remind the group that 5 minutes remain.)

j. (After the game has been played for 10 minutes, have all the students who earned more than 5 points stand up. Praise these players for doing a very good job.)
- (For each game that ran smoothly, tell the monitor:) Your group did a good job.

EXERCISE 2

READING CHECKOUTS

a. Today is a reading-checkout day. While you're writing answers, I'm going to call on you one at a time to read part of the story we read in lesson 9.

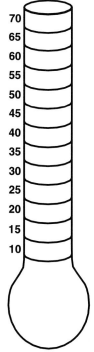

b. (Hold up a thermometer chart.) This is a thermometer chart. Write your name at the top of your thermometer chart. The numbers on the thermometer show the lessons for the checkouts from 10 through 70. The number at the bottom is 10. That's the checkout we'll do today. Touch the number 10. ✔
- When you pass a checkout, you color a space. Students who pass the checkout for lesson 10 today, get to color space 10 red.

c. You pass a checkout by reading the passage in less than a minute without making more than 2 mistakes.

Remember, less than a minute and no more than 2 errors. If you don't pass the checkout today, you can try again next time. But you can't color in the space for 10 until you pass checkout 10.
When I call on you to come and do your checkout, bring your thermometer chart.

d. (Call on individual students to read the portion of story 9 marked with ❀. Time the student. Note words that are missed and total number of words read.)
- (Teacher reference:)

> ❀ Old Henry explained. "We are behind a lot of other geese. Those geese fly through the air and leave a trail of wind that moves in the same direction the geese are moving. We're flying through that air, so we don't have to work as hard as the geese up [50] front."
> Tim said, "That's good for us, but I sure wouldn't want to be one of those geese up front."
> Henry said, "All the geese [75] that are up front take turns at being the first goose in the V. They fly at the point for an hour or more and [100] then change places with another goose."
> Then Henry noticed that his wing wasn't as sore ❀ [115] as it had been.

- (If the student reads the passage in one minute or less and makes no more than 2 errors, direct the student to color in the bottom segment of the thermometer chart.)

- (If the student makes any mistakes, point to each word that was misread and identify it.)
- (If the student does not meet the rate-error criterion for the passage, direct the student to practice reading the story with the assigned partner.)

TEST

a. **Find lesson 10, test 1 in your textbook.** ✓

- This lesson is a test. You'll work items you've done before.

b. Read the items and write the answers on your lined paper. Work carefully. Raise your hand when you've completed all the items.
(Observe students, but do not give feedback on errors.)

MARKING THE TEST

a. (Check students' work before beginning lesson 11. Refer to the Answer Key for the correct answers.)

b. (Record all test 1 results on the Test Summary Sheet and the Group Summary Sheet. Reproducible Summary Sheets are at the back of the Teacher's Guide.)

TEST REMEDIES

Provide any necessary remedies for test 1 before presenting lesson 11. Test remedies are discussed in the Teacher's Guide.)

Test 1 Firming Table

Test Item	Introduced in lesson	Test Item	Introduced in lesson	Test Item	Introduced in lesson
1	1	13	6	25	8
2	1	14	6	26	8
3	1	15	7	27	8
4	3	16	7	28	8
5	3	17	7	29	8
6	3	18	7	30	8
7	3	19	7	31	8
8	6	20	7	32	9
9	6	21	7	33	9
10	6	22	7	34	3
11	6	23	8	35	3
12	6	24	8		

(Present Language Arts lesson 10 after completing Reading lesson 10. See Language Arts Guide.)

(Present Literature lesson 1 after completing Reading lesson 10. See Literature Guide.)

Special Project

Note: After completing lesson 10, do this special project with the students. The project may be done at another time of day. For the project, reproduce the map in Appendix K of the Teacher's Guide. Color the dotted segment of the route red, and tape the map to the chalkboard or an easel.

Materials: Each student will need a piece of unlined paper, a regular pencil, and a marking pencil.

a. Find page 46 in your textbook. ✓
b. These are directions for a special project.
• (Call on individual students to read the first paragraph of the project.)
• (Teacher reference:)

Special Project

Some maps have a key that lets you figure out how far apart things are on the map. The map on page 47 is like maps you've seen before. It shows the path that the geese took from Canada to Florida. The key down at the bottom of the map shows how long 100 miles is on the map. Follow the steps below to learn how to use the key to figure out distances on the map.

c. You'll read the steps to me and I'll follow them. Watch how I do each step, because that's what you'll do.
• (Use the mounted map and a piece of unlined paper to demonstrate. Be sure students are able to see each step. Call on individual students to read steps 1 through 4. After each step is read, show the students how to do the step.)
• (Teacher reference:)

1. Place a piece of paper on the map so that one corner is on Big Trout Lake. Then hold the paper so that the edge is right next to the path that the geese took.
2. You're going to use your **marking** pencil to make three marks on the edge of your paper. Hold your paper very still and make the first mark at the first landing place.
3. Make the second mark at the landing place in Michigan.
4. Make the third mark at the landing place in Kentucky.

d. This time I'll read steps 1 through 4. You'll do them.
• (Read step 1.)
• Everybody, do step 1. (Observe students and give feedback.)
e. (Read step 2.)
• Everybody, do step 2. (Observe students and give feedback.)
f. (Read step 3.)
• Everybody, do step 3. (Observe students and give feedback.)
g. (Read step 4.)
• Everybody, do step 4. (Observe students and give feedback.)
h. For the rest of the steps, we'll use the key at the bottom of the map. It shows how long 100 miles is on the map. Everybody, touch the key. ✓
• How many miles does the key show? (Signal.) *100 miles.*
i. Now you'll read the rest of the steps to me and I'll do them.
(Call on individual students to read steps 5 through 9. After each step is read, show the students how to do the step.)

- (Teacher reference:)

> 5. Find the corner of your paper that shows where the path from Big Trout Lake started.
> 6. Hold that corner of your paper at the beginning of the line in the key. Use your **regular** pencil and mark the other end of the line.
> 7. Now move your paper so the mark you just made is at the beginning of the line in the key.
> 8. Mark the other end of the line.
> 9. Keep repeating steps 7 and 8 until you get to the last mark you made with your marking pencil.

  j. Now it's your turn. I'll read steps 5 through 9 and you'll do them. Remember, you have to hold your paper very still and in the right place when you make your marks.
- (Read step 5.)
- Everybody, do step 5. (Observe students and give feedback.)

  k. (Read step 6.)
- Everybody, do step 6. (Observe students and give feedback.)

  l. (Read step 7.)
- Everybody, do step 7. (Observe students and give feedback.)

  m. (Read step 8.)
- Everybody, do step 8. (Observe students and give feedback.)

  n. (Read step 9.)
- Everybody, do step 9. (Observe students and give feedback.)

  o. (Call on a student to read the next sentence.)
- (Teacher reference:)

> Figure out how many hundred miles it is from Big Trout Lake to the first landing place.

- Everybody, do it. Count the marks from Big Trout Lake to the first landing place. The first landing place is where you made the first mark with your **marking** pencil. (Observe students and give feedback.)
- About how many hundred miles is it from Big Trout Lake to the first landing place? (Signal.) *100 miles.*

  p. (Call on a student to read the next sentence.)
- (Teacher reference:)

> Figure out how many hundred miles it is from the first landing place to the landing place in Michigan.

- Everybody, do it. ✓
- About how many hundred miles is it from the first landing place to the landing place in Michigan? (Signal.) *200 miles.*

  q. (Call on a student to read the next sentence.)
- (Teacher reference:)

> Figure out how many hundred miles it is from the landing place in Michigan to the landing place in Kentucky.

- Everybody, do it. ✓
- About how many hundred miles is it from the landing place in Michigan to the landing place in Kentucky? (Signal.) *300 miles.*

Lessons 11–15 • Planning Page

Looking Ahead

	Lesson 11	Lesson 12	Lesson 13	Lesson 14	Lesson 15
Lesson Events	Reading Words Comprehension Passage Story Reading Paired Practice Written Items Independent Work Workcheck Language Arts	**Vocabulary Sentence** Reading Words Comprehension Passage Story Reading Paired Practice Written Items Independent Work Workcheck Language Arts	Vocabulary Sentence Reading Words Comprehension Passages Story Reading Paired Practice Written Items Independent Work Workcheck Language Arts	Vocabulary Sentences Reading Words Comprehension Passage Story Reading Paired Practice Written Items Independent Work Workcheck Language Arts	Vocabulary Sentence Reading Words Comprehension Passage Story Reading Reading Checkouts Written Items Independent Work Workcheck Language Arts
Vocabulary Sentence		#2: <u>Scientists</u> do **not ignore ordinary things.**	#2: <u>Scientists</u> do not <u>ignore</u> <u>ordinary</u> things.	sentence #1 sentence #2	#2: <u>Scientists</u> do not <u>ignore</u> <u>ordinary</u> things.
Reading Words: Word Types	modeled words compound words names of months words with endings mixed words	modeled words multi-syllable words mixed words	modeled words compound words words with endings mixed words	words with underlined part mixed words multi-syllable words	modeled words -ed words mixed words
New Vocabulary	Eskimo son	ice floe pebbled splatter	hind repeated Usk	nudged scrambled tumbling hitch ridge	no-see-ums speckled cliff swarming sloshing
Comprehension Passage	*The Tilt of the Earth*	*Facts About Eskimos*	*Animals in Alaska* *Where Oomoo and Oolak lived*	*The Dangerous Season*	*Florida, Canada, and Alaska*
Story	*The Flock Reaches Florida*	*Back to Canada*	*Oomoo*	*Usk, the Polar Bear*	*Playing with Usk*
Skill Items				Vocabulary sentence	Sequencing Vocabulary Sentences
Special Materials		*Materials for project			Thermometer charts
Special Projects/ Activities		Project after lesson 12		Activity after lessons 14–16	

*Road map with mileage key of students' state.

Lesson 11

READING WORDS

Column 1

a. **Find lesson 11 in your textbook.** ✓
  - Touch column 1. ✓
  - (Teacher reference:)

1. **Eskimo**	4. **ordinary**
2. **son**	5. **scientist**
3. **kayak**	

b. Word 1 is **Eskimo.** What word? (Signal.) *Eskimo.*
  - Spell **Eskimo.** Get ready. (Tap for each letter.) *E-S-K-I-M-O.*
  - Eskimos are native people that live in Alaska and Canada. You'll read a story about Eskimos that starts on the next lesson.
c. Word 2 is **son.** What word? (Signal.) *Son.*
  - Spell **son.** Get ready. (Tap for each letter.) *S-O-N.*
  - If parents have a male child, that child is the parents' **son.** Everybody, what do we call the parents' male child? (Signal.) *Son.*
  - Who knows what we call the parents' female child? (Call on a student.) *Daughter.*
d. Word 3 is **kayak.** What word? (Signal.) *Kayak.*
  - Spell **kayak.** Get ready. (Tap for each letter.) *K-A-Y-A-K.*
e. Word 4 is **ordinary.** What word? (Signal.) *Ordinary.*
  - Spell **ordinary.** Get ready. (Tap for each letter.) *O-R-D-I-N-A-R-Y.*
f. Word 5 is **scientist.** What word? (Signal.) *Scientist.*
g. Let's read those words again, the fast way.
  - Word 1. What word? (Signal.) *Eskimo.*
  - (Repeat for words 2–5.)
h. (Repeat step g until firm.)

Column 2

i. Find column 2. ✓
  - (Teacher reference:)

1. <u>any</u>more	4. <u>winter</u>time
2. <u>day</u>light	5. <u>rest</u>less
3. <u>day</u>time	

j. These words are compound words. The first part of each word is underlined.
k. Word 1. What's the underlined part? (Signal.) *any.*
  - What's the whole word? (Signal.) *Anymore.*
  - Word 2. What's the underlined part? (Signal.) *day.*
  - What's the whole word? (Signal.) *Daylight.*
  - Word 3. What's the underlined part? (Signal.) *day.*
  - What's the whole word? (Signal.) *Daytime.*
  - Word 4. What's the underlined part? (Signal.) *winter.*
  - What's the whole word? (Signal.) *Wintertime.*
  - Word 5. What's the underlined part? (Signal.) *rest.*
  - What's the whole word? (Signal.) *Restless.*
l. Let's read those words again, the fast way.
  - Word 1. What word? (Signal.) *Anymore.*
  - (Repeat for words 2–5.)
m. (Repeat step l until firm.)

Column 3

n. Find column 3. ✓
  - (Teacher reference:)

1. **January**	3. **December**
2. **March**	4. **February**

  - These words are the names of months.
o. Word 1. What word? (Signal.) *January.*
  - (Repeat for words 2–4.)
p. (Repeat step o until firm.)

Column 4

q. Find column 4. ✓

- (Teacher reference:)

1.	reaches	4.	splashing
2.	honking	5.	tilted
3.	friends		

- All these words have endings.
- r. Word 1. What word? (Signal.) *Reaches.*
- (Repeat for words 2–5.)
- s. (Repeat step r until firm.)

Column 5

- t. Find column 5. ✓
- (Teacher reference:)

1.	Newmans Lake	4.	constant
2.	seventy	5.	ignore
3.	sir	6.	spear

- u. Number 1. What words? (Signal.) *Newmans Lake.*
- Word 2. What word? (Signal.) *Seventy.*
- (Repeat for words 3–6.)
- v. (Repeat step u until firm.)

Individual Turns

(For columns 1–5: Call on individual students, each to read one to three words per turn.)

EXERCISE 2

COMPREHENSION PASSAGE

- a. Find part B in your textbook. ✓
- You're going to read the next story about Henry and Tim. First you'll read the information passage. It gives some facts about the earth.
- b. Everybody, touch the title. ✓
- (Call on a student to read the title.) *[The Tilt of the Earth.]*
- Everybody, what's the selection going to tell about? (Signal.) *The Tilt of the Earth.*
- c. (Call on individual students to read the passage, each student reading two or three sentences at a time. Ask the specified questions as the students read.)

The Tilt of the Earth
The earth is tilted. The poles are not straight up and down. Instead, they tilt.

- Everybody, are the poles of the earth **straight up and down** or **tilted**? (Signal.) *Tilted.*

Picture 1   Picture 2

- Picture 1 shows what the earth would look like if the poles were always straight up and down. Picture 2 shows what the earth looks like with poles that are tilted. Are the poles straight up and down in picture 2? (Signal.) *No.*
- Remember, the poles are tilted, not straight up and down.

And the poles tilt the same way as the earth circles the sun.

- Everybody, does the tilt change as the earth goes around the sun? (Signal.) *No.*
- The tilt is the same during all seasons.

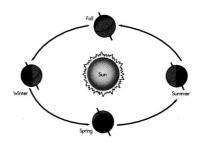

Picture 3 shows the tilt of the earth during the different seasons.
Touch the earth at wintertime.

- Everybody, do it. ✓

The North Pole tilts away from the sun during winter.

- Everybody, say that rule. Get ready. (Signal.) *The North Pole tilts away from the sun during winter.*
- Touch the North Pole during winter. ✓
- Is it tilting **toward** the sun or **away from** the sun? (Signal.) *Away from the sun.*
- Yes, the North Pole is tilted away from the sun during winter.

You can see that half of the earth is in shadow and half is in sunlight. But the North Pole is completely in shadow. That means that as the earth spins around and around during wintertime, there is no daylight at the

North Pole. There is constant darkness.

- Listen to that part again:
But the North Pole is completely in shadow. That means that as the earth spins around and around during wintertime, there is no daylight at the North Pole. There is constant darkness.
- If the North Pole is in darkness, there is no daytime. There is just nighttime throughout winter. Remember, when the North Pole tilts away from the sun, what season is it? (Signal.) *Winter.*
- And when it tilts away from the sun, is the North Pole in darkness all the time or daylight all the time? (Signal.) *Darkness.*

Touch the earth at summertime.

- Everybody, do it. ✓

The North Pole tilts toward the sun during summer.

- Everybody, say that rule. Get ready. (Signal.) *The North Pole tilts toward the sun during summer.*

Half the earth is in shadow and half is in sunlight. But the North Pole tilts toward the sun, so it is completely in sunlight. That means that at the North Pole during summer, there is no night. There is daylight all the time during summer. The sun never sets.

Remember, if the pole tilts away from the sun, it's wintertime at the pole and there is no daylight. If the pole tilts toward the sun, it is summertime and there is no night.

EXERCISE 3

STORY READING

a. Find part C in your textbook. ✓
The error limit for this story is 11 errors.
b. Everybody, touch the title. ✓
- (Call on a student to read the title.) *[The Flock Reaches Florida.]*
- Everybody, what's the title? (Signal.) *The Flock Reaches Florida.*
c. (Call on individual students to read the passage, each student reading two or three sentences at a time. Ask the specified questions as the students read.)

- (Correct errors: Tell the word. Direct the student to reread the sentence.)
- (If the group makes more than 11 errors, direct the students to reread the story.)

The Flock Reaches Florida
The next morning before the flock took off, Henry tried out his wing. He took off from the field and flew around the lake. When he landed, Tim came up to him and said, "I know what you were doing. You were trying to see if your wing is all right. Is it?"

"It feels pretty good," Henry said with a smile. "I can fly today."

And he did. The leader of the flock honked out directions to the goose that would be at the point of the V. Then, there were loud splashing and flapping sounds as more than eighty geese took off from Jackson Lake. Tim and Old Henry took their place near the back of the V and the flock went higher and higher.

"Why are we going so high?" Tim asked.

"When we're up high, we'll be able to ride some winds that are blowing toward Florida. We should be able to go far today without doing much work."

- Everybody, what state were the geese in? (Signal.) *Georgia.*
- What was the name of the lake they just left? (Signal.) *Jackson Lake.*
- How many geese were in the flock? (Call on a student. Idea: *More than eighty.*)
- Why did the flock fly so high? (Call on a student. Idea: *So they could ride some winds to Florida.*)
- Everybody, would the geese have to do **more work** or **less work** if the flock moved with the wind? (Signal.) *Less work.*

The winds blew and the flock flew. Around noon, Henry told Tim, "We're in Florida now."

"Wow," Tim said. "That means we're almost at Crooked Lake."

Henry laughed. "No, we still have a long way to go, and we won't get there today. It's more than two hundred miles to Crooked Lake."

Tim said, "So where will we spend tonight?"

"I don't know. Our flock always stops at Newmans Lake, which is about seventy miles from here. But I don't know where this flock lands."

Less than two hours later, Henry found out where the flock would land—at Newmans Lake.

- Everybody, what was the name of the lake that Henry's flock always landed at? (Signal.) *Newmans Lake.*
- What state is Newmans Lake in? (Signal.) *Florida.*
- Look at the map.
- Touch the lake where the geese spent the night. It's one of the dark blue lakes. ✓
- What's the name of that lake? (Signal.) *Jackson Lake.*
- Touch the lake where they are going to land. ✓
- What's the name of that lake? (Signal.) *Newmans Lake.*
- Touch the key on the map that shows the miles. ✓
- How many miles does the key show? (Signal.) *100.*
- Use the key on the map to figure out about how many miles it is from Jackson Lake to Newmans Lake. ✓
- About how many miles are between those lakes? (Call on a student. Idea: *About 300 miles.*)
- You can see where Crooked Lake is. It's a dark blue lake that is about 120 miles south of Newmans Lake.

There were lots and lots of geese around Newmans Lake. Tim said, "It looks like ✦ all the geese in the world are right here."

"There are a lot of geese here," Henry said. "But wait until you see how many geese there are near Crooked Lake."

The flock circled Newmans Lake and landed near a shore that was covered with geese. Some of them were honking and showing off by flapping their wings. Others were napping. The leader of the flock swam over to Old Henry and said, "We're going to spend tomorrow resting here. Then we'll go to Reedy Lake the next day. Do you plan to fly with us?"

Henry flapped his wings and said, "I do. I feel fine."

Tim smiled and said, "Me, too."

So two days later, Tim and Henry were flying high above Crooked Lake. Henry told Tim, "This is where we leave the flock. Our lake is right down there."

- Everybody, look at the map again. It's two days later and the big flock is over Crooked Lake. Touch where they are. ✓
- This is where Henry and Tim leave the flock. What's the name of the lake the flock is going to? (Signal.) *Reedy Lake.*
- You can find Reedy Lake right near Crooked Lake, but it's not a dark blue lake. Touch Reedy Lake. ✓

Old Henry flew up near the front of the great V and called to the leader. "Thank you, sir," Henry said. "You're a fine leader and you have a wonderful flock. We were glad to have the chance to fly with you."

"Good luck to both of you," the leader said. Then Henry and Tim swooped down from the flock. "I can't wait to see my mom and dad," Tim said.

Henry was also looking forward to seeing his old friends and his children and grandchildren. But he also felt a little sad. As the two geese swooped closer and closer to the beautiful blue lake below, Henry knew that he would miss flying with Tim. This trip was the first time in years that Henry felt that somebody really needed his help. That was a good feeling for Henry.

- Everybody, who did Henry talk to before he and Tim left the flock? (Signal.) *The leader.*
- Who was Tim looking forward to seeing? (Call on a student. Idea: *His parents.*)
- Who was Henry looking forward to seeing? (Call on a student. Idea: *Old friends, relatives.*)

- Why would Henry miss flying with Tim? (Call on a student. Idea: *Because he enjoyed feeling needed.*)

PAIRED PRACTICE

You're going to read aloud to your partner. First the **B** members will read. Then the **A** members will read from the star to the end of the story. (Observe students and give feedback. Praise teams that follow the rules.)

WRITTEN ITEMS

Comprehension Passage Items

a. **Find part A on your worksheet.** ✓
- The items in part A are about the tilt of the earth. I'll call on individual students to read the items. Don't say the answers. If an item has choices, read the choices.

b. (For each item: Call on a student to read the item.)
- Item 1. *[Write the number of the earth that has the North Pole tilting away from the sun.]*
- Item 2. *[Write the number of the earth that has the North Pole tilting toward the sun.]*
- Item 3. *[Write the number of the earth that has darkness all around the North Pole.]*
- Item 4. *[Write the number of the earth that has daylight all around the North Pole.]*
- Read the directions by the picture. *[Write which season each earth in the picture shows.]*
- Item 9. *[The picture shows the sun and two balls. **Fix up the balls so that half of each ball is in sunlight and half is in shadow.**]*
- Item 10. *[During winter at the North Pole, how often does the sun shine? Never, all the time.]*
- Item 11. *[During summer at the North Pole, how often does the sun shine? Never, all the time.]*
- Item 12. *[What season is it at the North Pole when the North Pole tilts **toward** the sun?]*
- Item 13. *[What season is it at the North Pole when the North Pole tilts **away from** the sun?]*

Story Items

c. Items 14 through 21 are about today's story. Don't say the answers.
- Item 14. *[In today's story, the flock started out at Jackson Lake in the state of <u>blank</u>.]*
- Item 15. *[The flock landed at Newmans Lake in the state of <u>blank</u>.]*
- Item 16. *[The flock rested for <u>blank</u>.]*
- Item 17. *[Then the flock flew to <u>blank</u> Lake in the state of <u>blank</u>.]*
- Item 18. *[The flock they were flying with went on to <u>blank</u> Lake.]*
- Item 19. *[**Underline** the geese Tim was looking forward to seeing. Children, friends, dad, grandchildren, mom.]*
- Item 20. *[**Underline** the geese Henry was looking forward to seeing. Children, friends, dad, grandchildren, mom.]*
- Item 21. *[What was Henry going to miss?]*

End-of-Lesson Activities

Now finish the written work for lesson 11. Do the worksheet first and then the textbook. Raise your hand when you're finished. (Observe students and give feedback.)

a. (Direct students to take out their marking pencils.)
- We're going to check your independent work. Remember, if you got an item wrong, make an **X** next to the item. Don't change any answers.

b. (For each item: Read the item. Call on a student to answer it. If the answer is wrong, say the correct answer. Refer to the Answer Key for the correct answers.)

c. Now use your marking pencil to fix up any items you got wrong. Remember, all mistakes must be fixed up before you hand in your independent work.

(Present Language Arts lesson 11 after completing Reading lesson 11. See Language Arts Guide.)

Note: A special project occurs after lesson 12. See page 71 for the materials you'll need.

EXERCISE 1

VOCABULARY

a. **Find page 352 in your textbook.** ✓
- Touch sentence 2. ✓
- This is a new vocabulary sentence. It says: Scientists do not ignore ordinary things. Everybody, read that sentence. Get ready. (Signal.) *Scientists do not ignore ordinary things.*
- Close your eyes and say the sentence. Get ready. (Signal.) *Scientists do not ignore ordinary things.*
- (Repeat until firm.)

b. Scientists are highly-trained people who study different things about the world. Some scientists study water. Some study the sun.
- Everybody, what do we call highly trained people who study different things about the world? (Signal.) *Scientists.*

c. When you don't pay attention to something, you **ignore** that thing. Everybody, what's another way of saying **She did not pay attention to the noisy children?** (Signal.) *She ignored the noisy children.*
- What's another way of saying **He did not pay attention to the teacher's directions?** (Signal.) *He ignored the teacher's directions.*

d. Things that you see all the time in different places are **ordinary** things. Everybody, what do you call trees that you see all the time? (Signal.) *Ordinary trees.*
- What do you call houses you see all the time? (Signal.) *Ordinary houses.*

e. Listen to the sentence again: *Scientists do not ignore ordinary things.*
- Everybody, say the sentence. Get ready. (Signal.) *Scientists do not ignore ordinary things.*

f. Everybody, what word means that you don't pay attention to something? (Signal.) *Ignore.*
- What do we call highly trained people who study different things about the world? (Signal.) *Scientists.*
- What word tells about things that you see all the time? (Signal.) *Ordinary.*

g. Listen: Do scientists pay attention to ordinary things? (Signal.) *Yes.*
- Yes, scientists do not ignore ordinary things. So they pay attention to those things and study those things.

EXERCISE 2

READING WORDS

Column 1

a. Find lesson 12 in your textbook. ✓
- Touch column 1. ✓
- (Teacher reference:)

1. polar bear	4. Oolak
2. ice floe	5. shoulder
3. Oomoo	

b. The words in line 1 are **polar bear.** What words? (Signal.) *Polar bear.*

c. The words in line 2 are **ice floe.** What words? (Signal.) *Ice floe.*
- An ice floe is a flat sheet of ice that floats in the ocean. It is like a flat iceberg.

d. Word 3 is **Oomoo.** What word? (Signal.) *Oomoo.*
- Spell **Oomoo.** Get ready. (Tap for each letter.) *O-O-M-O-O.*

e. Word 4 is **Oolak.** What word? (Signal.) *Oolak.*
- Spell **Oolak.** Get ready. (Tap for each letter.) *O-O-L-A-K.*
- Oomoo and Oolak are characters in a story you will read.

f. Word 5 is **shoulder.** What word? (Signal.) *Shoulder.*
- Spell **shoulder.** Get ready. (Tap for each letter.) *S-H-O-U-L-D-E-R.*

g. Let's read those words again, the fast way.
- Number 1. What words? (Signal.) *Polar bear.*
- Number 2. What words? (Signal.) *Ice floe.*
- Word 3. What word? (Signal.) *Oomoo.*
- (Repeat for words 4 and 5.)

h. (Repeat step g until firm.)

Column 2

i. Find column 2. ✓
- (Teacher reference:)

> 1. **pebbled**   3. **Alaskan**
> 2. **splatter**   4. **scattered**

j. These words have more than one syllable. The first part of each word is underlined.

k. Word 1. What's the underlined part? (Signal.) *pebble.*
- What's the whole word? (Signal.) *Pebbled.*
- Things that are pebbled are covered with small stones. A road that is covered with small stones is called a pebbled road. Everybody, what do we call a beach that is covered with small stones? (Signal.) *A pebbled beach.*
- Word 2. What's the underlined part? (Signal.) *splatt.*
- What's the whole word? (Signal.) *Splatter.*
- When wet things hit something, they **splatter** and spread out. Everybody, what happens to a wet snowball when it hits something? (Signal.) *It splatters and spreads out.*
- Word 3. What's the underlined part? (Signal.) *Alaska.*
- What's the whole word? (Signal.) *Alaskan.*
- Word 4. What's the underlined part? (Signal.) *scatter.*
- What's the whole word? (Signal.) *Scattered.*

l. Let's read those words again, the fast way.
- Word 1. What word? (Signal.) *Pebbled.*
- (Repeat for words 2–4.)

m. (Repeat step l until firm.)

Column 3

n. Find column 3. ✓
- (Teacher reference:)

> 1. **killer whale**   3. **spear**
> 2. **Eskimo**   4. **January**

o. Number 1. What words? (Signal.) *Killer whale.*
- Word 2. What word? (Signal.) *Eskimo.*
- (Repeat for words 3 and 4.)

p. (Repeat step o until firm.)

Column 4

q. Find column 4. ✓
- (Teacher reference:)

> 1. **walrus**   3. **son**
> 2. **kayak**   4. **restless**

r. Word 1. What word? (Signal.) *Walrus.*
- (Repeat for words 2–4.)

s. (Repeat step r until firm.)

Individual Turns

(For columns 1–4: Call on individual students, each to read one to three words per turn.)

EXERCISE 3

COMPREHENSION PASSAGE

a. Find part B in your textbook. ✓
- You're going to read the last story about Henry and Tim. First, you'll read the information passage. It gives some facts about Eskimos.

b. Everybody, touch the title. ✓
- (Call on a student to read the title.) *[Facts About Eskimos.]*
- Everybody, what's the selection going to tell about? (Signal.) *Facts About Eskimos.*

c. (Call on individual students to read the passage, each student reading two or three sentences at a time. Ask the specified questions as the students read.)

> **Facts About Eskimos**
> In the next lesson, you will read about Eskimos. The winters are very cold where Eskimos live.

- Everybody, if the winters are very cold, do Eskimos live close to the North Pole or close to the equator? (Signal.) *Close to the North Pole.*

> **Eskimos live near the North Pole in Canada and Alaska.**

- Where do they live? (Call on a student. Idea: *Near the North Pole in Canada and Alaska.*)

Alaska is a state of the United States, but it is far north of the main part of the United States. Touch Alaska on the map.

Picture 1

- Everybody, do it. ✓
- Does Alaska touch the other states of the United States? (Signal.) *No.*
- In what directions do you have to go from the main part of the United States to reach Alaska? (Call on a student.) *North and west.*
- Everybody, touch the letter **C** on the map. ✓
- Is that letter in Alaska? (Signal.) *No.*
- What country is that letter in? (Signal.) *Canada.*
- Remember, Eskimos live in that part of Canada and they live in Alaska.

Picture 2 shows an Eskimo with some of the things that Eskimos use.
   The Eskimo is holding a fishing pole in one hand.
   The Eskimo is holding a fishing spear in the other hand.

Picture 2

- Everybody, touch the fishing spear. ✓

The Eskimo is wearing warm clothes that are made from animal skins.

- Why do Eskimos need warm clothes? (Call on a student. Idea: *Because it gets very cold where they live.*)
- His coat is very warm. Look at what he is wearing on his feet. That footwear is very warm.

Near the Eskimo is a sled.

- Everybody, touch the sled.
- In what season do they use these sleds? (Signal.) *Winter.*
- They carry things on the sled and sometimes they ride on the sled.

The dogs that pull the sleds are called sled dogs.

- Everybody, touch a sled dog. ✓
- Those are strong dogs.

The boat that Eskimos use in the summer is called a kayak.

- Everybody, touch the kayak. ✓
- Why don't they use kayaks in the winter? (Call on a student. Idea: *Because all the water is frozen.*)

Make sure you can read these words:

Eskimo	Alaska
kayak	spear

- (Call on individual students to read all the words in the box.)

EXERCISE 4

STORY READING

a. Find part C in your textbook. ✓
- The error limit for this story is 13 errors.
b. Everybody, touch the title. ✓
- (Call on a student to read the title.) *[Back to Canada.]*
- Everybody, what's the title? (Signal.) *Back to Canada.*
c. (Call on individual students to read the story, each student reading two or three sentences at a time. Ask the specified questions as the students read.)

- (Correct errors: Tell the word. Direct the student to reread the sentence.)
- (If the group makes more than 13 errors, direct the students to reread the story.)

Back to Canada

There were hundreds of geese on Crooked Lake and in the fields around it. Henry and Tim circled the lake twice before Henry spotted their flock. Then he pointed his wing toward the south shore and said, "There's our flock right there."

- Everybody, on which shore was their flock? (Signal.) *The south shore.*

The two geese flew very low over the flock and honked loudly. As they made a sharp turn and headed back, Henry could hear some of the geese in the flock saying things like, "Who are those geese?" and "Doesn't that one goose look a lot like Henry?"

- Everybody, did the geese in the flock think that it really was Henry? (Signal.) *No.*
- Why not? (Call on a student. Idea: *Because they thought Henry was in Canada.*)

Tim and Henry landed right in the middle of the flock. Oh, how the geese honked and flapped their wings. Tim's mom flapped her wings so hard she sent little feathers flying all over the place. His dad rushed over and gave Tim a big old goose kiss. "My son," he said, "I didn't think we'd ever see you again."

Tim had tears in his eyes. As Tim ran off with his mom and dad, Henry's friends formed a big circle around him and honked so loudly that you could hear them for miles. A few minutes later, some of his children, grandchildren and great grandchildren came from their flocks to give Henry big old goose kisses.

- Who did Tim go off with after he and Henry landed? (Call on a student. Idea: *His parents.*)
- Everybody, were his mom and dad surprised to see him? (Signal.) *Yes.*
- Who were the first geese to give Henry a big welcome? (Call on a student. Idea: *Friends.*)

- It says that his children, grandchildren, and great grandchildren came from their flocks to welcome Henry. Those geese were not in Henry's flock. You'll read more about that later in this story.

One of Henry's grandchildren said, "We didn't think you were coming, but we knew we would see you next summer when we went north again."

"Yes," a great grandchild said, "but now you'll be able to fly back to Canada with us next spring."

Henry started to say, "Oh, I don't know," but then he smiled and said, "Sure. We'll all go back to Canada in the spring."

- Henry started to say, "Oh, I don't know." Why did he start to say that? (Call on a student. Idea: *He didn't know if he would be able to make the trip.*)
- Then what did he say? (Call on a student. Idea: *That they'd all go back to Canada in the spring.*)

And that's what happened. Henry spent the winter in the warm Florida sun, napping, eating, swimming and visiting with his friends and family. About two times every week, he would go flying with some of the geese who were less than a year old. He would always make sure that Tim went ★ with them. Henry would give the young geese practice at flying in a V. Henry would honk out orders as the V would swoop over Crooked Lake very low and very fast. Once in a while, Henry would have a sore wing after flying with the young geese, but his wing wasn't too bad.

- Name some of the things that Henry did during that winter. (Call on individual students. Ideas: *Napping; eating; swimming; visiting with friends; flying with the young geese.*)
- How old were the geese that he flew with? (Call on a student. Idea: *Less than a year old.*)
- What would those geese practice doing? (Call on a student. Ideas: *Flying in a V; swooping low and fast.*)

- How was Henry's wing after all that flying? (Call on a student. Idea: *It was a little sore after flying, but not too bad.*)

Henry wasn't really worried about his wing because the trip back north was a lot easier than the trip down to Florida. The trip north started in January, but the geese wouldn't reach Big Trout Lake in Canada until the middle of April.

- Everybody, when did the geese start going north again? (Signal.) *January.*
- When would the flock reach Big Trout Lake? (Signal.) *April.*
- Raise your hand when you know how many months that is.(Call on a student.) How many? (Ideas: *3; 4.*)

At the beginning of January, Tim, Henry and all the geese began feeling restless. They wanted to fly north. Two days later, the first flocks took off. Over the next few days, Henry watched hundreds and hundreds of flocks take off. Finally, Henry's flock was ready. It flew into the sky and joined other flocks that were leaving Crooked Lake, Reedy Lake and the other nearby lakes. The geese flew in four great Vs. The sky was filled with geese.

- Everybody, how did the geese start feeling at the beginning of January? (Signal.) *Restless.*
- In which direction did they want to go? (Signal.) *North.*
- Was Henry's flock one of the first flocks to take off? (Signal.) *No.*
- The geese that took off from the lakes around Crooked Lake formed how many great Vs? (Signal.) *4.*
- Look at the picture. It shows how many geese are in the sky when the geese start moving north.

Henry's flock followed the warm weather as it moved north. The flock would stay at a landing place long enough to make sure that the next landing place would not be frozen.

- How long did the flock stay at each landing place? (Call on a student. Idea: *Long enough to be sure the next landing place wasn't frozen.*)
- So they stayed at some landing places for weeks.

Finally, in the middle of April, the flock arrived at Big Trout Lake. There was honking and flapping as the geese met other flocks that stayed at Big Trout Lake during the summer.
Two days after the flock landed at Big Trout Lake, Tim and Henry said goodbye. It was time for Tim and the other geese that were almost a year old to form their own flock and fly off to Sandy Lake. The young geese would spend the summer at that lake.

- Listen to that part again:
  Two days after the flock landed at Big Trout Lake, Tim and Henry said goodbye. It was time for Tim and the other geese that were almost a year old to form their own flock and fly off to Sandy Lake. The young geese would spend the summer at that lake.
- Tim was going to be part of a new flock. What was unusual about all the geese in that flock? (Call on a student. Idea: *They were all almost a year old.*)
- That's why Henry's children and grandchildren were not in his flock. They were in their own flocks, and they first went into those flocks just before they were one year old.

Before Tim left, he gave Henry a big old goose kiss and said, "Thank you for everything you've done. And I hope that I'll see you next winter at Crooked Lake."
Henry said, "I'll be there."

- Who thinks that Tim will miss Henry?
- Who thinks that Henry will miss Tim?

PAIRED PRACTICE

You're going to read aloud to your partner. The **A** members will read first. Then the **B** members will read from the star to the end of the story.
(Observe students and give feedback. Praise teams that follow the rules.)

WRITTEN ITEMS

Comprehension Passage Items

a. **Find part A on your worksheet.** ✓
- The questions in part A are about Eskimos, Canada, and Alaska. I'll call on individual students to read the items. Don't say the answers. If an item has choices, read the choices.

b. (For each item: Call on a student to read the item.)
- Item 1. *[Which letter on the map shows Alaska?]*
- Item 2. *[Which letter shows Canada?]*
- Item 3. *[Which letter shows the main part of the United States?]*
- Item 4. *[Which 2 letters show where Eskimos live?]*
- Item 5. *[How warm is it during winter in Alaska?]*
- Items 6 through 11. Look at the picture below. **Write the name of each of these objects in the correct place:** Eskimo, fishing pole, sled, sled dogs, fishing spear, kayak.
- Item 12. *[What kind of boat do Eskimos use in the summer?]*
- Item 13. *[Why don't they use those boats in the winter?]*

Story Items

c. Items 14 through 26 are about today's story. Don't say the answers.
- Item 14. *[Who met Tim at Crooked Lake?]*
- Item 15. *[Why were they surprised to see Tim?]*
- Item 16. *[The first geese to greet Henry were his blank.]*
- Item 17. *[Were Henry's children, grandchildren, and great grandchildren in the same flock as Henry?]*
- Item 18. *[In the winter, Henry gave the young geese practice in flying in a blank.]*
- Item 19. *[The flocks started to fly north again in the month of blank.]*
- Item 20. *[They did not arrive at Big Trout Lake until the month of blank.]*
- Item 21. *[So it took them blank months to make the trip north.]*
- Item 22. *[After the flocks arrived at Big Trout Lake, blank and the other young geese left the flock.]*
- Item 23. *[How old were all these geese?]*
- Item 24. *[Where did those geese move to?]*
- Item 25. *[What lake would this flock go to in the fall?]*

End-of-Lesson Activities

Now finish the independent work for lesson 12. Do the worksheet first and then the textbook. Raise your hand when you're finished. (Observe students and give feedback.)

a. (Direct students to take out their marking pencils.)
- We're going to check your independent work. Remember, if you got an item wrong, make an **X** next to the item. Don't change any answers.

b. (For each item: Read the item. Call on a student to answer it. If the answer is wrong, say the correct answer. Refer to the Answer Key for the correct answers.)

c. Now use your marking pencil to fix any items you got wrong. Remember, all mistakes must be fixed before you hand in your independent work.

(Present Language Arts lesson 12 after completing Reading lesson 12. See Language Arts Guide.)

Special Projects

Note: After completing lesson 12, do these special projects with the students. You may do the projects during another part of the school day.

Materials: Road maps of your state

Project 1

a. Everybody, find page 59 in your textbook. ✓
- (Call on individual students to read the project, each student reading two to three sentences.)
- (Teacher reference:)

Special Project

Use a road map of your state to figure out how far it is between some of the cities in your state. Use the key to measure the distances.

Compare the distance you get using the key with the distance number that is shown on the map.

The distance numbers that are given on the map are often more than the distance you get by using the key. Why is that true?

Who would travel farther between two cities, a goose or a person driving on the road?

Why?

---

b. (Divide the class into groups of four or five.)
- (Provide each group with a road map that shows the distances between towns or cities as coded numbers on the map.)
- (Select two cities. Direct groups to ignore the roads and figure out the distance between the cities if someone went in a straight line. Direct groups to write their estimate of the straight-line distance between the cities.)
c. (Call on different groups to tell their distance estimates. Write the straight-line distances on the board.)
- (Repeat with two or three other examples.)
d. You've figured the straight-line distance between the cities, but the roads don't always go in a straight line between the cities.
- (Show the students how to find the distance number between cities on the map and how to add them together to find the total road distance between the cities.)
e. (Direct the groups to figure out the road distances between two pairs of cities for which they have found straight-line distances. Write the road distance on the board next to the straight-line distance for the pairs of cities.)
- Why are the road distances greater than the straight-line distances? (Call on a student. Idea: *Because the roads don't always go in straight lines.*)
- Who would travel farther between two cities, a goose or a person driving on the road? (Call on a student.) *A person driving on the road.*
- Why? (Call on a student. Idea: *Because the roads don't go in straight lines.*)

Project 2

a. Listen to the last part of the Old Henry story:
Two days after the flock landed at Big Trout Lake, Tim and Henry said goodbye. It was time for Tim and the other geese that were almost a year old to form their own flock and fly off to Sandy Lake. The young geese would spend the summer at the lake. Before Tim left, he gave Henry a big old goose kiss and said, "Thank you for everything you've done. And I hope that I'll see you next winter at Crooked Lake." Henry said, "I'll be there."

b. Henry is pretty old. Maybe he won't live through the summer. But maybe he will, and maybe he'll make the trip. Or maybe he will be alive in the fall, but maybe he won't be able to make the trip.
  • Raise your hand if you think he won't live through the summer.
  • Raise your hand if you think he will live through the summer and will make the trip.
  • Raise your hand if you think he'll live through the summer, but he won't be able to make the trip.
c. (Assign groups of four or five students based on their opinions. All members of a group should have the same opinion about what will happen in the fall.)
  • Each group is going to make up a story that tells what happens next fall. You'll tell about Tim and his flock. You'll tell about the flock that Old Henry is in. And you'll tell about Old Henry and what happens to him.
  • (Direct groups to write down some of the things they want their story to cover. Praise good suggestions.)
d. (After a group agrees on the story line, each member of the group is to write the story. Not all stories within a group have to be exactly the same.)
  • (Arrange for members of each group to read their story to the entire class.)
  • (Display the stories.)

VOCABULARY REVIEW

a. Here's the new vocabulary sentence: Scientists do not ignore ordinary things.
- Everybody, say the sentence. Get ready. (Signal.) *Scientists do not ignore ordinary things.*
- (Repeat until firm.)

b. Everybody, what word tells about things that you see all the time? (Signal.) *Ordinary.*
- What word means that you don't pay attention to something? (Signal.) *Ignore.*
- What do we call highly-trained people who study different things about the world? (Signal.) *Scientists.*
- (Repeat step b until firm.)

READING WORDS
Column 1

a. **Find lesson 13 in your textbook. ✓**
- Touch column 1. ✓
- (Teacher reference:)

1.	hind	4.	shoulder
2.	Alaskan	5.	jacket
3.	December	6.	icy

b. Word 1 is **hind.** What word? (Signal.) *Hind.*
- Spell **hind.** Get ready. (Tap for each letter.) *H-I-N-D.*
- Another word for the back part of animals is the **hind** part. Everybody, what do we call the back legs of an animal? (Signal.) *The hind legs.*

c. Word 2. What word? (Signal.) *Alaskan.*
- Spell **Alaskan.** Get ready. (Tap for each letter.) *A-L-A-S-K-A-N.*

d. Word 3. What word? (Signal.) *December.*
- Spell **December.** Get ready. (Tap for each letter.) *D-E-C-E-M-B-E-R.*

e. Word 4. What word? (Signal.) *Shoulder.*
- Spell **shoulder.** Get ready. (Tap for each letter.) *S-H-O-U-L-D-E-R.*

f. Word 5. What word? (Signal.) *Jacket.*

g. Word 6. What word? (Signal.) *Icy.*

h. Let's read those words again, the fast way.
- Word 1. What word? (Signal.) *Hind.*
- (Repeat for words 2–6.)

i. (Repeat step h until firm.)

Column 2

j. Find column 2. ✓
- (Teacher reference:)

1.	snowball	3.	snowdrift
2.	playmate	4.	slowpoke

k. These words are compound words. The first part of each word is underlined.

l. Word 1. What's the underlined part? (Signal.) *snow.*
- What's the whole word? (Signal.) *Snowball.*
- Word 2. What's the underlined part? (Signal.) *play.*
- What's the whole word? (Signal.) *Playmate.*
- Word 3. What's the underlined part? (Signal.) *snow.*
- What's the whole word? (Signal.) *Snowdrift.*
- Word 4. What's the underlined part? (Signal.) *slow.*
- What's the whole word? (Signal.) *Slowpoke.*

m. Let's read those words again, the fast way.
- Word 1. What word? (Signal.) *Snowball.*
- (Repeat for words 2–4.)

n. (Repeat step m until firm.)

Column 3

o. Find column 3. ✓
- (Teacher reference:)

1.	repeated	3.	dangerous
2.	playful	4.	walruses

p. All these words have endings. The first part of each word is underlined.

q. Word 1. What's the first part? (Signal.) *repeat.*
- What's the whole word? (Signal.) *Repeated.*

- When you **repeat** something, you do it again. How do you repeat a question? (Call on a student. Idea: *Say it again.*)
- Word 2. What's the first part? (Signal.) *play.*
- What's the whole word? (Signal.) *Playful.*
- Word 3. What's the first part? (Signal.) *danger.*
- What's the whole word? (Signal.) *Dangerous.*
- Word 4. What's the first part? (Signal.) *walrus.*
- What's the whole word? (Signal.) *Walruses.*

r. Let's read those words again, the fast way.
- Word 1. What word? (Signal.) *Repeated.*
- (Repeat for: **2. playful, 3. dangerous, 4. walruses.**)
s. (Repeat step r until firm.)

Column 4

t. Find column 4. ✓
- (Teacher reference:)

1. **killer whale**	4. **Oolak**
2. **polar bear**	5. **March**
3. **ice floe**	6. **splat**

u. Number 1. What words? (Signal.) *Killer whale.*
- (Repeat for numbers 2 and 3.)
v. Word 4. What word? (Signal.) *Oolak.*
- (Repeat for words 5 and 6.)
w. (Repeat steps u and v until firm.)

Column 5

x. Find column 5. ✓
- (Teacher reference:)

1. **Usk**	4. **February**
2. **Oomoo**	5. **scattered**
3. **pebbled**	6. **fur**

y. Word 1. What word? (Signal.) *Usk.*
- **Usk** is the name of a polar bear you'll read about.
z. Word 2. What word? (Signal.) *Oomoo.*
- (Repeat for words 3–6.)
a. Let's read those words again.
- Word 1. What word? (Signal.) *Usk.*
- (Repeat for words 2–6.)
b. (Repeat step a until firm.)

Individual Turns
(For columns 1–5: Call on individual students, each to read one to three words per turn.)

COMPREHENSION PASSAGES

Passage B

a. Find part B in your textbook. ✓
- You're going to start a new story about two Eskimo children. First, you'll read two information passages. The first one gives some facts about Alaskan animals.
b. Everybody, touch the title. ✓
- (Call on a student to read the title.) *[Animals in Alaska.]*
- Everybody, what's the title? (Signal.) *Animals in Alaska.*
c. (Call on individual students to read the passage, each student reading two or three sentences at a time. Ask the specified questions as the students read.)

Animals in Alaska
The picture below shows some of the animals that live in Alaska. Here are the names of the animals in the picture: polar bear, elephant seal, killer whale, walrus and wolf.

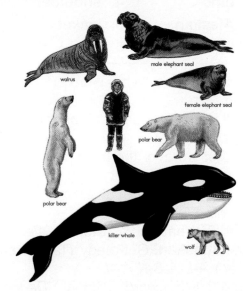

- (Call on individual students to reread the names in the sentence.)
- Everybody, touch one of the polar bears in the picture. ✓
- What color are those bears? (Signal.) *White.*

- You can see that polar bears can stand on their hind legs.
- Touch the two elephant seals. ✓
- Which seal is bigger, the male elephant seal or the female elephant seal? (Signal.) *The male elephant seal.*
- Yes, they don't look very much alike.
- Touch the killer whale. ✓
- You can see the teeth that this whale has. The killer whale is very smart and very dangerous.
- Touch one of the fins of the killer whale. ✓
- Touch the walrus. ✓
- The walrus has large tusks. Those tusks are big teeth. Touch the walrus's tusks. ✓
- Touch the wolf. ✓
- The wolf has long legs so it can go through the deep snow without getting stuck.

> **Tell which animal in the picture is the biggest and which animal is the smallest.**

- Everybody, which animal is the biggest? (Signal.) *The killer whale.*
- Which animal is the smallest? (Signal.) *The wolf.*

Passage C

a. Find part C in your textbook. ✓
- This information passage tells about where the next story takes place.
b. Everybody, touch the title. ✓
- (Call on a student to read the title.) [*Where Oomoo and Oolak Lived.*]
- Everybody, what's the title? (Signal.) *Where Oomoo and Oolak Lived.*
c. (Call on individual students to read the passage, each student reading two or three sentences at a time. Ask the specified questions as the students read.)

> **Where Oomoo and Oolak Lived**
> **In the next story, you will read about Oomoo and Oolak. They were Eskimos who lived in Alaska.**
> **Pictures 1, 2 and 3 show the place where Oomoo and Oolak lived.**
> **Pictures 1 and 2 show what their place looked like in the spring.**
> **Picture 1 shows how that place looks if you are standing on the beach.**
> **Picture 2 shows how that place looks**

> **if you are above that place looking down. Picture 2 is like a map of the place. You can see the ice floe in Picture 2.**

Picture 1

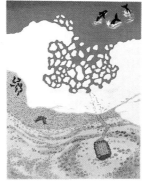

Picture 2   Picture 3

- The ice floe is the part of the ocean that is still covered with ice. Run your finger from one end of the ice floe in picture 2 to the other. ✓
- Pictures 1 and 2 show some of the same things. Everybody, touch the tent in both pictures.
  (Observe students and give feedback.)
- Picture 2 doesn't show how high above the beach the tent is. Touch the path down to the beach in pictures 1 and 2.
  (Observe students and give feedback.)

> **The pebbled beach shows where the sand ends and the ocean begins.**

- In picture 2, the pebbled beach is the part with animals on it. Everybody, run your finger from one end of the pebbled beach to the other end. ✓
- The beach is called a pebbled beach because it's covered with pebbles. What are pebbles? (Call on a student. Idea: *Small stones.*)
- Touch the path where it crosses the pebbled beach in picture 2. ✓

- Now follow the path across the ice floe and out to the water. ✓
- Remember where that path goes. You'll be reading about it.

> **Seals are on the pebbled beach, far from the tent.**

- Everybody, touch the seals in picture 2. ✓

> **Two walruses are closer on the pebbled beach. Near the end of the ice floe are killer whales.**

- Everybody, touch the two walruses in picture 2. ✓
- Touch the killer whales in the water near the end of the ice floe. ✓

> **The tent on top of the hill was Oomoo's summer home.**
> **Picture 3 shows how the same place looked at the end of summer.**

- Everybody, touch the picture that shows how the place looks at the end of summer. ✓

> **Compare the place in spring and at the end of the summer. Tell three things that have changed.**

- Look at pictures 2 and 3 and tell one thing that has changed by the end of summer. (Call on individual students. Ideas: *The seals are gone; the walruses are gone; there aren't many ice chunks;* etc.)

> **In summer, the seals and the walruses moved away before the water froze. The killer whales also moved away. These animals came back in the spring.**
> **Make sure you can read these words:**
>
> | seal | walrus | killer whale |
> | ice floe | slope | |

- (Call on individual students to read the words in the box.)

Note: Beginning with this lesson, students do not read the whole story out loud.

STORY READING

a. Find part D in your textbook. ✓
- This is the first part of a new story. The error limit for group reading is 11 errors.
b. Everybody, touch the title. ✓
- (Call on a student to read the title.) *[Oomoo.]*
- Everybody, what's the title? (Signal.) *Oomoo.*
c. (Call on individual students to read the story, each student reading two or three sentences at a time. Ask the specified questions as the students read.)

> - (Correct errors: Tell the word. Direct the student to reread the sentence.)
> - (If the group makes more than 11 errors, direct the students to reread the story.)

> **Oomoo**
> **Oomoo was an Eskimo girl who was twelve years old.**

- You know some things about Oomoo. Name two things you know about her. (Call on a student. Ideas: *She's an Eskimo; she is 12 years old.*)

> **Oomoo had a brother named Oolak. He was ten.**

- Everybody, how old was Oolak? (Signal.) *Ten.*
- Who was older, Oomoo or Oolak? (Signal.) *Oomoo.*

> **Oomoo and Oolak lived in Alaska, near the ocean. When our story starts, Oomoo and Oolak are very happy. They are happy because it is April.**

- Everybody, in what part of the world did they live? (Signal.) *Alaska.*
- Why were they happy? (Call on a student. Idea: *Because it was April.*)
- I wonder why April made them happy.

April is a very good time of the year for the Eskimos along the Alaskan coast because April is in spring. And in the spring, the days start getting longer and warmer.

- Everybody, what happens to the days in spring? (Signal.) *They get longer and warmer.*
- What season is April in? (Signal.) *Spring.*

In the spring, you can notice the days getting longer. The days get longer because the North Pole of the earth is tilting toward the sun. As the North Pole tilts more and more toward the sun, the days get longer and longer.

- Why do the days get longer in spring? (Call on a student. Idea: *The North Pole of the earth starts leaning toward the sun.*)

If you live in Alaska, the days get very short in the winter and very long in the summer. The picture of the globes shows why. Globe W shows how the earth looks on the first day of winter. The X marks the place where Oomoo and Oolak live. Half of the earth is dark all the time. The place where Oomoo and Oolak live is so close to the North Pole that it is in darkness all winter long.

- Everybody, touch globe **W.** ✓
- How do you know that this is the earth in wintertime? (Call on a student. Idea: *The North Pole is tilting away from the sun.*)
- Everybody, touch the place marked with an **X.** ✓
- That's where Oomoo and Oolak live. The little dotted line shows how that **X** moves when the earth turns around and around. The **X** never goes into the sunlight. It's always in the shadow. That means it is **always** dark in the winter where Oomoo and Oolak live.

During Oomoo's winter, there is no daytime. There is only nighttime. That nighttime lasts for weeks and weeks. Imagine not seeing the sun for weeks. Then imagine what it is like to see the sun start coming out for a longer time each day.
Look at globe S. It shows the earth on the first day of summer.

- Everybody, touch globe **S.** ✓
- How do you know that globe S shows the earth during summer? (Call on a student. Idea: *The North Pole is tilting toward the sun.*)
- Everybody, touch the place where Oomoo lives. ✓
- Is it in the **shadow** or the **sunlight**? (Signal.) *Sunlight.*
- So during the summertime, there is no darkness where Oomoo and Oolak live.

You can tell that globe S shows summer because the North Pole is tilting toward the sun. On the first day of summer, it doesn't get dark where Oomoo and Oolak live. They are so close to the North Pole that they can see the sun all the time. For weeks, there is no night—just daytime. Then the sun starts disappearing for a longer time each day.

- Everybody, in which season would the sun shine all the time where Oomoo lives? (Signal.) *Summer.*
- When the sun starts disappearing for longer times each day, what season is it? (Signal.) *Fall.*

Remember, in summer the sun shines all the time where Oomoo and Oolak live. In winter, the sun does not shine at all. If you understand these facts, you can see why Oomoo and Oolak were happy when it was April. During the months of December and January, they had not seen the sun. During the months of February and March, the days got

> longer and warmer. In April, the days were getting much longer. Now the sun was shining more than 12 hours each day.

- Everybody, how long was the sun shining each day in April? (Signal.) *More than 12 hours.*

> The little flowers were starting to pop out on hills near the ocean. Thousands of seals were beginning to appear along the shore. Now the days were beautiful. "The sun," Oomoo said to herself and held her hands up. "The beautiful sun." She took a deep breath and smiled at Oolak. He smiled. They were standing on a hill next to the ocean. Tiny white clouds were scattered in the blue sky. The ocean was blue and gray, and it looked very cold. There was still a lot of snow on the ground, but it was wet snow, the kind of snow that made good snowballs.

- Everybody, I'll read that part again. Close your eyes and get a picture of how Oomoo must have felt after that long, dark winter.
    The little flowers were starting to pop out on hills near the ocean. Thousands of seals were beginning to appear along the shore. Now the days were beautiful. "The sun," Oomoo said to herself and held her hands up. "The beautiful sun." She took a deep breath and smiled at Oolak. He smiled.
    They were standing on a hill next to the ocean. Tiny white clouds were scattered in the blue sky. The ocean was blue and gray, and it looked very cold. There was still a lot of snow on the ground, but it was wet snow, the kind of snow that made good snowballs.
- If you were Oomoo, tell me some things that you were feeling. (Call on individual students. Ideas: *Happy; excited.*)
- Imagine the flowers blooming while there is still snow on the ground.
- Read the rest of the story to yourself. Find out two things. Find out why Oomoo started to run away from Oolak. Also find out what made her stop running when she was on the ice chunks. Raise your hand when you're done.

> Oolak made a good snowball. Oomoo figured out what Oolak was going to do, so she started to run away. She ran down the slippery hill and onto the ice chunks. She heard a snowball splat next to her, but she didn't stop. She ran and hollered over her shoulder, "Missed again!" She was smiling as she jumped to the next chunk of ice. She heard another splat next to her.
>   Then she stopped. In front of her, a huge polar bear was climbing from the water onto the ice. The polar bear was no more than three meters from Oomoo.

- (After all students have raised their hand:)
- Why did Oomoo run from Oolak? (Call on a student. Idea: *Because he was going to throw a snowball at her.*)
- Where did she run? (Call on a student. Ideas: *Down the slippery hill; onto the ice chunks.*)
- What made her stop running when she was on the ice chunks? (Call on a student. Idea: *A huge polar bear was in front of her.*)
- How far was that polar bear from her? (Call on a student. Idea: *No more than three meters.*)
- Everybody, look at the picture. Oomoo is no longer on the ice floe. She is on the chunks of ice that have broken off the ice floe. Everybody, touch the polar bear in the picture. ✓
- I wonder what's going to happen next.

EXERCISE 5

PAIRED PRACTICE

You're going to read aloud to your partner. First the **B** members will read. Then the **A** members will read from the star to the end of the story.
(Observe students and give feedback. Praise teams that follow the rules.)

EXERCISE 6

WRITTEN ITEMS
Story Items
a. Find part E in your textbook. ✓

b. The items in part E are about today's story.

c. (For each item: Call on a student to read the item.)

- Item 1. *[When days get longer, is the North Pole tilting **toward the sun** or **away from the sun**?]*
- Item 2. *[When days get shorter, is the North Pole tilting **toward the sun** or **away from the sun**?]*
- Item 3. *[Oomoo and Oolak might have a hard time going to sleep at night in the summertime. Tell why.]*
- Item 4. *[In April, the sun shines for more than <u>blank</u> hours each day in Alaska.]*
- Item 5. *[What kind of animal did Oomoo see at the end of the story?]*
- Item 6. *[How far was Oomoo from that animal?]*
- Item 7. *[During Oomoo's winter, there is no <u>blank</u>. Daytime, nighttime.]*
- Item 8. *[Write the letter of the globe that shows how the earth looks on the first day of winter.]*
- Item 9. *[Write the letter of the globe that shows how the earth looks on the first day of summer.]*

Comprehension Passage Items

d. **Find part A on your worksheet.** ✓

- The items in part A are about Alaskan animals. I'll call on a student to read the items, but don't say the answers.
- Read the directions at the top of the box. *[Label each animal in the picture below.]*
- (Teacher reference:)

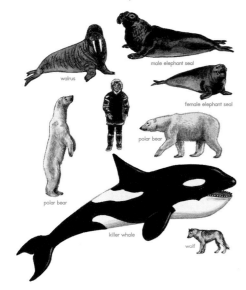

e. (For each item: Call on a student to read the item.)

- Item 7. *[Which animal in the picture is the biggest?]*

- Item 8. *[Which animal in the picture is the smallest?]*

f. The items in part B are about where Oomoo and Oolak live.

g. (For each item: Call on a student to read the item.)

- Read the directions above the map. *[Write these words in the correct places on the map.]*
- Read the words you'll put on the map. *[Pebbled beach, killer whales, summer home, path, ice floe, seals, walruses.]*
- Item 16. *[At the end of summer, the beach where Oomoo lived was different from the picture in 3 ways. What was different about the ice floe?]*
- Item 17. *[What was missing from the water?]*
- Item 18. *[What was missing from the beach?]*

End-of-Lesson Activities

INDEPENDENT WORK

Now finish your independent work for lesson 13. Do the worksheet first and then the textbook. Raise your hand when you're finished. (Observe students and give feedback.)

WORKCHECK

a. (Direct students to take out their marking pencils.)

- We're going to check your independent work. Remember, if you got an item wrong, make an **X** next to the item. Don't change any answers.

b. (For each item: Read the item. Call on a student to answer it. If the answer is wrong, say the correct answer. Refer to the Answer Key for the correct answers.)

c. Now use your marking pencil to fix up any items you got wrong. Remember, all mistakes must be fixed up before you hand in your independent work.

LANGUAGE ARTS

(Present Language Arts lesson 13 after completing Reading lesson 13. See Language Arts Guide.)

Lesson 14

VOCABULARY REVIEW

a. You learned a sentence that tells what the horses did.
  • Everybody, say that sentence. Get ready. (Signal.) *The horses became restless on the dangerous route.*
  • (Repeat until firm.)

b. Here's the last sentence you learned: Scientists do not ignore ordinary things.
  • Everybody, say that sentence. Get ready. (Signal.) *Scientists do not ignore ordinary things.*
  • (Repeat until firm.)

c. Everybody, what do we call highly trained people who study different things about the world? (Signal.) *Scientists.*
  • What word tells about things that you see all the time? (Signal.) *Ordinary.*
  • What word means that you don't pay attention to something? (Signal.) *Ignore.*

d. Once more. Say the sentence that tells what scientists do not do. Get ready. (Signal.) *Scientists do not ignore ordinary things.*

READING WORDS

Column 1

a. **Find lesson 14 in your textbook.** ✓
  • Touch column 1. ✓
  • (Teacher reference:)

1. nudged	4. tossing
2. scrambled	5. jacket
3. growling	6. playmate

b. These words have more than one part. The first part of each word is underlined.

c. Word 1. What's the underlined part? (Signal.) *nudge.*
  • What's the whole word? (Signal.) *Nudged.*
  • Spell **nudged.** Get ready. (Tap for each letter.) *N-U-D-G-E-D.*

  • When you **nudge** something, you give it a little push. Everybody, what word means **to give something a little push?** (Signal.) *Nudge.*
  • Word 2. What's the underlined part? (Signal.) *scramble.*
  • What's the whole word? (Signal.) *Scrambled.*
  • Spell **scrambled.** Get ready. (Tap for each letter.) *S-C-R-A-M-B-L-E-D.*
  • Things that are **scrambled** are all mixed up. Here's that sentence with the words scrambled: are that scrambled things up mixed all.
  • Word 3. What's the underlined part? (Signal.) *growl.*
  • What's the whole word? (Signal.) *Growling.*
  • Spell **growling.** Get ready. (Tap for each letter.) *G-R-O-W-L-I-N-G.*
  • Word 4. What's the underlined part? (Signal.) *toss.*
  • What's the whole word? (Signal.) *Tossing.*
  • Spell **tossing.** Get ready. (Tap for each letter.) *T-O-S-S-I-N-G.*
  • Word 5. What's the underlined part? (Signal.) *jack.*
  • What's the whole word? (Signal.) *Jacket.*
  • Word 6. What's the underlined part? (Signal.) *play.*
  • What's the whole word? (Signal.) *Playmate.*

d. Let's read those words again, the fast way.
  • Word 1. What word? (Signal.) *Nudged.*
  • (Repeat for words 2–6.)

e. (Repeat step d until firm.)

Column 2

f. Find column 2. ✓
  • (Teacher reference:)

1. tumbling	4. hind
2. hitch	5. fur
3. ridge	6. icy

g. Word 1. What word? (Signal.) *Tumbling.*
- When things tumble, they turn over and over and over. If a rock tumbles down a hill, it turns over and over as it comes down the hill.
h. Word 2. What word? (Signal.) *Hitch.*
- When you hitch two things together, you attach them to each other. When a farmer attaches a horse to a wagon, he hitches the horse to the wagon. Everybody, what does a woman do when she attaches a trailer to a truck? (Signal.) *She hitches the trailer to the truck.*
i. Word 3. What word? (Signal.) *Ridge.*
- A ridge is a long strip of land that is raised above the land around it. If you walk along the ridge, you walk on the long, raised strip. If you get off the ridge, you will go down one side or the other.
j. Word 4. What word? (Signal.) *Hind.*
  - (Repeat for words 5 and 6.)
k. Let's read those words again, the fast way.
  - Word 1. What word? (Signal.) *Tumbling.*
  - (Repeat for: **2. hitch, 3. ridge, 4. hind, 5. fur, 6. icy.**)
l. (Repeat step k until firm.)

Column 3
m. Find column 3. ✓
- (Teacher reference:)

1. **snowdrifts**	4. **repeated**
2. **dangerous**	5. **playful**
3. **slowpoke**	

n. Word 1. What word? (Signal.) *Snowdrifts.*
  - (Repeat for words 2–5.)
o. (Repeat step n until firm.)

Individual Turns

(For columns 1–3: Call on individual students, each to read one to three words per turn.)

EXERCISE 3

COMPREHENSION PASSAGE

a. Find part B in your textbook. ✓
- You're going to read the next story about Oomoo and Oolak. First you'll read the information passage. It gives some facts about spring in Alaska.
b. Everybody, touch the title. ✓
- (Call on a student to read the title.) *[The Dangerous Season.]*

- Everybody, what's the selection going to tell about? (Signal.) *The Dangerous Season.*
c. (Call on individual students to read the passage, each student reading two or three sentences at a time. Ask the specified questions as the students read.)

The Dangerous Season
The animals in Alaska are most dangerous in the spring. The male animals are ready to fight anything. The females have babies in the spring. After they have had babies, they will fight any animal that bothers their babies.

- Everybody, in which season are animals most dangerous in Alaska? (Signal.) *Spring.*
- Tell me about the male animals. (Call on a student. Idea: *They're ready to fight anything.*)
- Everybody, when do females have babies? (Signal.) *In the spring.*
- What makes females fight in the spring? (Call on a student. Idea: *When animals bother their babies.*)

Polar bears are dangerous. So are wolves and walruses. The picture shows two animals fighting on the beach.

- Everybody, what kind of animals are fighting in the picture? (Signal.) *Elephant seals.*
- Are those male elephant seals or female elephant seals? (Signal.) *Male elephant seals.*
- What are the females doing? (Call on a student. Idea: *Lying on the beach.*)

The winner of the fight will keep his place on the beach. The loser will have to find another spot on the beach. The loser will probably have to fight another seal.

- Tell me about the winner. (Call on a student. Idea: *He'll keep his place on the beach.*)
- Where will the loser have to go? (Call on a student. Idea: *To another spot on the beach.*)

- What will he probably have to do there? (Call on a student. Idea: *Fight another seal.*)

Remember, these animals are most dangerous in the spring.

- That fact is important in a story you're going to read.

STORY READING

> **Note:** Students read the end of the story silently.

a. Find part C in your textbook. ✓ The error limit for group reading is 12 errors.
b. Everybody, touch the title. ✓
- (Call on a student to read the title.) *[Usk, the Polar Bear.]*
- Everybody, what's the title? (Signal.) *Usk, the Polar Bear.*
- What happened at the end of the last story? (Call on a student. Idea: *Oomoo met a polar bear.*)
- Today's story starts with Oomoo standing on an ice chunk. In front of her is a huge polar bear.
c. (Call on individual students to read the passage, each student reading two or three sentences at a time. Ask the specified questions as the students read.)

> - (Correct errors: Tell the word. Direct the student to reread the sentence.)
> - (If the group makes more than 12 errors, direct the students to reread the story.)

Usk, the Polar Bear
"Usk," Oomoo shouted. "Usk, you big hill of white. Where have you been?"

- Everybody, does she know this polar bear? (Signal.) *Yes.*
- Does she seem to be afraid of the bear? (Signal.) *No.*
- What's the bear's name? (Signal.) *Usk.*

The huge polar bear stood up and wagged his head from side to side. He was nearly three meters tall when he stood up on his hind legs.

- Three meters is higher than the ceilings in most houses and apartments. Imagine an animal so big that it could not stand up straight in an ordinary room.

Oomoo started to run toward Usk, but then she stopped. She remembered what her father had told her last fall, when the days were starting to get short. Her father had told her that Usk was no longer a bear cub. He was a full-grown bear and full-grown bears are not pets.

- What had her father told her about Usk? (Call on a student. Idea: *Usk was a full-grown bear.*)
- What's a bear cub? (Call on a student. Idea: *A baby bear.*)
- What season was it when her father told her that? (Signal.) *Fall.*
- What season is it in the story now? (Signal.) *Spring.*

Now Oolak was standing on the ice chunk next to Oomoo. "Wow," he said, "Usk has grown a lot since last fall."
"Yes," Oomoo said. "Usk is beautiful." She was right.
Usk's coat was white-white, so bright in the sun that the color hurt Oomoo's eyes.

- Everybody, imagine that huge bear so white in the bright sun that the color hurts your eyes.

As she looked at Usk, she remembered the first time she had ever seen him. Hunters had shot Usk's mother three years ago. Usk was just a baby, no bigger than a puppy.

- Everybody, how long ago had she first seen Usk? (Signal.) *Three years ago.*
- What had happened to his mother? (Call on a student. Idea: *Hunters shot her.*)
- How big was Usk when Oomoo first saw him? (Call on a student. Idea: *No bigger than a puppy.*)

- Everybody, use your hands and show me how big Usk was when she first saw him. ✓

When Oomoo found Usk, he was very skinny and he could hardly move. For months she fed him milk from a bottle that she had made out of animal skins. Usk grew bigger and bigger. He became the best playmate that anybody ever had. He loved to run and wrestle in the snow. He slid down steep snowdrifts headfirst. He slid down them tail first. In fact, he would sometimes slide down them as he turned around and around, with his legs sticking out in all directions as he swept a wide path down the snowdrift.

- This part tells about what Usk had been like when he was a cub. Get a picture of him playing when he was about as big as a dog. I'll read that part again:

  When Oomoo found Usk, he was very skinny and he could hardly move. For months she fed him milk from a bottle that she had made out of animal skins. Usk grew bigger and bigger. He became the best playmate that anybody ever had. He loved to run and wrestle in the snow. He slid down steep snowdrifts headfirst. He slid down them tail first. In fact, he would sometimes slide down them as he turned around and around, with his legs sticking out in all directions as he swept a wide path down the snowdrift.

❀ **As Oomoo stood near the great bear, she found it hard to believe that this same bear used to fit inside her jacket or that this bear used to sleep on the floor of her winter home.**

- Why did she find that hard to believe? (Call on a student. Idea: *Because he was so big now.*)

Usk had been Oomoo's friend for over two years, but last fall something about him changed. He still liked to play sometimes, but ✦ at other times he didn't seem to be interested in Oomoo or in being with her.

- How did he change? (Call on a student. Ideas: *He stopped wanting to play; he wasn't interested in Oomoo.*)
- When had this change come about? (Call on a student. Ideas: *The third year; last fall.*)
- This change happened when Usk was over 2 years old.

Usk would go off by himself and walk along the high slopes, sometimes howling into the air like a dog. Sometimes he wouldn't come down to see Oomoo for three or four days at a ❀ time. And each time he came back, he didn't seem as playful as he had been the time before.

- When he went off by himself, how long would he be gone? (Call on a student. Idea: *Three or four days.*)
- And how was he different each time he came back? (Call on a student. Idea: *He wasn't as playful.*)
- Why do you think Usk was changing? (Call on individual students. Ideas: *He was getting older; he wanted to be with other bears.*)

One day late in the fall, another polar bear came over the hills. It was a young male, about the same size as Usk. Usk attacked that bear and drove it away. That was the day that Oomoo's father told her and Oolak not to go near the bear anymore. "Usk is a bear," her father had told them. "And bears do what bears do. They are not pets. Do not go near Usk anymore. He could hurt you."

- Everybody, was Usk behaving like a playful bear cub now? (Signal.) *No.*
- Why did he pick a fight with that other bear? (Call on a student. Idea: *He didn't want the other bear on his home ground.*)

Oomoo stood there on the ice chunk, looking up at Usk. She remembered what her father had told her.

- The story tells us where Oomoo is. Everybody, where is she? (Signal.) *On the ice chunk.*
- What season is it? (Signal.) *Spring.*

- She's remembering what her father had told her. What had he told her? (**Call on a student.** Idea: *To stay away from Usk.*)
- Everybody, when had her father told her that? (**Signal.**) *Last fall.*
- When had Usk fought with the other bear? (**Signal.**) *Last fall.*
- During this whole story, Oomoo has been standing on the ice chunk. She has been remembering different things. She has been remembering what Usk was like as a cub. She has been remembering what happened last fall.

> **Oomoo wanted to run over and give that great big bear a great big hug. She wanted to bury her face in his heavy white fur. She wanted to slide down the slopes with him. But she just stood there, smiling. "Hi, Usk," she said. Her brother repeated the greeting.**

- Why didn't Oomoo hug Usk? (**Call on a student.** Ideas: *She was afraid of Usk; her father told her to stay away from Usk.*)
- Everybody, what did Oolak say? (**Signal.**) *Hi, Usk.*

> **Usk dropped to all four legs and lowered his rear end, the way he always did when he wanted to play.**

- Have you ever seen dogs do that? They get their rear ends down and then they run really fast. That's what Usk was doing.
- Read the rest of the story to yourself. Find out two things. Find out what Oolak threw at Usk. Find out what Usk did. Raise your hand when you're done.

> **"Usk wants to play," Oolak hollered. Oolak was holding a wet snowball. He threw it at Usk and hit the bear in the shoulder. "Come on, Usk," he yelled, and ran back toward the shore.**
> **Oomoo was going to remind her brother that they should not play with Usk. But before she could say anything, the bear bumped into her, almost knocking her into the icy water. Usk ran past her after Oolak, who was running toward the beach**

> **and hollering, "Here I am, you big white slowpoke."**
> **Oomoo started running after the bear. She began to laugh.**

- (After all students have raised their hands:)
- Everybody, what did Oolak throw at Usk? (**Signal.**) *A snowball.*
- Then what did Usk do? (**Call on a student.** Idea: *Ran after Oolak.*)
- Was Usk mad? (**Signal.**) *No.*
- So they were running from the ice chunks toward the beach. Everybody, who was running first? (**Signal.**) *Oolak.*
- Who was running after Oolak? (**Signal.**) *Usk.*
- Who was running after Usk? (**Signal.**) *Oomoo.*
- How do you think Oomoo's father would feel about this game if he saw it? (**Call on a student.** Idea: *He wouldn't like it.*)

EXERCISE 5

PAIRED PRACTICE

You're going to read aloud to your partner. Today the **A** members will read first. Then the **B** members will read from the star to the end of the story.
(Observe students and give feedback. Praise teams that follow the rules.)

EXERCISE 6

WRITTEN ITEMS

Comprehension Passage Items

a. **Find part A on your worksheet.** ✓
- The items in part A are about the dangerous season in Alaska. I'll call on a student to read the items, but don't say the answers.

b. (For each item: Call on a student to read the item.)
- Item 1. *[In what season are animals most dangerous in Alaska?]*
- Item 2. *[During what season do female animals in Alaska have babies?]*
- Item 3. *[Female animals fight in the spring to protect <u>blank</u>.]*
- Item 4. *[Name 2 kinds of Alaskan animals that are dangerous in the spring.]*

Story Items

c. The items in part B are about today's story.

d. (For each item: Call on a student to read the item.)

- Item 5. *[What had happened to Usk's mother?]*
- Item 6. *[When Oomoo first saw Usk, Usk was no bigger than a <u>blank</u>.]*
- Item 7. *[About how tall was Usk when he stood up now?]*
- Item 8. *[Oomoo's father said, "Full-grown bears are not <u>blank</u>." Cubs, pets, dogs.]*
- Item 9. *[Usk had become less playful last <u>blank</u>.]*
- Item 10. *[Oomoo didn't run up and hug Usk because she remembered what <u>blank</u> had told her.]*
- Item 11. *[What did Oolak throw at Usk?]*
- Item 12. *[Why did Oolak do that?]*

Skill Items

e. The sentence above item 13 says: Scientists do not ignore ordinary things. Items 13 through 15 refer to that sentence.

- Item 13. *[What word means that you don't pay attention to something?]* Everybody, what word? (Signal.) *Ignore.*
- Item 14. *[What word tells about things that you see all the time?]* Everybody, what word? (Signal.) *Ordinary.*
- Item 15. *[What do we call highly trained people who study different things about the world?]* Everybody, what word? (Signal.) *Scientists.*

End-of-Lesson Activities

Now finish the independent work for lesson 14. Raise your hand when you're finished.

(Observe students and give feedback.)

a. (Direct students to take out their marking pencils.)

- We're going to check your independent work. Remember, if you got an item wrong, make an **X** next to the item. Don't change any answers.

b. (For each item: Read the item. Call on a student to answer it. If the answer is wrong, say the correct answer. Refer to the Answer Key for the correct answers.)

c. Now use your marking pencil to fix any items you got wrong. Remember, all mistakes must be fixed before you hand in your independent work.

(Present Language Arts lesson 14 after completing Reading lesson 14. See Language Arts Guide.)

(Present Activity 1 after completing Reading lessons 14-16. See Activities Across the Curriculum.)

Lesson 15

Materials: Each student will need their thermometer chart for exercise 6.

EXERCISE 1

VOCABULARY REVIEW

a. You learned a sentence that tells what scientists do not do.
- Everybody, say that sentence. Get ready. (Signal.) *Scientists do not ignore ordinary things.*
- (Repeat until firm.)

b. Everybody, what's the first word in the sentence? (Signal.) *Scientists.*

c. I'll say part of the sentence. When I stop, you say the next word. Listen: Scientists do not ignore . . . Everybody, what's the next word? (Signal.) *Ordinary.*

d. Listen: Scientists do not . . . Everybody, what's the next word? (Signal.) *Ignore.*
- Say the whole sentence. Get ready. (Signal.) *Scientists do not ignore ordinary things.*

EXERCISE 2

READING WORDS

Column 1

a. **Find lesson 15 in your textbook.** ✓
- Touch column 1. ✓
- (Teacher reference:)

1. mosquito	4. no-see-ums
2. actually	5. scientists
3. punish	6. ordinary

b. Word 1 is **mosquito.** What word? (Signal.) *Mosquito.*
- Spell **mosquito.** Get ready. (Tap for each letter.) *M-O-S-Q-U-I-T-O.*

c. Word 2 is **actually.** What word? (Signal.) *Actually.*
- Spell **actually.** Get ready. (Tap for each letter.) *A-C-T-U-A-L-L-Y.*

d. Word 3 is **punish.** What word? (Signal.) *Punish.*
- Spell **punish.** Get ready. (Tap for each letter.) *P-U-N-I-S-H.*

e. Word 4 is **no-see-ums.** What word? (Signal.) *No-see-ums.*
- No-see-ums are tiny biting insects that live in Alaska and Canada. No-see-ums feel like mosquitoes, but they are so small you can hardly see them.

f. Word 5. What word? (Signal.) *Scientists.*
- Word 6. What word? (Signal.) *Ordinary.*

g. Let's read those words again, the fast way.
- Word 1. What word? (Signal.) *Mosquito.*
- (Repeat for words 2–6.)

h. (Repeat step g until firm.)

Column 2

i. Find column 2. ✓
- (Teacher reference:)

1. speckled	3. scrambled
2. nudged	4. sliced

- All these words end with the letters **E–D.**

j. Word 1. What word? (Signal.) *Speckled.*
- Things that have small spots are speckled. Everybody, what do we call a chicken that has small spots? (Signal.) *A speckled chicken.*

k. Word 2. What word? (Signal.) *Nudged.*
- (Repeat for words 3 and 4.)

l. Let's read those words again.
- Word 1. What word? (Signal.) *Speckled.*
- (Repeat for words 2–4.)

m. (Repeat step l until firm.)

Column 3

n. Find column 3. ✓
- (Teacher reference:)

1. forth	4. hitch
2. cliff	5. enter
3. ignore	6. careless

o. Word 1. What word? (Signal.) *Forth.*
- Move your hand back and forth. ✓

p. Word 2. What word? (Signal.) *Cliff.*
- A cliff is like a side of a hill that goes almost straight up and down.

q. Word 3. What word? (Signal.) *Ignore.*
- (Repeat for words 4–6.)

r. (Repeat step q until firm.)

Column 4

s. Find column 4. ✓
- (Teacher reference:)

> 1. swarming   3. growling
> 2. sloshing   4. tumbling

- All these words end with the letters **I-N-G.**
t. Word 1. What word? (Signal.) *Swarming.*
- When insects swarm, hundreds of them fly very close to each other.
u. Word 2. What word? (Signal.) *Sloshing.*
- If you swing a bucket of water back and forth, the water sloshes around.
v. Word 3. What word? (Signal.) *Growling.*
w. Word 4. What word? (Signal.) *Tumbling.*
x. Let's read those words again, the fast way.
- Word 1. What word? (Signal.) *Swarming.*
- (Repeat for words 2–4.)
y. (Repeat step x until firm.)

EXERCISE 3

COMPREHENSION PASSAGE

a. Find part B in your textbook. ✓
- You're going to read the next story about Oomoo and Oolak. First you'll read the information passage. It reviews some facts you have learned.
b. Everybody, touch the title. ✓
- (Call on a student to read the title.) *[Florida, Canada, and Alaska.]*
- Everybody, what's the title? (Signal.) *Florida, Canada, and Alaska.*
c. (Call on individual students to read the passage, each student reading two or three sentences at a time. Ask the specified questions as the students read.)

> **Florida, Canada, and Alaska**
> You've read about places in Florida, Canada and Alaska. See what you remember about those places.
> Which place in Canada did you read about?

- Everybody, what's the answer? (Signal.) *Big Trout Lake.*

> **Who lived there?**

- What's the answer? (Call on a student. Idea: *Henry, Tim, and their friends and relatives.*)

> **Who lived in Alaska?**

- What's the answer? (Call on a student. Idea: *Oomoo, Oolak, Usk.*)

> **Which place is farthest south, Florida, Big Trout Lake or Alaska?**

- Everybody, what's the answer? (Signal.) *Florida.*

> **Which place is farthest north?**

- Everybody, what's the answer? (Signal.) *Alaska.*

> **Which place has the warmest winters?**

- Everybody, what's the answer? (Signal.) *Florida.*

> **Which place has the coldest winters?**

- Everybody, what's the answer? (Signal.) *Alaska.*

> **Here's a map that shows Canada and Alaska.**
> **You can see the route that goes from Big Trout Lake to where Oomoo and Oolak live.**

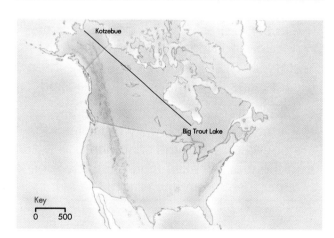

- Everybody, touch Big Trout Lake. ✓
- What country is that lake in? (Signal.) *Canada.*
- Touch the place where Oomoo and Oolak live. ✓
- That place is in the United States. What state of the United States is it in? (Signal.) *Alaska.*
- (Repeat until firm.)

Use the key to figure out about how far it is between these two places.

- Everybody, touch the key that shows miles. ✓
- How many miles does the key show? (Signal.) *500 miles.*
- Make marks on your paper and figure out about how many hundred miles it is from Big Trout Lake to the place where Oomoo and Oolak live. (Observe students and give feedback.)
- About how many miles is the route? (Call on a student. Idea: *2500 miles.*)

EXERCISE 4

STORY READING

a. Find part C in your textbook. ✓
- The error limit for group reading is 9 errors.
b. Everybody, touch the title. ✓
- (Call on a student to read the title.) *[Playing with Usk.]*
- Everybody, what's the title? (Signal.) *Playing with Usk.*
c. Where was Oolak at the end of the last story? (Call on a student. Ideas: *On an ice chunk; running toward the beach.*)
- Where was Usk? (Call on a student. Ideas: *On an ice chunk; behind Oolak.*)
- Where was Oomoo? (Call on a student. Ideas: *On an ice chunk; behind Usk.*)
d. (Call on individual students to read the story, each student reading two or three sentences at a time. Ask the specified questions as the students read.)

> - (Correct errors: Tell the word. Direct the student to reread the sentence.)
> - (If the group makes more than 9 errors, direct the students to reread the story.)

Playing with Usk
Oolak ran very fast, but Usk ran even faster. Usk caught up to Oolak just as Oolak reached the beach. Usk nudged Oolak with his nose, and Oolak went tumbling in the pebbles.

- Everybody, who was faster, Oolak or Usk? (Signal.) *Usk.*
- What does that mean, he went tumbling in the pebbles? (Call on a student. Idea: *He fell down.*)

Usk made a growling sound and shook his head, but Oomoo knew that he was just playing the way dogs sometimes do. Oolak got to his feet and started to stumble through the pebbles. Before he got two meters down the beach, however, Usk caught up to him again, gave him a nudge in the back, and down went Oolak.

- What happened this time when Oolak ran away from Usk? (Call on a student. Idea: *Usk knocked him down.*)

Oomoo ran to the edge of the beach where there was a snowdrift that was about a meter deep. She made a snowball and threw it at Usk. Splat! It hit him on the rear end. He turned around and stood up.
Usk made a growling sound and chased Oomoo. He caught up to her, grabbed her by the collar and pushed her over. She went face first into the snowdrift next to the pebbled beach.
She rolled over and laughed. Usk was sitting in the snow next to her, panting. With his big pink tongue hanging out, he looked like a great big white dog. She tossed some snow at his tongue. He licked his chops, and then started to pant again.

- Everybody, show me how you pant. ✓
- Show me how an animal licks its chops. ✓

"Hey," Oolak said. "Let's hitch him up to the sled."
Oomoo remembered the fun that she and Oolak ★ used to have sledding down the hills with Usk.

- Oomoo is starting to remember some things again. Where is she while she is thinking about these things? (Call on a student. Idea: *Lying in the snow; on the beach.*)
- What is she remembering about Usk? (Call on a student. Idea: *When he went sledding with her.*)

She used to hitch him to a dog sled and let him run down the hills. Sometimes he would stop halfway down and the sled would run into him. Then everybody would tumble down the hill.

- Why would the sled sometimes run into him? (Call on a student. Idea: *Because he would stop.*)

Sometimes he would run very fast and then make a turn at the bottom of the hill. The sled would slide in a great circle and then turn over, tossing Oomoo and Oolak into the snow.

- What did he do to make the sled turn over? (Call on a student. Idea: *He made a sharp turn.*)

Sometimes Usk would . . .

- The dots tell us that something is missing. Something made her stop thinking about Usk. We'll find out what made her stop.

"Oomoo," her father shouted.

- What made Oomoo stop thinking about Usk? (Call on a student. Idea: *Her dad shouted at her.*)

Oomoo stopped thinking of sledding with Usk and looked up on the top of the hill, where her father was standing.

- Everybody, where was her father? (Signal.) *On the top of the hill.*
- Do you think he's very happy with them? (Call on a student. Idea: *No.*)
- Why not? (Call on a student. Idea: *They're not supposed to play with Usk.*)

"Oomoo," he shouted again. "Oolak, come here now." Oomoo and Oolak scrambled up the slope through the wet snow.
The top of the hill was free of snow. Oomoo stamped the snow from her feet and looked down. She did not want to look at her father. She could feel that he was looking at her.

- Why did she not want to look at her father? (Call on a student. Ideas: *She was ashamed; she was afraid.*)
- What do you think he's going to tell them? (Call on a student. Idea: *They're not supposed to play with Usk.*)

"Oomoo, I am ashamed of you," he said. "What season of the year is it?" Oomoo answered quietly.

- Everybody, what season did she tell him? (Signal.) *Spring.*
- Read the rest of the story to yourself. Find out two things. Find out what her father said he would do if Oomoo and Oolak did not stay away from Usk. Find out what Oolak did when their father told them what he would do. Raise your hand when you're done.

> **Her father said, "And in what season are bears the most dangerous?"**
> **"Spring," she said.**
> **"And what did I tell you about playing with Usk?"**
> **Oomoo replied, "We should not go near him."**
> **Her father said, "If you cannot stay away from that bear, you will have to stay where he will not go."**

- (After all students have raised their hand:)
- What did Oomoo's father say would happen if they did not stay away from Usk? (Call on a student. Idea: *They'd have to stay where the bear cannot go.*)
- Where do you think they'll have to stay? (Call on a student. Student preference.)

Note: There is a reading checkout in this lesson; therefore, there is no paired practice.

READING CHECKOUTS

a. Today is a reading-checkout day. While you're writing answers to your worksheet and textbook items, I'm going to call on you one at a time to read part of the story we read in lesson 14.

b. (Hold up a thermometer chart.) ✓
- Remember, when you pass a checkout, you color that space red. Students who pass the checkout for lesson 15 get to color space 15 red.

c. You pass a checkout by reading the passage in less than a minute without making more than 2 mistakes. Remember, less than a minute and no more than 2 errors. If you don't pass the checkout today, you can try again next time. But you can't color in the space for 15 until you pass checkout 15. When I call on you to come and do your checkout, bring your thermometer chart.

d. (Call on individual students to read the portion of story 14 marked with 🌸.)
- (Time the student. Note words that are missed and total number of words read.)
- (Teacher reference:)

> 🌸 As Oomoo stood near the great bear, she found it hard to believe that this same bear used to fit inside her jacket or that this bear used to sleep on the floor of her winter home.
>
> Usk had been Oomoo's friend for over two years, [50] but last fall something about him changed. He still liked to play sometimes, but ★ at other times he didn't seem to be interested in Oomoo [75] or in being with her. Usk would go off by himself and walk along the high slopes, sometimes howling into the air like a dog. [100] Sometimes he wouldn't come down to see Oomoo for three or four days at a 🌸 [115] time.

- (If the student reads the passage in one minute or less and makes no more than 2 errors, direct the student to color in space 15 of the thermometer chart.)

> - (If the student does not meet the rate-error criterion for the pasage, direct the student to practice reading the story with the assigned partner.)
> - (If the student makes any mistakes, point to each word that was misread and identify it.)

WRITTEN ITEMS
Skill Items

a. Find part D in your textbook. ✓
b. I'll read the items. You follow along.
   Item 1: Write the letter of the event that happened near the beginning of the story.
   Item 2: Write the letter of the event that happened near the middle of the story.
   Item 3: Write the letter of the event that happened near the end of the story.
c. Here's event A: Her father said, "And in what season are bears the most dangerous?" Get ready to tell me if that event is from the **beginning** of the story, the **middle**, or the **end.** Everybody, which part of the story? (Signal.) *End.*
d. Here's event B: Oolak got to his feet and started to stumble through the pebbles. Get ready to tell me if that event is from the **beginning** of the story, the **middle**, or the **end.** Everybody, which part of the story? (Signal.) *Beginning.*
e. Here's event C: With his big pink tongue hanging out, he looked like a great big white dog. Get ready to tell me if that event is from the **beginning** of the story, the **middle**, or the **end.** Everybody, which part of the story? (Signal.) *Middle.*
f. Item 4. The horses became blank on the dangerous blank. Raise your hand when you know which vocabulary sentence that's supposed to be. (Call on a student.) Say the sentence. *[The horses became restless on the dangerous route.]*
- Everybody, say that sentence. Get ready. (Signal.) *The horses became restless on the dangerous route.*
- Item 5. Blank do not blank blank things. Raise your hand when you know which vocabulary sentence that's supposed to be. (Call on a student.) Say the sentence. *[Scientists do not ignore ordinary things.]*
- Everybody, say that sentence. Get ready. (Signal.) *Scientists do not ignore ordinary things.*
- Everybody, write the sentences for items 4 and 5. Be sure to spell all the words correctly.
   (Observe students and give feedback.)

Story Items

g. **Find part B on your worksheet.** ✓

h. Items 6 through 12 are about today's story.

i. (For each item: Call on a student to read the item.)

• Item 6. *[What happened when Usk nudged Oolak with his nose?]*

• Item 7. *[Usk started chasing Oomoo after* <u>*blank*</u>*.]*

• Item 8. *[When Usk caught up to Oomoo, what did he grab? Boot, collar.]*

• Item 9: *[Then what did Usk do to Oomoo?]*

• Item 10: *[Who made the children stop playing?]*

• Item 11: *[When Oomoo reached her father, she didn't look at him. Why?]*

• Item 12: *[Will the father let the children play with Usk?]*

End-of-Lesson Activities

INDEPENDENT WORK

Now finish your independent work for lesson 15. Raise your hand when you're finished. (Observe students and give feedback.)

WORKCHECK

a. (Direct students to take out their marking pencils.)

• We're going to check your independent work. Remember, if you got an item wrong, make an **X** next to the item. Don't change any answers.

b. (For each item: Read the item. Call on a student to answer it. If the answer is wrong, say the correct answer. Refer to the Answer Key for the correct answers.)

c. Now use your marking pencil to fix up any items you got wrong. Remember, all mistakes must be fixed up before you hand in your independent work.

LANGUAGE ARTS

(Present Language Arts lesson 15 after completing Reading lesson 15. See Language Arts Guide.)

Lessons 16–20 • Planning Page

	Lesson 16	Lesson 17	Lesson 18	Lesson 19	Lesson 20
Lesson Events	**Vocabulary Sentence** Reading Words Comprehension Passage Story Reading Paired Practice Written Items Independent Work Workcheck Language Arts	Vocabulary Sentence Reading Words Story Reading Paired Practice Written Items Independent Work Workcheck Language Arts	Vocabulary Sentences Reading Words Comprehension Passage Story Reading Paired Practice Written Items Independent Work Workcheck Language Arts	Vocabulary Sentence Reading Words Story Reading Paired Practice Written Items Independent Work Workcheck Language Arts	Fact Game Reading Checkouts Test Marking the Test Test Remedies Literature Lesson Language Arts
Vocabulary Sentence	**#3: She actually repeated that careless mistake.**	#3: She actually repeated that careless mistake.	sentence #1 sentence #2 sentence #3	#3: She actually repeated that careless mistake.	
Reading Words Word Types	modeled words words with endings -s words mixed words	modeled words mixed words	mixed words	words with underlined part mixed words	
New Vocabulary	numb shrank grinding glanced	surface current		kneeled	
Comprehension Passage	*Facts About Killer Whales*		*Facts About Drifting*		
Story	*The Beach*	*The Ice Floe*	*Drifting on an Ice Chunk*	*The Storm*	
Skill Items	Sequencing	Sequencing	Vocabulary sentence Sequencing	Vocabulary	Test: Vocabulary Sentences #2, 3
Special Materials					Thermometer charts, dice, Fact Game 20, Fact Game Answer Key, scorecard sheets, *materials for literature lesson
Special Projects/ Activities					

*Literature anthology; blackline master 2A; writing materials; drawing materials

VOCABULARY

a. **Find page 352 in your textbook.** ✓
- Touch sentence 3. ✓
- This is a new vocabulary sentence. It says: *She actually repeated that careless mistake.*
- Everybody, read that sentence. Get ready. (Signal.) *She actually repeated that careless mistake.*
- Close your eyes and say the sentence. Get ready. (Signal.) *She actually repeated that careless mistake.*
- (Repeat until firm.)

b. **Actually** means **really.** So, if she actually repeated that careless mistake, she **really** repeated that mistake.
- Everybody, what's another way of saying **That mean-looking dog is really a very nice dog?** (Signal.) *That mean-looking dog is actually a very nice dog.*
- What's another way of saying **I'm really not very thirsty?** (Signal.) *I'm actually not very thirsty.*

c. When you repeat something, you do it again and again and again. Everybody, what word did I repeat? (Signal.) *Again.*
- What word means **to do something again?** (Signal.) *Repeat.*

d. **Careless** is the opposite of **careful.** What word means the **opposite of careful?** (Signal.) *Careless.*
- So a careless mistake is one that happens because you are not careful.

e. Listen to the sentence again: She actually repeated that careless mistake. Everybody, say the sentence. Get ready. (Signal.) *She actually repeated that careless mistake.*

f. Everybody, what word means the opposite of **careful?** (Signal.) *Careless.*
- What word means **did something again?** (Signal.) *Repeated.*
- What word means **really?** (Signal.) *Actually.*
- (Repeat step f until firm.)

READING WORDS

Column 1

a. Find lesson 16 in your textbook. ✓
- Touch column 1. ✓
- (Teacher reference:)

1. **numb**	4. **sliced**
2. **shrank**	5. **cliff**
3. **ridge**	6. **itch**

b. Word 1 is **numb.** What word? (Signal.) *Numb.*
- Spell **numb.** Get ready. (Tap for each letter.) *N-U-M-B.*
- When part of your body gets numb, you don't have any feeling in that part.

c. Word 2 is **shrank.** What word? (Signal.) *Shrank.*
- Spell **shrank.** Get ready. (Tap for each letter.) *S-H-R-A-N-K.*
- Things that get smaller now **shrink;** things that got smaller yesterday **shrank.** Everybody, what do we say for things that get smaller now? (Signal.) *Shrink.*
- What do we say for things that got smaller yesterday? (Signal.) *Shrank.*

d. Word 3 is **ridge.** What word? (Signal.) *Ridge.*
- Spell **ridge.** Get ready. (Tap for each letter.) *R-I-D-G-E.*

e. Word 4. What word? (Signal.) *Sliced.*
- Spell **sliced.** Get ready. (Tap for each letter.) *S-L-I-C-E-D.*

f. Word 5. What word? (Signal.) *Cliff.*
- Word 6. What word? (Signal.) *Itch.*

g. Let's read those words again, the fast way.
- Word 1. What word? (Signal.) *Numb.*
- (Repeat for words 2–6.)

h. (Repeat step g until firm.)

Column 2

i. Find column 2. ✓
- (Teacher reference:)

1. **grinding**	4. **swarming**
2. **glanced**	5. **nicer**
3 **punishment**	6. **speckled**

j. All these words have an ending. The first part of each word is underlined.

k. Word 1. What's the underlined part? (Signal.) *grind.*
   - What's the whole word? (Signal.) *Grinding.*
   - When two hard things rub together, they grind, and they make a grinding sound.
   - Word 2. What's the underlined part? (Signal.) *glance.*
   - What's the whole word? (Signal.) *Glanced.*
   - When you glance at something, you give that thing a quick look. You don't stare at it; you just give it a quick look. Everybody, glance at the door. ✓
   - Word 3. What's the underlined part? (Signal.) *punish.*
   - What's the whole word? (Signal.) *Punishment.*
   - Word 4. What's the underlined part? (Signal.) *swarm.*
   - What's the whole word? (Signal.) *Swarming.*
   - Word 5. What's the underlined part? (Signal.) *nice.*
   - What's the whole word? (Signal.) *Nicer.*
   - Word 6. What's the underlined part? (Signal.) *speckle.*
   - What's the whole word? (Signal.) *Speckled.*

l. Let's read those words again, the fast way.
   - Word 1. What word? (Signal.) *Grinding.*
   - (Repeat for: **2. glanced, 3. punishment, 4. swarming, 5. nicer, 6. speckled.**)

m. (Repeat step l until firm.)

Column 3

n. Find column 3. ✓
   - (Teacher reference:)

1. **groans**	3. **mosquitoes**
2. **creaks**	4. **no-see-ums**

   - All these words end with the letter **S.**

o. Word 1. What word? (Signal.) *Groans.*
   - (Repeat for words 2–4.)

p. (Repeat step o until firm.)

Column 4

q. Find column 4. ✓
   - (Teacher reference:)

1. **ignore**	4. **forth**
2. **enter**	5. **schoolyard**
3. **sloshing**	

r. Word 1. What word? (Signal.) *Ignore.*
   - (Repeat for words 2–5.)
s. (Repeat step r until firm.)

Individual Turns

(For columns 1–4: Call on individual students, each to read one to three words per turn.)

EXERCISE 3

COMPREHENSION PASSAGE

a. Find part B in your textbook. ✓
   - You're going to read the next story about Oomoo and Oolak. First you'll read the information passage. It gives some facts about killer whales.
b. Everybody, touch the title. ✓
   - (Call on a student to read the title.) *[Facts About Killer Whales.]*
   - Everybody, what's the selection going to tell about? (Signal.) *Facts About Killer Whales.*
c. (Call on individual students to read the passage, each student reading two or three sentences at a time. Ask the specified questions as the students read.)

> **Facts About Killer Whales**
> **You'll be reading more about killer whales. Here are facts about killer whales:**
> **Killer whales are about 12 meters long. Most other whales are much longer than killer whales.**

   - Everybody, about how long are killer whales? (Signal.) *12 meters long.*
   - How do killer whales compare in size with other whales? (Call on a student. Idea: *Killer whales are smaller.*)

> **Killer whales are not fish. Fish are cold-blooded. Whales are warm-blooded, like bears, humans and dogs.**

   - Everybody, are killer whales fish? (Signal.) *No.*
   - How do you know they are not fish? (Call on a student. Idea: *Because they are not cold-blooded.*)
   - Name some other animals that are warm-blooded like killer whales. (Call on individual students. Ideas: *Cows, horses, cats,* etc.)

- Name some other animals that are cold-blooded like fish. (Call on individual students. Ideas: *Flies, ants, snakes, frogs*, etc.)

Killer whales are very smart.

- Everybody, say that fact. Get ready. (Signal.) *Killer whales are very smart.*
- (Repeat until firm.)

Some scientists think that killer whales are smarter than dogs. Killer whales hunt in packs.

- Everybody, say that fact. Get ready. (Signal.) *Killer whales hunt in packs.*
- (Repeat until firm.)
- What does that mean, they hunt in packs? (Call on a student. Idea: *They hunt in groups.*)

They kill larger whales, polar bears, seals or any other animal that is in the water.

- I don't think I would want to be near a pack of them.

EXERCISE 4

STORY READING

a. Find part C in your textbook. ✓
- The error limit for group reading is 12 errors.
b. Everybody, touch the title. ✓
- (Call on a student to read the title.) *[The Beach.]*
- Everybody, what's the title? (Signal.) *The Beach.*
c. (Call on individual students to read the passage, each student reading two or three sentences at a time. Ask the specified questions as the students read.)

- (Correct errors: Tell the word. Direct the student to reread the sentence.)
- (If the group make more than 12 errors, direct the students to reread the story.)

The Beach
Oomoo's father said, "You must stay away from Usk."
Then he ordered Oomoo and Oolak to stay near their summer house for two full days.

- Why did he order them to stay there? (Call on a student. Idea: *Because they disobeyed him and played with Usk.*)

Oomoo and Oolak were not to go down to the beach or on the ice floe or into the hills. Oomoo's family had just moved into their summer home, which was a tent on a ridge near the ocean.

- Everybody, what was their summer home? (Signal.) *A tent.*
- Where was it? (Call on a student. Idea: *On a ridge near the ocean.*)
- What could you see from their summer home? (Call on a student. Idea: *The ocean.*)

Their winter home was at the bottom of a cliff, right next to the beach. The winter home was a cave dug into the side of the cliff.

- Why would they want a cave for their winter home? (Call on a student. Idea: *It's warmer.*)

The screaming winter wind could not get inside the cave. The summer home was much nicer, and it was much larger than the cave. It was made from animal skins. The only problem with the summer home was the bugs.

- Everybody, what was the problem with the summer home? (Signal.) *The bugs.*

As soon as the snow starts to melt in Alaska, insects come out. Mosquitoes come out in clouds— millions and millions of them. The mosquitoes don't seem to bother the bears or the dogs, but they sure bother humans. There are also biting flies in Alaska. Biting flies look like ordinary flies, but they bite like mosquitoes. They leave red bumps that itch.

- When do insects first come out? (Call on a student. Idea: *When the snow starts to melt.*)
- How many mosquitoes are there? (Call on a student. Idea: *Millions of them.*)

- Everybody, what other kind of biting insect is there? (Signal.) *Biting flies.*

> There are other biting flies—very small ones. And there are also little insects so small that you have to look very carefully to see them. They come out when the sun goes down, and they bite. Their bites feel like mosquito bites, but they do not leave a red mark. These tiny bugs are called no-see-ums.

- Everybody, what are the very tiny biting bugs called? (Signal.) *No-see-ums.*

> Oomoo didn't like the bugs, but she managed to ignore them most of the time. And Oomoo's summer home was in a place where the wind blew hard. When the wind blew, the bugs stayed away.

- Everybody, what kept the bugs away? (Signal.) *The wind.*

> Oomoo was being punished, but she really didn't mind sitting there on the hill near her summer home, looking down at the beach. The beach was like a ✦circus that had a million different acts. There were acts from the elephant seals. They were swarming on the beach about half a mile from Oomoo's summer home. Male seals were fighting for the best places on the beach.

- Everybody, look at the picture. Touch Oomoo's summer home. ✓
- What is Oomoo doing in the picture? (Call on a student. Ideas: *Looking out at the ocean; sitting next to the tent.*)
- Everybody, touch the elephant seals. ✓
- Which seals were fighting? (Signal.) *Male seals.*

> Closer to Oomoo was another act. Two walruses were lying on a part of the beach that was speckled with thousands of birds. In the ocean were the killer whales, swimming back and forth just beyond the end of the ice floe. The killer whales were waiting for the seals to enter the water.

- Everybody, touch the walruses on the beach. ✓
- Touch the killer whales. ✓
- Why were they waiting for seals? (Call on a student. Idea: *They wanted to eat them.*)

> As Oomoo watched the killer whales, she remembered a time when she had been very close to them. She had been out in a kayak with her father. It was late spring and the ocean was very calm. Oomoo's father paddled the kayak past the end of the ice floe. Suddenly, three huge killer whales appeared in the water. The fins of the killer whales sliced through the water as they circled the boat. Then one of the whales lifted its head out of the water and seemed to look right at Oomoo. The whale opened its mouth and Oomoo could see the shiny white row of knives.

- What are those knives? (Call on a student. Idea: *The whale's teeth.*)
- Everybody, were the killer whales around when Oomoo and her father started out? (Signal.) *No.*
- When did they appear? (Call on a student. Idea: *When they were past the end of the ice floe.*)
- How do you think Oomoo felt? (Call on a student. Idea: *Very frightened.*)

The whale was only a few meters from the kayak. It looked at Oomoo for a few seconds, then slipped back into the water, making a sloshing sound. Oomoo and her father sat silently in the kayak. Oomoo was so frightened that her hands were shaking. Then slowly, the three killer whales moved away from the kayak.

• Read the rest of the story to yourself. Find out what Oomoo felt when she watched the killer whales from the ridge near her summer home. Find out what caught her attention and made her stop thinking about the whales. Raise your hand when you're done.

As Oomoo sat on the ridge looking out at the killer whales and thinking about what had happened, she could feel goose bumps on her arms. "I never want to be that close to killer whales again," she said to herself. Then the sounds on the beach caught her attention. Some of the birds near the walruses were fighting.

• (After all students have raised their hand:)
• Everybody, what did Oomoo feel on her arms as she watched the killer whales? (Signal.) *Goose bumps.*
• Why? (Call on a student. Idea: *Because she was thinking about being very close to killer whales.*)
• What caught her attention and made her stop thinking about whales? (Call on a student. Ideas: *The sounds on the beach; fighting birds.*)

EXERCISE 5

PAIRED PRACTICE

You're going to read aloud to your partner. The **B** members will read first. Then the **A** members will read from the star to the end of the story.
(Observe students and give feedback. Praise teams that follow the rules.)

EXERCISE 6

WRITTEN ITEMS

Story Items

a. **Find part B on your worksheet.** ✓
• The items in part B are about today's story.
b. (For each item: Call on a student to read the item.)
• Item 7. *[How long did Oomoo and Oolak have to stay near the summer house?]*
• Item 8. *[What kind of house was the summer house?]*
• Item 9. *[What kind of house was the winter house?]*
• Item 10. *[Which house was bigger?]*
• Item 11. *[What was the only problem with the summer house?]*
• Item 12. *[Name 3 kinds of biting insects that Alaska has in the spring.]*
• Item 13. *[Why was Oomoo's summer home in a place where the wind blew hard?]*
• Item 14. *[What were the male seals on the beach fighting for?]*
• Item 15. *[What were the killer whales waiting for?]*
• Item 16. *[What were Oomoo and her father in when the killer whales came close to them?]*
• Item 17. *[How many whales were there?]*

Skill Items

c. Touch the box below item 17. ✓
• I'll read the items. You follow along.
Item 18: Write the letter of the event that happened near the beginning of the story.
Item 19: Write the letter of the event that happened in the middle of the story.
Item 20: Write the letter of the event that happened near the end of the story.
d. Here's event A: They were swarming by the thousands on the beach about half a mile from Oomoo's summer home. Get ready to tell me if that event is from the **beginning** of the story, the **middle,** or the **end.** Everybody, which part of the story? (Signal.) *Middle.*
e. Here's event B: Then Oomoo's father ordered Oomoo to stay near their summer house for two full days. Get ready to tell me if that event is from the **beginning** of the story, the **middle,** or the **end.** Everybody, which part of the story? (Signal.) *Beginning.*

f. Here's event C: "I never want to be that close to killer whales again," she said to herself. Get ready to tell me if that event is from the **beginning** of the story, the **middle,** or the **end.** Everybody, which part of the story? (Signal.) *End.*

End-of-Lesson Activities

INDEPENDENT WORK

Now finish the independent work for lesson 16. Raise your hand when you're finished.
(Observe students and give feedback.)

WORKCHECK

a. (Direct students to take out their marking pencils.)

• We're going to check your independent work. Remember, if you got an item wrong, make an **X** next to the item. Don't change any answers.

b. (For each item: Read the item. Call on a student to answer it. If the answer is wrong, say the correct answer. Refer to the Answer Key for the correct answers.)

c. Now use your marking pencil to fix any items you got wrong. Remember, all mistakes must be fixed before you hand in your independent work.

LANGUAGE ARTS

(Present Language Arts lesson 16 after completing Reading lesson 16. See Language Arts Guide.)

VOCABULARY REVIEW

a. Here's the new vocabulary sentence: She actually repeated that careless mistake.
- Everybody, say that sentence. Get ready. (Signal.) *She actually repeated that careless mistake.*
- (Repeat until firm.)

b. Everybody, what word means **did something again?** (Signal.) *Repeated.*
- What word means **the opposite of careful?** (Signal.) *Careless.*
- What word means **really?** (Signal.) *Actually.*

READING WORDS

Column 1

a. **Find lesson 17 in your textbook.** ✓
- Touch column 1. ✓
- (Teacher reference:)

1. surface	4. schoolyard
2. current	5. punishment
3. careless	

b. Word 1 is **surface.** What word? (Signal.) *Surface.*
- Spell **surface.** Get ready. (Tap for each letter.) *S-U-R-F-A-C-E.*
- The surface of the water is the top of the water.

c. Word 2. What word? (Signal.) *Current.*
- Spell **current.** Get ready. (Tap for each letter.) *C-U-R-R-E-N-T.*
- A water current is a stream of water that moves in the same direction. Everybody, what do we call **wind** that moves in the same direction? (Signal.) *A wind current.*

d. Word 3. What word? (Signal.) *Careless.*
- Spell **careless.** Get ready. (Tap for each letter.) *C-A-R-E-L-E-S-S.*

e. Word 4. What word? (Signal.) *Schoolyard.*

f. Word 5. What word? (Signal.) *Punishment.*

g. Let's read those words again, the fast way.
- Word 1. What word? (Signal.) *Surface.*
- (Repeat for words 2–5.)

h. (Repeat step g until firm.)

Column 2

i. Find column 2. ✓
- (Teacher reference:)

1. creaks	4. numb
2. glanced	5. groans
3. shrank	6. grinding

j. Word 1. What word? (Signal.) *Creaks.*
- (Repeat for words 2–6.)

k. (Repeat step j until firm.)

Individual Turns

(For columns 1 and 2: Call on individual students, each to read one to three words per turn.)

STORY READING

a. Find part B in your textbook. ✓
- The error limit for group reading is 14 errors.

b. Everybody, touch the title. ✓
- (Call on a student to read the title.) *[The Ice Floe.]*
- Everybody, what's the title? (Signal.) *The Ice Floe.*
- What is this story going to tell about? (Call on a student. Idea: *The ice floe.*)
- Everybody, do ice floes cover the **land** or the **ocean?** (Signal.) *The ocean.*

c. (Call on individual students to read the story, each student reading two or three sentences at a time. Ask the specified questions as the students read.)

- (Correct errors: Tell the word. Direct the student to reread the sentence.)
- (If the group makes more than 14 errors, direct the students to reread the story.)

The Ice Floe

Ice floes melt in the spring. During the winter, parts of the ocean are covered with very thick ice. In some places, the ice is three meters thick. During the winter, you can walk far out on the frozen ocean. Then the spring comes and ice starts to melt. When it melts, chunks of ice break off and float into the ocean. Some of these chunks are as big as a schoolyard. Some are no bigger than a table.

- Everybody, how thick does the ice floe get in some places during the winter? (Signal.) *Three meters thick.*
- Why can you walk far out on the ocean in winter? (Call on a student. Idea: *Because it's frozen.*)
- How big are the very big chunks of ice that break off? (Call on a student. Idea: *As big as a schoolyard.*)
- The next part tells about sounds. Imagine those sounds when we read about them.

When an ice floe begins to break up in the spring, you can hear it. At night, as you lie in your summer home, you can hear many sounds. You can hear the sound of wolves and sometimes bears growling. You can hear a million buzzes from a million bugs that circle above you. You can hear the occasional bark of the seals. And you can hear the ice floe. It moans and groans. It creaks and it cracks. Sometimes, it squeaks and squeals. It's a sound that you'll never forget and that you learn to love.

- Make some of the sounds that the ice floe makes when it melts. (Call on a student. Check for at least two: *moaning, groaning, creaking, cracking, squeaking, squealing.*)

Ice floes also make noise in the winter. The ice floes creak and groan when the air is so cold that sweat freezes to your face. The air is so cold that a deep breath hurts and makes you cough.

- Have you ever been in that kind of cold air? (Call on individual students. Student preference.)
- Everybody, is spring the only time the ice floes make noise? (Signal.) *No.*

In the winter, the ice floes creak and groan because great sheets of ice are crowding together and there is not enough room for them. So the ice floes buckle. Sometimes great chunks of ice break off and are pushed over other chunks. The chunks make noise when they move around.

But the sound that the ice chunks make in the spring is different. Now the chunks are melting and sliding back into the water.

- Why do the ice chunks make noise in the spring? (Call on a student. Idea: *Because they're melting.*)
- Everybody, is that the same reason they make noise in the winter? (Signal.) *No.*
- Why do they make noise in the winter? (Call on a student. Ideas: *Because they are crowded together; because there's not enough room for them.*)

To Oomoo, the chunks sounded happy in the spring. They seemed to say, "I'm free to float into the ocean."

Oomoo loved to play on the ice chunks in the spring, but she knew that she had to be careful and follow the rule. The rule was that she could never go out to the chunks near the end of the ice floe. That was where the killer whales were.

- Which chunks was she supposed to stay away from? (Call on a student. Idea: *The chunks near the end of the ice floe.*)

During the spring there was always a small pack of whales waiting in the water just beyond the end of the ice floe.

- Where were the killer whales? (Call on a student. Idea: *Near the end of the ice floe.*)

⭐ **Here's why it was very dangerous to be on the ice chunks near the end of the ice floe. If the ice chunk that you were standing on drifted out into the ocean, you could not get back. Someone would have to save you. But you would be very far from shore—maybe more than a mile. Maybe the people from your village would not hear your calls for help. If they didn't, the chunk of ice would float farther and farther into the ocean. Then it would melt. It would get smaller and smaller. As it shrank, the killer whales would move closer and closer to the ice chunk. But even if the killer whales didn't attack you, you would die within minutes after you went into the water. The water is so cold that it would take only a few minutes for your arms and legs to become so numb that you could not move.**

• Listen to that part again and get ready to answer some questions.

Here's why it was very dangerous to be on the ice chunks near the end of the ice floe. If the ice chunk that you were standing on drifted out into the ocean, you could not get back. Someone would have to save you. But you would be very far from shore— maybe more than a mile. Maybe the people from your village would not hear your calls for help. If they didn't, the chunk of ice would float farther and farther into the ocean. Then it would melt. It would get smaller and smaller. As it shrank, the killer whales would move closer and closer to the ice chunk. But even if the killer whales didn't attack you, you would die within minutes after you went into the water. The water is so cold that it would take only a few minutes for your arms and legs to become so numb that you could not move.

• What could happen to an ice chunk near the end of the ice floe? (Call on a student. Idea: *It could drift out into the ocean.*)
• How could you get back to shore if that happened? (Call on a student. Idea: *Somebody would have to save you.*)

• If nobody saved you, what two things might happen? (Call on a student. Ideas: *You might freeze in the ocean; the killer whales might get you.*)
• Everybody, look at the picture on the next page that shows the ice floe. Touch the place where the killer whales are. ✓

• Touch the ice chunks closest to the killer whales. ✓
• That's the place that Oomoo cannot go because it is too dangerous. Now go back to page 85. The three dots show that part of the story is missing.

Oomoo's punishment was over.

• What was she being punished for? (Call on a student. Idea: *Playing with Usk.*)
• What did she have to do while she was being punished? (Call on a student. Idea: *Stay near her summer house for two days.*)
• Now that her punishment was over, what do you think she'll do? (Call on a student. Student preference.)

She had just finished lunch. She could see her breath as she ran along the pebbled beach. She listened to the grinding sound of the pebbles under her feet. "Here's a good one," Oolak shouted. He was on the ice floe, pointing to a chunk of ice that was right in front of him.

• What was he talking about? (Call on a student. Idea: *An ice chunk.*)
• What time of day was it? (Call on a student: Idea: *Just after lunchtime.*)
• How do you know it was cool outside? (Call on a student. Idea: *She could see her breath.*)

The chunk was a perfect size. It was about five meters across. Oomoo ran over to her brother. Then they jumped onto the ice chunk. The ice chunk rocked a little bit when they landed on it. ✓

- Everybody, about how big was the ice chunk? (Signal.) *Five meters across.*
- What did Oomoo and Oolak do? (Call on a student. Idea: *Jumped onto the ice chunk.*)
- Why do you think they did that? (Call on a student. Ideas: *To play on it; to ride on it.*)
- Everybody, show me with your hand what the ice chunk did when they landed on it. ✓

The ice floe was shaped like a giant letter C. The ice chunk that Oomoo and Oolak were on was near the bottom end of the C. Oolak pointed across the water to a place near the top of the C. He said, "The ice chunk will drift over there. Then we can walk back."

- The dotted line in the picture on the next page shows where Oolak pointed. Everybody, touch the ice chunk that Oomoo and Oolak are standing on. ✓

- Now follow the dotted line to the place where they are supposed to drift to. ✓
- Read the rest of the story to yourself. Find out two things. Find out why Oomoo thought it would be safe to drift on the ice chunk. Find out what she looked at in the ocean. Raise your hand when you're done.

For a moment, Oomoo was going to say, "That's a pretty long way to drift." Then she turned around and faced the wind. It was blowing from the east. If it kept on blowing, it would move the ice chunk to the place Oolak pointed to. She glanced at the killer whales just beyond the end of the ice floe. Then she said, "Okay, let's go." The ice chunk had already drifted a few meters.

- (After all students have raised their hand:)
- What made Oomoo think it would be safe to drift on the ice chunk? (Call on a student. Idea: *The way the wind was blowing.*)
- Everybody, which direction was the wind coming from? (Signal.) *The east.*
- So in which direction would it push the ice chunk? (Signal.) *West.*
- That would be safe. What did she look at in the ocean? (Signal.) *The killer whales.*
- What did she decide to do? (Call on a student. Idea: *Drift on the ice chunk.*)
- Everybody, start at the top of the giant C-shaped ice floe and trace around it. ✓
- Touch the part of the C they're supposed to drift to. ✓
- What part is that? (Call on a student. Idea: *The top part.*)
- Next time we'll see if that's where they drift.

EXERCISE 4

PAIRED PRACTICE

You're going to read aloud to your partner. The **A** members will read first. Then the **B** members will read from the star to the end of the story.
(Observe students and give feedback. Praise teams that follow the rules.)

EXERCISE 5

WRITTEN ITEMS

Skill Items

a. **Find part A on your worksheet.** ✓
b. I'll read the items. You follow along. Item 1: Write the letter of the event that happened near the beginning of the story.

Item 2: Write the letter of the event that happened in the middle of the story.
Item 3: Write the letter of the event that happened near the end of the story.

c. Here's event A: During the winter, you can walk far out on the frozen ocean. Get ready to tell me if that event is from the **beginning** of the story, the **middle,** or the **end.** Everybody, which part of the story? (Signal.) *Beginning.*

d. Here's event B: But even if the killer whales didn't attack you, you would die within a few minutes after you went into the water. Get ready to tell me if that event is from the **beginning** of the story, the **middle,** or the **end.** Everybody, which part of the story? (Signal.) *Middle.*

e. Here's event C: For a moment, Oomoo was going to say, "That's a pretty long way to drift." Get ready to tell me if that event is from the **beginning** of the story, the **middle,** or the **end.** Everybody, which part of the story? (Signal.) *End.*

End-of-Lesson Activities

INDEPENDENT WORK

Now finish your independent work for lesson 17. Raise your hand when you're finished. (Observe students and give feedback.)

WORKCHECK

a. (Direct students to take out their marking pencils.)
 • We're going to check your independent work. Remember, if you got an item wrong, make an **X** next to the item. Don't change any answers.
b. (For each item: Read the item. Call on a student to answer it. If the answer is wrong, say the correct answer. Refer to the Answer Key for the correct answers.)
c. Now use your marking pencil to fix up any items you got wrong. Remember, all mistakes must be fixed up before you hand in your independent work.

LANGUAGE ARTS

(Present Language Arts lesson 17 after completing Reading lesson 17. See Language Arts Guide.)

Lesson 18

EXERCISE 1

VOCABULARY REVIEW

a. You learned a sentence that tells what the horses did.
- Everybody, say that sentence. Get ready. (Signal.) *The horses became restless on the dangerous route.*
- (Repeat until firm.)

b. You learned a sentence that tells what scientists do not do.
- Say that sentence. Get ready. (Signal.) *Scientists do not ignore ordinary things.*
- (Repeat until firm.)

c. Here's the last sentence you learned: She actually repeated that careless mistake.
- Everybody, say that sentence. Get ready. (Signal.) *She actually repeated that careless mistake.*
- (Repeat until firm.)

d. What word means **really?** (Signal.) *Actually.*
- What word means **did something again?** (Signal.) *Repeated.*
- What word means **the opposite of careful?** (Signal.) *Careless.*

e. Once more. Say the sentence that tells what she repeated. Get ready. (Signal.) *She actually repeated that careless mistake.*

EXERCISE 2

READING WORDS

Column 1

a. **Find lesson 18 in your textbook.** ✓
- Touch column 1. ✓
- (Teacher reference:)

1. careless	4. surface
2. gripping	5. current
3. stung	6. drowned

b. Word 1. What word? (Signal.) *Careless.*
- (Repeat for words 2–6.)

c. (Repeat step b until firm.)

EXERCISE 3

COMPREHENSION PASSAGE

a. Find part B in your textbook. ✓
- You're going to read the next story about Oomoo and Oolak. First you'll read the information passage. It gives some facts about drifting.

b. Everybody, touch the title. ✓
- (Call on a student to read the title.) *[Facts About Drifting.]*
- Everybody, what's the selection going to tell about? (Signal.) *Facts About Drifting.*

c. (Call on individual students to read the passage, each student reading two or three sentences at a time. Ask the specified questions as the students read.)

> **Facts About Drifting**
> **You're reading about an ice chunk that is drifting. Here are facts about how things drift in the ocean:**
> **Winds make things drift.**

- Everybody, say that fact about winds. Get ready. (Signal.) *Winds make things drift.*

> **If the wind blows hard, the wind will push things and make them move. The wind will make things move in the same direction the wind blows.**

- Everybody, in which direction will you drift when you're in a big wind? (Signal.) *The same direction the wind blows.*

> **The picture shows wind blowing a cloud. Which direction is that wind coming from?**

- Everybody, what's the answer? (Signal.) *South.*
- In which direction is it moving? (Signal.) *North.*
- So in which direction will it push things? (Signal.) *North.*
- Touch ice chunk Z. ✓
- Show me the direction the wind will make that ice chunk move. ✓

Ocean currents also make things drift.

- **Everybody, say that fact. Get ready. (Signal.)** *Ocean currents also make things drift.*
- **(Repeat until firm.)**

Ocean currents are like great rivers of water within the ocean. An ocean current moves. If you are in an ocean current, you will move in the same direction the current moves.

- **Everybody, in which direction will you move when you're in a current? (Signal.)** *The same direction the current moves.*

The picture shows two ocean currents, A and B. In which direction is ocean current A moving?

- **Everybody, what's the answer? (Signal.)** *South.*

In which direction is ocean current B moving?

- **Everybody, what's the answer? (Signal.)** *West.*
- Touch the ice chunk in current A. ✓
- Show me the direction it will drift if there's no wind. ✓
- Touch the ice chunk in current B. ✓
- Show me the direction it will drift if there's no wind. ✓

Remember the facts about how things drift. Winds make things drift. Currents make things drift. Something in a wind moves in the direction the wind is moving. Something in a current moves in the direction the current is moving.

EXERCISE 4

STORY READING

a. Find part C in your textbook. ✓
- The error limit for group reading is 10 errors.
b. Everybody, touch the title. ✓
- (Call on a student to read the title.) *[Drifting on an Ice Chunk.]*

- **Everybody, what's the title? (Signal.)** *Drifting on an Ice Chunk.*
- **Where are Oomoo and Oolak? (Call on a student. Idea:** *On an ice chunk.)*
- **Everybody, the wind is blowing from which direction? (Signal.)** *East.*
- **In which direction is the wind blowing that ice chunk? (Signal.)** *West.*
c. (Call on individual students to read the passage, each student reading two or three sentences at a time. Ask the specified questions as the students read.)

- (Correct errors: Tell the word. Direct the student to reread the sentence.)
- (If the group makes more than 10 errors, direct the students to reread the story.)

Drifting on an Ice Chunk
The sun felt very warm as Oomoo and Oolak stood on the drifting chunk of ice. The flies and mosquitoes were thick near the shore, but when the ice drifted into the open water, the insects were not as thick.

- What does that mean, the insects were not as thick? (Call on a student. Idea: *There were not as many insects.*)
- The open water is where there is no ice. Everybody, where were the insects thick, near the shore or over the open water? (Signal.) *Near the shore.*

Soon there were very few insects bothering Oomoo and her brother.

- What does that tell you about how far they were from shore? (Call on a student. Idea: *They were pretty far.*)

Slowly, the ice drifted west, toward the other side of the C-shaped ice floe.
"Let's rock the ice," Oolak said, and began to jump up and down on one end of the ice chunk. Oomoo moved next to him and began to jump at the same time that Oolak jumped.
The ice began to rock more and more, making waves and a great sloshing sound. The cold ocean water swirled and jumped, sometimes coming over the surface of the ice.

- Why was the ocean water swirling and jumping? (Call on a student. Idea: *Because Oomoo and Oolak were jumping on the ice chunk and making it rock.*)
- Everybody, pretend that your hand is the ice chunk. Show me what it was doing. ✓
- What was making the ice chunk do that? (Call on a student. Idea: *Kids jumping up and down.*)
- Everybody, does it sound like Oomoo and Oolak are having fun? (Signal.) *Yes.*

Oomoo was looking at the water, careful not to get too close to the edge of the ice chunk. She did not want to fall into the ocean. Suddenly, she noticed that the water turned dark—from a sparkling blue to a purple, and her shoulders were no longer warm. Everything looked darker.

- What happened to the color of the water? (Call on a student. Idea: *It changed from blue to purple.*)
- What happened to her shoulders? (Call on a student. Idea: *They got colder.*)
- What could make everything look darker? (Call on a student. Idea: *The sun going behind the clouds.*)

She looked south to see the sun, but it was behind a cloud. The cloud was not the kind of cloud you see when the weather is nice. It was a low storm cloud, a fat cloud that had a bottom layer that looked almost green.

- Tell me two things about the cloud that covered the sun. (Call on a student. Ideas: *It was a low storm cloud; it was fat; its bottom layer looked almost green.*)

- Everybody, touch that cloud in the picture. ✓

Oomoo knew about these clouds. Her father and the other men of the village had told many stories of the green clouds and how they brought winds that could sweep a boat out into the ocean.

- Why were these clouds dangerous? (Call on a student. Ideas: *Because they brought very strong winds; because they could sweep a boat into the ocean.*)
- If the winds could sweep a boat out into the ocean, what do you think they could do to an ice chunk? (Call on a student. Idea: *Sweep it out into the ocean.*)

The men of the village told that anybody going into the ocean should look at the sky—always look at the sky.

- What should you look for in the sky if you went out onto the ocean? (Call on a student. Ideas: *Green clouds; storm clouds.*)

Oomoo knew that as soon as you spotted a green cloud, you should get to shore immediately. Even if that cloud seemed to be many miles away, ✦ you should not wait. The cloud would move in very fast, and when it did, it would bring terrible winds and rain. Oomoo had seen green clouds before. Once they came and almost destroyed Oomoo's tent. The winds blew so hard that they knocked down the strong posts that held up the tent. Oomoo remembered that she and Oolak stretched out on the tent and held onto the tent posts as hard as they could. If they had tried to stand up, the wind would have blown the tent into the ocean.

- How did they keep the tent from blowing away? (Call on a student. Idea: *By laying down on it.*)

Oomoo remembered those things. But as she looked up at the great cloud that had covered the sun, she realized that she and Oolak had been careless. They hadn't followed the rule about watching the sky.

- What had they done that was careless? (Call on a student. Idea: *Not watched the sky.*)

Suddenly, the wind tore across the ocean like a great rake. The wind made a dark path as it raced across the surface of the water.

- If you look carefully at the picture on the next page, you can see the dark place that the wind is making on the water. That place is dark because the wind is roughing up the surface of the water.

The water was smooth in front of the place where the wind touched down. Where the wind hit the water, the surface was rough with sprays of water blowing into the air.
"That wind will blow us north into the open water," Oomoo shouted. "Get down, Oolak, and find something to hang on to."

- Everybody, look at the picture. Touch the dark place where the wind is hitting the water. ✓
- Is the water **smooth** or **rough** in that place? (Signal.) *Rough.*
- Touch the water near the ice chunk that Oomoo is on. ✓
- Is that water **rough** or **smooth**? (Signal.) *Smooth.*

- Is the wind moving the rough water **toward Oomoo** or **away from Oomoo**? (Signal.) *Toward Oomoo.*
- If the wind is coming **from the shore**, which way will it push the ice chunk? (Call on a student. Ideas: *Away from the shore; north; to the open water.*)
- Read the rest of the story to yourself. Find out two things. Find out how fast the wind was moving. Find out what Oomoo held on to. Raise your hand when you're done.

Oomoo and Oolak got down and watched the wind moving from the shore. The wait seemed very long, but it was only a few seconds. The wind was moving about 40 miles per hour.
Suddenly, the wind hit them. With a whistling sound, it hit. Oomoo held on with one hand over the edge of the ice chunk. She stuck the other one in a hole on the surface of the chunk. The spray of the water hit them. More wind. More spray. Now bigger waves, blowing and washing over the top of the ice chunk. The water was icy, and the wind was blowing. The ice chunk was drifting straight north, out into the ocean.

- (After all students have raised their hand:)
- Everybody, how fast was the wind blowing? (Signal.) *About 40 miles per hour.*
- It came from shore. In which direction did it make the ice chunk move? (Call on a student. Ideas: *North; away from shore.*)
- Everybody, look at the picture on page **93**. It shows Oomoo and Oolak lying down on the ice chunk. The wind is blowing from the south. Point on the picture to show which direction the wind is pushing the ice chunk. ✓
- Show me the place where the ice chunk would drift if there was no big wind. ✓
- Show me the way the ice chunk will drift with the big wind pushing it. ✓
- How did Oomoo hold on to the ice chunk? (Call on a student. Ideas: *With one hand over the edge and the other stuck in a hole on the surface of the chunk.*)

- Listen to that part of the story again and imagine how it feels with the ice-cold water and the sounds of the waves and the wind:

> Oomoo and Oolak got down and watched the wind moving from the shore. The wait seemed very long, but it was only a few seconds. The wind was moving about 40 miles per hour. Suddenly, the wind hit them. With a whistling sound, it hit. Oomoo held on with one hand over the edge of the ice chunk. She stuck the other one in a hole on the surface of the chunk. The spray of the water hit them. More wind. More spray. Now bigger waves, blowing and washing over the top of the ice chunk. The water was icy, and the wind was blowing. The ice chunk was drifting straight north, out into the ocean.

EXERCISE 5

PAIRED PRACTICE

You're going to read aloud to your partner. The **B** members will read first. Then the **A** members will read from the star to the end of the story.
(Observe students and give feedback. Praise teams that follow the rules.)

EXERCISE 6

WRITTEN ITEMS

Skill Items

a. Find part D in your textbook. ✓
b. The sentence above item 1 says: She actually repeated that careless mistake. Items 1 through 3 refer to that sentence.

- Item 1: What word means **to do something again?** Everybody, what word? **(Signal.)** *Repeated.*
- Item 2: What word means the opposite of **careful?** Everybody, what word? **(Signal.)** *Careless.*
- Item 3: What word means **really?** Everybody, what word? **(Signal.)** *Actually.*

End-of-Lesson Activities

INDEPENDENT WORK

Now finish the independent work for lesson 18. Raise your hand when you're finished. **(Observe students and give feedback.)**

WORKCHECK

a. (Direct students to take out their marking pencils.)
- We're going to check your independent work. Remember, if you got an item wrong, make an **X** next to the item. Don't change any answers.
b. (For each item: Read the item. Call on a student to answer it. If the answer is wrong, say the correct answer. Refer to the Answer Key for the correct answers.)
c. Now use your marking pencil to fix any items you got wrong. Remember, all mistakes must be fixed before you hand in your independent work.

LANGUAGE ARTS

(Present Language Arts lesson 18 after completing Reading lesson 18. See Language Arts Guide.)

EXERCISE 1

VOCABULARY REVIEW

a. You learned a sentence that tells what she repeated.
- Everybody, say that sentence. Get ready. (Signal.) *She actually repeated that careless mistake.*
- (Repeat until firm.)

b. I'll say part of the sentence. When I stop, you say the next word. Listen: She actually . . . Everybody, what's the next word? (Signal.) *Repeated.*

c. Listen: She actually repeated that . . . Everybody, what's the next word? (Signal.) *Careless.*
- Say the whole sentence. Get ready. (Signal.) *She actually repeated that careless mistake.*

d. Listen: She . . . Everybody, what's the next word? (Signal.) *Actually.*

EXERCISE 2

READING WORDS

Column 1

a. **Find lesson 19 in your textbook.** ✓
- Touch column 1. ✓
- (Teacher reference:)

1. **kneeled**	4. **drowned**
2. **hailstone**	5. **playfully**
3. **gripping**	

b. These words have more than one part. The first part of each word is underlined.

c. Word 1. What's the underlined part? (Signal.) *kneel.*
- What's the whole word? (Signal.) *Kneeled.*
- The underlined part of the word **kneeled** is **knee.** When you kneel, you get down on your knees. Everybody, what are you doing when you get down on your knees? (Signal.) *Kneeling.*
- Word 2. What's the underlined part? (Signal.) *hail.*
- What's the whole word? (Signal.) *Hailstone.*

- Word 3. What's the underlined part? (Signal.) *gripp.*
- What's the whole word? (Signal.) *Gripping.*
- Word 4. What's the underlined part? (Signal.) *drown.*
- What's the whole word? (Signal.) *Drowned.*
- Word 5. What's the underlined part? (Signal.) *playful.*
- What's the whole word? (Signal.) *Playfully.*

d. Let's read those words again, the fast way.
- Word 1. What word? (Signal.) *Kneeled.*
- (Repeat for words 2–5.)

e. (Repeat step d until firm.)

Column 2

f. Find column 2. ✓
- (Teacher reference:)

1. **actually**	3. **marble**
2. **stung**	4. **dents**

g. Word 1. What word? (Signal.) *Actually.*
- (Repeat for words 2–4.)

h. (Repeat step g until firm.)

Individual Turns

(For columns 1 and 2: Call on individual students, each to read one to three words per turn.)

EXERCISE 3

STORY READING

a. Find part B in your textbook. ✓
- The error limit for group reading is 11 errors.

b. Everybody, touch the title. ✓
- (Call on a student to read the title.) *[The Storm.]*
- Everybody, what's the title? (Signal.) *The Storm.*

c. (Call on individual students to read the story, each student reading two or three sentences at a time. Ask the specified questions as the students read.)

The Storm
If the wind hadn't started to blow, Oomoo and Oolak would have drifted west to the other side of the C-shaped ice floe. But the wind blew them off course.

- What does that mean? (Call on a student. Ideas: *It blew them away from the top of the C-shaped ice flow; it made them go in a different direction.*)
- What would have happened if the wind hadn't started to blow? (Call on a student. Idea: *Oomoo and Oolak would have drifted toward the top of the C-shaped ice floe.*)

The wind was blowing from the shore, directly from the south. The wind blew everything north. The last place in the world that Oomoo and Oolak wanted to go was north.

- Everybody, in which direction was the wind blowing the ice chunk? (Signal.) *North.*
- What was in the ocean to the north? (Signal.) *The killer whales.*

Oomoo noticed that the ice chunk was already very close to the end of the ice floe. Once the ice chunk went past the ice floe, there were currents that would take it farther and farther into the ocean, where it would melt.

- Where would the currents take them? (Call on a student. Idea: *Farther into the ocean.*)
- What would happen then? (Call on a student. Ideas: *The killer whales would get them; the ice chink would melt; they would freeze in the water.*)

"Help! Help!" Oomoo shouted, but her voice was small against the sounds of the wind.
The wind howled. It whistled. It made great blowing sounds. And it threw water so hard that the drops stung when they hit.

- Everybody, could her voice be heard very far? (Signal.) *No.*
- Why not? (Call on a student. Idea: *Because the wind was much louder than her voice.*)
- How did the drops feel when they hit Oomoo? (Call on a student. Idea: *They stung.*)
- Why did they sting? (Call on a student. Idea: *Because they hit her very hard.*)

"Help!" Oomoo shouted.
The waves were crashing over the side of the chunk now, almost washing Oomoo into the ocean. She tried to keep her face turned toward shore. "Help!" she hollered.

- I'll read that part again. Imagine how Oomoo and Oolak must have felt.
  "Help! Help!" Oomoo shouted, but her voice was small against the sounds of the wind. The wind howled. It whistled. It made great blowing sounds. And it threw water so hard that the drops stung when they hit. "Help!" Oomoo shouted. The waves were crashing over the side of the chunk now, almost washing Oomoo into the ocean. She tried to keep her face turned toward shore. "Help!" she hollered.

Suddenly, she heard Oolak's voice behind her. It was almost drowned out by the sound of the wind.

- What does that mean, it was almost drowned out by the sound of the wind? (Call on a student. Idea: *She could barely hear his voice because the wind was so loud.*)

"Oomoo," he called. She turned around and looked at the ice chunk. But she couldn't see Oolak. He had been washed into the water. Then she saw his hands. They were gripping the top edge of the ice chunk.

- Where was Oolak? (Call on a student. Idea: *In the water.*)
- What do you think happened to make him fall into the water? (Call on a student. Ideas: *The wind knocked him off the ice chunk; a big wave hit him.*)

She slid over and looked down into the water. "I can't get up," he shouted.

She rolled on to her back and let her legs hang over the side of the ice chunk. "Grab my legs," she shouted.

Picture 1

Picture 2

Picture 3

- Picture 1 shows Oolak in the water and Oomoo on her back with her legs hanging over the side of the ice chunk. You can see how big the waves are. How is she going to try to get Oolak out of the water? (Call on a student. Ideas: *By pulling him up with her legs; by letting him climb up her legs.*)

He grabbed her legs. He started to climb up, but when he did, he almost pulled Oomoo into the water with him. She started to slide, and she probably would have slid into the water if that big wave hadn't hit the ice chunk.

- She probably would have slid into the water if something hadn't happened just then. What happened? (Call on a student. Idea: *A big wave hit the ice chunk.*)

Oolak was on the side of the ice chunk that faced the ocean.

- Everybody, was he on the side facing the shore? (Signal.) *No.*

- Which side was he on? (Signal.) *The side facing the ocean.*

The waves were coming from the shore side of the ✦ ice chunk. Just as Oomoo was sliding off, a huge wave hit the shore side of the ice chunk. It lifted up the shore side and then pushed it very hard. The wave actually slid the ice chunk right under Oomoo and Oolak. In fact, it moved the chunk so fast that Oomoo and Oolak ended up right in the middle of the chunk.

- Listen to that part again and get a picture of how the wave moved the ice chunk.

  The waves were coming from the shore side of the ice chunk. Just as Oomoo was sliding off, a huge wave hit the shore side of the ice chunk. It lifted up the shore side and then pushed it very hard. The wave actually slid the ice chunk right under Oomoo and Oolak. In fact, it moved the chunk so fast that Oomoo and Oolak ended up right in the middle of the chunk.

- Pictures 1, 2, and 3 show what happened. The arrow in each picture shows the direction the waves and the wind are moving. Everybody, touch picture 1. ✓
- The wave is just starting to reach the ice chunk. You can see Oomoo sliding into the water.
- Touch picture 2. ✓
- The wave is now under the ice chunk and the ice chunk is really tilted.
- Turn the page and touch picture 3. ✓
- Now the wave is carrying the ice chunk along. The chunk straightened out so fast that it flipped Oomoo and Oolak right in the middle of the ice chunk.

⚙ Oolak looked very frightened and cold. His eyes were wide. Oomoo tried to hold on to him and keep him from slipping off. "Are we going to die?" he shouted.

"No, we're okay," Oomoo said. She was lying. She didn't see any way that she and Oolak could survive.

Then suddenly the wind died.

- What does that mean? (Call on a student. Idea: *It stopped blowing.*)

The waves still rolled and continued to push the ice chunk beyond the floe. But the big wind had stopped. Rain and hail started to fall. The rain and hail made more noise than the wind had made. "Help!" Oomoo shouted. But she was starting to lose her voice.

- What does that mean, she was starting to lose her voice? (Call on a student. Idea: *She could hardly talk anymore.*)
- Everybody, would anyone be able to hear her anyway? (Signal.) *No.*
- Why not? (Call on a student. Ideas: *Because she was far from shore; because it was too noisy from the rain and hail.*)

"Let's shout together," she said to Oolak. "One, two, three: help!" ✿

- Say that the way they said it. (Call on two students. Students should sound desperate.)

They repeated the shout again and again, until they could not yell anymore. Still the rain and the hail pounded down. Even though the rain was cold, it was much warmer than the ocean water.

- Everybody, which was **warmer**, the rain or the ocean water? (Signal.) *The rain.*
- So which was **colder**? (Signal.) *The ocean water.*
- Read the rest of the story to yourself. Find out two things. Find out how long it rained hard. The story tells that Oomoo saw them, five or six of them. Find out what it was that she saw. Raise your hand when you're done.

After half an hour, the rain began to die down. When the rain had been coming down very hard, Oomoo had not been able to see more than a few meters. Now she could see where they were. The ice chunk was near the top of the C-shaped ice floe and it was still moving north. Oomoo looked to the ocean, past the ice floe, and she could see them—five or six of them. Sometimes they would roll out of the water so that she could

see the black-and-white marking around their heads. Sometimes they would move along with only their fins above the water. Oomoo saw the killer whales but she didn't say anything to Oolak.

- (After all students have raised their hand:)
- How long did it rain hard? (Call on a student. Idea: *About half an hour.*)
- The story said, Oomoo saw them. Everybody, what did she see? (Signal.) *Killer whales.*
- Where was the ice chunk when she saw them? (Call on a student. Idea: *Near the top of the C-shaped ice floe.*)
- Everybody, in which direction was it drifting? (Signal.) *North.*
- Did Oomoo tell Oolak that she saw the killer whales? (Signal.) *No.*
- Why do you think she didn't tell him? (Call on a student. Idea: *So that he wouldn't be afraid.*)

EXERCISE 4
PAIRED PRACTICE

You're going to read aloud to your partner. Today the **A** members will read first. Then the **B** members will read from the star to the end of the story.
(Observe students and give feedback. Praise teams that follow the rules.)

EXERCISE 5
WRITTEN ITEMS
Skill Items

a. Find part D in your textbook. ✓
b. Item 1. Blank do not blank blank things. Raise your hand when you know which vocabulary sentence that's supposed to be. (Call on a student.) Say the sentence. [*Scientists do not ignore ordinary things.*]
- Everybody, say that sentence. Get ready. (Signal.) *Scientists do not ignore ordinary things.*
c. Item 2. She blank blank that blank mistake. Raise your hand when you know which vocabulary sentence that's supposed to be. (Call on a student.) Say the sentence. [*She actually repeated that careless mistake.*]

- Everybody, say that sentence. Get ready. (Signal.) *She actually repeated that careless mistake.*

End-of-Lesson Activities

INDEPENDENT WORK

Now finish your independent work for lesson 19. Raise your hand when you're finished. (Observe students and give feedback.)

WORKCHECK

a. (Direct students to take out their marking pencils.)
   - We're going to check your independent work. Remember, if you got an item wrong, make an **X** next to the item. Don't change any answers.

b. (For each item: Read the item. Call on a student to answer it. If the answer is wrong, say the correct answer. Refer to the Answer Key for the correct answers.)

c. Now use your marking pencil to fix any items you got wrong. Remember, all mistakes must be fixed before you hand in your independent work.

LANGUAGE ARTS

(Present Language Arts lesson 19 after completing Reading lesson 19. See Language Arts Guide.)

Note: You will need to reproduce blackline masters for the Fact Game in lesson 20 (Appendix G in Teacher's Guide).

Materials for Lesson 20

Fact Game

For each team (4 or 5 students):
- pair of number cubes (or dice)
- copy of Fact Game 20

For each student:
- their copy of the scorecard sheet (at the end of workbook A)

For each monitor:
- a pencil
- Fact Game 20 answer key (at end of textbook A)

Reading Checkout

Each student needs their thermometer chart.

Literature Lesson 2

See Literature Guide for the materials you will need.

EXERCISE 1

FACT GAME

a. You're going to play the game that uses the facts you have learned. Remember the rules. The player rolls the number cubes, figures out the number of the question, reads that question out loud, and answers it. The monitor tells the player if the answer is right or wrong. If it's wrong, the monitor tells the right answer. If it's right, the monitor gives the player one point. Don't argue with the monitor. The number cubes go to the left and the next player has a turn. You'll play the game for 10 minutes.

b. (Divide students into groups of four or five. Assign monitors. Circulate as students play the game. Comment on groups that are playing well.)

c. (At the end of 10 minutes, have all students who earned more than 10 points stand up.)

- (Tell the monitor of each game that ran smoothly:) Your group did a good job.

EXERCISE 2

READING CHECKOUTS

a. Today is a test day and a reading-checkout day. While you're writing answers, I'm going to call on you one at a time to read part of the story we read in lesson 19.

- Remember, you pass the checkout by reading the passage in less than a minute without making more than 2 mistakes. And when you pass the checkout, you color the space for lesson 20 on your thermometer chart. When I call on you to come and do your checkout, bring your thermometer chart.

b. (Call on individual students to read the portion of story 19 marked with ❀.)

- (Time the student. Note words that are missed and total number of words read.)

- (Teacher reference:)

> ❀ Oolak looked very frightened and cold. His eyes were wide. Oomoo tried to hold on to him and keep him from slipping off. "Are we going to die?" he shouted.
>
> "No, we're okay," Oomoo said. She was lying. She didn't see any way that she and Oolak could survive.
>
> Then [50] suddenly the wind died. The waves still rolled and continued to push the ice chunk beyond the floe. But the big wind had stopped. [75] Rain and hail started to fall. The rain and hail made more noise than the wind had made. "Help!" Oomoo shouted. But she was starting [100] to lose her voice.
>
> "Let's shout together," she said to Oolak. "One, two, three: help!" ❀ [115]

- (If the student reads the passage in one minute or less and makes no more than 2 errors, direct the student to color in the space for lesson 20 on the thermometer chart.)

- (If the student makes any mistakes, point to each word that was misread and identify it.)
- (If the student does not meet the rate-error criterion for the passage, direct the student to practice reading the story with the assigned partner.)

TEST

a. **Find lesson 20, test 2 in your textbook.** ✓
- This lesson is a test. You'll work items you've done before.
b. Read the items and write the answers on your lined paper. Work carefully. Raise your hand when you've completed all the items.
(Observe students, but do not give feedback on errors.)

MARKING THE TEST

a. (Check students' work before beginning lesson 21. Refer to the Answer Key for the correct answers.)
b. (Record all test 2 results on the Test Summary Sheet and the Group Summary Sheet. Reproducible Summary Sheets are at the back of the Teacher's Guide.)

TEST REMEDIES

(Provide any necessary remedies for test 2 before presenting lesson 21. Test remedies are discussed in the Teacher's Guide.)

Test 2 Firming Table

Test Item	Introduced in lesson	Test Item	Introduced in lesson	Test Item	Introduced in lesson
1	11	11	13	21	18
2	11	12	13	22	18
3	12	13	14	23	18
4	12	14	14	24	16
5	12	15	16	25	12
6	12	16	16	26	16
7	12	17	16	27	12
8	13	18	16	28	16
9	13	19	18	29	12
10	13	20	18		

(Present Language Arts lesson 20 after completing Reading lesson 20. See Language Arts Guide.)

(Present Literature lesson 2 after completing Reading lesson 20. See Literature Guide.)

Lessons 21–25 • Planning Page

	Lesson 21	Lesson 22	Lesson 23	Lesson 24	Lesson 25
Lesson Events	**Vocabulary Sentence** Reading Words Comprehension Passage Story Reading Paired Practice Independent Work Workcheck Language Arts	Vocabulary Sentence Reading Words Comprehension Passage Story Reading Paired Practice Independent Work Workcheck Language Arts	Vocabulary Sentences Reading Words Story Reading Paired Practice Independent Work Workcheck Language Arts	Vocabulary Sentence Reading Words Comprehension Passage Story Reading Paired Practice Independent Work Workcheck Language Arts	**Vocabulary Sentence** Reading Words Story Reading Reading Checkouts Independent Work Workcheck Language Arts
Vocabulary Sentence	**#4: The smell <u>attracted</u> flies <u>immediately</u>.**	#4: The smell <u>attracted</u> flies <u>immediately</u>.	sentence #2 sentence #3 sentence #4	#4: The smell <u>attracted</u> flies <u>immediately</u>.	**#5: The <u>rim</u> of the <u>volcano</u> <u>exploded</u>.**
Reading Words: Word Types	modeled words words with endings mixed words	modeled words words with endings mixed words	modeled words multi-syllable words mixed words	multi-syllable words proper nouns mixed words	modeled words mixed words words with endings compound words
New Vocabulary	mukluks wrist gulped gently owed rose sight		Atlantic Ocean Africa armor	Andros Island Bermuda Triangle	seagulls first mate mast engineer galley stern
Comprehension Passage	*Facts About Clouds*	*Piles*		*Dinosaurs of the Mesozoic*	
Story	*The Killer Whales Wait*	*Usk and the Killer Whale*	*Layers of the Earth*	*Edna Parker*	*Looking for Something to Do*
Skill Items		Sequencing	Vocabulary sentence	Vocabulary Compare Sequencing	Vocabulary
Special Materials		*Materials for project			Thermometer charts
Special Projects/ Activities	Activity after lesson 21	Project after lesson 22	Activity after lessons 23–24	Activity after lessons 24–32	

*Reference materials (books on Alaska, books on Eskimos, encyclopedias, *National Geographic* magazines, *CD-ROMs)* and poster-making supplies (butcher paper or poster board, markers, crayons, paints, scissors, paste, note cards, drawing paper)

EXERCISE 1

VOCABULARY

a. **Find page 352 in your textbook.** ✓
- Touch sentence 4. ✓
- This is a new vocabulary sentence. It says: The smell attracted flies immediately. Everybody, say that sentence. Get ready. (Signal.) *The smell attracted flies immediately.*
- Close your eyes and say the sentence. Get ready. (Signal.) *The smell attracted flies immediately.*
- (Repeat until firm.)

b. The smell **attracted** flies. If the smell attracted flies, the smell really interested the flies and pulled them toward the smell. Everybody, what word means **really interested** the flies? (Signal.) *Attracted.*

c. The sentence says the smell attracted flies **immediately. Immediately** means **right now.** Everybody, what word means **right now?** (Signal.) *Immediately.*

d. Listen to the sentence again: The smell attracted flies immediately. Everybody, say that sentence. Get ready. (Signal.) *The smell attracted flies immediately.*

e. What word means **really interested** the flies? (Signal.) *Attracted.*
- What word means **right now?** (Signal.) *Immediately.*

EXERCISE 2

READING WORDS

Column 1

a. Find lesson 21 in your textbook. ✓
- Touch column 1. ✓
- (Teacher reference:)

1. mukluks	3. hailstone
2. wrist	4. playfully

b. Word 1 is **mukluks.** What word? (Signal.) *Mukluks.*
- Spell **mukluks.** Get ready. (Tap for each letter.) *M-U-K-L-U-K-S.*
- Mukluks are very warm boots that Eskimos wear.

c. Word 2 is **wrist.** What word? (Signal.) *Wrist.*
- Spell **wrist.** Get ready. (Tap for each letter.) *W-R-I-S-T.*
- Your wrist is the joint between your hand and your arm. Everybody, touch your wrist. ✓

d. Word 3. What word? (Signal.) *Hailstone.*

e. Word 4. What word? (Signal.) *Playfully.*

f. Let's read those words again, the fast way.
- Word 1. What word? (Signal.) *Mukluks.*
- (Repeat for words 2–4.)

g. (Repeat step f until firm.)

Column 2

h. Find column 2. ✓
- (Teacher reference:)

1. gulped	4. wavy
2. gently	5. kneeled
3. owed	6. dents

i. All these words have an ending.

j. Word 1. What word? (Signal.) *Gulped.*
- When you gulp something, you swallow it quickly. Here's another way of saying **She swallowed the water quickly: She gulped the water.**
- What's another way of saying **They swallowed their food quickly?** (Signal.) *They gulped their food.*
- Word 2. What word? (Signal.) *Gently.*
- Things that are gentle are the opposite of things that are rough. Everybody, what's the opposite of **a rough touch?** (Signal.) *A gentle touch.*
- What's the opposite of someone who behaves roughly? (Signal.) *Someone who behaves gently.*
- (Repeat until firm.)
- Word 3. What word? (Signal.) *Owed.*
- Something that you owe is something that you must pay. If you owe five dollars, you must pay five dollars. If you owe somebody a favor, you must pay that person a favor.

- Word 4. What word? (Signal.) *Wavy.*
- (Repeat for: **5. kneeled, 6. dents.**)

k. Let's read those words again, the fast way.
- Word 1. What word? (Signal.) *Gulped.*
- (Repeat for: **2. gently, 3. owed, 4. wavy, 5. kneeled, 6. dents.**)
l. (Repeat step k until firm.)

Column 3

m. Find column 3. ✓
- (Teacher reference:)

1. rose	3. marble
2. sight	4. dove

n. Word 1. What word? (Signal.) *Rose.*
- Something that moves up today rises. Something that moved up yesterday **rose.** Everybody, what do we say for something that moves up today? (Signal.) *Rises.*
- What do we say for something that moved up yesterday? (Signal.) *Rose.*
- Word 2. What word? *Sight.*
- A sight is something you see. A terrible sight is something terrible that you see. Everybody, what do we call something **wonderful** that you see? (Signal.) *A wonderful sight.*
- Word 3. What word? (Signal.) *Marble.*
- Word 4 rhymes with **stove.** What word? (Signal.) *Dove.*

o. Let's read those words again.
- Word 1. What word? (Signal.) *Rose.*
- (Repeat for words 2–4.)
p. (Repeat step o until firm.)

Individual Turns

(For columns 1–3: Call on individual students, each to read one to three words per turn.)

EXERCISE 3

COMPREHENSION PASSAGE

a. Find part B in your textbook. ✓
- You're going to read the next story about Oomoo and Oolak. First, you'll read the information passage. It gives some facts about clouds.
b. Everybody, touch the title. ✓
- (Call on a student to read the title.) [*Facts About Clouds.*]

- Everybody, what's the title? (Signal.) *Facts About Clouds.*
c. (Call on individual students to read the passage, each student reading two or three sentences at a time. Ask the specified questions as the students read.)

> **Facts About Clouds**
> You have read about a big storm cloud. Here are facts about clouds:
> Clouds are made up of tiny drops of water.

- Everybody, say that fact. Get ready. (Signal.) *Clouds are made up of tiny drops of water.*

> In clouds that are very high, the water drops are frozen. Here is how those clouds look.

Picture 1   Picture 2

- Everybody, in what kind of clouds are the water drops frozen? (Signal.) *In clouds that are very high.*
- Touch a high cloud. ✓
- Those clouds are very pretty in the sunlight because the light bounces off the tiny frozen drops.

> Some kinds of clouds may bring days of bad weather. These are low, flat clouds that look like bumpy blankets.

- Everybody, what kind of clouds may bring days of bad weather? (Signal.) *Low, flat clouds.*
- Does that kind of cloud pass over quickly? (Signal.) *No.*
- Touch a low, flat cloud. ✓
- How long may that kind of cloud be around? (Call on a student. Idea: *Days.*)

> Some clouds are storm clouds. They are flat on the bottom, but they go up very high. Sometimes they are five miles high.

- Tell me how a storm cloud looks. (Call on a student. Idea: *It's flat on the bottom and it goes up very high.*)
- Everybody, how high is the top of a big storm cloud sometimes? (Signal.) *Five miles.*

The arrows in picture 3 show how the winds move inside a storm cloud. The winds move water drops to the top of the cloud.

- Everybody, touch the number **1** that is inside the cloud. ✓
- That's where a drop of water starts. The wind blows it up to the top of the cloud. Everybody, follow the arrow to the top of the cloud and then stop. ✓
- Tell me about the temperature of the air at the top of the cloud. Get ready. (Signal.) *It's freezing cold.*
- So what's going to happen to the drop? (Call on a student. Idea: *It will freeze.*)

The drops freeze. When a drop freezes, it becomes a tiny hailstone.

- Everybody, what do we call a drop when it moves up and freezes? (Signal.) *A tiny hailstone.*

The tiny hailstone falls to the bottom of the cloud.

- Everybody, touch the number **2** in the cloud. ✓
- That's where the drop freezes. Now it falls down. Everybody, follow the arrow down. ✓
- What's the temperature like at the bottom of the cloud? (Signal.) *It's warm.*

At the bottom of the cloud, the tiny hailstone gets covered with more water. Then it goes up again and freezes again.

- Everybody, when it gets to the top of the cloud, what's going to happen to the water that is covering it? (Signal.) *It will freeze.*

Now the hailstone is a little bigger. It keeps going around and around in the cloud until it gets so heavy that it falls from the cloud. Sometimes it is as big as a baseball. Sometimes it is smaller than a marble.

- Everybody, touch the number **1** in the cloud. ✓
- Pretend that your finger is a drop. Show me a drop that goes around inside the cloud four times. Each time it goes through the top of the cloud, say: "It freezes." Go. ✓

If you want to see how many times a hailstone has gone to the top of the cloud, break the hailstone in half. You'll see rings.

- Everybody, what will you see inside the hailstone? (Signal.) *Rings.*

Each ring shows one trip to the top of the cloud. Count the rings and you'll know how many times the hailstone went through the cloud. Hailstone A went through the cloud three times.

- The rings are numbered. Everybody, count the rings in hailstone A out loud, starting with the center circle. Get ready. (Signal.) *One, two, three.*

How many times did Hailstone B go through the cloud?

- Everybody, figure out the answer. Remember to count the outside ring. (Wait.)
- How many times? (Signal.) *Seven.*

EXERCISE 4

STORY READING

a. Find part C in your textbook. ✓
- The error limit for group reading is 12 errors.
b. Everybody, touch the title. ✓
- (Call on a student to read the title.) *[The Killer Whales Wait.]*
- Everybody, what's the title? (Signal.) *The Killer Whales Wait.*

- Where were Oolak and Oomoo when we left them? (Call on a student. Idea: *Floating on an ice chunk.*)
c. (Call on individual students to read the story, each student reading two or three sentences at a time. Ask the specified questions as the students read.)

> - (Correct errors: Tell the word. Direct the student to reread the sentence.)
> - (If the group makes more than 12 errors, direct the students to reread the story.)

The Killer Whales Wait
Oomoo took off one of her boots. She kneeled down and slammed the boot against the surface of the ice.

- Why do you think she was doing that? (Call on a student. Idea: *She was trying to make noise so someone would hear her.*)
- Why didn't she yell? (Call on a student. Ideas: *She was losing her voice; nobody could hear her.*)

The boot made a loud spanking sound. Oolak watched for a moment, then took off one of his boots and slapped it against the surface of the ice. "Maybe they'll hear this," Oomoo said. "I hope they do," she added. But she knew that it was still raining a little bit and that the rain made noise. She also knew that she and Oolak were far from shore—too far. They were more than a mile from the tent. She guessed that the sounds they made with their boots were lost in the rain and the slight breeze that was still blowing from the south.

- Everybody, did she think that the people on the shore would hear the sounds? (Signal.) *No.*
- About how far away were these people? (Signal.) *Over a mile.*
- Why didn't she think they would hear the signal? (Call on a student. Idea: *Because the wind and rain were louder than the signal.*)

From time to time, Oomoo glanced to the ocean. She hoped that she would see the killer whales moving far away. She hoped that the sound

of the boots would scare them away. But each time she looked in their direction, she saw them moving back and forth, just past the top of the C-shaped ice floe.

- How do you think that made her feel? (Call on a student. Idea: *Afraid.*)

Suddenly, Oolak tugged on Oomoo's shoulder and pointed toward the whales. His eyes were wide. He looked as if he was ready to cry. "I know," Oomoo said.

- What does she mean when she says, "I know?" (Call on a student. Idea: *She knew the whales were there.*)

Her voice was almost a whisper. "Just keep trying to signal," she said. "Maybe the people on the shore will hear us."

- Everybody, had Oolak noticed the whales before? (Signal.) *No.*
- Why did he look as if he was ready to cry? (Call on a student. Idea: *Because he was afraid of the killer whales.*)

As she pounded her boot against the surface of the ice, she stared toward the shore. She wanted to see a kayak moving silently through the rain. She wanted to hear the signal of a bell ringing. She wanted to . . . .

- She stopped thinking about those things. I wonder why.

Suddenly, she saw something white moving through the water.

- What do you think it is? (Call on individual students. Ideas: *Another ice chunk; a boat; an animal;* etc.)

At first, she thought that it was a chunk of ice. But no, it couldn't be. It was not moving the way ice moves. It was very hard to tell what it was through the light rain. It wasn't a kayak. It wasn't a long boat. It was . . . Usk.

Usk ★ was swimming directly toward the ice chunk. And he was moving very fast.

"Usk!" Oomoo yelled as loudly as she could. "Usk!" She stood up and waved her arms.

The huge polar bear caught up to the ice chunk when it was not more than a hundred meters away from the killer whales. "Will they go after Usk?" Oolak asked.

- Everybody, who does he think might go after Usk? (Signal.) *The killer whales.*
- How close are they to the whales now? (Call on a student. Idea: *About 100 meters.*)

"They'll go after Usk if they're hungry," Oomoo replied. "We've got to get out of here fast."

The huge bear swam up to the ice chunk, put his huge paws on the surface, and started to climb onto it. When he tried that, he almost tipped it over.

- Why? (Call on a student. Idea: *Because he was so heavy.*)

"No," Oomoo said. "Stay down." She tried to push him back. He rolled into the water and made a playful circle. "Give me your laces," Oomoo said to Oolak. Oomoo and Oolak untied the laces from their boots. These laces were long, thick strips of animal skin. Oomoo tied all the laces together. Quickly, she glanced back. The ice chunk was less than a hundred meters from the killer whales.

She called Usk. He playfully swam around the ice chunk, rolling over on his back and slapping the water with his front paws.

- What does Usk want to do? (Call on a student. Idea: *Play.*)

Oomoo waited until Usk got close to the shore side of the ice chunk.

- Everybody, which side did he move to? (Signal.) *The shore side.*

- What do you think Oomoo's going to do? (Call on a student. Idea: *Get Usk to help them get back to shore.*)

Then she slipped the laces around his neck. "Hang on tight," she told Oolak, and handed him one end of the laces. She and Oolak sat down on the ice chunk and tried to dig their heels into dents in the surface of the ice.

"Play sled," she told Usk. "Play sled. Go home."

- Read the rest of the story to yourself. Find out two things. Find out what Usk did at first. Find out something he may have seen that made him stop being playful. Raise your hand when you're done.

At first, Usk just rolled over and almost got the laces tangled in his front paws. "Home," Oomoo repeated. "Play sled and go home."

Usk stayed next to the ice chunk, making a playful sound. "Home," Oomoo shouted again.

Then Usk seemed to figure out what he was supposed to do. Perhaps he saw the fins of the killer whales. He got low in the water and started to swim toward shore.

- (After all students have raised their hands:)
- What did Oomoo keep telling Usk to do? (Call on a student. Ideas: *Go home; play sled.*)
- Everybody, did Usk do that at first? (Signal.) *No.*
- What did he do? (Call on a student. Idea: *Rolled over.*)
- What may Usk have seen that made him stop being playful? (Call on a student. Idea: *The fins of the killer whales.*)
- What did Usk do then? (Call on a student. Idea: *Swam toward shore.*)
- Everybody, look at the picture. What are Oomoo and Oolak hanging on to? (Signal.) *The laces.*
- Point on the picture to show the direction Usk is moving. ✓

EXERCISE 5

PAIRED PRACTICE

You're going to read aloud to your partner. Today the **B** members will read first. Then the **A** members will read from the star to the end of the story.
(Observe students and give feedback.)

End-of-Lesson Activities

INDEPENDENT WORK

Now finish your independent work for lesson 21. Raise your hand when you're finished. (Observe students and give feedback.)

WORKCHECK

a. (Direct students to take out their marking pencils.)
- We're going to check your independent work. Remember, if you got an item wrong, make an **X** next to the item. Don't change any answers.

b. (For each item: Read the item. Call on a student to answer it. If the answer is wrong, say the correct answer. Refer to the Answer Key for the correct answers.)

c. Now use your marking pencil to fix up any items you got wrong. Remember, all mistakes must be fixed up before you hand in your independent work.

LANGUAGE ARTS

(Present Language Arts lesson 21 after completing Reading lesson 21. See Language Arts Guide.)

ACTIVITIES

(Present Activity 2 after completing Reading lessons 21. See Activities Across the Curriculum.)

> **Note:** A special project occurs after lesson 22. See page 128 for the materials you'll need.

VOCABULARY REVIEW

a. Here's the new vocabulary sentence: The smell attracted flies immediately.
- Everybody, say that sentence. Get ready. (Signal.) *The smell attracted flies immediately.*
- (Repeat until firm.)

b. What word means **right now?** (Signal.) *Immediately.*
- What word means **really interested** the flies? (Signal.) *Attracted.*

READING WORDS

Column 1

a. **Find lesson 22 in your textbook.** ✓
- Touch column 1. ✓
- (Teacher reference:)

1. **Mesozoic**	4. **Triceratops**
2. **dinosaur**	5. **Tyrannosaurus**
3. **skeleton**	

b. Word 1 is **Mesozoic.** What word? (Signal.) *Mesozoic.*
- Spell **Mesozoic.** Get ready. (Tap for each letter.) *M-E-S-O-Z-O-I-C.*

c. Word 2 is **dinosaur.** What word? (Signal.) *Dinosaur.*
- Spell **dinosaur.** Get ready. (Tap for each letter.) *D-I-N-O-S-A-U-R.*

d. Word 3 is **skeleton.** What word? (Signal.) *Skeleton.*
- Spell **skeleton.** Get ready. (Tap for each letter.) *S-K-E-L-E-T-O-N.*

e. Word 4 is **Triceratops.** What word? (Signal.) *Triceratops.*

f. Word 5 is **Tyrannosaurus.** What word? (Signal.) *Tyrannosaurus.*

g. Let's read those words again, the fast way.
- Word 1. What word? (Signal.) *Mesozoic.*
- (Repeat for words 2–5.)

h. (Repeat step g until firm.)

Column 2

i. Find column 2. ✓
- (Teacher reference:)

1. **earlier**	4. **gulped**
2. **mukluks**	5. **gently**
3. **wavy**	6. **owed**

- All these words have an ending.

j. Word 1. What word? (Signal.) *Earlier.*
- (Repeat for words 2–6.)

k. (Repeat step j until firm.)

Column 3

l. Find column 3. ✓
- (Teacher reference:)

1. **figure**	4. **dove**
2. **sight**	5. **wrist**
3. **rose**	

m. Word 1. What word? (Signal.) *Figure.*
- (Repeat for words 2–5.)

n. (Repeat step m until firm.)

Individual Turns

(For columns 1–3: Call on individual students, each to read one to three words per turn.)

COMPREHENSION PASSAGE

a. Find part B in your textbook. ✓
- You're going to read the last story about Oomoo and Oolak. First you'll read the information passage. It teaches a rule about piles.

b. Everybody, touch the title. ✓
- (Call on a student to read the title.) *[Piles.]*
- Everybody, what's the title? (Signal.) *Piles.*

c. (Call on individual students to read the passage, each student reading two or three sentences at a time. Ask the specified questions as the students read.)

Piles

Here's a rule about piles:
Things closer to the bottom of the pile went into the pile earlier.

- Everybody, what do we know about things closer to the bottom of a pile? (Signal.) *They went into the pile earlier.*
- Listen to the rule: Things closer to the bottom of the pile went into the pile earlier.
- Say the whole rule. Get ready. (Signal.) *Things closer to the bottom of the pile went into the pile earlier.*
- (Repeat until firm.)

Here's a pile:
Which thing is closest to the bottom of the pile?

- Everybody, touch the object that is closest to the bottom of the pile. ✓
- Name that object. Get ready. (Signal.) *Shoe.*

So the shoe went into the pile first.

- Everybody, which object went into the pile first? (Signal.) *The shoe.*
- We know that the shoe went into the pile earlier than the other objects because the shoe is closer to the bottom of the pile than any other object.

The shoe went into the pile before the bone went into the pile. The shoe went into the pile before the cup went into the pile.

- Everybody, touch the book and the bone. ✓
- Which object is closer to the bottom of the pile? (Signal.) *The book.*

- So which object went into the pile earlier? (Signal.) *The book.*

Look at the cup and the bone.

- Everybody, touch them. ✓

Which object is closer to the bottom of the pile?

- Everybody, what's the answer? (Signal.) *The bone.*

So which object went into the pile earlier?

- Everybody, what's the answer? (Signal.) *The bone.*

Look at the pencil and the rock.

- Everybody, touch them. ✓

Which object is closer to the bottom of the pile?

- Name that object. Get ready. (Signal.) *The pencil.*

So which object went into the pile earlier?

- Name that object. Get ready. (Signal.) *The pencil.*

The rule tells us that things closer to the bottom of the pile went into the pile earlier. Use this rule to figure out which object was the last one to go into the pile.

- Everybody, touch the object that went into the pile last. ✓
- Name that object. Get ready. (Signal.) *The rock.*

Use the rule to figure out which object went into the pile just after the shoe went into the pile.

- Everybody, name that object. Get ready (Signal.) *The book.*

Use the rule to figure out which object went into the pile just after the pencil went into the pile.

- Everybody, name the object. Get ready. (Signal.) *The knife.*

STORY READING

a. Find part C in your textbook. ✓
- The error limit for group reading is 12 errors.

b. Everybody, touch the title. ✓
- (Call on a student to read the title.) *[Usk and the Killer Whale.]*
- Everybody, what's the title? (Signal.) *Usk and the Killer Whale.*

c. (Call on individual students to read the story, each student reading two or three sentences at a time. Ask the specified questions as the students read.)

- (Correct errors: Tell the word. Direct the student to reread the sentence.)
- (If the group makes more than 12 errors, direct the students to reread the story.)

Usk and the Killer Whale
When Usk began to swim toward shore, he moved with so much power that he almost pulled Oomoo and Oolak off the ice. They leaned back and dug their heels in.

- What were they digging their heels into? (Call on a student. Idea: *The dents in the ice chunk.*)

They hung on to the laces as hard as they could hang on.
Oomoo looked over her shoulder. She saw a terrible sight.

- What does that mean, a terrible sight? (Call on a student. Idea: *Something scary.*)
- What do you think it was? (Call on a student. Idea: *The killer whales.*)

One of the fins was moving toward them. The fin rose out of the water, and she could see that the whale was looking at them. Its mouth was open and she could see the row of knives in its mouth.

- What were those knives? (Call on a student. Idea: *Teeth.*)

She clearly saw the wavy black-and-white markings on its body. Then it dove into the water. Its fin disappeared. But the whale was moving very fast.

Quickly, Oomoo tied the laces around her wrist so that she had a free hand. With that hand, she slapped the ice. "Maybe this sound will scare it off," she said to herself. "Oh, please go away," she said out loud. "Please."

She looked into the water and suddenly she saw the huge form of the whale pass under them. Her heart was pounding so hard that she seemed to shake all over. She kept looking down, but she didn't see anything for about a minute. Then she saw the whale roll out of the water about five meters in front of them.

- Listen to that part of the story again. She clearly saw the wavy black-and-white markings on its body. Then it dove into the water. Its fin disappeared. But the whale was moving very fast. Quickly, Oomoo tied the laces around her wrist so that she had a free hand. With that hand, she slapped the ice. "Maybe this sound will scare it off," she said to herself. "Oh, please go away," she said out loud. "Please." She looked into the water and suddenly she saw the huge form of the whale pass under them. Her heart was pounding so hard that she seemed to shake all over. She kept looking down, but she didn't see anything for about a minute. Then she saw the whale roll out of the water about five meters in front of them.
- The picture shows this part of the story. Everybody, about how close is the whale to the ice chunk? (Signal.) *5 meters.*
- How does Usk look? (Call on a student: Ideas: *Mean; mad.*)
- Everybody, what is Oomoo doing with her free hand? (Signal.) *Slapping the ice.*
- Why? (Call on a student. Idea: *To try to scare the whale.*)
- What's her other hand doing? (Call on a student. Idea: *Holding on to the laces.*)

The bear made a growling sound and pricked up his ears. For a moment, Usk stopped swimming. Then he continued.

"Oh, please go away," Oomoo repeated to herself. Again, the form of the great whale moved under them, making a slight turn to the right. Oomoo continued to slap the ice with her hand. Oolak was saying something, but Oomoo couldn't think about that. She thought about one thing—that whale.

- Everybody, how many things was she thinking about? (Signal.) *One.*
- What was that? (Call on a student. Idea: *The whale near them.*)

Suddenly, the whale rolled out of the water behind them. It seemed to be turning away, toward the other whales. "Please go away," Oomoo said. Usk swam, Oomoo and Oolak held on to the laces. And Oomoo kept looking behind to see what the whale would do next. Suddenly, she saw it ☀ roll out of the water again. It was more than sixty meters from them.

- Everybody, the whale was more than how many meters away? (Signal.) *60.*
- How close to the ice chunk had it been? (Signal.) *5 meters.*
- So what do you think that whale is doing? (Call on a student. Idea: *Moving away from the ice chunk.*)

That whale was moving toward the other whales.
• • •

- What do those dots mean? (Call on a student. Idea: *Part of the story is missing.*)

The mosquitoes were terrible. So were the biting flies.

- If the story is telling about flies and mosquitoes, where is Oomoo now? (Call on a student. Ideas: *On shore; home.*)

There was no breeze at all, and the bugs were thick. But Oomoo didn't mind. She and Oolak had to stay near the tent.

- Everybody, where is Oomoo now? (Signal.) *Near the tent.*

- Why do you think she has to stay near the tent? (Call on a student. Idea: *She's being punished.*)

Oomoo and Oolak couldn't go on the slopes or down the path to the beach. They couldn't play. Their father had told them they had to study the sky and the ocean so they would not make the kind of mistake they made before.

- What kind of mistake had they made? (Call on a student. Idea: *They hadn't watched the sky.*)
- So what do they have to study now? (Call on a student. Idea: *The sky and the ocean.*)
- What does that mean, study the sky? (Call on a student. Idea: *Look at it carefully.*)

"When you look at the sky," their father had told them, "face into the wind and look at the place where the sky meets the land or the ocean."

- What place do you look at? (Call on a student. Idea: *Where the sky meets the land or the ocean.*)
- Which way do you face when you study the sky? (Call on a student. Idea: *Into the wind.*)
- So you'll see all the clouds that are going to come your way.

The day was peaceful, with the wind blowing gently from the ocean.

- If they had to face into the wind, where was Oomoo looking? (Call on a student. Idea: *At the sky over the ocean.*)

Oomoo watched the sky and the ocean. From time to time, she looked at the killer whales. She wondered what that whale had thought, and why it hadn't attacked Usk. "You will never understand the whale," an old man of the village had told her.
    That afternoon, everyone in the village gathered at Oomoo's tent.

- Why do you think they did that? (Call on a student. Student preference.)

The people formed a great ring. They sang. Then Oomoo's father led Usk into the middle of the ring. Women brought him a large smoked fish—his favorite food. He gulped it down and wagged his head from side to side. Then Oomoo's father took blue paint and painted the outline of a whale on each side of Usk.

- Everybody, look at the picture on page 111. What is Oomoo's father doing? (Call on a student. Idea: *Painting a whale on Usk.*)
- Read the rest of the story to yourself. Find out what was going to happen to Usk. Find out if Oomoo and Oolak were allowed to play with Usk. Raise your hand when you're done.

"Let this bear live under the sign of the whale," her father said. "Let no hunter shoot this bear or bother this bear. If this bear needs food, feed this bear. We owe much to this bear. Let us thank him."

The people from the village cheered and danced. Oomoo and Oolak danced with the others. They were very, very proud of their bear. They knew that they should not play with him because he was a bear, not a playmate. But they also knew that they owed their lives to that huge, white, playful bear.

- (After all the students have raised their hand:)
- Name something that Oomoo's father said would happen to Usk. (Call on a student. Ideas: *Nobody would bother him; he would have food.*)

- What did the people of the village do after Oomoo's father said what would happen to Usk? (Call on a student. Idea: *Cheered and danced.*)
- Everybody, were Oomoo and Oolak allowed to play with Usk? (Signal.) *No.*
- Why not? (Call on a student. Idea: *Because he was a bear, not a playmate.*)
- Everybody, look at the picture again. Do the people look happy? (Signal.) *Yes.*
- Why are they thanking Usk? (Call on a student. Idea: *Because he saved the children.*)

EXERCISE 5

PAIRED PRACTICE

You're going to read aloud to your partner. Today the **A** members will read first. Then the **B** members will read from the star to the end of the story.
(Observe students and give feedback.)

End-of-Lesson Activities

INDEPENDENT WORK

Now finish your independent work for lesson 22. Raise your hand when you're finished. (Observe students and give feedback.)

WORKCHECK

a. (Direct students to take out their marking pencils.)
- We're going to check your independent work. Remember, if you got an item wrong, make an **X** next to the item. Don't change any answers.
b. (For each item: Read the item. Call on a student to answer it. If the answer is wrong, say the correct answer. Refer to the Answer Key for the correct answers.)
c. Now use your marking pencil to fix any items you got wrong. Remember, all mistakes must be fixed before you hand in your independent work.

LANGUAGE ARTS

(Present Language Arts lesson 22 after completing Reading lesson 22. See Language Arts Guide.)

Special Project

Note: After completing lesson 22, do this special project with the students. The project may be done at another time of day.

Materials: Reference materials (books on Alaska, books on Eskimos, encyclopedias, *National Geographic* magazines, CD-ROMs) and poster-making supplies (butcher paper or poster board, markers, crayons, paints, scissors, paste, note cards, drawing paper)

a. Everybody, find page 115 in your textbook. ✓
- These are instructions for a project that we will do about Eskimos. (Call on individual students to read the instructions.)
- (Teacher reference:)

Special Project

Make a wall chart that shows and tells about Eskimos.
- Make pictures of the things that they use and wear.
- Make pictures of the kinds of houses that they live in.
- Find out what mukluks look like. Make a picture of them.
- Find out another name for killer whales and another name for Eskimos.
- Find out what kind of food Eskimos eat in the wintertime.
- Find out what kind of food they eat in the summertime.
- Find out what kind of animal skins they use to make clothes.
  Write the facts about Eskimos on the chart. You may want to write other facts about Eskimos.

b. We should work together in making this chart, so we'll form four teams. Each team will be responsible for part of the project. One team will find facts and pictures about the different kinds of houses that Eskimos live in. One team will find out about the food that Eskimos eat. One team will find out about the things they wear and how they make their clothes. One team will find out about the things they use and how they make the things they use. All teams will find out what mukluks look like. All teams will also find out another name for killer whales and another name for Eskimos.

c. (Assign the students to the four different teams. Tell the teams that they should find good pictures and facts. They should write their facts on cards before putting them on the wall chart.)

d. (Help the teams find reference materials, for example books on Alaska, books on Eskimos, encyclopedias, *National Geographic* magazines, CD-ROMs.)

e. (After each team presents its pictures and facts, help the students design their part of the display. The display should be divided into parts with headings. Under each heading would be the appropriate pictures and facts.)

f. (When the display is completed, praise the teams. Then tell all the students to learn all the facts that are shown on the chart.)

g. (Test the students on the chart information. Possibly invite another class for a presentation on Eskimos. A representative from each team would tell about the topic that team researched.)

EXERCISE 1

VOCABULARY REVIEW

a. You learned a sentence that tells what scientists do not do.
- Everybody, say that sentence. Get ready. (Signal.) *Scientists do not ignore ordinary things.*
- (Repeat until firm.)

b. You learned a sentence that tells what she actually did.
- Everybody, say that sentence. Get ready. (Signal.) *She actually repeated that careless mistake.*
- (Repeat until firm.)

c. Here's the last sentence you learned: The smell attracted flies immediately.
- Everybody, say that sentence. Get ready. (Signal.) *The smell attracted flies immediately.*
- (Repeat until firm.)

d. What word means **really interested** the flies? (Signal.) *Attracted.*
- What word means **right now?** (Signal.) *Immediately.*

e. Once more. Say the sentence that tells what the smell attracted. Get ready. (Signal.) *The smell attracted flies immediately.*

EXERCISE 2

READING WORDS

Column 1

a. **Find lesson 23 in your textbook.** ✓
- Touch column 1. ✓
- (Teacher reference:)

1. **Atlantic Ocean**	4. **Africa**
2. **Bermuda Triangle**	5. **engineer**
3. **Andros Island**	

b. Number 1 is **Atlantic Ocean.** What words? (Signal.) *Atlantic Ocean.*
- The Atlantic Ocean is the ocean that touches the eastern shore of the United States.

c. Number 2 is **Bermuda Triangle.** What words? (Signal.) *Bermuda Triangle.*

d. Number 3 is **Andros Island.** What words? (Signal.) *Andros Island.*

e. Word 4 is **Africa.** What word? (Signal.) *Africa.*
- Spell **Africa.** Get ready. (Tap for each letter.) *A-F-R-I-C-A.*
- Africa is a large area of land that is bigger than North America. It is on the other side of the Atlantic Ocean.

f. Word 5 is **engineer.** What word? (Signal.) *Engineer.*
- Spell **engineer.** Get ready. (Tap for each letter.) *E-N-G-I-N-E-E-R.*

g. Let's read those words again, the fast way.
- Number 1. What words? (Signal.) *Atlantic Ocean.*
- Number 2. What words? (Signal.) *Bermuda Triangle.*
- Number 3. What words? (Signal.) *Andros Island.*
- Word 4. What word? (Signal.) *Africa.*
- Word 5. What word? (Signal.) *Engineer.*

h. (Repeat step g until firm.)

Column 2

i. Find column 2. ✓
- (Teacher reference:)

1. **armor**	4. **Tyrannosaurus**
2. **dinosaur**	5. **skeleton**
3. **layers**	

j. Word 1. What word? (Signal.) *Armor.*
- Armor is a hard covering that is made to protect anything inside. A ship could be covered with armor. The skin of some animals is like armor. Everybody, what do we call the hard covering that protects something? (Signal.) *Armor.*

k. Word 2. What word? (Signal.) *Dinosaur.*
- (Repeat for words 3–5.)

l. Let's read those words again.
- Word 1. What word? (Signal.) *Armor.*
- (Repeat for words 2–5.)

m. (Repeat step l until firm.)

Column 3

n. Find column 3. ✓
- (Teacher reference:)

1. earliest	4. Mesozoic
2. Triceratops	5. explaining
3. killers	

o. Word 1. What word? (Signal.) *Earliest.*
- (Repeat for words 2–5.)

p. Let's read those words again.
- Word 1. What word? (Signal.) *Earliest.*
- (Repeat for words 2–5.)

q. (Repeat step p until firm.)

Individual Turns

(For columns 1–3: Call on individual students, each to read one to three words per turn.)

EXERCISE 3

STORY READING

a. Find part B in your textbook. ✓
- The error limit for group reading is 8 errors. Read carefully.

b. Everybody, touch the title. ✓
- (Call on a student to read the title.) *[Layers of the Earth.]*
- Everybody, what's the title? (Signal.) *Layers of the Earth.*
- (Call on individual students to read the story, each student reading two or three sentences at a time. Ask the specified questions as the students read.)

- (Correct errors: Tell the word. Direct the student to reread the sentence.)
- (If the group makes more than 8 errors, direct the students to reread the story.)

Layers of the Earth
You learned a rule about piles. Which things went into the pile earlier?

- Everybody, what's the answer? (Signal.) *Things closer to the bottom of the pile.*
- Say the rule. Get ready. (Signal.) *Things closer to the bottom of the pile went into the pile earlier.*

We use the rule about piles to figure out how things happened a long time ago.
   Look at picture 1. It shows a large cliff. There are rows of stones and rocks and seashells. Each row is called a layer.

PICTURE 1

- Everybody, what is each row called? (Signal.) *A layer.*
- The layers are labeled A, B, C, and D. Touch layer D. ✓
- Is that at the **top** or the **bottom** of the pile? (Signal.) *Top.*

The layers are piled up. That means the layers closer to the bottom of the pile came earlier.
   Which layer went into the pile earlier, layer C or layer D?

- Everybody, touch layer C and layer D. ✓
- The layer closer to the bottom of the pile went into the pile earlier. Which layer is that? (Signal.) *Layer C.*
- Everybody, touch layer A and layer B. ✓
- Which layer went into the pile earlier? (Signal.) *Layer A.*
- How do you know that layer A went into the pile earlier? (Call on a student. Idea: *Because it's closer to the bottom of the pile.*)

When we look at the layers of rock, we find skeletons of animals and shells of animals. In layer B, we find strange fish and other animals that lived many millions of years ago.

- How long ago did these skeletons and shells go into the pile? (Call on a student. Idea: *Many millions of years ago.*)
- Everybody, touch some of the skeletons and shells in layer B. ✓
- These are skeletons and shells of animals that do not live on Earth anymore.

In layer D we find the skeletons of horses. Near the bottom of layer D, we find horses that are no bigger than dogs. Near the top of layer D, we find horses that are as big as the horses of today.

When we look at layer C, we find the skeletons of some very strange animals. These are dinosaurs.

- Everybody, touch the animals in layer C. ✓
- What are those skeletons of? (Signal.) *Dinosaurs.*
- Which came earlier, dinosaurs or horses? (Signal.) *Dinosaurs.*

Some of the dinosaurs were much bigger than elephants. Other dinosaurs had great spikes on their tails. No dinosaurs are alive today. The only place we find their bones is in one of the layers under ground. That is layer C. We can't find dinosaur bones in layer B. We can't find them in layer D.

- Everybody, what's the only layer where we find dinosaur skeletons? (Signal.) *Layer C.*
- Are any dinosaurs alive today? (Signal.) *No.*

The layers of ✦ rock tell us a great deal about things that happened millions and millions of years ago. They tell us what it was like when the great dinosaurs walked on Earth. There were no horses, bears, elephants or rabbits. There were no mice or cats. But there were many animals. Most of them were probably cold-blooded.

- Some relatives of dinosaurs are snakes and alligators. They're cold-blooded.

Some dinosaurs ate big animals. These dinosaurs were huge killers that could move fast. The ones that are found near the top of layer C stood almost 20 feet tall.

- Everybody, how tall were they? (Signal.) *Almost 20 feet.*

When we move above layer C, we find the beginning of animals that we know—horses, cats, bears, pigs. No layers show skeletons of humans. But if these skeletons were in the picture, they would be at the very top of the pile, in layer D.

- Everybody, touch the only place human skeletons would be. ✓
- You should be touching the top of layer D.

Here's another fact about the layers: When we dig a hole in any part of the world, we find the same layers. If we dig a hole in Africa or in Canada, we find skeletons of elephants near the top of the pile. We find dinosaurs in the next layer down.

The layer that has dinosaur skeletons is called the Mesozoic.

- Everybody, what's the name of the layer that has dinosaur skeletons? (Signal.) *Mesozoic.*
- Touch the Mesozoic in the picture. ✓

PICTURE 2

The layer that came after the Mesozoic is the top layer. The top layer has no skeletons of dinosaurs. This layer is still being laid down. We live at the top of the top layer.

- Everybody, touch the top layer in the picture. ✓
- Are there any dinosaur skeletons in that layer? (Signal.) *No.*

- But there are skeletons of a lot of other animals.
- Touch where you would find skeletons of humans. ✓
- You should be touching the top part of the top layer.

PAIRED PRACTICE

You're going to read aloud to your partner. The **B** members will read first. Then the **A** members will read from the star to the end of the story.
(Observe students and give feedback.)

End-of-Lesson Activities

INDEPENDENT WORK

Now finish your independent work for lesson 23. Raise your hand when you're finished. (Observe students and give feedback.)

WORKCHECK

a. (Direct students to take out their marking pencils.)
- We're going to check your workbook and textbook items. Remember, if you got an item wrong, make an **X** next to the item.
b. (For each item: Read the item. Call on a student to answer it. If the answer is wrong, say the correct answer. Refer to the Answer Key for the correct answers.)
c. Now use your marking pencil to fix any items you got wrong. Remember, all mistakes must be fixed before you hand in your work.

LANGUAGE ARTS

(Present Language Arts lesson 23 after completing Reading lesson 23. See Language Arts Guide.)

ACTIVITIES

(Present Activity 3 after completing Reading lessons 23-24. See Activities Across the Curriculum.)

EXERCISE 1

VOCABULARY REVIEW

a. You learned a sentence that tells what the smell attracted. Everybody, say that sentence. Get ready. (Signal.) *The smell attracted flies immediately.*

b. I'll say part of the sentence. When I stop, you say the next word. Listen: The smell . . . Everybody, what's the next word? (Signal.) *Attracted.*

c. Listen: The smell attracted flies . . . Everybody, what's the next word? (Signal.) *Immediately.*

• Say the whole sentence. Get ready. (Signal.) *The smell attracted flies immediately.*

EXERCISE 2

READING WORDS

Column 1

a. **Find lesson 24 in your textbook.** ✓
• Touch column 1. ✓
• (Teacher reference:)

1. **Florida**	4. **Carla**
2. **stormy**	5. **explaining**
3. **warning**	

• All these words have more than one syllable. The first syllable of each word is underlined.

b. Word 1. What's the first syllable? (Signal.) *flor.*
• What's the whole word? (Signal.) *Florida.*
• Spell **Florida.** Get ready. (Tap for each letter.) *F-L-O-R-I-D-A.*

c. Word 2. What's the first syllable? (Signal.) *storm.*
• What's the whole word? (Signal.) *Stormy.*
• Spell **stormy.** Get ready. (Tap for each letter.) *S-T-O-R-M-Y.*

d. Word 3. What's the first syllable? (Signal.) *warn.*
• What's the whole word? (Signal.) *Warning.*
• Spell **warning.** Get ready. (Tap for each letter.) *W-A-R-N-I-N-G.*

e. Word 4. What's the first syllable? (Signal.) *car.*
• What's the whole word? (Signal.) *Carla.*
• Spell **Carla.** Get ready. (Tap for each letter.) *C-A-R-L-A.*

f. Word 5. What's the first syllable? (Signal.) *ex.*
• What's the whole word? (Signal.) *Explaining.*

g. Let's read those words again.
• Word 1. What word? (Signal.) *Florida.*
• (Repeat for words 2–5.)

h. (Repeat step g until firm.)

Column 2

i. Find column 2. ✓
• (Teacher reference:)

1. **Andros Island**	3. **Atlantic Ocean**
2. **Bermuda Triangle**	4. **Edna Parker**

j. Number 1. What words? (Signal.) *Andros Island.*
• Andros Island is an island that is close to Florida.

k. Number 2. What words? (Signal.) *Bermuda Triangle.*
• The Bermuda Triangle is an area in the Atlantic Ocean where very strange things have happened to ships.

l. Number 3. What words? (Signal.) *Atlantic Ocean.*
• (Repeat for number 4.)

m. Let's read those words again.
• Number 1. What words? (Signal.) *Andros Island.*
• (Repeat for numbers 2–4.)

n. (Repeat step m until firm.)

Column 3

o. Find column 3. ✓
• (Teacher reference:)

1. **Mesozoic**	4. **Tyrannosaurus**
2. **armor**	5. **exciting**
3. **Triceratops**	6. **squawking**

p. Word 1. What word? (Signal.) *Mesozoic.*
• (Repeat for words 2–6.)

q. (Repeat step p until firm.)

Individual Turns

(For columns 1–3: Call on individual students, each to read one to three words per turn.)

EXERCISE 3

COMPREHENSION PASSAGE

a. Find part B in your textbook. ✓
- You're going to start a new story today. First you'll read the information passage. It gives some facts about dinosaurs.

b. Everybody, touch the title. ✓
- (Call on a student to read the title.) [Dinosaurs of the Mesozoic.]
- Everybody, what's the title? (Signal.) Dinosaurs of the Mesozoic.

c. (Call on individual students to read the passage, each student reading two or three sentences at a time. Ask the specified questions as the students read.)

Dinosaurs of the Mesozoic
You've read about the Mesozoic. What kind of animals lived in the Mesozoic?

- Everybody, what's the answer? (Signal.) Dinosaurs.

The picture shows two of the most important dinosaurs that lived in the Mesozoic.
    The huge killer that lived late in the Mesozoic is named Tyrannosaurus.

- Everybody, say that name. Get ready. (Signal.) Tyrannosaurus.

Tyrannosaurus was about 20 feet tall, twice as tall as an elephant.

- Everybody, touch the picture of Tyrannosaurus. ✓

The dinosaur with the horns and the armor is named Triceratops.

- Everybody, say that name. Get ready. (Signal.) Triceratops.
- Touch the picture of Triceratops. ✓

Tyrannosaurus did not have an easy time killing Triceratops.

- Why not? (Call on a student. Idea: Because Triceratops had horns and armor.)

- Everybody, touch Tyrannosaurus. ✓
- Touch Triceratops. ✓

EXERCISE 4

STORY READING

a. Find part C in your textbook. ✓
- The error limit for group reading is 7 errors. Read carefully.

b. Everybody, touch the title. ✓
- (Call on a student to read the title.) [Edna Parker.]
- Everybody, what's the title? (Signal.) Edna Parker.
- This is the first part of a new story. Everybody, who is this story about? (Signal.) Edna Parker.
- (Call on individual students to read the story, each student reading two or three sentences at a time. Ask the specified questions as the students read.)

- (Correct errors: Tell the word. Direct the student to reread the sentence.)
- (If the group makes more than 7 errors, direct the students to reread the story.)

Edna Parker
Edna Parker was thirteen years old. She had been out on her father's ship before. But this was the first time that her father, Captain Parker, let Edna bring a friend along.

- Everybody, who was Edna Parker's father? (Signal.) Captain Parker.
- Had Edna ever been on her father's ship before? (Signal.) Yes.
- What was going to be different about this trip? (Call on a student. Idea: Edna could bring a friend along.)

This was going to be a great trip for Edna.
    On other trips, Edna had a problem. She became bored. There was never anything for her to do on the ship after it left the harbor. Sometimes she would sweep up or help with the meals, but most of the time she just sat around and looked over the side of the ship at the swirling water. With Carla along, Edna would have fun.

• • •

- What was Edna's problem on other trips? (Call on a student. Idea: *She became bored.*)
- What does that mean, she became bored? (Call on a student. Idea: *She didn't have anything to do.*)
- How did Edna usually spend **most** of her time on the ship? (Call on a student. Idea: *Looking over the side of the ship at the swirling water.*)
- What was Edna's friend's name? (Signal.) *Carla.*
- Why would Edna have fun with Carla along? (Call on a student. Idea: *Because she would have someone to do things with.*)
- There are three dots in the story. What does that mean? (Call on a student. Idea: *Part of the story is missing.*)

❀ **Captain Parker was explaining the trip to the two girls. He pointed to a map of Florida and the Atlantic Ocean as he spoke.**

"We are starting from here," he said, pointing to the tip of Florida. "We are going to follow this dotted line to an island called Andros Island."

- Everybody, touch the part of Florida where the dotted line begins. ✓
- That's where the ship is now. Follow the line to Andros Island. ✓
- That's where they will go. Everybody, tell me the direction they will be going. Get ready. (Signal.) *East.*

Captain Parker continued, "That means we will pass through a place where hundreds of ships have sunk or been lost. It's called the Bermuda Triangle."

- Everybody, what's the name of the dangerous place? (Signal.) *The Bermuda Triangle.*

- What has happened in the Bermuda Triangle? (Call on a student. Idea: *Hundreds of ships have been lost or sunk.*)

Captain Parker continued, "Many sailors say the Bermuda Triangle is the most dangerous part of the ocean."
Carla's face seemed to drop.

- How did Carla feel when her face seemed to drop? (Call on a student. Ideas: *Afraid; surprised; worried.*)
- Everybody, I'll read what Captain Parker said. You make your face drop when you hear the bad news:
  Captain Parker continued, "That means we will pass through a place where hundreds of ships have sunk or been lost. It's called the Bermuda Triangle." Captain Parker continued, "Many sailors say the Bermuda Triangle is the most dangerous part of the ocean." (Students' faces should drop after ". . . the most dangerous part of the ocean.")

"Hey," Captain Parker said, and smiled. "Nothing's going to happen in a big ship like this. We ❀ are very ★ safe. And this is not the stormy season."

- Everybody, did Captain Parker think the trip would be dangerous? (Signal.) *No.*
- He gave two reasons. What were they? (Call on a student. Idea: *The ship was big and it wasn't the stormy season.*)

Carla asked, "Why is the Bermuda Triangle such a dangerous part of the ocean?"
"Bad seas," the captain answered. "There are huge waves and storms that come up without any warning. And there are whirlpools."

- What kinds of things do you find when the seas get bad in the Bermuda Triangle area? (Call on a student. Ideas: *Huge waves; unexpected storms; whirlpools.*)

Edna said, "You know what whirlpools are, don't you, Carla?"
"I think I know what they are," Carla replied.

Captain Parker said, "Let me explain. Did you ever watch water that was going down the drain? Sometimes it spins around and around and it makes the shape of an ice cream cone."

"I've seen those," Carla replied. "They suck water right down the drain."

"Yes," Captain Parker said. "Those are tiny whirlpools. The kind of whirlpools that you find in the Bermuda Triangle are just like those, except they are big enough to suck a ship down."

"Wow," Carla said.

- Read the rest of the story to yourself. Find out three things. Find out how far it is from Florida to Andros Island. Find out how long the trip will take. Find out what the girls should stay away from. Raise your hand when you're finished.

> Edna was trying to imagine a huge whirlpool.
> Captain Parker said, "Well, girls, Andros Island is only 120 miles from here, so we should arrive there in less than a day. We should have a smooth trip. The weather looks good. I am going to look over some maps now. You girls may play on deck, but stay away from the sides of the ship. And stay away from the lifeboats."
> "All right, Dad," Edna said, and the girls rushed onto the deck.

- (After all students have raised their hand:) Everybody, how far is it from Florida to Andros Island? (Signal.) *120 miles.*
- Everybody, how long will it take the ship to get there? (Signal.) *Less than a day.*
- Name one thing the girls should stay away from. (Call on a student. Ideas: *The sides of the ship; the lifeboats.*)
- Name something else the girls should stay away from. (Call on a student. Ideas: *The lifeboats; the sides of the ship.*)
- I sure hope those girls follow the rules.

- The picture shows Captain Parker's ship. The girls and Captain Parker were in the map room during this story. Everybody, touch the map room. ✓
- At the end of the story, the girls ran out on the deck. Everybody, touch the main deck. ✓
- Touch a lifeboat. ✓

EXERCISE 5

PAIRED PRACTICE

You're going to read aloud to your partner. The **A** members will read first. Then the **B** members will read from the star to the end of the story. (Observe students and give feedback.)

End-of-Lesson Activities

INDEPENDENT WORK

Now finish your independent work for lesson 24. Raise your hand when you're finished. (Observe students and give feedback.)

WORKCHECK

a. (Direct students to take out their marking pencils.)
- We're going to check your workbook and textbook items. Remember, if you got an item wrong, make an **X** next to the item.
b. (For each item: Read the item. Call on a student to answer it. If the answer is wrong, say the correct answer. Refer to the Answer Key for the correct answers.)
c. Now use your marking pencil to fix up any items you got wrong. Remember, all mistakes must be fixed up before you hand in your work.

LANGUAGE ARTS

(Present Language Arts lesson 24 after completing Reading lesson 24. See Language Arts Guide.)

ACTIVITIES

(Present Activity 4 after completing Reading lessons 24-32. See Activities Across the Curriculum.)

EXERCISE 1

VOCABULARY

a. **Find page 352 in your textbook.** ✓
- Touch sentence 5. ✓
- This is a new vocabulary sentence. It says: The rim of the volcano exploded. Everybody, say that sentence. Get ready. (Signal.) *The rim of the volcano exploded.*
- Close your eyes and say the sentence. Get ready. (Signal.) *The rim of the volcano exploded.*
- (Repeat until firm.)

b. A volcano is a mountain that is made from hot flowing rock that comes from inside the earth. Everybody, what do we call a mountain formed from flowing rock? (Signal.) *Volcano.*

c. The sentence says the **rim** exploded. Things with a thin top edge have a rim. The rim of the volcano is the top edge of the volcano.

d. When things **explode,** they make a loud bang and fly apart. If the rim exploded, it made a loud bang and flew apart.

e. Listen to the sentence again: The rim of the volcano exploded. Everybody, say that sentence. Get ready. (Signal.) *The rim of the volcano exploded.*

f. What word means it **made a bang and flew apart?** (Signal.) *Exploded.*
- What word means **a mountain formed from hot flowing rock?** (Signal.) *Volcano.*
- What word means **the top edge** of the volcano? (Signal.) *Rim.*
- (Repeat step f until firm.)

EXERCISE 2

READING WORDS

Column 1

a. Find lesson 25 in your textbook. ✓
- Touch column 1. ✓
- (Teacher reference:)

1. seagulls	4. pirates
2. elevator	5. instant
3. surface	6. handkerchief

b. Word 1 is **seagulls.** What word? (Signal.) *Seagulls.*
- Seagulls are birds that are seen around the ocean. They are sometimes called gulls.

c. Word 2 is **elevator.** What word? (Signal.) *Elevator.*
- Spell **elevator.** Get ready. (Tap for each letter.) E-L-E-V-A-T-O-R.

d. Word 3 is **surface.** What word? (Signal.) *Surface.*
- Spell **surface.** Get ready. (Tap for each letter.) S-U-R-F-A-C-E.

e. Word 4 is **pirates.** What word? (Signal.) *Pirates.*
- Spell **pirates.** Get ready. (Tap for each letter.) P-I-R-A-T-E-S.

f. Word 5 is **instant.** What word? (Signal.) *Instant.*
- Spell **instant.** Get ready. (Tap for each letter.) I-N-S-T-A-N-T.

g. Word 6 is **handkerchief.** What word? (Signal.) *Handkerchief.*

h. Let's read those words again.
- Word 1. What word? (Signal.) *Seagulls.*
- (Repeat for words 2–6.)

i. (Repeat step h until firm.)

Column 2

j. Find column 2. ✓
- (Teacher reference:)

1. first mate	3. engineer
2. mast	4. silent

k. Number 1. What words? (Signal.) *First mate.*
- The first mate is a crew member who is the captain's main helper.
- Word 2. What word? (Signal.) *Mast.*
- The mast on a ship is a tall pole. Some masts are used to hold sails in place.
- Word 3. What word? (Signal.) *Engineer.*
- The engineer on a ship is the crew member who makes sure that the engine is running well.
- Word 4. What word? (Signal.) *Silent.*

l. Let's read those words again.
- Number 1. What words? (Signal.) *First mate.*
- Word 2. What word? (Signal.) *Mast.*
- (Repeat for: **3. engineer, 4. silent.**)
m. (Repeat step l until firm.)

Column 3

n. Find column 3. ✓
- (Teacher reference:)

1. galley	4. pretend
2. stern	5. roughed
3. touch	

o. Word 1. What word? (Signal.) *Galley.*
- The galley is the kitchen on a plane or ship. Everybody, what do we call the kitchen on a ship? (Signal.) *Galley.*
p. Word 2. What word? (Signal.) *Stern.*
- The stern of a ship is the back of the ship. Everybody, what do we call the back of a ship? (Signal.) *Stern.*
q. Word 3. What word? (Signal.) *Touch.*
r. (Repeat for words 4 and 5.)
s. Let's read those words again.
- Word 1. What word? (Signal.) *Galley.*
- (Repeat for words 2–5.)
t. (Repeat step s until firm.)

Column 4

u. Find column 4. ✓
- (Teacher reference:)

1. exciting	3. squawking
2. powered	4. sliced

- All these words have an ending.
v. Word 1. What word? (Signal.) *Exciting.*
- (Repeat for words 2–4.)
w. Let's read those words again.
- Word 1. What word? (Signal.) *Exciting.*
- (Repeat for words 2–4.)
x. (Repeat step w until firm.)

Column 5

y. Find column 5. ✓
- (Teacher reference:)

1. <u>hail</u>stone	3. <u>tip</u>toe
2. <u>spy</u>glass	

- These words are compound words. The first part of each word is underlined.
z. Word 1. What's the underlined part? (Signal.) *hail.*
- What's the whole word? (Signal.) *Hailstone.*
a. Word 2. What's the underlined part? (Signal.) *spy.*
- What's the whole word? (Signal.) *Spyglass.*
b. Word 3. What's the underlined part? (Signal.) *tip.*
- What's the whole word? (Signal.) *Tiptoe.*
c. Let's read those words again.
- Word 1. What word? (Signal.) *Hailstone.*
- (Repeat for words 2 and 3.)
d. (Repeat step c until firm.)

Individual Turns

(For columns 1–5: Call on individual students, each to read one to three words per turn.)

STORY READING

a. Find part C in your textbook. ✓
- The error limit for group reading is 11 errors. Read carefully.
b. Everybody, touch the title. ✓
- (Call on a student to read the title.) *[Looking for Something to Do.]*
- Everybody, what's the title? (Signal.) *Looking for Something to Do.*
- (Call on individual students to read the story, each student reading two or three sentences at a time. Ask the specified questions as the students read.)

- (Correct errors: Tell the word. Direct the student to reread the sentence.)
- (If the group makes more than 11 errors, direct the students to reread the story.)

Looking for Something to Do
Edna and Carla had dashed out of the map room. They had run to the stern of the ship, where they watched the seagulls that followed the ship. The girls watched the waves roll off the stern of the ship.

- Everybody, where had they come from? (Signal.) *The map room.*
- Where were they now? (Signal.) *At the stern of the ship.*
- Is that the front of the ship or the back? (Signal.) *Back.*

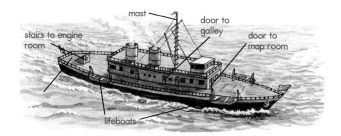

- Everybody, touch the stern of the ship on the on the next page. ✓

Then the girls ran to the galley. The cook was busy. They tried to talk to him, but the only thing he wanted to talk about was how much his new gold tooth hurt. After the girls spent about five minutes in the galley, they went to the engine room.

- First they were in the map room. Everybody, where did they go next? (Signal.) *The stern.*
- Where did they go next? (Signal.) *The galley.*
- What happens in the galley of a ship? (Call on a student. Idea: *Meals are prepared there.*)
- Why didn't they stay in the galley? (Call on a student. Idea: *The cook was complaining about his tooth.*)
- Everybody, where did they go next? (Signal.) *The engine room.*
- Turn back to page 125. ✓

The engine room in a ship is the place where the ship's engine is. Some ships have engines that are as big as a school room. The engine of Captain Parker's ship was not that big. It was about the size of a small truck.

The engineer looked at the girls and said, "What do you think you're doing here?"

They told him that they were looking around. He replied, "If you want to stay here, I'll put you to work. So if you don't want to work, get out."

- Say that the way the engineer said it. (Call on a student. Student should speak in an abrupt, impatient manner.)

The girls left the engine room. They walked around the front deck. They thought about climbing the ladder that went up to the top of the mast. But that seemed too scary.

- Why didn't the girls stay in the engine room? (Call on a student. Ideas: *They might be put to work; the engineer was mean.*)
- Where did they go after leaving the engine room? (Call on a student. Ideas: *To the front deck; the bow.*)
- They thought of climbing the mast. Everybody, turn the page and touch the mast in the picture. ✓
- Put your finger on the map room and move to the first place the girls went. (Students should touch the stern.)
- What place are you touching? (Signal.) *Stern.*
- Now go where the girls went next. (Students should touch the galley.)
- What place are you touching? (Signal.) *Galley.*
- Now go where the girls went next. (Students should touch the engine room.)
- What place are you touching? (Signal.) *Engine room.*
- Now go where they went next. (Students should touch the front deck.)
- What place are you touching? (Signal.) *Front deck.*
- (Repeat the sequence of the touching tasks until firm.)

At last the girls sat down on the front deck near a lifeboat. They sat and they sat and they sat. The girls tried to talk about different things. Edna studied the water. Then she realized that she was doing the same kinds of things that she used to do when she went alone on these trips. She was sitting in the sun watching the water. ⭐

The sea was very calm, like a sheet of glass. The ship sliced through the water and left waves that moved out in a giant V as far as Edna could see.

There were beads of sweat on Carla's forehead.

- What does that tell you about the temperature of the air? (Call on a student. Idea: *It was hot.*)

Carla said, "This Bermuda Triangle isn't as exciting as they say it is."

Edna nodded. "Yeah, this is boring."

For a moment, the girls were silent. Edna heard the squawking sound of the seagulls and the steady hum of the great engine that powered the ship. Then Carla said, "I wish we had our own boat. Then we could have some fun. I could be captain and you would be my first mate."

The girls looked at each other and smiled. Edna said, "Why don't we pretend that we have our own ship?"

- Read the rest of the story to yourself. Find out two things. Find out what Carla wanted to use for her ship. Find out what Edna first thought of Carla's idea. Raise your hand when you're finished.

> Carla said, "I see a boat we can use for our game." She pointed to a lifeboat that was hanging at the side of the ship. It was ready to be lowered into the water in case of trouble.
>
> Edna shook her head no. She said, "Remember what my dad told us? Stay away from the lifeboats."
>
> "Oh, come on, Edna. We won't get in trouble if we are careful. We won't touch anything. We'll just sneak into the lifeboat and play for a while."
>
> "No," Edna said slowly, looking at the lifeboat. Edna hadn't made up her mind to do it, but she looked around to see if any of the crew members could see them. She was just trying to figure out how hard it would be to sneak into the boat. No crew members were in sight.
>
> "Come on," Carla said with a big smile. "Come on, Edna."

- (After all students have raised their hand:) Everybody, what did Carla want to use for their pretend ship? (Signal.) *The lifeboat.*
- What did Edna first think of the idea of using the lifeboat? (Call on a student. Idea: *She didn't want to do it.*)
- How many crew members were watching? (Call on a student. Idea: *None.*)

- What do you think those girls will do? (Call on a student. Student preference.)

EXERCISE 4

> *Note:* There is a reading checkout in this lesson; therefore, there is no paired practice.

READING CHECKOUTS

a. Today is a reading-checkout day. While you're doing your independent work, I'm going to call on you one at a time to read part of the story from lesson 24. When I call you to come and do your checkout, bring your thermometer chart.

- Remember, you pass the checkout by reading the passage in less than a minute without making more than 2 mistakes. And when you pass the checkout, you'll color the space for lesson 25 on your thermometer chart.

b. (Call on individual students to read the portion of story 24 marked with ❁.)

- (Time the student. Note words that are missed and total number of words read.)
- (Teacher reference:)

> ❁ Captain Parker was explaining the trip to the two girls. He pointed to a map of Florida and the Atlantic Ocean as he spoke.
>
> "We are starting from here," he said, pointing to the tip of Florida. "We are going to follow this dotted line to an island called Andros [50] Island." Captain Parker continued, "That means we will pass through a place where hundreds of ships have sunk or been lost. It's called the Bermuda [75] Triangle." Captain Parker continued, "Many sailors say the Bermuda Triangle is the most dangerous part of the ocean."
>
> Carla's face seemed to drop.
>
> "Hey," Captain [100] Parker said, and smiled. "Nothing's going to happen in a big ship like this. We ❁ [115] are very safe."

- (If the student reads the passage in one minute or less and makes no more than 2 errors, direct the student to color in the space for lesson 25 on the thermometer chart.)

- (If the student makes any mistakes, point to each word that was misread and identify it.)
- (If the student does not meet the rate-error criterion for the passage, direct the student to practice reading the story with the assigned partner.)

End-of-Lesson Activities

INDEPENDENT WORK

Now finish your independent work for lesson 25. Raise your hand when you're finished. (Observe students and give feedback.)

WORKCHECK

a. (Direct students to take out their marking pencils.)
- We're going to check your workbook and textbook items. Remember, if you got an item wrong, make an **X** next to the item.
b. (For each item: Read the item. Call on a student to answer it. If the answer is wrong, say the correct answer. Refer to the Answer Key for the correct answers.)
c. Now use your marking pencil to fix up any items you got wrong. Remember, all mistakes must be fixed up before you hand in your work.

LANGUAGE ARTS

(Present Language Arts lesson 25 after completing Reading lesson 25. See Language Arts Guide.)

Lessons 26–30 · Planning Page

	Lesson 26	Lesson 27	Lesson 28	Lesson 29	Lesson 30
Lesson Events	Vocabulary Sentence Reading Words Story Reading Paired Practice Independent Work Workcheck Language Arts	Vocabulary Sentences Reading Words Comprehension Passage Story Reading Paired Practice Independent Work Workcheck Language Arts	Vocabulary Sentence Reading Words Story Reading Paired Practice Independent Work Workcheck Language Arts	**Vocabulary Sentence** Reading Words Story Reading Paired Practice Independent Work Workcheck Language Arts	Fact Game Reading Checkouts Test Marking the Test Test Remedies Literature Lesson Language Arts
Vocabulary Sentence	#5: The <u>rim</u> of the <u>volcano</u> <u>exploded</u>.	sentence #3 sentence #4 sentence #5	#5: The <u>rim</u> of the <u>volcano</u> <u>exploded</u>.	**#6: The new <u>exhibit</u> <u>displayed</u> <u>mysterious</u> fish.**	
Reading Words: Word Types	modeled words multi-syllable words words with endings	multi-syllable words mixed words	compound words multi-syllable words mixed words	modeled words words with endings mixed words	
New Vocabulary	shallow practice bow	moaned funnel-shaped stumbled	tangle gallon faint	breath shriek leathery clearing sense	
Comprehension Passage		*Facts About Whirlpools*			
Story	*The Lifeboat*	*A Giant Whirlpool*	*A Long Night*	*Footprints*	
Skill Items	Sequencing	Vocabulary Vocabulary sentence	Vocabulary Vocabulary sentences		Test: Vocabulary sentences #4, 5
Special Materials					Thermometer charts, dice, Fact Game 30, Fact Game Answer Key, scorecard sheets, * materials for literature lesson
Special Projects/ Activities					

*Literature anthology; blackline masters 3A, 3B, 3C, and 3D; lined paper

EXERCISE 1

VOCABULARY REVIEW

a. Here's the new vocabulary sentence: The rim of the volcano exploded.
  - Everybody, say that sentence. Get ready. (Signal.) *The rim of the volcano exploded.*
  - (Repeat until firm.)
b. What word means **a mountain formed from hot flowing rock?** (Signal.) *Volcano.*
  - What word means **the top edge** of the volcano? (Signal.) *Rim.*
  - What word means it **made a bang and flew apart?** (Signal.) *Exploded.*
  - (Repeat step b until firm.)

EXERCISE 2

READING WORDS

Column 1

a. **Find lesson 26 in your textbook.** ✓
  - Touch column 1. ✓
  - (Teacher reference:)

1. shallow	4. practice
2. tearing	5. bow
3. hind	

b. Word 1 is **shallow.** What word? (Signal.) *Shallow.*
  - Spell **shallow.** Get ready. (Tap for each letter.) *S-H-A-L-L-O-W.*
  - **Shallow** is the opposite of **deep.** Everybody, what's the opposite of **a deep bowl?** (Signal.) *A shallow bowl.*
  - What's the opposite of **a deep pond?** (Signal.) *A shallow pond.*
c. Word 2 rhymes with **caring.** What word? (Signal.) *Tearing.*
  - Spell **tearing.** Get ready. (Tap for each letter.) *T-E-A-R-I-N-G.*
d. Word 3 is **hind.** What word? (Signal.) *Hind.*
  - Spell **hind.** Get ready. (Tap for each letter.) *H-I-N-D.*
e. Word 4 is **practice.** What word? (Signal.) *Practice.*

- Spell **practice.** Get ready. (Tap for each letter.) *P-R-A-C-T-I-C-E.*
- When you practice something, you work on it. What's another way of saying **He worked on throwing a ball?** (Signal.) *He practiced throwing a ball.*
- What's another way of saying **They worked on the new song?** (Signal.) *They practiced the new song.*
f. Word 5 is **bow.** What word? (Signal.) *Bow.*
- The bow of a ship is the front of the ship. What do we call the front of a ship? (Signal.) *Bow.*
g. Let's read those words again.
  - Word 1. What word? (Signal.) *Shallow.*
  - (Repeat for words 2–5.)
h. (Repeat step g until firm)

Column 2

i. Find column 2. ✓
  - (Teacher reference:)

1. spyglass	4. besides
2. surface	5. lightning
3. instant	

- All these words have more than one syllable. The first syllable of each word is underlined.
j. Word 1. What's the first syllable? (Signal.) *spy.*
  - What's the whole word? (Signal.) *Spyglass.*
k. Word 2. What's the first syllable? (Signal.) *sur.*
  - What's the whole word? (Signal.) *Surface.*
l. Word 3. What's the first syllable? (Signal.) *in.*
  - What's the whole word? (Signal.) *Instant.*
m. Word 4. What's the first syllable? (Signal.) *be.*
  - What's the whole word? (Signal.) *Besides.*
n. Word 5. What's the first syllable? (Signal.) *light.*
  - What's the whole word? (Signal.) *Lightning.*

o. Let's read those words again.
- Word 1. What word? (Signal.) *Spyglass.*
- (Repeat for: **2. surface, 3. instant, 4. besides, 5. lightning.**)
p. (Repeat step n until firm.)

Column 3

q. Find column 3. ✓
- (Teacher reference:)

1. <u>el</u>evator	3. <u>hand</u>kerchief
2. <u>for</u>ty	4. <u>per</u>haps

- All these words have more than one syllable. The first syllable of each word is underlined.
r. Word 1. What's the first syllable? (Signal.) *el.*
- What's the whole word? (Signal.) *Elevator.*
s. Word 2. What's the first syllable? (Signal.) *for.*
- What's the whole word? (Signal.) *Forty.*
t. Word 3. What's the first syllable? (Signal.) *hand.*
- What's the whole word? (Signal.) *Handkerchief.*
u. Word 4. What's the first syllable? (Signal.) *per.*
- What's the whole word? (Signal.) *Perhaps.*
v. Let's read those words again.
- Word 1. What word? (Signal.) *Elevator.*
- (Repeat for words 2–4.)
w. (Repeat step v until firm.)

Column 4

x. Find column 4. ✓
- (Teacher reference:)

1. bailing	4. tiptoed
2. roughed	5. pirates
3. glassy	6. sloshed

- All these words have an ending.
y. Word 1. What word? (Signal.) *Bailing.*
- (Repeat for words 2–6.)
z. Let's read those words again.
- Word 1. What word? (Signal.) *Bailing.*
- (Repeat for words 2–6.)
a. (Repeat step z until firm.)

Individual Turns

(For columns 1–4: Call on individual students, each to read one to three words per turn.)

STORY READING

a. Find part B in your textbook. ✓
- The error limit for group reading is 12 errors. Read carefully.
b. Everybody, touch the title. ✓
- (Call on a student to read the title.) *[The Lifeboat.]*
- Everybody, what's the title? (Signal.) *The Lifeboat.*
- (Call on individual students to read the story, each student reading two or three sentences at a time. Ask the specified questions as students read.)

- (Correct errors: Tell the word. Direct the student to reread the sentence.)
- (If the group makes more than 12 errors, direct the students to reread the story.)

The Lifeboat
Carla and Edna were on the deck of Captain Parker's ship. Carla pretended to take out her spyglass and look around. "We're on an island," she said. "And there's our boat, pulled up on the beach." She pointed to the lifeboat. "I'm the captain and you're my first mate. So when I give an order, you carry it out."

- Everybody, is Carla talking about **real things** or **pretend things?** (Signal.) *Pretend things.*
- In this pretend game, what is Carla? (Signal.) *The captain.*
- What is Edna? (Signal.) *The first mate.*
- Who's going to be giving the orders in this pretend game—Carla or Edna? (Signal.) *Carla.*
- Who's going to carry out the orders? (Signal.) *Edna.*
- If somebody gives you an order, what do you do if you carry out the order? (Call on a student. Idea: *Do what you are told to do.*)

Edna pulled off her shoes and socks and rolled up her pants to the knees. She tied a handkerchief around her head. She felt like a sailor now. "Yes sir, Captain, sir," she said as she stood up. The deck felt very hot on Edna's feet.

- Everybody, is Edna going along with Carla's game? (Signal.) *Yes.*

**"Remember, we're on an island,"
Carla said. "We have to be very
careful when we sneak into our boat.
There are pirates on this island.
Follow me."**

- Everybody, where are the girls pretending to be? (Signal.) *On an island.*
- Where are they really? (Call on a student. Idea: *On the ship.*)
- What are pirates? (Call on a student. Ideas: *Sailors that steal from other ships; rough men that sail the seas looking for treasure.*)

**Carla crouched down and tiptoed
across the deck to the lifeboat. She
climbed in the front. "The coast is
clear," she said softly.
"Ouch, ouch, ouch," Edna
whispered as she tiptoed across the
deck.**

- Why did she say that? (Call on a student. Idea: *The deck was hot and burned her feet.*)

**Edna jumped into the lifeboat. It
rocked from side to side. It was held
in the air by ropes that were attached
to the bow and to the stern.**

- Everybody, touch Edna in the picture. ✓
- What does Edna have around her head? (Signal.) *A handkerchief.*
- Touch Carla in the picture. ✓
- Touch the rope that's attached to the bow of the lifeboat. ✓
- You should be touching the front of the lifeboat.
- Touch the rope that's attached to the stern of the lifeboat. ✓

- What do you think would happen if you fooled around with those ropes? (Call on a student. Idea: *The lifeboat could fall into the water.*)

**Edna knew that you did something
with the ropes to lower the boat into
the water, but she wasn't sure how to
do it. And she didn't want to find out.**

- Why not? (Call on a student. Ideas: *She didn't want to fall into the water; she didn't want her father to know that they had played in the lifeboat.*)

**For a moment, Edna had a bad
feeling. They were doing something
they shouldn't do. But then Edna
explained things to herself. There
wasn't anything else to do. None of
the crew members would talk to
them. And besides, they would be
very careful.**

- Edna is trying to talk herself into playing this game. Listen to what she's telling herself:
  There wasn't anything else to do. None of the crew members would talk to them. And besides, they would be very careful.
- What reasons does she give herself for playing this game? (Call on a student. Ideas: *There wasn't anything else to do; crew members wouldn't talk to them; they'd be careful.*)

**Suddenly the boat dropped. Carla
must have grabbed one of the ropes
at the front of the boat or perhaps
the rope just slipped. Edna didn't
know. All she knew was that the boat
was falling like a high-speed elevator.**

- Imagine how that must have felt. Look at the picture. You can see how far it is all the way to the water. You can imagine what it must have felt like to fall all that distance.

**The ropes were making a howling
sound as they ran through the
wheels that had been holding the
lifeboat.**

- You can see those wheels in the picture, right above the bow and the stern of the lifeboat. Everybody, touch them. ✓

Edna wanted to yell something, but her voice wouldn't work.

The bow of the boat hit the water before the stern. Edna held on to the side of the boat as hard as she could. But when the boat hit the water, Edna went flying forward, bumping into ⚹ Carla. A huge wave broke over the front of the lifeboat and sloshed around in the bottom of the boat. The boat bounced in the waves that the large ship was making. Another wave broke over the side of the boat. For an instant, Edna was amazed at how loud the waves were. From the deck the ocean seemed almost silent. But now there were rushing sounds, splashing sounds, sloshing sounds. The waves from the stern of the big ship hit the lifeboat and almost turned it over.

Carla tried to stand up. She was waving her arms and yelling. Edna yelled, too. "Help!" "Stop!" "Here we are!" they yelled.

- Who are they yelling to? (Call on a student. Idea: *The people on the ship*.)
- If the waves from the stern of the ship were already hitting the lifeboat, the ship had already passed them.

The girls waved their arms. They continued to wave as the large ship became smaller, smaller, smaller.

- Why did it seem to get smaller and smaller? (Call on a student. Idea: *It was getting farther and farther away*.)

Then the girls stopped waving and continued to watch the large ship. Now it was only a dot on the glassy water.

- Everybody, was the ship on its way back to the girls? (Signal.) *No*.
- How do you know? (Call on a student. Idea: *It was only a dot, so it was far away*.)

Suddenly, as the girls watched the dot, a very cool breeze hit them from behind. The air suddenly had a different smell. The wind roughed up the surface of the water.

- If the wind keeps roughing up the surface of the water, big waves will form.

Edna turned around and looked up. Behind the lifeboat was a great storm cloud. It rose up and up. "Oh no," Edna said. Then her mind started to work fast. "Let's start bailing water out of this boat. We're in for a storm."

- How did the water get in the boat? (Call on a student. Ideas: *When the lifeboat fell into the water, water splashed in; when the large ship passed, it made waves*.)
- What do you do when you bail water from a boat? (Call on a student. Idea: *Throw water out of the boat*.)
- Everybody, read the rest of the story to yourself and find out three things. Find out how big the waves got. Find out how fast the wind was blowing. Find out why the girls stopped bailing. Raise your hand when you're finished.

When the girls started bailing, there was about 5 inches of water in the bottom of the boat. The girls bailed and bailed. The waves got bigger and bigger. Now there was only about 3 inches of water in the boat, but the waves hitting the boat were very big and they were starting to splash over the side. The girls bailed and bailed and the waves splashed and splashed. Now there was about 4 inches of water in the boat.

The girls had to stop bailing when a terrible wind hit the boat. The waves were so large that Edna had to hang on to the side of the boat. She just kept hanging on and hoping that the storm would stop. But the waves were now over 20 feet high and the winds were moving forty miles per hour. The boat was going up and down the waves.

- (After all students have raised their hand:) Everybody, did the storm get worse? (Signal.) *Yes.*
- How big did the waves get? (Call on a student.) *Over 20 feet high.*
- That's as high as a two-story building. Everybody, how fast was the wind moving? (Signal.) *Forty miles per hour.*
- Why did the girls stop bailing? (Call on a student. Idea: *A big wind hit the boat and they had to hang on.*)
- How do you think they felt? (Call on a student. Ideas: *Afraid; wet.*)

EXERCISE 4

PAIRED PRACTICE

You're going to read aloud to your partner. The **B** members will read first. Then the **A** members will read from the star to the end of the story.
(Observe students and give feedback.)

End-of-Lesson Activities

INDEPENDENT WORK

Now finish your independent work for lesson 26. Raise your hand when you're finished. (Observe students and give feedback.)

WORKCHECK

a. (Direct students to take out their marking pencils.)
- We're going to check your workbook and textbook items. Remember, if you got an item wrong, make an **X** next to the item.
b. (For each item: Read the item. Call on a student to answer it. If the answer is wrong, say the correct answer. Refer to the Answer Key for the correct answers.)
c. Now use your marking pencil to fix up any items you got wrong. Remember, all mistakes must be fixed up before you hand in your work.

LANGUAGE ARTS

(Present Language Arts lesson 26 after completing Reading lesson 26. See Language Arts Guide.)

Lesson 27

EXERCISE 1

VOCABULARY REVIEW

a. You learned a sentence that tells what she actually did.
- Everybody, say that sentence. Get ready. (Signal.) *She actually repeated that careless mistake.*
- (Repeat until firm.)

b. You learned a sentence that tells what the smell attracted.
- Everybody, say that sentence. Get ready. (Signal.) *The smell attracted flies immediately.*
- (Repeat until firm.)

c. Here's the last sentence you learned: The rim of the volcano exploded.
- Everybody, say that sentence. Get ready. (Signal.) *The rim of the volcano exploded.*
- (Repeat until firm.)

d. What word refers to a mountain formed from hot flowing rock? (Signal.) *Volcano.*
- What word means it **made a bang and flew apart?** (Signal.) *Exploded.*
- What word means the **top edge** of the volcano? (Signal.) *Rim.*
- (Repeat step c until firm.)

e. Once more. Say the sentence that tells what the rim of the volcano did. Get ready. (Signal.) *The rim of the volcano exploded.*

EXERCISE 2

READING WORDS

Column 1

a. **Find lesson 27 in your textbook.** ✓
- Touch column 1. ✓
- (Teacher reference:)

1. thunder	4. somehow
2. shallow	5. lightning
3. blinding	

- All these words have more than one syllable. The first syllable of each word is underlined.

b. Word 1. What's the first syllable? (Signal.) *thun.*

- What's the whole word? (Signal.) *Thunder.*
- Spell **thunder.** Get ready. (Tap for each letter.) *T-H-U-N-D-E-R.*

c. Word 2. What's the first syllable? (Signal.) *Shall.*
- What's the whole word? (Signal.) *Shallow.*
- Spell **shallow.** Get ready. (Tap for each letter.) *S-H-A-L-L-O-W.*

d. Word 3. What's the first syllable? (Signal.) *blind.*
- What's the whole word? (Signal.) *Blinding.*
- Spell **blinding.** Get ready. (Tap for each letter.) *B-L-I-N-D-I-N-G.*

e. Word 4. What's the first syllable? (Signal.) *some.*
- What's the whole word? (Signal.) *Somehow.*
- Spell **somehow.** Get ready. (Tap for each letter.) *S-O-M-E-H-O-W.*

f. Word 5. What's the first syllable? (Signal.) *light.*
- What's the whole word? (Signal.) *Lightning.*

g. Let's read those words again.
- Word 1. What word? (Signal.) *Thunder.*
- (Repeat for words 2–5.)

h. (Repeat step g until firm.)

Column 2

i. Find column 2. ✓
- (Teacher reference:)

1. moaned	4. aloud
2. funnel-shaped	5. tearing
3. stumbled	

j. Word 1. What word? (Signal.) *Moaned.*
- A moan is a sound that people make when they are in pain. Here's a moan: aaaahhh. Everybody, what do you call a sound like aaaahhh? (Signal.) *Moan.*

k. Word 2. What word? (Signal.) *Funnel-shaped.*
- Things that are funnel-shaped are shaped like a funnel. A funnel is a round tube that is wide on one end and narrow on the other.

l. Word 3. What word? (Signal.) *Stumbled.*

- **Stumbled** is another word for **tripped.** Everybody, what's another way of saying **He tripped on the tree root?** (Signal.) *He stumbled on the tree root.*
m. Word 4. What word? (Signal.) *Aloud.*
n. Word 5. What word? (Signal.) *Tearing.*
o. Let's read those words again.
  - Word 1. What word? (Signal.) *Moaned.*
  - (Repeat for words: **2. funnel-shaped, 3. stumbled, 4. aloud, 5. tearing.**)
p. (Repeat step o until firm.)

Individual Turns

(For columns 1 and 2: Call on individual students, each to read one to three words per turn.)

EXERCISE 3

COMPREHENSION PASSAGE

a. Find part B in your textbook. ✓
  - You're going to read the next story about Edna and Carla. First you'll read the information passage. It gives some information about whirlpools.
b. Everybody, touch the title. ✓
  - (Call on a student to read the title.) *[Facts About Whirlpools.]*
  - Everybody, what's the title? (Signal.) *Facts About Whirlpools.*
c. (Call on individual students to read the passage, each student reading two or three sentences at a time. Ask the specified questions as the students read.)

> **Facts About Whirlpools**
> In today's story, you will read about a whirlpool. Here are facts about whirlpools:
> Whirlpools are made up of moving water.

- Everybody, say that fact. Get ready. (Signal.) *Whirlpools are made up of moving water.*
- (Repeat until firm.)

> **A whirlpool is shaped like a funnel. Here is a funnel. It is wide on top and narrow on the bottom.**

- Everybody, touch the funnel. ✓
- What do we use funnels for? (Call on a student. Idea: *To pour liquid from one container to another.*)

- Everybody, which part of a funnel is wide? (Signal.) *The top.*
- Which part is narrow? (Signal.) *The bottom.*

> **Here is a whirlpool. It is wide on top and narrow on the bottom.**

- Everybody, touch the whirlpool. ✓
- You can see it is the same shape as the funnel.

> **The water in a whirlpool spins around and around. Something caught in a whirlpool goes around and around as it moves down.**

- The object goes around and around as it goes down. Start at the back of the arrow and make a path that goes around and around as it goes down inside the whirlpool. ✓

EXERCISE 4

STORY READING

a. Find part C in your textbook. ✓
  - The error limit for group reading is 11 errors. Read carefully.
b. Everybody, touch the title. ✓
  - (Call on a student to read the title.) *[A Giant Whirlpool.]*
  - Everybody, what's the title? (Signal.) *A Giant Whirlpool.*
  - (Call on individual students to read the story, each student reading two or three sentences at a time. Ask the specified questions as the students read.)

- (Correct errors: Tell the word. Direct the student to reread the sentence.)
- (If the group makes more than 11 errors, direct the students to reread the story.)

> **A Giant Whirlpool**
> Now it was starting to rain. The small lifeboat was sliding up huge waves and then down the other side of the waves. Edna felt sick and dizzy.

- What was making her feel that way? (Call on a student. Ideas: *The boat rocking in the water; the waves.*)

Just then the boat reached the top of a wave, and Carla shouted, "I see land." She pointed.

The lifeboat slid down the wave and Edna could not see anything but water. Then the boat moved up, up, to the top of another wave. Now Edna could see what Carla had pointed to. But it wasn't land. It was a wave, much bigger than the other waves.

- Everybody, when could the girls see in the distance—when they were at the top of a wave or at the bottom of a wave? (Signal.) *At the top of a wave.*
- Had Carla really seen land? (Signal.) *No.*
- What did she think was land? (Call on a student. Idea: *A huge wave.*)

"Hang on," Edna shouted. "A giant wave is coming toward us."

For an instant, everything became bright as lightning shot through the sky. A boom of thunder followed. The huge wave was now very close to the boat. Edna looked up to the top of it. It was like a cliff of water with a white, foaming top.

Somehow, the boat moved up the huge wave—up, up, very fast. And now faster. The boat was moving so fast that Edna couldn't see what was happening. More lightning. Thunder. Edna had to close her eyes. She was dizzy. Dizzy.

- Things were happening very fast. Let me read that part again. Close your eyes and imagine how the girls felt.

  For an instant, everything became bright as lightning shot through the sky. A boom of thunder followed. The huge wave was now very close to the boat. Edna looked up to the top of it. It was like a cliff of water with a white, foaming top.
  Somehow, the boat moved up the huge wave—up, up, very fast. And now faster. The boat was moving so fast that Edna couldn't see what was happening. More lightning. Thunder. Edna had to close her eyes. She was dizzy. Dizzy.

The boat wasn't just moving up. It was moving around and around. The boat was moving so fast that Edna could hardly tell which direction was up and which direction was down. But she could see that the boat was on the top of a huge funnel-shaped cone of water. The boat was being sucked into a giant whirlpool.

Edna tried to say something, but her voice wouldn't work. She pointed down to the bottom of the whirlpool. It seemed to be hundreds of meters below the tiny boat.

- Everybody, touch the boat in the picture on the next page. ✓
- Move your finger to show how that boat is moving in the whirlpool. (Students should move their fingers in tight circles.)

The next things happened very fast. They happened so fast that Edna was never sure exactly what happened or why. First, there were large hailstones—hundreds of them. For an instant, Edna noticed them floating in the boat, which was quickly filling up with water. So much hail came down that everything seemed to be white. The hail was hitting the girls, but Edna couldn't even feel it. Suddenly, there was a great flash and a great spray of water.

- What could cause the great flash? (Call on a student. Idea: *Lightning.*)

The flash was blinding.

Later, Edna thought a lot about that flash and the splash. Later she talked to Carla about it. The girls figured out that the lightning must have hit the water right in front of their boat. The lightning must have hit with so much power that it sent the boat flying through the air.

- What do they think happened? (Call on a student. Idea: *The lightning hit the water so hard that the boat went flying through the air.*)
- Everybody, did they actually remember all this happening? (Signal.) *No.*
- The only thing Edna remembered was a splash and something else. What else? (Call on a student. Idea: *A flash.*)

After the flash was the giant splash. That must have been the splash that the boat made when it came down. The boat must have landed far from the whirlpool.

The hail continued to fall for a few minutes. Then it stopped, and a steady rain began to fall. For hours, the rain came down. The wind died down and the waves became smaller and smaller. Finally the rain stopped. Without any warning at all, it stopped. The sea was calm again, and Edna was sick. Edna didn't want to talk. She didn't want to move. She was dizzy. She was lying near the back of the boat. The boat was half-filled with water now. Edna moaned, "Ooooh." She wasn't sure she knew where she was anymore.

- Everybody, after the flash and the splash, was the boat near the whirlpool anymore? (Signal.) *No.*
- Everybody, read the rest of the story to yourself. Find out three things. Find out how far from land the boat was when Edna looked around. Find out how deep the water below the boat was. Find out what Edna did when she realized where the boat was. Raise your hand when you're finished.

Carla was in the front of the boat, talking to herself. "I don't believe this," she said over and over. "I don't believe this. I want to go home."

Edna looked over the side of the boat. But she didn't see deep blue water that seemed to go down forever. She saw shallow water and sand. The boat was now in water that was only about a meter deep. Slowly, Edna looked around. "Land," she said aloud. She pointed to a row of palm trees and a beach that was about half a mile away. "Land," she said again. She was standing up and stepping over the side of the boat.

"Land," she said and stumbled into the water. She fell down and got up and started to wade toward the trees. She wanted to be on land. She wanted to be on something that would not rock and bounce and make her dizzy. "Land," she said.

- (After all students have raised their hand:) Where did the boat end up? (Call on a student. Ideas: *Near land; in shallow water.*)
- Everybody, about how far from land was it? (Signal.) *Half a mile.*
- About how deep was the water where the boat was? (Signal.) *One meter.*
- What did Edna do when she saw the land? (Call on a student. Ideas: *She said "Land!"; she got out of the boat.*)
- Why did she want to get on land? (Call on a student. Ideas: *She wanted to be on firm ground; she was dizzy.*)
- She has a long way to wade through that water, about half a mile.

PAIRED PRACTICE

You're going to read aloud to your partner. First the **A** members will read. Then the **B** members will read from the star to the end of the story. (Observe students and give feedback.)

End-of-Lesson Activities

Now finish your independent work for lesson 27. Raise your hand when you're finished. (Observe students and give feedback.)

WORKCHECK

a. (Direct students to take out their marking pencils.)
   - We're going to check your workbook and textbook items. Remember, if you got an item wrong, make an **X** next to the item.

b. (For each item: Read the item. Call on a student to answer it. If the answer is wrong, say the correct answer. Refer to the Answer Key for the correct answers.)

c. Now use your marking pencil to fix any items you got wrong. Remember, all mistakes must be fixed before you hand in your work.

LANGUAGE ARTS

(Present Language Arts lesson 27 after completing Reading lesson 27. See Language Arts Guide.)

VOCABULARY REVIEW

a. You learned a sentence that tells what the rim of the volcano did. Everybody, say the sentence. Get ready. (Signal.) *The rim of the volcano exploded.*

b. I'll say part of the sentence. When I stop, you say the next word. Listen: The rim of the . . . Everybody, what's the next word? (Signal.) *Volcano.*

c. Listen: The rim of the volcano . . . Everybody, what's the next word? (Signal.) *Exploded.*

• Say the whole sentence. Get ready. (Signal.) *The rim of the volcano exploded.*

d. Listen: The . . . Everybody, what's the next word? (Signal.) *Rim.*

READING WORDS

Column 1

a. **Find lesson 28 in your textbook.** ✓

• Touch column 1. ✓

• (Teacher reference:)

1. **upright**	3. **anyone**
2. **overturned**	4. **aloud**

• All these words are compound words. The first part of each word is underlined.

b. Word 1. What's the underlined part? (Signal.) *up.*

• What's the whole word? (Signal.) *Upright.*

c. Word 2. What's the underlined part? (Signal.) *over.*

• What's the whole word? (Signal.) *Overturned.*

d. Word 3. What's the underlined part? (Signal.) *any.*

• What's the whole word? (Signal.) *Anyone.*

e. Word 4. What's the underlined part? (Signal.) *a.*

• What's the whole word? (Signal.) *Aloud.*

f. Let's read those words again.

• Word 1. What word? (Signal.) *Upright.*

• (Repeat for words 2–4.)

g. (Repeat step f until firm.)

Column 2

h. Find column 2. ✓

• (Teacher reference:)

1. **tangle**	4. **strangest**
2. **gallons**	5. **bending**
3. **ignore**	6. **crowded**

• All these words have more than one syllable. The first syllable of each word is underlined.

i. Word 1. What's the underlined part? (Signal.) *tang.*

• What's the whole word? (Signal.) *Tangle.*

• A tangle is a mixed-up mass. If your hair is tangled, it is mixed up. It's not all combed in the same direction. Here's another way of saying a mixed-up mass of vines: a tangle of vines. Everybody, what's another way of saying **a mixed-up mass of vines?** (Signal.) *A tangle of vines.*

• What's another way of saying **a mixed-up mass of string?** (Signal.) *A tangle of string.*

j. Word 2. What's the underlined part? (Signal.) *gal.*

• What's the whole word? (Signal.) *Gallons.*

• A gallon is a unit of measurement that is the same as four quarts. A large jug of milk is a gallon. Everybody, what unit equals four quarts? (Signal.) *Gallon.*

k. Word 3. What's the underlined part? (Signal.) *ig.*

• What's the whole word? (Signal.) *Ignore.*

l. Word 4. What's the underlined part? (Signal.) *strange.*

• What's the whole word? (Signal.) *Strangest.*

m. Word 5. What's the underlined part? (Signal.) *bend.*

• What's the whole word? (Signal.) *Bending.*

n. Word 6. What's the underlined part? (Signal.) *crowd.*

• What's the whole word? (Signal.) *Crowded.*

o. Let's read those words again.
- Word 1. What word? (Signal.) *Tangle.*
- (Repeat for: **2. gallons, 3. ignore, 4. strangest, 5. bending, 6. crowded.**)
p. (Repeat step o until firm.)

Column 3

q. Find column 3. ✓
- (Teacher reference:)

1. faint	5. terrible
2. hind	6. driven
3. tearing	7. groove
4. practice	

r. Word 1. What word? (Signal.) *Faint.*
- Spell **faint.** Get ready. (Tap for each letter.) *F-A-I-N-T.*
- If something is faint, it is very hard to hear or see. A faint sound is a sound you can hardly hear. Everybody, what do we call an image you can hardly see? (Signal.) *A faint image.*
s. Word 2. What word? (Signal.) *Hind.*
- Spell **hind.** Get ready. (Tap for each letter.) *H-I-N-D.*
t. Word 3. What word? (Signal.) *Tearing.*
- Spell **tearing.** Get ready. (Tap for each letter.) *T-E-A-R-I-N-G.*
u. Word 4. What word? (Signal.) *Practice.*
- Spell **practice.** Get ready. (Tap for each letter.) *P-R-A-C-T-I-C-E.*
v. Word 5. What word? (Signal.) *Terrible.*
w. (Repeat for words 6 and 7.)
x. Let's read those words again.
- Word 1. What word? (Signal.) *Faint.*
- (Repeat for words 2–7.)
y. (Repeat step x until firm.)

Individual Turns

(For columns 1–3: Call on individual students, each to read one to three words per turn.)

EXERCISE 3

STORY READING

a. Find part B in your textbook. ✓
- The error limit for group reading is 9 errors. Read carefully.

b. Everybody, touch the title. ✓
- (Call on a student to read the title.) *[A Long Night.]*
- Everybody, what's the title? (Signal.) *A Long Night.*
- (Call on individual students to read the story, each student reading two or three sentences at a time. Ask the specified questions as the students read.)

- (Correct errors: Tell the word. Direct the student to reread the sentence.)
- (If the group makes more than 9 errors, direct the students to reread the story.)

A Long Night
Carla called to Edna, "Help me get this boat on shore." Carla was pulling the lifeboat toward shore. She was a long way behind Edna. Edna waited for her. Then the girls pulled the lifeboat onto the beach and turned it over. Many gallons of salt water spilled out and ran back to the ocean.

- Everybody, where was the lifeboat now? (Signal.) *On the beach.*
- How did it get there? (Call on a student. Idea: *The girls dragged it there.*)
- What came out of it when they turned it over? (Call on a student. Idea: *Gallons of salt water.*)

The sky was starting to clear. In the distance were heavy clouds, but the waves on the ocean were small. Behind Edna and Carla was a heavy jungle. A great tangle of trees and vines crowded down to the beach. From the jungle came the sounds of birds and other animals. The whole beach was covered with red sand. Edna had never seen sand like that before.

- Everybody, close your eyes and get a picture of the land that Edna and Carla are on.

   The sky was starting to clear. In the distance were heavy clouds, but the waves on the ocean were small. Behind Edna and Carla was a heavy jungle. A great tangle of trees and vines crowded down to the beach. From the jungle came the sounds of birds and other animals. The whole beach was covered with red sand. Edna had never seen sand like that before.

- What was the ocean like? (Call on a student. Ideas: *Calm; the waves were small.*)
- Everybody, what was behind the beach? (Signal.) *A jungle.*
- What kinds of sounds could they hear? (Call on a student. Idea: *Birds and other animals.*)
- Where were the heavy clouds in the sky? (Call on a student. Ideas: *Far away; in the distance.*)
- What was strange about the beach? (Call on a student. Idea: *The red sand.*)

   Edna walked a few feet from the overturned lifeboat and sat down on the soft, red sand beach. "I'm sick," she said.

   "I'm sick, too," Carla said. She was lying down on the beach.

   A few minutes later, Carla was sleeping. Edna closed her eyes. The world seemed to be spinning around and around. The beach seemed to be rocking. "Oh," she said aloud. She kept her eyes closed and tried to ignore the terrible rocking and spinning.

• • •

- Everybody, were things **really** rocking and spinning? (Signal.) *No.*
- Why did Edna feel that they were? (Call on a student. Idea: *She was still dizzy.*)
- There are three dots in the story. What does that mean? (Call on a student. Idea: *Part of the story is missing.*)

   "BRRRRAAAAHHHH!"
   Edna sat up, her eyes wide. It was night. At first she didn't know where she was.

- Edna had been on the beach with her eyes closed. Now it is night. What must have happened? (Call on a student. Idea: *She fell asleep.*)

   "BRRRAAAHHH!"
   "What's making that noise?" Carla asked.

   Edna turned toward Carla's voice. It was so dark that Edna could hardly see her.

   Suddenly, as Edna looked in Carla's direction, she saw something moving out of the jungle. She heard it, too. It crashed through the vines and trees. There were breaking sounds and tearing sounds as small trees snapped and broke. Edna could see the faint outline of the trees being bent over and snapped down. Then she saw the faint outline of something else, something very large. An animal of some sort. "It can't be," Edna said aloud. The animal that she saw was too big. It was as big as some of the trees.

   Edna didn't have ★ much time to look at the animal because it stayed on the beach for only a few seconds. All Edna saw was a very faint outline. But she saw enough to know that she was looking at an animal like nothing she had ever seen before. It was big. It seemed to have a huge head. And it seemed to walk upright, on its hind legs.

- Everybody, could Edna see the animal clearly? (Signal.) *No.*
- What things did the animal do? (Call on a student. Ideas: *It made a noise; crashed through trees; came out on the beach.*)
- How long was the animal on the beach? (Call on a student. Idea: *A few seconds.*)
- Everybody, did the animal walk on **four** legs? (Signal.) *No.*
- How did it walk? (Call on a student. Idea: *On its hind legs.*)
- How big was the animal? (Call on a student. Ideas: *Very big; as big as trees.*)
- What kind of head did it have? (Call on a student. Ideas: *Huge; too big for an animal that size.*)

- Everybody, look at the picture. It shows Edna and Carla on the beach. If you look very carefully near the edge of the jungle you can see the faint outline of a huge animal walking on its hind legs. Do you have any ideas about what kind of animal that might be? (Call on individual students. Accept any large, upright-walking animal.)

> During the few seconds that Edna saw the animal, it seemed to throw its head back when it roared. Then it suddenly turned around and disappeared into the jungle. It left a trail of great crashing and bending sounds.
> "What was that?" Carla asked.
> "I don't know, but I'm scared," Edna answered.
> "Yeah," Carla said. "I think we should go stay under the lifeboat."
> "Good idea," Edna said.

- Everybody, where are they going to go? (Signal.) *Under the lifeboat.*
- Why? (Call on a student. Ideas: *To hide; to keep safe from the animal; they're scared.*)
- Do you think they'll be able to go to sleep again? (Call on individual students. Student preference.)

> So the girls crawled under the lifeboat and tried to sleep. But neither girl slept. One time, Edna was almost asleep when Carla moved her foot and made a noise. Edna sat up so suddenly that she hit her head on the inside of the lifeboat.

- Everybody, were the girls able to sleep well? (Signal.) *No.*
- What happened to Edna when there was a little sound? (Call on a student. Ideas: *She woke up; she sat up and hit her head.*)
- Read the rest of the story to yourself. Find out what the girls saw the next morning on the beach. Find out how big those things were. Raise your hand when you're finished.

> That was the longest night that Edna remembered. She kept waiting for the sky to become light. She wasn't sure which part would become light first, because she didn't know where east was. The first part to get light was over the jungle. Then it seemed that a year passed before it was light enough to see the ocean clearly. The sun was not up yet, but the birds were squawking and screaming in the jungle.
> At last, Edna and Carla crawled out from under the lifeboat. The first thing they did was walk to where they had seen the outline of the huge animal. As soon as they got close to the spot, they saw the animal's huge footprints in the red sand.
> When Edna looked at the footprints, she knew that there was an animal on this island that looked like no other living animal anyone had ever seen. It left footprints that were a yard long!

- (After all students have raised their hand:) Everybody, did the sky first get light **over the ocean** or **over the jungle**? (Signal.) *Over the jungle.*
- What direction was the part of the sky that got light first? (Signal.) *East.*
- What was the first thing the girls did after they crawled out from under the lifeboat? (Call on a student. Ideas: *Walked to where Edna had seen the huge animal; they walked toward the jungle.*)
- Everybody, what did they see in the sand? (Signal.) *Footprints.*
- How big were the footprints? (Call on a student. Ideas: *Huge; a yard long.*)
- Show me with your hands how long a footprint was. ✓

PAIRED PRACTICE

You're going to read aloud to your partner. The **B** members will read first. Then the **A** members will read from the star to the end of the story.

(Observe students and give feedback.)

End-of-Lesson Activities

INDEPENDENT WORK

Now finish your independent work for lesson 28. Raise your hand when you're finished. (Observe students and give feedback.)

WORKCHECK

a. (Direct students to take out their marking pencils.)
  • We're going to check your workbook and textbook items. Remember, if you got an item wrong, make an **X** next to the item.
b. (For each item: Read the item. Call on a student to answer it. If the answer is wrong, say the correct answer. Refer to the Answer Key for the correct answers.)
c. Now use your marking pencil to fix any items you got wrong. Remember, all mistakes must be fixed before you hand in your work.

LANGUAGE ARTS

(Present Language Arts lesson 28 after completing Reading lesson 28. See Language Arts Guide.)

Lesson 29

VOCABULARY

a. **Find page 352 in your textbook.** ✓
- Touch sentence 6. ✓
- This is a new vocabulary sentence. It says: The new exhibit displayed mysterious fish. Everybody, say that sentence. Get ready. (Signal.) *The new exhibit displayed mysterious fish.*
- Close your eyes and say the sentence. Get ready. (Signal.) *The new exhibit displayed mysterious fish.*
- (Repeat until firm.)

b. An exhibit has things arranged for people to see. An exhibit of rocks would have rocks arranged for people to see. What would an exhibit of fish have? (Call on a student. Idea: *Fish arranged for people to see.*)

c. Another word for **show** is **display.** When you show something, you display it. What's another way of saying **They showed their strength by lifting weights?** (Signal.) *They displayed their strength by lifting weights.*
- What's another way of saying **They showed the large pumpkins they had grown?** (Signal.) *They displayed the large pumpkins they had grown.*

d. The new exhibit displayed **mysterious** fish. Things that you do not understand are **mysterious.** A fish that you do not understand is a mysterious fish. Everybody, what would you call a volcano you do not understand? (Signal.) *A mysterious volcano.*
- What would you call a story you do not understand? (Signal.) *A mysterious story.*

e. Listen to the sentence again: The new exhibit displayed mysterious fish. Everybody, say the sentence. Get ready. (Signal.) *The new exhibit displayed mysterious fish.*

f. Everybody, what word means **showed?** (Signal.) *Displayed.*
- What word means **an arrangement of things for people to look at?** (Signal.) *Exhibit.*
- What word describes things we don't understand? (Signal.) *Mysterious.*
- (Repeat step f until firm.)

READING WORDS

Column 1

a. Find lesson 29 in your textbook. ✓
- Touch column 1. ✓
- (Teacher reference:)

1. breath	3. leathery
2. shriek	4. immediately

b. Word 1 is **breath.** What word? (Signal.) *Breath.*
- Spell **breath.** Get ready. (Tap for each letter.) *B-R-E-A-T-H.*
- Your breath is the air you take in or let out. If you hold your breath, you are not taking in air or letting it out. Everybody, what do we call the air you take in or let out? (Signal.) *Breath.*

c. Word 2 is **shriek.** What word? (Signal.) *Shriek.*
- Spell **shriek.** Get ready. (Tap for each letter.) *S-H-R-I-E-K.*
- A shriek is a very sharp scream. A shriek is not a nice sound. Everybody, what do we call a sharp scream? (Signal.) *Shriek.*

d. Word 3 is **leathery.** What word? (Signal.) *Leathery.*
- Spell **leathery.** Get ready. (Tap for each letter.) *L-E-A-T-H-E-R-Y.*
- If something is leathery, it looks or feels like leather. Here's another way of saying **The meat was like leather: The meat was leathery.** Everybody, what's another way of saying **His skin looked like leather?** (Signal.) *His skin was leathery.*

e. Word 4 is **immediately.** What word? (Signal.) *Immediately.*

f. Let's read those words again.
- Word 1. What word? (Signal.) *Breath.*
- (Repeat for: **2. shriek, 3. leathery, 4. immediately**.)
g. (Repeat step f until firm.)

Column 2

h. Find column 2. ✓
- (Teacher reference:)

1. clearing	4. practiced
2. dents	5. terrible
3. driven	6. terribly

i. Word 1. What word? (Signal.) *Clearing.*
- A clearing is a place in a forest or a jungle where there are no trees. Everybody, what word names a place in a forest where there are no trees? (Signal.) *Clearing.*
j. Word 2. What word? (Signal.) *Dents.*
- (Repeat for words 3–6.)
k. Let's read those words again.
- Word 1. What word? (Signal.) *Clearing.*
- (Repeat for words 2–6.)
l. (Repeat step k until firm.)

Column 3

m. Find column 3. ✓
- (Teacher reference:)

1. sense	4. thick
2. pond	5. spread
3. club	6. stared

n. Word 1. What word? (Signal.) *Sense.*
- If you have a good sense of sight, you can see well. If you have a good sense of hearing, you can hear well. Everybody, what's another way of saying **John can hear well?** (Signal.) *John has a good sense of hearing.*
o. Word 2. What word? (Signal.) *Pond.*
- (Repeat for words 3–6.)
p. Let's read those words again.
- Word 1. What word? (Signal.) *Sense.*
- (Repeat for words 2–6.)
q. (Repeat step p until firm.)

Column 4

r. Find column 4. ✓
- (Teacher reference:)

1. groove	4. stream
2. grove	5. tail
3. steam	6. trail

- These are tricky words. Don't get fooled.
s. Word 1 is **groove**. What word? (Signal.) *Groove.*
t. Word 2. What word? (Signal.) *Grove.*
- (Repeat for words 3–6.)
u. Let's read those words again.
- Word 1. What word? (Signal.) *Groove.*
- (Repeat for words 2–6.)
v. (Repeat step u until firm.)

Individual Turns

(For columns 1–4: Call on individual students, each to read one to three words per turn.)

EXERCISE 3

STORY READING

a. Find part B in your textbook. ✓
- The error limit for group reading is 12 errors. Read carefully.
b. Everybody, touch the title. ✓
- (Call on a student to read the title.) *[Footprints.]*
- Everybody, what's the title? (Signal.) *Footprints.*
- (Call on individual students to read the story, each student reading two or three sentences at a time. Ask the specified questions as the students read.)

- (Correct errors: Tell the word. Direct the student to reread the sentence.)
- (If the group makes more than 12 errors, direct the students to reread the story.)

Footprints
There was a row of footprints in the red sand. The footprints of the animal were a yard long. Each footprint had three toes. The size of the footprints told Edna something about the size of the animal.

- What would you know about the size of an animal that had footprints a yard long? (Call on a student. Idea: *It would be a big animal.*)

The footprints made very deep dents in the sand. These deep dents told Edna something about how much the animal weighed.

- What could the deep dents tell you? (Call on a student. Idea: *The animal weighed a lot.*)

- Everybody, which would make deeper dents, an animal that weighed **one hundred** pounds or an animal that weighed **one thousand** pounds? (Signal.) *An animal that weighed one thousand pounds.*

Between the footprints was a deep groove in the sand. Carla asked, "What could make that deep trail?"

- Everybody, touch the groove in the picture. ✓
- The groove goes where the footprints go. What could make that deep groove? (Call on individual students. Ideas: *A branch the animal was dragging; a tail;* etc.)
- Let's find out what made it.

Suddenly Edna shouted, "A tail. I'll bet a tail did that. That animal is walking on its hind legs. It's dragging a heavy tail behind it. The tail makes the groove in the sand."
For a while, the girls walked around the footprints and didn't say anything. Then they looked toward the jungle. The animal had left a huge path through the jungle. On either side of this path were thick vines and trees. But the path was almost clear. It looked as if somebody had driven a truck through the jungle and knocked down all the small trees and vines.

- Everybody, touch the path that goes into the jungle in the picture on page 143. ✓
- Can you see any trees that were knocked over when that animal went through the jungle? (Signal.) *Yes.*

✿Edna said, "I don't think we should go into that jungle."
"Yeah, we shouldn't do it," Carla said. The girls were silent for a few moments. They just stood there and looked at the great path that led

into the jungle. Then Carla said, "But we could follow that path for a little way. We don't have to go too far."

- Do you think they'll follow that path? (Call on individual students. Student preference.)

"I don't want to go in there," Edna said. But she wasn't telling Carla the truth. Part of her was frightened and wanted to run away. But part of her wanted to see what made those huge footprints. Her mind made pictures of that animal. In one of the pictures, the animal was chasing ✿ Carla and Edna. Edna was running as fast as she could, but the animal was getting closer and closer and . . .

- Edna stopped right in the middle of this thought. Let's find out why.

"Come on," Carla said. "Let's go just a little way."

- Why did Edna stop imagining what the animal was like? (Call on a student. Idea: *Carla started talking.*)

Now another part of Edna's mind was taking over. It wanted to see that animal. This part of Edna's mind was not terribly frightened. It made up pictures of Carla and Edna sneaking up on the animal. In these pictures, the animal did not see Edna ★ and Carla. "This animal is not very smart," Edna said to herself. "If it was a smart animal, it would have found us last night. Maybe it does not have a good sense of smell. Maybe it has poor eyes."

- Why didn't Edna think the animal was very smart? (Call on a student. Idea: *Because it didn't find them last night.*)
- What two things did Edna think might be wrong with the animal? (Call on a student. Idea: *It might have poor eyesight or a poor sense of smell.*)
- She thought the animal might have poor eyes. What does that mean? (Call on a student. Idea: *It could not see very well.*)

"Okay, let's follow the path," Edna said to Carla. "But just a little way."

Carla picked up a short, heavy branch. She practiced swinging it like a club. Edna picked up a branch too. They were easy to find in the path made by the animal.

- Why were they easy to find? (Call on a student. Idea: *The animal knocked branches off the trees.*)
- What do you think they planned to do with the clubs? (Call on a student. Idea: *Protect themselves.*)

So the girls started down the path into the jungle. They walked very slowly and carefully. They jumped each time a screech or a roar came from the jungle. They tried not to step on small branches that would make a cracking sound.

- Why? (Call on a student. Idea: *So the animal wouldn't hear them.*)

Slowly, they moved farther into the jungle. Soon, Edna could not see the beach behind her. The trees over them blocked out the light.

"This is far enough," Edna said after she realized that the girls had gone over a hundred meters into the jungle.

"Shhh," Carla said, and pointed straight ahead. Edna could see a clearing. In the middle of it was a small pond. From the pond, steam rose into the air. The girls moved forward. Now Edna could see a small stream flowing into the pond. And she saw tall grass.

- What things did Edna see in the clearing? (Call on a student. Ideas: *A pond with steam rising from it; a stream; tall grass.*)
- The picture shows the clearing. There are no trees in the clearing. Everybody, touch the pond. ✓
- Touch the steam that is rising into the air. ✓
- Touch the stream. ✓
- Touch the tall grass. ✓
- Read the rest of the story to yourself. I'm not going to tell you things to read for. So read it very carefully and be ready to answer some questions. Raise your hand when you're finished.

When the girls reached the edge of the clearing, Edna stopped. She noticed that the trees were very strange. She looked at a small tree on the edge of the clearing. "I saw a picture of a tree like this somewhere," she said. "But I can't remember where." She tried to remember. Suddenly, she did. And when she remembered, she wanted to run from the jungle as fast as she could. She had seen a picture of that tree in a book on dinosaurs. She had looked at the picture in the book many times. And she clearly remembered the tree. It was in a picture that showed Tyrannosaurus fighting with Triceratops.

Edna looked at the tree and remembered the huge footprints. "Oh no," she said aloud.

- (After all students have raised their hand:) Edna saw something next to the path that she recognized from a picture in a book. Everybody, what was that? (Signal.) *A tree.*
- What else was in the picture that showed the tree? (Call on a student. Ideas: *Dinosaurs; Tyrannosaurus fighting with Triceratops.*)
- When Edna remembered the picture, she thought of the footprints on the beach. Then she said, "Oh no," aloud. She had figured out something. What was that? (Call on a student. Idea: *Dinosaurs were on the island.*)

PAIRED PRACTICE

You're going to read aloud to your partner. The **A** members will read first. Then the **B** members will read from the star to the end of the story. (Observe students and give feedback.)

End-of-Lesson Activities

INDEPENDENT WORK

Now finish your independent work for lesson 29. Raise your hand when you're finished. (Observe students and give feedback.)

WORKCHECK

a. (Direct students to take out their marking pencils.)

- We're going to check your workbook and textbook items. Remember, if you got an item wrong, make an **X** next to the item.
b. (For each item: Read the item. Call on a student to answer it. If the answer is wrong, say the correct answer. Refer to the Answer Key for the correct answers.)
c. Now use your marking pencil to fix any items you got wrong. Remember, all mistakes must be fixed before you hand in your work.

LANGUAGE ARTS

(Present Language Arts lesson 29 after completing Reading lesson 29. See Language Arts Guide.)

> **Note:** You will need to reproduce blackline masters for the Fact Game in lesson 30. (Appendix G in Teacher's Guide).

Materials for Lesson 30

Fact Game

For each team (4 or 5 students):
- pair of number cubes (or dice)
- copy of Fact Game 30 (Reproducible blackline masters are at the back of the Teacher's Guide.)

For each student:
- their copy of the scorecard sheet (at end of workbook A)

For each monitor:
- a pencil
- Fact Game 30 answer key (at end of textbook A)

Reading Checkout

Each student needs their thermometer chart.

Literature Lesson 3

See Literature Guide for the materials you will need.

EXERCISE 1

FACT GAME

a. You're going to play the game that uses the facts you have learned. Remember the rules. The player rolls the number cubes, figures out the number of the question, reads that question out loud, and answers it. The monitor tells the player if the answer is right or wrong. If it's wrong, the monitor tells the right answer. If it's right, the monitor gives the player one point. Don't argue with the monitor. The number cubes go to the left and the next player has a turn. You'll play the game for 10 minutes.

b. (Divide students into groups of four or five. Assign monitors. Circulate as students play the game. Comment on groups that are playing well.)

c. (At the end of 10 minutes, have all students who earned more than 10 points stand up.)

- (Tell the monitor of each game that ran smoothly:) Your group did a good job.

EXERCISE 2

READING CHECKOUTS

a. Today is a test day and a reading-checkout day. While you're writing answers for the test, I'm going to call on you one at a time to read part of the story from lesson 29. When I call you to come and do your checkout, bring your thermometer chart.

- Remember, you pass the checkout by reading the passage in less than a minute without making more than 2 mistakes. And when you pass the checkout, you'll color the space for lesson 30 on your thermometer chart.

b. (Call on individual students to read the portion of story 29 marked with ✿.)

- (Time the student. Note words that are missed and number of words read.)

- (Teacher reference:)

> ✿Edna said, "I don't think we should go into that jungle."
> "Yeah, we shouldn't do it," Carla said. The girls were silent for a few moments. They just stood there and looked at the great path [50] that led into the jungle. Then Carla said, "But we could follow that path for a little way. We don't have to go too far."
> "I don't want to go in there," Edna said. But she wasn't telling Carla [75] the truth. Part of her was frightened and wanted to run away. But part of her wanted to see what made those huge footprints. Her [100] mind made pictures of that animal. In one of the pictures, the animal was chasing ✿ [115] Carla and Edna.

- (If the student reads the passage in one minute or less and makes no more than 2 errors, direct the student to color in the space for lesson 30 on the thermometer chart.)

- (If the student makes any mistakes, point to each word that was misread and identify it.)
- (If the student does not meet the rate-error criterion for the passage, direct the student to practice reading the story with the assigned partner.)

TEST

a. **Find page 148 in your textbook.** ✓
- This is a test. You'll work items you've done before.

b. Work carefully. Raise your hand when you've completed all the items. (Observe students but do not give feedback on errors.)

MARKING THE TEST

a. (Check students' work before beginning lesson 31. Refer to the Answer Key for the correct answers.)
b. (Record all test 3 results on the Test Summary Sheet and the Group Summary Sheet. Reproducible Summary Sheets are at the back of the Teacher's Guide.)

TEST REMEDIES

(Provide any necessary remedies for test 3 before presenting lesson 31. Test remedies are discussed in the Teacher's Guide.)

Test 3 Firming Table

Test Item	Introduced in lesson	Test Item	Introduced in lesson	Test Item	Introduced in lesson
1	21	13	23	25	24
2	21	14	23	26	24
3	21	15	23	27	24
4	21	16	23	28	27
5	22	17	23	29	27
6	22	18	23	30	27
7	22	19	23	31	29
8	22	20	23	32	29
9	22	21	23	33	21
10	22	22	23	34	21
11	22	23	23	35	21
12	23	24	23	36	21

LITERATURE BOOK

(Present Literature lesson 3 after completing Reading lesson 30. See Literature Guide.)

LANGUAGE ARTS

(Present Language Arts lesson 30 after completing Reading lesson 30. See Language Arts Guide.)

Lessons 31–35 • Planning Page

	Lesson 31	Lesson 32	Lesson 33	Lesson 34	Lesson 35
Lesson Events	Vocabulary Sentence Reading Words Story Reading Paired Practice Independent Work Workcheck Language Arts	Vocabulary Sentences Reading Words Vocabulary Story Reading Paired Practice Independent Work Workcheck Language Arts	Vocabulary Sentence **Vocabulary Sentence** Reading Words Comprehension Passage Story Reading Paired Practice Independent Work Workcheck Language Arts	Vocabulary Sentence Reading Words Comprehension Passage Story Reading Paired Practice Independent Work Workcheck Language Arts	Vocabulary Sentences Reading Words Story Reading Reading Checkouts Independent Work Workcheck Language Arts
Vocabulary Sentence	#6: The new exhibit <u>displayed</u> <u>mysterious</u> fish.	sentence #4 sentence #5 sentence #6	#6: The new exhibit <u>displayed</u> <u>mysterious</u> fish. **#7: She automatically arranged the flowers.**	#7: She <u>automatically</u> <u>arranged</u> the flowers.	sentence #5 sentence #6 sentence #7
Reading Words: Word Types	multi-syllable words words with an ending mixed words	modeled words mixed words	multi-syllable words mixed words	modeled words multi-syllable words mixed words	modeled words compound words words with endings multi-syllable words
New Vocabulary		adventure supplies remains	however swift quake hardened	approach blisters throat	museum character embarrassed directed divided
Comprehension Passage			_Volcanos and Earthquakes_	_Underlined Words_	
Story	_The Monster_	_Looking for Carla_	_Explosion_	_Back in the Lifeboat_	_Saved_
Skill Items	Sequencing	Vocabulary Vocabulary sentence	Vocabulary sentences	Vocabulary	Vocabulary sentence Sequencing
Special Materials					Thermometer charts, *materials for project
Special Projects/ Activities			Activity after lesson 33		Project after lesson 35

* Reference materials (books on dinosaurs, books on the Mesozoic era, encyclopedias, CD-ROMS); poster-making supplies (butcher paper or poster board, markers, crayons, paints, scissors, paste, magazines for pictures)

Lesson 31

EXERCISE 1

VOCABULARY REVIEW

a. Here's the new vocabulary sentence: The new exhibit displayed mysterious fish.
- Everybody, say the sentence. Get ready. (Signal.) *The new exhibit displayed mysterious fish.*
- (Repeat until firm.)

b. What word describes things we don't understand? (Signal.) *Mysterious.*
- What word means **an arrangement of things for people to look at?** (Signal.) *Exhibit.*
- What word means **showed?** (Signal.) *Displayed.*
- (Repeat step b until firm.)

EXERCISE 2

READING WORDS

Column 1

a. **Find lesson 31 in your textbook.** ✓
- Touch column 1. ✓
- (Teacher reference:)

1. **half-folded**	3. **forgot**
2. **eagle**	4. **monster**

- All these words have more than one syllable. The first syllable of each word is underlined.
b. Word 1. What's the first syllable? (Signal.) *half.*
- What's the whole word? (Signal.) *Half-folded.*
c. Word 2. What's the first syllable? (Signal.) *ēa.*
- What's the whole word? (Signal.) *Eagle.*
- Spell **eagle.** Get ready. (Tap for each letter.) *E-A-G-L-E.*
d. Word 3. What's the first syllable? (Signal.) *for.*
- What's the whole word? (Signal.) *Forgot.*
- Spell **forgot.** Get ready. (Tap for each letter.) *F-O-R-G-O-T.*
e. Word 4. What's the first syllable? (Signal.) *mon.*
- What's the whole word? (Signal.) *Monster.*
- Spell **monster.** Get ready. (Tap for each letter.) *M-O-N-S-T-E-R.*
f. Let's read those words again.
- Word 1. What word? (Signal.) *Half-folded.*
- (Repeat for words 2–4.)
g. (Repeat step f until firm.)

Column 2

h. Find column 2. ✓
- (Teacher reference:)

1. **leathery**	4. **mouthful**
2. **breaths**	5. **immediately**
3. **instantly**	6. **lying**

- All these words have an ending.
i. Word 1. What word? (Signal.) *Leathery.*
- (Repeat for words 2–6.)
j. Let's read those words again.
- Word 1. What word? (Signal.) *Leathery.*
- (Repeat for words 2–6.)
k. (Repeat step j until firm.)

Column 3

l. Find column 3. ✓
- (Teacher reference:)

1. **started**	4. **slid**
2. **stared**	5. **spread**
3. **sailed**	6. **attract**

- These words are tricky. Don't get fooled.
m. Word 1. What word? (Signal.) *Started.*
- (Repeat for words 2–6.)
n. Let's read those words again.
- Word 1. What word? (Signal.) *Started.*
- (Repeat for words 2–6.)
o. (Repeat step n until firm.)

Individual Turns

(For columns 1–3: Call on individual students, each to read one to three words per turn.)

EXERCISE 3

STORY READING

a. Find part B in your textbook. ✓
- The error limit for group reading is 12. Read carefully.
b. Everybody, touch the title. ✓

- (Call on a student to read the title.)
  [*The Monster.*]
- Everybody, what's the title? (Signal.)
  The Monster.
- What do you think the monster will turn out to be? (Call on a student. Idea: *A dinosaur.*)
- (Call on individual students to read the story, each student reading two or three sentences at a time. Ask the specified questions as the students read.)

- (Correct errors: Tell the word. Direct the student to reread the sentence.)
- (If the group makes more than 12 errors, direct the students to reread the story.)

The Monster
Just as Edna was going to tell Carla about the tree in the book, a loud flapping sound came from the sky.

- What was she going to say about the tree? (Call on a student. Idea: *It grew when dinosaurs were alive.*)
- Why didn't Edna tell about the tree? (Call on a student. Idea: *A loud flapping noise interrupted her.*)

A huge bird-like animal sailed down from above the jungle. It wasn't a bird because it didn't have feathers. It had large wings that looked like leather.

- Why wasn't it a bird? (Call on a student. Ideas: *It didn't have feathers; its wings were like leather.*)
- What covered the wings? (Call on a student. Idea: *Something that looked like leather.*)

The animal had large sharp teeth. As the animal got close to the ground, Edna could see that it was very big—bigger than an eagle. The animal flapped its leathery wings loudly as it landed in the middle of the clearing. When it landed, the girls could see it more clearly.
　　Carla whispered, "What is that thing?"
　　Edna said, "It's an animal that lived a hundred million years ago."

- Everybody, when did Edna say the animal had lived? (Signal.) *A hundred million years ago.*
- Not a million years ago. A **hundred** million years ago.

Edna and Carla stared at the animal. It was on a rock with its wings half-folded and its mouth open.

- Everybody, look at the picture of the animal on page 152. Are its wings flat against its body? (Signal.) *No.*
- How would you feel if you were close to that animal? (Call on a student. Ideas: *Scared; surprised.*)

　　"Let's get out of here," Edna said.
　　The girls began to sneak down the path toward the beach. Suddenly, the ground shook and there was a terrible crashing sound. The ground shook again. Edna couldn't tell where the sound was coming from. She ran from the path and hid behind a vine-covered tree. Then she realized that the crashing sound was moving closer and closer. It was coming from the beach and moving down the path toward the clearing. A small tree crashed to the ground right in front of Edna. Above her was the form of a monster. It was standing in the path that Edna and Carla had followed. Edna could smell the animal. It gave off a smell something like garbage. Edna instantly recognized the animal. Tyrannosaurus.

- Everybody, who was the animal? (Signal.) *Tyrannosaurus.*

- Let me read that part again. Imagine how Edna and Carla must have felt and what they must have seen and smelled. They were on the path going back toward the beach.

  "Let's get out of here," Edna said. The girls began to sneak down the path toward the beach. Suddenly, the ground shook and there was a terrible crashing sound. The ground shook again. Edna couldn't tell where the sound was coming from. She ran from the path and hid behind a vine-covered tree. Then she realized that the crashing sound was moving closer and closer. It was coming from the beach and moving down the path toward the clearing. A small tree crashed to the ground right in front of Edna. Above her was the form of a monster. It was standing in the path that Edna and Carla had followed. Edna could smell the animal. It gave off a smell something like garbage. Edna instantly recognized the animal. Tyrannosaurus.

  The monster moved so quickly that Edna could hardly believe it. Like lightning, it turned its head one way and then another. Its mouth was open and it seemed to be smiling with teeth as big as knives. The huge, bird-like animal in the clearing spread its wings and started to flap them. Immediately, Tyrannosaurus turned its head in the direction of the animal. An instant later, the monster was running toward the winged animal.

  With each step, the ground shook. As Tyrannosaurus ran toward the clearing, its huge tail followed. It hit the tree that Edna was standing behind. The tree cracked. Edna ✦ went flying into the soft plants that covered the floor of the jungle.

- What made Edna go flying onto the ground? (Call on a student. Idea: *Tyrannosaurus hit the tree she was hiding behind.*)

  Before Edna could stand up, she heard noises from the clearing. There was a leathery flapping sound.

- Who made that sound? (Call on a student. Idea: *The bird-like animal.*)

  Then there was a terrible crunching sound, like the sound of bones being crushed.

- What do you think made that sound? (Call on a student. Idea: *The dinosaur attacking the bird.*)

  There were three squawking sounds.

- Who do you think made those sounds? (Call on a student. Idea: *The bird-like animal.*)

  Then there were more crunching sounds.

  Edna got up and started to run. She ran down the path toward the beach. She made her legs move as fast as they could. And she kept telling them to move faster. She told herself, "Get out of here. Get out of here." She tripped and almost fell. "Don't fall," she told herself. "Run," she told herself. "Run and don't stop."

  She wasn't thinking about the noise she made as she ran. She wasn't thinking that Tyrannosaurus might hear her. She wasn't thinking about anything but running. "Run," she told herself. "Don't slow down."

- She is very frightened. She is so frightened that she is thinking about only one thing. What's that? (Call on a student. Idea: *Running away.*)

  She noticed that there was a large snake on the path right in front of her. It was yellow and black, and it was at least three meters long. But she didn't even slow down. With a great leap she jumped over the snake and kept on running. When the girls had gone into the jungle, the path had seemed long. Now it seemed longer. It seemed as if it would never end. "Run," she said out loud between her breaths. "Run. Run."

- What did Edna see on the path when she was running? (Call on a student. Idea: *A snake.*)

- Everybody, did she stop running? (Signal.) *No.*
- Did she try to go around that snake? (Signal.) *No.*
- What did she do? (Call on a student. Idea: *Jumped over the snake.*)
- Why wasn't she afraid of that snake? (Call on a student. Idea: *She was more worried about getting away from the dinosaur.*)
- Read the rest of the story to yourself and be ready to answer some questions. Raise your hand when you're finished.

Edna ran until she could see the beach ahead of her. Then her mind slowly began to work again. She stopped and turned around. There was nothing on the path behind her. Good. Good. Tyrannosaurus was making so much noise eating that flying animal that it couldn't hear Edna. Besides, Tyrannosaurus already had a meal. What would it want with a tiny animal like Edna? Edna wouldn't be much more than a mouthful for the monster. Edna was thinking now. She walked out onto the red sand of the beach.

She was out of breath. Now she began to realize how frightened she had been. She had been so frightened that she forgot about everything. She forgot about being careful. Suddenly, Edna turned all the way around. She had forgotten about Carla. Where was Carla?

Edna looked in all directions, but she couldn't see Carla.

- (After all students have raised their hand:) When did Edna's mind start working again? (Call on a student. Idea: *When she saw the beach.*)
- Why hadn't Tyrannosaurus heard Edna? (Call on a student. Idea: *It was too busy eating the flying animal.*)
- Why didn't Edna think that she would have made a very good meal for Tyrannosaurus? (Call on a student. Idea: *She was too small.*)

- After Edna was on the red sand beach, she realized that something was wrong. What was wrong? (Call on a student. Idea: *Carla was missing.*)

PAIRED PRACTICE

You're going to read aloud to your partner. First the **B** members will read. Then the **A** members will read from the star to the end of the story. (Observe students and give feedback.)

End-of-Lesson Activities

INDEPENDENT WORK

Now finish your independent work for lesson 31. Raise your hand when you're finished. (Observe students and give feedback.)

WORKCHECK

a. (Direct students to take out their marking pencils.)
- We're going to check your workbook and textbook items. Remember, if you got an item wrong, make an **X** next to the item.
b. (For each item: Read the item. Call on a student to answer it. If the answer is wrong, say the correct answer. Refer to the Answer Key for the correct answers.)
c. Now use your marking pencil to fix up any items you got wrong. Remember, all mistakes must be fixed up before you hand in your work.

LANGUAGE ARTS

(Present Language Arts lesson 31 after completing Reading lesson 31. See Language Arts Guide.)

Lesson 32

EXERCISE 1

VOCABULARY REVIEW

a. You learned a sentence that tells what the smell attracted.
- Everybody, say that sentence. Get ready. (Signal.) *The smell attracted flies immediately.*
- (Repeat until firm.)

b. You learned a sentence that tells what the rim of the volcano did.
- Everybody, say that sentence. Get ready. (Signal.) *The rim of the volcano exploded.*
- (Repeat until firm.)

c. Here's the last sentence you learned: The new exhibit displayed mysterious fish.
- Everybody, say that sentence. Get ready. (Signal.) *The new exhibit displayed mysterious fish.*
- (Repeat until firm.)

d. What word describes things we don't understand? (Signal.) *Mysterious.*
- What word means **an arrangement of things for people to look at?** (Signal.) *Exhibit.*
- What word means **showed?** (Signal.) *Displayed.*
- (Repeat step d until firm.)

e. Once more. Say the sentence that tells about the new exhibit. Get ready. (Signal.) *The new exhibit displayed mysterious fish.*

EXERCISE 2

READING WORDS

Column 1

a. Find lesson 32 in your textbook. ✓
- Touch column 1. ✓
- (Teacher reference:)

1. cough	4. neither
2. pour	5. adventure
3. volcano	6. supplies

b. Word 1 is **cough.** What word? (Signal.) *Cough.*

- Spell **cough.** Get ready. (Tap for each letter.) *C-O-U-G-H.*

c. Word 2 is **pour.** What word? (Signal.) *Pour.*
- Spell **pour.** Get ready. (Tap for each letter.) *P-O-U-R.*

d. Word 3 is **volcano.** What word? (Signal.) *Volcano.*
- Spell **volcano.** Get ready. (Tap for each letter.) *V-O-L-C-A-N-O.*

e. Word 4 is **neither.** What word? (Signal.) *Neither.*
- Spell **neither.** Get ready. (Tap for each letter.) *N-E-I-T-H-E-R.*

f. Word 5 is **adventure.** What word? (Signal.) *Adventure.*
- An adventure is a new, exciting experience. Everybody, what's another way of saying **They had a new, exciting experience in the forest?** (Signal.) *They had an adventure in the forest.*

g. Word 6 is **supplies.** What word? (Signal.) *Supplies.*
- The supplies you need for a job are the things you'll use up when you do that job. What supplies would you need to write a bunch of stories? (Call on a student. Ideas: *Paper, pens, pencils.*)

h. Let's read those words again.
- Word 1. What word? (Signal.) *Cough.*
- (Repeat for words 2–6.)

i. (Repeat step h until firm.)

Column 2

j. Find column 2. ✓
- (Teacher reference:)

1. remains	4. attract
2. shriek	5. safety
3. reason	

k. Word 1. What word? (Signal.) *Remains.*
- The remains of something are the parts that are left. Sometimes, the only remains of a dead animal is the skeleton. Everybody, what do we call the parts of something that are left? (Signal.) *Remains.*

l. Word 2. What word? (Signal.) *Shriek.*
- (Repeat for words 3–5.)

m. Let's read those words again.
- Word 1. What word? (Signal.) *Remains.*
- (Repeat for: **2. shriek, 3. reason, 4. attract, 5. safety.**)

n. (Repeat step m until firm.)

Column 3

o. Find column 3. ✓
- (Teacher reference:)

1. lying	4. breath
2. laying	5. pacing
3. breathe	6. packing

- These words are tricky. Don't get fooled.

p. Word 1 is **lying.** What word? (Signal.) *Lying.*

q. Word 2. What word? (Signal.) *Laying.*

r. Word 3 is **breathe.** What word? (Signal.) *Breathe.*

s. Word 4. What word? (Signal.) *Breath.*

t. Word 5 is **pacing.** What word? (Signal.) *Pacing.*

u. Word 6. What word? (Signal.) *Packing.*

v. Let's read those words again.
- Word 1. What word? (Signal.) *Lying.*
- (Repeat for words 2–6.)

w. (Repeat step v until firm.)

Column 4

x. Find column 4. ✓
- (Teacher reference:)

1. glanced	3. strangely
2. prancing	4. untangle

y. Word 1. What word? (Signal.) *Glanced.*
- (Repeat for words 2–4.)

z. Let's read those words again.
- Word 1. What word? (Signal.) *Glanced.*
- (Repeat for words 2–4.)

a. (Repeat step z until firm.)

Individual Turns

(For columns 1–4: Call on individual students, each to read one to three words per turn.)

<hr>

EXERCISE 3

STORY READING

a. Find part B in your textbook. ✓
- The error limit for group reading is 11 errors. Read carefully.

b. Everybody, touch the title. ✓
- (Call on a student to read the title.) *[Looking for Carla.]*
- Everybody, what's the title? (Signal.) *Looking for Carla.*
- (Call on individual students to read the story, each student reading two or three sentences at a time. Ask the specified questions as the students read.)

- (Correct errors: Tell the word. Direct the student to reread the sentence.)
- (If the group makes more than 11 errors, direct the students to reread the story.)

Looking for Carla
Carla was not in sight.

- What does that mean? (Call on a student. Idea: *Edna couldn't see Carla anywhere.*)

That meant that Carla was still back there in the jungle. Edna took a couple of steps into the jungle. She stopped and looked down the path. She couldn't see anything. Part of her mind told her, "Don't go back there. You'll get killed." Then another part of her mind said, "You've got to help Carla. Go back."

- Which part do you think is going to win? (Call on a student. Student preference.)
- What did the first part think? (Call on a student. Ideas: *Don't go back there; you'll get killed.*)
- What did another part think? (Call on a student. Ideas: *Go back; you've got to help Carla.*)

For a moment Edna thought of calling to Carla. But then she realized that the sound of her voice would attract the monster.
Suddenly, she noticed that she was walking back toward the clearing. She had decided to try to help her friend.

- What is she going to do? (Call on a student. Idea: *Help Carla.*)

She crouched over and kept near the side of the path. She was ready to duck behind a tree as soon as she spotted Tyrannosaurus.

- What was she going to do if she saw Tyrannosaurus? (Call on a student. Ideas: *Duck behind a tree; hide.*)

She couldn't hear anything except her breath and the sounds of her feet moving through the green plants. Step, step, step—she moved down the path.

She noticed a beautiful flower growing in the middle of the path. She noticed that the birds in the jungle were not squawking. "Why are they silent?" she asked herself.

She answered, "They probably flew away when Tyrannosaurus ran into the clearing."

Then once again she noticed how quiet it was. Step, step, step.

- What did she see growing in the path? (Call on a student. Idea: *A flower.*)
- What did she notice about the birds? (Call on a student. Idea: *They weren't squawking.*)
- Why did she think that the birds were quiet? (Call on a student. Idea: *She thought they flew away when Tyrannosaurus ran into the clearing.*)

Edna was nearly all the way back to the clearing when she heard Tyrannosaurus. She could smell the dinosaur, too, but she couldn't see it.

- How did Edna know that Tyrannosaurus was nearby? (Call on a student. Idea: *She could hear him and smell him.*)

Edna ducked behind a tree on the side of the path. Now her mind started to think about the things that might have happened.

Maybe Tyrannosaurus had already found Carla and maybe Tyrannosaurus . . .

- What do you think Tyrannosaurus would have done if it had found Carla? (Call on a student. Idea: *Eaten her.*)

"No," she told herself. "Don't think about things like that. Carla is all right."

- Why was she telling herself that Carla was all right? (Call on a student. Ideas: *So she wouldn't be afraid; because she wanted Carla to be okay.*)

Edna stayed behind the tree for a minute or two. Tyrannosaurus didn't seem to be moving toward her. So, slowly she snuck back onto the path and moved toward the sound of the breathing. Closer and closer. Then she saw Carla lying near the path. Her leg was ✦ tangled up in some vines. She was lying very still.

Part of Edna's mind said this: "Carla is not moving, so she is dead."

Another part of Edna's mind said this: "No. She is not dead, and she is not hurt. She is lying very still because Tyrannosaurus is very near and she doesn't want to move."

- What did the first part of Edna's mind think about Carla? (Call on a student. Ideas: *She is dead; she's not moving because she is dead.*)
- What did the other part think? (Call on a student. Ideas: *She's not dead; she's not hurt; she's not moving because Tyrannosaurus is near.*)
- Which part do you think is right? (Call on individual students. Student preference.)
- If Tyrannosaurus is very near, Edna had better be careful.

Edna snuck up a little closer. Now she could see Tyrannosaurus. The dinosaur was at the edge of the clearing, looking in the direction of Carla. But the dinosaur was not standing still. It was pacing and turning its head from one side to another, as if it was looking for something.

Edna looked at Carla. She was all right.

On the far end of the clearing were the remains of the flying dinosaur. For some reason, Tyrannosaurus was not eating them.

Suddenly, Edna got an idea of how to save Carla. The plan was very dangerous, but Edna felt strangely brave. She felt that she had to try to help Carla. Edna's plan was to catch the dinosaur's attention. She would go into the jungle and make a lot of noise. Tyrannosaurus would come after the noise. When the dinosaur followed the noise, Carla would be able to free herself and run to safety.

- Edna planned to catch Tyrannosaurus's attention. What does that mean? (Call on a student. Idea: *Make Tyrannosaurus notice her.*)
- How did she plan to catch the dinosaur's attention? (Call on a student. Idea: *By making a lot of noise in the jungle.*)
- When the dinosaur went after Edna, what would Carla do? (Call on a student. Idea: *Get free and run to safety.*)
- Read the rest of the story to yourself and be ready to answer some questions. Raise your hand when you're finished.

Edna's heart was pounding. She knew that she would have to be very fast. She remembered how fast Tyrannosaurus moved through the jungle.

Suddenly, Tyrannosaurus turned around. Three Triceratops dinosaurs came into the clearing. They held their heads down as they moved toward Tyrannosaurus. Tyrannosaurus ran toward them and then stopped. It opened its mouth very wide and let out a terrible shriek.

"Now," Edna told herself. She ran toward Carla, who was already sitting up and trying to untangle her leg.

Edna grabbed the vines and tried to pull them free. It seemed to take forever. Carla didn't say anything. The girls tugged at the vines and tried to get Carla's leg free. The dinosaurs were very close to them.

- (After all students have raised their hand:) Everybody, did Edna carry out her plan about catching Tyrannosaurus's attention? (Signal.) *No.*

- Why not? (Call on a student. Idea: *Three Triceratops attracted its attention.*)
- When the Triceratops came into the clearing, what did Tyrannosaurus do? (Call on a student. Idea: *Ran toward them, stopped, and shrieked.*)
- When Tyrannosaurus was paying attention to the Triceratops, what did Edna do? (Call on a student. Idea: *Ran to Carla and tried to free her.*)
- Everybody, what did the girls talk about? (Signal.) *Nothing.*
- What was wrapped around Carla's leg? (Signal.) *Vines.*
- Did they get Carla's leg free at the end of the story? (Signal.) *No.*

- Look at the picture. You can see how close the girls are to the edge of the clearing.
- What does it look like those dinosaurs are getting ready to do? (Call on a student. Idea: *Fight.*)

EXERCISE 4

PAIRED PRACTICE

You're going to read aloud to your partner. The **A** members will read first. Then the **B** members will read from the star to the end of the story. (Observe students and give feedback.)

End-of-Lesson Activities

Now finish your independent work for lesson 32. Raise your hand when you're finished. (Observe students and give feedback.)

a. (Direct students to take out their marking pencils.)

• We're going to check your workbook and textbook items. Remember, if you got an item wrong, make an **X** next to the item.

b. (For each item: Read the item. Call on a student to answer it. If the answer is wrong, say the correct answer. Refer to the Answer Key for the correct answers.)

c. Now use your marking pencil to fix up any items you got wrong. Remember, all mistakes must be fixed up before you hand in your work.

(Present Language Arts lesson 32 after completing Reading lesson 32. See Language Arts Guide.)

EXERCISE 1

VOCABULARY REVIEW

a. You learned a sentence that tells about the new exhibit.
- Everybody, say the sentence. Get ready. (Signal.) *The new exhibit displayed mysterious fish.*

b. I'll say part of the sentence. When I stop, you say the next word. Listen: The new exhibit . . . Everybody, what's the next word? (Signal.) *Displayed.*

c. Listen: The new exhibit displayed . . . Everybody, what's the next word? (Signal.) *Mysterious.*
- Say the whole sentence. Get ready. (Signal.) *The new exhibit displayed mysterious fish.*

d. Listen: The new . . . Everybody, what's the next word? (Signal.) *Exhibit.*

EXERCISE 2

VOCABULARY SENTENCE

a. **Find page 352 at the back of your textbook. ✓**
- Touch sentence 7. ✓
- This is a new vocabulary sentence. It says: She automatically arranged the flowers. Everybody, say that sentence. Get ready. (Signal.) *She automatically arranged the flowers.*
- Close your eyes and say the sentence. Get ready. (Signal.) *She automatically arranged the flowers.*
- (Repeat until firm.)

b. She **arranged** the flowers. That means she put each flower where she wanted it.

c. She did that **automatically.** Things that happen automatically don't require any thought.

d. Listen to the sentence again: She automatically arranged the flowers. Everybody, say that sentence. Get ready. (Signal.) *She automatically arranged the flowers.*

e. What word means that she put things where she wanted them? (Signal.) *Arranged.*
- What word means **without thinking?** (Signal.) *Automatically.*

EXERCISE 3

READING WORDS

Column 1

a. Find lesson 33 in your textbook. ✓
- Touch column 1. ✓
- (Teacher reference:)

1. **however**	4. **volcano**
2. **explodes**	5. **coughing**
3. **underwater**	

- All these words have more than one syllable. The first part of each word is underlined.

b. Word 1. What's the underlined part? (Signal.) *how.*
- What's the whole word? (Signal.) *However.*
- Another word for **but** is **however.** Here's another way of saying **She ate, but she did not feel well: She ate; however, she did not feel well.**
- Everybody, what's another way of saying **She ate, but she did not feel well?** (Signal.) *She ate; however, she did not feel well.*

c. Word 2. What's the underlined part? (Signal.) *ex.*
- What's the whole word? (Signal.) *Explodes.*

d. Word 3. What's the underlined part? (Signal.) *under.*
- What's the whole word? (Signal.) *Underwater.*

e. Word 4. What's the underlined part? (Signal.) *vol.*
- What's the whole word? (Signal.) *Volcano.*

f. Word 5. What's the underlined part? (Signal.) *cough.*
- What's the whole word? (Signal.) *Coughing.*

g. Let's read those words again.
- Word 1. What word? (Signal.) *However.*
- (Repeat for words 2–5.)

h. (Repeat step g until firm.)

Column 2

i. Find column 2. ✓

• (Teacher reference:)

1. **swift**	4. **pours**
2. **glanced**	5. **directed**
3. **thud**	

j. Word 1. What word? (Signal.) *Swift.*
• Spell **swift**. Get ready. (Tap for each letter.) *S-W-I-F-T.*
• Something that is **swift** is very fast. What's another way of saying **The horse was very fast?** (Signal.) *The horse was swift.*

k. Word 2. What word? (Signal.) *Glanced.*
• Spell **glanced.** Get ready. (Tap for each letter.) *G-L-A-N-C-E-D.*

l. Word 3. What word? (Signal.) *Thud.*
• Spell **thud.** Get ready. (Tap for each letter.) *T-H-U-D.*
• (Repeat for words 4 and 5.)

m. Let's read those words again.
• Word 1. What word? (Signal.) *Swift.*
• (Repeat for words 2–5.)

n. (Repeat step m until firm.)

Column 3

o. Find column 3. ✓
• (Teacher reference:)

1. **quake**	4. **prancing**
2. **hardened**	5. **divided**
3. **explosion**	

p. Word 1. What word? (Signal.) *Quake.*
• When something quakes, it shakes very hard.

q. Word 2. What word? (Signal.) *Hardened.*
• Something that becomes hard is called hardened. Everybody, what do you call **ice cream** that becomes hard? (Signal.) *Hardened ice cream.*

r. Word 3. What word? (Signal.) *Explosion.*
• (Repeat for words 4 and 5.)

s. Let's read those words again.
• Word 1. What word? (Signal.) *Quake.*
• (Repeat for words 2–5.)

t. (Repeat step s until firm.)

Individual Turns

(For columns 1–3: Call on individual students, each to read one to three words per turn.)

COMPREHENSION PASSAGE

a. Find part B in your textbook. ✓
• You're going to read the next story about Edna and Carla. First you'll read the information passage. It gives some facts about volcanos and earthquakes.

b. Everybody, touch the title. ✓
• (Call on a student to read the title.) *[Volcanos and Earthquakes.]*
• Everybody, what's the title? (Signal.) *Volcanos and Earthquakes.*

c. (Call on individual students to read the passage, each student reading two or three sentences at a time. Ask the specified questions as the students read.)

Volcanos and Earthquakes
You will be reading about volcanos and earthquakes. A volcano is a mountain that is made of hot melted rock. That rock comes from inside the earth.

• Everybody, what is a volcano made of? (Signal.) *Hot melted rock.*
• Where does the melted rock come from? (Signal.) *Inside the earth.*

The picture shows what a volcano would look like if it were cut in half and we could see the inside.
There is a layer of melted rock in the earth far below the volcano.

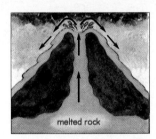

melted rock

• Everybody, touch the words **melted rock** in the picture. ✓

The melted rock moves up to the surface of the earth. When the melted rock pours out onto the surface of the earth, the rock cools and becomes hard. More melted rock piles up on top of the hardened rock. The volcano keeps growing in the shape of a cone.

- Everybody, what's the shape of a volcano? (Signal.) *Cone.*
- The melted rock pours out of the volcano. Then what happens to the rock? (Call on a student. Idea: *The rock cools and gets hard.*)
- Everybody, touch the words **melted rock.** ✓
- Follow the arrows up inside the volcano to the top of the volcano. ✓
- The rock is still melted. Where does it go now? (Call on a student. Idea: *Down the sides of the volcano.*)
- Everybody, use two fingers and follow the melted rock down both sides of the volcano. ✓
- What's happening to it as it moves down the sides of the volcano? (Call on a student. Idea: *It's getting cold and hard.*)

The volcano may pour out great clouds of smoke.

- Everybody, touch the smoke in the picture. ✓

Sometimes a volcano explodes. Sometimes there are earthquakes around volcanos.

| EXERCISE 5 |

STORY READING

a. Find part C in your textbook. ✓
- The error limit for group reading is 12 errors. Read carefully.
b. Everybody, touch the title. ✓
- (Call on a student to read the title.) *[Explosion.]*
- Everybody, what's the title? (Signal.) *Explosion.*
- (Call on individual students to read the story, each student reading two or three sentences at a time. Ask the specified questions as the students read.)

- (Correct errors: Tell the word. Direct the student to reread the sentence.)
- (If the group makes more than 12 errors, direct the students to reread the story.)

Explosion
Carla and Edna were tugging at the vines that were tangled around Carla's leg. The vines were like thick,

sticky ropes that wouldn't let go. Occasionally, Edna glanced up and looked at what was happening in the clearing. The three Triceratops dinosaurs were lined up, waiting for Tyrannosaurus. The giant Tyrannosaurus was prancing around with its mouth wide open. It would move toward the Triceratops dinosaurs and then it would back away. From time to time, it would let out a terrible shriek.

- Why didn't Tyrannosaurus just attack those Triceratops? (Call on a student. Ideas: *There were too many of them; the Triceratops were lined up; the Triceratops had horns and armor.*)
- This next part tells what Edna was thinking and noticing.

The leg is free! Take her hand and help her up. Now run. Keep an eye on her. Let her run in front of you. Push her on the back so that she runs faster. Is that as fast as she can run? Let's get out of here. Keep running. Look, there's the beach. Run. Right down to the edge of the water. Stop. Turn around. Look back. They're not coming after you. Safe. Safe.

- Listen to that part again. Pretend that you are Edna. These are the things you're thinking about:

The leg is free! Take her hand and help her up. Now run. Keep an eye on her. Let her run in front of you. Push her on the back so that she runs faster. Is that as fast as she can run? Let's get out of here. Keep running. Look, there's the beach. Run. Right down to the edge of the water. Stop. Turn around. Look back. They're not coming after you. Safe. Safe.

The girls stood near the edge of the water for a few minutes, listening to the sounds that came from the jungle. The sounds told them that a terrible fight was going on. Tyrannosaurus would shriek from time to time. Then there would be a great thud.

- What could make a great thud? (Call on a student. Idea: *Something heavy falling to the ground.*)

After a few minutes, the shriek of Tyrannosaurus turned into a cry.

- Do you think Tyrannosaurus is winning the fight? (Call on a student. Idea: *No.*)
- Why not? (Call on a student. Idea: *Its shriek turned into a cry, as if it was hurt.*)

Just then the whole island seemed to shake.
 The tops of the trees began to shake. They shook so hard that coconuts fell to the ground. The birds left the island. They were flying to the west. Suddenly the ground shook with such force that Edna fell down. The red beach moved up and then down. It rocked to one side and then to the other.
 "Earthquake!" Carla yelled.

- Why did Edna fall down? (Call on a student. Idea: *Because the ground kept moving.*)

Some trees near the edge of the jungle fell over. As Edna sat up, she noticed a great cloud of smoke over the top of the island. "Volcano," she shouted.
 The smoke boiled and billowed into the air with great speed. Within a few seconds, it had covered the whole eastern part of the sky. And still the smoke cloud was growing.

- Everybody, touch the smoke cloud in the picture on page 162. ✓
- Look at the way those billows of smoke seem to be boiling.

"Come on," Edna shouted. She ran toward the boat. The beach suddenly shook. She stumbled, fell, and slid through the red sand. She got up and ran. The sky was now becoming dark, as the enormous cloud continued to grow.
 The girls reached the boat and turned it over. They pushed it into the shallow water. When they were a few meters from the shore, a terrible quake shook the island.

- What is a terrible quake? (Call on a student. Idea: *When the ground moves a lot.*)

It made a large crack in the sand beach. That crack moved out into the water, right under the boat. Suddenly, Edna noticed that the sand under her feet had disappeared.

- Why did the sand disappear? (Call on a student. Idea: *It fell into a crack.*)

She slipped underwater. The currents were very swift and she felt her feet being pulled into the current.

- What does that mean, the currents were very swift? (Call on a student. Idea: *They were very fast.*)
- The picture shows what happened to Edna. Everybody, is Edna in **deep** or **shallow** water? (Signal.) *Deep.*
- Why? (Call on a student. Idea: *She fell into the crack.*)
- Everybody, did Carla fall into the crack the earthquake made? (Signal.) *No.*
- Touch the crack. ✓
- Edna looks like she's in big trouble.

Edna reached up and tried to grab something. Her hand grabbed a rope that was attached to the front of the boat. She held on to the rope with all her might. The currents were spinning her around, but she kept a tight grip on the rope. Slowly she pulled herself up to the boat. She came out of the water coughing.

- Why was she coughing? (Call on a student. Idea: *She swallowed water.*)

As soon as she caught her breath, she called, "Carla, Carla!" She had salt water in her eyes, so she couldn't see well.

"I'm here," Carla answered.

Edna rubbed her eyes with one hand and looked in the direction of the voice. Carla was sitting in the boat. She helped Edna get into the boat. The sky was so dark now that it was almost like night.

- What was making the sky dark? (Call on a student. Idea: *Smoke from the volcano.*)
- Read the rest of the story to yourself and be ready to answer some questions. Raise your hand when you're finished.

Suddenly, there was a terrible explosion. The explosion had so much force that it seemed to press the air against Edna's face. This pressing feeling came before the sound of the explosion. The sound was like nothing that Edna had ever heard. It was so loud that her ears rang for hours. That explosion had so much force that it knocked down all the trees on the island.

The girls began to row away from the island. "Where are we going to go?" Carla asked.

"I don't know," Edna replied. "I don't know." She did know one thing, however. She knew that she didn't want to be near that island.

- (After all students have raised their hand:) What happened to the volcano? (Call on a student. Idea: *It exploded.*)
- Before Edna **heard** the explosion, she felt something. What did she feel? (Call on a student. Ideas: *A pressing feeling; air pressing against her face.*)

- How loud was the explosion? (Call on a student. Idea: *Very loud.*)
- The story said the explosion was so loud that Edna's ears rang for hours. Your ears actually ring after you hear a very loud sound. You will hear a ringing sound in your head.
- What did the explosion do to the island? (Call on a student. Idea: *Knocked down all the trees.*)
- Everybody, did the girls know where they were going to go? (Signal.) *No.*

EXERCISE 6

PAIRED PRACTICE

You're going to read aloud to your partner. The **B** members will read first. Then the **A** members will read from the star to the end of the story. (Observe students and give feedback.)

End-of-Lesson Activities

INDEPENDENT WORK

Finish your independent work for lesson 33. Raise your hand when you're finished. (Observe students and give feedback.)

WORKCHECK

a. (Direct students to take out their marking pencils.)
- We're going to check your workbook and textbook items. Remember, if you got an item wrong, make an **X** next to the item.
b. (For each item: Read the item. Call on a student to answer it. If the answer is wrong, say the correct answer. Refer to the Answer Key for the correct answers.)
c. Now use your marking pencil to fix up any items you got wrong. Remember, all mistakes must be fixed up before you hand in your work.

LANGUAGE ARTS

(Present Language Arts lesson 33 after completing Reading lesson 33. See Language Arts Guide.)

ACTIVITIES

(Present Activity 5 after completing Reading lesson 33. See Activities Across the Curriculum.)

Lesson 34

VOCABULARY REVIEW

a. Here's the new vocabulary sentence: She automatically arranged the flowers.
- Everybody, say that sentence. Get ready. (Signal.) *She automatically arranged the flowers.*
- (Repeat until firm.)

b. What word means **without thinking?** (Signal.) *Automatically.*
- What word means that she put things where she wanted them? (Signal.) *Arranged.*

READING WORDS

Column 1

a. **Find lesson 34 in your textbook.** ✓
- Touch column 1. ✓
- (Teacher reference:)

1.	approach	4. stomach
2.	bandage	5. mysterious
3.	laundry	6. Tuesday

b. Word 1 is **approach.** What word? (Signal.) *Approach.*
- Spell **approach.** Get ready. (Tap for each letter.) *A-P-P-R-O-A-C-H.*
- When you approach something, you move toward it. Everybody, what's another way of saying **They moved toward the counter?** (Signal.) *They approached the counter.*
- What's another way of saying **They moved toward the lake?** (Signal.) *They approached the lake.*

c. Word 2 is **bandage.** What word? (Signal.) *Bandage.*
- Spell **bandage.** Get ready. (Tap for each letter.) *B-A-N-D-A-G-E.*

d. Word 3 is **laundry.** What word? (Signal.) *Laundry.*
- Spell **laundry.** Get ready. (Tap for each letter.) *L-A-U-N-D-R-Y.*

e. Word 4 is **stomach.** What word? (Signal.) *Stomach.*

- Spell **stomach.** Get ready. (Tap for each letter.) *S-T-O-M-A-C-H.*

f. Word 5 is **mysterious.** What word? (Signal.) *Mysterious.*

g. Word 6 is **Tuesday.** What word? (Signal.) *Tuesday.*

h. Let's read those words again.
- Word 1. What word? (Signal.) *Approach.*
- (Repeat for words 2–6.)

i. (Repeat step h until firm.)

Column 2

j. Find column 2. ✓
- (Teacher reference:)

1.	blisters	4. neither
2.	adventure	5. shadow
3.	unreal	6. supplies

- All these words have more than one syllable. The first syllable of each word is underlined.

k. Word 1. What's the first syllable? (Signal.) *blis.*
- What's the whole word? (Signal.) *Blisters.*
- Blisters are sore bubbles that form from rubbing or burning. You can get blisters on your feet if your shoes do not fit well.

l. Word 2. What's the first syllable? (Signal.) *ad.*
- What's the whole word? (Signal.) *Adventure.*

m. Word 3. What's the first syllable? (Signal.) *un.*
- What's the whole word? (Signal.) *Unreal.*

n. Word 4. What's the first syllable? (Signal.) *nei.*
- What's the whole word? (Signal.) *Neither.*

o. Word 5. What's the first syllable? (Signal.) *shad.*
- What's the whole word? (Signal.) *Shadow.*

p. Word 6. What's the first syllable? (Signal.) *supp.*
- What's the whole word? (Signal.) *Supplies.*

q. Let's read those words again.
- Word 1. What word? (Signal.) *Blisters.*
- (Repeat for words 2–6.)

r. (Repeat step q until firm.)

Column 3

s. Find column 3. ✓
- (Teacher reference:)

1. **throat**	4. **rim**
2. **chew**	5. **beneath**
3. **nor**	6. **honestly**

t. Word 1. What word? (Signal.) *Throat.*
- The front of your neck is sometimes called your throat. Everybody, touch your throat. ✓

u. Word 2. What word? (Signal.) *Chew.*
- (Repeat for words 3–6.)

v. Let's read those words again.
- Word 1. What word? (Signal.) *Throat.*
- (Repeat for words 2–6.)

w. (Repeat step v until firm.)

Individual Turns

(For columns 1–3: Call on individual students, each to read one to three words per turn.)

EXERCISE 3

COMPREHENSION PASSAGE

a. Find part B in your textbook. ✓
- You're going to read the next part of the story about Edna and Carla. First you'll read the information passage. It gives some information about reading underlined words.

b. Everybody, touch the title. ✓
- (Call on a student to read the title.) [*Underlined Words.*]
- Everybody, what's the title? (Signal.) *Underlined Words.*

c. (Call on individual students to read the passage, each student reading two or three sentences at a time. Ask the specified questions as the students read.)

Underlined Words
   Some of the words in stories you will read must be spoken loudly. Here's the rule about words that must be spoken louder than other words: The words that must be spoken louder are underlined.

- Listen to that rule again: The words that must be spoken louder are underlined.
- Everybody, say that rule. Get ready. (Signal.) *The words that must be spoken louder are underlined.*
- (Repeat until firm.)

To the right are sentences with underlined words. Say the underlined words in a loud voice. Say the other words in a soft voice.

- I'll read the first sentence: That is **wrong**.
- Everybody, read that sentence. Get ready. (Signal.) *That is **wrong**.*
- I'll call on you to read the sentences. Remember to say the words that are underlined very loudly. (Call on individual students to read sentences b–i. Students should say the underlined words louder than the other words.)

b. You are a **crook**.
c. I am **not** a crook.
d. I'm **tired** of reading.
e. My name is **Sam**.
f. **My** name is Sam, **too**.
g. This book is **hard**.
h. If you think **your** book is hard, try reading **this** book.
i. You sure like to **talk**.

EXERCISE 4

STORY READING

a. Find part C in your textbook. ✓
- The error limit for group reading is 10 errors. Read carefully.

b. Everybody, touch the title. ✓
- (Call on a student to read the title.) [*Back in the Lifeboat.*]
- Everybody, what's the title? (Signal.) *Back in the Lifeboat.*
- (Call on individual students to read the story, each student reading two or three sentences at a time. Ask the specified questions as the students read.)

- (Correct errors: Tell the word. Direct the student to reread the sentence.)
- (If the group makes more than 10 errors, direct the students to reread the story.)

Back in the Lifeboat
The lifeboat was floating on a bright, shining sea. The sea was so calm that it looked almost as if it was made of glass. When Edna looked down, she could see different colors. Where the water was not very deep, the color was green. Deeper spots were blue, with the deepest spots dark blue.

- Everybody, what color were the shallow places? (Signal.) *Green.*
- What color were the deepest places? (Signal.) *Dark blue.*

The sun pounded down on the girls. Edna had blisters on her hands from rowing, but she was not rowing now. She was just sitting.

- Why would rowing give you blisters? (Call on a student. Idea: *The oars rub against your hands.*)

In the far distance, a billowing cloud rose high into the sky.

- Everybody, what was making that billowing cloud? (Signal.) *The volcano.*

Edna could no longer see the island.
  As she sat there in the lifeboat, she realized that they didn't have supplies.

- What kinds of supplies would they need if they were going to stay on the ocean for very much time? (Call on a student. Ideas: *Fresh water; food; hats to shade them from the sun; etc.*)

There were no other islands in sight. The boat seemed to be drifting in a current, and the current was taking the boat to the west. But how long would it be before the girls spotted another island? What would they do if they didn't find land soon? Edna was already starting to feel thirsty. She tried not to think about it, but when she swallowed, she noticed that her throat was dry.

- Why didn't she just drink water from the ocean? (Call on a student. Ideas: *Ocean water is too salty to drink; it's bad for you.*)

Neither Edna nor Carla had said anything for a long time. The adventure they had on the island was so unreal that Edna didn't know what to say.
  Suddenly, Edna noticed that the boat was drifting faster. When she looked to the west, she got a very sick feeling. In the distance, she could see the rim of a whirlpool.
  The boat was moving toward it, speeding faster and faster, through the green water.

- Everybody, what did Edna see that made her feel sick? (Signal.) *A whirlpool.*
- Was the water here deep or shallow? (Signal.) *Shallow.*
- How do you know? (Call on a student. Idea: *Because the water was green.*)

The rushing sounds got louder and louder. Now the boat was moving over the rim of the whirlpool. "Hang on," Edna shouted, as she grabbed on to the side of the boat. She hung on with all her might. The boat sped around and around and around. Edna looked up at the sky. The clouds seemed to be spinning around and around. The boat was going ✦ deeper and deeper into the whirlpool.
  Now Edna could see a great cone of water above the boat. The boat was spinning so fast that its force pressed Edna against the bottom of the boat. She felt sick and dizzy. She squeezed her eyes closed as tightly as she could. Then the sounds seemed to fade away and everything went dark.

● ● ●

- Listen to that part of the story again:
    The rushing sounds got louder and louder. Now the boat was moving over the rim of the whirlpool. "Hang on," Edna shouted, as she grabbed on to the side of the boat. She hung on with all her might. The boat sped around

and around and around. Edna looked up at the sky. The clouds seemed to be spinning around and around. The boat was going deeper and deeper into the whirlpool.

Now Edna could see a great cone of water above the boat. The boat was spinning so fast that its force pressed Edna against the bottom of the boat. She felt sick and dizzy. She squeezed her eyes closed as tightly as she could. Then the sounds seemed to fade away and everything went dark.

- I think everything went dark because she passed out. Everybody, was the boat very far down in the whirlpool when she passed out? (Signal.) *Yes.*
- How fast was it moving? (Call on a student. Ideas: *So fast it pressed Edna against the bottom of the boat; very fast.*)
- Everybody, what do the three dots in the story tell you? (Signal.) *Part of the story is missing.*

Heat. Terrible heat. "Where am I?" Edna said aloud. Then she realized that she was lying in the bottom of the lifeboat. The sun was beating down on her face. The boat was not moving. As she sat up, she realized that there was some water in the bottom of the boat. The water was very warm.

- Everybody, was the boat in the whirlpool now? (Signal.) *No.*
- How fast was it moving? (Call on a student. Idea: *It wasn't moving.*)
- Why was there water in the bottom of the boat? (Call on a student. Idea: *Water from the whirlpool got in the boat.*)
- That water was warm because it had been sitting in the bottom of the boat for a long time.

Edna looked over at Carla. "Are you okay?" Edna asked.

Carla looked very sick. "I think so," she said. "What happened?"

"I don't know," Edna answered. "We were in a whirlpool. That's the last thing I remember. Are we dead?"

- Why would Edna think that they were dead? (Call on a student. Ideas: *She thought they drowned in the whirlpool; because she had passed out; the last thing they remembered was the whirlpool.*)

"I don't think we're dead," Carla replied. "But I don't remember how we got out of the whirlpool. I passed out."

❀"I passed out, too," Edna said. Slowly, she turned around and looked at the ocean. It was perfectly calm. She didn't see any signs of whirlpools. And she didn't see any billowing clouds that marked the island. "We must be far from the island," Edna said.

- What do you do when you pass out? (Call on a student. Ideas: *You faint; everything goes black and silent.*)
- Why did she think they were far from the island? (Call on a student. Idea: *She didn't see any billowing clouds.*)
- Read the rest of the story to yourself and be ready to answer some questions. Raise your hand when you're finished.

Edna looked over the side of the boat, into the water. It was very dark blue. She could see some fish swimming around beneath the boat. They seemed to like staying in the shadow of the boat. As Edna looked at the fish, she remembered something she had once read. Fish have a lot of fresh water in them. If you chew on raw fish, you can squeeze the water ❀ out. Edna didn't like the idea of chewing on raw fish, but she knew that without water, she and Carla would not last for more than a few more hours in the hot sun.

- (After all students have raised their hand:) What fact had Edna remembered about fish? (Call on a student. Idea: *They contain a lot of fresh water.*)
- How could someone get that fresh water out of the fish? (Call on a student. Idea: *Chew on a raw fish.*)

- Everybody, did Edna look forward to chewing on raw fish? **(Signal.)** *No.*
- If Edna and Carla are going to chew on raw fish, what will they have to do first? **(Call on a student. Idea:** *Catch the fish.***)**
- I wonder how they plan to do that.

EXERCISE 5
PAIRED PRACTICE

You're going to read aloud to your partner. The **A** members will read first. Then the **B** members will read from the star to the end of the story.
(Observe students and give feedback.)

End-of-Lesson Activities

INDEPENDENT WORK

Now finish your independent work for lesson 34. Raise your hand when you're finished. **(Observe students and give feedback.)**

WORKCHECK

a. **(Direct students to take out their marking pencils.)**
- We're going to check your workbook and textbook items. Remember, if you got an item wrong, make an **X** next to the item.
b. **(For each item: Read the item. Call on a student to answer it. If the answer is wrong, say the correct answer. Refer to the Answer Key for the correct answers.)**
c. Now use your marking pencil to fix up any items you got wrong. Remember, all mistakes must be fixed up before you hand in your work.

LANGUAGE ARTS

(Present Language Arts lesson 34 after completing Reading lesson 34. See Language Arts Guide.)

> *Note:* A special project occurs after lesson 35. See page 190 for the materials you'll need.

VOCABULARY REVIEW

a. You learned a sentence that tells what the rim of the volcano did.
- Everybody, say that sentence. Get ready. (Signal.) *The rim of the volcano exploded.*
- (Repeat until firm.)

b. You learned a sentence that tells about the new exhibit.
- Everybody, say that sentence. Get ready. (Signal.) *The new exhibit displayed mysterious fish.*
- (Repeat until firm.)

c. Here's the last sentence you learned: She automatically arranged the flowers.
- Everybody, say that sentence. Get ready. (Signal.) *She automatically arranged the flowers.*
- (Repeat until firm.)

d. What word means that she put things where she wanted them? (Signal.) *Arranged.*
- What word means **without thinking?** (Signal.) *Automatically.*

e. Once more. Say the sentence that tells about what she automatically did. Get ready. (Signal.) *She automatically arranged the flowers.*

READING WORDS

Column 1

a. **Find lesson 35 in your textbook.** ✓
- Touch column 1. ✓
- (Teacher reference:)

1. **actually**	4. **Leonard**
2. **exhibit**	5. **character**
3. **museum**	6. **embarrassed**

b. Word 1 is **actually.** What word? (Signal.) *Actually.*
- Spell **actually.** Get ready. (Tap for each letter.) *A-C-T-U-A-L-L-Y.*

c. Word 2 is **exhibit.** What word? (Signal.) *Exhibit.*

- Spell **exhibit.** Get ready. (Tap for each letter.) *E-X-H-I-B-I-T.*

d. Word 3 is **museum.** What word? (Signal.) *Museum.*
- Spell **museum.** Get ready. (Tap for each letter.) *M-U-S-E-U-M.*

- A museum is a place with many different kinds of exhibits—rocks, fish, and hundreds of other things. Everybody, what do we call a place that has many different kinds of exhibits? (Signal.) *Museum.*

e. Word 4 is **Leonard.** What word? (Signal.) *Leonard.*
- Spell **Leonard.** Get ready. (Tap for each letter.) *L-E-O-N-A-R-D.*

f. Word 5 is **character.** What word? (Signal.) *Character.*
- When you say that somebody is a character, you mean the person is unusual. Everybody, what's another way of saying **Millie is unusual?** (Signal.) *Millie is a character.*
- What's another way of saying **The boy was unusual?** (Signal.) *The boy was a character.*

g. Word 6 is **embarrassed.** What word? (Signal.) *Embarrassed.*
- When you are embarrassed, you feel foolish or silly. If you drop your cake at a party, you might feel embarrassed.

h. Let's read those words again.
- Word 1. What word? (Signal.) *Actually.*
- (Repeat for words 2–6.)

i. (Repeat step h until firm.)

Column 2

j. Find column 2. ✓
- (Teacher reference:)

1. **underwater**	3. **somehow**
2. **overboard**	4. **automobile**

- All these words are compound words.

k. Word 1. What word? (Signal.) *Underwater.*
- (Repeat for words 2–4.)

l. Let's read those words again.
- Word 1. What word? (Signal.) *Underwater.*
- (Repeat for words 2–4.)

m. (Repeat step l until firm.)

Column 3

n. Find column 3. ✓
- (Teacher reference:)

1. directed	5. sandwiches
2. divided	6. honestly
3. bandages	7. handful
4. approached	

- All these words have endings.
o. Word 1. What word? (Signal.) *Directed.*
- When you direct people to do something, you order them to do it. Everybody, what's another way of saying **He ordered them to leave the room?** (Signal.) *He directed them to leave the room.*
p. Word 2. What word? (Signal.) *Divided.*
- Things that are divided are separated into parts. If the money was separated into four parts, the money was divided into four parts. Everybody, what's another way of saying **The pie was separated into six parts?** (Signal.) *The pie was divided into six parts.*
q. Word 3. What word? (Signal.) *Bandages.*
- (Repeat for words 4–7.)
r. Let's read those words again.
- Word 1. What word? (Signal.) *Directed.*
- (Repeat for words 2–7.)
s. (Repeat step r until firm.)

Column 4

t. Find column 4. ✓
- (Teacher reference:)

1. Monday	5. stomach
2. laundry	6. Tuesday
3. yesterday	7. possible
4. mysterious	

u. Word 1. What word? (Signal.) *Monday.*
- (Repeat for words 2–7.)
v. Let's read those words again.
- Word 1. What word? (Signal.) *Monday.*
- (Repeat for words 2–7.)
w. (Repeat step v until firm.)

Individual Turns

(For columns 1–4: Call on individual students, each to read one to three words per turn.)

STORY READING

a. Find part B in your textbook. ✓
- The error limit for group reading is 13 errors. Read carefully.
b. Everybody, touch the title. ✓
- (Call on a student to read the title.) [*Saved.*]
- Everybody, what's the title? (Signal.) *Saved.*
- (Call on individual students to read the story, each student reading two or three sentences at a time. Ask the specified questions as the students read.)

- (Correct errors: Tell the word. Direct the student to reread the sentence.)
- (If the group makes more than 13 errors, direct the students to reread the story.)

Saved

Edna realized that she and Carla needed water. Without it, they would not last for more than a few more hours. Edna moved to the front of the boat and started to look for fishing gear. But then she noticed a slim line of smoke in the distance. It wasn't the billowing smoke that came from the island. "A ship," Edna said as she stood up. "I think there's a ship over there." She pointed.

Carla stood up. "You're right. I can see it, and I think it's coming in this direction."

- What kind of smoke did Edna see in the distance? (Call on a student. Ideas: *Smoke from the ship; a slim line.*)
- How did she know that it wasn't the smoke from the island? (Call on a student. Idea: *Because it wasn't a billowing cloud.*)

The next hour seemed longer than any hour Edna ever remembered. Edna didn't do anything but watch the approaching ship. She felt that if she stopped watching it, it would disappear. As it got closer, she recognized the ship. "That's Dad's ship," she shouted. "They're coming back for us."

• • •

- Everybody, how long did Edna and Carla watch the ship? (Signal.) *An hour.*
- What was the only thing Edna did during that hour? (Call on a student. Idea: *Watched the approaching ship.*)
- Whose ship was it? (Call on a student. Idea: *Captain Parker's.*)
- Everybody, what do those three dots tell you? (Signal.) *A part of the story is missing.*

The crew members helped Edna and Carla onto the deck of the ship.

- What part of the story is missing? (Call on a student. Idea: *The ship reaching the lifeboat.*)

Captain Parker put his arms around the girls. Then Edna started to cry. She didn't want to cry. During the whole adventure, she hadn't cried. But now, as her dad hugged her, she couldn't help it. Tears started to run down her cheeks. "Dad," she said. She was so glad to be back, and she was ashamed for not paying attention to what her father had said.

- What did she do that made her ashamed? (Call on a student. Ideas: *She played in the lifeboat; she didn't pay attention to what her father said.*)

"I'm glad we found you," Captain Parker said. "Now let's get you taken care of."

- The girls had been in the lifeboat for a while. What kinds of things would need to be taken care of? (Call on individual students. Ideas: *They needed water; food; medicine for blisters and sunburn;* etc.)

Both girls had blisters on their hands from rowing. They were both badly sunburned. And they were very hungry and thirsty. But within an hour, they were fixed up. Now the girls had burn cream on their noses. They had little bandages on their hands. And they had full stomachs. Edna drank three glasses of juice. She ate two sandwiches. And she almost finished a huge piece of pie.

But she couldn't make it through that pie. She pushed herself away from the table and stood up. "I'm full," she said.

"I'd like to talk with you girls," Captain Parker said.

- What do you think he wants to talk about? (Call on a student. Idea: *What happened to the girls.*)

The girls followed him to the map room. Captain Parker told them to sit down. "All right," he said. "What happened?"

"I know we shouldn't have been playing around with the lifeboat," Carla said. "But I'm the one to blame. Edna didn't ✦ want to do it. It was my idea."

"Just tell me what happened," Captain Parker said. So the girls told the whole story: how the boat fell into the water, how they got sucked into the whirlpool, how they found the mysterious island, and what happened on the island. After the girls had finished telling about the second whirlpool, Carla said, "I don't know how we got out of the whirlpool, but we did, somehow. Then the next thing we knew, your ship was coming back toward us."

"That's some story," Captain Parker said. "Do you honestly think all those things happened?"

- Everybody, does he sound as if he believes the story? (Signal.) *No.*

"Oh yeah," Edna said. "We're not making it up. It really happened, the whole thing."

Then Carla said, "Don't you believe us?"

Captain Parker smiled. "From the way you tell the story, I think you believe it. But I'm not sure it really happened that way."

"It did happen, Dad," Edna said. "It really did. Everything we told you is true."

"Well then, tell me this," Captain Parker said. "What day of the week was it when you went overboard?"

"Monday," Edna said.

"And you spent a night on the island. Is that correct?"

"Yes," Edna agreed.

Captain Parker said, "So what day would that make today?"

"Today is Tuesday," Edna said.

Captain Parker opened a door and said to a crew member, "Tell these girls what day today is."

The man looked a little puzzled. "Monday," he said.

- How could it still be Monday? (Call on a student. Ideas: *None of what the girls said was true; don't know.*)

"Monday?" Edna said. "No, that was yesterday. Today is Tuesday."

The young crew member smiled and said, "What is this, some kind of joke?"

Captain Parker said, "No, everything is all right. Thank you."

- Read the rest of the story to yourself and be ready to answer some questions. Raise your hand when you're finished.

Carla said to Edna, "It can't be Monday."

"But it is Monday," Captain Parker said. "You may have had too much sun out there. But it has only been five hours since you left the ship."

"But it really happened, Dad," Edna said.

Later that afternoon, Edna was taking her wet clothes to the laundry room. As she approached the laundry room, she checked the pockets of her pants. She turned one pocket inside out and suddenly she stopped. About a handful of wet red sand fell onto the deck of the ship. If the adventure hadn't happened, how did that sand get into her pocket?

Edna never found the answer to that question.

- (After all students have raised their hand:) Something happened to make Edna think that the adventure really did happen. What was that? (Call on a student. Idea: *She found red sand in her pocket.*)
- Everybody, where is the only place she could have gotten that sand? (Signal.) *The island.*
- So if the sand was in her pocket, what does that mean? (Call on a student. Idea: *She was on the island.*)
- Everybody, did she ever find out the answer to how the sand got in her pocket? (Signal.) *No.*
- This story was a real mystery.

- Look at the picture. ✓
- What is that strange little animal in the picture and where do you think it came from? (Call on a student. Idea: *A tiny dinosaur from the island.*)

EXERCISE 4

READING CHECKOUTS

> **Note:** There is a reading checkout in this lesson; therefore, there is no paired practice.

a. Today is a reading-checkout day. While you're doing your independent work, I'm going to call on you one at a time to read part of the story from lesson 34. When I call you to come and do your checkout, bring your thermometer chart.

• Remember, you pass the checkout by reading the passage in less than a minute without making more than 2 mistakes. And when you pass the checkout, you'll color the space for lesson 35 on your thermometer chart.

b. (Call on individual students to read the portion of story 34 marked with ✿.)

• (Time the student. Note words that are missed and total number of words read.)

• (Teacher reference:)

> ✿ **"I passed out, too," Edna said. Slowly, she turned around and looked at the ocean. It was perfectly calm. She didn't see any signs of whirlpools. And she didn't see any billowing clouds that marked the island. "We must be far from the island," Edna said.**
>
> **Edna looked over the [50] side of the boat, into the water. It was very dark blue. She could see some fish swimming around beneath the boat. They seemed to [75] like staying in the shadow of the boat. As Edna looked at the fish, she remembered something she had once read. Fish have a lot [100] of fresh water in them. If you chew on raw fish, you can squeeze the ✿ [115] water out.**

• (If the student reads the passage in one minute or less and makes no more than 2 errors, direct the student to color in the space for lesson 35 on the thermometer chart.)

• (If the student makes any mistakes, point to each word that was misread and identify it.)

• (If the student does not meet the rate-error criterion for the passage, direct the student to practice reading the story with the student's assigned partner.)

End-of-Lesson Activities

INDEPENDENT WORK

Now finish your independent work for lesson 35. Raise your hand when you're finished. (Observe students and give feedback.)

WORKCHECK

a. (Direct students to take out their marking pencils.)

• We're going to check your workbook and textbook items. Remember, if you got an item wrong, make an **X** next to the item.

b. (For each item: Read the item. Call on a student to answer it. If the answer is wrong, say the correct answer. Refer to the Answer Key for the correct answers.)

c. Now use your marking pencil to fix up any items you got wrong. Remember, all mistakes must be fixed up before you hand in your work.

LANGUAGE ARTS

(Present Language Arts lesson 35 after completing Reading lesson 35. See Language Arts Guide.)

Special Project

Materials: Reference materials (books on dinosaurs, books on the Mesozoic era, encyclopedias, CD-ROMs) and poster-making supplies (butcher paper or poster board, markers, crayons, paints, scissors, paste, magazines for pictures)

a. Everybody, find page 178 in your textbook. ✓
  • Touch the underlined word near the end of the passage. ✓
  • That word is **Apatosaurus.** What word? (Signal.) *Apatosaurus.*
  • We're going to read these instructions for a dinosaur project. (Call on individual students to read the instructions.)
  • (Teacher reference:)

Special Project

For today's lesson, you will do a project on dinosaurs. You will make a wall chart that shows some of the great dinosaurs.

Dinosaurs lived during the Mesozoic. The Mesozoic was divided into three parts: The early Mesozoic, the middle Mesozoic, and the late Mesozoic. Tyrannosaurus lived in the late Mesozoic.

Make your chart show three layers. In the bottom layer, show pictures of some dinosaurs that lived in the early Mesozoic. Try to find at least two dinosaurs from the early Mesozoic. Write facts about the dinosaurs that you show on your chart. Tell each dinosaur's name, what it ate, and how big it was.

Do the same thing for the dinosaurs of the middle Mesozoic. Find at least four dinosaurs. One of them may be Apatosaurus, which was much, much bigger than Tyrannosaurus or Triceratops. Put their pictures in the middle layer of the chart. Write facts that tell their names, what they ate, and how big they were.

Do the same thing for the dinosaurs of the late Mesozoic. Find facts and pictures for at least four dinosaurs.

---

b. We'll form teams for this project and each team will be responsible for part of the project. One team will find facts and pictures about the different dinosaurs that lived in the early Mesozoic. One team will find out about the dinosaurs that lived in the middle Mesozoic. One team will find out about the dinosaurs that lived in the late Mesozoic.
c. (Assign the students to the different teams. The teams should write their facts on cards before putting them on the wall chart.)
d. (Help the teams find reference materials [CD-ROMs, books on dinosaurs, books on the Mesozoic era, encyclopedias, *National Geographic* magazines].)
e. (After each team presents its pictures and facts, help the students design their part of the display. The display should be divided into three layers. Each layer should contain the appropriate pictures and facts.)
f. (When the display is complete, praise the teams. Then tell all the students to learn the facts that are shown on the chart. Test the students on the chart information.)
g. (Possibly invite another class for a presentation on dinosaurs. A representative from each team would tell about the part of the Mesozoic that team researched.)

	Lesson 36	**Lesson 37**	**Lesson 38**	**Lesson 39**	**Lesson 40**
Lesson Events	**Vocabulary Sentence** Vocabulary Sentence Reading Words Comprehension Passage Story Reading Paired Practice Independent Work Language Arts	Vocabulary Sentence Reading Words Story Reading Paired Practice Study Item Independent Work Workcheck Language Arts	Vocabulary Sentences Reading Words Story Reading Paired Practice Study Item Independent Work Workcheck Language Arts	**Vocabulary Sentence** Vocabulary Sentence Reading Words Story Reading Paired Practice Independent Work Workcheck Language Arts	Fact Game Reading Checkouts Test Marking the Test Test Remedies Literature Lesson Language Arts
Vocabulary Sentence	**#8: They were impressed by her large vocabulary.** #7: She automatically arranged the flowers.	#8: They were impressed by her large vocabulary.	sentence #6 sentence #7 sentence #8	**#9: He responded to her clever solution.** #8: They were impressed by her large vocabulary.	
Reading Words: Word Types	modeled words multi-syllable words mixed words	multi-syllable words compound words words with endings mixed words	modeled words multi-syllable words	modeled words multi-syllable words mixed words	
New Vocabulary	electricity expression possible darted invent pace	sharp-minded	invisible suggest explanation chuckled	assignment arithmetic checker	
Comprehension Passage	*Inventing*				
Story	*Grandmother Esther*	*Grandmother Esther's Inventions*	*Trying to Discover Needs*	*Bad Ideas*	
Skill Items	Vocabulary Vocabulary sentences		Vocabulary sentence	Sequencing Vocabulary sentences	Test: Vocabulary sentences # 6, 7, 8
Special Materials		Reference materials	Reference materials		Thermometer charts, dice, Fact Game 40, Fact Game Answer Key, scorecard sheets, *materials for literature lesson
Special Projects/ Activities	Activity after lesson 36				

* Literature anthology; blackline masters 4A, 4B, 4C, and 4D; lined paper; drawing materials. Optional: Research resources (computer, encyclopedia, etc.).

Lesson 36

VOCABULARY

a. **Find page 352 in your textbook.** ✓
- Touch sentence 8. ✓
- This is a new vocabulary sentence. It says: They were impressed by her large vocabulary. Everybody, say that sentence. Get ready. (Signal.) *They were impressed by her large vocabulary.*
- Close your eyes and say the sentence. Get ready. (Signal.) *They were impressed by her large vocabulary.*
- (Repeat until firm.)

b. The sentence says they were **impressed** by something. When you're impressed by something, you think it is very good.

c. They were impressed by her large **vocabulary.** A person's vocabulary is all the words the person knows. The sentence says she had a **large** vocabulary. That means she knew a large number of words. Everybody, what word refers to all the words a person knows? (Signal.) *Vocabulary.*

d. Listen to the sentence again: They were impressed by her large vocabulary. Everybody, say that sentence. Get ready. (Signal.) *They were impressed by her large vocabulary.*

e. What word refers to all the words a person knows? (Signal.) *Vocabulary.*
- What word means they thought her vocabulary was very good? (Signal.) *Impressed.*

EXERCISE 2

VOCABULARY REVIEW

a. You learned a sentence that tells what she automatically did.
- Everybody, say that sentence. Get ready. (Signal.) *She automatically arranged the flowers.*
- (Repeat until firm.)

b. I'll say part of that sentence. When I stop, you say the next word. Listen: She automatically . . . Everybody, what's the next word? (Signal.) *Arranged.*

c. Listen: She . . . Everybody, what's the next word? (Signal.) *Automatically.*
- Say the whole sentence. Get ready. (Signal.) *She automatically arranged the flowers.*

EXERCISE 3

READING WORDS

Column 1

a. Find lesson 36 in your textbook. ✓
- Touch column 1. ✓
- (Teacher reference:)

1. arrange	4. Esther
2. magazine	5. electricity
3. material	6. expression

b. Word 1 is **arrange.** What word? (Signal.) *Arrange.*
- Spell **arrange.** Get ready. (Tap for each letter.) *A-R-R-A-N-G-E.*

c. Word 2 is **magazine.** What word? (Signal.) *Magazine.*
- Spell **magazine.** Get ready. (Tap for each letter.) *M-A-G-A-Z-I-N-E.*

d. Word 3 is **material.** What word? (Signal.) *Material.*
- Spell **material.** Get ready. (Tap for each letter.) *M-A-T-E-R-I-A-L.*

e. Word 4 is **Esther.** What word? (Signal.) *Esther.*
- Spell **Esther.** Get ready. (Tap for each letter.) *E-S-T-H-E-R.*

f. Word 5 is **electricity.** What word? (Signal.) *Electricity.*
- Electricity is the power that runs appliances like washing machines and televisions. Everybody, what's the name of the power that runs televisions? (Signal.) *Electricity.*

g. Word 6 is **expression.** What word? (Signal.) *Expression.*
- The expression on your face shows what you're feeling. A puzzled expression means that you are puzzled or not sure. A happy expression means that you're happy.

h. Let's read those words again, the fast way.
- Word 1. What word? (Signal.) *Arrange.*
- (Repeat for: **2. magazine, 3. material, 4. Esther, 5. electricity, 6. expression.**)
i. (Repeat step h until firm.)

Column 2

j. Find column 2. ✓
- (Teacher reference:)

1. <u>poss</u>ible	4. <u>auto</u>mobile
2. <u>every</u>one	5. <u>dis</u>play
3. <u>grand</u>mother	6. <u>ex</u>hibit

- All these words have more than one syllable. The first part of each word is underlined.
k. Word 1. What's the underlined part? (Signal.) *poss.*
- What's the whole word? (Signal.) *Possible.*
- Things that are possible are things that could happen. Everybody, is it possible for you to stand up and clap your hands? (Signal.) *Yes.*
- Is it possible for you to spread your arms and fly like a bird? (Signal.) *No.*
l. Word 2. What's the underlined part? (Signal.) *every.*
- What's the whole word? (Signal.) *Everyone.*
m. Word 3. What's the underlined part? (Signal.) *grand.*
- What's the whole word? (Signal.) *Grandmother.*
n. Word 4. What's the underlined part? (Signal.) *auto.*
- What's the whole word? (Signal.) *Automobile.*
o. Word 5. What's the underlined part? (Signal.) *dis.*
- What's the whole word? (Signal.) *Display.*
p. Word 6. What's the underlined part? (Signal.) *ex.*
- What's the whole word? (Signal.) *Exhibit.*
q. Let's read those words again.
- Word 1. What word? (Signal.) *Possible.*
- (Repeat for words 2–6.)
r. (Repeat step q until firm.)

Column 3

s. Find column 3. ✓
- (Teacher reference:)

1. embarrassed	5. outing
2. darted	6. pencils
3. actually	7. crazier
4. hurrying	

t. Word 1. What word? (Signal.) *Embarrassed.*
u. Word 2. What word? (Signal.) *Darted.*
- When something darts around, it moves like a dart, very fast and straight.
v. Word 3. What word? (Signal.) *Actually.*
- (Repeat for words 4–7.)
w. Let's read those words again.
- Word 1. What word? (Signal.) *Embarrassed.*
- (Repeat for words 2–7.)
x. (Repeat step w until firm.)

Column 4

y. Find column 4. ✓
- (Teacher reference:)

1. invent	4. Leonard
2. pace	5. museum
3. character	6. speech

z. Word 1 is **invent.** What word? (Signal.) *Invent.*
- When a person makes an object for the very first time, the person **invents** the object.
a. Word 2. What word? (Signal.) *Pace.*
- The pace of something is the speed of that thing. If something is fast, it moves at a fast pace.
b. Word 3. What word? (Signal.) *Character.*
- (Repeat for words 4–6.)
c. Let's read those words again.
- Word 1. What word? (Signal.) *Invent.*
- (Repeat for words 2–6.)
d. (Repeat step c until firm.)

Individual Turns

(For columns 1–4: Call on individual students, each to read one to three words per turn.)

COMPREHENSION PASSAGE

a. Find part B in your textbook. ✓
- You're going to start a new story about a boy named Leonard. First you'll read the information passage. It gives some facts about inventing.

b. Everybody, touch the title. ✓
- (Call on a student to read the title.) [Inventing.]
- Everybody, what's the title? (Signal.) *Inventing.*

c. (Call on individual students to read the passage, each student reading two or three sentences at a time. Ask the specified questions as the students read.)

Inventing

You live in a world that is filled with things that are made by humans. In this world are cars and airplanes and telephones and books. There are chairs and tables and stoves and dishes. There are thousands of things that you use every day.

Each of these things was <u>invented</u>. That means that somebody <u>made</u> the object for the first time.

- When a person invents something, what does that person do? (Call on a student. Idea: *Makes an object for the first time.*)

The person who made the first automobile invented the automobile. The person who made the first television invented the television. Remember, when somebody makes an object for the first time, the person invents that object. The object the person makes is called the invention. The first airplane was an invention. The first telephone was an invention.

- Everybody, what do we call the object that is made for the first time? (Signal.) *Invention.*
- When a person makes that object for the first time, what do we say the person did? (Signal.) *Invented the object.*
- Name some things that were invented. (Call on individual students. Ideas: *Car, refrigerator, telephone, light bulb,* etc.)

Everything that is made by humans was invented by somebody. At one time, there were no cars, light bulbs or glass windows. People didn't know how to make these things, because nobody had invented them yet.

Most of the things that you use every day were invented after the year 1800. Here are just some of the things that people did not have before 1800: trains, trucks, cars, airplanes, bicycles, telephones, radios, televisions, movies, tape recorders, computers, electric appliances like washing machines, toasters, refrigerators or dishwashers.

- Everybody, most of the things we use every day were invented after what year? (Signal.) *1800.*
- Name some of the things you wouldn't have if you lived before 1800. (Call on individual students. Ideas: *Radio, tape recorder, dishwasher,* etc.)

STORY READING

a. Find part C in your textbook. ✓
- The error limit for group reading is 10 errors. Read carefully.

b. Everybody, touch the title. ✓
- (Call on a student to read the title.) [Grandmother Esther.]
- Everybody, what's the title? (Signal.) *Grandmother Esther.*
- Everybody, who is going to be in this story? (Signal.) *Grandmother Esther.*
- (Call on individual students to read the story, each student reading two or three sentences at a time. Ask the specified questions as the students read.)

- (Correct errors: Tell the word. Direct the student to reread the sentence.)
- (If the group makes more than 10 errors, direct the students to reread the story.)

Grandmother Esther

The year was 1980. Leonard was 12 years old. He was at the museum with his grandmother.

- Everybody, in what year did this story take place? (Signal.) *1980.*
- Is that year in the **past** or the **future?** (Signal.) *Past.*
- How old was Leonard in 1980? (Signal.) *12.*
- Where were Leonard and his grandmother? (Signal.) *At the museum.*
- What kinds of things do you see in a museum? (Call on individual students. Ideas: *Paintings; jewelry; pottery; animal skeletons; things from many years ago; exhibits; displays;* etc.)

Going places with Grandmother Esther was fun, but it was also embarrassing. It was embarrassing because Grandmother Esther had a lot to say, and she talked in a very loud voice. She talked the loudest and the longest about inventing. So when Leonard went to the museum with Grandmother Esther, he was ready to hear a lot of loud talk about inventing.

- What was Grandmother Esther going to talk about? (Call on a student. Idea: *Inventing.*)

In the museum, they spent a little time looking at the displays of wild animals and the dinosaurs. Leonard wanted to spend more time here, but Grandmother Esther kept hurrying Leonard along. She would say, "Let's keep moving or we won't see all the things we want to look at in the other parts of the museum."

- What do you think was in the parts of the museum that she wanted to see? (Call on a student. Ideas: *Inventions; the first cars; the first radios;* etc.)

Leonard knew what parts of the museum his grandmother was talking about—the displays of the first automobiles, the first airplanes, the first computers and other things, such as the first radios.

- Name some of the displays Grandmother Esther was interested in. (Call on a student. Ideas: *Early cars, planes, computers, radios,* etc.)

So Grandmother Esther swept Leonard through the display of Egypt 4 thousand years ago.

- Everybody, did they spend much time looking at this display? (Signal.) *No.*

She darted through the exhibit of the cave people and through the display of horses. She slowed her pace as the two approached the display of the first airplanes.

- Everybody, did she like the display of horses and the cave people? (Signal.) *No.*
- How do you know? (Call on a student. Idea: *She hurried through them.*)
- Everybody, did she like the display of the first airplanes? (Signal.) *Yes.*
- How do you know? (Call on a student. Idea: *She slowed down to look at them.*)

As they walked through the large doorway of the exhibit hall, she announced, "Here is where we see the work of the most important people in the world—the inventors."
Leonard listened to his grandmother's speech about inventors. He nodded and very quietly said, "Yes." He was hoping that she might talk more softly if he talked softly, so he spoke in a voice that was almost a whisper. But it didn't work. Grandmother Esther's voice echoed across the large display hall.

- Why did he speak in a voice that was almost a whisper? (Call on a student. Idea: *He was hoping that if he whispered, his grandmother would whisper, too.*)
- Everybody, did his plan work? (Signal.) *No.*
- How do you know her voice was very loud? (Call on a student. Idea: *It echoed.*)

"Without inventors there would be nothing," she said. Other people were starting to look at her and Leonard. Leonard could feel his ears getting hot from embarrassment.
"Where would we be today without inventors?" ★ **she asked herself**

> **loudly. Then she answered her own question: "We would have no planes because nobody would invent them. We would have no electric lights, no radios. We would not be able to build buildings like this one. We would still be living in <u>caves</u>!"**

- Say that last sentence the way she said it. (Call on a student. Student should emphasize the word **caves** and speak in a loud voice.)
- Everybody, who does she think changed things so that we don't live in caves anymore? (Signal.) *Inventors.*

> **Grandmother Esther said the word <u>caves</u> so loudly that a guard at the other end of the exhibit hall turned around and stared at her. She marched to the display of the first airplane and pointed to it. "This was a great invention," she announced. "The two men who invented it knew that a machine could fly through the air. But other people didn't believe them. They said the inventors were <u>crazy</u> for working on a flying machine. But the inventors didn't give up. They invented a machine that actually flew. Once others saw that it was possible for machines to fly, they began inventing better flying machines. They invented faster machines and bigger machines. <u>Look</u> at them!" She waved her arm in the direction of the other airplanes on display. Nearly everyone in the hall looked at the rows of planes.**

- The picture on page 181 shows Grandmother Esther and Leonard in the exhibit hall.
- Everybody, touch the earliest airplane on display. ✓
- Touch the guard at the far end of the exhibit hall. ✓

- Who are all the people listening to? (Signal.) *Grandmother Esther.*
- How does Leonard feel? (Call on a student. Idea: *Embarrassed.*)
- Everybody, touch the first plane and move down the row. Look at how the planes changed. ✓
- Read the rest of the story to yourself and be ready to answer some questions. Raise your hand when you're finished.

> **Grandmother Esther marched down the center aisle of the display. In a great voice, she said, "But none of these later planes would be possible without the first one. And the first one would not have been possible without the inventors— those brave men who didn't listen to other people but who <u>knew</u> that we don't have to stand with our feet stuck in the mud. We can fly with the birds!"**
>
> **The sound of her voice echoed through the hall. Then, one of the people who had been listening to her began to clap. Then others clapped. Soon there was a loud sound of clapping. Even the guard was clapping. Leonard was very embarrassed, but he didn't want to be the only one not clapping. So he clapped, too. He said to himself, "My grandmother is a real character."**

- (After all students have raised their hand:) Grandmother Esther made a big speech about the men who invented the first airplane. Everybody, then what did the people who were listening do? (Signal.) *Clapped.*
- Who was the last person to start clapping? (Signal.) *Leonard.*
- How did he feel? (Call on a student. Idea: *Embarrassed.*)
- He said to himself, "My grandmother is a real character." What does that mean? (Call on a student. Ideas: *She is different from other people; she has a strong personality.*)
- Grandmother Esther was trying to persuade people to think about inventors in a certain way. What did she want them to believe about inventors? (Call on a student. Idea: *That they're the most important people in the world.*)

- She did at least 2 things to try to persuade the people who could hear her. Here's one thing she did: She tried to persuade them with **the way** she talked. What way was that? (Call on a student. Idea: *Loudly.*)
- Why could speaking loudly be better at persuading than speaking in a soft voice? (Call on a student. Idea: *The speaker sounds more convinced of what she says.*)
- You don't usually want to argue with somebody who speaks loudly.
- Another thing Grandmother Esther did to persuade the people was to use words to describe inventors. She made them sound very special. Here's one thing she said: "Here's where we see the work of the most important people in the world— the inventors." What part of that sentence makes inventors sound very special? (Call on a student. Idea: *The most important people in the world.*)
- Do you think everybody would agree that inventors are the most important people in the world? (Call on a student. Idea: *No.*)
- Can you think of anything else that Grandmother Esther said or did to persuade people that inventors are the most important people? (Call on individual students. Ideas: *She gave a lot of examples; she talked as if she was very sure of herself; she used gestures; she said things like "Look at them!"; she emphasized words; she said colorful things like, ". . . we don't have to stand with our feet stuck in the mud. We can **fly** with the **birds.**"*)

EXERCISE 6

PAIRED PRACTICE

You're going to read aloud to your partner. The **B** members will read first. Then the **A** members will read from the star to the end of the story. (Observe students and give feedback.)

End-of-Lesson Activities

INDEPENDENT WORK

Now finish your independent work for lesson 36. Raise your hand when you're finished. (Observe students and give feedback.)

WORKCHECK

a. (Direct students to take out their marking pencils.)
   - We're going to check your workbook and textbook items. Remember, if you got an item wrong, make an **X** next to the item.
b. (For each item: Read the item. Call on a student to answer it. If the answer is wrong, say the correct answer. Refer to the Answer Key for the correct answers.)
c. Now use your marking pencil to fix up any items you got wrong. Remember, all mistakes must be fixed up before you hand in your work.

LANGUAGE ARTS

(Present Language Arts lesson 36 after completing Reading lesson 36. See Language Arts Guide.)

ACTIVITIES

(Present Activity 6 after completing Reading lesson 36. See Activities Across the Curriculum.)

Note: Students will need access to reference materials at the end of lesson 37. See page 201 for details.

Lesson 37

EXERCISE 1

VOCABULARY REVIEW

a. Here's the new vocabulary sentence: They were impressed by her large vocabulary.
 • Everybody, say that sentence. Get ready. (Signal.) *They were impressed by her large vocabulary.*
 • (Repeat until firm.)
b. What word means they thought her vocabulary was very good? (Signal.) *Impressed.*
 • What word refers to all the words a person knows? (Signal.) *Vocabulary.*

EXERCISE 2

READING WORDS

Column 1

a. **Find lesson 37 in your textbook. ✓**
 • Touch column 1. ✓
 • (Teacher reference:)

1. <u>sharp</u>-minded	3. <u>hard</u>-boiled
2. <u>ex</u>hibit	4. <u>my</u>self

 • All these words have more than one syllable. The first syllable of each word is underlined.
b. Word 1. What's the first syllable? (Signal.) *sharp.*
 • What's the whole word? (Signal.) *Sharp-minded.*
 • A person who is sharp-minded has a quick mind or a smart mind. Everybody, what do we call a person who has a quick mind? (Signal.) *Sharp-minded.*
c. Word 2. What's the first syllable? (Signal.) *ex.*
 • What's the whole word? (Signal.) *Exhibit.*
d. Word 3. What's the first syllable? (Signal.) *hard.*
 • What's the whole word? (Signal.) *Hard-boiled.*
e. Word 4. What's the first syllable? (Signal.) *my.*
 • What's the whole word? (Signal.) *Myself.*

f. Let's read those words again.
 • Word 1. What word? (Signal.) *Sharp-minded.*
 • (Repeat for words 2–4.)
g. (Repeat step f until firm.)

Column 2

h. Find column 2. ✓
 • (Teacher reference:)

1. <u>out</u>doors	3. <u>stair</u>way
2. <u>rail</u>road	4. <u>under</u>stand

 • All these words are compound words. The first part of each word is underlined.
i. Word 1. What's the underlined part? (Signal.) *out.*
 • What's the whole word? (Signal.) *Outdoors.*
j. Word 2. What's the underlined part? (Signal.) *rail.*
 • What's the whole word? (Signal.) *Railroad.*
k. Word 3. What's the underlined part? (Signal.) *stair.*
 • What's the whole word? (Signal.) *Stairway.*
l. Word 4. What's the underlined part? (Signal.) *under.*
 • What's the whole word? (Signal.) *Understand.*
m. Let's read those words again.
 • Word 1. What word? (Signal.) *Outdoors.*
 • (Repeat for words 2–4.)
n. (Repeat step m until firm.)

Column 3

o. Find column 3. ✓
 • (Teacher reference:)

1. arranged	4. stuffed
2. crazier	5. coughed
3. choked	6. expression

 • All these words have endings.
p. Word 1. What word? (Signal.) *Arranged.*
 • Spell **arranged.** Get ready. (Tap for each letter.) *A-R-R-A-N-G-E-D.*
q. Word 2. What word? (Signal.) *Crazier.*
 • Spell **crazier.** Get ready. (Tap for each letter.) *C-R-A-Z-I-E-R.*

r. Word 3. What word? (Signal.) *Choked.*
- Spell **choked.** Get ready. (Tap for each letter.) *C-H-O-K-E-D.*
s. Word 4. What word? (Signal.) *Stuffed.*
- Spell **stuffed.** Get ready. (Tap for each letter.) *S-T-U-F-F-E-D.*
t. Word 5. What word? (Signal.) *Coughed.*
- (Repeat for word 6.)
u. Let's read those words again.
- Word 1. What word? (Signal.) *Arranged.*
- (Repeat for words: **2. crazier, 3. choked, 4. stuffed, 5. coughed, 6. expression.**)
v. (Repeat step u until firm.)

Column 4

w. Find column 4. ✓
- (Teacher reference:)

1. **material**	4. **ceiling**
2. **electricity**	5. **invention**
3. **magazine**	6. **inventors**

x. Word 1. What word? (Signal.) *Material.*
- (Repeat for words 2–6.)
y. Let's read those words again.
- Word 1. What word? (Signal.) *Material.*
- (Repeat for words 2–6.)
z. (Repeat step y until firm.)

Individual Turns

(For columns 1–4: Call on individual students, each to read one to three words per turn.)

STORY READING

a. Find part B in your textbook. ✓
- The error limit for group reading is 11 errors. Read carefully.
b. Everybody, touch the title. ✓
- (Call on a student to read the title.) [*Grandmother Esther's Inventions.*]
- Everybody, what's the title? (Signal.) *Grandmother Esther's Inventions.*
- (Call on individual students to read the story, each student reading two or three sentences at a time. Ask the specified questions as the students read.)

- (Correct errors: Tell the word. Direct the student to reread the sentence.)
- (If the group makes more than 11 errors, direct the students to reread the story.)

Grandmother Esther's Inventions
Leonard and his grandmother had been in the museum all morning. Now they were sitting outdoors, on the wide stairway that led from the museum. Grandmother Esther was pulling things from her lunch bag and setting them on the stair. And she was still talking. Leonard thought that she would never stop.

- Where were they sitting? (Call on a student. Ideas: *Outdoors; on the stairway.*)
- What time of day was it? (Call on a student. Idea: *Lunchtime.*)
- What had they done all morning? (Call on a student. Idea: *Looked at things in the museum.*)
- What were they going to do now? (Call on a student. Idea: *Eat lunch.*)

"Yes," she said, "I was an inventor myself." Leonard had heard this story many times. He could say the whole thing as well as she could.
"Yes," she repeated. "But things were different back then. Nobody wanted to listen to a <u>woman</u> inventor. Everybody used to think that inventors were a crazy bunch anyhow. But they thought that a <u>woman</u> inventor had to be even crazier than the other inventors. So nobody listened to me. And so some great inventions were never made."

- Why did she think that nobody listened to her? (Call on a student. Ideas: *People thought inventors were crazy; no one listened to a woman inventor.*)

She took a bite from a hard-boiled egg. Leonard thought she might stop talking while she ate, but she talked with her mouth full. "Yes," she said. "I actually invented the first water bed years before anybody else did. But you couldn't get good material back then. So it leaked a little bit, and everybody said it was a crazy idea."

- Everybody, what had she invented? (Signal.) *The water bed.*

- Why didn't people like her invention? (Call on a student. Idea: *It leaked*.)
- She said that you couldn't get good material back then. What kind of material was she talking about? (Call on a student. Ideas: *Rubber; heavy vinyl cloth; plastic*.)

She continued, "I also invented the folding bicycle. You could fold it up and carry it with you. Just because there were a few little problems with it, people thought it was crazy. But I could have fixed those problems. With just a little more work, I could have made a bike that wouldn't fold up when you were riding it."

- What was the problem with her folding bicycle? (Call on a student. Idea: *It folded up when you rode it*.)
- How would you like to have a bike that did that? (Call on a student. Idea: *Wouldn't like it*.)
- She said that she was a good inventor, but does it sound to you as if she made very good inventions? (Call on a student. Idea: *No*.)

Leonard wanted to invent things, too. But what could he invent? Almost without thinking, he said, "Well, the trouble with being an inventor is that everything has already been invented."

- What did Leonard think the problem was? (Call on a student. Idea: *Everything was already invented*.)

Grandmother Esther started to cough. While she was still coughing, she said, "Leonard, what kind of talk is that?" She pointed to the large hall behind her. "Think of how the world looked to people a hundred years ago. They said, 'We've got horse carts and buildings. We have railroads and ⭐ ships. We must have everything. There is nothing more to invent.' But a few sharp-minded people could see that people <u>didn't</u> have everything."

- Leonard thought that everything had already been invented. Grandmother Esther pointed out that most people who lived a hundred years ago thought that everything had been invented then.
- Everybody, did the people who lived a hundred years ago have all the inventions that we have today? (Signal.) *No*.
- Do you think most people who lived a hundred years ago had any idea of the kinds of things that we have today? (Signal.) *No*.

Leonard realized that she was right. The people who lived in caves thought that everything had been invented. They didn't know about radios and automobiles and planes and televisions.

Grandmother Esther was still talking as she ate her sandwich. "The inventor sees things that are not there yet. The inventor thinks about how things could be. Everybody else just sees things as they are now."

Leonard nodded his head. For a moment he thought about what she said. Then he asked, "But how do you think about things that haven't been invented? What do you do, just think of make-believe things?"

She coughed and then she shouted, "Make-believe? Inventors don't deal in make-believe. They deal in what people <u>need</u>. That's where the invention starts. The inventor looks around and notices that people have trouble doing some things. The inventor sees a need that people have." Grandmother Esther stuffed the rest of her sandwich in her mouth. In an instant, she continued talking. "After the inventor sees a need, the inventor figures out how to meet that need."

- What's the first thing an inventor does? (Call on a student. Ideas: *Looks around and notices that people have trouble doing some things; sees a need*.)
- What's the next thing an inventor does? (Call on a student. Idea: *Figures out how to meet the need*.)

"I don't understand," Leonard said.

- Read the rest of the story to yourself and be ready to answer some questions. Raise your hand when you're finished.

> **She pointed back toward the exhibit hall and said, "The two men who invented the airplane saw a need. They saw that people could get places faster if they could fly in a straight line rather than going around on roads. They said to themselves, 'Let's make something that will let people go places faster.' So they invented a flying machine."**
>
> **She continued, "The person who invented the car saw a need. That person saw that horses were a lot of work. People spent a lot of time feeding them and taking care of them. With a car, people would save a lot of time. With a car they could also go faster from place to place."**
>
> **She pointed her finger at Leonard. "Remember, if you want to be an inventor, start with a need. Then figure out how to meet that need."**

- (After all students have raised their hand:) Grandmother Esther told Leonard that inventors always start with a need. What need did the men who invented the first plane start with? (Call on a student. Idea: *The need for people to get from one place to another faster.*)
- What kind of need was there for the first automobile? (Call on a student. Ideas: *To get places faster; save time not taking care of horses.*)
- Name at least two problems with horses. (Call on a student. Ideas: *Horses were a lot of work; horses were slow; horses had to be fed; horses had to be taken care of.*)

EXERCISE 4

PAIRED PRACTICE

You're going to read aloud to your partner. The **A** members will read first. Then the **B** members will read from the star to the end of the story.
(Observe students and give feedback.)

EXERCISE 5

STUDY ITEM

a. Find part C in your textbook. ✓
- Touch item 21. ✓
b. Follow along as I read the item: Today's story mentions the two men who invented the first airplane. Look in a book on airplanes, in an encyclopedia, or on a computer and see if you can find out the names of these two men.
c. If you finish your independent work early, raise your hand and I'll tell you how you can look up the answer to that study item.
d. (When students raise their hand, direct them to **airplanes** in an encyclopedia, on a computer, or in a book on airplanes.)

End-of-Lesson Activities

INDEPENDENT WORK

Now finish your independent work for lesson 37. Raise your hand when you're finished. (Observe students and give feedback.)

WORKCHECK

a. (Direct students to take out their marking pencils.)
- We're going to check your workbook and textbook items. Remember, if you got an item wrong, make an **X** next to the item.
b. (For each item: Read the item. Call on a student to answer it. If the answer is wrong, say the correct answer. Refer to the Answer Key for the correct answers.)
c. Now use your marking pencil to fix up any items you got wrong. Remember, all mistakes must be fixed up before you hand in your work.

LANGUAGE ARTS

(Present Language Arts lesson 37 after completing Reading lesson 37. See Language Arts Guide.)

> ***Note:*** Students will need access to reference materials at the end of lesson 38. See page 205 for details.

Lesson 38

EXERCISE 1

VOCABULARY REVIEW

a. You learned a sentence that tells about the new exhibit.

- Everybody, say that sentence. Get ready. (Signal.) *The new exhibit displayed mysterious fish.*
- (Repeat until firm.)

b. You learned a sentence that tells what she automatically did.

- Everybody, say that sentence. Get ready. (Signal.) *She automatically arranged the flowers.*
- (Repeat until firm.)

c. Here's the last sentence you learned: They were impressed by her large vocabulary.

- Everybody, say that sentence. Get ready. (Signal.) *They were impressed by her large vocabulary.*
- (Repeat until firm.)

d. What word means they thought her vocabulary was very good? (Signal.) *Impressed.*

- What word refers to all the words a person knows? (Signal.) *Vocabulary.*

e. Once more. Say the sentence that tells what they were impressed by. Get ready. (Signal.) *They were impressed by her large vocabulary.*

EXERCISE 2

READING WORDS

Column 1

a. **Find lesson 38 in your textbook.** ✓
- Touch column 1. ✓
- (Teacher reference:)

1. invisible	4. explanation
2. suggest	5. vocabulary
3. protection	6. automatically

b. Word 1 is **invisible.** What word? (Signal.) *Invisible.*

- If something is invisible, you can't see it. Everybody, what word means you can't see it? (Signal.) *Invisible.*

c. Word 2 is **suggest.** What word? (Signal.) *Suggest.*

- When you suggest a plan, you tell about a possible plan. It may not be the only plan, but it's possible. What do you do when you suggest a place to go? (Call on a student. Idea: *Tell about a possible place to go.*)

d. Word 3 is **protection.** What word? (Signal.) *Protection.*

- Protection is something that protects.

e. Word 4 is **explanation.** What word? (Signal.) *Explanation.*

- When you give an explanation, you tell how something works.

f. Word 5. What word? (Signal.) *Vocabulary.*

g. Word 6. What word? (Signal.) *Automatically.*

h. Let's read those words again.
- Word 1. What word? (Signal.) *Invisible.*
- (Repeat for words 2–6.)

i. (Repeat step h until firm.)

Column 2

j. Find column 2. ✓
- (Teacher reference:)

1. chuckled	4. magazine
2. ceiling	5. expression
3. repeated	

k. Word 1. What word? (Signal.) *Chuckled.*
- A chuckle is a little laugh.

l. Word 2. What word? (Signal.) *Ceiling.*
- (Repeat for words 3–5.)

m. Let's read those words again.
- Word 1. What word? (Signal.) *Chuckled.*
- (Repeat for words 2–5.)

n. (Repeat step m until firm.)

Individual Turns

(For columns 1 and 2: Call on individual students, each to read one to three words per turn.)

EXERCISE 3

STORY READING

a. Find part B in your textbook. ✓

- The error limit for group reading is 12 errors. Read carefully.
b. Everybody, touch the title. ✓
- (Call on a student to read the title.) *[Trying to Discover Needs.]*
- Everybody, what's the title? (Signal.) *Trying to Discover Needs.*
- (Call on individual students to read the story, each student reading two or three sentences at a time. Ask the specified questions as the students read.)

- (Correct errors: Tell the word. Direct the student to reread the sentence.)
- (If the group makes more than 12 errors, direct the students to reread the story.)

Trying to Discover Needs

Leonard tried to think like an inventor, but the job was a lot harder than Leonard thought it would be. At first, Leonard had a lot of trouble trying to figure out things that people might need. He tried to remember what Grandmother Esther had said. "Start with a need," she had said. "Then figure out how to meet that need."

- Everybody, what's the first thing you do when you think like an inventor? (Signal.) *Start with a need.*
- What's the next thing you do? (Signal.) *Figure out how to meet that need.*
- What does that mean, to meet the need? (Call on a student. Idea: *Solve the problem.*)

But figuring out what people need was a big problem.

Leonard started out by asking people, "What do you need?" First, he asked his father. "Say, Dad, I'm thinking of inventing some things. What do you need?"

His dad was reading a paper. He looked up at Leonard and smiled.

"Well," his dad said as he put the paper down. "Well," he repeated. "Let me see." He looked up at the ceiling. "Let me see."

- Everybody, does it sound like his dad has any good ideas? (Signal.) *No.*
- I don't know that Leonard's father thinks like an inventor.

Leonard's dad chuckled. "I could use more money. Maybe you can invent a tree that grows money."

Leonard smiled. Then he waited.

His dad said, "It would be nice to have less traffic on the road. Maybe you could invent a way to take traffic off the road."

- Everybody, was his dad giving **good ideas** or just **silly wishes?** (Signal.) *Silly wishes.*
- What was the first silly wish? (Call on a student. Idea: *A tree that grows money.*)
- What was the next silly wish? (Call on a student. Idea: *A way to take traffic off the road.*)

Leonard didn't even smile over his dad's last idea. "Come on, Dad," he said. "I'm not kidding around. I need some ideas about things I might be able to invent. But I have to start with a <u>need</u>."

"Well, let me see," his father said, and looked down at the paper again. "There are probably a lot of things that people need. I just can't think of one right now."

"Okay," Leonard said. "Thanks anyhow." To himself, he was saying, "My dad just doesn't have the mind of an inventor."

Next, Leonard talked to his mother. "Mom," he said, "I need ideas for inventions." He explained his problem to her. She was working at her desk.

"Oh, dear," she said. "Every time I go somewhere I can think of a million things that would make good inventions. Let me see . . . ." She rubbed her chin and looked off into space.

- Everybody, show me what she did. ✓

"Let me see," she repeated. "Oh, yes," she said after a few moments. "I would like to have something that automatically made up the grocery list. You know, when the refrigerator gets low on milk, the ★ word <u>milk</u> automatically goes on the list. Or when we run out of peanut butter, <u>peanut butter</u> goes on the list."

- What kind of thing does she want to see invented? (Call on a student. Idea: *A machine that makes up a grocery list.*)
- How would that invention help people? (Call on a student. Ideas: *They'd always know what they needed to shop for; it would save time.*)

> "Yeah," Leonard said. "That sounds pretty good. But how would that work?"
>
> His mother looked at him with a puzzled expression.

- Everybody, show me a puzzled expression. ✓

> "Leonard," she said, "I'm not the inventor. You asked if I knew of something that should be invented. You didn't ask me how to invent it. If you want to know how to invent it, go ask your grandmother."
>
> So Leonard asked his grandmother. He first explained his mother's idea. Then he said, "But I don't know how to invent that kind of list."
>
> Grandmother Esther was reading a car magazine. She looked up over her glasses and shook her head no. She said, "Your mother has had that crazy idea about the list for twenty years. She must have tried to get me to invent that list fifty times. And I must have told her five thousand times that I don't know how to invent a list that automatically writes down things when you get low on them. But every time I turn around, here she is again, talking about that same invention. I think your mother's problem is that she hates to go grocery shopping and she doesn't like to make up grocery lists. Now I'm not saying that it's impossible to invent something that would make up lists. I'm just saying that you're looking at one inventor who doesn't know how to do it."

- Everybody, is his mother's idea for the list a new idea for her? (Signal.) *No.*
- How long has she been talking about it? (Signal.) *Twenty years.*

- Does Grandmother Esther know how to invent it? (Signal.) *No.*
- Read the rest of the story to yourself and be ready to answer some questions. Raise your hand when you're finished.

> "Okay," Leonard said. "Thanks anyhow." As he left the room, Grandmother Esther was looking at her magazine, talking to herself. She was saying, "Again and again and again I kept telling her, I don't know how to do it. But she kept coming back with the same idea, that silly list writer."
>
> During the week that followed, Leonard talked to nearly everybody about things they thought should be invented. At the end of the week, he didn't have any good ideas for inventions. But he had discovered something. People just don't seem to be very good at telling about things that they need. Leonard said to himself, "Maybe the hardest part of being an inventor is finding something to invent."

- (After all students have raised their hand:) What did Leonard discover during the next week? (Call on a student. Idea: *People aren't good at telling about what they need.*)
- What seemed to be the hardest part of being an inventor? (Call on a student. Idea: *Finding something to invent.*)
- How many good ideas for inventions did Leonard have at the end of the week? (Call on a student. Idea: *None.*)

EXERCISE 4

PAIRED PRACTICE

You're going to read aloud to your partner. The **B** members will read first. Then the **A** members will read from the star to the end of the story. (Observe students and give feedback.)

EXERCISE 5

STUDY ITEM

a. Find part C in your textbook. ✓
- Touch item 24. ✓

b. Follow along as I read the item: The two-wheeled bicycle is not very old. It was probably hard for somebody to get the idea of a two-wheeled bicycle because it seemed impossible for somebody to move along on two wheels without falling over. Find out when J. K. Starley invented his two-wheeled *Ariel* bicycle.

c. If you finish your independent work early, raise your hand and I'll tell you how you can look up the answer to that study item.

d. (When students raise their hand, direct them to **bicycles** in an encyclopedia, on a computer, or in a book on bicycles.)

End-of-Lesson Activities

INDEPENDENT WORK

Now finish your independent work for lesson 38. Raise your hand when you're finished. (Observe students and give feedback.)

WORKCHECK

a. (Direct students to take out their marking pencils.)

• We're going to check your workbook and textbook items. Remember, if you got an item wrong, make an **X** next to the item.

b. (For each item: Read the item. Call on a student to answer it. If the answer is wrong, say the correct answer. Refer to the Answer Key for the correct answers.)

c. Now use your marking pencil to fix up any items you got wrong. Remember, all mistakes must be fixed up before you hand in your work.

LANGUAGE ARTS

(Present Language Arts lesson 38 after completing Reading lesson 38. See Language Arts Guide.)

Lesson 39

EXERCISE 1

VOCABULARY

a. **Find page 352 in your textbook.** ✓
- Touch sentence 9. ✓
- This is a new vocabulary sentence. It says: He responded to her clever solution. Everybody, say that sentence. Get ready. (Signal.) *He responded to her clever solution.*
- Close your eyes and say the sentence. Get ready. (Signal.) *He responded to her clever solution.*
- (Repeat until firm.)

b. The **solution** is what she did to solve a problem. What word refers to solving a problem? (Signal.) *Solution.*

c. **Responded** is another word for **reacted.** If you respond to something, you react to it.

d. Her solution was **clever.** That means it was very smart.

e. Listen to the sentence again: He responded to her clever solution. Everybody, say that sentence. Get ready. (Signal.) *He responded to her clever solution.*

f. What word means **reacted?** (Signal.) *Responded.*
- What word refers to solving a problem? (Signal.) *Solution.*
- What word means **very smart?** (Signal.) *Clever.*
- (Repeat step f until firm.)

EXERCISE 2

VOCABULARY REVIEW

a. You learned a sentence that tells what they were impressed by.
- Everybody, say that sentence. Get ready. (Signal.) *They were impressed by her large vocabulary.*
- (Repeat until firm.)

b. I'll say part of the sentence. When I stop, you say the next word. Listen: They were . . . Everybody, what's the next word? (Signal.) *Impressed.*

c. Listen: They were impressed by her large . . . Everybody, what's the next word? (Signal.) *Vocabulary.*

- Say the whole sentence. Get ready. (Signal.) *They were impressed by her large vocabulary.*

EXERCISE 3

READING WORDS

Column 1

a. Find lesson 39 in your textbook. ✓
- Touch column 1. ✓
- (Teacher reference:)

1. assignment	4. empty
2. solution	5. electricity
3. arithmetic	

b. Word 1 is **assignment.** What word? (Signal.) *Assignment.*
- A job that somebody gives you to do is called an assignment. If the job is to write something, it is a writing assignment.
- Everybody, if the job is to read something, what is it called? (Signal.) *A reading assignment.*

c. Word 2 is **solution.** What word? (Signal.) *Solution.*

d. Word 3 is **arithmetic.** What word? (Signal.) *Arithmetic.*
- Arithmetic is another word for **math.**

e. Word 4. What word? (Signal.) *Empty.*

f. Word 5. What word? (Signal.) *Electricity.*

g. Let's read those words again.
- Word 1. What word? (Signal.) *Assignment.*
- (Repeat for words 2–5.)

h. (Repeat step g until firm.)

Column 2

i. Find column 2. ✓
- (Teacher reference:)

1. <u>col</u>lar	4. <u>ped</u>al
2. <u>check</u>er	5. <u>sub</u>tract
3. <u>mud</u>dy	6. <u>in</u>visible

- All these words have more than one syllable. The first part of each word is underlined.

j. Word 1. What's the underlined part?

j. Word 1. What's the underlined part? (Signal.) *col.*
  • What's the whole word? (Signal.) *Collar.*
  • Spell **collar.** Get ready. (Tap for each letter.) *C-O-L-L-A-R.*
k. Word 2. What's the underlined part? (Signal.) *check.*
  • What's the whole word? (Signal.) *Checker.*
  • Spell **checker.** Get ready. (Tap for each letter.) *C-H-E-C-K-E-R.*
  • A person that checks things is called a checker. A machine that checks things is also called a checker. Everybody, what do we call a person or machine that checks things? (Signal.) *Checker.*
l. Word 3. What's the underlined part? (Signal.) *mud.*
  • What's the whole word? (Signal.) *Muddy.*
  • Spell **muddy.** Get ready. (Tap for each letter.) *M-U-D-D-Y.*
m. Word 4. What's the underlined part? (Signal.) *ped.*
  • What's the whole word? (Signal.) *Pedal.*
  • Spell **pedal.** Get ready. (Tap for each letter.) *P-E-D-A-L.*
n. Word 5. What's the underlined part? (Signal.) *sub.*
  • What's the whole word? (Signal.) *Subtract.*
o. Word 6. What's the underlined part? (Signal.) *in.*
  • What's the whole word? (Signal.) *Invisible.*
p. Let's read those words again.
  • Word 1. What word? (Signal.) *Collar.*
  • (Repeat for: **2. checker, 3. muddy, 4. pedal, 5. subtract, 6. invisible.**)
q. (Repeat step p until firm.)

Column 3
r. Find column 3. ✓
  • (Teacher reference:)

1. Frank	4. Sarah
2. mess	5. towels
3. Rita	6. suggested

s. Word 1. What word? (Signal.) *Frank.*
  • (Repeat for words 2–6.)
t. Let's read those words again.
  • Word 1. What word? (Signal.) *Frank.*
  • (Repeat for words 2–6.)
u. (Repeat step t until firm.)

Individual Turns
(For columns 1–3: Call on individual students, each to read one to three words per turn.)

EXERCISE 4
STORY READING

a. Find part B in your textbook. ✓
  • The error limit for group reading is 12 errors. Read carefully.
b. Everybody, touch the title. ✓
  • (Call on a student to read the title.) [*Bad Ideas.*]
  • Everybody, what's the title? (Signal.) *Bad Ideas.*
  • (Call on individual students to read the story, each student reading two or three sentences at a time. Ask the specified questions as the students read.)

  • (Correct errors: Tell the word. Direct the student to reread the sentence.)
  • (If the group makes more than 12 errors, direct the students to reread the story.)

Bad Ideas
   Leonard had tried asking people about things that they thought he could invent. But the people he asked weren't very good about giving him good ideas. One of Leonard's friends, Frank, suggested inventing a vacation that lasted all year long.

  • Everybody, who made that suggestion? (Call on a student. Ideas: *Frank; one of Leonard's friends.*)
  • Was that a **serious idea** for an invention or was it **another silly wish?** (Signal.) *Another silly wish.*

   Another friend, Teddy, wanted a machine that made ice cream from dirt. Ann wanted something to put on her teeth so she would never have to brush them.
   Rita wanted a pair of wings so she could fly. Sarah wanted something that would make her invisible. Freddie wanted a bicycle that you didn't have to pedal. You'd just sit on the thing and it would take you places. All these people had ideas about things that they wanted, but most of these ideas were dreams.

"Dreams are a problem," Grandmother Esther told Leonard. He had just told her that he was thinking about giving up the idea of being an inventor. And he had told her why.

- Why did he want to give up? (Call on a student. Ideas: *All the ideas for inventions seemed like silly dreams; he couldn't come up with any idea.*)

"Yes, dreams are a problem," she repeated. "Here's why, young man. There are dreams that are wishes. And there are dreams that an inventor has. The line between these dreams is not always clear."

- Everybody, listen to that part again:
  "Yes, dreams are a problem," she repeated. "Here's why, young man. There are dreams that are wishes. And there are dreams that an inventor has. The line between these dreams is not always clear."
- What two kinds of dreams are there? (Call on a student. Idea: *Dreams that are wishes and dreams that an inventor has.*)
- Which kind does Leonard want? (Call on a student. Idea: *Dreams that an inventor has.*)
- Which kind had people been giving him? (Call on a student. Idea: *Dreams that are wishes.*)
- Grandmother Esther said that **the line** between these dreams is not always clear. What does that mean? (Call on a student. Idea: *It's hard to tell the difference between them.*)

Grandmother Esther continued, "Think of the men who invented the first plane. They had a dream, a crazy dream. They wanted to fly. Men with legs who had stood on the ground from the time they were born wanted to fly with the birds. That was a dream as crazy as the dream of becoming invisible or the dream of making ice cream from dirt. And I can't help you out. You'll have to find out which dreams are just empty wishes and which dreams may turn into inventions."

"Okay," Leonard said and left the room.
Grandmother Esther was talking to herself about dreams. "Where would we be without dreams? The inventor must have them. And who is to say that a dream is crazy? It was a crazy dream to have lights that ran by electricity or machines that could add and subtract. It was a crazy dream to . . ."

- Everybody, who is she talking to? (Signal.) *Herself.*
- The dots tell you that Leonard can no longer hear her. She just keeps talking. Listen to that part again:
  Grandmother Esther was talking to herself about dreams. "Where would we be without dreams? The inventor must have them. And who is to say that a dream is crazy? It was a crazy dream to have lights that ran by electricity or machines that could add and subtract. It was a crazy dream to . . ."

❀ Leonard was ✦ ready to forget about being an inventor. But then something happened that changed the way he looked at the problem. As he walked into the kitchen, he noticed that he had mud on the bottom of his shoes. He hadn't noticed it before. Now it was too late. He had made tracks all over the house. If only he had noticed that his shoes were dirty. For a moment, he felt very dumb for tracking mud all over the house. He could almost hear what his mother was going to say: "You should always check your shoes before coming into the house."
Leonard tiptoed over to the outside door and took off his ❀ muddy shoes. He got some paper towels and started to clean up the mess. Then, when he had almost cleaned the last footprint on the kitchen floor, an idea hit him. It hit him so hard that it put a smile on his face. Just like that, he knew how to think like an inventor. He said out loud, "I need a shoe checker. I know I need it because when I don't have one, I don't do a good job of checking my shoes."

- He got the idea of how to think like an inventor. How did that idea make him feel? (Call on a student. Ideas: *Happy, excited.*)
- How did he know that he had a need for a shoe checker? (Call on a student. Idea: *Because he always forgot to check if his shoes were dirty.*)
- So that need tells Leonard about something that he might invent.

> A shoe checker wasn't a bad idea for an invention. But the idea wasn't the most important thing to Leonard. The way he got the idea was the important thing.

- Everybody, what was the most important thing to Leonard? (Signal.) *The way he got the idea.*

He didn't do something well. Then he figured out that he needed something to help him do it well.

- What didn't he do well? (Call on a student. Idea: *Check his shoes.*)
- Remember how he figured out the need. He didn't do something well. That told him that he needed something to help him do it well. When he didn't do it well, he knew that he had a need.
- Read the rest of the story to yourself and be ready to answer some questions. Raise your hand when you're finished.

> That's how to figure out things to invent. You don't ask people. You do things. And when you do them, you pay attention to problems that you have. Each of the problems that you have tells you about something that you could invent to solve the problem.
> Leonard's mother walked into the kitchen and saw Leonard smiling. "This is the first time I've seen you have a good time while you clean up a mess," she said.
> "That's because I like this mess," Leonard said.
> His mother shook her head. "He must take after his grandmother," she said to herself.

- (After all students have raised their hand:) Everybody, is asking people the best way to get ideas for an invention? (Signal.) *No.*
- The best way is to do things. And when you do them, you pay attention to something. What is that something? (Call on a student. Idea: *Problems.*)
- What does each problem tell you? (Call on a student. Ideas: *About something you could invent to solve the problem; about a need.*)
- Why was Leonard smiling when his mother walked into the kitchen? (Call on a student. Ideas: *He was happy; he had a great idea.*)
- Everybody, did she know why he was smiling? (Signal.) *No.*
- She said, "He must take after his grandmother." What does that mean, take after his grandmother? (Call on a student. Idea: *He is like his grandmother.*)
- In what way did she think he was the same as Grandmother Esther? (Call on a student. Ideas: *He's unusual; says unusual things.*)

EXERCISE 5

PAIRED PRACTICE

You're going to read aloud to your partner. The **A** members will read first. Then the **B** members will read from the star to the end of the story. (Observe students and give feedback.)

End-of-Lesson Activities

INDEPENDENT WORK

Now finish your independent work for lesson 39. Raise your hand when you're finished. (Observe students and give feedback.)

WORKCHECK

a. (Direct students to take out their marking pencils.)
- We're going to check your workbook and textbook items. Remember, if you got an item wrong, make an **X** next to the item.

b. (For each item: Read the item. Call on a student to answer it. If the answer is wrong, say the correct answer. Refer to the Answer Key for the correct answers.)

c. Now use your marking pencil to fix up any items you got wrong. Remember, all mistakes must be fixed up before you hand in your work.

(Present Language Arts lesson 39 after completing Reading lesson 39. See Language Arts Guide.)

Note: You will need to reproduce blackline masters for the Fact Game in lesson 40. (Appendix G in Teacher's Guide).

Materials for Lesson 40

Fact Game

For each team (4 or 5 students):
- pair of number cubes (or dice)
- copy of Fact Game 40 (Reproducible blackline masters are at the back of the Teacher's Guide.)

For each student:
- their copy of the scorecard sheet (at end of workbook A)

For each monitor:
- a pencil
- Fact Game 40 answer key (at end of textbook A)

Reading Checkout

Each student needs their thermometer chart.

Literature Lesson 4

See Literature Guide for the materials you will need.

EXERCISE 1

FACT GAME

a. You're going to play the game that uses the facts you have learned. Remember the rules. The player rolls the number cubes, figures out the number of the question, reads that question out loud, and answers it. The monitor tells the player if the answer is right or wrong. If it's wrong, the monitor tells the right answer. If it's right, the monitor gives the player one point. Don't argue with the monitor. The number cubes go to the left and the next player has a turn. You'll play the game for 10 minutes.

b. (Divide students into groups of four or five. Assign monitors. Circulate as students play the game. Comment on groups that are playing well.)

c. (At the end of 10 minutes, have all students who earned more than 10 points stand up.)

- (Tell the monitor of each game that ran smoothly:) Your group did a good job.

EXERCISE 2

READING CHECKOUTS

a. Today is a test day and a reading-checkout day. While you're writing answers, I'm going to call on you one at a time to read part of the story from lesson 39. When I call you to come and do your checkout, bring your thermometer chart.

- Remember, you pass the checkout by reading the passage in less than a minute without making more than 2 mistakes. And when you pass the checkout, you'll color the space for lesson 40 on your thermometer chart.

b. (Call on individual students to read the portion of story 39 marked with ✿ .)

- (Time the student. Note words that are missed and total number of words read.)
- (Teacher reference:)

✿ **Leonard was ready to forget about being an inventor. But then something happened that changed the way he looked at the problem. As he walked into the kitchen, he noticed that he had mud on the bottom of his shoes. He hadn't noticed it before. Now it was too late. [50] He had made tracks all over the house. If only he had noticed that his shoes were dirty. For a moment, he felt very dumb [75] for tracking mud all over the house. He could almost hear what his mother was going to say: "You should always check your shoes before [100] coming into the house."**

Leonard tiptoed over to the outside door and took off his ✿[115] muddy shoes.

- (If the student reads the passage in one minute or less and makes no more than 2 errors, direct the student to color in the space for lesson 40 on the thermometer chart.)

- (If the student makes any mistakes, point to each word that was misread and identify it.)
- (If the student does not meet the rate-error criterion for the passage, direct the student to practice reading the story with the student's assigned partner.)

EXERCISE 3

TEST

a. **Find page 199 in your textbook.** ✓
- This is a test. You'll work items you've done before.
- Work carefully. Raise your hand when you've completed all the items. (Observe students but do not give feedback on errors.)

EXERCISE 4

MARKING THE TEST

a. (Check students' work before beginning lesson 41. Refer to the Answer Key for the correct answers.)
b. (Record all test 4 results on the Test Summary Sheet and the Group Summary Sheet. Reproducible Summary Sheets are at the back of the Teacher's Guide.)

EXERCISE 5

TEST REMEDIES

(Provide any necessary remedies for test 4 before presenting lesson 41. Test remedies are discussed in the Teacher's Guide.)

Test 4 Firming Table

Test Item	Introduced in lesson	Test Item	Introduced in lesson	Test Item	Introduced in lesson
1	31	7	36	13	29
2	33	8	36	14	29
3	33	9	36	15	36
4	33	10	37	16	33
5	36	11	38	17	29
6	36	12	38	18	36

LITERATURE

(Present Literature lesson 4 after completing Reading lesson 40. See Literature Guide.)

LANGUAGE ARTS

(Present Language Arts lesson 40 after completing Reading lesson 40. See Language Arts Guide.)

Lessons 41–45 · Planning Page

Looking Ahead

	Lesson 41	Lesson 42	Lesson 43	Lesson 44	Lesson 45
Lesson Events	Vocabulary Sentence Reading Words Story Reading Paired Practice Independent Work Workcheck Language Arts	Vocabulary Sentences Reading Words Story Reading Paired Practice Independent Work Workcheck Language Arts	**Vocabulary Sentence** Vocabulary Sentence Reading Words Story Reading Paired Practice Independent Work Workcheck Language Arts	Vocabulary Sentence Reading Words Story Reading Paired Practice Study Items Independent Work Workcheck Language Arts	Vocabulary Sentences Reading Words Vocabulary Sentence Story Reading Reading Checkouts Independent Work Workcheck Language Arts
Vocabulary Sentence	#9: He responded to her clever solution.	sentence #7 sentence #8 sentence #9	**#10: The patent attorney wrote an agreement.** #9: He responded to her clever solution.	#10: The patent attorney wrote an agreement.	sentence #8 sentence #9 sentence #10
Reading Words: Word Types	modeled words compound words words with an ending mixed words	multi-syllable words words with an ending mixed words	2-syllable words mixed words	compound words words with an ending mixed words	modeled words mixed words
New Vocabulary	example energy device mentioned sternly	expect	tone	shaft whether	diagram lawyer purchase
Comprehension Passage					
Story	*A Plan for Inventing*	*The Electric Eye*	*A Good Idea*	*One Way*	*Another Problem*
Skill Items		Vocabulary sentence	Vocabulary sentences		Sequencing Vocabulary sentence
Special Materials				Reference materials	Thermometer charts
Special Projects/ Activities	Activity after lessons 41–43				Activity after lessons 45–46

Lesson 41

VOCABULARY REVIEW

a. Here's the new vocabulary sentence: He responded to her clever solution.
  • Everybody, say that sentence. Get ready. (Signal.) *He responded to her clever solution.*
  • (Repeat until firm.)
b. What word refers to solving a problem? (Signal.) *Solution.*
  • What word means **reacted?** (Signal.) *Responded.*
  • What word means **very smart?** (Signal.) *Clever.*

READING WORDS

Column 1

a. **Find lesson 41 in your textbook.** ✓
  • Touch column 1. ✓
  • (Teacher reference:)

1. example	3. device
2. energy	4. respond

b. Word 1 is **example.** What word? (Signal.) *Example.*
  • Spell **example.** Get ready. (Tap for each letter.) *E-X-A-M-P-L-E.*
  • A dog is an example of an animal. What's another example of an animal? (Call on a student. Ideas: *Cat, elephant, cow,* etc.)
  • What's an example of a piece of furniture? (Call on a student. Ideas: *Couch, table, chair,* etc.)
c. Word 2 is **energy.** What word? (Signal.) *Energy.*
  • Spell **energy.** Get ready. (Tap for each letter.) *E-N-E-R-G-Y.*
  • The amount of work something can do depends on how much energy it has. A battery with a lot of energy can light a flashlight for a long time. A person with a lot of energy can be very active for long periods of time.
d. Word 3 is **device.** What word? (Signal.) *Device.*
  • Spell **device.** Get ready. (Tap for each letter.) *D-E-V-I-C-E.*

• A device is something that is made by people. It may be a machine or a fixture. Everybody, what's another way of saying **He made a machine for picking grapes?** (Signal.) *He made a device for picking grapes.*
  • What's another way of saying **That fixture holds hats?** (Signal.) *That device holds hats.*
e. Word 4. What word? (Signal.) *Respond.*
  • Spell **respond.** Get ready. (Tap for each letter.) *R-E-S-P-O-N-D.*
f. Let's read those words again.
  • Word 1. What word? (Signal.) *Example.*
  • (Repeat for words 2–4.)
g. (Repeat step f until firm.)

Column 2

h. Find column 2. ✓
  • (Teacher reference:)

1. whenever	4. bedtime
2. shopkeeper	5. bathtub
3. earmuffs	

• All these words are compound words. The first part of each word is underlined.
i. Word 1. What's the underlined part? (Signal.) *when.*
  • What's the whole word? (Signal.) *Whenever.*
j. Word 2. What's the underlined part? (Signal.) *shop.*
  • What's the whole word? (Signal.) *Shopkeeper.*
k. Word 3. What's the underlined part? (Signal.) *ear.*
  • What's the whole word? (Signal.) *Earmuffs.*
l. Word 4. What's the underlined part? (Signal.) *bed.*
  • What's the whole word? (Signal.) *Bedtime.*
m. Word 5. What's the underlined part? (Signal.) *bath.*
  • What's the whole word? (Signal.) *Bathtub.*
n. Let's read those words again.
  • Word 1. What word? (Signal.) *Whenever.*
  • (Repeat for words 2–5.)
o. (Repeat step n until firm.)

Column 3

p. Find column 3. ✓
- (Teacher reference:)

1. impressed	4. buzzer
2. forgetting	5. automatically
3. explanation	

- All these words have an ending.

q. Word 1. What word? (Signal.) *Impressed.*
- (Repeat for words 2–5.)

r. Let's read those words again.
- Word 1. What word? (Signal.) *Impressed.*
- (Repeat for words 2–5.)

s. (Repeat step r until firm.)

Column 4

t. Find column 4. ✓
- (Teacher reference:)

1. mentioned	4. protection
2. sternly	5. unfolded
3. matching	6. bakery

- All these words have an ending.

u. Word 1. What word? (Signal.) *Mentioned.*
- When you mention something, you quickly tell about it. Everybody, what's another way of saying **quickly tell?** (Signal.) *Mention.*

v. Word 2. What word? (Signal.) *Sternly.*
- A stern expression is a frowning expression. Here's a stern expression. (Frown.)

w. Word 3. What word? (Signal.) *Matching.*
- (Repeat for words 4–6.)

x. Let's read those words again.
- Word 1. What word? (Signal.) *Mentioned.*
- (Repeat for words 2–6.)

y. (Repeat step x until firm.)

Column 5

z. Find column 5. ✓
- (Teacher reference:)

1. collar	4. plastic
2. difficult	5. raise
3. hood	6. vocabulary

a. Word 1. What word? (Signal.) *Collar.*
- (Repeat for words 2–6.)

b. Let's read those words again.
- Word 1. What word? (Signal.) *Collar.*
- (Repeat for words 2–6.)

c. (Repeat step b until firm.)

Individual Turns

(For columns 1–5: Call on individual students, each to read one to three words per turn.)

EXERCISE 3

STORY READING

a. Find part B in your textbook. ✓
- The error limit for group reading is 12 errors. Read carefully.

b. Everybody, touch the title. ✓
- (Call on a student to read the title.) *[A Plan for Inventing.]*
- Everybody, what's the title? (Signal.) *A Plan for Inventing.*
- (Call on individual students to read the story, each student reading two or three sentences at a time. Ask the specified questions as the students read.)

- (Correct errors: Tell the word. Direct the student to reread the sentence.)
- (If the group makes more than 12 errors, direct the students to reread the story.)

A Plan for Inventing
Thinking like an inventor was difficult for Leonard until he figured out this plan: He did different things. And he noticed each time he had a problem. When he noticed a problem, he knew that he had a <u>need.</u> He needed something that would solve that problem. The thing he needed to solve the problem was an invention.

- When he did different things, what did he notice? (Call on a student. Ideas: *Problems; a need.*)
- Each problem told him about something. What did it tell him? (Call on a student. Ideas: *That he needed something to solve the problem; about something he could invent.*)

After Leonard worked out his plan for finding needs, he tried to do all kinds of things. He washed the car, washed the windows, and washed the dog. He washed the floors and the walls and the dishes. He helped his dad fix a table. He helped the man who lived next door change a tire on his car.

- Why was he doing all these things? (Call on a student. Ideas: *To discover needs; to find problems.*)

All the time Leonard did these things, his mind was working. He tried to see where he had problems. For three weeks he did things and noticed the problems that he had. And at the end of three weeks, he had a big list of things that he might invent. Some of the ideas were pretty good.

- Everybody, how long did he try to find different problems? (Signal.) *Three weeks.*

Leonard had found out that he wasn't very good at cracking raw eggs, and he thought of an invention that would crack egg shells. Leonard had found out that he was always forgetting to hang up his clothes when he took them off at night. Then his mother would come in and say, "Leonard, Leonard, look at your clothes, all over the place." Leonard figured out that what he needed was a tape that would come on just before bedtime. The voice on the tape would say, "Leonard, Leonard, hang up your clothes. Don't just drop them under your nose."

- How did Leonard know that he had a need for an egg cracker? (Call on a student. Idea: *He wasn't good at cracking eggs.*)
- What problem did he have with his clothes at bedtime? (Call on a student. Idea: *He forgot to hang them up.*)
- What kind of invention did he think could solve that need? (Call on a student. Idea: *A tape that would remind him to hang up his clothes.*)

Leonard had a problem each time it rained. Leonard hated umbrellas, so he never took one with him. But then he would be caught in the rain without an umbrella. He would get soaked.

He thought of a way to meet his need for some protection from the rain. Why not invent a coat that has a special hood? When the hood is not being used, it looks like a big collar. But when the hood is unfolded, ✦ it becomes a little umbrella.

- What problem did Leonard have when it rained? (Call on a student. Ideas: *He forgot his umbrella; he would get soaked.*)
- What kind of invention did he think might solve that problem? (Call on a student. Idea: *A coat with a hood that turned into an umbrella.*)
- Is that a pretty good idea? (Call on a student. Student preference.)

Leonard discovered that he had a great problem when he tried to wash his dog. The problem was that Leonard got all wet. If he tried to wash the dog in the bathtub, the dog would jump out in the middle of the bath and shake. The room would then be covered with water. Leonard would then have to spend a lot of time cleaning up the mess. If Leonard washed the dog outside, the problem was not as great, but Leonard still got soaked.

- Why wasn't the problem as great outside? (Call on a student. Idea: *Because it didn't matter if the dog got the ground wet.*)

He thought of an invention to meet this need. The invention was a large plastic box with holes in it. First you would fill a tub with water. Then you'd put the dog in the tub. Next, you'd put the plastic box over the tub. The dog would stick its head out through one of the holes. You could reach through the other holes and wash the dog and you wouldn't get wet while you were washing the dog. "Not bad," Leonard said to himself when he got this idea. "Not bad at all."

Leonard made pictures of some of his ideas. He showed them to the members of his family and he explained how they worked. His father said, "Leonard, I'm impressed."

- What does that mean: I'm impressed? (Call on a student. Ideas: *He thought Leonard was smart; had done well.*)

> **Leonard's mother said, "Leonard, those are very good ideas. But did you ever think of inventing a machine that would automatically write out the things that you need at the grocery store?"**

- Everybody, is she still talking about that list? (Signal.) *Yes.*
- Read the rest of the story to yourself and be ready to answer some questions. Raise your hand when you're finished.

> **When Leonard's mother mentioned the list-making machine, Grandmother Esther said, "Stop talking about that crazy invention. Leonard seems to have some good ideas here. They show that the boy has been thinking like an inventor. Now he needs to stop thinking and start inventing." She looked sternly at Leonard.**
> **Leonard smiled and said, "But I still don't know which thing I should invent."**
> **"They're all pretty good," his father said.**
> **His mother said, "I like the machine that makes up a list of things to buy."**
> **Leonard said, "I'm not sure I've found the right idea yet."**
> **Leonard shook his head. He was becoming very tired of trying to be an inventor.**

- (After all students have raised their hand:) Which invention did Leonard's dad think he should work on? (Call on a student. Ideas: *All of them; he wasn't sure.*)
- Which invention did Leonard's mother like the best? (Call on a student. Idea: *The machine that made grocery lists.*)
- What did Grandmother Esther think he should do? (Call on a student. Idea: *He should stop thinking and start inventing.*)
- Why wasn't Leonard ready to do that? (Call on a student. Idea: *He wasn't sure he'd found the right thing to invent.*)

- Why was Leonard becoming tired of trying to be an inventor? (Call on a student. Idea: *Because he couldn't think of what to invent.*)
- What do you think is going to happen? Will Leonard invent one of those things, will he give up, or will he find something better to invent? (Call on individual students. Student preference.)

EXERCISE 4

PAIRED PRACTICE

You're going to read aloud to your partner. The **B** members will read first. Then the **A** members will read.
(Observe students and give feedback.)

End-of-Lesson Activities

INDEPENDENT WORK

Now finish your independent work for lesson 41. Raise your hand when you're finished. (Observe students and give feedback.)

WORKCHECK

a. (Direct students to take out their marking pencils.)
- We're going to check your workbook and textbook items. Remember, if you got an item wrong, make an **X** next to the item.
b. (For each item: Read the item. Call on a student to answer it. If the answer is wrong, say the correct answer. Refer to the Answer Key for the correct answers.)
c. Now use your marking pencil to fix up any items you got wrong. Remember, all mistakes must be fixed up before you hand in your work.

LANGUAGE ARTS

(Present Language Arts lesson 41 after completing Reading lesson 41. See Language Arts Guide.)

ACTIVITIES

(Present Activity 7 after completing Reading lessons 41-43. See Activities Across the Curriculum.)

Lesson 42

EXERCISE 1

VOCABULARY REVIEW

a. You learned a sentence that tells what she automatically did.
   - Everybody, say that sentence. Get ready. (Signal.) *She automatically arranged the flowers.*
   - (Repeat until firm.)

b. You learned a sentence that tells what they were impressed by.
   - Everybody, say that sentence. Get ready. (Signal.) *They were impressed by her large vocabulary.*
   - (Repeat until firm.)

c. Here's the last sentence you learned: He responded to her clever solution.
   - Everybody, say that sentence. Get ready. (Signal.) *He responded to her clever solution.*
   - (Repeat until firm.)

d. What word means **reacted?** (Signal.) *Responded.*
   - What word means **very smart?** (Signal.) *Clever.*
   - What word refers to solving a problem? (Signal.) *Solution.*
   - (Repeat step d until firm.)

e. Once more. Say the sentence that tells what he responded to. Get ready. (Signal.) *He responded to her clever solution.*

EXERCISE 2

READING WORDS

Column 1

a. **Find lesson 42 in your textbook.** ✓
   - Touch column 1. ✓
   - (Teacher reference:)

1. interest	3. Grandma
2. aside	4. energy

   - All these words have more than one syllable. The first part of each word is underlined.

b. Word 1. What's the underlined part? (Signal.) *inter.*
   - What's the whole word? (Signal.) *Interest.*

- Spell **interest.** Get ready. (Tap for each letter.) *I-N-T-E-R-E-S-T.*
- If you have an interest in something, you pay attention to that thing.

c. Word 2. What's the underlined part? (Signal.) *a.*
   - What's the whole word? (Signal.) *Aside.*
   - Spell **aside.** Get ready. (Tap for each letter.) *A-S-I-D-E.*

d. Word 3. What's the underlined part? (Signal.) *grand.*
   - What's the whole word? (Signal.) *Grandma.*
   - Spell **Grandma.** Get ready. (Tap for each letter.) *G-R-A-N-D-M-A.*

e. Word 4. What's the underlined part? (Signal.) *en.*
   - What's the whole word? (Signal.) *Energy.*
   - Spell **energy.** Get ready. (Tap for each letter.) *E-N-E-R-G-Y.*

f. Let's read those words again.
   - Word 1. What word? (Signal.) *Interest.*
   - (Repeat for words 2–4.)

g. (Repeat step f until firm.)

Column 2

h. Touch column 2. ✓
   - (Teacher reference:)

1. example	3. excuse
2. expect	4. clever

   - All these words have more than one syllable. The first part of each word is underlined.

i. Word 1. What's the underlined part? (Signal.) *ex.*
   - What's the whole word? (Signal.) *Example.*

j. Word 2. What's the underlined part? (Signal.) *ex.*
   - What's the whole word? (Signal.) *Expect.*
   - When you **think** something will happen, you **expect** it to happen. Here's another way of saying **I think Tim will call: I expect Tim to call.** Everybody, what's another way of saying **I think that dog will bark?** (Signal.) *I expect that dog to bark.*

k. Word 3. What's the underlined part? (Signal.) *ex.*

- What's the whole word? (Signal.) *Excuse.*
- l. Word 4. What's the underlined part? (Signal.) *clev.*
  - What's the whole word? (Signal.) *Clever.*
- m. Let's read those words again.
  - Word 1. What word? (Signal.) *Example.*
  - (Repeat for: **2. expect, 3. excuse, 4. clever.**)
- n. (Repeat step m until firm.)

Column 3

o. Find column 3. ✓
  - (Teacher reference:)

1. counter	4. traced
2. kneeling	5. serves
3. blocking	

- All these words have an ending.
- p. Word 1. What word? (Signal.) *Counter.*
- q. Word 2. What word? (Signal.) *Kneeling.*
  - When you are on your knees, you are kneeling.
- r. Word 3. What word? (Signal.) *Blocking.*
  - (Repeat for words 4 and 5.)
- s. Let's read those words again.
  - Word 1. What word? (Signal.) *Counter.*
  - (Repeat for words 2–5.)
- t. (Repeat step s until firm.)

Column 4

u. Find column 4. ✓
  - (Teacher reference:)

1. beam	4. she'd
2. dance	5. target
3. respond	

- v. Word 1. What word? (Signal.) *Beam.*
  - (Repeat for words 2–5.)
- w. Let's read those words again.
  - Word 1. What word? (Signal.) *Beam.*
  - (Repeat for words 2–5.)
- x. (Repeat step w until firm.)

Individual Turns

(For columns 1–4: Call on individual students, each to read one to three words per turn.)

EXERCISE 3

STORY READING

a. Find part B in your textbook. ✓
  - The error limit for group reading is 12 errors. Read carefully.

b. Everybody, touch the title. ✓
  - (Call on a student to read the title.) *[The Electric Eye.]*
  - Everybody, what's the title? (Signal.) *The Electric Eye.*
  - (Call on individual students to read the story, each student reading two or three sentences at a time. Ask the specified questions as the students read.)

- (Correct errors: Tell the word. Direct the student to reread the sentence.)
- (If the group makes more than 12 errors, direct the students to reread the story.)

The Electric Eye

Leonard was walking to school. Grandmother Esther was on her way to her exercise class. The exercise class was held near Leonard's school, so she was walking with him. Whenever she walked, she talked, and talked, and talked. And when she talked about inventing, she talked very loudly. Leonard knew that she wasn't shouting at him. He knew that she wasn't mad when she pointed her finger and raised her voice. He knew these things. But the other people who were walking along the street didn't know. They stopped and stared at Grandmother Esther. To them, it must have seemed that she was yelling at Leonard.

- What did the people on the street think was happening? (Call on a student. Idea: *She was yelling at Leonard.*)
- What made them think she was yelling at him? (Call on a student. Idea: *She talked loudly and pointed her finger.*)

Leonard was very embarrassed, but he didn't know what to say. As she talked, Leonard thought about an invention he needed.

- He's embarrassed. Why? (Call on a student. Ideas: *Because everyone was looking at him; because his grandmother was talking so loudly.*)
- **That's** his problem. What does he need? (Call on a student. Idea: *An invention to make his Grandmother stop talking so loudly.*)

What about a pair of thick earmuffs? If he wore them, he wouldn't be able to hear her. No, that wouldn't work. She'd just talk louder. What about a buzzer? The buzzer could buzz louder when she talked louder. If she wanted the buzzer to stop, she'd have to talk softly.

- What would the buzzer do when she talked louder? (Call on a student. Idea: *Buzz louder.*)
- So what would she have to do to make the buzzer stop? (Call on a student. Idea: *Talk more softly.*)
- That might be a good invention.

"Now there's an invention," she said, pointing to something. She and Leonard were in front of a bakery. The window was filled with things that looked so good to eat that Leonard tried not to look at them.

- Why did he try not to look at them? (Call on a student. Ideas: *They made him hungry; he wanted to eat them.*)

Grandmother Esther seemed to be pointing at the door. "Yes, a very simple invention, but a very clever one."
"What invention is that?" Leonard asked.
"The electric eye, of course," she said. Leonard didn't know what she was talking about. "The electric what?" he asked.
"The electric eye. Don't tell me you don't know what an electric eye is."
Before he could respond, she opened the door to the bakery. She pointed to a tiny light that was on one side of the door, about half a meter from the floor. "There it is," she said. "The electric eye."

- You can see the electric eye in the picture. The dotted line shows a tiny beam of light coming from it. Everybody, touch the electric eye. ✓

"What does it do?" Leonard asked. "It tells the shopkeeper that you're coming into the shop. Watch." She held her hand in front of the little beam of light that came from the electric eye. As soon as she did that a buzzer sounded in the back of the bakery. "That's just what happens when you walk into the store."

- What happens when you walk into the store? (Call on a student. Idea: *A buzzer sounds in the back of the store.*)

She explained how the electric eye worked. The beam of light went from one side of the door to the other. As long as the beam reached a little target on the other side of the door, nothing happened. But when something got in the way of that beam of light and kept it from reaching the target, the buzzer sounded.

- Listen to that part again and look at the picture:
    She explained how the electric eye worked. The beam of light went from one side of the door to the other. As long as the beam reached a little target on the other side of the door, nothing happened. But when something got in the way of that beam of light and kept it from reaching the target, the buzzer sounded.
- Everybody, touch the electric eye and follow the beam of light from the electric eye to the target on the other side of the door. ✓
- As long as the beam of light reaches the target, nothing happens. What happens when something stops that beam from reaching the target? (Call on a student. Idea: *A buzzer sounds.*)

She explained that the buzzer kept sounding as long as the beam was broken. So when somebody walked in the door, the body would stop the beam of light from reaching the

target. When the body stopped the beam, the buzzer sounded. That buzzer told the shopkeeper that somebody was going through the door.

- Read the rest of the story to yourself and be ready to answer some questions. Raise your hand when you're finished.

> **Grandmother Esther was kneeling in front of the doorway as she explained how the beam worked. Several people were trying to get into the bakery. They waited as she explained the electric eye. The shopkeeper was standing behind the counter, looking at her. When she finished her explanation of the electric eye, she said, "This is a good example of a clever invention. The electric eye is a simple invention, but it has many, many uses."**
>
> **One of the people who was trying to get into the store said, "Very interesting."**
>
> **The other person said, "Yes, very interesting."**
>
> **The shopkeeper said, "Excuse me, could you stand aside and let these people come in?"**
>
> **Leonard said, "Come on, Grandma, you're blocking the doorway."**
>
> **And Grandmother Esther said, "Of course, the electric eye is not as great an invention as the airplane or the electric light. But the electric eye serves many needs."**
>
> **The shopkeeper said, "Yes, it does."**
>
> **Leonard said, "Come on, Grandma, I've got to go to school."**

- (After all students have raised their hand:) Everybody, look at the picture. Touch the counter. ✓
- Who is that behind the counter? (Signal.) *The shopkeeper.*
- Who was trying to get into the bakery? (Call on a student. Idea: *Some people.*)
- Why couldn't they get in? (Call on a student. Idea: *Grandmother Esther was kneeling in front of the doorway.*)
- Did they say they found Grandmother Esther's talk interesting? (Call on a student. Idea: *Yes.*)

- How did the shopkeeper feel? (Call on a student. Ideas: *He just wanted the customers to come into his shop; he wanted Grandmother Esther to go away.*)
- How do you think Leonard felt? (Call on a student. Ideas: *Embarrassed; in a hurry to go.*)
- What did he say to get her to move out of the doorway? (Call on a student. Idea: *Come on, Grandma, I've got to go to school*)

EXERCISE 4

PAIRED PRACTICE

You're going to read aloud to your partner. The **A** members will read first. Then the **B** members will read from the star to the end of the story.
(Observe students and give feedback.)

End-of-Lesson Activities

INDEPENDENT WORK

Now finish your independent work for lesson 42. Raise your hand when you're finished. (Observe students and give feedback.)

WORKCHECK

a. (Direct students to take out their marking pencils.)
- We're going to check your workbook and textbook items. Remember, if you got an item wrong, make an **X** next to the item.
b. (For each item: Read the item. Call on a student to answer it. If the answer is wrong, say the correct answer. Refer to the Answer Key for the correct answers.)
c. Now use your marking pencil to fix up any items you got wrong. Remember, all mistakes must be fixed up before you hand in your work.

LANGUAGE ARTS

(Present Language Arts lesson 42 after completing Reading lesson 42. See Language Arts Guide.)

EXERCISE 1

VOCABULARY

a. **Find the vocabulary sentences on page 352 in your textbook.** ✓
- Touch sentence 10. ✓
- This is a new vocabulary sentence. It says: The patent attorney wrote an agreement. Everybody, say that sentence. Get ready. (Signal.) *The patent attorney wrote an agreement.*
- Close your eyes and say the sentence. Get ready. (Signal.) *The patent attorney wrote an agreement.*
- (Repeat until firm.)

b. A **patent** is a license that says that only one person can make a particular product. New inventions are patented so that not everybody can make the product.

c. A patent **attorney** is a lawyer whose special job is getting patents for new inventions.

d. The sentence says the patent attorney wrote an **agreement.** An agreement is a paper that tells what two people promise to do. If people make an agreement, they shouldn't break the agreement. They should keep their promises.

e. Listen to the sentence again: The patent attorney wrote an agreement. Everybody say that sentence. Get ready. (Signal.) *The patent attorney wrote an agreement.*

f. Everybody, what word means **lawyer?** (Signal.) *Attorney.*
- What word names a license for somebody to be the only person who can make a product? (Signal.) *Patent.*
- What do we call a lawyer whose special job is getting patents for new inventions? (Signal.) *Patent attorney.*
- What word means **a promise made by people?** (Signal.) *Agreement.*
- (Repeat step f until firm.)

EXERCISE 2

VOCABULARY REVIEW

a. You learned a sentence that tells what he responded to.

- Everybody, say that sentence. Get ready. (Signal.) *He responded to her clever solution.*
- (Repeat until firm.)

b. I'll say part of the sentence. When I stop, you say the next word. Listen: He . . . Everybody, what's the next word? (Signal.) *Responded.*

c. Listen: He responded to her clever . . . Everybody, what's the next word? (Signal.) *Solution.*
- Say the whole sentence. Get ready. (Signal.) *He responded to her clever solution.*

d. Listen: He responded to her . . . Everybody, what's the next word? (Signal.) *Clever.*

EXERCISE 3

READING WORDS

Column 1

a. Find lesson 43 in your textbook. ✓
- Touch column 1. ✓
- (Teacher reference:)

| 1. clearer | 3. supper |
| 2. device | 4. outfit |

- All these words have more than one syllable. The first part of each word is underlined.

b. Word 1. What's the underlined part? (Signal.) *clear.*
- What's the whole word? (Signal.) *Clearer.*
- Spell **clearer.** Get ready. (Tap for each letter.) *C-L-E-A-R-E-R.*

c. Word 2. What's the underlined part? (Signal.) *de.*
- What's the whole word? (Signal.) *Device.*
- Spell **device.** Get ready. (Tap for each letter.) *D-E-V-I-C-E.*

d. Word 3. What's the underlined part? *Supp.*
- What's the whole word? (Signal.) *Supper.*
- Spell **supper.** Get ready. (Tap for each letter.) *S-U-P-P-E-R.*

e. Word 4. What's the underlined part? (Signal.) *out.*
- What's the whole word? (Signal.) *Outfit.*

- Spell **outfit.** Get ready. (Tap for each letter.) *O-U-T-F-I-T.*
f. Let's read those words again.
  - Word 1. What word? (Signal.) *Clearer.*
  - (Repeat for: **2. device, 3. supper, 4. outfit.**)
g. (Repeat step f until firm.)

Column 2

h. Find column 2. ✓
  - (Teacher reference:)

1. tone	4. solution
2. arithmetic	5. giggled
3. stinks	

i. Word 1. What word? (Signal.) *Tone.*
  - Your tone of voice tells what you are feeling. I can say "What are you doing?" so it sounds like a question or so it sounds like I'm scolding you. Which tone of voice do you want to hear? (Call on a student. Student preference.)
  - (Say "What are you doing?" using the selected tone of voice.)
j. Word 2. What word? (Signal.) *Arithmetic.*
  - (Repeat for words 3–5.)
k. Let's read those words again.
  - Word 1. What word? (Signal.) *Tone.*
  - (Repeat for words 2–5.)
l. (Repeat step k until firm.)

Column 3

m. Find column 3. ✓
  - (Teacher reference:)

1. assignment	4. sour
2. drawings	5. practicing
3. enter	6. realizing

n. Word 1. What word? (Signal.) *Assignment.*
  - (Repeat for words 2–6.)
o. Let's read those words again.
  - Word 1. What word? (Signal.) *Assignment.*
  - (Repeat for words 2–6.)
p. (Repeat step o until firm.)

Individual Turns

(For columns 1–3: Call on individual students, each to read one to three words per turn.)

STORY READING

a. Find part B in your textbook. ✓
  - The error limit for group reading is 11 errors. Read carefully.
b. Everybody, touch the title. ✓
  - (Call on a student to read the title.) *[A Good Idea.]*
  - Everybody, what's the title? (Signal.) *A Good Idea.*
  - (Call on individual students to read the story, each student reading two or three sentences at a time. Ask the specified questions as the students read.)

- (Correct errors: Tell the word. Direct the student to reread the sentence.)
- (If the group makes more than 11 errors, direct the students to reread the story.)

A Good Idea
The next evening, after supper, it happened. Leonard had no warning that it would happen. But it did. Everything in his mind suddenly came together and he had the idea for a great invention.

- What happened that evening? (Call on a student. Idea: *Leonard got an idea for a great invention.*)
- Everybody, did Leonard know that this would happen? (Signal.) *No.*

Here's how it happened: After supper, he went to his room to get a pencil. He was going to make some more drawings of ideas for inventions. When he started back to the kitchen, Grandmother Esther hollered at him, "Turn off the light in your room. Remember to save energy."
Leonard turned around, went back to his room, turned off the light, and stood there in the dark room. He felt the idea coming into his head. It got bigger and clearer and . . . "Hot dog!" he shouted.

- Why did he shout? (Call on a student. Ideas: *He was excited; he had an idea.*)
- How did he feel? (Call on a student. Ideas: *Happy, excited.*)

He shouted, "What an idea for an invention! Hot dog!"

He ran into the kitchen. "I've got it. What an idea! This is the best idea anybody ever had for an invention!"

His mother smiled. "I'll bet it's a machine that makes up a list of things you need at the store."

"Stop talking about that stupid machine," Grandmother Esther yelled from the other room. She ran into the kitchen. She was wearing her exercise outfit.

- Look at the picture on the next page. ✓
- What is Grandmother Esther wearing? (Call on a student. Ideas: *Her exercise outfit; purple sweatsuit.*)

Grandmother Esther asked, "What's your idea, Leonard?"

Leonard said, "Let me explain how it's going to work. It's dark outside. And it's dark in the living room of your house. But when you walk through the door to the living room, the light goes on automatically. The light stays on as long as you're in the living room. But when you leave the living room, the light goes off."

- Leonard explained how the invention would work. Listen to that part again:
  Leonard said, "Let me explain how it's going to work. It's dark outside. And it's dark in the living room of your house. But when you walk through the door to the living room, the light goes on automatically. The light stays on as long as you're in the living room. But when you leave the living room, the light goes off."
- What happens when you walk **into** the room? (Call on a student. Idea: *The light goes on.*)

- What happens when you **leave** the room? (Call on a student. Idea: *The light goes off.*)
- What kind of thing could make the lights go on and off automatically? (Call on a student. Idea: *An electric eye.*)

Leonard's mother shook her head. "That sounds far too difficult."

Grandmother Esther said, "It sounds difficult to you because you don't know how the electric eye works."

- Everybody, did Grandmother Esther know how Leonard was thinking of making the lights go on and off? (Signal.) *Yes.*
- What was he going to use? (Signal.) *An electric eye.*

"The electric eye?" Leonard's mother asked.

Leonard said, "Here's how it works, Mom. There's a little beam of light that goes across the doorway to the living room. When you enter the room, you break the beam. When you break that ✦ beam, the light turns on. Then when you leave the room, you break the beam and the light goes off."

"Oh, my," Leonard's mother said. He could tell from her tone of voice that she didn't understand what he said.

"Good thinking," Grandmother Esther said, and slapped Leonard on the back. "That's a fine idea for an invention, a fine idea."

"Thank you," Leonard said.

- Everybody, do you think she feels that the electric eye invention is the right idea? (Signal.) *Yes.*

Grandmother Esther made a sour looking face. Slowly she said, "There's one big problem with being a good inventor. You have to think of all the things that could go wrong."

"What could go wrong?" Leonard asked.

Grandmother Esther explained. "When you break the beam one time, the light goes on. When you break the beam the next time, the light goes off. When you break the beam the next time, the light goes on."

"Right," Leonard said.

"That's the problem," Grandmother Esther said. "What if two people walk into a dark room? When the first one goes into the room, the light will go on. Now the second person goes into the room. What happens to the light?"

"It goes off," Leonard said very sadly. He shook his head. "Now both people are in the dark, and my invention stinks."

- What happens when the first person enters the room? (Call on a student. Idea: *The light goes on.*)
- What happens when the second person enters the room? (Call on a student. Idea: *The light goes off.*)
- Everybody, is that the way Leonard wants it to work? (Signal.) *No.*
- Read the rest of the story to yourself and be ready to answer some questions. Remember, Leonard has just said that he thinks his invention stinks. Raise your hand when you're finished.

"Wrong!" Grandmother Esther shouted. "Both people are in the dark, but your invention does not stink. Every invention has problems. An inventor has to look at these problems and try to solve them. But you must remember that inventing something is more than just getting an idea. You must work on that idea until it is a good idea. Then you must take that good idea and make it into a good invention. Just because there's a problem doesn't mean that you give up. You've got a great idea."

Leonard's mother said, "I have a great idea for an invention. It's a machine that . . ."

"Not now," Grandmother Esther said. "We're close to a <u>real</u> invention."

Leonard said, "I'll just have to think about the problem and try to figure out how to solve it."

- (After all students have raised their hand:) Why did Leonard think that his invention stinks? (Call on a student. Idea: *Because it has problems.*)
- Everybody, did Grandmother Esther think it stinks? (Signal.) *No.*
- She told him that every new invention has problems. So what does the inventor have to do? (Call on a student. Idea: *Solve the problems.*)
- Leonard's mother said she had a great idea for an invention. What do you think it was? (Call on a student. Idea: *The automatic grocery list-writer.*)
- Everybody, is Leonard going to give up? (Signal.) *No.*
- What is he going to do? (Call on a student. Idea: *Think about the problem and try to solve it.*)

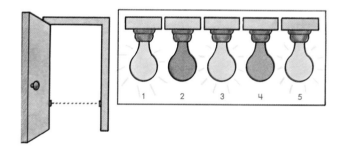

- Everybody, look at the picture. The picture shows Leonard's invention. The lights in the box show what will happen each time the beam of light is broken. When we start out, the light is **not on.** What will happen when the beam is broken **one time?** (Signal.) *The light will go on.*
- What happens when the beam is broken two times? (Signal.) *The light will go off.*
- Look at the picture in the box and get ready to tell me what will happen when the beam is broken **five** times. (Pause.) Get ready. (Signal.) *The light will go on.*
- Everybody, get ready to tell me what will happen when the beam is broken **four** times. (Pause.) Get ready. (Signal.) *The light will go off.*
- Can you figure out what will happen when the beam is broken **six** times? (Call on a student. Idea: *The light will go off.*)

EXERCISE 5

PAIRED PRACTICE

You're going to read aloud to your partner. The **B** members will read first. Then the **A** members will read from the star to the end of the story.
(Observe students and give feedback.)

End-of-Lesson Activities

INDEPENDENT WORK

Now finish your independent work for lesson 43. Raise your hand when you're finished. (Observe students and give feedback.)

WORKCHECK

a. (Direct students to take out their marking pencils.)
 • We're going to check your workbook and textbook items. Remember, if you got an item wrong, make an **X** next to the item.
b. (For each item: Read the item. Call on a student to answer it. If the answer is wrong, say the correct answer. Refer to the Answer Key for the correct answers.)
c. Now use your marking pencil to fix up any items you got wrong. Remember, all mistakes must be fixed up before you hand in your work.

LANGUAGE ARTS

(Present Language Arts lesson 43 after completing Reading lesson 43. See Language Arts Guide.)

Note: Students will need access to reference materials at the end of lesson 44. See page 231 for details.

EXERCISE 1

VOCABULARY REVIEW

a. Here's the new vocabulary sentence: The patent attorney wrote an agreement.
  - Everybody, say that sentence. Get ready. (Signal.) *The patent attorney wrote an agreement.*
  - (Repeat until firm.)
b. Everybody, what word means **lawyer?** (Signal.) *Attorney.*
  - What word means **a promise made by people?** (Signal.) *Agreement.*
  - What do we call a lawyer whose special job is getting patents for new inventions? (Signal.) *Patent attorney.*
  - What word names a license for somebody to be the only person who can make a product? (Signal.) *Patent.*
  - (Repeat step b until firm.)

EXERCISE 2

READING WORDS

Column 1

a. **Find lesson 44 in your textbook.** ✓
  - Touch column 1. ✓
  - (Teacher reference:)

1. **bath**room	3. **home**work
2. **one**-way	4. **out**fit

  - All these words are compound words. The first part of each word is underlined.
b. Word 1. What's the underlined part? (Signal.) *bath.*
  - What's the whole word? (Signal.) *Bathroom.*
c. Word 2. What's the underlined part? (Signal.) *one.*
  - What's the whole word? (Signal.) *One-way.*
d. Word 3. What's the underlined part? (Signal.) *home.*
  - What's the whole word? (Signal.) *Homework.*
e. Word 4. What's the underlined part? (Signal.) *out.*
  - What's the whole word? (Signal.) *Outfit.*
f. Let's read those words again.
  - Word 1. What word? (Signal.) *Bathroom.*
  - (Repeat for words 2–4.)
g. (Repeat step f until firm.)

Column 2

h. Find column 2. ✓
  - (Teacher reference:)

1. **entering**	3. **practicing**
2. **drums**	4. **realizing**

  - All these words have an ending.
i. Word 1. What word? (Signal.) *Entering.*
  - (Repeat for words 2–4.)
j. Let's read those words again.
  - Word 1. What word? (Signal.) *Entering.*
  - (Repeat for words 2–4.)
k. (Repeat step j until firm.)

Column 3

l. Find column 3. ✓
  - (Teacher reference:)

1. **shaft**	3. **drew**
2. **whether**	4. **goose**

m. Word 1. What word? (Signal.) *Shaft.*
  - Spell **shaft.** Get ready. (Tap for each letter.) *S-H-A-F-T.*
  - The shaft of a pencil is the part with long straight sides. The shaft of an arrow is the part with long straight sides.
n. Word 2. What word? (Signal.) *Whether.*
  - Spell **whether.** Get ready. (Tap for each letter.) *W-H-E-T-H-E-R.*
  - In some sentences, **whether** means **if.** Here's another way of saying **He decided if he would go: He decided whether he would go.**
  - Everybody, what's another way of saying **He wondered if his mother would call?** (Signal.) *He wondered whether his mother would call.*
o. Word 3. What word? (Signal.) *Drew.*
  - Spell **drew.** Get ready. (Tap for each letter.) *D-R-E-W.*
p. Word 4. What word? (Signal.) *Goose.*
  - Spell **goose.** Get ready. (Tap for each letter.) *G-O-O-S-E.*

q. Let's read those words again.
- Word 1. What word? (Signal.) *Shaft.*
- (Repeat for: **2. whether, 3. drew, 4. goose.**)

r. (Repeat step q until firm.)

Individual Turns

(For columns 1–3: Call on individual students, each to read one to three words per turn.)

STORY READING

a. Find part B in your textbook. ✓
- The error limit for group reading is 14 errors. Read carefully.

b. Everybody, touch the title. ✓
- (Call on a student to read the title.) *[One Way.]*
- Everybody, what's the title? (Signal.) *One Way.*
- (Call on individual students to read the story, each student reading two or three sentences at a time. Ask the specified questions as the students read.)

- (Correct errors: Tell the word. Direct the student to reread the sentence.)
- If the group makes more than 14 errors, direct the students to reread the story.)

One Way
Leonard said to himself, "Figure out how to solve that problem."

- What problem was he telling himself about? (Call on a student. Idea: *How to keep the light from turning off when a second person came into the room.*)

It was a real problem. Every time the beam is broken, the lights change. If they are on, they go off. So if somebody is in a room with the lights on and somebody else comes into the room, the beam is broken and the lights go off.

- That's the problem. When somebody is in the room with the lights on and somebody else comes into the room, what happens? (Call on a student. Idea: *The lights go off.*)

He was on his way to school. He walked past the bakery. For a moment he remembered how embarrassed he had been when Grandmother Esther blocked the people who were trying to come into the store.

From time to time his mind would notice other things around him, but most of the time it was busy with the problem. "Think."

Then Leonard realized that he was looking at a sign. "One way," the sign said. And it had an arrow. "One way." Although Leonard didn't figure out the answer to his problem at that moment, he had a very strange feeling, as if he were very close to the answer.

- There was something about that arrow and the words **one way** that gave him the start of an idea about solving the problem.

Leonard said, "My device has to know which way you are going. It has to know if you are entering the room or leaving the room." Leonard crossed the street. Then he stopped and said out loud, "But one electric eye can't tell whether you're coming in or going out."

Two boys who were walking to school giggled and pointed at Leonard.

- Why were they doing that? (Call on a student. Idea: *Because Leonard was talking to himself.*)

When Leonard saw them pointing, he realized how crazy he must have looked as he talked to himself.

Later that day in school, Leonard was supposed to be doing his arithmetic homework. He liked arithmetic and he was good at it, but he couldn't seem to work on it that day. He kept thinking of the problem and the one-way sign. Without realizing what he was doing, he drew the sign on his paper.

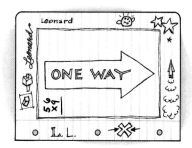

- The picture on the next page shows the sign with the arrow that Leonard drew. It's trying to tell Leonard something.

✿ He studied the arrow. He traced it with his pencil three or four times. Then he traced over the letters in the sign. Then he put two dots next to each other on ✦ the shaft of the arrow.

- Everybody, touch the straight line along the bottom edge of the arrow. That shows the shaft. Hold your fingers on that line where he might have made two dots. (Accept side-by-side positions on the shaft.)

Suddenly, he felt goose bumps all over his face and down his back. He almost jumped out of his seat. "Wow!" he shouted. "I've got it!"

- He figured out something. Listen to that part again and imagine how he must have felt:

    Then he put two dots next to each other on the shaft of the arrow. Suddenly, he felt goose bumps all over his face and down his back. He almost jumped out of his seat. "Wow!" he shouted. "I've got it!"

- What did he do when he figured out the solution? (Call on a student. Ideas: *He almost jumped out of his seat; he shouted; he got goose bumps.*)

Everybody in the class was looking at him. He could feel his face becoming very hot. He cleared his throat and coughed. Then he looked down at his paper. He could still feel the eyes of everybody in the room looking at him.

- Did you ever get that feeling that somebody is looking at you even though you can't see the person? (Call on individual students. Student preference.)

Then he heard the teacher's voice. "Is anything ✿ wrong, Leonard?"

Leonard looked up. "No, no. I just figured out the solution to a problem I've been working on."

The teacher said, "I'm glad to see that you are so excited about solving your arithmetic problems, but when you work out the solution to the next problem, try to be a little more quiet about it."

• • •

- Everybody, what kind of problem did Leonard's teacher think he had worked out? (Signal.) *Arithmetic problem.*
- Do you think Leonard will tell the teacher that he wasn't really working on arithmetic? (Call on a student. Idea: *No.*)

After school that day, Leonard ran home. It felt great to run. Sometimes when he ran he felt heavy, but as he went home that afternoon, he felt very light and very fast. He could feel the wind on his face. He raced with the cars when they started out from stop signs. He could stay with them for more than half a city block.

When he got home, he ran into the house. "Grandma!" he shouted. "I've got it!" Grandmother Esther was practicing on her drums. Leonard's mother was in the hall. She was wearing earmuffs.

- Why? (Call on a student. Ideas: *Because Grandmother Esther was playing the drums; it was noisy.*)

Leonard told Grandmother Esther how to solve the problem. "On the side of the door we put two electric eyes, not one."

- Pay close attention to this solution so that you understand it. What's the first part of the solution? (Call on a student. Idea: *Two electric eyes are put up instead of one.*)
- Everybody, so if there are two electric eyes, how many beams will go across the doorway? (Signal.) *Two.*

Leonard continued, "The electric eyes are side by side. When somebody goes through the door, they will break one beam first, then the second beam. If the outside beam is broken first and the inside beam is broken next, the person is moving into the room."

- Listen to that part again:
    Leonard continued, "The electric eyes are side by side. When somebody goes through the door, they will break one beam first, then the second beam. If the outside beam is broken first and the inside beam is broken next, the person is moving into the room."
- Everybody, when a person goes into the room, which beam gets broken first, the outside beam or the inside beam? (Signal.) *The outside beam.*
- When a person **leaves** the room, which beam gets broken first? (Signal.) *The inside beam.*

Leonard continued to explain, "If the inside beam is broken first and the outside beam is broken next, the person is moving out of the room. We make the electric eye device turn on the light if somebody goes into the room and turn off the light if somebody goes out of the room."

- (Teacher reference:)

A

- The picture shows Leonard's solution to the problem. There are four doors in the picture. You can see the two electric eyes on each door. Everybody, touch door A. ✓
- The **1** shows which beam is broken first. The **2** shows the beam that is broken next. The arrow shows which way the

person has to be moving. The person has to move in the direction that would break beam 1 first and beam 2 next. That person would be moving out of the room.

- (Teacher reference:)

B

- Everybody, touch door B. ✓
- Point your finger in the direction that would break beam 1 first and beam 2 next. ✓
- Your finger should be pointing into the room.
- (Teacher reference:)

C

- Touch door C. ✓
- Point your finger in the direction that would break beam 1 first and beam 2 next. ✓
- Is your finger pointing into the room or out of the room? (Signal.) *Into the room.*

- (Teacher reference:)

D

- Touch door D. ✓
- Point your finger in the direction that would break beam 1 first and beam 2 next. ✓
- Is your finger pointing into the room or out of the room? (Signal.) *Out of the room.*
- Leonard's solution to the problem is really smart, isn't it? If a person goes one way, the lights go on. If a person goes the other way, the lights go off. I can see where he got the idea from the one-way sign.

EXERCISE 4

PAIRED PRACTICE

You're going to read aloud to your partner. The **A** members will read first. Then the **B** members will read from the star to the end of the story. (Observe students and give feedback.)

EXERCISE 5

STUDY ITEMS

a. Find study items 25 and 26 at the end of your textbook lesson. ✓
b. Follow along as I read: Grandmother Esther talked about what a great invention the electric light bulb is. The man who invented it was named Thomas Alva Edison. Item 25: Find out when he invented the electric light bulb. Item 26: Find out 2 other things that he invented.
c. If you finish your independent work early, raise your hand and I'll tell you how you can look up the answers to those study items.
d. (When students raise their hand, direct them to a book on Edison or to **Edison** in an encyclopedia or on a computer.)

End-of-Lesson Activities

INDEPENDENT WORK

Now finish your independent work for lesson 44. Raise your hand when you're finished. (Observe students and give feedback.)

WORKCHECK

a. (Direct students to take out their marking pencils.)
- We're going to check your workbook and textbook items. Remember, if you got an item wrong, make an **X** next to the item.
b. (For each item: Read the item. Call on a student to answer it. If the answer is wrong, say the correct answer. Refer to the Answer Key for the correct answers.)
c. Now use your marking pencil to fix up any items you got wrong. Remember, all mistakes must be fixed up before you hand in your work.

LANGUAGE ARTS

(Present Language Arts lesson 44 after completing Reading lesson 44. See Language Arts Guide.)

Lesson 45

EXERCISE 1

VOCABULARY REVIEW

a. You learned a sentence that tells what they were impressed by.
- Everybody, say that sentence. Get ready. (Signal.) *They were impressed by her large vocabulary.*
- (Repeat until firm.)

b. You learned a sentence that tells what he responded to.
- Everybody, say that sentence. Get ready. (Signal.) *He responded to her clever solution.*
- (Repeat until firm.)

c. Here's the last sentence you learned: The patent attorney wrote an agreement.
- Everybody, say that sentence. Get ready. (Signal.) *The patent attorney wrote an agreement.*
- (Repeat until firm.)

d. What word means **a promise made by people?** (Signal.) *Agreement.*
- What word means **lawyer?** (Signal.) *Attorney.*
- What word names a license for somebody to be the only person who can make a product? (Signal.) *Patent.*
- What words name a lawyer whose special job is getting patents for new inventions? (Signal.) *Patent attorney.*
- (Repeat step d until firm.)

e. Once more. Say the sentence that tells what the patent attorney wrote. Get ready. (Signal.) *The patent attorney wrote an agreement.*

EXERCISE 2

READING WORDS

Column 1

a. **Find lesson 45 in your textbook.** ✓
- Touch column 1. ✓
- (Teacher reference:)

1. **diagram**	4. **attorney**
2. **lawyer**	5. **permission**
3. **purchase**	6. **electrical**

b. Word 1 is **diagram.** What word? (Signal.) *Diagram.*
- Spell **diagram.** Get ready. (Tap for each letter.) *D-I-A-G-R-A-M.*
- A diagram is a picture that is something like a map. It doesn't show the way things really look, but it shows the important parts very clearly.

c. Word 2 is **lawyer.** What word? (Signal.) *Lawyer.*
- Spell **lawyer.** Get ready. (Tap for each letter.) *L-A-W-Y-E-R.*
- People who need help with the law go to a lawyer.

d. Word 3 is **purchase.** What word? (Signal.) *Purchase.*
- Spell **purchase.** Get ready. (Tap for each letter.) *P-U-R-C-H-A-S-E.*
- **Purchase** is another word for **buy.** When you buy something, you purchase that thing.

e. Word 4 is **attorney.** What word? (Signal.) *Attorney.*
- Spell **attorney.** Get ready. (Tap for each letter.) *A-T-T-O-R-N-E-Y.*

f. Word 5 is **permission.** What word? (Signal.) *Permission.*

g. Word 6 is **electrical.** What word? (Signal.) *electrical.*

h. Let's read those words again.
- Word 1. What word? (Signal.) *Diagram.*
- (Repeat for words 2–6.)

i. (Repeat step h until firm.)

Column 2

j. Find column 2. ✓
- (Teacher reference:)

1. **secret**	3. **shame**
2. **rapped**	4. **booming**

k. Word 1. What word? (Signal.) *Secret.*
- (Repeat for words 2–4.)

l. Let's read those words again.
- Word 1. What word? (Signal.) *Secret.*
- (Repeat for words 2–4.)

m. (Repeat step l until firm.)

Column 3

n. Find column 3. ✓
- (Teacher reference:)

1. snappy	3. company
2. sighed	4. patent

o. Word 1. What word? (Signal.) *Snappy.*
- (Repeat for words 2–4.)

p. Let's read those words again.
- Word 1. What word? (Signal.) *Snappy.*
- (Repeat for words 2–4.)

q. (Repeat step p until firm.)

Individual Turns

(For columns 1–3: Call on individual students, each to read one to three words per turn.)

EXERCISE 3

STORY READING

a. Find part B in your textbook. ✓
- The error limit for group reading is 15 errors. Read carefully.

b. Everybody, touch the title. ✓
- (Call on a student to read the title.) *[Another Problem.]*
- Everybody, what's the title? (Signal.) *Another Problem.*
- (Call on individual students to read the story, each student reading two or three sentences at a time. Ask the specified questions as the students read.)

- (Correct errors: Tell the word. Direct the student to reread the sentence.)
- (If the group makes more than 15 errors, direct the students to reread the story.)

Another Problem
"That's a great solution," Grandmother Esther said.

- What solution is she talking about? (Call on a student. Idea: *Using two electric eyes instead of one.*)

Leonard had just explained his idea. Instead of one electric eye on the side of the door, he would use two of them. When somebody walked into the room, the body would break one beam before the other beam. If the outside beam was broken first, the person was moving into the room. If the inside beam was broken first, the person was moving out of the room.

- Everybody, which way would a person be moving if the **outside** beam was broken first? (Signal.) *Into the room.*
- Which way would a person be moving if the **inside** beam was broken first? (Signal.) *Out of the room.*

Leonard explained, "As soon as I saw that arrow on the one-way sign, I knew that I was close to the solution."
"Good job," Grandmother Esther said and rapped out a snappy drum roll.

- Everybody, use your hands to show me a snappy drum roll. ✓

Grandmother Esther continued, "But there is still one problem."
"Oh, no," Leonard said. "Not another problem."
Grandmother Esther hit the biggest drum. Then she said, "Your machine can tell whether somebody comes into the room or goes out of the room. And your machine turns off the lights when somebody leaves the room."
Then she said, "But what would happen if three people were sitting in the room reading and one of them left the room?"

- What would happen if somebody left the room? (Call on a student. Idea: *The lights would go off.*)
- How would those people who are reading in the room feel about that? (Call on a student. Idea: *They wouldn't like it.*)
- It seems that Leonard still has a big problem.

Leonard sighed and said, "The light would go off."
Leonard felt dumb for not seeing this problem before his grandmother pointed it out. The electric eye device that he had imagined couldn't count. It couldn't tell if one person was in the room or if ten were in the room.

- What can't his device do? (Call on a student. Idea: *Count.*)
- So how would you change the device so it would work better? (Call on a student. Idea: *Make it count.*)

The only thing Leonard's device knew how to do was to turn the lights on if somebody came into the room and turn them off if somebody left the room. But the device didn't know how many people were in the room.

Grandmother Esther said, "Your invention has to know how to count people in the room." Then she made a long drum roll and ended it with a terribly loud boom. "So, make it count," she said.

"How do I do that?" Leonard asked.

She responded, "What if you had a counter on your device? When a person went into the room, the counter would count one. When the next person went into the room, the counter would count again—two. With a counter, your device would know how many people are in the room. ★ It wouldn't shut off the lights until the last person left the room."

- Everybody, what would the counter count to if there were six people in the room? (Signal.) *Six.*
- Here's a new problem: Would the lights go off if there were three people in the room and one person left the room? (Signal.) *No.*
- When would the counter turn off the lights? (Call on a student. Idea: *When the last person left the room.*)

For a few moments, Leonard thought about what she said. Then he said, "I get it. The lights wouldn't go off if there were still some people in the room." Then he added, "But I don't know how to make the device count."

"Think, think, think," she said and began to tap on the smallest drum. "Think, Leonard, think," she repeated.

Leonard knew that she wasn't going to tell him any more about how to make the device count, so he left the room and began to think.

For nearly the rest of the day, Leonard's mind kept hearing his grandmother say, "Think, think, think." But the problem was much harder for Leonard than she made it sound. He thought and thought.

Just before supper, he went into the bathroom. He filled the sink with water and washed his hands. When he started to let the water out of the sink, he got the idea. The water would keep going out of the sink until the sink was empty. The water kept going out until there was <u>zero</u> water in the sink. That was the secret. "Count to zero," he said out loud.

- Everybody, what did he think the counter had to do? (Signal.) *Count to zero.*

He ran to his room and got some paper. Then he made a little drawing that showed how the device could count. Look at the drawing that he made.

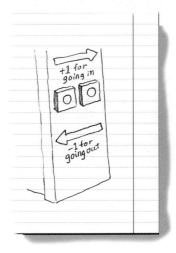

- Everybody, look at the picture. Touch the two electric eyes in the middle. ✓
- Touch the arrow **above** the electric eyes. ✓
- What does it say for that arrow? (Signal.) *Plus one for going in.*
- Every time somebody **goes in,** what does the counter do? (Call on a student. Ideas: *Adds one; plusses one.*)
- So if three people go in, how many will the counter plus? (Signal.) *Three.*
- Touch the arrow **below** the electric eyes. ✓
- What does it say for that arrow? (Signal.) *Minus one for going out.*

- Every time somebody **goes out of** the room, what does the counter do? (Call on a student. Ideas: *Subtracts one; minuses one.*)
- If three people go into the room and three people leave the room, what number will the counter end up at? (Signal.) *Zero.*
- If six people go into the room and six people leave the room, what number will the counter end up at? (Signal.) *Zero.*

> **Leonard ran into the kitchen. Grandmother Esther was starting to eat her salad. He showed her the drawing and explained. "The device can tell each time somebody goes into the room and each time somebody goes out. So we make a counter that counts <u>forward</u> each time somebody goes into the room. If four people go into the room, the counter counts one, two, three, four. Each time somebody leaves the room, the counter counts <u>backward</u>. So if three people leave, the counter counts backward: three, two, one. But the lights don't go off until the counter counts back to zero."**

- That's the big rule. Everybody, when do the lights go off? (Signal.) *When the counter counts back to zero.*
- So the lights stay on as long as somebody is in the room.

> **Leonard continued to explain, "When the last person leaves the room, the counter counts back to zero. Now the lights go off."**
> **Grandmother Esther jumped out of her chair, threw her arms around Leonard, and gave him a kiss.**

- How did she feel? (Call on a student. Ideas: *Happy, proud, excited.*)
- The pictures show what happens when people go into the room. Remember, the lights only go off when the counter counts back to zero.

A

- Everybody, touch picture A. ✓
- Each **solid** arrow shows that a person **went into** the room. Everybody, how many people went into the room? (Signal.) *Two.*
- So what does the counter count forward to? (Signal.) *Two.*
- Each **dotted** arrow shows that a person **left** the room. Everybody, how many people left the room? (Signal.) *Two.*
- So how many does the counter minus? (Signal.) *Two.*
- The counter plussed two and minused two. So what number does the counter end up at? (Signal.) *Zero.*
- And what happens to the lights? (Signal.) *They go off.*

B

- Touch picture B. ✓
- Count up the solid arrows and get ready to tell me how many people went **into** the room. (Pause.) How many? (Signal.) *Five.*
- Now count the number of people who left the room. (Pause.) How many? (Signal.) *Four.*
- How many more people would have to leave before the lights went off? (Signal.) *One.*

C

- Touch picture C. ✓
- How many people went into the room? (Signal.) *One.*
- How many people left the room? (Signal.) *One.*
- So what number does the counter end up at? (Signal.) *Zero.*
- Are the lights off? (Signal.) *Yes.*

D

- Touch picture D. ✓
- How many people went into the room? (Signal.) *Four.*
- How many people left the room? (Signal.) *Four.*
- So what number does the counter end up at? (Signal.) *Zero.*
- Are the lights off? (Signal.) *Yes.*

EXERCISE 4

READING CHECKOUTS

Note: There is a reading checkout in this lesson; therefore, there is no paired practice.

a. Today is a reading-checkout day. While you're doing your independent work, I'm going to call on you one at a time to read part of the story from lesson 44.
- Remember, you pass the checkout by reading the passage in less than a minute without making more than 2 mistakes. And when you pass the checkout, you'll color the space for lesson 44 on your thermometer chart.

b. (Call on individual students to read the portion of story 44 marked with ❀.)
- (Time the student. Note words that are missed and number of words read.)
- (Teacher reference:)

> ❀ **He studied the arrow. He traced it with his pencil three or four times. Then he traced over the letters in the sign. Then he put two dots next to each other on the shaft of the arrow. Suddenly, he felt goose bumps all over his face and down his [50] back. He almost jumped out of his seat. "Wow!" he shouted. "I've got it!"**
>
> **Everybody in the class was looking at him. He could feel [75] his face becoming very hot. He cleared his throat and coughed. Then he looked down at his paper. He could still feel the eyes of [100] everybody in the room looking at him. Then he heard the teacher's voice. "Is anything ❀ [115] wrong, Leonard?"**

- (If the student reads the passage in one minute or less and makes no more than 2 errors, direct the student to color in the space for lesson 45 on the thermometer chart.)

- (If the student made any mistakes, point to each word that was misread and identify it.)
- (If the student does not meet the rate-error criterion for the passage, direct the student to practice reading the story with the assigned partner.)

End-of-Lesson Activities

INDEPENDENT WORK

Now finish your independent work for lesson 45. Raise your hand when you're finished. (Observe students and give feedback.)

WORKCHECK

a. (Direct students to take out their marking pencils.)

• We're going to check your workbook and textbook items. Remember, if you got an item wrong, make an **X** next to the item.

b. (For each item: Read the item. Call on a student to answer it. If the answer is wrong, say the correct answer. Refer to the Answer Key for the correct answers.)

c. Now use your marking pencil to fix up any items you got wrong. Remember, all mistakes must be fixed up before you hand in your work.

LANGUAGE ARTS

(Present Language Arts lesson 45 after completing Reading lesson 45. See Language Arts Guide.)

ACTIVITIES

(Present Activity 8 after completing Reading lessons 45-46. See Activities Across the Curriculum.)

Lessons 46–50 • Planning Page

	Lesson 46	Lesson 47	Lesson 48	Lesson 49	Lesson 50
Lesson Events	**Vocabulary Sentence** Vocabulary Sentence Reading Words Story Reading Paired Practice Independent Work Workcheck Language Arts	Vocabulary Sentence Reading Words Story Reading Paired Practice Independent Work Workcheck Language Arts	Vocabulary Sentences Reading Words Story Reading Paired Practice Independent Work Workcheck Language Arts	**Vocabulary Sentence** Vocabulary Sentence Reading Words Story Reading Paired Practice Independent Work Workcheck Language Arts	Fact Game Reading Checkouts Test Marking the Test Test Remedies Literature Lesson Language Arts
Vocabulary Sentence	**#11: The <u>applause</u> <u>interrupted</u> his speech.** #10: The <u>patent</u> <u>attorney</u> wrote an <u>agreement</u>.	#11: The <u>applause</u> <u>interrupted</u> his speech.	sentence #9 sentence #10 sentence #11	**#12: She <u>selected</u> a <u>comfortable</u> seat.** #11: The <u>applause</u> <u>interrupted</u> his speech.	
Reading Words: Word Types	modeled words multi-syllable words words with an ending mixed words	compound words words with an ending mixed words	modeled words mixed words	2-syllable words words with an ending mixed words	
New Vocabulary	business manufacturer	disappointed	hesitated excellent	products nudged	
Comprehension Passage					
Story	*Leonard's Model*	*An Invention Fair*	*The Manufacturers at the Fair*	*Deals*	
Skill Items	Vocabulary sentences		Vocabulary sentence	Vocabulary sentences	Test: Vocabulary sentences
Special Materials					Thermometer charts, dice, Fact Game 50, Fact Game Answer Key, scorecard sheets, * materials for literature lesson
Special Projects/ Activities	Activity after lessons 45–46		Activity after lessons 48–51		

* Literature anthology; blackline masters 5A, 5B, and 5C; drawing materials; lined
  paper; "read to" copy of *Little House on the Prairie*

EXERCISE 1

VOCABULARY

a. **Find the vocabulary sentences on page 352 in your textbook.** ✓
- Touch sentence 11. ✓
- This is a new vocabulary sentence. It says: The applause interrupted his speech. Everybody, say that sentence. Get ready. (Signal.) *The applause interrupted his speech.*
- Close your eyes and say the sentence. Get ready. (Signal.) *The applause interrupted his speech.*
- (Repeat until firm.)

b. When people clap, they applaud. Their clapping is called **applause.**

c. The sentence says their applause interrupted something. **Interrupt** means **break into.** If the applause interrupted the speech, the applause broke into the speech.

d. Listen to the sentence again: The applause interrupted his speech. Everybody, say that sentence. Get ready. (Signal.) *The applause interrupted his speech.*

e. Everybody, what word means **the clapping?** (Signal.) *Applause.*
- What word means **broke into?** (Signal.) *Interrupted.*

EXERCISE 2

VOCABULARY REVIEW

a. You learned a sentence that tells what the patent attorney wrote.
- Everybody, say that sentence. Get ready. (Signal.) *The patent attorney wrote an agreement.*
- (Repeat until firm.)

b. I'll say part of the sentence. When I stop, you say the next word. Listen: The . . . Everybody, what's the next word? (Signal.) *Patent.*

c. Listen: The patent attorney wrote an . . . Everybody, what's the next word? (Signal.) *Agreement.*
- Say the whole sentence. Get ready. (Signal.) *The patent attorney wrote an agreement.*

d. Listen: The patent . . . Everybody, what's the next word? (Signal.) *Attorney.*

EXERCISE 3

READING WORDS

Column 1

a. Find lesson 46 in your textbook. ✓
- Touch column 1. ✓
- (Teacher reference:)

1. business	4. flood
2. manufacturer	5. turner-off-er
3. disappointed	

b. Word 1 is **business.** What word? (Signal.) *Business.*
- If you sell flowers, you are in the business of selling flowers. Here's another way of saying **She sells baskets: She's in the business of selling baskets.** Your turn. What's another way of saying **She sells baskets?** (Signal.) *She's in the business of selling baskets.*

c. Word 2 is **manufacturer.** What word? (Signal.) *Manufacturer.*
- Somebody who makes a product manufactures the product. The person is called a manufacturer. Everybody, what do we call a person who makes a product? (Signal.) *Manufacturer.*

d. Word 3 is **disappointed.** What word? (Signal.) *Disappointed.*

e. Word 4 is **flood.** What word? (Signal.) *Flood.*

f. Word 5 is **turner-off-er.** What word? (Signal.) *Turner-off-er.*

g. Let's read those words again.
- Word 1. What word? (Signal.) *Business.*
- (Repeat for words 2–5.)

h. (Repeat step g until firm.)

Column 2

i. Find column 2. ✓
- (Teacher reference:)

1. model	4. supply
2. patent	5. automatic
3. purchase	

- All these words have more than one syllable. The first part of each word is underlined.
j. Word 1. What's the underlined part? (Signal.) *mod.*
- What's the whole word? (Signal.) *Model.*
- Spell **model.** Get ready. (Tap for each letter.) *M-O-D-E-L.*
k. Word 2. What's the underlined part? (Signal.) *pat.*
- What's the whole word? (Signal.) *Patent.*
- Spell **patent.** Get ready. (Tap for each letter.) *P-A-T-E-N-T.*
l. Word 3. What's the underlined part? (Signal.) *pur.*
- What's the whole word? (Signal.) *Purchase.*
- Spell **purchase.** Get ready. (Tap for each letter.) *P-U-R-C-H-A-S-E.*
m. Word 4. What's the underlined part? (Signal.) *supp.*
- What's the whole word? (Signal.) *Supply.*
- Spell **supply.** Get ready. (Tap for each letter.) *S-U-P-P-L-Y.*
n. Word 5. What's the underlined part? (Signal.) *auto.*
- What's the whole word? (Signal.) *Automatic.*
o. Let's read those words again.
- Word 1. What word? (Signal.) *Model.*
- (Repeat for: **2. patent, 3. purchase, 4. supply, 5. automatic.**)
p. (Repeat step o until firm.)

Column 3
q. Find column 3. ✓
- (Teacher reference:)

1. **electrical**	4. **lawyers**
2. **connected**	5. **announcer**
3. **diagrams**	

- All these words have an ending.
r. Word 1. What word? (Signal.) *Electrical.*
- (Repeat for words 2–5.)
s. Let's read those words again.
- Word 1. What word? (Signal.) *Electrical.*
- (Repeat for words 2–5.)
t. (Repeat step s until firm.)

Column 4
u. Find column 4. ✓
- (Teacher reference:)

1. **owe**	3. **company**
2. **attorney**	4. **permission**

v. Word 1. What word? (Signal.) *Owe.*
- (Repeat for words 2–4.)
w. Let's read those words again.
- Word 1. What word? (Signal.) *Owe.*
- (Repeat for words 2–4.)
x. (Repeat step w until firm.)

Individual Turns
(For columns 1–4: Call on individual students, each to read one to three words per turn.)

EXERCISE 4
STORY READING
a. Find part B in your textbook. ✓
- The error limit for group reading is 13 errors. Read carefully.
b. Everybody, touch the title. ✓
- (Call on a student to read the title.) *[Leonard's Model.]*
- Everybody, what's the title? (Signal.) *Leonard's Model.*
- What would Leonard make a model of? (Call on a student. Idea: *His electric-eye invention.*)
- (Call on individual students to read the story, each student reading two or three sentences at a time. Ask the specified questions as the students read.)

- (Correct errors: Tell the word. Direct the student to reread the sentence.)
- (If the group makes more than 13 errors, direct the students to reread the story.)

Leonard's Model
It's easy to say that the invention will count things, but it's a much harder job to build a device that counts. Grandmother Esther was a big help for this part of the job. She knew a lot about electricity.

- Everybody, what runs the electric eye? (Signal.) *Electricity.*
- What will run the counter? (Signal.) *Electricity.*
- You'd have to know something about how to connect wires and work with electricity to make such a device.

Grandmother Esther got books for Leonard that showed him where to buy electric eyes and how to hook electric wires up to make the electric eyes work. These books also showed where to purchase electric counters. After Leonard and his grandmother decided which type of electric eyes they wanted, she made a few phone calls, took Leonard with her in her jeep, and bought the supplies that they needed to build a model of his invention.

- Everybody, what kind of vehicle does Grandmother Esther drive? (Signal.) *A jeep.*
- She plays the drums and she drives a jeep. She is not an ordinary grandmother. What else does she do that is unusual? (Call on individual students. Ideas: *She goes to exercise classes; knows about electricity; invents things;* etc.)

"Now remember, Leonard," she said as they left the electrical supply store. "You owe me ninety dollars. When you start making money from your invention, just remember that I'm giving up my fishing trip so that you can build your invention."

- Listen to that part again:
  "Now remember, Leonard," she said as they left the electrical supply store. "You owe me ninety dollars. When you start making money from your invention, just remember that I'm giving up my fishing trip so that you can build your invention."
- Everybody, who paid for the supplies? (Signal.) *Grandmother Esther.*
- How much did they cost? (Signal.) *Ninety dollars.*
- What had Grandmother Esther planned to do with the money that she spent on the supplies? (Call on a student. Idea: *Go fishing.*)
- When will Leonard be able to pay her back? (Call on a student. Idea: *When he starts making money on his invention.*)

"You shouldn't give up your fishing trip, Grandmother," he said. "I'll get the money . . . ."

"I'm kidding you," she said. "I'd much rather invent something than go fishing any time."

- Everybody, did she mind giving up the fishing trip? (Signal.) *No.*
- Why not? (Call on a student. Idea: *She'd rather be working on an invention.*)

She started up the jeep and made the engine roar loudly. Suddenly, the jeep jumped forward, snapping Leonard's head back. And off they went to their home.

- Everybody, is she a **slow, easy** driver or a **little bit wild**? (Signal.) *A little bit wild.*
- How do you know? (Call on a student. Ideas: *Because the jeep's engine roared; because it jumped forward; because Leonard's head snapped back.*)

Leonard and his grandmother built a model of the electric eye device. The model was a little room with a doorway that was about one meter tall. There was a light bulb connected to the top of the doorway.

To show how the model worked, Leonard used a large teddy bear and large dolls. Leonard moved these objects through the doorway. An object would break the outside beam first, then the inside beam.

- What's going to happen to the light if the outside beam is broken first? (Call on a student. Idea: *It will turn on.*)

As soon as the first object broke both beams, the light went on. Leonard would move more objects through the doorway and the light would stay on.

Then Leonard would begin to move the objects the other way. The light would stay on until the last object went back through the doorway. Then the light would go off.

- The picture shows a model of the room with a doorway. Some objects are already in the room and Leonard is moving another object into the room. The arrow shows the direction the doll is moving.
- Everybody, is the light **on** or **off**? (Signal.) *On.*
- What's going to happen to the light when Leonard moves that big sailor doll through the doorway? (Call on a student. Ideas: *Nothing; it will stay on.*)
- Everybody, after that sailor doll is inside the room, how many objects will be in the room? (Signal.) *Four.*
- How many will have to leave the room before the light goes off? (Signal.) *Four.*

"This device works!" Leonard shouted after he and his grandmother had tested it four times. ☆ "It works. We've invented an automatic light turner-off-er!"

- Everybody, what did Leonard call his invention? (Signal.) *An automatic light turner-off-er.*

But Leonard's work was not finished. He had a model of the invention, and that model worked. But now he had to protect his invention.

- Everybody, what did he have to do now? (Signal.) *Protect his invention.*
- I wonder what that means, protect the invention.

An invention needs protection from people who copy it and say that it is their invention.

- What does the invention need protection from? (Call on a student. Ideas: *From people who would steal the idea; from people who would copy it and say they made it first.*)

To protect an invention, the inventor gets a patent.

- Everybody, what does the inventor get to protect the invention? (Signal.) *A patent.*

When an invention is patented, the only person who can make copies of that invention is the inventor. If other people want to make copies of it, they have to get permission from the inventor.

- Everybody, when an inventor has a patent on an invention, who is the only person who can make copies of that invention? (Signal.) *The inventor.*
- What if other people want to make copies? (Call on a student. Idea: *They must get permission from the inventor.*)

The inventor may tell somebody that it is all right to make copies of the invention. But the inventor doesn't usually <u>give</u> somebody this right. The inventor <u>sells</u> the right.

- Everybody, what does the inventor usually do? (Signal.) *Sells the right.*

The inventor may say this to the person who wants to make copies: "Each time you make a copy, you must give me so much money."

- If the person agrees to this deal, what would the person have to do? (Call on a student. Idea: *Give the inventor money for each copy that is made.*)

Maybe the person has to pay five dollars for each copy that is built. Maybe the inventor sells the whole patent to a company that wants to make copies of the invention.

- Listen to that sentence again: Maybe the inventor sells the whole patent to a company that wants to make copies of the invention.

- The inventor may make a deal so that the person who makes copies gives the inventor so much money for each copy.
- What's the other thing the inventor may do? (Call on a student. Idea: *Sell the patent to a company.*)

If the invention is good, the inventor may make a lot of money from that invention.

- Let's say the inventor gets one dollar for each copy and the person who makes copies sells one million copies. Everybody, how much money would the inventor make? (Signal.) *One million dollars.*

But the first step is to get a patent. Without a patent, the inventor has no protection against people who want to make copies of the invention. Getting a patent is very difficult. There are special lawyers who do nothing but get patents for inventors. These lawyers are called patent attorneys.

- What do patent attorneys do? (Call on a student. Idea: *Get patents for inventors.*)

Grandmother Esther explained patents and patent attorneys to Leonard. Then she phoned a patent attorney and told her that Leonard wanted to patent his invention.
Leonard and his grandmother had three meetings with the patent attorney. The attorney answered hundreds of questions. Leonard and Grandmother Esther made diagrams of the invention for her.

- Everybody, how many meetings did they have with the patent attorney? (Signal.) *Three.*
- Look at the diagram on the next page. ✓
- It shows Leonard's invention and the wires that are needed to make it work.
- That device looks very complicated to me.

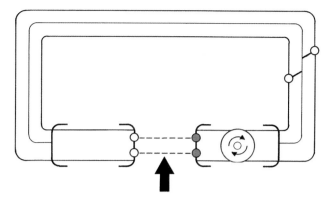

- Read the rest of the story to yourself and be ready to answer some questions. Find out how much the patent attorney cost them. Raise your hand when you're finished.

When they finally finished their meetings with the patent attorney, Grandmother Esther said, "Now you owe me another three thousand dollars. If your invention doesn't start making some money, I'll have to give up my flying lessons."
"You're great, Grandma," Leonard said. "You're just great."
"Oh, stop it," Grandmother Esther said and slapped Leonard on the back.

- (After all students have raised their hand:) Everybody, how much did the patent attorney cost? (Signal.) *Three thousand dollars.*
- Who paid for the patent attorney? (Signal.) *Grandmother Esther.*
- What did Grandmother Esther say she would have to give up to pay for the patent attorney? (Signal.) *Flying lessons.*
- What did Leonard say that made Grandmother Esther feel embarrassed? (Call on a student. Idea: *You're great, Grandma.*)

EXERCISE 5

PAIRED PRACTICE

You're going to read aloud to your partner. The **B** members will read first. Then the **A** members will read from the star to the end of the story. (Observe students and give feedback.)

End-of-Lesson Activities

Now finish your independent work for lesson 46. Raise your hand when you're finished. (Observe students and give feedback.)

a. (Direct students to take out their marking pencils.)
 • We're going to check your workbook and textbook items. Remember, if you got an item wrong, make an **X** next to the item.

b. (For each item: Read the item. Call on a student to answer it. If the answer is wrong, say the correct answer. Refer to the Answer Key for the correct answers.)
c. Now use your marking pencil to fix up any items you got wrong. Remember, all mistakes must be fixed up before you hand in your work.

(Present Language Arts lesson 46 after completing Reading lesson 46. See Language Arts Guide.)

EXERCISE 1

VOCABULARY REVIEW

a. Here's the new vocabulary sentence: The applause interrupted his speech.
- Everybody, say that sentence. Get ready. (Signal.) *The applause interrupted his speech.*
- (Repeat until firm.)

b. Everybody, what word means **broke into?** (Signal.) *Interrupted.*
- What word means **the clapping?** (Signal.) *Applause.*

EXERCISE 2

READING WORDS

Column 1

a. **Find lesson 47 in your textbook.** ✓
- Touch column 1. ✓
- (Teacher reference:)

1. basketball	3. notebook
2. loudspeaker	4. meantime

- All these words are compound words. The first part of each word is underlined.

b. Word 1. What's the underlined part? (Signal.) *basket.*
- What's the whole word? (Signal.) *Basketball.*

c. Word 2. What's the underlined part? (Signal.) *loud.*
- What's the whole word? (Signal.) *Loudspeaker.*

d. Word 3. What's the underlined part? (Signal.) *note.*
- What's the whole word? (Signal.) *Notebook.*

e. Word 4. What's the underlined part? (Signal.) *mean.*
- What's the whole word? (Signal.) *Meantime.*

f. Let's read those words again, the fast way.
- Word 1. What word? (Signal.) *Basketball.*
- (Repeat for words 2–4.)

g. (Repeat step f until firm.)

Column 2

h. Find column 2. ✓
- (Teacher reference:)

1. disappointed	4. manufacturers
2. announcer	5. charges
3. smoking	

- All these words have an ending.

i. Word 1. What word? (Signal.) *Disappointed.*
- When something you want does not happen, you feel disappointed. Everybody, how would you feel if you wanted to take a vacation and found out that you couldn't? (Signal.) *Disappointed.*

j. Word 2. What word? (Signal.) *Announcer.*
- (Repeat for words 3–5.)

k. Let's read those words again.
- Word 1. What word? (Signal.) *Disappointed.*
- (Repeat for words 2–5.)

l. (Repeat step k until firm.)

Column 3

m. Find column 3. ✓
- (Teacher reference:)

1. cloth	4. business
2. Friday	5. cost
3. prize	6. forth

n. Word 1. What word? (Signal.) *Cloth.*
- Spell **cloth.** Get ready. (Tap for each letter.) *C-L-O-T-H.*

o. Word 2. What word? (Signal.) *Friday.*
- Spell **Friday.** Get ready. (Tap for each letter.) *F-R-I-D-A-Y.*

p. Word 3. What word? (Signal.) *Prize.*
- Spell **prize.** Get ready. (Tap for each letter.) *P-R-I-Z-E.*

q. Word 4. What word? (Signal.) *Business.*
- Spell **business.** Get ready. (Tap for each letter.) *B-U-S-I-N-E-S-S.*

r. Word 5. What word? (Signal.) *Cost.*

s. Word 6. What word? (Signal.) *Forth.*

t. Let's read those words again.
- Word 1. What word? (Signal.) *Cloth.*
- (Repeat for words 2–6.)

u. (Repeat step t until firm.)

Individual Turns

(For columns 1–3: Call on individual students, each to read one to three words per turn.)

STORY READING

a. Find part B in your textbook. ✓
  • The error limit for group reading is 13 errors. Read carefully.
b. Everybody, touch the title. ✓
  • (Call on a student to read the title.) [An Invention Fair.]
  • Everybody, what's the title? (Signal.) *An Invention Fair.*
  • (Call on individual students to read the story, each student reading two or three sentences at a time. Ask the specified questions as the students read.)

> • (Correct errors: Tell the word. Direct the student to reread the sentence.)
> • (If the group makes more than 13 errors, direct the students to reread the story.)

An Invention Fair
  Leonard had found out a lot about inventing things. He found out that you have to start with a need. Then you get an idea for an invention that meets that need. Then you have to build a model of the invention and show that it works. Once you have a model, you must go to a patent attorney and get a patent for your invention. If your invention is the first one of its kind, you'll get a patent. Once you have a patent, you have protection for that invention. Nobody can make copies of the device that you have patented. You can give other people permission to make copies of the invention, but you can charge them for the right to make the copies.

  • Let's go through the steps that Leonard took in inventing the electric eye device. When he thought like an inventor, what did he start with? (Call on a student. Ideas: *A need; a problem.*)

  • Then he got an idea to meet that need. Then he had to make something. What was that? (Call on a student. Idea: *A model of the invention.*)
  • Everybody, after he had a model, what did he have to get? (Signal.) *A patent.*
  • Why did he need a patent? (Call on a student. Idea: *To protect his invention.*)
  • If you have a patent, who is the only person who can make copies of the invention? (Call on a student. Ideas: *Me; people I've given permission to.*)

But Leonard was not finished learning about inventions. Once you have patented an invention, you must sell it to somebody who is in the business of making things. Businesses that make things are called manufacturers.

  • Everybody, what are businesses that make things called? (Signal.) *Manufacturers.*
  • Leonard has an invention. Manufacturers build things. So Leonard is going to try to sell his invention to a manufacturer.

Grandmother Esther explained, "There are different ways that we can get in touch with manufacturers. We can take our model and go visit manufacturers who make things for houses. We can call them on the phone and see if they are interested in our invention. We can take out an ad in a magazine that manufacturers read." She shook her head no.

  • Everybody, did she like any of those ideas? (Signal.) *No.*
  • How do you know? (Call on a student. Idea: *She shook her head.*)
  • Name the ideas that she didn't like. (Call on a student. Ideas: *Visiting manufacturers, calling them on the phone, taking out ads in a magazine.*)

Then she smiled and continued. "But there's a better way. We can put our invention in an invention fair."

  • What's the better way? (Call on a student. Idea: *Put the invention in an invention fair.*)

"What's an invention fair?" Leonard asked.

His grandmother explained. "An invention fair is a place where inventors and manufacturers get together. The inventors bring their inventions. The manufacturers go to the fair to see if they want any of these new inventions. At the fair there are prizes for the best inventions."

"How soon can we enter an invention fair?" Leonard asked.

Grandmother Esther tossed a magazine to Leonard. It was opened to a large ad.

- What do you think that ad tells about? (Call on a student. Idea: *An invention fair.*)

The top of the ad announced, "World's Largest Invention Fair!" The rest of the ad told about the prizes and the fair. The first prize was twenty thousand dollars. The second prize was ten thousand dollars. And the third prize was five thousand dollars. There were also special prizes for inventions that were clever.

The fair would start on Friday at noon. Then it would run all day Saturday. It didn't cost inventors anything to show their inventions at the fair. ★ Thousands of people were expected to visit the fair.

- Listen to that part again:
  The top of the ad announced, "World's Largest Invention Fair!" The rest of the ad told about the prizes and the fair. The first prize was twenty thousand dollars. The second prize was ten thousand dollars. And the third prize was five thousand dollars. There were also special prizes for inventions that were clever.
  The fair would start on Friday at noon. Then it would run all day Saturday. It didn't cost inventors anything to show their inventions at the fair. Thousands of people were expected to visit the fair.
- Everybody, what is first prize? (Signal.) *Twenty thousand dollars.*

- What is second prize? (Signal.) *Ten thousand dollars.*
- On what day does the fair start? (Signal.) *Friday.*
- How much would you have to pay if you wanted to show your invention at that fair? (Signal.) *Nothing.*
- Were many people expected to go to the fair? (Signal.) *Yes.*

Leonard read the ad three times. Each time he read it, the fair sounded greater and greater.

"Can we win?" Leonard asked his grandmother.

"First prize," she said, smiling. "First prize."

- Everybody, what did she think they would win? (Signal.) *First prize.*
- How much money would that mean for them? (Signal.) *Twenty thousand dollars.*
- And that's only the money that they get as a prize for having the best invention. They can still sell the invention to a manufacturer.

Leonard slowly stood up. "You mean we can get twenty thousand dollars for our invention?" Leonard could not even imagine how much money that was. He once saved one hundred dollars. But that wasn't even close to one thousand dollars. As Leonard started to think about twenty <u>thousand</u> dollars, he became a little dizzy. "Twenty thousand dollars," he said over and over.

• • •

- Close your eyes and start thinking of dollar bills. Think of one . . . Now imagine ten. . . . Now try to imagine a pile of one hundred . . . Now a thousand . . . Now think of twenty piles that high.
- Everybody, look at the three dots in the story. What do they tell you? (Call on a student. Idea: *Part of the story is missing.*)

The invention fair took place in a huge hall. Leonard and his grandmother got there early in the morning. The fair opened at noon. Before noon, the inventors had to set up their displays.

- What kind of display would Leonard have to show his invention? (Call on a student. Ideas: *A room with a doorway and electric eyes, a light, and some objects; his model.*)

> **No inventor could get into the hall before that morning because there had been a basketball game in the hall the evening before.**

- Why couldn't the inventors get in and set up their displays the night before? (Call on a student. Idea: *There was a basketball game going on.*)

> **So the inventors were lined up at the door the next morning, ready to set up their displays. Some of them complained about the basketball game. An old man standing near Leonard and his grandmother told them that it would take him six hours to set up his display and he didn't know how he would have it ready when the fair opened.**

- Everybody, when was the fair going to be open to the public? (Signal.) *At noon.*

> **The old man said, "I'll just have to keep working on it while the fair is going on."**

- The picture shows Leonard and some of the other inventors waiting to get inside the hall. What is Grandmother Esther carrying? (Call on a student. Ideas: *The display; a bag with the toys in it.*)

- Which person had Leonard and Grandmother Esther been talking to? (Call on a student. Idea: *The old man.*)
- Everybody, do any of those inventors look a little crazy? (Signal.) *Yes.*
- I wonder what that man's invention could be.
- Read the rest of the story to yourself and be ready to answer some questions. You will read about where Leonard's table is in the hall. You can look at the big diagram of the hall and find his table. Raise your hand when you're finished.

> The doors opened and the inventors went into the hall. Other large doors opened and trucks moved into the hall. Men jumped from the trucks and began setting up rows and rows of tables. The men covered the tables with blue cloth. Every now and then a voice came over the loudspeaker and made announcements. One announcement was, "No smoking in the hall." Another announcement told the inventors where their tables were. Each inventor had a blue piece of paper that had a letter and a number on it. The announcer explained to the inventors that all slips that had the letter A would be in the first aisle, that the Bs would be in the next aisle, that the Cs would be in the next aisle, and so forth. Here's what it said at the top of Leonard's slip: F16.
>
> As Leonard and his grandmother walked to the aisle, Leonard said, "This is the biggest hall I've ever seen in my life."

- (After all students have raised their hand:) Everybody, each inventor got a blue slip of paper. What did it say on Leonard's slip? (Signal.) *F16.*
- So what table did he have to go to? (Signal.) *F16.*
- What aisle is that? (Signal.) *F.*
- How many places from the beginning of the aisle is F16? (Signal.) *16.*
- Touch the A aisle at the top of the diagram on page 233. ✓

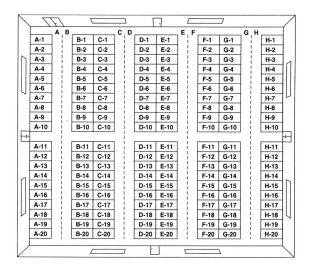

A	B		C	D		E	F		G	H	
A-1	B-1	C-1	D-1	E-1		F-1	G-1		H-1	
A-2	B-2	C-2	D-2	E-2		F-2	G-2		H-2	
A-3	B-3	C-3	D-3	E-3		F-3	G-3		H-3	
A-4	B-4	C-4	D-4	E-4		F-4	G-4		H-4	
A-5	B-5	C-5	D-5	E-5		F-5	G-5		H-5	
A-6	B-6	C-6	D-6	E-6		F-6	G-6		H-6	
A-7	B-7	C-7	D-7	E-7		F-7	G-7		H-7	
A-8	B-8	C-8	D-8	E-8		F-8	G-8		H-8	
A-9	B-9	C-9	D-9	E-9		F-9	G-9		H-9	
A-10	B-10	C-10	D-10	E-10		F-10	G-10		H-10	
A-11	B-11	C-11	D-11	E-11		F-11	G-11		H-11	
A-12	B-12	C-12	D-12	E-12		F-12	G-12		H-12	
A-13	B-13	C-13	D-13	E-13		F-13	G-13		H-13	
A-14	B-14	C-14	D-14	E-14		F-14	G-14		H-14	
A-15	B-15	C-15	D-15	E-15		F-15	G-15		H-15	
A-16	B-16	C-16	D-16	E-16		F-16	G-16		H-16	
A-17	B-17	C-17	D-17	E-17		F-17	G-17		H-17	
A-18	B-18	C-18	D-18	E-18		F-18	G-18		H-18	
A-19	B-19	C-19	D-19	E-19		F-19	G-19		H-19	
A-20	B-20	C-20	D-20	E-20		F-20	G-20		H-20	

- Now move across until you come to the aisle that Leonard and his grandmother went to. ✓
- Now go down that aisle until you come to Leonard's table. ✓
- See if you can find this table: C13. ✓
- See if you can find this table: H9. ✓

EXERCISE 4

PAIRED PRACTICE

You're going to read aloud to your partner. The **A** members will read first. Then the **B** members will read from the star to the end of the story. (Observe students and give feedback.)

End-of-Lesson Activities

INDEPENDENT WORK*

Now finish your independent work for lesson 47. Raise your hand when you're finished. (Observe students and give feedback.)

WORKCHECK

a. (Direct students to take out their marking pencils.)
  - We're going to check your workbook and textbook items. Remember, if you got an item wrong, make an **X** next to the item.
b. (For each item: Read the item. Call on a student to answer it. If the answer is wrong, say the correct answer. Refer to the Answer Key for the correct answers.)
c. Now use your marking pencil to fix up any items you got wrong. Remember, all mistakes must be fixed up before you hand in your work.

LANGUAGE ARTS

(Present Language Arts lesson 47 after completing Reading lesson 47. See Language Arts Guide.)

Lesson 48

EXERCISE 1

VOCABULARY REVIEW

a. You learned a sentence that tells what he responded to.
  - Everybody, say that sentence. Get ready. (Signal.) *He responded to her clever solution.*
  - (Repeat until firm.)

b. You learned a sentence that tells what the patent attorney wrote.
  - Everybody, say that sentence. Get ready. (Signal.) *The patent attorney wrote an agreement.*
  - (Repeat until firm.)

c. Here's the last sentence you learned: The applause interrupted his speech.
  - Everybody, say that sentence. Get ready. (Signal.) *The applause interrupted his speech.*
  - (Repeat until firm.)

d. What word means **broke into**? (Signal.) *Interrupted.*
  - What word means **the clapping?** (Signal.) *Applause.*

e. Once more. Say the sentence that tells what the applause interrupted. Get ready. (Signal.) *The applause interrupted his speech.*

EXERCISE 2

READING WORDS

Column 1

a. **Find lesson 48 in your textbook.** ✓
  - Touch column 1. ✓
  - (Teacher reference:)

1. hesitated	4. operator
2. during	5. introduced
3. applause	6. excellent

b. Word 1 is **hesitated.** What word? (Signal.) *Hesitated.*
  - When you **hesitate,** you **pause for a moment.** Everybody, what's another way of saying **She paused for a moment?** (Signal.) *She hesitated.*

- What's another way of saying **Before running across the street, they paused for a moment?** (Signal.) *Before running across the street, they hesitated.*

c. Word 2 is **during.** What word? (Signal.) *During.*
  - Spell **during.** Get ready. (Tap for each letter.) *D-U-R-I-N-G.*

d. Word 3. What word? (Signal.) *Applause.*
  - Spell **applause.** Get ready. (Tap for each letter.) *A-P-P-L-A-U-S-E.*

e. Word 4 is **operator.** What word? (Signal.) *Operator.*
  - Spell **operator.** Get ready. (Tap for each letter.) *O-P-E-R-A-T-O-R.*

f. Word 5 is **introduced.** What word? (Signal.) *Introduced.*

g. Word 6 is **excellent.** What word? (Signal.) *Excellent.*
  - Something that is very, very good is excellent. Everybody, what's another way of saying **Her story was very, very good?** (Signal.) *Her story was excellent.*
  - What's another way of saying **He gave a very, very good report?** (Signal.) *He gave an excellent report.*

h. Let's read those words again.
  - Word 1. What word? (Signal.) *Hesitated.*
  - (Repeat for words 2–6.)

i. (Repeat step h until firm.)

Column 2

j. Find column 2. ✓
  - (Teacher reference:)

1. interrupted	5. disappointed
2. praised	6. wandering
3. flood	7. nudged
4. notebooks	

k. Word 1. What word? (Signal.) *Interrupted.*

l. Word 2. What word? (Signal.) *Praised.*
  - (Repeat for words 3–7.)

m. Let's read those words again.
  - Word 1. What word? (Signal.) *Interrupted.*
  - (Repeat for words 2–7.)

n. (Repeat step m until firm.)

(For columns 1 and 2: Call on individual students, each to read one to three words per turn.)

EXERCISE 3

STORY READING

a. Find part B in your textbook. ✓
 • The error limit for group reading is 15 errors. Read carefully.
b. Everybody, touch the title. ✓
 • (Call on a student to read the title.) [The Manufacturers at the Fair.]
 • Everybody, what's the title? (Signal.) The Manufacturers at the Fair.
 • (Call on individual students to read the story, each student reading two or three sentences at a time. Ask the specified questions as the students read.)

> • (Correct errors: Tell the word. Direct the student to reread the sentence.)
> • (If the group makes more than 15 errors, direct the students to reread the story.)

The Manufacturers at the Fair
Leonard was very disappointed when the fair opened at noon. He expected to see thousands of people pour into the hall. He imagined that there would be crowds of people looking at his display. But when the fair opened at noon, only a very few people came into the hall.

• What had Leonard expected to happen? (Call on a student. Idea: *Thousands of people would come to the fair.*)
• What actually happened when the fair opened? (Call on a student. Idea: *Only a few people came.*)

Only three of the people who came into the hall stopped at Leonard's exhibit. As soon as one of them stopped, Leonard showed how the device worked. For his display he had brought the little room with the doorway. He moved his dolls and stuffed animals into the room. Then he moved them out. He showed how the device worked and explained how the light stays on until everybody has left the room.

• Everybody, look at the picture on the next page. Is the light on in the picture? (Signal.) *Yes.*
• How many objects are in the room? (Signal.) *One.*
• What's going to happen when the teddy bear leaves the room? (Call on a student. Idea: *The light will turn off.*)

But none of the people who stopped at the display that afternoon seemed to be very impressed. Two of them nodded and said, "Very interesting." Then they walked down the F aisle to the next exhibit. The third person who stopped at Leonard's display was a slim woman wearing a gray coat. She didn't say anything. She just looked, listened, nodded her head, and walked away.

• What did she do when Leonard explained the device? (Call on a student. Ideas: *She didn't say anything; she just looked, listened, nodded, walked away.*)
• She doesn't seem very polite at all.

Grandmother Esther told Leonard that these people were manufacturers. "They don't seem very interested in the invention," Leonard said.
His grandmother said, "Smart manufacturers will never let you know that they're interested in your invention. They know that you'll want more money for your invention if they're very interested. So they'll act as if they're not very interested. Don't let them fool you. The ones that seem the most interested are the ones who will never want to buy your invention."

- Listen to what she says again:
  "Smart manufacturers will never let you know that they're interested in your invention. They know that you'll want more money for your invention if they're very interested. So they'll act as if they're not very interested. Don't let them fool you. The ones that seem the most interested are the ones who will never want to buy your invention."
- Why don't smart manufacturers act interested in the inventions that they want? (Call on a student. Idea: *So they don't have to pay much money for the inventions.*)
- If a manufacturer seems very interested, what does that mean? (Call on a student. Idea: *The manufacturer doesn't want to buy the invention.*)
- If a manufacturer doesn't seem interested at all, what could that mean? (Call on a student. Idea: *That the manufacturer does want to buy your invention.*)

"Another thing," his grandmother continued. "A smart manufacturer will try to stay far away from your display. Here's why. The manufacturer doesn't want a crowd to gather in front of your display. The more people who show that they are interested in your invention, the more money the manufacturers will have to pay for your invention.

- Why wouldn't the manufacturer want a crowd to gather? (Call on a student. Idea: *The manufacturer would have to pay more money.*)

Remember, manufacturers want good inventions, but they don't want to pay any more money than they have to. So they're going to do everything they can to make you think that they're not interested."
After supper, great crowds of people flooded the hall.

- What does that mean, flooded the hall? (Call on a student. Ideas: *Lots of people poured into the hall; people filled the hall.*)

During most of the evening there was a group of people around Leonard's invention. ★ The people smiled and praised Leonard for his invention.

- Would these people be interested in manufacturing the invention? (Call on a student. Idea: *No.*)

Grandmother Esther explained, "The people who flood the fair after supper are not manufacturers. These are people who have other jobs. But they want to look at the new inventions. They're coming to the fair after work. The manufacturers have been at this fair since it opened. Being at the fair is part of their job."

- Listen to that part again:
  Grandmother Esther explained, "The people who flood the fair after supper are not manufacturers. These are people who have other jobs. But they want to look at the new inventions. They're coming to the fair after work. The manufacturers have been at this fair since it opened. Being at the fair is part of their job."
- If people are manufacturers, what would they do as part of their job? (Call on a student. Idea: *Be at the fair since it opened.*)
- If they weren't at the fair since it opened, what do we know about them? (Call on a student. Idea: *They aren't manufacturers.*)

"You're really smart, Grandmother," Leonard said.
Grandmother Esther said, "Those people you saw wandering around here this afternoon are the real manufacturers. They're the important ones."

- Everybody, were there a lot of people wandering around earlier? (Signal.) *No.*
- But how important were those people? (Call on a student. Idea: *Very important.*)

When the fair closed at ten that night, Leonard was very tired. "I never talked so much in my whole life," he explained to his grandmother.

The fair continued on the next day, Saturday. There weren't many people looking at the exhibits early in the morning. Grandmother Esther explained, "Most of the people you see here now are manufacturers. If you watch some of them, you'll see that they're writing things in little notebooks." Leonard watched two people, but neither person wrote anything. Then he spotted the slim woman in the gray coat. She was walking down the G aisle.

- Everybody, tell me the letter of the aisle Leonard's display was on. Get ready. (Signal.) *F.*
- How close was the G aisle? (Call on a student. Idea: *One aisle away.*)
- Who did he see walking down that aisle? (Call on a student. Idea: *The slim woman in the gray coat.*)

When the woman got to the end of the aisle, she took out a little book and wrote something. Then she walked to the E aisle and talked to two men. She talked only for a moment. Then the men went one way and she went another way.

- Everybody, do you think she is a manufacturer? (Signal.) *Yes.*
- Name some things she did that make you think she's a manufacturer. (Call on individual students. Ideas: *She was at the fair since it opened; she didn't seem interested in his invention; she wrote things in a book.*)

"This is really interesting," Leonard said.

Around 11 o'clock that morning, Grandmother Esther said, "Now the manufacturers will have to start making their deals with the inventors."

- Everybody, around what time in the morning is it now? (Signal.) *11 o'clock.*
- What does Grandmother Esther say is going to start happening? (Call on a student. Idea: *Manufacturers will start making deals with inventors.*)

"Why do they have to make their deals now?" Leonard asked.

Grandmother Esther explained. "First of all, they want to make their deals before the prizes are announced this evening. If the manufacturers think that an invention will win a prize, they know that they can make a much better deal before it gets the prize. Once an invention is a first-prize invention, the inventor can get much more money for the invention."

- Why would they want to make their deals before the prizes are announced? (Call on a student. Idea: *If the invention wins a prize, they will have to pay more for it.*)
- Read the rest of the story to yourself and be ready to answer some questions. Find out the two reasons manufacturers do things the way they do them. Raise your hand when you're finished.

Leonard said, "But Grandmother, why don't the manufacturers wait until later this afternoon before making deals with the inventors?"

Grandmother Esther said, "Here's the first reason. There will be many people here this afternoon. That means the inventors will be busy explaining their inventions. The second reason is that the manufacturers need at least three hours to make their deals with the inventors."

- (After all students have raised their hand:) Leonard asked a question. What did he ask? (Call on a student. Idea: *Why don't manufacturers wait until later to make their deals?*)
- Grandmother Esther gave two reasons that the manufacturers did not wait until the afternoon. What was the first reason? (Call on a student. Idea: *Later there will be many people talking to the inventors.*)
- What was the second reason? (Call on a student. Idea: *The manufacturers will need at least three hours to make their deals.*)

PAIRED PRACTICE

You're going to read aloud to your partner. The **B** members will read first. Then the **A** members will read from the star to the end of the story. (Observe students and give feedback.)

End-of-Lesson Activities

INDEPENDENT WORK

Now finish your independent work for lesson 48. Raise your hand when you're finished. (Observe students and give feedback.)

WORKCHECK

a. (Direct students to take out their marking pencils.)
 • We're going to check your workbook and textbook items. Remember, if you got an item wrong, make an **X** next to the item.
b. (For each item: Read the item. Call on a student to answer it. If the answer is wrong, say the correct answer. Refer to the Answer Key for the correct answers.)
c. Now use your marking pencil to fix up any items you got wrong. Remember, all mistakes must be fixed up before you hand in your work.

LANGUAGE ARTS

(Present Language Arts lesson 48 after completing Reading lesson 48. See Language Arts Guide.)

LANGUAGE ARTS

(Present Activity 9 after completing Reading lessons 48-51. See Activities Across the Curriculum.)

EXERCISE 1

VOCABULARY

a. **Find the vocabulary sentences on page 352 in your textbook.** ✓
- Touch sentence 12.
- This is a new vocabulary sentence. It says: She selected a comfortable seat. Everybody, say that sentence. Get ready. (Signal.) *She selected a comfortable seat.*
- Close your eyes and say the sentence. Get ready. (Signal.) *She selected a comfortable seat.*
- (Repeat until firm.)

b. **Selected** means **chose.** So if she selected a seat, she chose a seat. Everybody, what's another way of saying **They chose partners?** (Signal.) *They selected partners.*

c. She selected a **comfortable** seat. Things that are comfortable feel very pleasant. So a comfortable seat is one where she feels very pleasant.

d. Listen to the sentence again: She selected a comfortable seat. Everybody, say that sentence. Get ready. (Signal.) *She selected a comfortable seat.*

e. Everybody, what word means **chose?** (Signal.) *Selected.*
- What word tells that the seat felt pleasant? (Signal.) *Comfortable.*

EXERCISE 2

VOCABULARY REVIEW

a. You learned a sentence that tells what the applause interrupted.
- Everybody, say that sentence. Get ready. (Signal.) *The applause interrupted his speech.*
- (Repeat until firm.)

b. I'll say part of the sentence. When I stop, you say the next word. Listen: The . . . Everybody, what's the next word? (Signal.) *Applause.*

c. Listen: The applause . . . Everybody, what's the next word? (Signal.) *Interrupted.*
- Say the whole sentence. Get ready. (Signal.) *The applause interrupted his speech.*

EXERCISE 3

READING WORDS

Column 1

a. Find lesson 49 in your textbook. ✓
- Touch column 1. ✓
- (Teacher reference:)

1. **during**	4. **involve**
2. **elbow**	5. **meantime**
3. **hurry**	6. **remind**

- All these words have more than one syllable. The first part of each word is underlined.

b. Word 1. What's the underlined part? (Signal.) *dur.*
- What's the whole word? (Signal.) *During.*

c. Word 2. What's the underlined part? (Signal.) *el.*
- What's the whole word? (Signal.) *Elbow.*

d. Word 3. What's the underlined part? (Signal.) *hurr.*
- What's the whole word? (Signal.) *Hurry.*

e. Word 4. What's the underlined part? (Signal.) *in.*
- What's the whole word? (Signal.) *Involve.*

f. Word 5. What's the underlined part? (Signal.) *mean.*
- What's the whole word? (Signal.) *Meantime.*

g. Word 6. What's the underlined part? (Signal.) *re.*
- What's the whole word? (Signal.) *Remind.*

h. Let's read those words again.
- Word 1. What word? (Signal.) *During.*
- (Repeat for words 2–6.)

i. (Repeat step h until firm.)

Column 2

j. Find column 2. ✓
- (Teacher reference:)

1. **products**	4. **introduced**
2. **nudged**	5. **reasons**
3. **interrupted**	6. **shorter**

- All these words have an ending.
k. Word 1. What word? (Signal.) *Products.*
- Things that are made by people are products. Pencils, cars, cups, and motorboats are products.
l. Word 2. What word? (Signal.) *Nudged.*
- When you nudge something, you gently poke it. You can nudge somebody with your elbow or your shoulder or your hand.
m. Word 3. What word? (Signal.) *Interrupted.*
- (Repeat for: **4. introduced, 5. reasons, 6. shorter.**)
n. Let's read those words again.
- Word 1. What word? (Signal.) *Products.*
- (Repeat for: **2. nudged, 3. interrupted, 4. introduced, 5. reasons, 6. shorter.**)
o. (Repeat step n until firm.)

Column 3

p. Find column 3. ✓
- (Teacher reference:)

1. **bald**	4. **kindergarten**
2. **boss**	5. **information**
3. **eleven**	6. **businesslike**

q. Word 1. What word? (Signal.) *Bald.*
- (Repeat for words 2–6.)
r. Let's read those words again.
- Word 1. What word? (Signal.) *Bald.*
- (Repeat for words 2–6.)
s. (Repeat step r until firm.)

Column 4

t. Find column 4.
- (Teacher reference:)

1. **stage**	4. **judge**
2. **spotlight**	5. **deciding**
3. **paused**	

u. Word 1. What word? (Signal.) *Stage.*
- (Repeat for words 2–5.)
v. Let's read those words again.
- Word 1. What word? (Signal.) *Stage.*
- (Repeat for words 2–5.)
w. (Repeat steps v until firm.)

Individual Turns

(For columns 1–4: Call on individual students, each to read one to three words per turn.)

STORY READING

a. Find part B in your textbook. ✓
- The error limit for group reading is 13 errors. Read carefully.
b. Everybody, touch the title. ✓
- (Call on a student to read the title.) *[Deals.]*
- Everybody, what's the title? (Signal.) *Deals.*
- Who is going to be making deals? (Call on a student. Idea: *Manufacturers and inventors.*)
- When the manufacturers deal, how much money do they want to pay for the inventions? (Call on a student. Ideas: *Not much; as little as possible.*)
- When the inventors deal, how much money do they want to get for the inventions? (Call on a student. Ideas: *A lot; as much as possible.*)
- So these deals are going to be like games with the inventors and the manufacturers each trying to get the best possible deal.
- (Call on individual students to read the story, each student reading two or three sentences at a time. Ask the specified questions as the students read.)

- (Correct errors: Tell the word. Direct the student to reread the sentence.)
- (If the group makes more than 13 errors, direct the students to reread the story.)

Deals

Grandmother Esther had just given two reasons why the manufacturers would try to make deals with inventors before noon. The first reason was that the inventors would be very busy at their displays during the afternoon. The second reason was that it would take time for the inventor and the manufacturer to make a deal.

Just as she finished telling Leonard about what would happen, Leonard noticed that the slim woman in the gray coat was walking toward Leonard's display.

- Do you think that woman is interested in trying to make a deal? (Call on a student. Idea: *Yes.*)

She was with a man who was shorter than she was. They stopped at the display next to Leonard's and smiled as they looked at it.

- They're smiling at that display. What does that tell you about how interested they are in that display? (Call on a student. Idea: *They're not very interested in it.*)

Grandmother Esther whispered, "Leonard, they're going to try to make a deal with us. Let me do all the talking."

- Why do you think she didn't want Leonard to make the deal? (Call on a student. Idea: *She knew more about how to bargain with the manufacturers.*)

❀ The man and woman approached Leonard's display. They stopped. They didn't smile. They just stood there. "Hello," Leonard said at last.
The woman said, "Do you have a patent on this device?"
"Yes," Leonard replied.
The woman said nothing for a few moments. Then she said, "I'm with ABC Home Products."

- Everybody, does she work for a manufacturer? (Signal.) *Yes.*
- What's the name of that manufacturer? (Signal.) *ABC Home Products.*

The woman continued, "I don't think many people would be interested in an invention like yours. But I may be able to talk my boss into working out a deal. But that deal must not involve a lot of money."

- Listen to what she says again:
  "I don't think many people would be interested in an invention like yours. But I may be able to talk my boss into working out a deal. But that deal must not involve a lot of money."
- She says that not many people would be interested in the invention. Everybody, does she really think that? (Signal.) *No.*

- Why is she saying it? (Call on a student. Idea: *So Leonard will sell his invention for a low price.*)
- Then she says that if she works out a deal it must not involve a lot of money. Do you think that is true? (Call on a student. Idea: *No.*)
- If it's not true, why would she say it? (Call on a student. Idea: *So Leonard will sell his invention for a low price.*)

Grandmother Esther pointed to the large clock in the center of the hall. "It's already after eleven o'clock," she announced loudly. "This afternoon we're ❀ going to be very busy. This evening we're going to win first prize and there will be many manufacturers who are interested in this invention. If you want to make a deal, you'd better start talking about a lot of money and you'd better start right now."

- Raise your hand if you can read that speech the way Grandmother Esther said it. She's talking very tough. (Call on a student. Student should talk loudly.)
  "It's already after eleven o'clock. This afternoon we're going to be very busy. This evening we're going to win first prize and there will be many manufacturers who are interested in this invention. If you want to make a deal, you'd better start talking about a lot of money and you'd better start right now!"

The woman's eyes opened wide. For a moment she didn't seem to know what to say. Then she turned to the man who was with her. He said, "ABC Home Products is a good company to be with. We have a very good name and very good products. That should be important to any inventor."

- He's trying to make the company sound very good so that an inventor would want to go with that company even though there isn't much money for the invention. Everybody, do you think that Grandmother Esther will be tricked by this kind of talk? (Signal.) *No.*

"We're in no hurry to make a deal," Grandmother Esther said. Then she said, "In fact, I would just as soon wait until after the prizes are announced this evening."

- Why would she want to wait? (Call on a student. Idea: *Because if they win a prize, the invention will be worth more money.*)

"But what if you don't win first prize?" the man said. "There are some very exciting ⭐ inventions at this fair. I've looked at ten inventions that could take first prize."

"Well, that's fine," Grandmother Esther said. "You just go and make a deal for one of those inventions. But if you want to talk to us, you can always wait until after we win first prize."

- Everybody, does she think that there are ten inventions that can win first prize? (Signal.) *No.*
- Which invention does she think will win? (Call on a student. Idea: *Leonard's.*)

The woman in the gray coat nudged the man with her elbow.

- You do that when you want to call somebody's attention to something. Show me how you could nudge somebody with your elbow. (Call on a student.)

The man said, "We're going over to talk to the man we work for. Maybe we'll be back in a few minutes."

The man and woman left. Leonard watched them. They walked very fast toward the C aisle, where another man was standing. In the meantime, three men who had been standing at the head of the F aisle approached Leonard's display. A tall bald man walked up and introduced himself and the two men who were with him. Then he smiled and said, "It's just a shame that our company can't buy your device. I think it's very clever. But we've got too many inventions already. That's a real shame."

- What reason does this man give for his company not being interested in Leonard's device? (Call on a student. Idea: *They have too many inventions already.*)
- Everybody, do you believe him? (Signal.) *No.*

One of the other men said to the tall bald man, "Do you think that we might be able to take this invention if we didn't have to pay very much for it?"

The bald man said, "Well, I don't know. I just hadn't thought of that."

The third man said, "I'll bet that we could probably talk our boss into taking it if we didn't have to pay more than a few hundred dollars for it."

The bald man said, "That's an idea I hadn't thought of. Maybe you're right. Maybe we could do that."

- I think these men are acting. Listen to what they are saying:

One of the other men said to the tall bald man, "Do you think that we might be able to take this invention if we didn't have to pay very much for it?"

The bald man said, "Well, I don't know. I just hadn't thought of that."
The third man said, "I'll bet that we could probably talk our boss into taking it if we didn't have to pay more than a few hundred dollars for it."

The bald man said, "That's an idea I hadn't thought of. Maybe you're right. Maybe we could do that."

- Everybody, do you believe that they hadn't thought about trying to buy it for very little money? (Signal.) *No.*
- Read the rest of the story to yourself and be ready to answer some questions. Find out the lie that Grandmother Esther tells the bald man. Raise your hand when you're finished.

Grandmother Esther said, "Who do you think we are, a couple of kindergarten children? You're not going to steal this invention. You're going to tell us the name of the company you're with. You're going to give us your business card. You're going to tell us your best deal. And then we're going to see if that deal is better than the deal ABC Home Products wants to make."

"But Grandma," Leonard said. He was going to remind her that ABC Home Products had not told about the deal they wanted to make.

She interrupted Leonard and said, "I know what you're thinking, Leonard. You want to go with ABC Home Products. But we have to give these other manufacturers a chance, too."

- (After all students have raised their hand:) What was the first lie Grandmother Esther told the bald man? (Call on a student. Idea: *That ABC Home Products wants to make a deal.*)
- Leonard was going to correct what she said. What was he going to say? (Call on a student. Idea: *That ABC Home Products hadn't told about a deal.*)
- Why didn't he say that? (Call on a student. Idea: *Grandmother Esther interrupted him.*)
- She told another lie. What was that? (Call on a student. Idea: *That Leonard wants to go with ABC Home Products.*)
- She knew that Leonard wasn't thinking that at all. She just wanted to make him stop talking.

EXERCISE 5

PAIRED PRACTICE

You're going to read aloud to your partner. The **A** members will read first. Then the **B** members will read from the star to the end of the story. (Observe students and give feedback.)

End-of-Lesson Activities

INDEPENDENT WORK

Now finish your independent work for lesson 49. Raise your hand when you're finished. (Observe students and give feedback.)

WORKCHECK

a. (Direct students to take out their marking pencils.)
  - We're going to check your workbook and textbook items. Remember, if you got an item wrong, make an **X** next to the item.
b. (For each item: Read the item. Call on a student to answer it. If the answer is wrong, say the correct answer. Refer to the Answer Key for the correct answers.)
c. Now use your marking pencil to fix up any items you got wrong. Remember, all mistakes must be fixed up before you hand in your work.

LANGUAGE ARTS

(Present Language Arts lesson 49 after completing Reading lesson 49. See Language Arts Guide.)

> ***Note:*** Students will need access to a telephone directory Yellow Pages for lesson 51.
>
> You will need to reproduce blackline masters for the Fact Game in lesson 50 (Appendix G in Teacher's Guide).

Lesson 50

Materials for lesson 50

Fact Game

For each team (4 or 5 students):
- pair of number cubes (or dice)
- copy of Fact Game 50 (Reproducible blackline masters are at the back of the Teacher's Guide.)

For each student:
- their copy of the scorecard sheet (at end of workbook A)

For each monitor:
- a pencil
- Fact Game 50 answer key (at end of textbook A)

Reading Checkout

Each student needs their thermometer chart.

Literature Lesson 5

See Literature Guide for the materials you will need.

EXERCISE 1

FACT GAME

a. You're going to play the game that uses the facts you have learned. Remember the rules. The player rolls the number cubes, figures out the number of the question, reads that question out loud, and answers it. The monitor tells the player if the answer is right or wrong. If it's wrong, the monitor tells the right answer. If it's right, the monitor gives the player one point. Don't argue with the monitor. The number cubes go to the left and the next player has a turn. You'll play the game for 10 minutes.

b. (Divide students into groups of four or five. Assign monitors. Circulate as students play the game. Comment on groups that are playing well.)

c. (At the end of 10 minutes, have all students who earned more than 10 points stand up.)

- (Tell the monitor of each game that ran smoothly:) Your group did a good job.

EXERCISE 2

READING CHECKOUTS

a. Today is a test day and a reading-checkout day. While you're writing answers, I'm going to call on you one at a time to read part of the story we read in lesson 49.

- Remember, you pass the checkout by reading the passage in less than a minute without making more than 2 mistakes. And when you pass the checkout, you color the space for lesson 50 on your thermometer chart.

b. (Call on individual students to read the portion of story 49 marked with ❀.)

- (Time the student. Note words that are missed and the number of words read.)

- (Teacher reference:)

> ❀ The man and woman approached Leonard's display. They stopped. They didn't smile. They just stood there. "Hello," Leonard said at last.
>
> The woman said, "Do you have a patent on this device?"
>
> "Yes," Leonard replied.
>
> The woman said nothing for a few moments. Then she said, "I'm with ABC Home [50] Products." The woman continued, "I don't think many people would be interested in an invention like yours. But I may be able to talk my [75] boss into working out a deal. But that deal must not involve a lot of money."
>
> Grandmother Esther pointed to the large clock in the [100] center of the hall. "It's already after eleven o'clock," she announced loudly. "This afternoon we're ❀ [115] going to be very busy."

- (If the student reads the passage in one minute or less and makes no more than 2 errors, direct the student to color in the space for lesson 50 on the thermometer chart.)

- (If the student makes any mistakes, point to each word that was misread and identify it.
- (If the student does not meet the rate-error criterion for the passage, direct the student to practice reading the story with the assigned partner.

EXERCISE 3

TEST

a. **Find page 247 in your textbook.** ✓
- This is a test. You'll work items you've done before.
b. Work carefully. Raise your hand when you've completed all the items.
(Observe students but do not give feedback on errors.)

EXERCISE 4

MARKING THE TEST

a. (Check students' work before beginning lesson 51. Refer to the Answer Key for the correct answers.)
b. (Record all test 5 results on the Test Summary Sheet and the Group Summary Sheet. Reproducible Summary Sheets are at the back of the Teacher's Guide.)

EXERCISE 5

TEST REMEDIES

(Provide any necessary remedies for test 5 before presenting lesson 51. Test remedies are discussed in the Teacher's Guide.)

Test 5 Firming Table

Test Item	Introduced in lesson	Test Item	Introduced in lesson	Test Item	Introduced in lesson
1	43	13	45		
2	43	14	45		
3	43	15	45	25	47
4	44	16	45	26	47
5	44	17	45	27	47
6	44	18	45	28	39
7	44	19	45	29	43
8	44	20	45	30	43
9	44	21	45	31	46
10	45	22	46	32	39
11	45	23	46	33	43
12	45	24	47	34	39

LITERATURE

(Present Literature lesson 5 after completing Reading lesson 50. See Literature Guide.)

LANGUAGE ARTS

(Present Language Arts lesson 50 after completing Reading lesson 50. See Language Arts Guide.)

Note: Students will need access to reference materials at the end of lesson 51. See page 266 for details.

Lessons 51–55 · Planning Page

	Lesson 51	Lesson 52	Lesson 53	Lesson 54	Lesson 55
Lesson Events	Vocabulary Sentence Reading Words Story Reading Paired Practice Study Items Independent Work Workcheck Language Arts	Vocabulary Sentences Reading Words Comprehension Passage Story Reading Paired Practice Independent Work Workcheck Language Arts	**Vocabulary Sentence** Vocabulary Sentence Reading Words Comprehension Passage Story Reading Paired Practice Independent Work Workcheck Language Arts	Vocabulary Sentence Reading Words Comprehension Passage Story Reading Paired Practice Independent Work Workcheck Language Arts	Vocabulary Sentences Reading Words Fact Review Story Reading Reading Checkouts Independent Work Workcheck Language Arts
Vocabulary Sentence	#12: She <u>selected</u> a <u>comfortable</u> seat.	sentence #10 sentence #11 sentence #12	**#13: Without <u>gravity</u>, they were <u>weightless</u>.** #12: She <u>selected</u> a <u>comfortable</u> seat.	#13: Without <u>gravity</u>, they were <u>weightless</u>.	sentence #11 sentence #12 sentence #13
Reading Words: Word Types	modeled words multi-syllable words words with an ending mixed words	modeled words mixed words multi-syllable words	modeled words –ed words planet names multi-syllable words	multi-syllable words numbers modeled words mixed words	modeled words 2-syllable words words with an ending
New Vocabulary		solar system suppose	planet concluded	day-dreaming section	Tokyo pressure
Comprehension Passage		*Facts About Japan*	*Facts About the Solar System*	*Past, Present, and Future*	
Story	*The First-Prize Winner*	*Your Turn*	*An Important Test*	*The Test Questions*	*Waiting for a Letter*
Skill Items	Sequencing	Vocabulary sentence	Vocabulary sentences	Deduction	Vocabulary sentence
Special Materials	Telephone directory Yellow Pages	*Materials for project			Thermometer charts
Special Projects/ Activities		Project after lesson 52; Activity after lesson 53			

*Crayons, colored pencils, lined paper, and workbook A, page 94.

Materials: Telephone directory Yellow Pages for textbook study items 21 and 22.

EXERCISE 1
VOCABULARY REVIEW

a. Here's the new vocabulary sentence you learned: She selected a comfortable seat.
   - Everybody, say that sentence. Get ready. (Signal.) *She selected a comfortable seat.*
   - (Repeat until firm.)
b. Everybody, what word means **chose?** (Signal.) *Selected.*
   - What word tells that the seat felt pleasant? (Signal.) *Comfortable.*

EXERCISE 2
READING WORDS

Column 1

a. **Find lesson 51 in your textbook.** ✓
   - Touch column 1. ✓
   - (Teacher reference:)

1. young	4. judges
2. guess	5. remained
3. student	6. information

b. Word 1 is **young.** What word? (Signal.) *Young.*
   - Spell **young.** Get ready. (Tap for each letter.) *Y-O-U-N-G.*
c. Word 2 is **guess.** What word? (Signal.) *Guess.*
   - Spell **guess.** Get ready. (Tap for each letter.) *G-U-E-S-S.*
d. Word 3 is **student.** What word? (Signal.) *Student.*
   - Spell **student.** Get ready. (Tap for each letter.) *S-T-U-D-E-N-T.*
e. Word 4. What word? (Signal.) *Judges.*
   - Spell **judges.** Get ready. (Tap for each letter.) *J-U-D-G-E-S.*
f. Word 5. What word? (Signal.) *Remained.*
g. Word 6. What word? (Signal.) *Information.*

h. Let's read those words again.
i. Word 1. What word? (Signal.) *Young.*
   - (Repeat for words 2–6.)
j. (Repeat step h until firm.)

Column 2

k. Find column 2. ✓
   - (Teacher reference:)

1. agreement	4. spotlight
2. businesslike	5. excellent
3. offer	

   - All these words have more than one syllable. The first part of each word is underlined.
l. Word 1. What's the underlined part? (Signal.) *agree.*
   - What's the whole word? (Signal.) *Agreement.*
m. Word 2. What's the underlined part? (Signal.) *business.*
   - What's the whole word? (Signal.) *Businesslike.*
n. Word 3. What's the underlined part? (Signal.) *off.*
   - What's the whole word? (Signal.) *Offer.*
o. Word 4. What's the underlined part? (Signal.) *spot.*
   - What's the whole word? (Signal.) *Spotlight.*
p. Word 5. What's the underlined part? (Signal.) *ex.*
   - What's the whole word? (Signal.) *Excellent.*
q. Let's read those words again.
   - Word 1. What word? (Signal.) *Agreement.*
   - (Repeat for words 2–5.)
r. (Repeat step q until firm.)

Column 3

s. Find column 3. ✓
   - (Teacher reference:)

1. deciding	4. paused
2. dimmed	5. hesitated
3. flatly	6. concluded

   - All these words have an ending.
t. Word 1. What word? (Signal.) *Deciding.*

- (Repeat for: **2. dimmed, 3. flatly,
  4. paused, 5. hesitated, 6. concluded.**)
u. Let's read those words again.
- Word 1. What word? (Signal.) *Deciding.*
- (Repeat for words 2–6.)
v. (Repeat step u until firm.)

Column 4

w. Find column 4. ✓
- (Teacher reference:)

1. applause	4. operator
2. item	5. key
3. stage	

x. Word 1. What word? (Signal.) *Applause.*
- (Repeat for words 2–5.)
y. Let's read those words again.
- Word 1. What word? (Signal.) *Applause.*
- (Repeat for words 2–5.)
z. (Repeat step y until firm.)

Individual Turns

(For columns 1–4: Call on individual
students, each to read one to three words
per turn.)

EXERCISE 3

STORY READING

a. Find part B in your textbook. ✓
- The error limit for group reading is 13
  errors. Read carefully.
b. Everybody, touch the title. ✓
- (Call on a student to read the title.)
  [The First-Prize Winner.]
- Everybody, what's the title? (Signal.)
  The First-Prize Winner.
- Who do you think that's going to be?
  (Call on individual students. Student
  preference.)
- (Call on individual students to read the
  story, each student reading two or three
  sentences at a time. Ask the specified
  questions as the students read.)

- (Correct errors: Tell the word. Direct the
  student to reread the sentence.)
- (If the group makes more than 13 errors,
  direct the students to reread the story.)

The First-Prize Winner
**The woman in the gray coat came
back to Leonard's display with two
men. The other group of men had just
left. The woman's voice was very flat**

**and businesslike when she said, "I
will make one offer. We will pay you
ten thousand dollars in cash for your
invention and one dollar for every
copy that we sell."**

- Everybody, how much cash will they
  pay? (Signal.) *Ten thousand dollars.*
- How much will they pay for each copy?
  (Signal.) *One dollar.*

**Leonard listened to the offer and
could hardly believe what he heard.
He wanted to shout out, "Yes, we'll
take it!"**

- Everybody, did he think it was a good
  offer? (Signal.) *Yes.*
- How do you think Grandmother Esther
  will feel about it? (Call on individual
  students. Student preference.)

**But his grandmother said, "I'll
make <u>you</u> one offer. <u>You</u> will pay us
<u>fifteen</u> thousand dollars in cash and
<u>two</u> dollars for every device that you
sell."**

- The woman offered **ten** thousand dollars
  in cash. Everybody, how much did
  Grandmother Esther want? (Signal.)
  $15,000.
- The woman offered **one** dollar for each
  device that was sold. How much did
  Grandmother Esther want for each
  device? (Signal.) *Two dollars.*

**"Can't pay that much," the woman
said flatly. "Here's the best I can do.
Ten thousand dollars and two dollars
for every copy we sell."**

- What's the offer? (Call on a student.
  Idea: *They will pay Leonard $10,000 in
  cash and $2 for every copy they sell.*)
- Everybody, is that better than the
  woman's first offer? (Signal.) *Yes.*
- Is her latest offer as good as the deal
  that Grandmother Esther wanted?
  (Signal.) *No.*
- Do you think Grandmother Esther will
  take the offer? (Call on individual
  students. Student preference.)

Grandmother Esther said, "Write it down and sign it. You've got a deal."

Leonard jumped up and shouted, "We did it!"

Suddenly the woman in the gray coat smiled. She looked very nice when she smiled. She held out her hand and Leonard shook it. Her voice seemed to change and she sounded very pleasant. "I think this will be a very good deal for all of us."

- How did the woman change after she made the deal? (Call on a student. Ideas: *She smiled; her voice changed; she seemed nicer.*)
- So she isn't always a businesslike person. She just acts that way sometimes.

At two o'clock in the afternoon, Leonard and his grandmother were signing papers.

- They made the deal with the woman shortly after 11 o'clock. Now it was almost three hours later.

Grandmother Esther had called their patent attorney and the attorney had come down to read the agreement. The attorney said that it looked good. So Leonard and his grandmother signed the papers.

- The deal isn't finished until they sign the papers. When they sign, then everybody has to do what they agreed to do. What does ABC Home Products have to do? (Call on a student. Idea: *Pay $10,000 in cash and $2 for every copy they sell.*)

The afternoon went by very fast. Large crowds of people gathered in front of Leonard's display. A lot of people who watched how the invention worked shook hands with Leonard and said things like this: "That's a good energy saver." "We could use a device like that in our house."

That evening at 8:30 the lights in the hall were dimmed. A large spotlight came on and a beam of bright blue-white light fell on a man who stood on a small stage. "It's time for the prizes," he announced. People from all over the hall began to crowd close to the stage.

"Should we go over there, Grandmother?" Leonard asked.

"Of course," she replied. "We want to be right there when they announce the winner of the first prize."

So ⭐ they walked over near the stage. The man explained, "It was a very, very hard job deciding on a first-prize winner. There were many excellent inventions. The first and second prize winners were so close that it might have been a good idea to give them both first prize. But . . ." he hesitated and raised one hand. "Ladies and gentlemen. The winner of the first prize is . . ."

- Here it comes. The man is going to announce the winner of the first prize. This is the moment that Leonard has been waiting for.

The man paused again. "The winner is Ronald Hogan and his automatic list-writer."

- Everybody, who won first prize? (Signal.) *Ronald Hogan.*
- What was his invention? (Call on a student. Idea: *An automatic list-writer.*)

"What?" Grandmother Esther shouted. "<u>We</u> win first prize!"

- Everybody, she's saying that but did they actually win first prize? (Signal.) *No.*

Some of the people standing near Leonard turned around and looked at Grandmother Esther. The man on the stage continued, "For those of you who didn't see Mr. Hogan's great invention, I'll explain how it works. It fits on the side of your refrigerator. You give this machine information about what should be in the refrigerator. When the refrigerator gets low on anything, the machine automatically writes the name of that item on a list."

"Let's go home," Grandmother Esther said to Leonard. "This is like a bad dream."

"No, Grandma," Leonard said. "Let's stick around. Maybe we'll get one of the other prizes."

The man on the stage called Mr. Hogan to the stage and gave him a check for twenty thousand dollars. Grandmother Esther said, "This is enough to make you sick."

Then the announcer said, "Ladies and gentlemen. The second prize winner lost to the list-writer by only a hair."

- Everybody, did the second prize lose to the list-writer by very much? (Signal.) *No.*
- I wonder who won this prize.

The man continued, "This prize goes to Leonard Mathis for his automatic light operator. Leonard, come on up here and get your check for ten thousand dollars."

- Wow, Leonard got second prize.
- Read the rest of the story to yourself and be ready to answer some questions. Raise your hand when you're finished.

People were clapping like crazy. The spotlight swung over and the beam was on Leonard. His grandmother was pushing him. "Go on. Get your prize."

He grabbed her arm. "You're coming with me," he shouted. He had to shout, because the applause was so loud.

"No," she said and tried to push him away.

"You come, or I'm not going up there," he said.

So she went with him. They stood on the stage. The light was almost blinding. The man asked Leonard some questions and he answered them. But he could hardly remember what was happening. The next thing he knew, he was holding a check, and people were clapping again.

- (After all students have raised their hand:) Why did Leonard have to shout when he said things to his grandmother? (Call on a student. Idea: *People were clapping so loudly.*)

- What did he want Grandmother Esther to do? (Call on a student. Idea: *Go on stage with him.*)
- Why do you think he wanted her to go on the stage with him? (Call on a student. Ideas: *Because she helped him make the invention; because he was nervous.*)
- Everybody, did she want to go on the stage? (Signal.) *No.*
- Did he get her to go with him? (Signal.) *Yes.*
- Did Leonard remember much about what happened on the stage? (Signal.) *No.*

PAIRED PRACTICE

You're going to read aloud to your partner. The **B** members will read first. Then the **A** members will read from the star to the end of the story.
(Observe students and give feedback.)

STUDY ITEMS

a. Find items 21 and 22 in your textbook. ✓
- These are study items. Follow along as I read them: Look in the Yellow Pages of your phone book to find out 2 things.
- Item 21: Find out if there are any electric-equipment manufacturers. The word **manufacturer** may be written like this in the Yellow Pages: **mfr.** If the Yellow Pages list any electric-equipment manufacturers, write down the name of one manufacturer. That would be the kind of company that would make copies of Leonard's invention.
- Item 22: Also look up the names of stores that might sell the copies that are manufactured. These are stores that would be listed under a heading like this: **Electric Equipment and Supplies— Retail.** The name **retail** tells you that you can buy things at that store. Write the name of an electric-equipment-and-supply retail store.

b. If you finish your independent work early, raise your hand and I'll tell you how you can look up the answers to those study items.

c. (When students raise their hand, direct them to the Yellow Pages of a phone book. If necessary, help the students find the answers to the study items.)

End-of-Lesson Activities

INDEPENDENT WORK

Now finish your independent work for lesson 51. Raise your hand when you're finished. (Observe students and give feedback.)

WORKCHECK

a. (Direct students to take out their marking pencils.)
- We're going to check your workbook and textbook items. Remember, if you got an item wrong, make an **X** next to the item.

b. (For each item: Read the item. Call on a student to answer it. If the answer is wrong, say the correct answer. Refer to the Answer Key for the correct answers.)

c. Now use your marking pencil to fix up any items you got wrong. Remember, all mistakes must be fixed up before you hand in your work.

LANGUAGE ARTS

(Present Language Arts lesson 51 after completing Reading lesson 51. See Language Arts Guide.)

Note: A special project occurs after lesson 52. See page 274 for the materials you'll need.

Lesson 52

VOCABULARY REVIEW

a. You learned a sentence that tells what the patent attorney wrote.
- Everybody, say that sentence. Get ready. (Signal.) *The patent attorney wrote an agreement.*
- (Repeat until firm.)

b. You learned a sentence that tells what the applause interrupted.
- Everybody, say that sentence. Get ready. (Signal.) *The applause interrupted his speech.*
- (Repeat until firm.)

c. Here's the last sentence you learned: She selected a comfortable seat.
- Everybody, say that sentence. Get ready. (Signal.) *She selected a comfortable seat.*
- (Repeat until firm.)

d. What word tells that the seat felt pleasant? (Signal.) *Comfortable.*
- What word means **chose?** (Signal.) *Selected.*

e. Once more. Say the sentence that tells what she selected. Get ready. (Signal.) *She selected a comfortable seat.*

EXERCISE 2

READING WORDS

Column 1

a. **Find lesson 52 in your textbook.** ✓
- Touch column 1. ✓
- (Teacher reference:)

1. solar system	4. report
2. Jupiter	5. parents
3. Uranus	

b. Number 1 is **solar system.** What words? (Signal.) *Solar system.*
- The solar system is the group of planets and moons that move around the sun. Our Earth is part of the solar system.

c. Word 2 is **Jupiter.** What word? (Signal.) *Jupiter.*
- Spell **Jupiter.** Get ready. (Tap for each letter.) *J-U-P-I-T-E-R.*

d. Word 3 is **Uranus.** What word? (Signal.) *Uranus.*
- Spell **Uranus.** Get ready. (Tap for each letter.) *U-R-A-N-U-S.*

e. Word 4. What word? (Signal.) *Report.*
- Spell **report.** Get ready. (Tap for each letter.) *R-E-P-O-R-T.*

f. Word 5. What word? (Signal.) *Parents.*
- Spell **parents.** Get ready. (Tap for each letter.) *P-A-R-E-N-T-S.*

g. Let's read those words again.
- Number 1. What words? (Signal.) *Solar system.*

h. Word 2. What word? (Signal.) *Jupiter.*
- (Repeat for words 3–5.)

i. (Repeat step g until firm.)

Column 2

j. Find column 2. ✓
- (Teacher reference:)

1. key	4. student
2. headline	5. appear
3. fancy	6. young

k. Word 1. What word? (Signal.) *Key.*
- (Repeat for words 2–6.)

l. Let's read those words again.
- Word 1. What word? (Signal.) *Key.*
- (Repeat for words 2–6.)

m. (Repeat step l until firm.)

Column 3

n. Find column 3. ✓
- (Teacher reference:)

1. suppose	4. booklet
2. Wendy	5. gray-haired
3. chosen	

- All these words have more than one syllable. The first syllable of each word is underlined.

o. Word 1. What's the underlined part? (Signal.) *supp.*
- What's the whole word? (Signal.) *Suppose.*
- Another word for **believe** or **think** is **suppose.** Here's another way of saying **I think she is Al's sister: I suppose she is Al's sister.**

- Everybody, what's another way of saying **I believe you know the answer?** (Signal.) *I suppose you know the answer.*

p. Word 2. What's the underlined part? (Signal.) *wen.*
- What's the whole word? (Signal.) *Wendy.*

q. Word 3. What's the underlined part? (Signal.) *chose.*
- What's the whole word? (Signal.) *Chosen.*

r. Word 4. What's the underlined part? (Signal.) *book.*
- What's the whole word? (Signal.) *Booklet.*

s. Word 5. What's the underlined part? (Signal.) *gray.*
- What's the whole word? (Signal.) *Gray-haired.*

t. Let's read those words again.
- Word 1. What word? (Signal.) *Suppose.*
- (Repeat for: **2. Wendy, 3. chosen, 4. booklet, 5. gray-haired.**)

u. (Repeat step t until firm.)

Column 4

v. Find column 4. ✓
- (Teacher reference:)

1. **Pacific Ocean**	4. **Mercury**
2. **San Francisco**	5. **Neptune**
3. **million**	6. **Pluto**

w. Number 1. What place? (Signal.) *Pacific Ocean.*
- Number 2. What place? (Signal.) *San Francisco.*

x. Word 3. What word? (Signal.) *Million.*
- (Repeat for words 4–6.)

y. Let's read those words again.
- Number 1. What place? (Signal.) *Pacific Ocean.*
- Number 2. What place? (Signal.) *San Francisco.*

z. Word 3. What word? (Signal.) *Million.*
- (Repeat for words 4–6.)

a. (Repeat steps y and z until firm.)

Individual Turns

(For columns 1–4: Call on individual students, each to read one to three words per turn.)

EXERCISE 3
COMPREHENSION PASSAGE

a. Find part B in your textbook. ✓

- You're going to read a story about Japan. First, you'll read the information passage. It gives some facts about Japan.

b. Everybody, touch the title. ✓
- (Call on a student to read the title.) *[Facts About Japan]*
- Everybody, what's the title? (Signal.) *Facts About Japan.*

c. (Call on individual students to read the passage, each student reading two or three sentences at a time. Ask the specified questions as the students read.)

> **Facts About Japan**
> **In a few lessons, you're going to read a story that takes place in Japan.**
> **Here are some facts about Japan:**
> **Japan is a country that is west of the United States.**

- Everybody, in which direction would you go to get from the United States to Japan? (Signal.) *West.*

> **The United States is on one side of the Pacific Ocean and Japan is on the other side of the Pacific Ocean. The map shows that if you flew west from San Francisco, you would cross the Pacific Ocean and reach Japan.**

- Everybody, touch San Francisco on the map. ✓
- That's a city that's in the United States. Keep touching San Francisco with one hand. Follow the arrow from San Francisco to Japan with the other hand. ✓
- In which direction did you go from San Francisco? (Signal.) *West.*
- Which ocean did you cross? (Signal.) *Pacific.*
- What country did you reach? (Signal.) *Japan.*
- You can see that Japan is a small island.

> **Japan is much smaller than the state of Alaska.**

- Everybody, say that fact. Get ready. (Signal.) *Japan is much smaller than the state of Alaska.*
- Touch Japan with one finger and Alaska with another. ✓

- Which is bigger? (Signal.) *Alaska.*
- Yes, Alaska is four times bigger than Japan.

About 127 million people live in Japan.

- Everybody, say that fact. Get ready. (Signal.) *About 127 million people live in Japan.*
- That's a lot of people for such a small country.

Japan manufactures many products that are used in the United States and Canada.

- Everybody, say that fact. Get ready. (Signal.) *Japan manufactures many products that are used in the United States and Canada.*

Some of Japan's more famous products are automobiles, TVs, and CD players.

- Who can name some automobiles that are manufactured in Japan? (Call on individual students. Ideas: *Nissan, Toyota, Mazda,* etc.)
- Who can name some TV brands that are manufactured in Japan? (Call on individual students. Ideas: *Sony, Sanyo, Samsung,* etc.)
- What are CD players? (Call on a student. Idea: *A machine that can play music off a small disk.*)

EXERCISE 4

STORY READING

a. Find part C in your textbook. ✓
- The error limit for group reading is 12 errors. Read carefully.
b. Everybody, touch the title. ✓
- (Call on a student to read the title.) [*Your Turn.*]
- Everybody, what's the title? (Signal.) *Your Turn.*
- That's a strange title. I wonder what this story is about.
- (Call on individual students to read the story, each student reading two or three sentences at a time. Ask the specified questions as the students read.)

- (Correct errors: Tell the word. Direct the student to reread the sentence.)
- (If the group makes more than 12 errors, direct the students to reread the story.)

Your Turn
Three months had gone by since the invention fair, but Leonard was still not used to the idea that he was really an inventor.

- Everybody, how long has it been since the invention fair? (Signal.) *Three months.*

He still had trouble thinking about the money that he had won for second prize in the fair.

- Everybody, how much money was that? (Signal.) *Ten thousand dollars.*

But he sure felt good.
He noticed that a lot of kids in school wanted to be his friend now. And he noticed that he didn't seem to have as much free time as he used to have. Nearly every day he talked on the phone to somebody at ABC Home Products.

- Name one reason that he didn't have as much time now that he was an inventor. (Call on a student. Idea: *He had to talk to ABC Home Products on the phone every day.*)

The people at ABC Home Products were making up ads that told about the invention. They gave it a fancy name: Mr. Light Saver.

- Everybody, what's the name ABC Home Products gave to Leonard's invention? (Signal.) *Mr. Light Saver.*

For their ads, they had pictures of a funny-looking man who had a head that was a lightbulb. Mr. Light Saver told how he would save fuel, save electricity, and save money.

- What three things would Mr. Light Saver save? (Call on a student. Idea: *Fuel, electricity, and money.*)

ABC Home Products had sent Leonard copies of the ads that were going to appear in the newspapers.

Mr. Light Saver turns lights on and off **AUTOMATICALLY**.
No more leaving lights on.
No more running around turning them off.
No more wasted money. Instead, big savings.
Do your part to save energy.
See your ABC Home Products dealer today and ask about the low-cost plan for putting Mr. Light Saver in your home.
Look in the Yellow Pages under Electrical Equipment and Supplies—Retail.

Walk in and lights go on.
Walk out and lights go off.
new from ABC HOME PRODUCTS

SAVE THOSE ENERGY DOLLARS BY PUTTING **MR. LIGHT SAVER** IN EVERY ROOM OF YOUR HOUSE.

- There's a copy of an ad in your book. Everybody, what is that funny-looking man called? (Signal.) *Mr. Light Saver.*
- What do you think of him? (Call on a student. Student preference.)
- Let's read what that ad says. Start with the title. (Call on a student:)

> **Mr. Light Saver says—**

- Read the words in the bubble. (Call on a student:)

> **Save those energy dollars by putting MR. LIGHT SAVER in every room of your house.**

- How many Mr. Light Savers do they want you to put in your house? (Call on a student. Idea: *One in every room.*)
- That's a lot of light savers.
- (Call on individual students to read the boxed part of the ad:)

> **Mr. Light Saver turns your lights on and off AUTOMATICALLY.**
> **No more leaving lights on.**
> **No more running around turning them off.**
> **No more wasted money. Instead, big savings.**
> **Do your part to save energy.**
> **See your ABC Home Products dealer today and ask about the low-cost plan for putting Mr. Light Saver in your home.**
> **Look in the Yellow Pages under Electric Equipment and Supplies— Retail.**

- Where do they want you to look for the name of a store that sells Mr. Light Saver? (Call on a student. Ideas: *In the Yellow Pages; under Electric Equipment and Supplies—Retail.*)
- (Call on a student to read the rest of the ad:)

> **Walk in and lights go on.**
> **Walk out and lights go off.**
> **New from ABC Home Products**

- If you saw this ad, would you think that Mr. Light Saver is something you should have? (Call on a student. Idea: *Yes.*)
- That's what the ad is supposed to do. It's supposed to make everybody think that Mr. Light Saver is something they need.

Leonard kept these ads in a notebook. He also kept copies of newspaper reports on the invention fair. The best newspaper report filled almost one whole page of the newspaper. It came out the day after the fair.

   At the top of this report was a headline: "Young Student Wins Prize for Invention." Beneath the headline was another headline: "Leonard Mathis Gets Check for Ten Thousand Dollars for his Clever Energy Saver."

   Leonard had four other reports in his notebook. They told how he invented the device, how his grandmother helped him, and what he planned to do with the money. One report told about Grandmother Esther.

   Leonard had money in the bank. He had paid back the money that Grandmother Esther paid to the patent attorney and to the electrical supply store. ⭐

- How much money did the electrical supplies cost? (Call on a student. Idea: *Ninety dollars.*)
- How much did it cost to get the patent? (Call on a student. Idea: *Three thousand dollars.*)

Leonard wanted to pay Grandmother Esther more than he owed her, but she wouldn't take it. "You're the one who did the hard work on this invention," she told him. "All I did was keep you going in the right direction."

- She kept him going in the right direction by pointing out problems and giving him information when he needed it.

Everybody was happy, even Leonard's parents. They were proud of Leonard. His mother was happy for another reason. She bought one of the first list-writers that came out.

- Everybody, does that surprise you? (Signal.) *No.*

She said, "Now grocery shopping is easy."
But Leonard noticed one problem she had when she went shopping. Here's what happened: Leonard was with his mother at the grocery store. They were going back to the car with the groceries when Leonard noticed the problem. He and his mother were each carrying two large bags. His mother approached the trunk of the car. She wanted to put the bags into the trunk. But she had a problem.

- Everybody, look at the picture on the next page. Touch the trunk of the car. ✓
- Try to figure out the problem that his mother might have if she were carrying bags of groceries.

She needed to use her hands to get her key out and open the trunk. But her hands were busy hanging on to the bags of groceries.

- What was her problem? (Call on a student. Idea: *She couldn't get her keys with her hands full of groceries.*)

She said, "Oh my," and put the bags down while she hunted for her keys.
Leonard said to himself, "Here's a problem. That means there is a need that could be filled with an invention."

- He's thinking like an inventor now.

He looked at the back of the car. Then he walked over to the car and set the grocery bags down. The car was dusty. He drew two little circles in the dust. One circle was on each side. Then he looked at his mother, smiled, and said, "I have figured out an invention that will solve your problem."

- Leonard already has an idea for an invention that will solve the problem. His first invention took him weeks and weeks. This idea took only one minute. How is that possible? (Call on a student. Ideas: *It involves electric eyes; he's thinking like an inventor.*)
- Yes, he probably couldn't think up a new invention that fast, but he might be able to use information he already has.
- Everybody, look at the picture again. Touch the circles that he made in the dust. ✓

Now it is your turn to think like an inventor. See if you can figure out the device that Leonard was thinking about when he told his mother that he could solve her problem with an invention.

- I wonder if his idea has to do with an electric eye. Don't say anything yet. Just think. Think about the problem. The trunk won't open automatically. Think of the kind of invention that might solve that problem. Then look at the picture. Leonard drew those two circles. They mean something. Think of what might go where those two circles are. Think of all these things, but don't talk to each other about them yet.

PAIRED PRACTICE

You're going to read aloud to your partner. The **A** members will read first. Then the **B** members will read from the star to the end of the story.
(Observe students and give feedback.)

End-of-Lesson Activities

INDEPENDENT WORK

Now finish your independent work for lesson 52. Raise your hand when you're finished. (Observe students and give feedback.)

WORKCHECK

a. (Direct students to take out their marking pencils.)
• We're going to check your workbook and textbook items. Remember, if you got an item wrong, make an **X** next to the item.
b. (For each item: Read the item. Call on a student to answer it. If the answer is wrong, say the correct answer. Refer to the Answer Key for the correct answers.)
c. Now use your marking pencil to fix up any items you got wrong. Remember, all mistakes must be fixed up before you hand in your work.

LANGUAGE ARTS

(Present Language Arts lesson 52 after completing Reading lesson 52. See Language Arts Guide.)

Special Project

Note: After completing lesson 52, do the special project with the students. You may do this project during another part of the school day.

Materials: Crayons, colored pencils, lined paper, and workbook A, page 94

a. Today we're going to start on a project. I'm going to divide you into groups for this project.
• (Assign a leader and three or four students to each group.)
• The students in each group are going to work together to figure out an invention. First the leader will call on each student to explain an idea for the trunk-opening device. After all students in the group have told their ideas about how the invention could work, the group is going to work together to draw a diagram showing how the invention works. The group will also write an explanation of how the invention works.
b. Everybody, find page 94 in your workbook. ✓
c. (Call on individual students to read two or three sentences, starting with the title.)
• (Teacher reference:)

Special Project
Use the picture below and your lined paper to explain how Leonard's new invention works. Your group may make arrows on the picture to show which parts will move. Your group may use dotted lines and words to name the parts or show how the parts of the invention work. Don't be afraid to write on the picture.

• You're going to add lines or arrows or words to this picture to show how the invention works. You can also use crayons or colored pencils.
• (Teacher reference:)

Then use lined paper to tell how your group's invention will work.

• What is the group leader going to write on lined paper? (Call on a student. Idea: *How the invention will work.*)
• (Teacher reference:)

Try to think about the different problems that there might be with the invention. Talk about these problems. Try to solve the problems. When you're finished, have someone from your group read your report to the class.

• What's going to happen after you write your report? (Call on a student. Idea: *Someone from the group will read it to the class.*)
d. During your group's discussion, students must raise their hands and the leader will call on them. The group must agree on the invention before the leader writes the report. Each group will write only one report and draw one picture of the invention. That report and picture will have the ideas that everybody in the group agrees on. The leader will write the report, but the group will tell the leader what to write. Remember, you must raise your hand during the discussion of the invention.
e. Here's a summary of what will happen. First the leader calls on each student and every student tells how to solve the problem. Then the group discusses the best ideas. The group discusses how to make a diagram of the invention and how to explain the invention. Then the leader writes a report for the group. But the group tells the leader exactly what to write and what to show in the diagram.

EXERCISE 1

VOCABULARY

a. **Find the vocabulary sentences on page 352 in your textbook.** ✓
- Touch sentence 13. ✓
- This is a new vocabulary sentence. It says: Without gravity, they were weightless. Everybody, say that sentence. Get ready. (Signal.) *Without gravity, they were weightless.*
- Close your eyes and say the sentence. Get ready. (Signal.) *Without gravity, they were weightless.*
- (Repeat until firm.)

b. The sentence talks about **gravity.** Gravity is the force that pulls things back to Earth. When you throw a ball in the air, gravity pulls it back. If there were no gravity, the ball you throw would continue forever. Everybody, what's the name of the force that pulls things back to Earth? (Signal.) *Gravity.*

c. The sentence says that they were **weightless.** If they were weightless, they would just float in space. There would be no gravity to pull them down.

d. Listen to the sentence again: Without gravity, they were weightless. Everybody, say that sentence. Get ready. (Signal.) *Without gravity, they were weightless.*

e. Everybody, what word names the force that pulls things back to Earth? (Signal.) *Gravity.*
- What word means that something has no weight? (Signal.) *Weightless.*

EXERCISE 2

VOCABULARY REVIEW

a. You learned a sentence that tells what she selected.
- Everybody, say that sentence. Get ready. (Signal.) *She selected a comfortable seat.*
- (Repeat until firm.)

b. I'll say part of the sentence. When I stop, you say the next word. Listen: She . . . Everybody, what's the next word? (Signal.) *Selected.*

c. Listen: She selected a . . . Everybody, what's the next word? (Signal.) *Comfortable.*
- Say the whole sentence. Get ready. (Signal.) *She selected a comfortable seat.*

EXERCISE 3

READING WORDS

Column 1

a. Find lesson 53 in your textbook. ✓
- Touch column 1. ✓
- (Teacher reference:)

1. comfortable	4. cover
2. planet	5. score
3. solar system	6. spaceship

b. Word 1. What word? (Signal.) *Comfortable.*

c. Word 2. What word? (Signal.) *Planet.*
- The Earth that we live on is a planet. A planet is a huge object that is the shape of a ball.

d. Number 3. What words? (Signal.) *Solar system.*

e. Word 4. What word? (Signal.) *Cover.*

f. (Repeat for words 5 and 6.)

g. Let's read those words again.
- Word 1. What word? (Signal.) *Comfortable.*
- Word 2. What word? (Signal.) *Planet.*
- Number 3. What words? (Signal.) *Solar system.*
- Word 4. What word? (Signal.) *Cover.*
- (Repeat for words 5 and 6.)

h. (Repeat step g until firm.)

Column 2

i. Find column 2. ✓
- (Teacher reference:)

1. concluded	3. lettered
2. selected	4. guessed

- All these words end with the letters **E-D.** Those letters make different sounds in the words.

j. Word 1. What word? (Signal.) *Concluded.*
- Spell **concluded.** Get ready. (Tap for each letter.) *C-O-N-C-L-U-D-E-D.*
- **Conclude** is another word for **finish.** When you conclude something, you finish it. Everybody, what's another way of saying **He finished his speech?** (Signal.) *He concluded his speech.*

k. Word 2. What word? (Signal.) *Selected.*
- Spell **selected.** Get ready. (Tap for each letter.) *S-E-L-E-C-T-E-D.*

l. Word 3. What word? (Signal.) *Lettered.*
- Spell **lettered.** Get ready. (Tap for each letter.) *L-E-T-T-E-R-E-D.*

m. Word 4. What word? (Signal.) *Guessed.*
- Spell **guessed.** Get ready. (Tap for each letter.) *G-U-E-S-S-E-D.*

n. Let's read those words again.
- Word 1. What word? (Signal.) *Concluded.*
- (Repeat for: **2. selected, 3. lettered, 4. guessed.**)
o. (Repeat step n until firm.)

Column 3

p. Find column 3. ✓
- (Teacher reference:)

1. **Mars**	5. **Mercury**
2. **Pluto**	6. **Neptune**
3. **Jupiter**	7. **Venus**
4. **Saturn**	8. **Uranus**

- All these words are the names of planets.
q. Word 1. What word? (Signal.) *Mars.*
- (Repeat for words 2–8.)
r. Let's read those words again.
- Word 1. What word? (Signal.) *Mars.*
- (Repeat for words 2–8.)
s. (Repeat step r until firm.)

Column 4

t. Find column 4. ✓
- (Teacher reference:)

1. **final**	4. **section**
2. **magnetic**	5. **twenty-five**
3. **nervous**	6. **written**

u. Word 1. What word? (Signal.) *Final.*
- (Repeat for words 2–6.)
v. Let's read those words again.
- Word 1. What word? (Signal.) *Final.*
- (Repeat for words 2–6.)
w. (Repeat step v until firm.)

Individual Turns

(For columns 1–4: Call on individual students, each to read one to three words per turn.)

COMPREHENSION PASSAGE

a. Find part B in your textbook. ✓
- You're going to read a story about traveling through the solar system. First you'll read the information passage. It gives some facts about the solar system.
b. Everybody, touch the title. ✓
- (Call on a student to read the title.) [*Facts About the Solar System.*]
- Everybody, what's the title? (Signal.) *Facts About the Solar System.*
c. (Call on individual students to read the passage, each student reading two or three sentences at a time. Ask the specified questions as the students read.)

> **Facts About the Solar System**
> **The story that you will read tells about going to different parts of the solar system. Here are facts about the solar system:**
> **The solar system is made up of the sun and nine planets.**

- Everybody, say that fact. Get ready. (Signal.) *The solar system is made up of the sun and nine planets.*
- (Repeat until firm.)
- How many planets are in the solar system? (Signal.) *Nine.*
- How many suns are in the solar system? (Signal.) *One.*

> **Most of those planets have moons. Earth, the planet that we live on, is one of the nine planets in the solar system.**

- Everybody, name the planet that we live on. Get ready. (Signal.) *Earth.*

> **The sun is in the middle of the solar system.**

- Everybody, say that fact. Get ready. (Signal.) *The sun is in the middle of the solar system.*
- (Repeat until firm.)

- The sun is in the middle and the planets circle around the sun.

The sun is the only part of the solar system that is burning.

- Everybody, are the planets and their moons burning? (Signal.) *No.*
- What's the only part that's burning? (Signal.) *The sun.*
- And where is the sun? (Signal.) *In the middle of the solar system.*

The sun gives heat and light to all the planets of the solar system.

- The sun is burning and it gives off the heat and light that the planets receive.

So our Earth gets heat and light from the sun.
Picture 1 shows the sun and the nine planets. The arrows show that the planets move around the sun. The planet with the dotted arrow is our Earth.

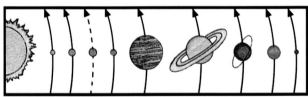

PICTURE 1

- Everybody, touch the planet with the dotted arrow. ✓
- Is Earth the planet that is closest to the sun? (Signal.) *No.*
- Is Earth farthest from the sun? (Signal.) *No.*

Here are the names of the planets: Mercury, Venus, Earth, Mars, Jupiter, Saturn, Uranus, Neptune, Pluto.

- Everybody, let's read those names together slowly, starting with Mercury. Get ready. Mercury (pause), Venus (pause), Earth (pause), Mars (pause), Jupiter (pause), Saturn (pause), Uranus (pause), Neptune (pause), Pluto.
- Study the names. Practice saying the names of the planets from Mercury through Jupiter until you can say them without looking at the names. (Pause.)

Mercury is closest to the sun. Pluto is farthest from the sun.

- Everybody, which planet is closest to the sun? (Signal.) *Mercury.*
- Which planet is farthest from the sun? (Signal.) *Pluto.*

Picture 2 shows that the sun is much larger than any planet. The sun is one hundred times larger than Earth.

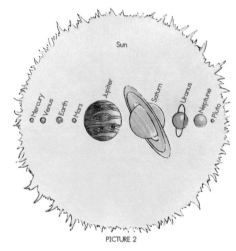

PICTURE 2

- The picture shows the sun. It's the large circle behind all the planets. Everybody, touch the sun in the picture. ✓
- Now touch Earth. ✓
- That is how big Earth would be if it were right in front of the sun.
- Everybody, how many times larger than Earth is the sun? (Signal.) *100.*
- Remember that fact.

But Earth is not the largest planet. The largest planet is Jupiter.

- Everybody, touch the planet that's the largest. ✓
- What's its name? (Signal.) *Jupiter.*

Which planet is next-largest?

- Everybody, what's the answer? (Signal.) *Saturn.*

STORY READING

a. Find part C in your textbook. ✓
- The error limit for group reading is 7 errors. Read carefully.
b. Everybody, touch the title. ✓

- (Call on a student to read the title.)
  [An Important Test.]
- Everybody, what's the title? (Signal.)
  An Important Test.
- (Call on individual students to read the story, each student reading two or three sentences at a time. Ask the specified questions as the students read.)

- (Correct errors: Tell the word. Direct the student to reread the sentence.)
- (If the group makes more than 7 errors, direct the students to reread the story.)

An Important Test

Wendy Chan's hand shook as she picked up the pencil. This test was the most important one she had ever taken. She didn't even want to think about what would happen if she failed it. Instead, she kept telling herself: "If you do well on this test, you will go on a trip across the solar system."

- This story starts right in the middle and we have to figure out what is happening. We know that somebody is taking a test. Everybody, who is that? (Signal.) *Wendy Chan.*
- Do we know what will happen if she does well on the test? (Signal.) *Yes.*
- What will happen? (Call on a student. Idea: *She will go on a trip across the solar system.*)
- Everybody, is it really possible for people to go across the solar system? (Signal.) *No.*
- So this story is make-believe. Maybe it's a story that takes place many years in the future when people will be able to go across the solar system. We'll have to read more and find out when this story is taking place.

A woman with gray hair was standing in front of the room. Wendy was seated with about thirty other students. The students had come from different parts of Canada.

- Everybody, get a picture of the room. How many students are in the room? (Signal.) *About 30.*
- Who is in the front of the room? (Call on a student. Idea: *A woman with gray hair.*)
- Everybody, what country were these students from? (Signal.) *Canada.*

Only ten students would be selected to go on the trip. Those would be the students with the highest test scores.

- How many students get to go on the trip? (Signal.) *Ten.*
- This sounds like a very tough test. I can see why Wendy would be nervous. What happens if she doesn't do better than most of the other students? (Call on a student. Idea: *She won't go on the trip.*)
- What happens if she gets one of the highest scores on the test? (Call on a student. Idea: *She will go on the trip across the solar system.*)

The gray-haired woman in front of the room smiled and said, "I think that you are all ready for this test. Am I correct?"

"Yes," the students agreed. Some of them laughed. They knew what would be covered in the test and they all wanted to go on the trip. So they had done just what Wendy had done for the past three months—studied.

She had studied every night, every Saturday, every Sunday. She had thought about the test when she ate, and she had even dreamed about the test. She kept thinking about one date—the date of the test. That was the most important date in her life—November 5, 2230.

- Now we know when this story is taking place. Everybody, in what year is the story taking place? (Signal.) *2230.*
- What year is it now? (Signal.) (Accept appropriate response.)
- So the year 2230 won't come around for over two hundred years.

Yes, she was ready for the test—really ready.

The gray-haired woman explained. "I suppose that you know these rules as well as I do, but let's go over them one more time. The test will take four hours. You'll have a five-minute break at the end of each hour.

- Everybody, how long will the test take? (Signal.) *Four hours.*

- How much break time will the students get? (Call on a student. Idea: *Five minutes every hour.*)

  You may not talk about the test during these breaks, but you may walk around or get something ✦ to drink. The questions on the test will cover facts about our planet and the other planets in the solar system. It will also cover facts about the spaceships that we use to travel through the solar system."

- What will the test cover? (Call on a student. Ideas: *Facts about Earth and the other planets in the solar system; facts about spaceships.*)

  The woman paused and smiled again. "I know that not all of you will be chosen for this trip. And I'm sorry that not everybody can go. But I would like to remind you that even if you don't go, this test has made you a smarter person. You have learned facts that you can use for the rest of your lives."

  For a moment, Wendy felt like crying. She felt very sorry for students who would not be able to go on the trip. The woman concluded by saying, "Good luck to all of you. You're a fine group of students."

  She was right. Only the best students from different parts of Canada were selected to take the test.

  The gray-haired woman said, "All right. You may begin the test. Open your test booklets and start."

  Wendy turned her booklet over and opened it to item 1. The item showed a map of the world. The instruction said, "Label the lettered parts on this map."

  "That's easy," she said to herself, and quickly wrote in the name for each letter.

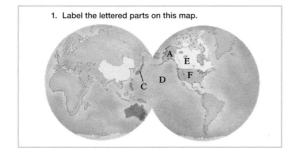

1. Label the lettered parts on this map.

- Look at the map. That map was on the test. Let's see if we can name the lettered parts.
- Everybody, touch **A**. ✓
- What place does **A** show? (Signal.) *Alaska.*
- Touch **C**. ✓
- What place does **C** show? (Signal.) *Japan.*
- Touch **D**. ✓
- What place does **D** show? (Signal.) *Pacific Ocean.*
- Touch **E**. ✓
- What place does **E** show? (Signal.) *Canada.*
- Touch **F**. ✓
- What place does **F** show? (Signal.) *United States.*

  Wendy looked at item 2. That item appears below.

- (Call on a student to read the questions.)

  2. What kind of animals are in the picture?

- Everybody, what's the answer? (Signal.) *Geese.*

  In what country are most wild ones born?

- Everybody, what's the answer? (Signal.) *Canada.*

  What is a group of these animals called?

- Everybody, what's the answer? (Signal.) *A flock.*

  How long do most of them live?

- Everybody, what's the answer? (Signal.) *30 years.*

- Read the rest of the story to yourself and be ready to answer some questions. Raise your hand when you're finished.

> **Wendy wrote answers to the questions and moved to the next item. She read the item and started to feel a little sick. She couldn't remember the answer. She knew that if she missed more than one or two items on this whole test, she would not go on the trip.**
> **Here was that item: Which planet has more moons, Jupiter or Saturn?**

- (After all students have raised their hand:) How did Wendy feel when she read the item at the end of the story? (Call on a student. Ideas: *Scared; sick.*)
- Why? (Call on a student. Idea: *Because she didn't remember the answer.*)
- What did the item ask? (Call on a student.) *[Which planet has more moons, Jupiter or Saturn?]*
- I hope she knows the answer.

EXERCISE 6

PAIRED PRACTICE

You're going to read aloud to your partner. The **B** members will read first. Then the **A** members will read from the star to the end of the story.
(Observe students and give feedback.)

End-of-Lesson Activities

INDEPENDENT WORK

Now finish your independent work for lesson 53. Raise your hand when you're finished. (Observe students and give feedback.)

WORKCHECK

a. (Direct students to take out their marking pencils.)
- We're going to check your workbook and textbook items. Remember, if you got an item wrong, make an **X** next to the item.
b. (For each item: Read the item. Call on a student to answer it. If the answer is wrong, say the correct answer. Refer to the Answer Key for the correct answers.)
c. Now use your marking pencil to fix up any items you got wrong. Remember, all mistakes must be fixed up before you hand in your work.

LANGUAGE ARTS

(Present Language Arts lesson 53 after completing Reading lesson 53. See Language Arts Guide.)

ACTIVITIES

(Present Activity 10 after completing Reading lesson 53. See Activities Across the Curriculum.)

EXERCISE 1

VOCABULARY REVIEW

a. Here's the new vocabulary sentence: Without gravity, they were weightless.
- Everybody, say that sentence. Get ready. (Signal.) *Without gravity, they were weightless.*
- (Repeat until firm.)

b. Everybody, what word means that something has no weight? (Signal.) *Weightless.*
- What word names the force that pulls things back to Earth? (Signal.) *Gravity.*

EXERCISE 2

READING WORDS

Column 1

a. **Find lesson 54 in your textbook.** ✓
- Touch column 1. ✓
- (Teacher reference:)

1. message	3. magnetic
2. improvement	4. equipment

b. Word 1 is **message.** What word? (Signal.) *Message.*

c. Word 2 is **improvement.** What word? (Signal.) *Improvement.*

d. Word 3 is **magnetic.** What word? (Signal.) *Magnetic.*

e. Word 4 is **equipment.** What word? (Signal.) *Equipment.*

f. Let's read those words again.
- Word 1. What word? (Signal.) *Message.*
- (Repeat for words 2–4.)

g. (Repeat step f until firm.)

Column 2

h. Find column 2. ✓
- (Teacher reference:)

1. eighteen	4. twenty-five
2. hundred	5. twelve
3. thirty	

- All these words tell about numbers.

i. Word 1. What word? (Signal.) *Eighteen.*
- (Repeat for words 2–5.)

j. Let's read those words again.
- Word 1. What word? (Signal.) *Eighteen.*
- (Repeat for words 2–5.)

k. (Repeat step j until firm.)

Column 3

l. Find column 3. ✓
- (Teacher reference:)

1. day-dreaming	4. latest
2. section	5. snack
3. comfortable	

m. Word 1. What word? (Signal.) *Day-dreaming.*
- When you daydream, you think about things that you would like to be doing. You could daydream about what you'll do on your vacation.

n. Word 2. What word? (Signal.) *Section.*
- **Section** is another word for **part.** Everybody, what's another way of saying **He read a part of the book?** (Signal.) *He read a section of the book.*

o. Word 3. What word? (Signal.) *Comfortable.*
- (Repeat for words 4 and 5.)

p. Let's read those words again.
- Word 1. What word? (Signal.) *Day-dreaming.*
- (Repeat for words 2–5.)

q. (Repeat step p until firm.)

Column 4

r. Find column 4. ✓
- (Teacher reference:)

1. streak	4. written
2. traveler	5. nervous
3. final	6. uncovered

s. Word 1. What word? (Signal.) *Streak.*
- Spell **streak.** Get ready. (Tap for each letter.) *S-T-R-E-A-K.*

t. Word 2. What word? (Signal.) *Traveler.*
- Spell **traveler.** Get ready. (Tap for each letter.) *T-R-A-V-E-L-E-R.*

u. Word 3. What word? (Signal.) *Final.*
- Spell **final.** Get ready. (Tap for each letter.) *F-I-N-A-L.*

v. Word 4. What word? (Signal.) *Written.*
- Spell **written.** Get ready. (Tap for each letter.) *W-R-I-T-T-E-N.*
w. Word 5. What word? (Signal.) *Nervous.*
x. Word 6. What word? (Signal.) *Uncovered.*
y. Let's read those words again.
- Word 1. What word? (Signal.) *Streak.*
- (Repeat for: **2. traveler, 3. final, 4. written, 5. nervous, 6. uncovered.**)
z. (Repeat step y until firm.)

Column 5

a. Find column 5. ✓
- (Teacher reference:)

---

1. office	4. worried
2. certainly	5. correctly
3. spaceship	

---

b. Word 1. What word? (Signal.) *Office.*
- (Repeat for words 2–5.)
c. Let's read those words again.
- Word 1. What word? (Signal.) *Office.*
- (Repeat for words 2–5.)
d. (Repeat step c until firm.)

Individual Turns

(For columns 1–5: Call on individual students, each to read one to three words per turn.)

EXERCISE 3

COMPREHENSION PASSAGE

a. Find part B in your textbook. ✓
- You're going to read the next story about Wendy. First you'll read the information passage. It gives some facts about time.
b. Everybody, touch the title. ✓
- (Call on a student to read the title.) *[Past, Present, and Future.]*
- Everybody, what's the title? (Signal.) *Past, Present, and Future.*
c. (Call on individual students to read the passage, each student reading two or three sentences at a time. Ask the specified questions as the students read.)

Past, Present, and Future
Things that are happening now are in the present time.

- Everybody, say that fact. Get ready. (Signal.) *Things that are happening now are in the present time.*

Things that <u>will</u> happen are in the future time.

- Everybody, say that fact. Get ready. (Signal.) *Things that <u>will</u> happen are in the future time.*
- (Teacher reference:)

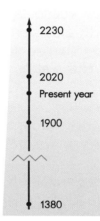

Look at the dates on the time line. Some dates on the time line are in the past and some are in the future. What is the present year?

- Everybody, what's the answer? (Signal.) (Accept appropriate response.)

What is the earliest year shown on the time line?

- Everybody, read the earliest year shown on the time line. Get ready. (Signal.) *1380.*

What is the future year that is closest to the present year?

- Everybody, start at the present year on the time line and go up into the future until you come to the first future year that is shown. ✓
- What year? (Signal.) *2020.*

What is the future year that is farthest in the future?

- Everybody, read that year. Get ready. (Signal.) *2230.*

Touch each year on the time line and tell if it's in the past or in the future.

- Everybody, touch 1380. ✓
  Past or future? (Signal.) *Past.*
- Touch 1900. ✓
  Past or future? (Signal.) *Past.*
- Touch 2020. ✓
  Past or future? (Signal.) *Future.*
- Touch 2230. ✓
  Past or future? (Signal.) *Future.*

EXERCISE 4

STORY READING

a. Find part C in your textbook. ✓
- The error limit for group reading is 9 errors. Read carefully.
b. Everybody, touch the title. ✓
- (Call on a student to read the title.) *[The Test Questions.]*
- Everybody, what's the title? (Signal.) *The Test Questions.*
- (Call on individual students to read the story, each student reading two or three sentences at a time. Ask the specified questions as students read.)

> - (Correct errors: Tell the word. Direct the student to reread the sentence.)
> - (If the group makes more than 9 errors, direct the students to reread the story.)

The Test Questions
Wendy started to feel sick because she couldn't remember the answer to the question.

- What question? (Call on a student. Idea: *Which planet has more moons, Jupiter or Saturn?*)

Then she said to herself, "Well, figure out the answer."
So she thought. And she remembered:
"Jupiter has sixteen moons.
Saturn has eighteen moons."

- Everybody, how many moons does Jupiter have? (Signal.) *16.*
- How many moons does Saturn have? (Signal.) *18.*
- Which planet has more moons? (Signal.) *Saturn.*

Wendy wrote the answer to the question. She knew it was correct.
The next items on the test asked facts about different places in the world. Here are the items:
If you went west from San Francisco, what is the name of the country you would reach first?

- Everybody, what country? (Signal.) *Japan.*

If you go west from the United States, what ocean do you cross?

- Everybody, what's the answer? (Signal.) *Pacific.*

Which is larger in size, Japan or Alaska?

- Everybody, what's the answer? (Signal.) *Alaska.*

Which has colder winter temperatures, the United States or Canada?

- Everybody, what's the answer? (Signal.) *Canada.*

In which direction would you go from Canada to reach the main part of the United States?

- Everybody, what's the answer? (Signal.) *South.*

Wendy answered the questions quickly.
The next question asked about spaceships. The item showed a picture of Traveler Four, the latest spaceship. The instructions said, "Label the lettered parts."
Here's what Wendy wrote:

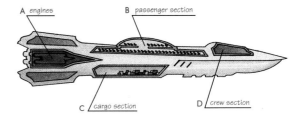

- Everybody, look at the picture. You can see the things that Wendy wrote on the diagram of the spaceship.
- Everybody, what does the letter **A** show in the picture? (Signal.) *Engines.*
- What does the letter **B** show? (Signal.) *Passenger section.*
- What does the letter **C** show? (Signal.) *Cargo section.*
- What does the letter **D** show? (Signal.) *Crew section.*
- Study that picture, because you will have questions about Traveler Four.

There were more items about Traveler Four. Here are those items and Wendy's answers:
    How long is Traveler Four? <u>405 feet</u>.

- Everybody, what's the answer? (Signal.) *405 feet.*
- That's longer than a football field.

How much weight can Traveler Four carry? <u>600 thousand pounds</u>.

- Everybody, what's the answer? (Signal.) *600,000 pounds.*
- And how long is Traveler Four? (Signal.) *405 feet.*
- Picture this tremendous spaceship. It is over 400 feet long. Everybody, and how much weight can it carry? (Signal.) *600,000 pounds.*
- That's more than 50 elephants weigh.

How many people are in the crew? <u>30</u>.
    How many passengers does Traveler Four hold? <u>200</u>.

- Imagine. There are 30 people on the crew. It takes that many people to run this spaceship.
- Everybody, how many passengers does the spaceship carry? (Signal.) *200.*

How fast can Traveler Four travel? <u>1 thousand miles per second</u>.

- Everybody, how fast does that spaceship travel? (Signal.) *1,000 miles per second.*

- Think about that. At that speed it could go all the way across the United States in two-and-a-half seconds. Remember, the speed tells about how many miles the ship can go in **one second**. You have to remember the whole answer: **One thousand miles per second.**
- Everybody, say that answer. Get ready. (Signal.) *One thousand miles per second.*

After Wendy answered the last question about Traveler Four, she thought about that ship. Imagine moving through space at the speed of one thousand miles per second. At that speed, you could go across the United States in two-and-a-half seconds. You could go around the world in only twenty-five seconds. You could go from Earth to the moon in only four minutes.

- Everybody, how long would it take to go around the world? (Signal.) *25 seconds.*
- How long would it take to go to the moon? (Signal.) *4 minutes.*

Wendy's mind moved away from the test. It began imagining what it must be like to be in Traveler Four. Imagine sitting in a comfortable passenger section that holds two hundred passengers. Imagine sitting there, eating a snack and talking to the person next to you as you streak through space at one thousand miles each second. The idea was so strange and impossible and exciting that Wendy could feel goose bumps forming on her arms. Imagine going from Earth to Jupiter in only four-and-a-half days. In that time, the spaceship would travel almost 400 million miles. Imagine!

- I don't blame her for getting goose bumps. That sounds fantastic.

Suddenly, Wendy said to herself, "If you want to go on that trip, you'd better do a good job on this test. So stop day-dreaming and start working."

- Read the rest of the story to yourself and be ready to answer some questions. Study the facts at the end of the story. Raise your hand when you're finished.

> **Wendy went back to the test. The next questions asked about the planets in the solar system. The questions asked how much they weighed, how fast they turned around, how long it took them to circle the sun, how many moons they had, and how far from the sun they were. These questions were easy for Wendy. She knew many facts about the planets. Of course, she knew the most about the planet Earth. But the planet that interested her most was Jupiter. Wendy found it interesting because it was the biggest planet in the solar system.**
>
> **Make sure that you know the answers to these questions:**
>
> **How fast does Traveler Four travel? <u>1 thousand miles per second</u>.**
>
> **How long would it take Traveler Four to go across the United States? <u>Two-and-a-half seconds</u>.**
>
> **How long would it take Traveler Four to go to the moon? <u>4 minutes</u>.**
>
> **How long would it take Traveler Four to go to Jupiter? <u>Four-and-a-half days</u>.**
>
> **How far is it from Earth to Jupiter? <u>400 million miles</u>.**

- (After all students have raised their hand:) Everybody, which planet did Wendy know the most about? (Signal.) *Earth.*
- Which planet did she find most interesting? (Signal.) *Jupiter.*
- Why? (Call on a student. Idea: *Because it is the biggest planet in the solar system.*)
- Don't look at the answers in your book. Say the answers to these questions.

Remember to say all the words for the answer, not just the numbers.
- Everybody, how fast does Traveler Four travel? (Signal.) *1,000 miles per second.*
- How far is it from Earth to Jupiter? (Signal.) *400 million miles.*
- (Repeat the last two questions until firm.)

EXERCISE 5

PAIRED PRACTICE

You're going to read aloud to your partner. The **A** members will read first. Then the **B** members will read from the star to the end of the story.
(Observe students and give feedback.)

End-of-Lesson Activities

INDEPENDENT WORK

Now finish your independent work for lesson 54. Raise your hand when you're finished. (Observe students and give feedback.)

WORKCHECK

a. (Direct students to take out their marking pencils.)
- We're going to check your workbook and textbook items. Remember, if you got an item wrong, make an **X** next to the item.

b. (For each item: Read the item. Call on a student to answer it. If the answer is wrong, say the correct answer. Refer to the Answer Key for the correct answers.)

c. Now use your marking pencil to fix up any items you got wrong. Remember, all mistakes must be fixed up before you hand in your work.

LANGUAGE ARTS

(Present Language Arts lesson 54 after completing Reading lesson 54. See Language Arts Guide.)

Lesson 55

VOCABULARY REVIEW

a. You learned a sentence that tells what the applause interrupted.
- Everybody, say that sentence. Get ready. (Signal.) *The applause interrupted his speech.*
- (Repeat until firm.)

b. You learned a sentence that tells what she selected.
- Everybody, say that sentence. Get ready. (Signal.) *She selected a comfortable seat.*
- (Repeat until firm.)

c. Here's the last sentence you learned: Without gravity, they were weightless.
- Everybody, say that sentence. Get ready. (Signal.) *Without gravity, they were weightless.*
- (Repeat until firm.)

d. Everybody, what word means that something has no weight? (Signal.) *Weightless.*
- What word names the force that pulls things back to Earth? (Signal.) *Gravity.*

e. Once more. Say the sentence that tells about being without gravity. Get ready. (Signal.) *Without gravity, they were weightless.*

READING WORDS

Column 1

a. **Find lesson 55 in your textbook.** ✓
- Touch column 1. ✓
- (Teacher reference:)

1. Tokyo	4. pressure
2. oxygen	5. adult
3. guest	6. guy

b. Word 1 is **Tokyo.** What word? (Signal.) *Tokyo.*
- Spell **Tokyo.** Get ready. (Tap for each letter.) *T-O-K-Y-O.*
- Tokyo is the largest city in Japan.

- Everybody, what's the name of the largest city in Japan? (Signal.) *Tokyo.*

c. Word 2 is **oxygen.** What word? (Signal.) *Oxygen.*
- Spell **oxygen.** Get ready. (Tap for each letter.) *O-X-Y-G-E-N.*

d. Word 3 is **guest.** What word? (Signal.) *Guest.*
- Spell **guest.** Get ready. (Tap for each letter.) *G-U-E-S-T.*

e. Word 4 is **pressure.** What word? (Signal.) *Pressure.*
- Pressure is a push. Press your hands together. ✓
- Pressure is the force that you feel. If you press harder, you feel more pressure.

f. Word 5. What word? (Signal.) *Adult.*

g. Word 6. What word? (Signal.) *Guy.*

h. Let's read those words again.
- Word 1. What word? (Signal.) *Tokyo.*
- (Repeat for words 2–6.)

i. (Repeat step h until firm.)

Column 2

j. Find column 2. ✓
- (Teacher reference:)

1. classroom	4. office
2. failure	5. spaceship
3. message	6. Sidney

- All these words have more than one syllable. The first syllable of each word is underlined.

k. Word 1. What's the first syllable? (Signal.) *class.*
- What's the whole word? (Signal.) *Classroom.*

l. Word 2. What's the first syllable? (Signal.) *fail.*
- What's the whole word? (Signal.) *Failure.*

m. Word 3. What's the first syllable? (Signal.) *mess.*
- What's the whole word? (Signal.) *Message.*

n. Word 4. What's the first syllable? (Signal.) *off.*
- What's the whole word? (Signal.) *Office.*

o. Word 5. What's the first syllable?
(Signal.) *space.*
- What's the whole word?
(Signal.) *Spaceship.*
p. Word 6. What's the first syllable?
(Signal.) *sid.*
- What's the whole word? (Signal.) *Sidney.*
q. Let's read those words again.
- Word 1. What word?
(Signal.) *Classroom.*
- (Repeat for: **2. failure, 3. message, 4. office, 5. spaceship, 6. Sidney.**)
r. (Repeat step q until firm.)

Column 3

s. Find column 3. ✓
- (Teacher reference:)

1. **certainly**	4. **improvement**
2. **underlined**	5. **worried**
3. **correctly**	

- All these words have an ending.
t. Word 1. What word? (Signal.) *Certainly.*
- (Repeat for words 2–5.)
u. Let's read those words again.
- Word 1. What word? (Signal.) *Certainly.*
- (Repeat for words 2–5.)
v. (Repeat step u until firm.)

Individual Turns

(For columns 1–3: Call on individual students, each to read one to three words per turn.)

EXERCISE 3

FACT REVIEW

a. Let's review some facts you have learned. First we'll go over the facts together. Then I'll call on individual students to do some facts.

b. Everybody, tell me which direction you go to get from the main part of the United States to Canada. (Pause.) Get ready. (Signal.) *North.*
- Tell me how fast Traveler Four travels. (Pause.) Get ready. (Signal.) *1,000 miles per second.*
- Tell me how far it is from Earth to Jupiter. (Pause.) Get ready. (Signal.) *400 million miles.*
- Name the planets, starting with Mercury. (Pause.) Get ready. (Signal.) *Mercury, Venus, Earth, Mars, Jupiter, Saturn, Uranus, Neptune, Pluto.*
- (Repeat step b until firm.)
c. Tell me which planet is the largest. (Pause.) Get ready. (Signal.) *Jupiter.*
- Tell me how many moons Jupiter has. (Pause.) Get ready. (Signal.) *Sixteen.*
- Tell me how many moons Saturn has. (Pause.) Get ready. (Signal.) *Eighteen.*
- Tell me which direction you go to get from Canada to the main part of the United States. (Pause.) Get ready. (Signal.) *South.*
- (Repeat step c until firm.)

Individual Turns
d. Now I'm going to call on individual students to do some facts.
e. (Call on individual students to do the set of facts in step b or step c.)

EXERCISE 4

STORY READING

a. Find part B in your textbook. ✓
- The error limit for group reading is 13 errors. Read carefully.
b. Everybody, touch the title. ✓
- (Call on a student to read the title.) *[Waiting for a Letter.]*
- Everybody, what's the title? (Signal.) *Waiting for a Letter.*
- (Call on individual students to read the story, each student reading two or three sentences at a time. Ask the specified questions as the students read.)

- (Correct errors: Tell the word. Direct the student to reread the sentence.)
- (If the group makes more than 13 errors, direct the students to reread the story.)

Waiting for a Letter
Wendy's fingers were sore from writing. She had spent most of the last four hours writing answers to test items. Now she was reading over her answers a final time. The woman with gray hair walked to the front of the room. "All right," she said. "The time is up. Stop writing. Turn your test booklet over. Make sure that your name is on it. And pass it forward."

- How long had Wendy been writing? (Call on a student. Idea: *About four hours.*)
- Everybody, what part of Wendy was sore? (Signal.) *Fingers.*

Suddenly, Wendy felt very frightened. Had she answered all the questions correctly? There were a couple of items that she wasn't sure about. She wasn't sure how fast Traveler Three went or when it was built.

- Everybody, tell me the name of the spaceship that can go to the moon in four minutes. (Signal.) *Traveler Four.*
- That's the latest spaceship. We know that there were some Travelers that were earlier than Traveler Four. What do you think they were called? (Call on a student. Idea: *Traveler One, Two, and Three.*)
- Everybody, which do you think was made first, Traveler Two or Traveler Three? (Signal.) *Traveler Two.*

Wendy knew many facts about Traveler One, Traveler Two, and Traveler Three. Traveler One held two hundred passengers, but it was a very slow ship compared to Traveler Four. Traveler One could go only one mile per second.

- Everybody, what was the name of the first Traveler? (Signal.) *Traveler One.*
- How many passengers did Traveler One carry? (Signal.) *200.*
- How many passengers does Traveler Four carry? (Signal.) *200.*
- They both carry the same number of people. What's the big difference between Traveler Four and Traveler One?

(Call on a student. Idea: *How fast they can go.*)
- Everybody, how fast could Traveler One go? (Signal.) *One mile per second.*
- At that rate, it would take 25 thousand seconds to go around the world. Who remembers how many seconds it takes Traveler Four to go around the world? (Call on a student. Idea: *25 seconds.*)
- That's a lot faster.

Traveler One took almost twelve years to go from Earth to Jupiter. Traveler Four could make the same trip in four-and-a-half days.
　　Traveler Two could go faster than Traveler One. Traveler Three could go faster yet. But Wendy wasn't sure how fast Traveler Three could go. She had written that it could go 45 miles per second, and she hoped her answer was right.
　　"You'll be getting a letter within a few weeks," the gray-haired woman said.

- The story was telling about the Travelers. Now it switched back to something else. Where is the story taking place now? (Call on a student. Idea: *The testing room.*)
- The test is over and the woman is talking.

The woman continued, "Your letter will tell you either that you have been selected to go on the trip or that you haven't been selected."

- The letter that they receive will tell the students one of two things. What are those things? (Call on a student. Idea: *Whether or not they've been selected to go on the trip.*)

Then the woman said, "I found out just this morning where the trip will go. If you're selected, you'll go to the planet Jupiter and spend nearly a week there."

- Everybody, did Wendy know before this time that the trip would go to Jupiter? (Signal.) *No.*

Wendy listened to the words, but she didn't feel excited. She still felt worried about answering the questions correctly.

The woman continued, "I know that the letter will disappoint most of you."

- Everybody, how many students will be selected for the trip? (Signal.) *Ten.*
- How many took the test? (Signal.) *About thirty.*
- So most of them will be disappointed, because they won't go.

The woman said, "Just remember that you have had a chance to learn a great deal, and you certainly should not feel like a failure if you aren't selected."

Wendy turned around and looked at the faces of the other students in the room. Some were smiling. Most were serious. The girl directly behind Wendy looked very sad. "What's wrong?" Wendy asked.

"I blew it," she said, "I just blew it. I thought I knew this stuff, but my mind seemed to go blank and I . . ." She covered her face with her hands.

- What does that mean, she thought she blew it? (Call on a student. Idea: *She didn't do well.*)
- She said her mind went blank. What does that mean? (Call on a student. Idea: *She couldn't remember anything.*)

Wendy turned around and put her hand on the girl's shoulder. "Hey," she said. "Maybe you did better than you think."

"Yeah," the girl said and uncovered her face. She tried to smile.

The woman in the front of the room said, "Good luck and thank you."

Everybody stood up and started talking at the same time. A lot of students were asking questions like, "What was the answer to the question about the mountains in Japan?"

Wendy turned to the girl who had been sitting behind her. Wendy said, "What's your name?"

"Sidney Miller," she said.

"Listen," Wendy said. "When they send the list of people who are going on the trip, I'll look for your name. Maybe we'll both make it."

"Thanks," Sidney said.

• • •

- What do the dots mean? (Call on a student. Idea: *Part of the story is missing.*)

The mail usually came to Wendy's house about 11 each ✦ morning.

- The story tells about the mail reaching Wendy's home. So Wendy must be back in her hometown now. When did the mail come to her house? (Call on a student. Idea: *Around 11:00.*)

By 11:15, Wendy's math class was over, so she ran to the phone and called her home. For the last five days, she had called home at 11:15 each morning. "Hi, Mom," she would say each day. She didn't have to tell her mother why she was calling. Her mother would say, "It hasn't come yet."

- What hasn't come yet? (Call on a student. Idea: *The letter.*)

"Oh," Wendy would say. Each time her mother told her that the letter hadn't come, Wendy felt glad and sad. She felt sad because she hadn't found out whether she was going on the trip. She felt a little glad because she didn't want the letter to come if it said she wasn't going.

- Why was she sad about the letter not coming? (Call on a student. Idea: *Because she hadn't found out if she was going on the trip.*)
- Why was she a little bit glad? (Call on a student. Idea: *Because she was afraid it might say she wasn't going on the trip.*)
- Read the rest of the story to yourself and be ready to answer some questions. Raise your hand when you're finished.

Then on November 19, Wendy's math teacher walked over to her desk just before the class was over. He bent over and said that there was an important message for her, and she should go to the office.

She felt so nervous that she hardly remembered leaving the classroom and going down the hall to the office. She was almost in a dream. The phone felt very heavy. She quickly moved it to her ear. "Mom," she said.

"You did it, honey," her mother said. "You're going."

- (After all students have raised their hand:) Where was Wendy when she got the message to go to the office? (Call on a student. Idea: *In math class.*)
- How did she feel when she went to the office? (Call on a student. Ideas: *Nervous; like in a dream.*)
- What message did her mother have for her? (Call on a student. Idea: *She was going on the trip.*)

EXERCISE 5

READING CHECKOUTS

Note: There is a reading checkout in this lesson; therefore, there is no paired practice.

a. Today is a reading-checkout day. While you're doing your independent work, I'm going to call on you one at a time to read part of the story from lesson 54.
- Remember, you pass the checkout by reading the passage in less than a minute without making more than 2 mistakes. And when you pass the checkout, you'll color the space for lesson 55 on your thermometer chart.
b. (Call on individual students to read the portion of story 54 marked with ❀.)
- (Time the student. Note words that are missed and number of words read.)
- (Teacher reference:)

❀ Wendy's mind moved away from the test. It began imagining what it must be like to be in Traveler Four. Imagine sitting in a comfortable passenger section that holds two hundred passengers. Imagine sitting there, eating a snack and talking to the

person next to you as you streak through [50] space at one thousand miles each second. The idea was so strange and impossible and exciting that Wendy could feel goose bumps forming on her [75] arms. Imagine going from Earth to Jupiter in only four-and-a-half days. In that time, the spaceship would travel almost 400 million miles. Imagine!

Suddenly [100] Wendy said to herself, "If you want to go on that trip, you'd better do ❀ [115] good job on this test."

- (If the student reads the passage in one minute or less and makes no more than 2 errors, direct the student to color in the space for lesson 55 on the thermometer chart.)
- (If the student makes any mistakes, point to each word that was misread and identify it.)
- (If the student does not meet the rate-error criterion for the passage, direct the student to practice reading the story with the assigned partner.)

End-of-Lesson Activities

INDEPENDENT WORK

Now finish your independent work for lesson 55. Raise your hand when you're finished. (Observe students and give feedback.)

WORKCHECK

a. (Direct students to take out their marking pencils.)
- We're going to check your workbook and textbook items. Remember, if you got an item wrong, make an **X** next to the item.
b. (For each item: Read the item. Call on a student to answer it. If the answer is wrong, say the correct answer. Refer to the Answer Key for the correct answers.)
c. Now use your marking pencil to fix up any items you got wrong. Remember, all mistakes must be fixed up before you hand in your work.

LANGUAGE ARTS

(Present Language Arts lesson 55 after completing Reading lesson 55. See Language Arts Guide.)

Note: You will need a globe for lesson 56.

Lessons 56–60 · Planning Page

	Lesson 56	Lesson 57	Lesson 58	Lesson 59	Lesson 60
Lesson Events	**Vocabulary Sentence** Vocabulary Sentence Reading Words Comprehension Passage Globe Story Reading Fact Review Paired Practice Independent Work Workcheck Language Arts	Vocabulary Sentence Reading Words Story Reading Paired Practice Independent Work Workcheck Language Arts	Vocabulary Sentences Reading Words Comprehension Passage Story Reading Paired Practice Independent Work Workcheck Language Arts	**Vocabulary Sentence** Vocabulary Sentence Reading Words Story Reading Paired Practice Independent Work Workcheck Language Arts	Fact Game Reading Checkouts Test Marking the Test Test Remedies Literature Lesson Language Arts
Vocabulary Sentence	**#14: She demonstrated how animals use oxygen.** #13: Without gravity, they were weightless.	#14: She demonstrated how animals use oxygen.	sentence #12 sentence #13 sentence #14	**#15: Lava erupted from the volcano's crater.** #14: She demonstrated how animals use oxygen.	
Reading Words: Word Types	multi-syllable words words with an ending mixed words	multi-syllable words modeled words words with an ending mixed words 2-syllable words	modeled words compound words multi-syllable words	modeled words words with an ending mixed words	
New Vocabulary		tremble palms survive	appeared	lo surround incredible	
Comprehension Passage	*More About Japan*		*Gravity*		
Story	*A Surprise at the Space Station*	*Traveler Four*	*The Gravity Device*	*Jupiter*	
Skill Items	Sequencing Vocabulary Vocabulary sentences		Vocabulary sentence	Vocabulary Vocabulary sentences	Test: Vocabulary sentences
Special Materials	Globe				Thermometer charts, dice, Fact Game 60, Fact Game Answer Key, scorecard sheets, *materials for literature lesson
Special Projects/ Activities	Activity after lesson 56				

*Literature anthology; blackline masters **(6A, 6B, and 6C; "Read to" copy of *Little House on the Prairie;* lined paper; optional: drawing materials)**

Lesson 56

Materials: You will need a globe for exercise 5.

EXERCISE 1

VOCABULARY

a. **Find the vocabulary sentences on page 352 in your textbook.** ✓
- Touch sentence 14. ✓
- This is a new vocabulary sentence. It says: She demonstrated how animals use oxygen. Everybody, say that sentence. Get ready. (Signal.) *She demonstrated how animals use oxygen.*
- Close your eyes and say the sentence. Get ready. (Signal.) *She demonstrated how animals use oxygen.*
- (Repeat until firm.)

b. The sentence says she **demonstrated** something. When you demonstrate something, you **show** it. Everybody, what's another way of saying **They showed how the bridge worked?** (Signal.) *They demonstrated how the bridge worked.*
- What's another way of saying **They showed their magic tricks?** (Signal.) *They demonstrated their magic tricks.*

c. She demonstrated how animals use **oxygen.** Oxygen is the part of the air your body needs to survive. If there's no oxygen in the air, you die. Everybody, what's the part of the air your body needs to survive? (Signal.) *Oxygen.*

d. Listen to the sentence again: She demonstrated how animals use oxygen. Everybody, say that sentence. Get ready. (Signal.) *She demonstrated how animals use oxygen.*

e. Everybody, what word means **showed?** (Signal.) *Demonstrated.*
- What word names the part of the air you need to survive? (Signal.) *Oxygen.*

EXERCISE 2

VOCABULARY REVIEW

a. You learned a sentence that tells about being without gravity.

- Everybody, say that sentence. Get ready. (Signal.) *Without gravity, they were weightless.*
- (Repeat until firm.)

b. I'll say part of the sentence. When I stop, you say the next word. Listen: Without . . . Everybody, what's the next word? (Signal.) *Gravity.*

c. Listen: Without gravity, they were . . . Everybody, what's the next word? (Signal.) *Weightless.*
- Say the whole sentence. Get ready. (Signal.) *Without gravity, they were weightless.*

EXERCISE 3

READING WORDS

Column 1

a. Find lesson 56 in your textbook. ✓
- Touch column 1. ✓
- (Teacher reference:)

1. <u>wel</u>come	4. <u>tooth</u>brush
2. <u>a</u>board	5. <u>under</u>lined
3. <u>bagg</u>age	

- All these words have more than one syllable. The first part of each word is underlined.

b. Word 1. What's the underlined part? (Signal.) *wel.*
- What's the whole word? (Signal.) *Welcome.*
- Spell **welcome.** Get ready. (Tap for each letter.) *W-E-L-C-O-M-E.*

c. Word 2. What's the underlined part? (Signal.) *a.*
- What's the whole word? (Signal.) *Aboard.*
- Spell **aboard.** Get ready. (Tap for each letter.) *A-B-O-A-R-D.*

d. Word 3. What's the underlined part? (Signal.) *bagg.*
- What's the whole word? (Signal.) *Baggage.*
- Spell **baggage.** Get ready. (Tap for each letter.) *B-A-G-G-A-G-E.*

e. Word 4. What's the underlined part? (Signal.) *tooth.*
- What's the whole word? (Signal.) *Toothbrush.*
f. Word 5. What's the underlined part? (Signal.) *under.*
- What's the whole word? (Signal.) *Underlined.*
g. Let's read those words again.
- Word 1. What word? (Signal.) *Welcome.*
- (Repeat for: **2. aboard, 3. baggage, 4. toothbrush, 5. underlined.**)
h. (Repeat step g until firm.)

Column 2

i. Find column 2. ✓
- (Teacher reference:)

1. **boarded**	4. **adults**
2. **clothing**	5. **provided**
3. **checkered**	

- All these words have an ending.
j. Word 1. What word? (Signal.) *Boarded.*
- (Repeat for words 2–5.)
k. Let's read those words again.
- Word 1. What word? (Signal.) *Boarded.*
- (Repeat for words 2–5.)
l. (Repeat step k until firm.)

Column 3

m. Find column 3. ✓
- (Teacher reference:)

1. **eleventh**	3. **questioned**
2. **remembering**	4. **scientists**

- All these words have an ending.
n. Word 1. What word? (Signal.) *Eleventh.*
- (Repeat for words 2–4.)
o. Let's read those words again.
- Word 1. What word? (Signal.) *Eleventh.*
- (Repeat for words 2–4.)
p. (Repeat step o until firm.)

Column 4

q. Find column 4. ✓
- (Teacher reference:)

1. **doctor**	4. **Tokyo**
2. **guy**	5. **packed**
3. **route**	6. **suit**

r. Word 1. What word? (Signal.) *Doctor.*
- (Repeat for words 2–6.)

s. Let's read those words again.
- Word 1. What word? (Signal.) *Doctor.*
- (Repeat for words 2–6.)
t. (Repeat step s until firm.)

Individual Turns

(For columns 1–4: Call on individual students, each to read one to three words per turn.)

<hr>
EXERCISE 4

COMPREHENSION PASSAGE

a. Find part B in your textbook. ✓
- You're going to read the next story about Wendy. First you'll read the information passage. It gives some facts about Japan.
b. Everybody, touch the title. ✓
- (Call on a student to read the title.) *[More About Japan.]*
- Everybody, what's the title? (Signal.) *More About Japan.*
c. (Call on individual students to read the passage, each student reading two or three sentences at a time. Ask the specified questions as the students read.)

More About Japan

In today's story, you will read about Wendy in Japan.
The map shows the route that her jet plane took to Japan. Name the country the jet left from.

- Everybody, name that country. Get ready. (Signal.) *Canada.*

In which direction did the jet fly?

- The plane took off from Canada. The **X** on the map shows where the flight started. The plane landed in Japan. It landed in the city of Tokyo. Get ready to tell the direction Wendy's plane took. Everybody, what direction? (Signal.) *West.*

- Trace the route that her jet took. ✓

The jet landed in a city in Japan. Name that city.

- Everybody, name that city. Get ready. (Signal.) *Tokyo.*
- Before we read the story, make sure that you can answer some questions without looking.
- Everybody, what **country** did Wendy leave from? (Signal.) *Canada.*
- What **country** did she go to? (Signal.) *Japan.*
- What **city** in Japan did she go to? (Signal.) *Tokyo.*
- In which direction did she travel to go from Canada to Japan? (Signal.) *West.*

<hr>

EXERCISE 5

GLOBE

a. (Present a globe. Touch Vancouver, Canada.)
- Here's where the jet left from. Everybody, what country is this? (Signal.) *Canada.*
- (Trace the route from Vancouver to Tokyo.)
- Here's where the jet landed. Everybody, what city is this? (Signal.) *Tokyo.*

b. My turn. I'm going to spin the globe around and around and then see if I can find the place the jet took off from.
- (Spin the globe. Touch Vancouver.) Here's the place the jet took off from. Your turn.

c. (Spin the globe. Call on a student.)
- See if you can find the place the jet took off from. ✓
- Now find Tokyo. ✓
- (Repeat step c with other students.)

<hr>

EXERCISE 6

STORY READING

a. Find part C in your textbook. ✓
- The error limit for group reading is 11 errors. Read carefully.

b. Everybody, touch the title. ✓
- (Call on a student to read the title.) [*A Surprise at the Space Station.*]
- Everybody, what's the title? (Signal.) *A Surprise at the Space Station.*
- The space station is the place where people go to get on a spaceship. It's near Tokyo.

- (Call on individual students to read the story, each student reading two or three sentences at a time. Ask the specified questions as the students read.)

- (Correct errors: Tell the word. Direct the student to reread the sentence.)
- (If the group makes more than 11 errors, direct the students to reread the story.)

A Surprise at the Space Station
From the space station, Wendy could see the city of Tokyo, the largest city in Japan.

- Everybody, in what country is Tokyo? (Signal.) *Japan.*
- We don't know how she got to the space station, but she's already there.

The space station was about twenty miles from Tokyo. Wendy stood in front of the large window and looked down at the beautiful city. She had traveled by jet from Canada to Japan. She had landed at the Tokyo airport. Five other students who were going on the trip to Jupiter were on Wendy's flight.

- Where did the jet land? (Call on a student. Idea: *At the Tokyo airport.*)
- Everybody, which country did it come from? (Signal.) *Canada.*
- Everybody, did **all** the students who are going to Jupiter come to Tokyo on the same flight? (Signal.) *No.*

Newspaper reporters met the students at the Tokyo airport. They questioned the students about how they felt about being selected to go on this trip. Wendy said that it was the most important thing that had ever happened to her.
At the airport, Wendy and the other students had boarded a special bus that took them from the airport to the space station.

- Everybody, how did Wendy and the other five students get from the airport to the space station? (Signal.) *On a bus.*

As Wendy looked out of the window, she wondered if she had packed everything she would need on the trip. Part of the letter that told her that she had been selected was a list of things that she should take with her. The list named things like toothbrush and clothing. Part of the letter was underlined: "Your baggage must not weigh more than 100 pounds."

- Everybody, what was the weight limit for the baggage? (Signal.) *100 pounds.*
- Why couldn't people take as much baggage as they wanted to? (Call on a student. Idea: *Because it would make the spaceship too heavy.*)

Wendy had her camera, three books, paper, and pencils. She didn't have room for her computer and some of the other things she had wanted to take. In fact, before she packed, she had her room filled with things that she wanted to take. But she had to leave most of them behind.

She walked from the window and sat down next to one of the boys who was going on the trip. His name was Bob. She said, "Do you have your list of students?"

"Yeah," he said. He opened a little bag and pulled out the list. She didn't know any of the other students who were going. Sidney's name was not on the list.

- Who is Sidney? (Call on a student. Idea: *The girl who sat behind Wendy during the test.*)
- Everybody, if her name is not on the list, is she going on the trip? (Signal.) *No.*

For a moment Wendy felt sad, remembering how Sidney looked after the test. Wendy imagined how Sidney must have felt today, knowing that the other students were going on the trip.

Wendy told herself not to think about Sidney. She asked Bob, "Do you know any of the other kids who are going on this trip?"

"Well, I did," he said. "Tim Mallory was supposed to go, but he's very sick and he can't make it. That poor guy."

"That must be terrible," Wendy said.

"I'm here!" a voice shouted from behind Wendy. "I'm here!"

Wendy turned around and looked. She couldn't believe what she saw. There was Sidney, standing in a checkered coat with her arms stretched out from her sides. She was laughing. "I'm here!" she repeated.

- That's strange. Everybody, was her name on the list? (Signal.) *No.*
- The story gave a clue about why Sidney was going on the trip. Can you figure out why she might be at the space station even though her name is not on the list? (Call on a student. Idea: *She's taking the place of the sick student.*)

Wendy jumped up, ran over to Sidney, and threw her arms around her. "Wow," Wendy said. "I can't believe it."

"Me neither," Sidney said. "But I'm here."

"But your name is not on the list," Wendy said.

"That's because I shouldn't be here," Sidney said. "I guess I had the eleventh-highest score."

- Everybody, how many can go on the trip? (Signal.) *Ten.*
- If somebody couldn't go, who would be the next person in line? (Call on a student. Ideas: *Sidney; the eleventh.*)

Sidney explained, "They called me last night and told me that somebody got sick and couldn't go. They asked if I could go. Could I go? Could I go?" She laughed. "Could I go? You bet I could."

- Read the rest of the story to yourself and be ready to answer some questions. Raise your hand when you're finished.

She grabbed Wendy's shoulders and started to dance and laugh. "What a joke. Could I go? I'm here." The space station was filled with people. Many of them were smiling at Wendy and Sidney.

Suddenly, a voice over the loudspeaker said, "Traveler Four will be leaving for Jupiter in fifteen minutes."

Wendy ran over and picked up her bag. She opened it and pulled out her papers. One of the things she had to do before she took the test was to get a report from her doctor. The report told that she was in good health.

She lined up with the other passengers. Most of them were scientists. People did not go to Jupiter for vacations. In fact, very few people went there. Only the most important people had that chance, and only adults had gone in the past. Wendy was in the first group of young people to make the trip.

The voice over the loudspeaker said, "Welcome aboard Traveler Four."

- (After all students have raised their hand:) What did the doctor's report say about Wendy's health? (Call on a student. Idea: *She was in good health.*)
- Most of the other passengers on the trip were not young people like Wendy. Everybody, who were they? (Signal.) *Scientists.*
- How many young people had made this trip before Wendy and the other students in her group? (Call on a student. Idea: *None.*)

EXERCISE 7

FACT REVIEW

- Everybody, name the planets, starting with Mercury. Get ready. (Tap for each name.) *Mercury, Venus, Earth, Mars, Jupiter, Saturn, Uranus, Neptune, Pluto.*
- (Repeat until firm.)

EXERCISE 8

PAIRED PRACTICE

You're going to read aloud to your partner. The **B** members will read first. Then the **A** members will read from the star to the end of the story.
(Observe students and give feedback.)

End-of-Lesson Activities

INDEPENDENT WORK

Now finish your independent work for lesson 56. Raise your hand when you're finished. (Observe students and give feedback.)

WORKCHECK

a. (Direct students to take out their marking pencils.)
- We're going to check your workbook and textbook items. Remember, if you got an item wrong, make an **X** next to the item.
b. (For each item: Read the item. Call on a student to answer it. If the answer is wrong, say the correct answer. Refer to the Answer Key for the correct answers.)
c. Now use your marking pencil to fix up any items you got wrong. Remember, all mistakes must be fixed up before you hand in your work.

LANGUAGE ARTS

(Present Language Arts lesson 56 after completing Reading lesson 56. See Language Arts Guide.)

ACTIVITIES

(Present Activity 11 after completing Reading lessons 56. See Activities Across the Curriculum.)

EXERCISE 1

VOCABULARY REVIEW

a. Here's the new vocabulary sentence: She demonstrated how animals use oxygen.
- Everybody, say that sentence. Get ready. (Signal.) *She demonstrated how animals use oxygen.*
- (Repeat until firm.)

b. Everybody, what word names the part of the air you need to survive? (Signal.) *Oxygen.*
- What word means **showed?** (Signal.) *Demonstrated.*

EXERCISE 2

READING WORDS

Column 1

a. **Find lesson 57 in your textbook.** ✓
- Touch column 1. ✓
- (Teacher reference:)

1. demonstrate	4. aisle
2. computer	5. gravity
3. breakfast	

b. Word 1 is **demonstrate.** What word? (Signal.) *Demonstrate.*

c. Word 2 is **computer.** What word? (Signal.) *Computer.*

d. Word 3 is **breakfast.** What word? (Signal.) *Breakfast.*

e. Word 4 is **aisle.** What word? (Signal.) *Aisle.*

f. Word 5. What word? (Signal.) *Gravity.*

g. Let's read those words again.
- Word 1. What word? (Signal.) *Demonstrate.*
- (Repeat for words 2–5.)

h. (Repeat step g until firm.)

Column 2

i. Find column 2. ✓
- (Teacher reference:)

1. tremble	4. oxygen
2. cabinet	5. equipment
3. darkness	6. keyboard

- All these words have more than one syllable. The first part of each word is underlined.

j. Word 1. What's the underlined part? (Signal.) *trem.*
- What's the whole word? (Signal.) *Tremble.*
- Spell **tremble.** Get ready. (Tap for each letter.) *T-R-E-M-B-L-E.*
- Something that trembles shakes a little. What's another way of saying **The building began to shake?** (Signal.) *The building began to tremble.*

k. Word 2. What's the underlined part? (Signal.) *cab.*
- What's the whole word? (Signal.) *Cabinet.*
- Spell **cabinet.** Get ready. (Tap for each letter.) *C-A-B-I-N-E-T.*

l. Word 3. What's the underlined part? (Signal.) *dark.*
- What's the whole word? (Signal.) *Darkness.*
- Spell **darkness.** Get ready. (Tap for each letter.) *D-A-R-K-N-E-S-S.*

m. Word 4. What's the underlined part? (Signal.) *ox.*
- What's the whole word? (Signal.) *Oxygen.*
- Spell **oxygen.** Get ready. (Tap for each letter.) *O-X-Y-G-E-N.*

n. Word 5. What's the underlined part? (Signal.) *equip.*
- What's the whole word? (Signal.) *Equipment.*

o. Word 6. What's the underlined part? (Signal.) *key.*
- What's the whole word? (Signal.) *Keyboard.*

p. Let's read those words again.
- Word 1. What word? (Signal.) *Tremble.*
- (Repeat for words 2–6.)

q. (Repeat step p until firm.)

Column 3

r. Find column 3. ✓
- (Teacher reference:)

1. **palms**	4. **partly**
2. **gaining**	5. **helmets**
3. **guests**	6. **provided**

- All these words have an ending.
s. Word 1. What word? (Signal.) *Palms.*
- The insides of your hands are called palms. Touch the palm of your hand. ✓
t. Word 2. What word? (Signal.) *Gaining.*
- (Repeat for words 3–6.)
u. Let's read those words again.
- Word 1. What word? (Signal.) *Palms.*
- (Repeat for words 2–6.)
v. (Repeat step u until firm.)

Column 4

w. Find column 4. ✓
- (Teacher reference:)

1. **survive**	3. **waist**
2. **pressure**	4. **suit**

x. Word 1. What word? (Signal.) *Survive.*
- If you survive, you live. If you don't survive, you die. If you live through an earthquake, you survive the earthquake.
y. Word 2. What word? (Signal.) *Pressure.*
- (Repeat for words 3 and 4.)
z. Let's read those words again.
- Word 1. What word? (Signal.) *Survive.*
- (Repeat for words 2–4.)
a. (Repeat step z until firm.)

Column 5

b. Find column 5. ✓
- (Teacher reference:)

1. **liquid**	3. **weightless**
2. **baggage**	4. **fastened**

c. Word 1. What word? (Signal.) *Liquid.*
- (Repeat for words 2–4.)
d. Let's read those words again.
- Word 1. What word? (Signal.) *Liquid.*
- (Repeat for words 2–4.)
e. (Repeat step d until firm.)

Individual Turns

(For columns 1–5: Call on individual students, each to read one to three words per turn.)

STORY READING

a. Find part B in your textbook. ✓
- The error limit for group reading is 13 errors. Read carefully.
b. Everybody, touch the title. ✓
- (Call on a student to read the title.) *[Traveler Four.]*
- Everybody, what's the title? (Signal.) *Traveler Four.*
- (Call on individual students to read the story, each student reading two or three sentences at a time. Ask the specified questions as the students read.)

- (Correct errors: Tell the word. Direct the student to reread the sentence.)
- (If the group makes more than 13 errors, direct the students to reread the story.)

Traveler Four
The inside of Traveler Four was beautiful. It looked even better than the pictures Wendy had seen. The seats were dark red and very comfortable. You could lean them all the way back to form a bed. In front of every pair of seats was a cabinet. Inside the cabinet were two space suits and two space helmets. There was also a little table for writing just below the computer keyboard. And there was even a little TV screen. You could select movies by pressing a button. Or you could just press a button for computer games.

- Everybody, look at the picture on the next page. It shows a pair of passenger seats and the cabinet with all the things in it.
- Touch a space suit. ✓
- Touch a space helmet. ✓
- Touch the TV screen. ✓
- Touch the writing table. ✓
- That looks pretty comfortable.

Sidney sat next to Wendy. They kept looking at each other and smiling, but Wendy felt very nervous. She noticed that the palms of her hands were sweaty. And the inside of her mouth felt very dry.

- Everybody, show me your palms. ✓
- How did Wendy's palms feel? (Call on a student. Idea: *Sweaty.*)
- Why were her palms sweaty? (Call on a student. Idea: *Because she was nervous.*)

Suddenly, a sharp screeching noise came from below. Then a voice came over the loudspeaker. "You'll hear some strange noises," the voice said. "The one you just heard was the elevator in the cargo section below you."

- What would that elevator be used for? (Call on a student. Idea: *To load cargo onto the ship.*)

Wendy noticed that a flight attendant was standing in front of the passenger section. He said, "I will tell you about the equipment on this spaceship. As you know, there is no oxygen in space. And there is none on Jupiter."

- What is oxygen? (Call on a student. Ideas: *A gas in the air; the part of the air that we use when we breathe.*)

The flight attendant continued, "Each passenger has a space suit and all the special equipment needed to survive in space."

- What does that mean, survive in space? (Call on a student. Idea: *Stay alive in space.*)

The attendant said, "When we get close to Jupiter, I'll show you how to work your space suits and your tanks of oxygen. Until then do not take your suit from the cabinet."
A loud blowing sound seemed to come from behind the passenger section. The flight attendant said, "Those are the engines. We're ready to take off. So lean your seats halfway back. Fasten the seat belts around your waist and across your shoulders."

- What two things were the passengers supposed to do? (Call on a student. Idea: *Lean their seats back and fasten their seatbelts.*)
- Show me where the seatbelt around your waist would go. ✓

The flight attendant said, "You will feel a great deal of pressure when the ship takes off because the spaceship is picking up speed very fast. You'll feel as if you're being pressed very hard into your seat. The pressure is no more than you would feel if somebody were sitting ✦ on your chest. The pressure lasts for only a few minutes."

- Everybody, who was talking? (Signal.) *The flight attendant.*
- Would it feel very comfortable to have somebody sitting on your chest? (Signal.) *No.*
- That's a lot of pressure.

The flight attendant said, "Remember, when the pressure starts fading, you'll be able to sit up and look out of the window."

- You wouldn't be able to sit up and look out of the window before the pressure faded even if you weren't wearing seatbelts. Why? (Call on a student. Idea: *Because the pressure would push you back in your seat.*)

The flight attendant concluded, "If this is your first trip, you'll be very impressed with what you see when you look out of the window."
Wendy leaned her seat halfway back. She fastened the belts around her waist and across her shoulders. Her lips felt very dry. The blowing sound was becoming very loud now, very unpleasant. A voice was saying something over the loudspeaker, but Wendy couldn't hear it over the blowing sound.

The blowing sound was now a roar that seemed to make the spaceship tremble. Then the roar got so loud that Wendy wanted to hold her hands over her ears. Then she felt as if something was pushing her back in her seat. The ship was moving very fast. It had taken off. The roar was even louder. The ship was trembling. For an instant, Wendy was afraid that it might fall apart. But then she told herself that the spaceship was probably going through layers of air so fast that it felt like a car going over a bumpy road.

- Wendy had an idea about why the ship was shaking. What was her idea? (Call on a student. Idea: *It was going through layers of air.*)
- Why didn't she just look out of the window to see what was happening? (Accept reasonable responses.)

Wendy guessed that the ship was probably already fifteen or twenty miles from Earth and gaining more speed. The pressure was not as great. And the roaring sound suddenly disappeared. Everything was silent. That meant that the ship was now moving faster than the speed of sound.

- Why did the roaring sound disappear? (Call on a student. Idea: *The ship was moving faster than the speed of sound.*)

The engines were in the back of the ship. But their sound could not catch up to the front of the ship where Wendy was. So there was no roaring. No noise. And the trembling stopped.

- Listen to that part again. It tells why there was no noise in the passenger section of the ship:
    The engines were in the back of the ship. But their sound could not catch up to the front of the ship where Wendy was. So there was no roaring. No noise. And the trembling stopped.

- Everybody, where were the engines? (Signal.) *In the back of the ship.*
- Why didn't the sound from the engines reach the passenger section? (Call on a student. Ideas: *The sound they made couldn't catch up to the front of the ship; the ship was moving faster than the speed of sound.*)
- Read the rest of the story to yourself and be ready to answer some questions. Raise your hand when you're finished.

A voice over the loudspeaker said, "Ladies, gentlemen, and special guests, if you want to see the planet Earth as you've never seen it before, look out the window."
Wendy leaned forward and looked out the window. She saw the most beautiful sight she had ever seen. There was a huge green and blue ball, partly covered with white streaks. Part of the ball was in darkness. It was Earth.

- (After all students have raised their hand:) Everybody, what planet did Wendy see out of the window? (Signal.) *Earth.*
- Tell about the colors that Wendy saw. (Call on a student. Idea: *Green and blue with white streaks.*)
- What do you think made the white streaks? (Call on a student. Idea: *Clouds.*)
- What time of day was it for the people who were on the dark side of Earth? (Signal.) *Nighttime.*
- The picture shows what Wendy saw. Do you think that's a beautiful sight? (Call on a student.)

PAIRED PRACTICE

You're going to read aloud to your partner. The **A** members will read first. Then the **B** members will read from the star to the end of the story.
(Observe students and give feedback.)

End-of-Lesson Activities

INDEPENDENT WORK

Now finish your independent work for lesson 57. Raise your hand when you're finished. (Observe students and give feedback.)

WORKCHECK

a. (Direct students to take out their marking pencils.)
- We're going to check your workbook and textbook items. Remember, if you got an item wrong, make an **X** next to the item.

b. (For each item: Read the item. Call on a student to answer it. If the answer is wrong, say the correct answer. Refer to the Answer Key for the correct answers.)

c. Now use your marking pencil to fix up any items you got wrong. Remember, all mistakes must be fixed up before you hand in your work.

LANGUAGE ARTS

(Present Language Arts lesson 57 after completing Reading lesson 57. See Language Arts Guide.)

Lesson 58

EXERCISE 1

VOCABULARY REVIEW

a. You learned a sentence that tells what she selected.
- Everybody, say that sentence. Get ready. (Signal.) *She selected a comfortable seat.*
- (Repeat until firm.)

b. You learned a sentence that tells about being without gravity.
- Everybody, say that sentence. Get ready. (Signal.) *Without gravity, they were weightless.*
- (Repeat until firm.)

c. Here's the last sentence you learned: She demonstrated how animals use oxygen.
- Everybody, say that sentence. Get ready. (Signal.) *She demonstrated how animals use oxygen.*
- (Repeat until firm.)

d. Everybody, what word names the part of the air you need to survive? (Signal.) *Oxygen.*
- What word means **showed?** (Signal.) *Demonstrated.*

e. Once more. Say the sentence that tells what she demonstrated. Get ready. (Signal.) *She demonstrated how animals use oxygen.*

EXERCISE 2

READING WORDS

Column 1

a. **Find lesson 58 in your textbook.** ✓
- Touch column 1. ✓
- (Teacher reference:)

1. upside	4. workout
2. bathroom	5. weightless
3. outside	6. sideways

- All these words are compound words. The first part of each word is underlined.

b. Word 1. What's the underlined part? (Signal.) *up.*
- What's the whole word? (Signal.) *Upside.*
- Spell **upside.** Get ready. (Tap for each letter.) *U-P-S-I-D-E.*

c. Word 2. What's the underlined part? (Signal.) *bath.*
- What's the whole word? (Signal.) *Bathroom.*
- Spell **bathroom.** Get ready. (Tap for each letter.) *B-A-T-H-R-O-O-M.*

d. Word 3. What's the underlined part? (Signal.) *out.*
- What's the whole word? (Signal.) *Outside.*
- Spell **outside.** Get ready. (Tap for each letter.) *O-U-T-S-I-D-E.*

e. Word 4. What's the underlined part? (Signal.) *work.*
- What's the whole word? (Signal.) *Workout.*
- Spell **workout.** Get ready. (Tap for each letter.) *W-O-R-K-O-U-T.*

f. Word 5. What's the underlined part? (Signal.) *weight.*
- What's the whole word? (Signal.) *Weightless.*

g. Word 6. What's the underlined part? (Signal.) *side.*
- What's the whole word? (Signal.) *Sideways.*

h. Let's read those words again.
- Word 1. What word? (Signal.) *Upside.*
- (Repeat for words 2–6.)

i. (Repeat step h until firm.)

Column 2

j. Find column 2. ✓
- (Teacher reference:)

1. unfastened	4. aimed
2. appeared	5. brightly
3. rocketing	

- All these words have an ending.

k. Word 1. What word? (Signal.) *Unfastened.*
- When you unfasten something, you undo it.

l. Word 2. What word? (Signal.) *Appeared.*
- Something appears when it first comes into sight. When a person first comes into sight, the person appears. Everybody, what's another way of saying **The animals first came into sight?** (Signal.) *The animals appeared.*

m. Word 3. What word? (Signal.) *Rocketing.*
  • (Repeat for: **4. aimed, 5. brightly.**)
n. Let's read those words again.
  • Word 1. What word? (Signal.) *Unfastened.*
  • (Repeat for: **2. appeared, 3. rocketing, 4. aimed, 5. brightly.**)
o. (Repeat step n until firm.)

Column 3

p. Find column 3. ✓
  • (Teacher reference:)

1. demonstrate	4. tank
2. shower	5. liquid
3. gravity	

q. Word 1. What word? (Signal.) *Demonstrate.*
  • (Repeat for words 2–5.)
r. Let's read those words again.
  • Word 1. What word? (Signal.) *Demonstrate.*
  • (Repeat for words 2–5.)
s. (Repeat step r until firm.)

Column 4

t. Find column 4. ✓
  • (Teacher reference:)

1. complained	4. incredible
2. exercise	5. computer
3. completed	

u. Word 1. What word? (Signal.) *Complained.*
  • (Repeat for words 2–5.)
v. Let's read those words again.
  • Word 1. What word? (Signal.) *Complained.*
  • (Repeat for words 2–5.)
w. (Repeat step v until firm.)

Individual Turns

(For columns 1–4: Call on individual students, each to read one to three words per turn.)

EXERCISE 3

COMPREHENSION PASSAGE

a. Find part B in your textbook. ✓
  • You're going to read the next story about Wendy. First you'll read the information passage. It gives some facts about gravity.
b. Everybody, touch the title. ✓

  • (Call on a student to read the title.) *[Gravity.]*
  • Everybody, what's the title? (Signal.) *Gravity.*
c. (Call on individual students to read the passage, each student reading two or three sentences at a time. Ask the specified questions as the students read.)

> **Gravity**
> **In today's story, you will read about gravity.**
> **Gravity is the force that pulls things back to a planet.**

  • Everybody, listen to that fact again: Gravity is the force that pulls things back to a planet.
  • Say that fact. Get ready. (Signal.) *Gravity is the force that pulls things back to a planet.*
  • (Repeat until firm.)

> **When you drop something, gravity pulls it down to Earth.**

  • Everybody, what pulls it back to Earth? (Signal.) *Gravity.*
  • What does gravity do to a ball if you throw it straight up in the air as hard as you can? (Call on a student. Idea: *Pulls it back to Earth.*)
  • What would that ball do if there was no gravity on Earth? (Call on a student. Ideas: *Float away; keep going out into space.*)

> **Not all planets have the same amount of gravity.**

  • Everybody, say that fact. Get ready. (Signal.) *Not all planets have the same amount of gravity.*
  • (Repeat until firm.)

> **Things weigh more on planets with stronger gravity.**

  • Everybody, would a ball weigh more on a planet that has **stronger** gravity than Earth, or on a planet with **weaker** gravity than Earth? (Signal.) *Stronger.*

If the planet has gravity that is twice as strong as the gravity on Earth, you would weigh two times as much on that planet. A person who weighs 100 pounds on Earth would weigh 200 pounds on that planet.

- Everybody, if a person weighs 100 pounds on planet A and 200 pounds on planet B, which planet has stronger gravity? (Signal.) *Planet B.*
- If a person weighs 100 pounds on planet A and 20 pounds on planet B, which planet has stronger gravity? (Signal.) *Planet A.*

Our moon has gravity that is much less than the gravity on Earth. A person who weighs 100 pounds on Earth would weigh only 17 pounds on the moon. Remember, the stronger the gravity of a planet, the more you weigh on that planet.

- Everybody, which has a stronger gravity, Earth or the moon? (Signal.) *Earth.*

The planets that have the greatest gravity are the very large planets. On Jupiter, a 100-pound person would weigh more than 200 pounds.

- Everybody, which has stronger gravity, Earth or Jupiter? (Signal.) *Jupiter.*
- Where would you weigh more, on Earth or Jupiter? (Signal.) *Jupiter.*

EXERCISE 4

STORY READING

a. Find part C in your textbook. ✓
- The error limit for group reading is 9 errors. Read carefully.
b. Everybody, touch the title. ✓
- (Call on a student to read the title.) [The Gravity Device.]
- Everybody, what's the title? (Signal.) *The Gravity Device.*
- A gravity device is something that makes spaceships have gravity like Earth.
- (Call on individual students to read the story, each student reading two or three sentences at a time. Ask the specified questions as students read.)

- (Correct errors: Tell the word. Direct the student to reread the sentence.)
- (If the group makes more than 9 errors, direct the students to reread the story.)

The Gravity Device
The people on the spaceship looked out their windows at Earth. They watched it get smaller as the spaceship streaked off into space.

- Why did Earth appear to get smaller? (Call on a student. Idea: *The ship was getting farther and farther away from it.*)

The sky in all directions was black now, but the sun was shining brightly. Wendy knew why there was no blue sky. She knew that the sky around Earth looked blue because there was a layer of air around Earth.

- Everybody, why does the sky look blue when you're on Earth? (Signal.) *Because there's a layer of air around Earth.*
- Yes, the air makes the sky look blue.

The spaceship was above the layer of air around Earth. Now there was nothing outside the spaceship, just empty space.

- Everybody, was the ship in a layer of air now? (Signal.) *No.*
- If there was no air around the spaceship now, would the sky look blue? (Signal.) *No.*
- What was the color outside the spaceship? (Signal.) *Black.*

Because there was no air, the spaceship did not have to use its engines anymore. The pilot just aimed the spaceship in the direction it was supposed to go and then turned off the engines. The spaceship continued to move in that direction. It didn't slow down because there was no air outside to slow it down.

- Why didn't the spaceship slow down? (Call on a student. Idea: *There was no air to slow it down.*)

- Air drags against things when they go fast. But if there is no air, there is nothing to drag against the ship and slow it down.

There was no strong gravity to pull the spaceship back toward Earth.

- Everybody, did the gravity of Earth pull the spaceship back down toward Earth anymore? (Signal.) *No.*

A flight attendant appeared in front of the passenger section. She said, "The Traveler Four has a new invention that has not been on any of the earlier Travelers. This invention is a gravity device. It makes you feel just like you do on Earth. If you drop something inside this spaceship, the object falls down. You can stand up and walk on the floor because the gravity device will always pull you down."

- The spaceship has gravity just like Earth. What happens if you drop something inside the spaceship? (Call on a student. Idea: *It falls to the floor.*)
- Why can you walk on the floor? (Call on a student. Idea: *The gravity device pulls you down.*)

The flight attendant continued, "But when the gravity device is not turned on, there is no gravity. And things float without falling. I'll show you how that works."

- She's going to turn off the gravity device. What will things do when she turns it off? (Call on a student. Idea: *Float in the air.*)

Wendy heard a high buzzing sound for an instant. Then she felt a little different. She looked at the flight attendant at the front of the passenger section and she could hardly believe what she saw. The flight attendant was not standing on the floor. She was floating in the air about a meter off the floor.

- Everybody, look at the picture. You can see the flight attendant at the front of the passenger section. Is the gravity device turned on in this picture? (Signal.) *No.*
- Is the flight attendant the only person floating around in this picture? (Signal.) *No.*

"I'll give you ★ a chance to see what it feels like to be weightless. But I would like to warn you about liquids. Let me demonstrate."
The flight attendant held up a paper cup that was covered. She took the cover off and slowly moved the cup downward, leaving a blob of orange juice floating in the air. It was in the same shape it had been when it was in the cup. Now the flight attendant blew on the blob very gently. The blob began to change shape and move away from her. She said, "If I hit this liquid, it will break into a million tiny drops. That's dangerous, because it will make breathing very difficult."

- What would happen if she broke the liquid into tiny drops? (Call on a student. Idea: *It would be difficult to breathe.*)

She took a large bag and caught all but a little part of the floating liquid. Then she said, "Watch." And she hit the little blob. It turned into something like a cloud of dust.

- Read the rest of the story to yourself and be ready to answer some questions. Raise your hand when you're finished.

> "Okay," she said to the passengers. "Take off your seat belts and float around. Don't try to move too fast, or you may hurt yourself."
>
> Wendy had already unfastened her seat belts. She pushed up and floated out of her seat. She looked around. There was Sidney, upside down, floating near the ceiling of the spaceship. And there were the other passengers, floating this way and that way, just like a bunch of fish in a fish tank.
>
> Wendy laughed.
>
> A couple of students were dancing in space. People were bumping into each other.
>
> After a few minutes, the flight attendant said, "Okay, we're going to turn on the gravity device very slowly. You'll find yourself sinking slowly to the floor."
>
> As soon as she finished talking, Wendy felt herself falling slowly to the floor. She stood up. Then she felt herself getting heavier and heavier until she felt like she always did when she stood on Earth. "Wow," she said to Sidney. "That was great."

- (After all students have raised their hand:) Everybody, did the gravity device come on **fast** or **slowly?** (Signal.) *Slowly.*
- Before it came on, what were people doing? (Call on a student. Idea: *Floating in the air.*)
- After Wendy was standing up, she kept feeling heavier and heavier. Why? (Call on a student. Idea: *The gravity was getting greater and greater.*)
- When the gravity device was on all the way, how did she feel? (Call on a student. Idea: *Like she did when she was on Earth.*)

PAIRED PRACTICE

You're going to read aloud to your partner. The **B** members will read first. Then the **A** members will read from the star to the end of the story.

(Observe students and give feedback.)

End-of-Lesson Activities

INDEPENDENT WORK

Now finish your independent work for lesson 58. Raise your hand when you're finished. (Observe students and give feedback.)

WORKCHECK

a. (Direct students to take out their marking pencils.)
- We're going to check your workbook and textbook items. Remember, if you got an item wrong, make an **X** next to the item.

b. (For each item: Read the item. Call on a student to answer it. If the answer is wrong, say the correct answer. Refer to the Answer Key for the correct answers.)

c. Now use your marking pencil to fix up any items you got wrong. Remember, all mistakes must be fixed up before you hand in your work.

LANGUAGE ARTS

(Present Language Arts lesson 58 after completing Reading lesson 58. See Language Arts Guide.)

EXERCISE 1
VOCABULARY

a. **Find the vocabulary sentences on page 352 in your textbook.** ✓
- Touch sentence 15. ✓
- This is a new vocabulary sentence. It says: Lava erupted from the volcano's crater. Everybody, say that sentence. Get ready. (Signal.) *Lava erupted from the volcano's crater.*
- Close your eyes and say the sentence. Get ready. (Signal.) *Lava erupted from the volcano's crater.*
- (Repeat until firm.)

b. The sentence says that **lava** erupted. Lava is hot melted rock.

c. When lava **erupts** from a volcano, the lava is spit out or coughed out. Everybody, when lava is spit out or coughed out of a volcano, what is the volcano doing? (Signal.) *Erupting.*

d. A volcano's **crater** is the enormous dent in the top of the volcano. Everybody, what do we call the enormous dent? (Signal.) *Crater.*

e. Listen to the sentence again: Lava erupted from the volcano's crater. Everybody, say that sentence. Get ready. (Signal.) *Lava erupted from the volcano's crater.*

f. Everybody, what word means **melted rock?** (Signal.) *Lava.*
- What do we call the enormous dent at the top of a volcano? (Signal.) *Crater.*
- What word means **coughed out** or **spit out?** (Signal.) *Erupted.*
- (Repeat step f until firm.)

EXERCISE 2
VOCABULARY REVIEW

a. You learned a sentence that tells what she demonstrated.
- Everybody, say that sentence. Get ready. (Signal.) *She demonstrated how animals use oxygen.*

b. I'll say part of the sentence. When I stop, you say the next word. Listen: She . . . Everybody, what's the next word? (Signal.) *Demonstrated.*

c. Listen: She demonstrated how animals use . . . Everybody, what's the next word? (Signal.) *Oxygen.*
- Say the whole sentence. Get ready. (Signal.) *She demonstrated how animals use oxygen.*

EXERCISE 3
READING WORDS
Column 1

a. Find lesson 59 in your textbook. ✓
- Touch column 1. ✓
- (Teacher reference:)

1. **Io**	4. **view**
2. **surround**	5. **area**
3. **instead**	

b. Word 1 is **Io (EYE-oh).** What word? (Signal.) *Io.*
- Spell **Io.** Get ready. (Tap for each letter.) *I-O.*
- Io is a large moon that circles Jupiter.

c. Word 2 is **surround.** What word? (Signal.) *Surround.*
- Spell **surround.** Get ready. (Tap for each letter.) *S-U-R-R-O-U-N-D.*
- If something surrounds you, it is all the way around you. Everybody, what's another way of saying **The wall goes all the way around the city?** (Signal.) *The wall surrounds the city.*

d. Word 3 is **instead.** What word? (Signal.) *Instead.*
- Spell **instead.** Get ready. (Tap for each letter.) *I-N-S-T-E-A-D.*

e. Word 4 is **view.** What word? (Signal.) *View.*
- Spell **view.** Get ready. (Tap for each letter.) *V-I-E-W.*

f. Word 5 is **area.** What word? (Signal.) *Area.*

g. Let's read those words again.
- Word 1. What word? (Signal.) *Io.*
- (Repeat for words 2–5.)

h. (Repeat step g until firm.)

Column 2

i. Find column 2. ✓
- (Teacher reference:)

> 1. circling   4. bathrooms
> 2. completed   5. rocketing
> 3. complained

- All these words have an ending.

j. Word 1. What word? (Signal.) *Circling.*
- (Repeat for words 2–5.)

k. Let's read those words again.
- Word 1. What word? (Signal.) *Circling.*
- (Repeat for words 2–5.)

l. (Repeat step k until firm.)

Column 3

m. Find column 3. ✓
- (Teacher reference:)

> 1. snored   4. striped
> 2. showers   5. exercises
> 3. serving   6. erupting

- All these words have an ending.

n. Word 1. What word? (Signal.) *Snored.*
- (Repeat for words 2–6.)

o. Let's read those words again.
- Word 1. What word? (Signal.) *Snored.*
- (Repeat for words 2–6.)

p. (Repeat step o until firm.)

Column 4

q. Find column 4. ✓
- (Teacher reference:)

> 1. incredible   4. outside
> 2. aisle   5. sideways
> 3. breakfast   6. workout

r. Word 1. What word? (Signal.) *Incredible.*
- Something that is **incredible** is **amazing.** What's another way of saying **They saw an amazing sight?** (Signal.) *They saw an incredible sight.*

s. Word 2. What word? (Signal.) *Aisle.*
- (Repeat for words 3–6.)

t. Let's read those words again.
- Word 1. What word? (Signal.) *Incredible.*
- (Repeat for words 2–6.)

u. (Repeat step t until firm.)

Column 5

v. Find column 5. ✓

- (Teacher reference:)

> 1. we're   3. we'll
> 2. were   4. well

- These words are easy to confuse. One word in each pair is a contraction. It's made up of two words that are stuck together.

w. Word 1. What word? (Signal.) *We're.*
- Yes, that's a contraction for **we are. We're** going to the store.

x. Word 2. What word? (Signal.) *Were.*
- Yes, that's the word **were.** They **were** going to the store.

y. Word 3. What word? (Signal.) *We'll.*
- That's a contraction for **we will. We'll** go to the store.

z. Word 4. What word? (Signal.) *Well.*
- Yes, we feel **well.**

a. Let's read those words again.
- Word 1. What word? (Signal.) *We're.*
- (Repeat for words 2–4.)

b. (Repeat step a until firm.)

Individual Turns

(For columns 1–5: Call on individual students, each to read one to three words per turn.)

EXERCISE 4

STORY READING

a. Find part B in your textbook. ✓
- The error limit is 11. Read carefully.

b. Everybody, touch the title. ✓
- (Call on a student to read the title.) *[Jupiter.]*
- Everybody, what's the title? (Signal.) *Jupiter.*
- (Call on individual students to read the story, each student reading two or three sentences at a time. Ask the specified questions as the students read.)

> - (Correct errors: Tell the word. Direct the student to reread the sentence.)
> - (If the group makes more than 11 errors, direct the students to reread the story.)

> **Jupiter**
> **By dinner time of the first day, Traveler Four had traveled over forty million miles.**

- Everybody, how far had it traveled in less than a day? (Signal.) *Over forty million miles.*

The spaceship had gone past the planet Mars. That planet looked red. It didn't have many clouds around it, like Earth does. The flight attendant told the passengers about Mars. But Wendy already knew everything the flight attendant said.

Wendy knew that Mars is smaller than Earth. It is also colder because it is much farther from the sun than Earth is.

- Everybody, what color did Mars look? (Signal.) *Red.*
- Tell me about the colors of Earth when you see it from space. (Call on a student. Idea: *It's green, blue, and streaked with white.*)
- Everybody, which planet has more clouds around it, Earth or Mars? (Signal.) *Earth.*
- Which planet is hotter? (Signal.) *Earth.*
- Why is Mars colder? (Call on a student. Idea: *It's farther from the sun.*)

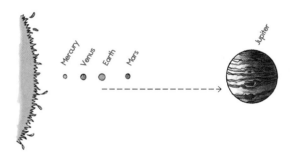

- Everybody, look at the map of the planets on the next page. ✓
- The dotted arrow shows the path that Traveler Four took. Everybody, is it going **toward the sun** or **away from the sun?** (Signal.) *Away from the sun.*
- If the planets are colder as you get farther from the sun, what's Jupiter going to be like? (Call on a student. Idea: *Very cold.*)

Sleeping on a spaceship was comfortable enough, but Wendy didn't sleep much that first night. It was very quiet in the spaceship. Nearly all the lights were turned off.

Wendy had moved her seat all the way back so that it became a bed. The only sounds in the spaceship were the buzzing sounds of the gravity device and the sounds of people snoring. Sidney snored very loudly.

- Show me what Sidney sounded like. (Call on a student.)

From time to time, Wendy went to sleep, but then she would wake up, feeling strange. For a moment, she wouldn't remember where she was. Then she would look around and remember that she was over fifty million miles from Earth, rocketing through space at one thousand miles per second.

Outside the spaceship, the sun shined brightly, but the sun was getting smaller, because the spaceship was moving away from it.

- Why did the sun appear to get smaller? (Call on a student. Idea: *The ship was getting farther away from it.*)
- It didn't really become night for Wendy and the others. They just knew it was night by what time it was. They could see the sun all the time.

At 7 the next morning, the lights came on inside the spaceship and people got up. People had to wait in line to use the bathrooms. They took showers, brushed their teeth, and changed their clothes. Then they exercised. Not everybody could exercise at the same time because there wasn't enough room. The flight attendants divided the passengers into three groups. The people in the front of the passenger section were in the first group. Wendy was in the second group. The first group got out in the aisles and did their exercises. They jumped up and down one hundred times. They did as many push-ups as they could. They did sit-ups. They ran in place. They did stretching exercises. Some of the passengers complained.

"You need this exercise," the flight attendant in front of the passenger section said. "We're going to be in this ship for a long time, and you'll get weak if you just sit all that time."

- Why did they need the exercise? (Call on a student. Ideas: *They'd get weak if they sat all the way to Jupiter; they were going to be on the ship for a long time.*)
- Name some exercises they did. (Call on individual students. Ideas: *Sit-ups; push-ups; running in place; jumping.*)

> Now the first ✦ group sat down and Wendy's group got up. "Now we'll show you how to do it," one of the men in Wendy's group said. "We can do better than the first group."

- They sound like they're going to have fun doing their exercises.

> "Yeah," some of the other people in group two shouted.
>
> So Wendy and the others worked very hard at their exercises. After each exercise, somebody would shout, "We're number one!"
>
> Some of the people in the first group were saying things like, "Boo for group two." But they weren't serious. Everybody was laughing. Some people in the third group said things like, "We can beat both those other groups."
>
> Wendy was tired when the exercises were finished. Her heart was pounding and she was sweating. Sidney said, "That was a good workout."
>
> Now the third group was doing their exercises. "Booooo!" Sidney shouted. "We were twice as good as that group!"

- Everybody, was she really mad at the third group? (Signal.) *No.*
- Read the rest of the story to yourself and be ready to answer some questions. Raise your hand when you're finished.

> ❁After the exercises were completed, the flight attendants served a big breakfast. As soon as the attendants started serving the people in front of Wendy, she realized that she was very hungry.

> Wendy ate her breakfast very fast. Sidney didn't eat her roll, so she gave it to Wendy. "I don't know why I'm so hungry," Wendy said, "but I could eat a horse."
>
> Wendy slept well that night. The next day she got up, did her exercises, studied, ate lunch, studied some more, and took a nap in the afternoon. When she woke up, the pilot was talking over the loudspeaker. She said, "We're going to turn the spaceship sideways so that you can ❁ see Jupiter. It is quite a sight."
>
> Slowly, the ship turned. It continued to move in the same direction it had been moving, but it was now moving sideways. Wendy pressed close to the window. And there it was, the largest planet in the solar system—Jupiter. It looked huge. Wendy could clearly see four moons. She knew that there were twelve others, but she couldn't see them. The planet looked like a great striped ball, with the stripes circling the planet. Some stripes were dark brown, some were orange, and some were white. For a moment, Wendy couldn't talk. She heard the other passengers saying things like, "Isn't that beautiful?" and "Incredible!"

- (After all students have raised their hand:) Everyone, which group ate first, group one or group three? (Signal) *Group one.*
- Where was Wendy sitting? (Call on a student. Ideas: *With the second group; in the middle.*)
- So when did she get served? (Call on a student. Ideas: *Second; next.*)
- The story said that Wendy could eat a horse. What does that mean? (Call on a student. Idea: *She could eat a lot.*)
- How did Wendy sleep on the second night? (Call on a student. Idea: *Well.*)
- Name some things she did the next day. (Call on individual students. Ideas: *Exercised; studied; ate lunch; took a nap.*)
- What did the pilot do to the spaceship that afternoon? (Call on a student. Idea: *She turned it sideways.*)

- Everybody, show me how the ship was moving when it was sideways. ✓
- Describe how Jupiter looked. (Call on individual students. Ideas: *It was huge; you could see four moons; it had red, brown, and white stripes; it was beautiful.*)
- Everybody, how many moons could Wendy see? (Signal.) *Four.*

- Look at the picture. It shows how Jupiter looked.

EXERCISE 5

PAIRED PRACTICE

You're going to read aloud to your partner. The **A** members will read first. Then the **B** members will read from the star to the end of the story.
(Observe students and give feedback.)

End-of-Lesson Activities

INDEPENDENT WORK

Now finish your independent work for lesson 59. Raise your hand when you're finished. (Observe students and give feedback.)

WORKCHECK

a. (Direct students to take out their marking pencils.)
- We're going to check your workbook and textbook items. Remember, if you got an item wrong, make an **X** next to the item.
b. (For each item: Read the item. Call on a student to answer it. If the answer is wrong, say the correct answer. Refer to the Answer Key for the correct answers.)
c. Now use your marking pencil to fix up any items you got wrong. Remember, all mistakes must be fixed up before you hand in your work.

LANGUAGE ARTS

(Present Language Arts lesson 59 after completing Reading lesson 59. See Language Arts Guide.)

> *Note:* You will need to reproduce blackline masters for the Fact Game in lesson 60 (Appendix G in Teacher's Guide).

Lesson 60

EXERCISE 1

FACT GAME

a. You're going to play the game that uses the facts you have learned. Remember the rules. The player rolls the number cubes, figures out the number of the question, reads that question out loud, and answers it. The monitor tells the player if the answer is right or wrong. If it's wrong, the monitor tells the right answer. If it's right, the monitor gives the player one point. Don't argue with the monitor. The number cubes go to the left and the next player has a turn. You'll play the game for 10 minutes.

b. (Divide students into groups of four or five. Assign monitors. Circulate as students play the game. Comment on groups that are playing well.)

c. (At the end of 10 minutes, have all students who earned more than 10 points stand up.)

  - (Tell the monitor of each game that ran smoothly:) Your group did a good job.

EXERCISE 2

READING CHECKOUTS

a. Today is a test day and a reading-checkout day. While you're writing answers, I'm going to call on you one at a time to read part of the story we read in lesson 59.

  - Remember, you pass the checkout by reading the passage in less than a minute without making more than 2 mistakes. And when you pass the checkout, you color the space for lesson 60 on your thermometer chart.

b. (Call on individual students to read the portion of story 59 marked with ❀.)

  - (Time the student. Note words that are missed and number of words read.)

  - (Teacher reference:)

> ❀ **After the exercises were completed, the flight attendants served a big breakfast. As soon as the attendants started serving the people in front of Wendy, she realized that she was very hungry. Wendy ate her breakfast very fast. Sidney didn't eat her roll, so she gave it to Wendy. "I [50] don't know why I'm so hungry," Wendy said, "but I could eat a horse."**
>
> **Wendy slept well that night. The next day she got up, [75] did her exercises, studied, ate lunch, studied some more, and took a nap in the afternoon. When she woke up, the pilot was talking over [100] the loudspeaker. She said, "We're going to turn the spaceship sideways so that you can ❀ [115] see Jupiter.**

  - (If the student reads the passage in one minute or less and makes no more than 2 errors, direct the student to color in the space for lesson 60 on the thermometer chart.)

- (If the student makes any mistakes, point to each word that was misread and identify it.)
- (If the student does not meet the rate-error criterion for the passage, direct the student to practice reading the story with the assigned partner.)

EXERCISE 3

TEST

a. **Find page 301 in your textbook.** ✓
- This is a test. You'll work items you've done before.
b. Work carefully. Raise your hand when you've completed all the items.
(Observe students but do not give feedback on errors.)

EXERCISE 4

MARKING THE TEST

a. (Check students' work before beginning lesson 61. Refer to the Answer Key for the correct answers.)
b. (Record all test 6 results on the Test Summary Sheet and the Group Summary Sheet. Reproducible Summary Sheets are at the back of the Teacher's Guide.)

EXERCISE 5

TEST REMEDIES

(Provide any necessary remedies for test 6 before presenting lesson 61. Test remedies are discussed in the Teacher's Guide.)

Test 6 Firming Table

Test Item	Introduced in lesson	Test Item	Introduced in lesson	Test Item	Introduced in lesson
1	53	13	53	25	59
2	53	14	53	26	59
3	53	15	53	27	59
4	53	16	52	28	59
5	53	17	52	29	58
6	56	18	52	30	58
7	53	19	52	31	49
8	53	20	58	32	53
9	53	21	58	33	49
10	54	22	58	34	53
11	54	23	58	35	56
12	54	24	58	36	56

LITERATURE

(Present Literature lesson 6 after completing Reading lesson 60. See Literature Guide.)

LANGUAGE ARTS

(Present Language Arts lesson 60 after completing Reading lesson 60. See Language Arts Guide.)

Lessons 61–65 · Planning Page

	Lesson 61	Lesson 62	Lesson 63	Lesson 64	Lesson 65
Lesson Events	Fact Review Vocabulary Sentence Reading Words Story Reading Paired Practice Independent Work Workcheck Language Arts	Vocabulary Sentences Reading Words Comprehension Passage Story Reading Paired Practice Independent Work Workcheck Language Arts	Vocabulary Sentence Reading Words Story Reading Paired Practice Independent Work Workcheck Language Arts	**Vocabulary Sentence** Reading Words Fact Review Story Reading Paired Practice Independent Work Workcheck Language Arts	Vocabulary Sentence Reading Words Story Reading Reading Checkouts Study Items Independent Work Workcheck Language Arts
Vocabulary Sentence	#15: <u>Lava</u> <u>erupted</u> from the volcano's <u>crater</u>.	sentence #13 sentence #14 sentence #15	#15: <u>Lava</u> <u>erupted</u> from the volcano's <u>crater</u>.	**#16: The <u>incredible</u> whales made them <u>anxious</u>.**	#16: The <u>incredible</u> whales made them <u>anxious</u>.
Reading Words: Word Types	modeled words words with an ending mixed words	2-syllable words words with an ending mixed words	modeled words compound words mixed words	multi-syllable words mixed words words with an ending	mixed words
New Vocabulary	assigned telescope equipped gases dome		manage		slumped pale
Comprehension Passage		*Planets and Gravity*			
Story	*Io*	*The Space Station on Io*	*A Trip to the Volcano*	*Help*	*Sidney*
Skill Items		Vocabulary sentence	Vocabulary sentences Sequencing		
Special Materials					Reference materials Thermometer charts
Special Projects/ Activities	Activity after lessons 61–62			Activity after lessons 64–66	

Lesson 61

EXERCISE 1
FACT REVIEW

a. Let's review some facts you have learned. First we'll go over the facts together. Then I'll call on individual students to do some facts.
b. Everybody, tell me how far it is from Earth to Jupiter. (Pause.) Get ready. (Signal.) *400 million miles.*
 • Tell me how fast Traveler Four travels. (Pause.) Get ready. (Signal.) *1,000 miles per second.*
 • Tell me how many planets there are in the solar system. (Pause.) Get ready. (Signal.) *Nine.*
 • (Repeat step b until firm.)
c. Tell me how many suns are in the solar system. (Pause.) Get ready. (Signal.) *One.*
 • Name the largest city in Japan. (Pause.) Get ready. (Signal.) *Tokyo.*
 • Tell me in which direction you would fly to get from Vancouver to Tokyo. (Pause.) Get ready. (Signal.) *West.*
 • (Repeat step c until firm.)
d. Name the planets in order, starting with Mercury. (Pause.) Get ready. (Tap for each name.) *Mercury, Venus, Earth, Mars, Jupiter, Saturn, Uranus, Neptune, Pluto.*
 • (Repeat step d until firm.)

Individual Turns
 • Now I'm going to call on individual students to do some facts.
 • (Call on individual students to do the set of facts in step b, c, or d.)

EXERCISE 2
VOCABULARY REVIEW

a. Here's the new vocabulary sentence: Lava erupted from the volcano's crater.
 • Everybody, say that sentence. Get ready. (Signal.) *Lava erupted from the volcano's crater.*
 • (Repeat until firm.)

b. Everybody, what word means **melted rock?** (Signal.) *Lava.*
 • What word means **coughed out** or **spit out?** (Signal.) *Erupted.*
 • What do we call the enormous dent at the top of a volcano? (Signal.) *Crater.*
 • (Repeat step b until firm.)

EXERCISE 3
READING WORDS
Column 1

a. **Find lesson 61 in your textbook.** ✓
 • Touch column 1. ✓
 • (Teacher reference:)

| 1. receive | 3. telescope |
| 2. assigned | 4. lava |

b. Word 1 is **receive.** What word? (Signal.) *Receive.*
 • Spell **receive.** Get ready. (Tap for each letter.) *R-E-C-E-I-V-E.*
c. Word 2 is **assigned.** What word? (Signal.) *Assigned.*
 • Spell **assigned.** Get ready. (Tap for each letter.) *A-S-S-I-G-N-E-D.*
 • A person who is assigned a book is the only person who can use the book. Someone who is assigned a room is the only one who can use the room.
d. Word 3 is **telescope.** What word? (Signal.) *Telescope.*
 • Spell **telescope.** Get ready. (Tap for each letter.) *T-E-L-E-S-C-O-P-E.*
 • A telescope is a device that makes distant things look large. We use telescopes to look at the stars. Everybody, what's the name of the device that makes distant things look large? (Signal.) *Telescope.*
e. Word 4 is **lava.** What word? (Signal.) *Lava.*
 • Spell **lava.** Get ready. (Tap for each letter.) *L-A-V-A.*
f. Let's read those words again.
 • Word 1. What word? (Signal.) *Receive.*
 • (Repeat for: **2. assigned, 3. telescope, 4. lava.**)
g. (Repeat step f until firm.)

Column 2

h. Find column 2. ✓
- (Teacher reference:)

> 1. equipped   4. surrounded
> 2. gases   5. towers
> 3. erupting   6. impressive

- All these words have an ending.
i. Word 1. What word? (Signal.) *Equipped.*
- When you're well equipped for doing something, you have all the supplies you need to do the job. How would you be well equipped to go out in very cold weather? (Call on a student. Ideas: *Warm clothes, gloves, hat,* etc.)
j. Word 2. What word? (Signal.) *Gases.*
- Gases float in the air. Oxygen is a gas.
k. Word 3. What word? (Signal.) *Erupting.*
- (Repeat for words 4–6.)
l. Let's read those words again.
- Word 1. What word? (Signal.) *Equipped.*
- (Repeat for words 2–6.)
m. (Repeat step l until firm.)

Column 3

n. Find column 3. ✓
- (Teacher reference:)

> 1. dome   4. view
> 2. restless   5. soup
> 3. instead   6. program

o. Word 1. What word? (Signal.) *Dome.*
- Another word for a **rounded ceiling** is a **dome.** Everybody, what do we call a rounded ceiling? (Signal.) *Dome.*
p. Word 2. What word? (Signal.) *Restless.*
q. Word 3. What word? (Signal.) *Instead.*
- r. (Repeat for words 4–6.)
s. Let's read those words again.
- Word 1. What word? (Signal.) *Dome.*
- (Repeat for words 2–6.)
t. (Repeat step s until firm.)

Individual Turns

(For columns 1–3: Call on individual students, each to read one to three words per turn.)

EXERCISE 4

STORY READING

a. Find part B in your textbook. ✓
- The error limit for group reading is 12 errors. Read carefully.
b. Everybody, touch the title. ✓
- (Call on a student to read the title.) *[Io.]*
- Everybody, what's the title? (Signal.) Io.
- (Call on individual students to read the story, each student reading two or three sentences at a time. Ask the specified questions as the students read.)

> - (Correct errors: Tell the word. Direct the student to reread the sentence.)
> - (If the group makes more than 12 errors, direct the students to reread the story.)

> **Io**
> **The last two days of the trip went slowly. Wendy didn't sleep well on the last night.**

- Everybody, how long does the trip from Earth to Jupiter take? (Signal.) *Four-and-a-half-days.*
- How did Wendy sleep on the first night? (Call on a student. Idea: *Not well.*)
- How did she sleep on the next night? (Call on a student. Ideas: *Well; okay.*)
- How did she sleep on the last night? (Call on a student. Idea: *Not well.*)
- How many more nights will she sleep on Traveler Four before it reaches Jupiter? (Call on a student. Idea: *None.*)

> **Wendy was getting very restless. She could hardly wait to get to Jupiter. Actually, the spaceship would not land on Jupiter. It would land on one of Jupiter's larger moons, named Io.**

- Everybody, would the spaceship land on Jupiter? (Signal.) *No.*
- Name the place it would land. Get ready. (Signal.) Io.

> **Jupiter has a gravity that is much stronger than that of Earth.**
> **A large man weighs about 200 pounds on Earth. That same man would weigh 500 pounds on Jupiter.**

- Everybody, where would a man be heavier, on Earth or Jupiter? (Signal.) *Jupiter.*

316 *Lesson 61*

- How much would a 200-pound man weigh on Jupiter? (Signal.) *500 pounds.*

That man would weigh so much on Jupiter that he could hardly stand up. He would feel as if he were carrying two people on his back.

- How easily would you move if you had to carry two people on your back all day long? (Call on a student. Idea: *Not easily.*)
- That's how it would feel on Jupiter.

There was another reason that the spaceship would not land on the surface of Jupiter. The planet is surrounded by a thick layer of gas. The surface of the planet is dark. Even with bright lights, it is impossible to see more than a few meters.

- What surrounds Jupiter? (Call on a student. Idea: *A thick layer of gas.*)
- So how do things look on the surface? (Call on a student. Idea: *Dark.*)

So instead of landing on the surface of Jupiter, Traveler Four would land on Io, a moon about as big as our moon.

- Everybody, about how big is Io? (Signal.) *As big as our moon.*

Io is very close to the surface of Jupiter. There are no gases surrounding Io. In fact, there is nothing but empty space surrounding Io. Io floats through space. And it moves around Jupiter very fast. Io goes all the way around Jupiter in about two days.

- Everybody, about how long does it take Io to circle all the way around Jupiter? (Signal.) *Two days.*
- Remember that fact.

The last morning on Traveler Four was very busy. The flight attendants showed the passengers how to put on their space suits. "Remember," one of the flight attendants said, "there is no oxygen on Io. There is oxygen inside the space station, but when you go outside, you must wear your space suit, or you'll die."

- Everybody, how much oxygen is there on the surface of Io? (Signal.) *None.*
- What do you have to do when you walk around on Io? (Call on a student. Idea: *Wear a space suit.*)

The attendant continued, "When you leave the space station, you must go with another person. Your space suit is equipped with an automatic radio that tells you where you are and how to get back to the space station. The radio also tells you how much more air you have in your oxygen tanks."

- What things does the automatic radio in the space suit tell you? (Call on a student. Ideas: *Where you are; how to get back to the space station; how much air you have in your oxygen tanks.*)

The space suit was very heavy. The flight attendants helped Wendy and the other passengers get into their suits. Two large tanks were attached to the back of each space suit. These tanks held oxygen that the person would breathe.
Look at the picture of the space suit.

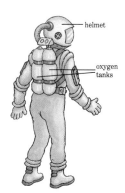

- Everybody, do it. Touch the two oxygen tanks on the back. ✓
- Touch the helmet. ✓

The passengers could hardly walk in their space suits.

- Why? (Call on a student. Idea: *The suits were so heavy.*)

"Don't worry," the flight attendant said. "Io is quite a bit smaller than Earth. So the gravity on Io is less than it is on Earth. That means that you won't feel very heavy ✦ in your space suit when you walk around on Io. In fact, you should be able to jump 8 feet high on Io. That should make you feel like a super basketball player."

- Everybody, would their space suits feel heavy on Io? (Signal.) *No.*
- Why? (Call on a student. Idea: *Because there's not much gravity.*)
- Everybody, how high can you jump on Io? (Signal.) *Eight feet.*
- Show me how high one foot is. ✓
- Imagine jumping eight feet high. That's higher than I can reach.

After the passengers walked around in their space suits, they took them off and put them away.

- Where are the space suits kept on Traveler Four? (Call on a student. Idea: *In cabinets.*)

In the middle of the afternoon, the engines of the spaceship started up.

- Everybody, had the engines been running all the time? (Signal.) *No.*
- Why not? (Call on a student. Idea: *They didn't need the engines in space.*)

"The engines are slowing us down," a flight attendant explained. "It will take us about three hours to slow to the same speed that Io is going."
    The view outside the window was incredible. The planet Jupiter was so huge that it seemed to cover half the sky. From time to time, the flight attendant pointed out interesting facts about the planet. At one time she said, "If you look at the lower half of the planet, you'll see a part that looks something like an eye."

Wendy could see it clearly. The attendant said, "That eye is two times as big as Earth."
    Wendy shook her head. "Incredible," she said.

- Everybody, touch the eye in the picture of Jupiter on page 305. ✓
- How big is that eye? (Signal.) *Two times as big as Earth.*
- So you can imagine how big the planet is.
- Read the rest of the story to yourself and be ready to answer some questions. Raise your hand when you're finished.

As the spaceship got close to Io, the attendant said, "If you look closely, you'll see that there are volcanos on Io. New volcanos erupt all the time. There is a volcano near the top of the moon that is erupting right now."
    Wendy looked closely at the moon. Near the top of it, she could see a very thin line of smoke moving up from one of the volcanos. The engines started to slow the ship with greater force. It felt as if something was pulling the ship backward very hard. But the ship was still moving faster than the moon.
    Now Wendy could see the space station on the moon. It was a large dome with three towers next to it. Sidney said, "It must have been a hard job to build that station."
    Wendy agreed. The spaceship was now getting ready to land on Io.

- (After all students have raised their hand:) Everybody, what was the thin line of smoke from? (Signal.) *A volcano.*
- Why was the pilot running the engines? (Call on a student. Idea: *To slow down the spaceship.*)
- What did the space station look like? (Call on a student. Idea: *A large dome with three towers next to it.*)
- Everybody, touch the dome. That's the round part in the center. ✓
- Touch the towers. ✓

EXERCISE 5

PAIRED PRACTICE

You're going to read aloud to your partner. The **B** members will read first. Then the **A** members will read from the star to the end of the story.
(Observe students and give feedback.)

End-of-Lesson Activities

INDEPENDENT WORK

Now finish your independent work for lesson 61. Raise your hand when you're finished. (Observe students and give feedback.)

WORKCHECK

a. (Direct students to take out their marking pencils.)
  - We're going to check your workbook and textbook items. Remember, if you got an item wrong, make an **X** next to the item.
b. (For each item: Read the item. Call on a student to answer it. If the answer is wrong, say the correct answer. Refer to the Answer Key for the correct answers.)
c. Now use your marking pencil to fix up any items you got wrong. Remember, all mistakes must be fixed up before you hand in your work.

LANGUAGE ARTS

(Present Language Arts lesson 61 after completing Reading lesson 61. See Language Arts Guide.)

ACTIVITIES

(Present Activity 12 after completing Reading lessons 61-62. See Activities Across the Curriculum.)

Lesson 62

VOCABULARY REVIEW

a. You learned a sentence that tells about being without gravity.
- Everybody, say that sentence. Get ready. (Signal.) *Without gravity, they were weightless.*
- (Repeat until firm.)

b. You learned a sentence that tells what she demonstrated.
- Everybody, say that sentence. Get ready. (Signal.) *She demonstrated how animals use oxygen.*
- (Repeat until firm.)

c. Here's the last sentence you learned: Lava erupted from the volcano's crater.
- Everybody, say that sentence. Get ready. (Signal.) *Lava erupted from the volcano's crater.*
- (Repeat until firm.)

d. What do we call the enormous dent at the top of a volcano? (Signal.) *Crater.*
- What word means **coughed out** or **spit out?** (Signal.) *Erupted.*
- What word means **melted rock?** (Signal.) *Lava.*
- (Repeat step d until firm.)

e. Once more. Say the sentence that tells what lava did. Get ready. (Signal.) *Lava erupted from the volcano's crater.*

READING WORDS

Column 1

a. **Find lesson 62 in your textbook.** ✓
- Touch column 1. ✓
- (Teacher reference:)

1. suitcase	4. receive
2. crunchy	5. Samson
3. program	6. close-up

- All these words have more than one syllable. The first syllable of each word is underlined.

b. Word 1. What's the first syllable? (Signal.) *suit.*

- What's the whole word? (Signal.) *Suitcase.*
- Spell **suitcase.** Get ready. (Tap for each letter.) *S-U-I-T-C-A-S-E.*

c. Word 2. What's the first syllable? (Signal.) *crunch.*
- What's the whole word? (Signal.) *Crunchy.*
- Spell **crunchy.** Get ready. (Tap for each letter.) *C-R-U-N-C-H-Y.*

d. Word 3. What's the first syllable? (Signal.) *pro.*
- What's the whole word? (Signal.) *Program.*
- Spell **program.** Get ready. (Tap for each letter.) *P-R-O-G-R-A-M.*

e. Word 4. What's the first syllable? (Signal.) *re.*
- What's the whole word? (Signal.) *Receive.*
- Spell **receive.** Get ready. (Tap for each letter.) *R-E-C-E-I-V-E.*

f. Word 5. What's the first syllable? (Signal.) *sam.*
- What's the whole word? (Signal.) *Samson.*

g. Word 6. What's the first syllable? (Signal.) *close.*
- What's the whole word? (Signal.) *Close-up.*

h. Let's read those words again.
- Word 1. What word? (Signal.) *Suitcase.*
- (Repeat for words 2–6.)

i. (Repeat step h until firm.)

Column 2

j. Find column 2. ✓
- (Teacher reference:)

1. assigned	4. telescopes
2. impressive	5. unpacked
3. zipped	6. bubbling

- All these words have an ending.

k. Word 1. What word? (Signal.) *Assigned.*
- (Repeat for words 2–6.)

l. Let's read those words again.
- Word 1. What word? (Signal.) *Assigned.*
- (Repeat for words 2–6.)

m. (Repeat step l until firm.)

Column 3

n. Find column 3. ✓
- (Teacher reference:)

1. overhang	4. crater
2. crackle	5. warned
3. splattered	

o. Word 1. What word? (Signal.) *Overhang.*
p. (Repeat for words 2–5.)
q. Let's read those words again.
- Word 1. What word? (Signal.) *Overhang.*
- (Repeat for words 2–5.)
r. (Repeat step q until firm.)

Column 4

s. Find column 4. ✓
- (Teacher reference:)

1. film	4. leak
2. area	5. soup
3. lava	

t. Word 1. What word? (Signal.) *Film.*
- (Repeat for words 2–5.)
u. Let's read those words again.
- Word 1. What word? (Signal.) *Film.*
- (Repeat for words 2–5.)
v. (Repeat step u until firm.)

Individual Turns

(For columns 1–4: Call on individual students, each to read one to three words per turn.)

EXERCISE 3

COMPREHENSION PASSAGE

a. Find part B in your textbook. ✓
- You're going to read the next story about Wendy. First you'll read the information passage. It reviews some facts you've learned.
b. Everybody, touch the title. ✓
- (Call on a student to read the title.) *[Planets and Gravity.]*
- Everybody, what's the title? (Signal.) *Planets and Gravity.*
c. (Call on individual students to read the passage, each student reading two or three sentences at a time. Ask the specified questions as the students read.)

Planets and Gravity
You've learned a lot of facts about planets. Here are some of the more important facts.
Bigger planets have stronger gravity. Smaller planets have weaker gravity.
The stronger the gravity on a planet, the more somebody would weigh on that planet.

- Everybody, which planets have stronger gravity, big planets or small planets? (Signal.) *Big planets.*

If a person weighs 100 pounds on Earth, the person will weigh more than 100 pounds on planets that have stronger gravity than Earth. The person will weigh less than 100 pounds on planets that have weaker gravity than Earth.

- Everybody, which planet is bigger, Earth or Saturn? (Signal.) *Saturn.*
- So which planet has stronger gravity? (Signal.) *Saturn.*
- Which planet is bigger, Jupiter or Mars? (Signal.) *Jupiter.*
- So which planet has stronger gravity? (Signal.) *Jupiter.*
- Where would you weigh more, on Earth or on Jupiter? (Signal.) *On Jupiter.*
- Where would you weigh more, on Saturn or on Mars? (Signal.) *On Saturn.*
- A person weighs 100 pounds on planet A and 30 pounds on planet B. Which planet has stronger gravity? (Signal.) *Planet A.*
- Something weighs 20 pounds on planet Z and 30 pounds on planet B. Which planet has stronger gravity? (Signal.) *Planet B.*

A person who weighs 100 pounds on Earth weighs over twice as much on Jupiter but weighs only 17 pounds on our moon.
Saturn has 18 moons. Jupiter has 16 moons. Earth has one moon.

- Everybody, which planet has 18 moons? (Signal.) *Saturn.*
- Which planet has 16 moons? (Signal.) *Jupiter.*
- Which planet has one moon? (Signal.) *Earth.*

Io is the moon that is closest to Jupiter.

It takes about 2 days for Io to go all the way around Jupiter.

There is no oxygen around Io and no oxygen around our moon.

A person can jump 8 feet high on Io.

- Everybody, what's the name of the moon closest to Jupiter? (Signal.) *Io.*
- About how long does it take for Io to go all the way around Jupiter? (Signal.) *2 days.*
- How high could you jump on Io? (Signal.) *8 feet.*

EXERCISE 4

STORY READING

a. Find part C in your textbook. ✓
- The error limit for group reading is 11 errors. Read carefully.
b. Everybody, touch the title. ✓
- (Call on a student to read the title.) *[The Space Station on Io.]*
- Everybody, what's the title? (Signal.) *The Space Station on* Io.
- (Call on individual students to read the story, each student reading two or three sentences at a time. Ask the specified questions as students read.)

> - (Correct errors: Tell the word. Direct the student to reread the sentence.)
> - (If the group makes more than 11 errors, direct the students to reread the story.)

The Space Station on Io

As Traveler Four approached Io, the engines came on with great force.

- Why? (Call on a student. Idea: *They were slowing the ship.*)

The engines didn't sound the way they sounded near Earth because there was no air around Io. So Wendy didn't hear the great roaring sounds of the engines. But she felt the engines buzzing and making everything inside the spaceship tremble.

Traveler Four floated slowly down to the surface of the moon, right between two towers. When it landed, the passengers clapped and cheered. Wendy could hardly wait to leave the ship.

- I can imagine why the passengers cheered and why they were glad to leave the ship. Everybody, how long had they been on it? (Signal.) *Four-and-a-half days.*
- How would you feel after being on that ship for four-and-a-half days? (Call on a student. Ideas: *Cramped; tired; restless.*)

The flight attendants helped the passengers get into their space suits. The attendants checked everybody to make sure that they had zipped up the suit so that no air would leak out.

One flight attendant announced that the suits would not feel heavy because the pilot had turned off the gravity device. With the gravity device turned off, Wendy felt much lighter than she did on Earth.

- Everybody, tell me which has stronger gravity, Io or Earth. Get ready. (Signal.) *Earth.*
- So even in her space suit, Wendy didn't feel very heavy on Io.

The flight attendant talked to the passengers over the radio that was in their helmets. "Go directly into the space station. Inside you will receive information about Io. You will also receive a map of the places you may visit on Io. You can pick up your baggage inside the space station."

The attendant continued, "We're going to let the air out of the spaceship now. You may feel a little dizzy for a few seconds. Take your time and walk slowly to the space station."

Wendy waited with the other passengers as the air was let out of Traveler Four. Then the doors opened and the passengers walked outside.

Wendy felt very light as she left the spaceship. The ground was crunchy. She took a couple of steps on it.

- How would it feel if it was crunchy? (Call on a student. Ideas: *Like walking on dry leaves; walking on eggshells; walking on ice;* etc.)

Then she decided to take a little jump. She jumped about five feet high.

- Show me how high five feet is. (Call on a student.)
- Wendy thought she would take a little jump. Everybody, is five feet high a little jump? (Signal.) *No.*
- Why can she jump so high? (Call on a student. Idea: *There is not much gravity.*)

She started to laugh and was ready to jump again when she heard a voice over her radio. "Take it easy," the voice said. "Just walk to the space station."

Before walking inside the space station, Wendy turned around and looked at Io. She could see three volcanos but they were not erupting. One was very close to the space station. The sky was almost completely covered by Jupiter. It was the biggest thing that Wendy had ever seen. And it was beautiful. The sight of Jupiter was so impressive that she just stood there, looking.

"Keep moving," a voice said over the radio. "There will ★ be lots of time to look at Jupiter later on."

The inside of the space station looked very strange. There was a large meeting area in the middle of the dome. Around one side were tiny rooms. Each passenger was assigned one of these rooms. Wendy's room was right next to Sidney's room. The rooms were so small that there was just enough space inside for a bed and a chair. Wendy hung her space suit in the closet and unpacked her suitcase. She took out her camera and made sure that there was film in it. Then she went out into the meeting area.

- How big was Wendy's room? (Call on a student. Idea: *Very small.*)
- Everybody, who had the room right next to her? (Signal.) *Sidney.*
- Name some things Wendy did in her room before she went to the meeting area. (Call on a student. Ideas: *Took off her space suit; unpacked her suitcase; took out her camera; made sure there was film in her camera.*)

A very tall man told the passengers to sit down. "Welcome to Io," he said. "My name is Rod Samson. I know that most of you will be busy during most of the day, but everybody will have time to look around. Everybody will get a map that shows the places you might visit."

- Everybody, what's the name of the man who is talking? (Signal.) *Rod Samson.*
- Read the rest of the story to yourself and be ready to answer some questions. Raise your hand when you're finished.

Rod Samson continued, "The favorite spot that people visit is a volcano about half a mile away. We call it Soup Pot because it has a large lake of lava just inside the cone. And the lava boils and bubbles like a great pot of boiling soup. It's safe to walk around the rim of Soup Pot because it has given no signs that it will erupt. But be careful when you walk around the rim. If you fall inside, there won't be much left of you."

"Let's go there," Sidney said. "I've never seen the inside of a volcano."

"Me, neither," Wendy said.

Rod Samson told about other things that people might look at on Io. Then he pointed to a row of telescopes near the windows of the space station. "Of course, you may want to look at Jupiter. Through those telescopes you can get a close-up view of the clouds that surround the great planet. Also, we have thousands of pictures of Jupiter. And we have hundreds of books and CD-ROMs that show and tell everything we know about the

planet. If you look on the back of your map, you'll find a list of the more important facts about Jupiter. The planet is bigger than all the other planets in the solar system put together. It spins around one time every ten hours. The gases that surround it are poisonous."

When the meeting was over, Sidney said, "Let's go see the volcano."

- (After all students have raised their hand:) What place did Sidney want to visit? (Call on a student. Ideas: *The volcano; Soup Pot.*)
- Everybody, about how far from the space station is Soup Pot? (Signal.) *Half a mile.*
- How big is Jupiter compared to the other planets in the solar system? (Call on a student. Ideas: *It's the biggest; bigger than all the others put together.*)
- Everybody, how long does it take for Jupiter to spin around one time? (Signal.) *Ten hours.*
- What kind of instruments were lined up around the dome? (Signal.) *Telescopes.*
- What could you look at through those telescopes? (Call on a student. Ideas: *Jupiter; Jupiter's clouds.*)

EXERCISE 5

PAIRED PRACTICE

You're going to read aloud to your partner. The **A** members will read first. Then the **B** members will read from the star to the end of the story. (Observe students and give feedback.)

End-of-Lesson Activities

INDEPENDENT WORK

Now finish your independent work for lesson 62. Raise your hand when you're finished. (Observe students and give feedback.)

WORKCHECK

a. (Direct students to take out their marking pencils.)
  - We're going to check your workbook and textbook items. Remember, if you got an item wrong, make an **X** next to the item.
b. (For each item: Read the item. Call on a student to answer it. If the answer is wrong, say the correct answer. Refer to the Answer Key for the correct answers.)
c. Now use your marking pencil to fix up any items you got wrong. Remember, all mistakes must be fixed up before you hand in your work.

LANGUAGE ARTS

(Present Language Arts lesson 62 after completing Reading lesson 62. See Language Arts Guide.)

EXERCISE 1

VOCABULARY REVIEW

a. You learned a sentence that tells what lava did.
- Everybody, say that sentence. Get ready. (Signal.) *Lava erupted from the volcano's crater.*
- (Repeat until firm.)

b. Everybody, what's the first word of the sentence? (Signal.) *Lava.*

c. I'll say part of the sentence. When I stop, you say the next word. Listen: Lava erupted from the volcano's . . . Everybody, what's the next word? (Signal.) *Crater.*

d. Listen: Lava . . . Everybody, what's the next word? (Signal.) *Erupted.*
- Say the whole sentence. Get ready. (Signal.) *Lava erupted from the volcano's crater.*

EXERCISE 2

READING WORDS

Column 1

a. **Find lesson 63 in your textbook.** ✓
- Touch column 1. ✓
- (Teacher reference:)

1. **manage**	3. **swallow**
2. **numb**	4. **vehicle**

b. Word 1 is **manage.** What word? (Signal.) *Manage.*
- Spell **manage.** Get ready. (Tap for each letter.) *M-A-N-A-G-E.*
- If you manage to do something, you work hard until you do it. Here's another way of saying **She worked hard until she fixed the pipe: She managed to fix the pipe.** Everybody, what's another way of saying **She worked hard until she climbed the rope?** (Signal.) *She managed to climb the rope.*

c. Word 2 is **numb.** What word? (Signal.) *Numb.*
- Spell **numb.** Get ready. (Tap for each letter.) *N-U-M-B.*

d. Word 3 is **swallow.** What word? (Signal.) *Swallow.*
- Spell **swallow.** Get ready. (Tap for each letter.) *S-W-A-L-L-O-W.*

e. Word 4 is **vehicle.** What word? (Signal.) *Vehicle.*
- Spell **vehicle.** Get ready. (Tap for each letter.) *V-E-H-I-C-L-E.*

f. Let's read those words again.
- Word 1. What word? (Signal.) *Manage.*
- (Repeat for words 2–4.)

g. (Repeat step f until firm.)

Column 2

h. Find column 2. ✓
- (Teacher reference:)

1. **overhang**	4. **suitcase**
2. **close-up**	5. **red-hot**
3. **restless**	6. **butterflies**

- All these words are made up of two smaller words. The first part of each word is underlined.

i. Word 1. What's the underlined part? (Signal.) *over.*
- What's the whole word? (Signal.) *Overhang.*

j. Word 2. What's the underlined part? (Signal.) *close.*
- What's the whole word? (Signal.) *Close-up.*

k. Word 3. What's the underlined part? (Signal.) *rest.*
- What's the whole word? (Signal.) *Restless.*

l. Word 4. What's the underlined part? (Signal.) *suit.*
- What's the whole word? (Signal.) *Suitcase.*

m. Word 5. What's the underlined part? (Signal.) *red.*
- What's the whole word? (Signal.) *Red-hot.*

n. Word 6. What's the underlined part? (Signal.) *butter.*
- What's the whole word? (Signal.) *Butterflies.*

o. Let's read those words again.
- Word 1. What word? (Signal.) *Overhang.*
- (Repeat for: **2. close-up, 3. restless, 4. suitcase, 5. red-hot, 6. butterflies.**)
p. (Repeat step o until firm.)

Column 3

q. Find column 3. ✓
- (Teacher reference:)

1. crater	5. crackle
2. splattered	6. warned
3. strings	7. tingles
4. bubbling	

r. Word 1. What word? (Signal.) *Crater.*
- (Repeat for words 2–7.)
s. Let's read those words again.
- Word 1. What word? (Signal.) *Crater.*
- (Repeat for words 2–7.)
t. (Repeat step s until firm.)

Individual Turns

(For columns 1–3: Call on individual students, each to read one to three words per turn.)

EXERCISE 3

STORY READING

a. Find part B in your textbook. ✓
- The error limit for group reading is 13 errors. Read carefully.
b. Everybody, touch the title. ✓
- (Call on a student to read the title.) *[A Trip to the Volcano.]*
- Everybody, what's the title? (Signal.) *A Trip to the Volcano.*
- (Call on individual students to read the story, each student reading two or three sentences at a time. Ask the specified questions as the students read.)

- (Correct errors: Tell the word. Direct the student to reread the sentence.)
- (If the group makes more than 13 errors, direct the students to reread the story.)

A Trip to the Volcano
The temperature outside the space station was almost 200 degrees below zero.

- What would that temperature do to you if you weren't wearing a space suit? (Call on a student. Idea: *Freeze you.*)

But Wendy was warm inside her space suit. She could look out through the helmet. She walked with Sidney toward the volcano. Little red flags were lined up along the path to mark the way to the volcano rim. The ground was crunchy and Wendy could feel it crackle under her feet as she walked along. Then she suddenly thought about running. She wondered how it would feel to run where you weigh much less than you weigh on Earth.

- Everybody, will she be able to run **faster** or **slower** than she can run on Earth? (Signal.) *Faster.*

So she began running. Her first step must have covered nine feet. In a moment, she must have been running faster than a deer could run on Earth. And she wasn't even trying to go as fast as she could. She leaped high above the surface of Io and landed as softly as a feather. "Wow," she said into her helmet, "this is great."

Sidney's voice answered, "Yeah. Watch this."

Wendy turned her head and saw Sidney running next to her. Sidney was leaping very high. Then suddenly she did a somersault above the surface of the ground and landed on her feet. "That's great," Wendy said.

- Everybody, look at the picture on the next page. You can see the girls doing their tricks. Touch Sidney. ✓
- What is Sidney doing? (Call on a student. Idea: *Somersault.*)
- What is Wendy doing? (Call on a student. Idea: *Leaping high.*)
- Would you like to do those things? (Call on a student. Idea: *Yes.*)

"You are using up your oxygen too fast," a voice said over Wendy's radio. "If you keep using it this fast, your oxygen will last only 35 minutes."

- That voice told Wendy how long her oxygen would last. How long? (Signal.) *35 minutes.*
- It takes more oxygen to exercise.

"I'd better take it easy," Wendy said. The voice that warned her about the oxygen was part of the space suit. It was the automatic radio that told how much oxygen was left.

Sidney said, "When we exercise very hard like that, we're using up much more oxygen than we do when we take it easy."

The girls slowed to a walk and continued toward the volcano. The red flags marked a path that circled around the right side of the volcano. The rim of the volcano was over half a mile above the surface of Io, but the climb was not difficult.

- Why would the climb be easy even if it was very steep? (Call on a student. Idea: *Because the low gravity makes it easy to climb, run,* etc.)

Within half an hour the girls were standing on the huge rim that circled the volcano. They looked down inside the cone-shaped crater of the volcano. Sidney said, "Now I see why they call it Soup Pot."

About one hundred meters below the rim was lava. Most of it looked gray. There were cracks running through it. The cracks went this way and that way.

There were a few huge bubbling places. The bubbling lava was not gray. It was bright orange. And it boiled up slowly, making huge bubbles that burst slowly and splattered great strings of lava on the gray surface. These strings would slowly turn color as they cooled. They would first turn ✦ a brown color. Then they would become more and more gray until you couldn't see them anymore.

- Tell how the orange hot strings of lava looked when they turned colors. (Call on a student. Idea: *They turned brown, then gray.*)
- The picture shows the girls looking down into Soup Pot. Everybody, touch the path that goes around the rim of the volcano. ✓
- Inside the volcano are gray parts with cracks running this way and that way. Everybody, touch one of those gray parts. ✓
- Touch a part that is bubbling. ✓
- What color is the lava in the bubbling parts? (Signal.) *Orange.*
- Which lava is hotter, the gray lava or the orange lava? (Signal.) *The orange lava.*
- Yes, the boiling lava is orange because it's so hot.

Wendy knew that the lava was melted rock. When it cooled, it hardened into gray rock again. When it was boiling hot, it was like red-hot mud.

The crater of the volcano was very large. A city block could easily fit inside the volcano crater.

- How large was the inside of the volcano? (Call on a student. Ideas: *Bigger than a city block; very large.*)

The girls stood on the rim for a few minutes, watching the lava boil and splatter. Then they started to walk around the rim. The path was marked with red flags. As they started to walk, the voice came over Wendy's radio. "Your oxygen supply will last 45 minutes if you keep using it as fast as you are using it."

- Everybody, how long will her oxygen last if she keeps using it as fast as she is using it now? (Signal.) *45 minutes.*

- Before, the voice told her that she had only 35 minutes of oxygen left. Now it says that she has 45 minutes left. Why does she have so much more oxygen left now? (Call on a student. Ideas: *She's been using less oxygen; she's walking instead of running.*)

> **Wendy thought, "If we have 45 minutes of oxygen, we should have plenty of time to walk around the rim and get back to the space station."**
>
> **The girls walked around the rim until they came to a place where there was an overhang. The overhang was like a little shelf that stuck out about three meters over the rim. Sidney pointed to the overhang. "Let's stand out on the end of that overhang," she said.**

- Everybody, you can see the overhang in the picture. Touch it. ✓
- Read the rest of the story to yourself and be ready to answer some questions. Raise your hand when you're finished.

> **The overhang looked scary. Wendy thought for a moment, then said, "Okay, let's go out there."**
>
> **So the girls walked onto the overhang. They walked to the end of it and looked down. They were almost above the lava. When Wendy looked down, she got a little dizzy looking at the boiling hot rock. Then suddenly, she felt the ground move. She quickly turned around and saw that the overhang was cracking off and starting to fall into the crater. She started to run back to the rim, but it was too late. The overhang broke off with Wendy and Sidney standing on it. Wendy reached out and grabbed a rock on the edge of the rim. She felt Sidney behind her, trying to grab on to her. But Sidney could not hold on. She fell. Wendy could hear her yelling something over the radio, but Wendy couldn't turn around. She was hanging on to the rock with all her might.**

- (After all students have raised their hand:) What happened to the overhang when the girls were standing on the end of it? (Call on a student. Idea: *It broke off.*)
- What did Wendy do? (Call on a student. Idea: *She grabbed a rock on the edge of the rim.*)
- What happened to Sidney? (Call on a student. Idea: *She fell.*)
- Why didn't Wendy turn around and see what happened to Sidney? (Call on a student. Idea: *She was trying to hang on to the rock.*)

EXERCISE 4

PAIRED PRACTICE

You're going to read aloud to your partner. The **B** members will read first. Then the **A** members will read from the star to the end of the story. (Observe students and give feedback.)

End-of-Lesson Activities

INDEPENDENT WORK

Now finish your independent work for lesson 63. Raise your hand when you're finished. (Observe students and give feedback.)

WORKCHECK

a. (Direct students to take out their marking pencils.)
- We're going to check your workbook and textbook items. Remember, if you got an item wrong, make an **X** next to the item.
b. (For each item: Read the item. Call on a student to answer it. If the answer is wrong, say the correct answer. Refer to the Answer Key for the correct answers.)
c. Now use your marking pencil to fix up any items you got wrong. Remember, all mistakes must be fixed up before you hand in your work.

LANGUAGE ARTS

(Present Language Arts lesson 63 after completing Reading lesson 63. See Language Arts Guide.)

Lesson 64

EXERCISE 1

VOCABULARY

a. **Find the vocabulary sentences on page 352 of your textbook.** ✓
- Touch sentence 16. ✓
- This is a new vocabulary sentence. It says: The incredible whales made them anxious. Everybody, say that sentence. Get ready. (Signal.) *The incredible whales made them anxious.*
- Close your eyes and say the sentence. Get ready. (Signal.) *The incredible whales made them anxious.*
- (Repeat until firm.)

b. **Incredible** is another word for **amazing.** Everybody, what's another way of saying **The birds were amazing?** (Signal.) *The birds were incredible.*

c. The sentence says the **whales** were incredible. Whales are warm-blooded animals. They look like huge fish, but they are not fish.

d. The sentence says that they were **anxious. Anxious** is another word for **nervous** or **scared.** If you're anxious about something, you're nervous or scared. Everybody, what word means **nervous** or **scared?** (Signal.) *Anxious.*

e. Listen to the sentence again: The incredible whales made them anxious. Everybody, say that sentence. Get ready. (Signal.) *The incredible whales made them anxious.*

f. Everybody, what word means **amazing?** (Signal.) *Incredible.*
- What word means **nervous** or **scared?** (Signal.) *Anxious.*
- What word names warm-blooded animals that look like fish? (Signal.) *Whales.*
- (Repeat step f until firm.)

EXERCISE 2

READING WORDS

Column 1

a. Find lesson 64 in your textbook. ✓
- Touch column 1. ✓

- (Teacher reference:)

1. **tingles**	3. **managed**
2. **purple**	4. **butterflies**

- All these words have more than one syllable. The first syllable of each word is underlined.

b. Word 1. What's the first syllable? (Signal.) *ting.*
- What's the whole word? (Signal.) *Tingles.*

c. Word 2. What's the first syllable? (Signal.) *pur.*
- What's the whole word? (Signal.) *Purple.*

d. Word 3. What's the first syllable? (Signal.) *man.*
- What's the whole word? (Signal.) *Managed.*

e. Word 4. What's the first syllable? (Signal.) *butt.*
- What's the whole word? (Signal.) *Butterflies.*

f. Let's read those words again.
- Word 1. What word? (Signal.) *Tingles.*
- (Repeat for words 2–4.)

g. (Repeat step f until firm.)

Column 2

h. Find column 2. ✓
- (Teacher reference:)

1. **numb**	3. **vehicle**
2. **swallow**	4. **shapes**

i. Word 1. What word? (Signal.) *Numb.*
- Spell **numb.** Get ready. (Tap for each letter.) *N-U-M-B.*

j. Word 2. What word? (Signal.) *Swallow.*
- Spell **swallow.** Get ready. (Tap for each letter.) *S-W-A-L-L-O-W.*

k. Word 3. What word? (Signal.) *Vehicle.*
- Spell **vehicle.** Get ready. (Tap for each letter.) *V-E-H-I-C-L-E.*

l. Word 4. What word? (Signal.) *Shapes.*
- Spell **shapes.** Get ready. (Tap for each letter.) *S-H-A-P-E-S.*

m. Let's read those words again.
- Word 1. What word? (Signal.) *Numb.*
- (Repeat for words 2–4.)

n. (Repeat step m until firm.)

Column 3

o. Find column 3. ✓
   • (Teacher reference:)

1. slumped	3. attaching
2. scariest	4. smoked

   • All these words have an ending.
p. Word 1. What word? (Signal.) *Slumped.*
   • (Repeat for words 2–4.)
q. Let's read those words again.
   • Word 1. What word? (Signal.) *Slumped.*
   • (Repeat for words 2–4.)
r. (Repeat step q until firm.)

Individual Turns

(For columns 1–3: Call on individual students, each to read one to three words per turn.)

EXERCISE 3

FACT REVIEW

a. Let's review some facts you have learned. First we'll go over the facts together. Then I'll call on individual students to do some facts.
b. Everybody, tell me how long it takes Jupiter to spin around one time. (Pause.) Get ready. (Signal.) *10 hours.*
   • Tell me how much a 100-pound person would weigh on our moon. (Pause.) Get ready. (Signal.) *17 pounds.*
   • Tell me how far it is from Earth to Jupiter. (Pause.) Get ready. (Signal.) *400 million miles.*
   • (Repeat step b until firm.)
c. Tell me how fast Traveler Four travels. (Pause.) Get ready. (Signal.) *1,000 miles per second.*
   • Tell me how many times larger than Earth the sun is. (Pause.) Get ready. (Signal.) *100.*
   • Tell me about how long it takes Io to go all the way around Jupiter. Get ready. (Signal.) *2 days.*
   • (Repeat step c until firm.)
d. Tell me whether gravity is stronger on a **large planet** or on a **small planet.** (Pause.) Get ready. (Signal.) *Large planet.*
   • Tell me whether you would weigh **more** or weigh **less** on a very large planet. (Pause.) Get ready. (Signal.) *More.*

   • Tell me whether you would weigh **more** or weigh **less** on a very small planet. (Pause.) Get ready. (Signal.) *Less.*
   • (Repeat step d until firm.)
e. Tell me which has stronger gravity, Earth or Mars. (Pause.) Get ready. (Signal.) *Earth.*
   • Tell me which has stronger gravity, Earth or Saturn. (Pause.) Get ready. (Signal.) *Saturn.*
   • Tell me which has stronger gravity, Earth or our moon. (Pause.) Get ready. (Signal.) *Earth.*
   • (Repeat step e until firm.)
f. Everybody, say the names of the planets, starting with the planet closest to the sun. Get ready. (Tap for each name.) *Mercury, Venus, Earth, Mars, Jupiter, Saturn, Uranus, Neptune, Pluto.*
   • (Repeat step f until firm.)

Individual Turns

   • Now I'm going to call on individual students to do some facts.
   • (Call on individual students to do the set of facts in step b, c, d, e, or f.)

EXERCISE 4

STORY READING

a. Find part B in your textbook. ✓
   • The error limit for group reading is 10 errors. Read carefully.
b. Everybody, touch the title. ✓
   • (Call on a student to read the title.) [Help.]
   • Everybody, what's the title? (Signal.) *Help.*
   • Where did we leave Wendy? (Call on a student. Idea: *Hanging near the rim of the volcano.*)
   • (Call on individual students to read the story, each student reading two or three sentences at a time. Ask the specified questions as the students read.)

   • (**Correct errors**: Tell the word. Direct the student to reread the sentence.)
   • (If the group makes more than 10 errors, direct the students to reread the story.)

Help
The overhang fell into the crater. Wendy had managed to grab the rim and hang on. She easily pulled herself up and stood up on the rim.

- Why was it easy for her to pull herself up? (Call on a student. Idea: *There wasn't much gravity.*)

She turned around and looked down into the crater. She could see the overhang sticking out of the lava. It was slowly sinking down. But where was Sidney?

- Everybody, did she see Sidney? (Signal.) *No.*
- What was the overhang doing? (Call on a student. Idea: *Sinking into the lava.*)

Wendy looked at the surface of the lava. No Sidney. Then she looked near the edge of the lava. There was Sidney. She wasn't in the lava. She was hanging on to a rock and her feet were only a couple of meters above the lava.
"Help," Sidney shouted over the radio. "I think I'm slipping. Help me."
Wendy didn't know what to do. She couldn't climb down to where Sidney was, because the inside wall of the crater was almost straight up and down. Wendy didn't have a rope or any way to reach Sidney and pull her out.
"You just hang on," Wendy said. "I'll be right back."

- What do you think Wendy is going to do to help Sidney? (Call on a student. Idea: *Get help at the space station.*)

Wendy started to run back to the space station. And this time, she ran as fast as she could go. Down the side of the volcano she went. She took steps that were four and five meters long. She leaped down the side of the mountain like a deer. The automatic voice came over her radio.

- What's it going to say? (Call on a student. Idea: *She's using too much oxygen.*)

"You are using your oxygen too fast. You will be out of oxygen in two minutes."
"I don't care," Wendy said and ran faster.
She reached the bottom of the volcano and ran toward the space station. When she was about 200 meters from the space station, another voice came over her radio. "Wendy, what's wrong?" the voice said. "You shouldn't be running that fast."

- Everybody, is that the automatic voice? (Signal.) *No.*
- I'll bet it's somebody from the space station who is watching her run.

It was Rod Samson's voice.
"Sidney!" Wendy shouted. "She fell off the rim. She's almost in the lava. She . . . she . . . she can't hang on much longer."
"Stop right there," Rod shouted. "Just sit down and rest. We'll be there in less than a minute."
The automatic voice came over her radio. "You have fifteen seconds of oxygen left."

- Everybody, when will she run out of oxygen? (Signal.) *In 15 seconds.*
- Will the people from the space station be able to get there in 15 seconds? (Signal.) *No.*
- She'll run out of oxygen before they can get there. What will happen to Wendy then? (Call on a student. Ideas: *She won't be able to breathe; she might die; she might faint.*)

Wendy stopped running. She was breathing so hard that she ★ couldn't catch her breath. "Sidney's in trouble," she yelled over her radio. "Help her . . . Help . . ."
"Don't say anything," Rod said over the radio. "Just sit down and take it easy."
"You are out of oxygen," the automatic voice said. ✿ Wendy sat down and realized that it was very hard to breathe.

- Why? (Call on a student. Idea: *There was no oxygen left in her tanks.*)

> **The harder she tried, the less she could breathe. She started to see spots in front of her eyes. Things were becoming purple and spotted. Her hands felt numb. She couldn't tell if she was sitting down or standing up.**

- Everybody, were the spots she saw real? (Signal.) *No.*
- What's happening to her? (Call on a student. Idea: *She's starting to faint.*)

> **She wanted to cry. "Sidney," she said. "She's caught in the volcano. Help . . . her . . ." She shook her head and tried to clear the spots away. Her hands and arms were covered with tingles. Her mouth was dry. She tried to swallow but she couldn't. She tried to talk but nothing happened. Her voice wasn't working. She started to see butterflies—purple ones. She . . .** ❀
>
> • • •

- Listen to that part again. Try to imagine how she felt when she couldn't get oxygen:

  > The harder she tried, the less she could breathe. She started to see spots in front of her eyes. Things were becoming purple and spotted. Her hands felt numb. She couldn't tell if she was sitting down or standing up. She wanted to cry. "Sidney," she said. "She's caught in the volcano. Help . . . her . . ." She shook her head and tried to clear the spots away. Her hands and arms were covered with tingles. Her mouth was dry. She tried to swallow but she couldn't. She tried to talk but nothing happened. Her voice wasn't working. She started to see butterflies—purple ones. She . . .

> **Wendy suddenly saw the shapes of people. "Help," she said.**
> **"Be quiet," a woman's voice said. Wendy realized that she was inside a vehicle that was bouncing over the surface of Io.**

- Where was she when she passed out? (Call on a student. Idea: *On the ground.*)
- Where is she now? (Call on a student. Idea: *Inside a vehicle.*)
- What must have happened in the part of the story that's missing? (Call on a student. Idea: *Somebody put her in the vehicle.*)
- Read the rest of the story to yourself and be ready to answer some questions. Raise your hand when you're finished.

> **Wendy's helmet was off. There was air inside the vehicle. Rod Samson was driving the vehicle. Another man was sitting next to him. A woman was in back with Wendy. The woman was attaching fresh oxygen tanks to Wendy's space suit.**
> **Wendy tried to sit up, but the woman gently pushed her back down. The woman said, "Take it easy. We'll be up at the top of Soup Pot in just a minute."**
> **"You've got to get there fast," Wendy said. "Sidney is just hanging on. She's . . ."**
> **"We're going as fast as we can," the woman said. "Everything is going to be all right."**
> **Wendy looked at the woman's face. The woman looked worried.**
> **The woman said, "I'll put your helmet back on. You have fresh tanks of oxygen now."**
> **Rod said to the woman, "Fasten her helmet. We're almost there."**
> **The woman helped Wendy put on the helmet. The vehicle stopped. Wendy looked outside. The vehicle had stopped on the rim of Soup Pot, right near the place where the overhang had been.**

- (After all students have raised their hand:) Everybody, how many people were in the vehicle with Wendy? (Signal.) *Three.*

- Who was driving? (Signal.) *Rod Samson.*
- What did the woman put on the back of Wendy's space suit? (Call on a student. Idea: *Oxygen tanks.*)
- Where did the vehicle stop? (Call on a student. Ideas: *On the rim of Soup Pot; near where the overhang had been.*)

EXERCISE 5
PAIRED PRACTICE

You're going to read aloud to your partner. The **A** members will read first. Then the **B** members will read from the star to the end of the story. (Observe students and give feedback.)

End-of-Lesson Activities

INDEPENDENT WORK

Now finish your independent work for lesson 64. Raise your hand when you're finished. (Observe students and give feedback.)

WORKCHECK

a. (Direct students to take out their marking pencils.)
- We're going to check your workbook and textbook items. Remember, if you got an item wrong, make an **X** next to the item.
b. (For each item: Read the item. Call on a student to answer it. If the answer is wrong, say the correct answer. Refer to the Answer Key for the correct answers.)
c. Now use your marking pencil to fix up any items you got wrong. Remember, all mistakes must be fixed up before you hand in your work.

LANGUAGE ARTS

(Present Language Arts lesson 64 after completing Reading lesson 64. See Language Arts Guide.

ACTIVITIES

(Present Activity 13 after completing Reading lessons 64-66. See Activities Across the Curriculum.)

Note: Students will need access to reference materials at the end of lesson 65. See page 337 for details.

Lesson 65

EXERCISE 1

VOCABULARY REVIEW

a. Here's the new vocabulary sentence: The incredible whales made them anxious.
  • Everybody, say that sentence. Get ready. (Signal.) *The incredible whales made them anxious.*
  • (Repeat until firm.)

b. Everybody, what word means **nervous** or **scared?** (Signal.) *Anxious.*
  • What word means **amazing?** (Signal.) *Incredible.*
  • What word names warm-blooded animals that look like fish? (Signal.) *Whales.*
  • (Repeat step b until firm.)

EXERCISE 2

READING WORDS

a. **Find lesson 65 in your textbook. ✓**
  • Touch word 1. ✓
  • (Teacher reference:)

1. **slumped**	5. **smoked**
2. **pale**	6. **tea**
3. **sipped**	7. **Terry**
4. **scariest**	

b. Word 1. What word? (Signal.) *Slumped.*
  • Spell **slumped.** Get ready. (Tap for each letter.) *S-L-U-M-P-E-D.*
  • When people slump, they slouch and do not sit up straight or stand up straight. Everybody, what word describes people when they don't sit or stand up straight? (Signal.) *Slump.*

c. Word 2. What word? (Signal.) *Pale.*
  • Spell **pale.** Get ready. (Tap for each letter.) *P-A-L-E.*
  • This word does not refer to a bucket. It refers to things that are whiter than they normally are. If the sky is pale blue, the blue is whiter than it normally is. Everybody, what word means **whiter than normal?** (Signal.) *Pale.*

d. Word 3. What word? (Signal.) *Sipped.*
  • Spell **sipped.** Get ready. (Tap for each letter.) *S-I-P-P-E-D.*

e. Word 4. What word? (Signal.) *Scariest.*

  • Spell **scariest.** Get ready. (Tap for each letter.) *S-C-A-R-I-E-S-T.*

f. Word 5. What word? (Signal.) *Smoked.*
  • (Repeat for words 6 and 7.)

g. Let's read those words again.
  • Word 1. What word? (Signal.) *Slumped.*
  • (Repeat for words 2–7.)

h. (Repeat step g until firm.)

EXERCISE 3

STORY READING

a. Find part B in your textbook. ✓
  • The error limit for group reading is 12 errors. Read carefully.

b. Everybody, touch the title. ✓
  • (Call on a student to read the title.) *[Sidney.]*
  • Everybody, what's the title? (Signal.) *Sidney.*
  • (Call on individual students to read the story, each student reading two or three sentences at a time. Ask the specified questions as the students read.)

  • (Correct errors: Tell the word. Direct the student to reread the sentence.)
  • (If the group makes more than 12 errors, direct the students to reread the story.)

Sidney

"Where is she?" the woman asked as Wendy and the others got out of the vehicle.

  • Everybody, who is the woman asking about? (Signal.) *Sidney.*
  • Which person is the woman talking to? (Signal.) *Wendy.*

Wendy led the way to the edge of the rim. She pointed down. "She's right there," Wendy said and pointed. But Sidney was not where she had been.

  • Where had she been when Wendy left her? (Call on a student. Idea: *Hanging on to a rock just above the lava.*)

Wendy could see the rock that Sidney had been hanging on to. But Sidney was no longer hanging on to that rock.

"Sidney," Wendy yelled over the radio. "Where are you? Sidney!"

The others started to call. Then Rod said, "Be quiet and listen." Nobody said anything. The only sounds that came over the radio were the sounds of people breathing.

Then suddenly a small voice came over the radio. "Help," it said.

It was Sidney's voice.

- Everybody, could she be calling for help if she was in the lava? (Signal.) *No.*

"There," Rod shouted and pointed straight down. Just above the rock that Sidney had been hanging on to was a little cave. A foot and leg of a space suit were sticking out of that cave. Sidney must have climbed up the rock and into that cave.

"Fasten the rope to the front of the vehicle," Rod told the other man. "I'm going down."

The other man took one end of the rope and tied it to the front of the vehicle. Then Rod tossed the rest of the rope over the rim. Down and down it fell. The end of the rope reached the surface of the lava. It touched a part that was bright orange. The end of the rope smoked for a second. Wendy could see that the end had burned off.

- Everybody, what color was the lava where the rope touched it? (Signal.) *Orange.*
- Was that lava **hotter** or **cooler** than the gray parts? (Signal.) *Hotter.*
- What happened to the end of the rope? (Call on a student. Idea: *It burned off.*)

Rod slid down the rope very fast. For a moment, it seemed as if he would slide right into the lava. He was swinging back and forth just a few meters above it. Some of the huge bubbles that were breaking sent strings of lava very close to him. He kept swinging until he was able to swing right into the little

could not see him now. She saw Sidney's leg disappear and she could hear Rod talking to Sidney.

"Are you hurt?" he asked.

"Just a little bit," she said. "But I'm very scared."

"I don't blame you," Rod said. "Climb onto my back and put your arms around my neck. . . . There. That's good. Now just hang on tight and I'll get you out of here."

Rod then called, "Terry, back the vehicle up slowly. Back ✸ away from the rim."

- Everybody, what's the name of the man Rod is talking to? (Signal.) *Terry.*
- What's Terry going to do? (Call on a student. Idea: *Back up the vehicle.*)
- If Rod and Sidney hang on to the rope, what will happen to them when the vehicle backs up? (Call on a student. Idea: *They'll get pulled up to the rim.*)

Terry ran to the vehicle and got in. A moment later, the vehicle began to move backward. The rope that was attached to it started to move up. Now Wendy could see Rod and Sidney. They swung out of the little cave and they were slowly swinging over the lava.

- Everybody, look at the picture. Point to show which way the vehicle is moving. ✓
- Which way do Sidney and Rod move when the vehicle moves away from the rim? (Signal.) *Up.*
- How do you think Sidney feels hanging on to Rod's back and swinging over the lava? (Call on a student. Ideas: *Scared; anxious.*)

Slowly, Rod and Sidney moved up as the vehicle continued to back up. Up, up, up. Now they were almost at the rim.

"Okay, stop it there," Rod called. "We'll climb up the rest of the way."

Rod reached over the rim and began pulling himself up. Sidney was hanging tightly on to his neck. The woman helped pull Rod and Sidney onto the rim. Then she grabbed Sidney and helped her stand up. Sidney's face looked very pale. Wendy hugged her. "I'm so glad that you're okay," Wendy said.

"Me, too," Sidney said. "That was the scariest thing that ever happened to me. But I'm so glad that Rod . . ."

Everybody got into the vehicle. The vehicle moved slowly down the side of the volcano and along the row of flags back to the space station.

- Was the vehicle moving as fast as it could go now? (Signal.) *No.*
- Why not? (Call on a student. Idea: *They weren't in a hurry.*)

A door opened in the space station and the vehicle went inside. The door closed behind the vehicle.

- Read the rest of the story to yourself and be ready to answer some questions. Raise your hand when you're finished.

The woman helped Sidney from the vehicle. Then the others got out. They walked through a door to the meeting place in the space station. When they were inside, they took off their helmets. The woman helped Sidney to one of the chairs. Sidney slumped into the chair.

"I don't feel scared anymore," Sidney said. Then she added, "But am I ever tired. I feel as if I've been working for a hundred years."

Wendy said, "When we came back to the volcano and didn't see you, I thought I was going to die. I thought you had fallen into that lava."

"I was close," Sidney said. "I was hanging on to that rock. Then after a while I got one foot into a little crack in the rocks and I pushed up. I climbed into that cave."

"I'm glad," Wendy said.

Rod handed Sidney a cup of tea. "Sip this," he said. "Watch out. It's hot."

Sidney sipped the tea, looked up, and smiled. Then she said, "Oh, am I glad to be back here."

- (After all students have raised their hand:) How did Sidney feel when she got inside the space station? (Call on a student. Ideas: *Tired; glad.*)
- How did she manage to get into the cave? (Call on a student. Idea: *She climbed in.*)
- Everybody, what did Rod give Sidney to drink? (Signal.) *Tea.*

EXERCISE 4

Note: There is a reading checkout in this lesson; therefore, there is no paired practice.

READING CHECKOUTS

a. Today is a reading-checkout day. While you're doing your independent work, I'm going to call on you one at a time to read part of the story from lesson 64.
- Remember, you pass the checkout by reading the passage in less than a minute without making more than 2 mistakes. And when you pass the checkout, you'll color the space for lesson 65 on your thermometer chart.
b. (Call on individual students to read the portion of story 64 marked with ❀.)
- (Time the student. Note words that are missed and number of words read.)
- (Teacher reference:)

❀ Wendy sat down and realized that it was very hard to breathe. The harder she tried, the less she could breathe. She started to see spots in front of her eyes. Things were becoming purple and spotted. Her hands felt numb. She couldn't tell if she was sitting down or [50] standing up. She wanted to cry. "Sidney," she said. "She's caught in the volcano.

Help . . . her . . ." She shook her head and tried to clear the [75] spots away. Her hands and arms were covered with tingles. Her mouth was dry. She tried to swallow but she couldn't. She tried to talk [100] but nothing happened. Her voice wasn't working. She started to see butterflies—purple ones. She . . . 🌸[115]

- (If the student reads the passage in one minute or less and makes no more than 2 errors, direct the student to color in the space for lesson 65 on the thermometer chart.)

- (If the student makes any mistakes, point to each word that was misread and identify it.)
- (If the student does not meet the rate-error criterion for the passage, direct the student to practice reading the story with the assigned partner.)

EXERCISE 5
STUDY ITEMS

a. Find study items 18 and 19 at the end of your textbook lesson. ✓
b. Follow along as I read: Today's story told about a vehicle that goes on the surface of Io. No people have gone to Io yet. But people have gone from Earth to the moon. They have taken a vehicle with them. See if you can find out some facts about that vehicle.
   Item 18: Find out what makes it run.
   Item 19: Find out the name of the vehicle.
c. If you finish your independent work early, raise your hand and I'll tell you how you can look up the answers to those study items.
d. (When students raise their hands, direct them to **space exploration** in an encyclopedia, on a computer, or to a book on space exploration.)

End-of-Lesson Activities

INDEPENDENT WORK

Now finish your independent work for lesson 65. Raise your hand when you're finished. (Observe students and give feedback.)

WORKCHECK

a. (Direct students to take out their marking pencils.)
   - We're going to check your workbook and textbook items. Remember, if you got an item wrong, make an **X** next to the item.
b. (For each item: Read the item. Call on a student to answer it. If the answer is wrong, say the correct answer. Refer to the Answer Key for the correct answers.)
c. Now use your marking pencil to fix up any items you got wrong. Remember, all mistakes must be fixed up before you hand in your work.

LANGUAGE ARTS

(Present Language Arts lesson 65 after completing Reading lesson 65. See Language Arts Guide.)

Note: You will need materials for a special project that occurs after lesson 66. See page 344 for details.

Lessons 66–70 • Planning Page

Looking Ahead

	Lesson 66	Lesson 67	Lesson 68	Lesson 69	Lesson 70
Lesson Events	Vocabulary Sentences Reading Words Story Reading Paired Practice Independent Work Workcheck Language Arts	Vocabulary Sentence **Vocabulary Sentence** Reading Words Fact Review Comprehension Passage Story Reading Paired Practice Independent Work Workcheck Language Arts	Vocabulary Sentence Reading Words Story Reading Paired Practice Independent Work Workcheck Language Arts	Vocabulary Sentences Reading Words Comprehension Passage Story Reading Paired Practice Independent Work Workcheck Language Arts	Fact Game Reading Checkouts Test Marking the Test Test Remedies Literature Lesson Language Arts
Vocabulary Sentence	sentence #14 sentence #15 sentence #16	#16: The <u>incredible whales</u> made them <u>anxious</u>. **#17: The <u>boring speaker disturbed</u> the <u>audience</u>.**	#17: The <u>boring</u> speaker <u>disturbed</u> the <u>audience</u>.	sentence #15 sentence #16 sentence #17	
Reading Words: Word Types	modeled words **ea** words multi-syllable words mixed words	modeled words words with an ending mixed words	modeled words mixed words	words with an ending multi-syllable words mixed words	
New Vocabulary	ridiculous serious gather prepare	solve	deliver		
Comprehension Passage		*Kinds of Animals*		*Training Animals*	
Story	*Back to Earth*	*Waldo's Cooking*	*A Problem*	*Waldo Gets a Job*	
Skill Items	Vocabulary sentence	Vocabulary sentences	Sequencing	Vocabulary sentence	Test: Vocabulary sentences #15, 16, 17
Special Materials	*Materials for project				Thermometer charts, dice, Fact Game 70, Fact Game Answer Key, scorecard sheets, **materials for literature lesson
Special Projects/ Activities	Project after lesson 66			Activity after lesson 69	

*Reference materials (books on the solar system, encyclopedias, CD-ROMs); poster-making supplies (butcher paper or poster board, markers, crayons, paints, scissors, paste, magazine for pictures).

**Literature anthology; blackline masters 7A,7B, and 7C; lined paper; drawing materials

EXERCISE 1

VOCABULARY REVIEW

a. You learned a sentence that tells what she demonstrated.
  • Everybody, say that sentence. Get ready. (Signal.) *She demonstrated how animals use oxygen.*
  • (Repeat until firm.)

b. You learned a sentence that tells what lava did.
  • Everybody, say that sentence. Get ready. (Signal.) *Lava erupted from the volcano's crater.*
  • (Repeat until firm.)

c. Here's the last sentence you learned: The incredible whales made them anxious.
  • Everybody, say that sentence. Get ready. (Signal.) *The incredible whales made them anxious.*
  • (Repeat until firm.)

d. What word names warm-blooded animals that look like fish? (Signal.) *Whales.*
  • What word means **amazing?** (Signal.) *Incredible.*
  • What word means **nervous** or **scared?** (Signal.) *Anxious.*
  • (Repeat step d until firm.)

e. Once more. Say the sentence that tells how the incredible whales made them feel. Get ready. (Signal.) *The incredible whales made them anxious.*

EXERCISE 2

READING WORDS

Column 1

a. **Find lesson 66 in your textbook.** ✓
  • Touch column 1. ✓
  • (Teacher reference:)

1. pigeon	5. ridiculous
2. giraffe	6. Michael
3. squirrel	7. serious
4. spaghetti	

b. Word 1 is **pigeon.** What word? (Signal.) *Pigeon.*
  • Spell **pigeon.** Get ready. (Tap for each letter.) *P-I-G-E-O-N.*

c. Word 2 is **giraffe.** What word? (Signal.) *Giraffe.*
  • Spell **giraffe.** Get ready. (Tap for each letter.) *G-I-R-A-F-F-E.*

d. Word 3 is **squirrel.** What word? (Signal.) *Squirrel.*

e. Word 4 is **spaghetti.** What word? (Signal.) *Spaghetti.*

f. Word 5 is **ridiculous.** What word? (Signal.) *Ridiculous.*
  • When you think something is **really silly,** you think it is **ridiculous.**
  • Everybody, what's another way of saying **I think that party was really silly?** (Signal.) *I think that party was ridiculous.*
  • What's another way of saying **I think that movie was really silly?** (Signal.) *I think that movie was ridiculous.*

g. Word 6 is **Michael.** What word? (Signal.) *Michael.*

h. Word 7 is **serious.** What word? (Signal.) *Serious.*
  • The opposite of something funny is something serious. Everybody, what's the opposite of **a funny movie?** (Signal.) *A serious movie.*
  • What's the opposite of **a funny expression?** (Signal.) *A serious expression.*

i. Let's read those words again, the fast way.
  • Word 1. What word? (Signal.) *Pigeon.*
  • (Repeat for words 2–7.)

j. (Repeat step i until firm.)

Column 2

k. Find column 2. ✓
  • (Teacher reference:)

1. great	4. least
2. meals	5. earn
3. ready	6. clean

  • All these words have the letters **e-a** in them. But be careful, because **e-a** makes different sounds in the words.

l. Word 1. What word? (Signal.) *Great.*
- (Repeat for: **2. meals, 3. ready, 4. least, 5. earn, 6. clean.**)
m. (Repeat step l until firm.)

Column 3

n. Find column 3. ✓
- (Teacher reference:)

1. gather	**4. hamburger**
2. enjoying	**5. parrot**
3. meow	**6. hometown**

o. Word 1. What word? (Signal.) *Gather.*
- When you pick up things from different places and put them in one place, you **gather** those things. Here's another way of saying **She picked flowers from different places and put them in one place: She gathered flowers.**
- Your turn. What's another way of saying **She picked flowers from different places and put them in one place?** (Signal.) *She gathered flowers.*
- (Repeat until firm.)

p. Word 2. What word? (Signal.) *Enjoying.*
- (Repeat for words 3–6.)

q. Let's read those words again.
- Word 1. What word? (Signal.) *Gather.*
- (Repeat for words 2–6.)
r. (Repeat step q until firm.)

Column 4

s. Find column 4. ✓
- (Teacher reference:)

1. prepare	**3. zebra**
2. kitchen	**4. yeah**

t. Word 1. What word? (Signal.) *Prepare.*
- When you get ready for something, you prepare for that thing.
- Everybody, what's another way of saying **She got ready for school?** (Signal.) *She prepared for school.*
- What's another way of saying **He got ready for playing football?** (Signal.) *He prepared for playing football.*
- What's another way of saying **She got ready for school?** (Signal.) *She prepared for school.*
- (Repeat until firm.)
u. Word 2. What word? (Signal.) *Kitchen.*
- (Repeat for words 3 and 4.)
v. Let's read those words again.
- Word 1. What word? (Signal.) *Prepare.*
- (Repeat for words 2–4.)
w. (Repeat step v until firm.)

Individual Turns

(For columns 1–4: Call on individual students, each to read one to three words per turn.)

STORY READING

a. Find part B in your textbook. ✓
- The error limit for group reading is 13 errors. Read carefully.
b. Everybody, touch the title. ✓
- (Call on a student to read the title.) [*Back to Earth.*]
- Everybody, what's the title? (Signal.) *Back to Earth.*
- (Call on individual students to read the story, each student reading two or three sentences at a time. Ask the specified questions as the students read.)

- (Correct errors: Tell the word. Direct the student to reread the sentence.)
- (If the group makes more than 13 errors, direct the students to reread the story.)

Back to Earth
Wendy and Sidney and the other students stayed on Io for five days. They went with the scientists who were studying the rocks on Io. They went on a land vehicle that took them two hundred miles from the space station to a place where there were big volcanos—much bigger than Soup Pot. One of these big volcanos was erupting. The girls and the other students took pictures of the things they saw. Wendy took over two hundred pictures. She even took some pictures through a telescope. She attached her camera to one end of the telescope and took pictures of the eye of Jupiter. She also took pictures of some of the other parts of the huge planet. She took one picture of a small moon that looked as if it was almost touching the surface of Jupiter.

- Name some things that Wendy did during her five days on Jupiter. (Call on a student. Ideas: *She visited volcanos; traveled on a land vehicle; took pictures; went with some scientists to study rocks.*)

- You can see two pictures that Wendy took. The huge volcano is over two miles high. The other picture shows the enormous clouds that are swirling around to form the eye.

  The five days seemed to pass very quickly. Then it was time to go back to Earth. Wendy felt both happy and sad.

- Why would she feel happy? (Call on a student. Idea: *Because she was going home.*)
- Why would she feel sad? (Call on a student. Idea: *Because she was leaving Io and her new friends.*)

  She was looking forward to getting back and telling her friends and her family about the things she had seen. She could hardly wait to show her pictures to her friends. She could almost hear what they would say when they saw some of the pictures. She imagined that their eyes would get big and they would say things like "Wow," and "That's incredible."

- These were the things that made her happy. Listen to that part again:
  She was looking forward to getting back and telling her friends and her family about the things she had seen. She could hardly wait to show her pictures to her friends. She could almost hear what they would say when they saw some of the pictures. She imagined that their eyes would get big and they would say things like, "Wow," and "That's incredible."
- Name some things that made her happy about leaving. (Call on a student. Ideas: *She could tell her friends and family about her trip; she could show her pictures.*)

  On the day that Traveler Four was to leave for Earth, Wendy and Sidney went back to Soup Pot. They felt very strange walking up the path to the rim of the volcano.

- Why? (Call on a student. Idea: *Because they had both almost died the last time they were there.*)

But they wanted to take one more look at the place where they had their most frightening adventure. They didn't plan to stay long this time, just long enough to take some pictures. They wanted pictures of the place where the overhang had been and pictures of the inside of the crater.

- What two things did they want pictures of? (Call on a student. Idea: *Where the overhang had been and the inside of the crater.*)

Wendy wanted these pictures more than any of the others.

- Why? (Call on a student. Ideas: *Because that was where her most frightening adventure had happened; because she'd be telling the story of her adventure.*)

  She took six pictures. For the last one that she took, she got down on her belly and leaned over the rim to take a picture of the crater. Sidney said, "Be careful. We don't want to have to save you." Wendy was careful.

  • • •

- There are dots in the story. What does that mean? (Call on a student. Idea: *Part of the story is missing.*)

  As the girls entered the space station again, the automatic voice inside Wendy's helmet said, "You have forty minutes of oxygen left."

- Everybody, did she have that much oxygen left the last time she tried to get to the space station? (Signal.) *No.*
- What happened to her oxygen supply last time? (Call on a student. Idea: *It ran out.*)
- Why does she have so much oxygen left this time? (Call on a student. Ideas: *She isn't running; she's not using as much oxygen.*)

Later that day, the students and most of the passengers who had come to Jupiter with them boarded Traveler Four.

- What does that mean, they boarded Traveler Four? (Call on a student. Idea: *They got on the ship*.)

Some of the scientists stayed on Io. And some of the scientists that had been on Io for months left with Wendy ✦ and the other students. Two of these scientists had been on Io for over a year.

- How long had two of the scientists been there? (Call on a student. Idea: *Over a year*.)
- Everybody, had those scientists come to Io on Wendy's flight? (Signal.) *No.*

Wendy and Sidney hugged Rod. They knew him very well by now. He was a scientist, a very smart one. He was also a very nice person.

During the time the girls were on Io, he had explained things to them, had eaten with them, and had been a good friend. For Wendy, it was sad to say goodbye to him. After she hugged him, she had to turn away, because she didn't want him to see that she had tears in her eyes.

- That must have been sad.

The trip back to Earth on Traveler Four didn't seem to take as long as the trip out to Jupiter. In fact, the four-and-a-half days seemed to go by quickly. Wendy read a lot and made plans about things that she would do when she got back to her hometown. When Traveler Four landed at the space station in Japan, the sun was just starting to come up.

- Everybody, what time of day was it in Japan when they landed? (Signal.) *Morning.*

Everybody cheered when the huge spaceship landed. Then the students said goodbye to each other. Sidney and Wendy made a lot of plans. They planned to see each other the following year. They planned to write to each other. They planned to phone each other and to send each other good pictures.

- Name some things they planned to do. (Call on individual students. Ideas: *See each other; write each other; phone each other; send pictures*.)
- Read the rest of the story to yourself and be ready to answer some questions. Raise your hand when you're finished.

As Wendy and Sidney got out of the bus at the airport in Japan, Wendy realized that she had a lot to tell Sidney and not much time to tell those things. So she talked very fast. Sidney did too. The girls seemed to say the same things over and over. "I'll never forget that day on Io," Sidney said for about the tenth time.

"Me, neither," Wendy said.

Then the girls said goodbye to each other. They hugged each other. They cried more. Then Sidney went to her plane and Wendy went to hers.

Wendy felt sad for the first hour of the plane trip back to her hometown. Slowly, she started to feel better as she looked forward to getting home. Suddenly, she noticed that the woman next to her was reading a book about the solar system. The woman was reading a page that had pictures of Jupiter and Io. When the woman noticed that Wendy was looking at the book, the woman said, "Our solar system is incredible."

Wendy agreed.

Then the woman said, "I was just reading the most amazing facts about Jupiter. Did you know that one of the moons near Jupiter has volcanos on it?"

Wendy laughed and said, "Yes, I do." Then she told the woman about her frightening adventure.

- (After all students have raised their hand:) Everybody, did Wendy and Sidney get on the same plane? (Signal.) *No.*
- Wendy noticed that the woman next to her was reading a book. What was that book about? (Signal.) *The solar system.*

- The woman asked Wendy something that made Wendy laugh. What did the woman ask about? (Call on a student. Idea: *If Wendy knew that one of Jupiter's moons had volcanos on it.*)
- Why did Wendy laugh? (Call on a student. Idea: *Because she had an adventure with a volcano on Io.*)
- Listen to that last part. It's the ending to the whole story about Wendy:

> Then the girls said goodbye to each other. They hugged each other. They cried more. Then Sidney went to her plane and Wendy went to hers. Wendy felt sad for the first hour of the plane trip back to her hometown. Slowly, she started to feel better as she looked forward to getting home. Suddenly, she noticed that the woman next to her was reading a book about the solar system. The woman was reading a page that had pictures of Jupiter and Io. When the woman noticed that Wendy was looking at the book, the woman said, "Our solar system is incredible."
> Wendy agreed.
> Then the woman said, "I was just reading the most incredible facts about Jupiter. Did you know that one of the moons near Jupiter has volcanos on it?"
> Wendy laughed and said, "Yes, I do." Then she told the woman about her frightening adventure.

PAIRED PRACTICE

You're going to read aloud to your partner. First the **B** members will read first. Then the **A** members will read from the star to the end of the story. (Observe students and give feedback.)

End-of-Lesson Activities

INDEPENDENT WORK

Now finish your independent work for lesson 66. Raise your hand when you're finished. (Observe students and give feedback.)

WORKCHECK

a. (Direct students to take out their marking pencils.)
  - We're going to check your workbook and textbook items. Remember, if you got an item wrong, make an **X** next to the item.
b. (For each item: Read the item. Call on a student to answer it. If the answer is wrong, say the correct answer. Refer to the Answer Key for the correct answers.)
c. Now use your marking pencil to fix up any items you got wrong. Remember, all mistakes must be fixed up before you hand in your work.

LANGUAGE ARTS

(Present Language Arts lesson 66 after completing Reading lesson 66. See Language Arts Guide.)

Special Project

Note: After completing lesson 66, do this special project with the students. You may do this project during another part of the school day.

Materials: Reference materials (books on the solar system, encyclopedias, CD-ROMs) and poster-making supplies (butcher paper or poster board, markers, crayons, paints, scissors, paste, magazine for pictures)

a. Everybody, find page 331 in your textbook. ✓
   * (Call on individual students to read two or three sentences.)
   * (Teacher reference:)

> **Special Project**
> Make a wall chart that shows these planets:
> Mercury, Venus, Earth, Mars, Jupiter.
> For each planet, find the answers to these questions:
> * How big is the planet?
> * How many hours does it take to turn around?
>   (How long is a day on that planet?)
> * How long does it take to circle the sun?
> * How many moons does it have?
> * How far from the sun is it?

   * When you're finding out the facts about these planets, think about how we can make the chart look very impressive.
b. (Direct the group to make a large wall chart that shows Wendy's trip and these five planets of the solar system: Mercury, Venus, Earth, Mars, and Jupiter.)
c. (Divide the group into subgroups, each of which is responsible for finding out information about one or two planets. Use encyclopedias, computers or books [such as *World Book*] to get information that answers the questions about each planet.)
d. (Help each group find the information needed for the chart. After the students have looked up the information, ask the group for ideas about how to display the information: **How can we make the chart look really impressive?** Praise students for finding interesting facts and for offering ideas about how to display information.) Show the students what the chart should look like when it is finished. Note that the information is recorded about each planet.)
e. (After the chart is finished, arrange a presentation to another classroom, with each of the subgroups presenting the information it was responsible for.)

Note: The Special Project following lesson 106 will require students to modify their chart by adding the last four planets: Saturn, Uranus, Neptune, Pluto.

EXERCISE 1

VOCABULARY REVIEW

a. You learned a sentence that tells how the incredible whales made them feel.

- Everybody, say that sentence. Get ready. (Signal.) *The incredible whales made them anxious.*
- (Repeat until firm.)

b. I'll say part of the sentence. When I stop, you say the next word. Listen: The incredible . . . Everybody, what's the next word? (Signal.) *Whales.*

c. Listen: The incredible whales made them . . . Everybody, what's the next word? (Signal.) *Anxious.*

- Say the whole sentence. Get ready. (Signal.) *The incredible whales made them anxious.*

d. Listen: The . . . Everybody, what's the next word? (Signal.) *Incredible.*

EXERCISE 2

VOCABULARY

a. **Find page 352 in your textbook.** ✓
- Touch sentence 17. ✓
- This is a new vocabulary sentence. It says: The boring speaker disturbed the audience. Everybody, read that sentence. Get ready. (Signal.) *The boring speaker disturbed the audience.*
- Close your eyes and say the sentence. Get ready. (Signal.) *The boring speaker disturbed the audience.*
- (Repeat until firm.)

b. The sentence says: The boring speaker disturbed the audience. **Boring** is the opposite of **interesting.** Everybody, what's the opposite of **an interesting speech?** (Signal.) *A boring speech.*

- What's the opposite of an interesting book? (Signal.) *A boring book.*
- What's the opposite of an interesting TV program? (Signal.) *A boring TV program.*

c. The sentence says that the speaker disturbed the audience. When you bother something, you disturb it. Everybody, what's another way of saying **She bothered her brother?** (Signal.) *She disturbed her brother.*

- What's another way of saying **The way she laughs bothers me?** (Signal.) *The way she laughs disturbs me.*
- What's another way of saying **I was bothered by the foul smell?** (Signal.) *I was disturbed by the foul smell.*

d. The sentence talks about the audience. All the people who watch an event are the people in the audience. Name some events that have an audience. (Call on individual students. Ideas: *TV shows, sporting events, movies, plays,* etc.)

e. Listen to the sentence again: The boring speaker disturbed the audience. Everybody, say the sentence. Get ready. (Signal.) *The boring speaker disturbed the audience.*

f. Everybody, what word is the opposite of **interesting?** (Signal.) *Boring.*
- What do we call all the people who watch an event? (Signal.) *Audience.*
- What's another word for **bothered?** (Signal.) *Disturbed.*
- (Repeat step f until firm.)

EXERCISE 3

READING WORDS

Column 1

a. Find lesson 67 in your textbook. ✓
- Touch column 1. ✓
- (Teacher reference:)

1. Waldo Greem	4. kitchen
2. solve	5. hamster
3. serious	

b. Number 1 is a name: **Waldo Greem.** What name? (Signal.) *Waldo Greem.*

c. Word 2 is **solve.** What word? (Signal.) *Solve.*
- Spell **solve.** Get ready. (Tap for each letter.) *S-O-L-V-E.*
- When you solve a problem, you figure out the answer to that problem. Everybody, what's a person doing when she figures out the answer to a math problem? (Signal.) *Solving a math problem.*

- What's a person doing when he figures out the answer to a health problem? (Signal.) *Solving a health problem.*
d. Word 3. What word? (Signal.) *Serious.*
- Spell **serious**. Get ready. (Tap for each letter.) *S-E-R-I-O-U-S.*
e. Word 4. What word? (Signal.) *Kitchen.*
- Spell **kitchen**. Get ready. (Tap for each letter.) *K-I-T-C-H-E-N.*
f. Word 5. What word? (Signal.) *Hamster.*
- Spell **hamster**. Get ready. (Tap for each letter.) *H-A-M-S-T-E-R.*
g. Let's read those words again, the fast way.
- Number 1. What name? (Signal.) *Waldo Greem.*
- Word 2. What word? (Signal.) *Solve.*
- (Repeat for: **3. serious, 4. kitchen, 5. hamster.**)
h. (Repeat step g until firm.)

Column 2
i. Find column 2. ✓
- (Teacher reference:)

1. zebras	4. fainted
2. trainer	5. screeching
3. parrots	

- All these words have an ending.
j. Word 1. What word? (Signal.) *Zebras.*
- (Repeat for words 2–5.)
k. Let's read those words again.
- Word 1. What word? (Signal.) *Zebras.*
- (Repeat for words 2–5.)
l. (Repeat step k until firm.)

Column 3
m. Find column 3. ✓
- (Teacher reference:)

1. **Fran**	4. **zoo**
2. **world's**	5. **disturb**
3. **prepare**	

n. Word 1. What word? (Signal.) *Fran.*
- (Repeat for words 2–5.)
o. Let's read those words again.
- Word 1. What word? (Signal.) *Fran.*
- (Repeat for words 2–5.)
p. (Repeat step o until firm.)

Column 4
q. Find column 4. ✓
- (Teacher reference:)

1. **elephants**	4. **trucks**
2. **yeah**	5. **audience**
3. **pigeons**	

r. Word 1. What word? (Signal.) *Elephants.*
- (Repeat for words 2–5.)
s. Let's read those words again.
- Word 1. What word? (Signal.) *Elephants.*
- (Repeat for words 2–5.)
t. (Repeat step s until firm.)

Individual Turns
(For columns 1–4: Call on individual students, each to read one to three words.)

EXERCISE 4

FACT REVIEW
a. Let's review some facts you have learned. First we'll go over the facts together. Then I'll call on individual students to do some facts.
b. Everybody, tell me how much oxygen is on Io. (Pause.) Get ready. (Signal.) *None.*
- Tell me how long it takes Io to go all the way around Jupiter. **Less than...** (Pause.) Get ready. (Signal.) *2 days.*
- Tell me which has **more** gravity—**Jupiter** or **Io.** (Pause.) Get ready. (Signal.) *Jupiter.*
- Tell me where you can jump three meters high—on Jupiter or on Io. (Pause.) Get ready. (Signal.) *On Io.*
- (Repeat step b until firm.)
c. Tell me which is **smaller** than Earth— **Jupiter** or **Io.** (Pause.) Get ready. (Signal.) *Io.*
- If you are **very heavy** on a planet, that planet has lots of... (Pause.) Get ready. (Signal.) *Gravity.*
- Tell me if you would feel **light** or **heavy** on Io. (Pause.) Get ready. (Signal.) *Light.*
- Let's say an object weighed 10 pounds on Earth. Tell me if the object would weigh **more** than 10 pounds **on the moon.** (Pause.) Get ready. (Signal.) *No.*
- (Repeat step c until firm.)

COMPREHENSION PASSAGE

a. Find part B in your textbook. ✓
- You're going to start a new story. First you'll read the information passage. It gives some facts about animals.

b. Everybody, touch the title. ✓
- (Call on a student to read the title.) *[Kinds of Animals.]*
- Everybody, what's the title? (Signal.) *Kinds of Animals.*

c. (Call on individual students to read the passage, each student reading two or three sentences at a time. Ask the specified questions as the students read.)

> **Kinds of Animals**
> **The pictures below show some of the animals that you'll be reading about. Read the name for each animal.**

- I'll say the letter for each animal. You read the name.
- A. Get ready. (Signal.) *Elephant.*
- B. Get ready. (Signal.) *Zebra.*
- C. Get ready. (Signal.) *Squirrel.*
- D. Get ready. (Signal.) *Parrot.*
- E. Get ready. (Signal.) *Rabbit.*
- F. Get ready. (Signal.) *Tiger.*
- G. Get ready. (Signal.) *Sheep.*
- H. Get ready. (Signal.) *Pigeon.*
- I. Get ready. (Signal.) *Hamster.*
- J. Get ready. (Signal.) *Goat.*
- K. Get ready. (Signal.) *Giraffe.*
- (Repeat until firm.)

> **The story that you'll read will also talk about an elephant's trunk. Touch that part of the elephant.**

- Everybody, do it. ✓

STORY READING

a. Find part C in your textbook. ✓
- This is the first part of a new story.
- The error limit for group reading is 12 errors.

b. Everybody, touch the title. ✓
- (Call on a student to read the title.) *[Waldo's Cooking.]*
- Everybody, what's the title? (Signal.) *Waldo's Cooking.*
- We're going to read a new series of stories. Everybody, what is that series going to tell about? (Signal.) *Waldo's cooking.*

c. (Call on individual students to read the story, each student reading two or three sentences at a time. Ask the specified questions as the students read.)

- (Correct errors: Tell the word. Direct the student to reread the sentence.)
- (If the group makes more than 12 errors, direct the students to reread the story.)

> **Waldo's Cooking**
> **Waldo Greem became the world's greatest animal trainer because of his cooking.**

- Everybody, what made Waldo the world's greatest animal trainer? (Signal.) *His cooking.*
- That sounds very strange but we'll find out how it happened.

> **Waldo cooked from the time he was ten years old. He loved to cook eggs and big meals like spaghetti. There was one serious problem with the things he cooked—nobody could stand them.**

- What does that mean, nobody could stand them? (Call on a student. Idea: *Nobody liked to eat the things he cooked.*)
- That would be a big problem.
- Everybody, when did he start cooking? (Signal.) *When he was ten years old.*

> **His mother and father didn't want to make him feel bad about his cooking, so they tried to eat the things that he cooked. They tried to pretend that they were enjoying his**

hamburgers or his spaghetti, but they didn't enjoy anything that Waldo cooked.

- Everybody, show me how you would look if you were trying to pretend that you liked something that tasted really bad. ✓

Waldo's brother Michael and his sister Fran wouldn't eat anything that Waldo cooked. When they found out that he had cooked something, they would just say, "Ugh, I'm not hungry." Instead of eating one of his meals, they would eat a peanut butter sandwich.

Waldo didn't give up.

- What does that mean, he didn't give up? (Call on a student. Idea: *He kept cooking.*)

He kept trying to be a better cook, but no matter how hard he tried to make better meals, people couldn't stand his cooking. Sometimes his school would have a party and Waldo would bring something that he fixed. When the party was over, everything that the other students brought for the party would be gone. Everything that Waldo brought would still be on the table.

- Why? (Call on a student. Idea: *Because no one could stand the things he cooked.*)
- Why would other people's food be gone? (Call on a student. Idea: *Because people ate it.*)

For years Waldo cooked and for years nobody could stand his cooking—at least, no human could stand his cooking. Animals were different. Every time Waldo cooked, many animals would gather around his house—usually more than twenty animals. They didn't just like Waldo's cooking. They loved it. Cats, dogs, birds, squirrels, rabbits, sheep, goats and even cows and horses would come into the yard and stand near the kitchen window.

- Why did they stand near the kitchen window? (Call on a student. Idea: *They smelled Waldo's cooking.*)

When Waldo fixed big meals that took a long time to prepare, over a hundred animals would gather in the yard. The dogs would howl; the cats would meow; the other animals would make other noises. "This has got to stop," Waldo's father said after Waldo had fixed a huge meal. "Our yard is like a zoo every time Waldo cooks."

On that day, the yard really did look like a zoo. It was a warm day and the windows in the kitchen were open. The smell of his cooking must have drifted to the other side of the town where a circus was being held. As soon as the smell reached the circus animals, they went crazy and ran from the circus. They followed their noses to Waldo's yard.

- They followed their noses. What were their noses telling them? (Call on a student. Ideas: *That Waldo's cooking smelled good; where his food was.*)

Just as Waldo was getting ★ ready to put his meal on the table, he noticed that there was a large elephant trunk coming through the window. He looked outside and almost fainted. Elephants, zebras, monkeys, parrots, and all the other animals from the circus were in the yard. The animal trainers from the circus were also in the yard. They were tugging and pulling at the animals, trying to lead them into trucks and take them from the yard. But the animals would not move. They were crowding around the windows, howling and screeching and making all kinds of noises.

That day was a very bad one for Waldo, but it was also a very good one, because that was the day that Waldo found out how to train any animal.

- Why was that day a good one for Waldo? (Call on a student. Idea: *He found out how to train any animal.*)
- Do you have any idea of how he might train them? (Call on a student. Idea: *Use his cooking for rewards.*)

When the people in Waldo's family saw the animals in the yard, they became very angry. His sister Fran said, "Make Waldo stop cooking. This is ridiculous." His brother Michael said, "Yeah, make Waldo stop cooking." His mother said, "Waldo, I think you had better not cook anymore."

- Read the rest of the story to yourself. Raise your hand when you're done.

One of the trainers from the circus was leaning in the window. She said, "What do you have in there that's making the animals go crazy?"

Another trainer appeared at the window. "How are we going to get them into the trucks?" he said. "They just won't move."

Waldo looked at the meal he had made. He felt very sad. Then he said, "I'll help you get them back into the truck."

Waldo dumped some of the meal into a large bowl. Then he walked outside with the bowl. The animals crowded around him. Then he walked to the truck. All the animals followed. The circus animals followed and so did all the cats and dogs and squirrels and goats that usually came around the house when Waldo cooked.

Waldo climbed into the truck and all the animals followed. Then he gave all the circus animals a little bit of food. That seemed to make them very happy. One of the trainers said, "That's amazing. He just gives them a little bite of food and they're happy."

Waldo jumped out of the truck and all the animals that had not been fed followed him—the dogs and cats and squirrels and birds. He gave each of these animals a little bite of food and they were happy. A trainer said to Waldo, "I don't know what you put in that food, but I've never seen anything like this before."

- (After all students have raised their hand:) How did Waldo get the animals into the truck? (Call on a student. Idea: *He took food on the truck; the animals followed him; and he fed them.*)
- Everybody, did only the circus animals follow him on the truck? (Signal.) *No.*

- How did he get the animals that did not belong to the circus to leave the truck? (Call on a student. Idea: *He took food out of the truck and fed them.*)
- Now I think I understand why Waldo's cooking helped him become the world's greatest animal trainer. What do you think he'll do to become such a great trainer? (Call on a student. Idea: *Get them to do what he wants by feeding them his cooking.*)
- Everybody, look at the picture. It shows Waldo carrying his food toward the truck. See if you can find some of the animals that I name. Zebra . . . elephant . . . squirrel . . . parrot . . . rabbit . . . goat . . . sheep . . . giraffe . . . tiger. What other animals do you see in the picture? (Call on individual students. Ideas: *Lion, pig, horse, cow, dogs,* etc.)

EXERCISE 7

PAIRED PRACTICE

You're going to read aloud to your partner. The **A** members will read first. Then the **B** members will read from the star to the end of the story. (Observe students and give feedback.)

End-of-Lesson Activities

INDEPENDENT WORK

Now finish the independent work for lesson 67. Raise your hand when you're finished. (Observe students and give feedback.)

WORKCHECK

a. (Direct students to take out their marking pencils.)
- We're going to check your independent work. Remember, if you got an item wrong, make an **X** next to the item.
b. (For each item: Read the item. Call on a student to answer it. If the answer is wrong, say the correct answer. Refer to the Answer Key for the correct answers.)
c. Now use your marking pencil to fix up any items you got wrong. Remember, all mistakes must be fixed up before you hand in your independent work.

LANGUAGE ARTS

(Present Language Arts lesson 67 after completing Reading lesson 67. See Language Arts Guide.)

Lesson 68

VOCABULARY REVIEW

a. Here's the new vocabulary sentence: The boring speaker disturbed the audience.
- Everybody, say the sentence. Get ready. (Signal.) *The boring speaker disturbed the audience.*
- (Repeat until firm.)

b. Everybody, what do we call the people who watch an event? (Signal.) *Audience.*
- What word is the opposite of **interesting?** (Signal.) *Boring.*
- What's another word for **bothered?** (Signal.) *Disturbed.*

EXERCISE 2

READING WORDS

Column 1

a. **Find lesson 68 in your textbook.** ✓
- Touch column 1. ✓
- (Teacher reference:)

1. deliver	3. cute
2. folks	4. applaud

b. Word 1 is **deliver.** What word? (Signal.) *Deliver.*
- Spell **deliver.** Get ready. (Tap for each letter.) *D-E-L-I-V-E-R.*
- When you bring something to a place, you deliver it to that place.
- Everybody, what's another way of saying **They brought a pizza to our school?** (Signal.) *They delivered a pizza to our school.*
- What's another way of saying **The mail carrier brought a package?** (Signal.) *The mail carrier delivered a package.*

c. Word 2 is **folks.** What word? (Signal.) *Folks.*
- Spell **folks.** Get ready. (Tap for each letter.) *F-O-L-K-S.*

d. Word 3 is **cute.** What word? (Signal.) *Cute.*
- Spell **cute.** Get ready. (Tap for each letter.) *C-U-T-E.*

e. Word 4. What word? (Signal.) *Applaud.*
- Spell **applaud.** Get ready. (Tap for each letter.) *A-P-P-L-A-U-D.*

f. Let's read those words again, the fast way.
- Word 1. What word? (Signal.) *Deliver.*
- (Repeat for words 2–4.)

g. (Repeat step f until firm.)

Column 2

h. Find column 2. ✓
- (Teacher reference:)

1. funniest	3. solve
2. answering	4. fried

i. Word 1. What word? (Signal.) *Funniest.*
- (Repeat for words 2–4.)

j. Let's read those words again.
- Word 1. What word? (Signal.) *Funniest.*
- (Repeat for words 2–4.)

k. (Repeat step j until firm.)

Individual Turns

(For columns 1 and 2: Call on individual students, each to read one to three words per turn.)

EXERCISE 3

STORY READING

a. Find part B in your textbook. ✓
- The error limit for group reading is 12 errors.

b. Everybody, touch the title. ✓
- (Call on a student to read the title.) [A Problem.]
- Everybody, what's the title? (Signal.) *A Problem.*

c. (Call on individual students to read the story, each student reading two or three sentences at a time. Ask the specified questions as the students read.)

- (Correct errors: Tell the word. Direct the student to reread the sentence.)
- (If the group makes more than 12 errors, direct the students to reread the story.)

A Problem

Many people had gathered in the yard when the circus animals had crowded around the kitchen windows. Most of those people remained in the yard after the circus truck left with the circus animals.

- Everybody, did the people leave when the circus animals left? (Signal.) *No.*

The people stayed because more animals were gathering in the yard. People laughed and pointed at all the dogs and cats and birds and squirrels that were trying to stay close to Waldo. There were so many animals around him that you couldn't see any part of Waldo from his waist down to his feet.

- What part of Waldo couldn't you see? (Call on a student. Idea: *From his waist to his feet.*)

When he moved, all the animals moved. When he stopped, all the animals stopped.

Waldo's father tried to get close to Waldo, but he couldn't.

- Why not? (Call on a student. Idea: *Animals were all around him.*)

"Waldo," he shouted, "You're just going to have to stop cooking things."

The people who were watching laughed.

His brother and sister said, "Yeah, stop cooking."

Waldo was going to say, "But I love to cook." Just as he started to talk, a large dog jumped up and licked him on the face. Waldo turned his head away. A bird landed on his head. As he brushed the bird away, a squirrel climbed up his leg. "But," Waldo said, "I love . . ."

- What is Waldo trying to say? (Call on a student. Idea: *I love to cook.*)

The people who were watching Waldo laughed harder and harder. One person said, "This is the funniest show I've ever seen. Look at those animals."

Waldo's mother said, "Waldo, you better go inside so these animals will go away."

Waldo walked up the back steps of his house and the crowd of animals followed him. He reached into the bowl and grabbed a little handful of food. He threw the food as far as he could.

- Why do you think he did that? (Call on a student. Ideas: *So the animals would chase it; so he could get away from the animals.*)

The whole crowd of animals went after the food. Birds were flying. Rabbits were leaping. Dogs and cats and horses were running. The people who were watching laughed and laughed. Then they began to applaud. Waldo smiled and waved. He felt embarrassed but he didn't know what to say.

- The people watching acted like they were seeing a very funny show. What did they do to show that they really enjoyed the show? (Call on a student. Idea: *Laughed and clapped.*)

Waldo went inside. His father followed him. "Waldo," he said. "This has to stop."

Waldo felt very sad as he slowly slumped into a kitchen chair. "Yes, Waldo," his mother said. "We are not running a zoo here. Every time you cook a large meal, more than a hundred animals appear in the yard."

"Yeah," his brother Michael said. "Every time you cook, the phone rings all evening long. Everybody wants to know if we've seen ★ their dog or their cat."

"Yeah," his sister Fran said. "I'm getting tired of answering the phone. Some of those calls are ridiculous. I hate it when somebody asks if I've seen a striped cat. I tell them I've seen a whole yard full of striped cats."

- Listen to that part again.

  Waldo went inside. His father followed him. "Waldo," he said. "This has to stop."

  Waldo felt very sad as he slowly slumped into a kitchen chair. "Yes, Waldo," his mother said. "We are not running a zoo here. Every time you cook a large meal, more than a hundred animals appear in the yard."

  "Yeah," his brother Michael said. "Every time you cook, the phone rings all evening long. Everybody wants to know if we've seen their dog or their cat."

  "Yeah," his sister Fran said. "I'm getting tired of answering the phone. Some of those calls are ridiculous. I hate it when somebody asks if I've seen a striped cat. I tell them I've seen a whole yard full of striped cats."

- Why did people from all over call Waldo's home? (Call on a student. Idea: *They wondered where their pets were.*)
- Where do you think the missing dogs and cats were? (Call on a student. Idea: *At Waldo's house.*)
- Why did Waldo's sister think it was ridiculous when somebody asked if she had seen a striped cat? (Call on a student. Idea: *Because her yard was full of striped cats.*)

Waldo's brother said, "We see more than striped cats. We see black cats and brown cats and yellow cats and cats with one eye and cats with . . ."

"All right," Waldo's mother said. "That's enough."

- Say that the way his mother said it to make Waldo's brother stop talking. (Call on a student. Student should speak in a commanding tone.)

"And cats with long hair and cats with no hair and cats with . . ."

- Everybody, who's talking? (Signal.) *Waldo's brother.*
- Did he pay attention when his mother said, "That's enough?" (Signal.) *No.*

"I said, that's enough!"

- Everybody, who said that? (Signal.) *Waldo's mother.*

Waldo covered his face with his hands and started to cry. "I don't want to make any trouble," he said. "I just love to cook and I love animals . . ."

Waldo's father patted him on the back. "I know how you feel, son. But you can see that we've got a big problem here."

"Yes, Dad," Waldo said.

"Make him stop cooking," his sister said. "Make him stop."

His brother said, "Yeah, make him stop. Or make him answer all the phone calls."

- Why did his brother think Waldo should answer the phone? (Call on a student. Idea: *Because it's Waldo's fault that all the animals are there.*)
- Read the rest of the story to yourself and be ready to answer some questions. Raise your hand when you're done.

"That's enough from you two," Waldo's mother said. She continued, "Waldo is a good boy. We just have to figure out some way to solve this problem."

His sister said, "I know how to solve the problem. We could make Waldo . . ."

"Go into the other room," Waldo's mother said. Then his mother added, "We'll work out a solution to this problem."

So Waldo, his mother, and his father sat in the kitchen and talked about the problem. There were still many animals outside. Two big dogs were standing on their hind legs, looking through the kitchen window.

One of them kept howling. The phone was ringing in the other room. Every now and then, one of the neighbors would yell something like, "Get out of here. Go home."

After Waldo and his parents talked for a while, Waldo's father said, "I don't see any solution except one. You're going to have to stop cooking."

Waldo's mother said, "I'm afraid that's right. It costs a lot of money to cook all that food. Then nobody can eat it except those animals."

Waldo said, "But I'll pay for the food. I'll get a job and make enough to pay for my own food. And I'll . . ."

"I'm sorry, son," his father said. "I think you'll just have to stop cooking."

- (After all students have raised their hand:) How did Waldo plan to pay for the food? (Call on a student. Idea: *Get a job.*)
- Everybody, did his parents agree with his solution? (Signal.) *No.*
- What decision did Waldo's parents make? (Call on a student. Idea: *Waldo had to stop cooking.*)
- Why do you think the phone was ringing while Waldo and his parents talked? (Call on a student. Idea: *People were looking for their pets.*)

PAIRED PRACTICE

You're going to read aloud to your partner. The **B** members will read first. Then the **A** members will read from the star to the end of the story. (Observe students and give feedback.)

End-of-Lesson Activities

INDEPENDENT WORK

Now finish the independent work for lesson 68. Raise your hand when you're finished. (Observe students and give feedback.)

WORKCHECK

a. (Direct students to take out their marking pencils.)
- We're going to check your independent work. Remember, if you got an item wrong, make an **X** next to the item.
b. (For each item: Read the item. Call on a student to answer it. If the answer is wrong, say the correct answer. Refer to the Answer Key for the correct answers.)
c. Now use your marking pencil to fix up any items you got wrong. Remember, all mistakes must be fixed up before you hand in your independent work.

LANGUAGE ARTS

(Present Language Arts lesson 68 after completing Reading lesson 68. See Language Arts Guide.)

Lesson 69

EXERCISE 1
VOCABULARY REVIEW

a. You learned a sentence that tells what lava did.
- Everybody, say that sentence. Get ready. (Signal.) *Lava erupted from the volcano's crater.*
- (Repeat until firm.)

b. You learned a sentence that tells what made them anxious.
- Say that sentence. Get ready. (Signal.) *The incredible whales made them anxious.*
- (Repeat until firm.)

c. Here's the last sentence you learned: The boring speaker disturbed the audience.
- Everybody, say that sentence. Get ready. (Signal.) *The boring speaker disturbed the audience.*
- (Repeat until firm.)

d. Everybody, what's another word for **bothered?** (Signal.) *Disturbed.*
- What do we call all the people who watch an event? (Signal.) *Audience.*
- What word is the opposite of **interesting?** (Signal.) *Boring.*

e. Once more. Say the sentence that tells what the speaker did. Get ready. (Signal.) *The boring speaker disturbed the audience.*

EXERCISE 2
READING WORDS

Column 1

a. Find lesson 69 in your textbook. ✓
- Touch column 1. ✓
- (Teacher reference:)

1. **fried**	4. **folks**
2. **masks**	5. **delivering**
3. **mobbed**	

- All these words have an ending.
b. Word 1. What word? (Signal.) *Fried.*
- Spell **fried.** Get ready. (Tap for each letter.) *F-R-I-E-D.*

c. Word 2. What word? (Signal.) *Masks.*
- Spell **masks.** Get ready. (Tap for each letter.) *M-A-S-K-S.*
d. Word 3. What word? (Signal.) *Mobbed.*
- Spell **mobbed.** Get ready. (Tap for each letter.) *M-O-B-B-E-D.*
e. Word 4. What word? (Signal.) *Folks.*
- Spell **folks.** Get ready. (Tap for each letter.) *F-O-L-K-S.*
f. Word 5. What word? (Signal.) *Delivering.*
g. Let's read those words again.
- Word 1. What word? (Signal.) *Fried.*
- (Repeat for words 2–5.)
h. (Repeat step g until firm.)

Column 2

i. Find column 2. ✓
- (Teacher reference:)

1. **backyard**	4. **owner**
2. **wagging**	5. **cleaning**
3. **attracting**	

j. These words have more than one syllable. The first part of each word is underlined.
k. Word 1. What's the underlined part? (Signal.) *back.*
- What's the whole word? (Signal.) *Backyard.*
- Word 2. What's the underlined part? (Signal.) *wagg.*
- What's the whole word? (Signal.) *Wagging.*
- Word 3. What's the underlined part? (Signal.) *attract.*
- What's the whole word? (Signal.) *Attracting.*
- Word 4. What's the underlined part? (Signal.) *own.*
- What's the whole word? (Signal.) *Owner.*
- Word 5. What's the underlined part? (Signal.) *clean.*
- What's the whole word? (Signal.) *Cleaning.*
l. Let's read those words again, the fast way.
- Word 1. What word? (Signal.) *Backyard.*
- (Repeat for words 2–5.)
m. (Repeat step l until firm.)

Column 3

n. Find column 3. ✓
  • (Teacher reference:)

1. **dust**	4. **wore**
2. **whew**	5. **screech**
3. **cage**	6. **cute**

o. Word 1. What word? (Signal.) *Dust.*
  • (Repeat for words 2–6.)
p. Let's read those words again.
  • Word 1. What word? (Signal.) *Dust.*
  • (Repeat for words 2–6.)
q. (Repeat step p until firm.)

Individual Turns

(For columns 1–3: Call on individual students, each to read one to three words per turn.)

EXERCISE 3

COMPREHENSION PASSAGE

a. Find part B in your textbook. ✓
  • You're going to read the next story about Waldo. First you'll read the information passage. It gives some facts about training animals.
b. Everybody, touch the title. ✓
  • (Call on a student to read the title.) [*Training Animals.*]
  • Everybody, what's the title? (Signal.) *Training Animals.*
  • What does this passage tell about? (Signal.) *Training animals.*
c. (Call on individual students to read the passage, each student reading two or three sentences at a time. Ask the specified questions as the students read.)

> **Training Animals**
> **You're going to read about how animals are trained to do tricks.**
> **Here's how to train animals:**
> **First, you tell the animal what to do.**

  • Everybody, what's the first thing you do? (Signal.) *Tell the animal what to do.*

> **If the animal does what you tell it to do, you reward the animal.**

  • What do you do if the animal does what you tell it do? (Call on a student. Idea: *Reward it.*)

> **You reward the animal by giving it something it likes.**

  • Name some things you would give a dog to reward it for doing what you tell it to do. (Call on individual students. Ideas: *A bone; some food; a pat on the head;* etc.)

> **If the animal does not do what you tell it to do, you do not reward the animal.**

  • That's important. When don't you reward the animal? (Call on a student. Idea: *When it doesn't do what you tell it to do.*)

> **You may have to wait a long time before the animal does the trick you want it to do. But if you reward the animal the right way, the animal will learn that the only way to get the reward is to do the trick.**

  • What's the only way the animal can get the reward? (Call on a student. Idea: *Do the trick.*)

> **The animal wants the reward, so the animal does the trick.**
> **Remember: Reward the animal each time the animal does the trick. Do not reward the animal if the animal does not do the trick.**

  • Remember that rule for training animals. Everybody, what do you do each time the animal does the trick? (Signal.) *Reward the animal.*

EXERCISE 4

STORY READING

a. Find part C in your textbook. ✓
  • This is the next part of Waldo's story.
  • The error limit for group reading is 15 errors.

b. Everybody, touch the title. ✓
- (Call on a student to read the title.) *[Waldo Gets a Job.]*
- Everybody, what's the title? (Signal.) *Waldo Gets a Job.*

c. (Call on individual students to read the story, each student reading two or three sentences at a time. Ask the specified questions as the students read.)

- (Correct errors: Tell the word. Direct the student to reread the sentence.)
- (If the group makes more than 15 errors, direct the students to reread the story.)

Waldo Gets a Job

After all those circus animals came to Waldo's house, his parents told him that he had to stop cooking. After they told him what they had decided, he tried to think of ways that he could cook without attracting animals. He thought about closing all the windows in the house when he cooked, but he knew that his brother and sister would not like this plan. They were always complaining about the smell of Waldo's cooking, even when the windows were open.

- What was Waldo's plan? (Call on a student. Idea: *To close all the windows when he cooked.*)
- How would closing all the windows keep the animals from gathering by the kitchen? (Call on a student. Idea: *Because the smell wouldn't get outside where the animals could smell it.*)
- Why didn't he think his brother and sister would like the plan? (Call on a student: Idea: *Because they complained about how Waldo's cooking smelled even when the windows were open.*)

He thought of giving them masks they could wear, but he didn't think they would like that plan.

After Waldo hadn't cooked for two months, he came up with a plan that he thought would work. He decided to get a job and earn money so that he could pay for the food that he cooked. That was part of his plan, but not all of it. He also planned to fix up the garage so that he could cook there and sleep there. Then he could have animals around to eat his cooking, but they wouldn't disturb the neighbors or disturb his parents.

- His plan had two parts. What was the first part? (Call on a student. Idea: *Make money for the food he cooked.*)
- What was the second part? (Call on a student. Idea: *Fix up the garage so he could stay there and the animals wouldn't disturb his parents or the neighbors.*)

Waldo didn't tell anybody about his plan. He just put his plan into action.

- What does that mean, put it into action? (Call on a student. Idea: *Started doing it.*)

First, he got a job. Actually, he tried three jobs before he found one that he liked.
⚙ Waldo's first job was delivering newspapers. He didn't like that job because he had to get up very early in the morning.

- Why didn't he like to deliver papers? (Call on a student. Idea: *He had to get up early in the morning.*)

The second job that he got was cleaning up in a shoe store. He hated that job. All he did was take boxes of shoes from the shelves and dust the boxes. Then he would sweep the floor in the back room. It was the most boring job in the world, but Waldo would have kept that job if he hadn't found the third job. He would have kept working in the shoe store because he liked earning money more than he hated dusting boxes.

- Listen to that sentence again: He would have kept working in the shoe store because he liked earning money more than he hated dusting boxes. Everybody, did he hate to dust boxes? (Signal.) *Yes.*

So he dusted boxes and dusted boxes and ⚙ dusted boxes. The box dusting went on for two weeks.

Then, one day after work, he was walking home thinking about the terrible job he had. Suddenly, he heard a dog barking. He turned toward the barking and noticed that he was in front of a pet shop. Waldo looked at the dog that was barking. He said to himself, "I have seen that dog in my yard before."

- Why would that dog have been in Waldo's yard? (Call on a student. Idea: *He smelled Waldo's cooking.*)

The dog continued to bark. At last the owner of the pet store went over to the dog's cage. "Stop that barking," the ✦ owner shouted. But the dog didn't stop.

Waldo walked inside the pet shop. The dog began wagging his tail. Waldo looked at the owner, and before he knew what he was saying, he said, "I can help you keep those animals happy."

- What would Waldo do to make those animals happy? (Call on a student. Idea: *Cook for them.*)
- Everybody, look at the picture. You can see the owner of the pet shop and Waldo. You can also see the dog that is wagging its tail.

The owner looked at Waldo. She was a tall woman who wore glasses. "What did you say?" she asked.

"I said that I can help you make these animals happy," Waldo said. Then he kept on talking. He hadn't planned to make a big speech, but the speech came out. He told the owner that people like to buy happy pets, not pets that bark or cry. He told her that more people would stop and look in the window if the animals looked friendly and did funny tricks. Then he told her that he knew how to make the animals happy.

- Waldo told the owner what kind of animals people like to buy. Everybody, do they like to buy pets that bark or cry? (Signal.) *No.*
- Why not? (Call on a student. Idea: *Pets that bark or cry aren't any fun.*)
- Everybody, do people like to buy pets that look friendly and do funny tricks? (Signal.) *Yes.*
- Do you think Waldo could make those animals look friendly and do funny tricks? (Call on a student. Idea: *Yes.*)

"How can you do that?" she asked.

He said, "If I show you how, could you give me a job working with these animals?"

"Maybe," she said. "But first you'll have to show me what you can do."

Waldo asked, "Do you have a kitchen in the back of this pet shop?"

"Yes, I do," she said. "But I don't understand what . . ."

Waldo asked, "Do you have some food that I can cook?"

"Yes, I do," she said. "But I don't understand what . . ."

"Let me cook up some stuff and I'll show you what I can do."

So the owner led Waldo into the kitchen and showed him where the food was. Waldo went to work. He fried things. He boiled things. He cooked things in the oven.

- How do you fry things? (Call on a student. Idea: *You put them in a pan with some oil.*)
- How do you boil things? (Call on a student. Idea: *You put them in boiling water.*)
- What kind of things would you cook in the oven? (Call on a student. Ideas: *Breads, cakes, casseroles, roasts, etc.*)

Then he mixed things together. When he was done, the owner said, "Whew, that stuff stinks."

- Read the rest of the story to yourself and be ready to answer some questions. Raise your hand when you're done.

Waldo didn't say anything. He dumped all the things he had cooked into a large bowl. The owner opened the windows in the kitchen and stood near one of the windows, holding her nose.

Outside, the animals were beginning to gather. "This is strange," she said to Waldo, as she held her nose. "There are three goats in the backyard. I wonder where they came from. And look at the squirrels."

"Close the window," Waldo said, "or they'll come inside."

"I've never seen anything like this," the owner said.

The animals inside the pet shop were starting to howl and screech and run around in circles and jump up and down. The owner of the pet shop said "My, my. I've never seen anything like this in my whole life."

Waldo smiled and said, "Just wait and see what they do when I bring the food out to them."

- (After all students have raised their hand:)
- Why did the owner open the windows? (Call on a student. Idea: *Waldo's cooking smelled bad; to let the stink out.*)
- What happened outside the pet shop? (Call on a student. Idea: *Animals were gathering.*)
- What were the animals inside the pet shop doing? (Call on a student. Idea: *Making noise and running around.*)
- How did the owner of the pet shop feel about the things that were going on? (Call on a student. Idea: *She was surprised.*)

EXERCISE 5

PAIRED PRACTICE

You're going to read aloud to your partner. The **A** members will read first. Then the **B** members will read from the star to the end of the story. (Observe students and give feedback.)

End-of-Lesson Activities

INDEPENDENT WORK

Now finish the independent work for lesson 69. Raise your hand when you're finished. (Observe students and give feedback.)

WORKCHECK

a. (Direct students to take out their marking pencils.)
- We're going to check your independent work. Remember, if you got an item wrong, make an **X** next to the item.
b. (For each item: Read the item. Call on a student to answer it. If the answer is wrong, say the correct answer. Refer to the Answer Key for the correct answers.)
c. Now use your marking pencil to fix up any items you got wrong. Remember, all mistakes must be fixed up before you hand in your independent work.

LANGUAGE ARTS

(Present Language Arts lesson 69 after completing Reading lesson 69. See Language Arts Guide.)

ACTIVITIES

(Present Activity 14 after completing Reading lessons 69. See Activities Across the Curriculum.)

Note: You will need to reproduce blackline masters for the Fact Game in lesson 70 (Appendix G in Teachers Guide).

Test 7

Materials for Lesson 70
Fact Game
For each team (4 or 5 students):
- pair of number cubes (or dice)
- copy of Fact Game 70 (Reproducible blackline masters are at the back of the Teacher's Guide.)

For each student:
- their copy of the scorecard sheet (at end of workbook A)

For each monitor:
- a pencil
- Fact Game 70 answer key (at end of textbook A)

Reading Checkout
Each student needs their thermometer chart.

Literature Lesson 7
See Literature Guide for the materials you will need.

EXERCISE 1

FACT GAME

a. (Divide students into groups of four or five. Assign monitors.)
b. You'll play the fact game for 10 minutes.
- (Circulate as students play the game. Comment on groups that are playing well.)
c. (At the end of 10 minutes, have all students who earned more than 10 points stand up.)
- (Tell the monitor of each game that ran smoothly:) Your group did a good job.

EXERCISE 2

READING CHECKOUTS

a. Today is a test day and a reading-checkout day. While you're writing answers, I'm going to call on you one at a time to read part of the story we read in lesson 69.

- Remember, you pass the checkout by reading the passage in less than a minute without making more than 2 mistakes. And when you pass the checkout, you color the space for lesson 70 on your thermometer chart.
b. (Call on individual students to read the portion of story 69 marked with ❀.)
- (Time the student. Note words that are missed and number of words read.)
- (Teacher reference:)

> ❀ **Waldo's first job was delivering newspapers. He didn't like that job because he had to get up very early in the morning. The second job that he got was cleaning up in a shoe store. He hated that job. All he did was take boxes of shoes from the shelves [50] and dust the boxes. Then he would sweep the floor in the back room. It was the most boring job in the world, but Waldo [75] would have kept that job if he hadn't found the third job. He would have kept working in the shoe store because he liked earning [100] money more than he hated dusting boxes. So he dusted boxes and dusted boxes and ❀ [115] dusted boxes.**

- (If the student reads the passage in one minute or less and makes no more than 2 errors, direct the student to color in the space for lesson 70 on the thermometer chart.)

- (If the student makes any mistakes, point to each word that was misread and identify it.)
- (If the student does not meet the rate-error criterion for the passage, direct the student to practice reading the story with the assigned partner.)

EXERCISE 3

TEST

a. **Find page 346 in your textbook.** ✓
- This is a test. You'll work items you've done before.

b. Work carefully. Raise your hand when you've completed all the items. (Observe students but do not give feedback on errors.)

LITERATURE

(Present Literature lesson 7 after completing Reading lesson 70. See Literature Guide.)

LANGUAGE ARTS

(Present Language Arts lesson 70 after completing Reading lesson 70. See Language Arts Guide.)

EXERCISE 4

MARKING THE TEST

a. (Check students' work before beginning lesson 71. Refer to the Answer Key for the correct answers.)

b. (Record all test 7 results on the Test Summary Sheet and the Group Summary Sheet. Reproducible Summary Sheets are at the back of the Teacher's Guide.)

EXERCISE 5

TEST REMEDIES

(Provide any necessary remedies for test 7 before presenting lesson 71. Test remedies are discussed in the Teacher's Guide.)

Test 7 Firming Table

Test Item	Introduced in lesson	Test Item	Introduced in lesson	Test Item	Introduced in lesson
1	61	13	61	25	67
2	61	14	61	26	67
3	61	15	63	27	69
4	61	16	63	28	69
5	61	17	63	29	69
6	61	18	63	30	59
7	61	19	63	31	64
8	61	20	63	32	64
9	61	21	67	33	67
10	61	22	67	34	59
11	61	23	67	35	64
12	61	24	67	36	67